Charles Freshman

The Jews and the Israelites

Their religion, philosophy, traditions, and literature

Charles Freshman

The Jews and the Israelites
Their religion, philosophy, traditions, and literature

ISBN/EAN: 9783337131500

Printed in Europe, USA, Canada, Australia, Japan

Cover: Foto ©Lupo / pixelio.de

More available books at **www.hansebooks.com**

היהודים ומקוה ישראל

THE

JEWS AND THE ISRAELITES:

THEIR

RELIGION, PHILOSOPHY, TRADITIONS,

AND LITERATURE,

IN CONNECTION WITH THEIR PAST AND PRESENT CONDITION,
AND THEIR FUTURE PROSPECTS.

BY

REV. C. FRESHMAN, D. D.

TORONTO:
A. DREDGE & CO.
1870.

TORONTO :
THE DAILY TELEGRAPH PRINTING HOUSE,
CORNER KING AND BAY STREETS.

I AFFECTIONATELY

INSCRIBE

ERRATA.

On page 19, read מדוש not פרוש
" 59, " הבו not הבן
" 308, " עולם not עולם
" 332, " טויא not טרויא

I AFFECTIONATELY

INSCRIBE

THIS WORK TO THE

Rev. W. M. Punshon, M. A.

THE HONORED PRESIDENT

OF THE

Wesleyan Methodist Conference in Canada,

IN ESTEEM FOR

HIS MANY VIRTUES AND DISTINGUISHED TALENTS.

THE AUTHOR.

PREFACE.

BY THE REV. G. R. SANDERSON.

Since nations began to exist, up to the present hour—all through the history of our race—no nation has ever had a being which has gathered around itself an interest half so profound as that which attaches to the Jewish people. Nor *attached* alone! It is interwoven with their very existence and circumstances in all periods. Like the life-blood of the heart permeating every particle of the physical system, interest pervades everything relating to the ancient people of God.

It is incorporated with their origin, perpetuity and ultimate destiny; runs through their captivities and emancipations; their exultations and depressions; their gatherings and dispersions; their victories and defeats; their opulence and poverty; their decimations and increase; their fidelity and apostacy; felt in the marvellous interposition of Jehovah in their behalf, in the honors bestowed and the scourges inflicted by a hand equally righteous in all its ways.

A people of profoundest interest! The receivers of the Divine Law, and, for ages the sole depository of the revealed will of Heaven, with a religion and a polity alike from God: the people whence sprung the world's only hope—a people on whose sin-darkened sky arose the bright, the morning star; a people who, though now scattered and peeled, and torn, are yet to be brought in with the fulness of the Gentiles.

As the diamond, once flashing in its own brightness on the coronet of beauty and power, but displaced and lost amid the dust of earth, yet again recovered and cleansed from the gathered obscurations of many years, shall yet again flash forth in the sunlight of heaven with an unrivalled splendour, so shall the once exalted, but long and still depressed Jewish nation, be lifted up by an Almighty power to an altitude of grandeur, such as prophetic lips alone would dare to utter.

HA-JEHUDIM AND MIKVEH ISRAEL supplies a want long felt by the student of this wonderful people. Many ponderous tomes are sometimes searched in vain for a single fact or circumstance relative to the Jew or Judaism. Here, within a reasonable compass, is brought together a mass of information such as many volumes would be sifted in vain to furnish. Unquestionably, many learned and devoted men have written on the subject, and yet have failed to accomplish all that the present volume has achieved.

For such a work the learned and accomplished author has enjoyed special qualifications. Satisfactorily and successfully has he performed it. Himself for many years a devoted Jew, a distinguished Rabbi, a profound scholar, a tireless student to this hour, DR. FRESHMAN possessed abilities, qualities and facilities for the work undertaken, such as few men, in any land, could claim.

And it is surprising how much is crowded into a volume of less than five hundred pages! *Everything*, apparently, relating to the Jewish people, their manners, customs, religion, language, literature, practices, belief, temple, money, schools, chirurgery, lost tribes, Rabbies, traditions, is given in the volume, so that to the reader the marvel is, how so much is found within so small a compass.

To the theological student, whether old or young, but especially to the latter, this volume will be a priceless treasure. No such student *can afford* to be without it. No Minister's library will be complete if HA-JEHUDIM be not there.

The lover of Jewish literature will find the following pages a mine of gold to him. Not a mine where now and then a little gold may be found; and that, after much labour, but gold all through the mine and inviting acceptance.

The devout Christian will, as he reads, be constantly reminded of the purity and goodness, the truth and justice of his Heavenly Father. His sympathies for the Jew and for humanity will grow stronger, and his love for his God will grow warmer as he reads HA-JEHUDIM AND MIKVEH ISRAEL.

The richest blessing of heaven is invoked on the Book, the Reader, and the Author.

BELLEVILLE, *Nov.* 23rd, 1869.

INTRODUCTION.

In one of the grandest works that mortal mind has created, there stands the record, "*Si monumentum quaris circumspice.*" With how much more justice such words might be prefixed to the Jews, it were needless to prove.

Amid all the vicissitudes of time and the revolutions of empires, Judaism has remained permanent, the only vestige of the remote past which has entirely defied decay or dissolution. Mightier people than Israel have appeared on the great stage of humanity, but they have vanished like the shadowy figures of a phantasmagoria. On their ruins other people have arisen, but conquest and admixture have so modified them, that beyond a few centuries no man can trace a certain ancestry. Why is it that three thousand three hundred years have passed and have left but this one verdant line amidst an immensity of desert; this one solitary star in a firmament of darkness?

When of old, men raised their vast structures of physical power, they employed none but human materials. The elements which alone could give stability—principles of eternal right derived from their eternal source—were altogether wanting. Time, therefore, did its work. By the ordinary process of waste, of antagonism, of brute force, the gigantic fabrics, which already contained the germs of decomposition, common to them with their founders, was swept from the earth. Nations suffered this fate so completely, that their very existence is to be traced rather to their conquerors than to themselves. In the era which separates ancient from modern history, a new chaos supervened, as though to show man that his works stand in vain against the laws which regulate him and them. The dark ages, as this era is called, and out of which modern civilization grew, as the original earth grew out of the first chaos, not only effectually covered with its veil all that antiquity had created by merely human agencies, but it enveloped in an impenetrable shroud the origin of all that modern times were to know from that same source. Three things survived the general wreck, and formed connecting links between the past and the futrue.

First, the literature of old struggled through the storm. When the strongest and most mighty peoples perished, nor left a vestige behind, the small voice of their immortal minds was borne on the air-waves of time to an eternal future. Over this emanation from the Divine, that which could annihilate mortal works, however substantial, passed harmlessly. Some fragments of papyrus or parchment were consumed, and with them a few stray ideas were lost; but the great truths which genius had investigated and recorded; the sublime language in which the soul of one man in one age had spoken to the souls of all men in all ages; the lofty conceptions by which morality had proved its connection with an imperishable and heavenly origin, these no physical convulsions could destroy, they were above and beyond such accidents.

Secondly, Christianity survived the fiery ordeal, because that too owed its existence to the eternal revelation of Sinai, and man could only modify, not extirpate. It did not pass through the flames unscathed, because it contained mortal elements, but its morality, its God-teaching, remained intact. In the battle which it had been compelled to maintain against the barbarous forces of northern and eastern idolatry, it had fought on terms so unequal that it had been necessitated to call in strategy to its aid. The luxurious easterns were best ruled through their passions; the uncouth northerns transplanted to the genial south were best governed by their fears. Those followed the patriarch of the Greek Church, these the father of the Roman Church. But in both churches what had been abstract faith—that is, the tie which binds man to forms and modes of belief—became concrete religion. This result was arrived at through the agency of those who had recourse to strategy, and who, in adopting expedients themselves, by their profession and practice sought to prove their efficacy. Priestcraft was, what had been Christianity; a change, and a sad one, but there is hope while vitality was not destroyed, that some future elementary revolution may restore the original combination. Then charity, which in the doctrine of abstract faith, means love for universal mankind, shall cease to be what concrete religion made it, love only for self and self's imitators. Then man shall acknowledge that true God-worship consists not in observance of any particular customs, but in the humble, zealous cultivation of those qualities by which the Eternal has made Himself known to the world. The members of one creed shall not arrogate to themselves peculiar morality and peculiar salvation, denying both to the members of other creeds, but they shall learn that morality and salvation are the cause and effect of all earnest endeavours to rise to the knowledge of revelation. Men shall cease to attempt the substitution of one set of forms for another set of forms; they shall satisfy themselves with being honest and dignified exponents of their own mode of belief, and shall not seek to coerce what heaven itself has left unfettered—the rights of conscience. They shall strive to remove all obstacles to the spread of God-worship, by showing how superior are the happiness, the intellectuality, the virtue of its professors; but they shall stop there; not even for the sake of securing their object, preferring their own faith for that of another. This was the original combination under which Christianity was called into existence; this was the power which enabled it to survive the shock which had destroyed all else, and to this must it return before its mission can be perfectly accomplished. What the teachings of Sinai were to the children of Abraham, the teachings of the other mount were to be to the rest of the world; one was not to supersede the other, but to render it accessible.

Thirdly, Judaism and the Jews escaped the general wreck. Not quite purely, because Rabbinism from within, and persecution from without, did partially what priestcraft did entirely; but with enough of the Divine left to withstand what must have proved fatal to anything less imbued with the spirit of the Eternal. While nation contended with nation, and race with race, all made common cause against the people of God. Diversity of religion knew of no harmony but that which taught scorn of Israel. Men, through their various forms and tenets, looked with less fidelity to heaven than to those spots of earth which held Jews as objects for persecution. If they differed in all else, they were unanimous in hatred. While the doctrine of faith had failed to inculcate love, they had found excuses for contempt and cruelty. But through all, Judaism and the Jews remained. Over the fair face of nature there passes a convulsion; heaven sends its flooding rains, its searing lightnings; earth appears by volcanic agency, opened to entomb, and the sea, carried beyond its boundaries, engulfs the ruins spared from earth and heaven. Desolation holds undisputed sway, and seems to threaten that there, at least, life is forever extinct, vitality for ever annihilated. But the spirit of God still shines in the glorious sun, in the new forms of existence that permeate wave, earth, and air, in the elasticity with which all recovers itself in obedience to the Divine law. " Day and night, summer and winter, shall never cease." So it has been with Judaism. What physical convulsions do for nature, human brutality has done for Judaism, and with like effect. The essence of eternal existence has never been eradicated, and still from ruin, from desolation, from despair, new life has gushed with unabated vigour, new vitality soared with pinion ever sublime. And why? Because in Judaism the Eternal implanted the germs from which salvation is ultimately to spring; because, no matter what form religion may since have been, for wise purposes, permitted to assume, all that it contains of holy and pure is identical with the holiness and purity of Judaism, as taught by Moses and the Prophets. Meanwhile, the brooklet that took its rise in the valley of the Euphrates, runs eternally on towards the illimitable ocean It defies mortal attempts to dam its course; it disdains to mingle with adjacent waters. Clouds at times obscure its day, but the sun of its guidance still penetrates to illuminate. And why is this? Because the spring that supplies the brooklet wells from an omnipotent source; because the waters of its bosom are the waters of life everlasting; because the works of man only are perishable, while the works of God are as the hills that change not.

"In what light does the world now appear to the Jew? Let us try to look at it as it presents itself to him. Is there much in it fitted, at first sight at least, to shake his faith in the religion which he has received from his ancestors? When he surveys the systems around him, and compares his own with them, what is there to make him conclude that his is less pure, less elevated, less Divine? In pagan lands, what does he behold but idols, grim, uncouth, and monstrous, adored by a worship that is childish, immoral or bloody, and connected with dogmas which are ridiculous, incredible, or revolting. Is it for the system of Brahminism or Budhism, that the Jew is to forsake the institute of Moses? Is it for such notions as the Shasters can give him of Vishnu, that he is to renounce the simple, yet sublime and spiritual idea which the Old Testament presents of Jehovah? Is he to turn away from him that sits between the cherubim to bow before Juggernaut? The Jew is not likely to exchange even the Talmud, foolish and absurd as its teaching is, for the sacred books of the Brahmin. Modern Judaism, corrupt as it is, placed beside the gross and sensual system of Hindooism, appears a spiritual and heavenly conception. In Mohammedan countries, the Jew meets just as little to open his eyes to the errors of his creed. He looks around in that vast empire for the fruits that ought to accompany the religion of heaven. He sees them nowhere; neither social virtue, nor public justice. He himself encounters only contumely and wrong. He goes back to his former creed, and clings to it with fonder reverence than ever.

"When the Jew passes from Mohammedan into Popish lands, he is sensible of no change for the better. He beholds on all sides pomps, temples and idols. Everything is loved and served save God. Since his return from Babylon, the Jew has cherished a deeply-rooted aversion to idols; and to abandon Judaism, and become a Romanist, he feels would be to renounce Jehovah and become a worshipper of idols. To the Jew living at Rome, at Florence, or at Vienna, in what light can Christianity possibly appear but as a revival of Paganism? Do not Jupiter and Venus under other names, still reign throughout Christendom? Why, then, should the Jew change his faith? Is he not better as he is?

"But, it may be said, in Protestant lands, at least, the Jew has an opportunity of seeing genuine Christianity. Here, at least, it is not confounded with idolatry. Granting this, still how small a portion of true Chistianity do we find, and how few Jews comparatively live in these lands? And even as regards those who do reside among us, how seldom do they come in contact with a living example of the gospel? Where are the humility, the uprightness, the self-denial, the love of man, and the reverence of God, which ought to flow from Christianity? The Jew casts his eye over society, and sees wealth and pleasure eagerly pursued; the Sabbath desecrated; the holy name of God profaned, and frauds and crimes of frequent occurrence. Are the fruits of Christianity he asks, better than those of Judaism? What will it advantage me that I exchange the synagogue for the church? Thus, the inconsistencies of real Christians, or the ungodliness of merely nominal ones, in the opinion of the Jew, completely justify him in his rejection of the gospel, and adherence to Judaism."—*Record, F. C.*

By a singular fatality, the character of the Jew has been assailed by the infidel not less than by the bigot. Between the two, the condition of the luckless Hebrew has been not unlike that of the lion in the fable. Men of all ages have indulged in bitter hatred against, and in malignant sneers at the Jew, and have falsified the opinions of the Jew, and held up his teachers to unmerited scorn. The Jew has been, and still is, entirely misunderstood; and even the converted Jew has to suffer the consequences. But that time is fast going by. The Hebrew Christians are now taking the pen in their hands, lifting up their voices, and protesting with their whole hearts against the injustice done them by the ignorant as well as the bigoted, and fully expect that good men of every creed and every lineage will bid them " God-speed."

When all this is borne in mind, it will not appear strange if this volume on " Judaism," written by a Hebrew Christian, may not be exactly in accordance with what the public has been accustomed to read. We highly prize the privilege of living in a country where, and at a time when liberty and progress of mind is the order of the day. The past, with its manifold recollections; the future, with its boundless anticipations; the derision in which the Jew is still held, the suspicion and jealousy exhibited towards the converted Jew; all these have exercised their legitimate influence on the mind of the Author.

The kind reader, will, therefore, allow me to indulge the hope that the hands of every true and honest man will be strengthened who endeavors to break down that icy barrier which pride and ignorance, bigotry and prejudice, has raised between those who are children of one Father, creatures of one God.

The Author cannot allow this volume to go into the hands of the public, without acknowledging his indebtedness to the "Israelite," of Cincinnatti, and the "Israelite Indeed," of New York, from which sources the Author derived a great deal of information. Also, the obligations under which he is placed to the Rev. Dr. Nelles, President of Victoria College, who kindly gave himself the trouble of perusing the MS. And to Rev. Prof. Burwash, M. A., for his many valuable and important suggestions in the treatment of the different parts. And imperfect as this volume still is, it had been much more so, if the whole had not, in its first shape, passed through the hands of my friend, the Rev. George Cochran, who is equally distinguished for the correctness of his taste, and his extensive acquaintance with literature.

May the Lord be pleased to look with favor upon this effort to explain and defend truth.

THE AUTHOR.

BRIGHTON, *Nov.* 22*nd*, 1869.

RECOMMENDATIONS.

To the Editor of the *Christian Guardian.*

DR. FRESHMAN'S NEW WORK.

DEAR SIR,—I was pleased to see in the *Guardian*, the recent commendatory notices of Dr. Freshman's new work. Having been permitted to examine a portion of the manuscript, I desire to bear testimony to the great interest and value of the production. Perhaps few men living are so well qualified as Dr. Freshman to treat of the subject he has selected. His Hebrew origin and training, his conversion to Christianity, his fine talents, his extensive learning, and his deep sympathy with his Jewish brethren, all seem especially to fit him for the task he has undertaken.

Many Christians are earnestly looking for the time when "the blindness that has happened to Israel" shall disappear. To such persons this book will be most welcome as tending to draw the attention of Christendom more fully toward this important field of evangelical labour; while to the general reader, nothing can be uninteresting that throws light on the past history, or present condition, of so remarkable a people. Whether we subscribe the phenomena of Judaism to the operation of general laws, or to special interpositions of Providence; whether we read the facts in the light of reason or in the better light of the Cross, we have in either case a marvellous story of power and of weakness, of faith and of unbelief, of glory and of shame. Ethnology, psychology, philology, theology, all have a problem in the Jew; alone among the nations, and yet the means by which all are being gathered into one!

The Doctor's treatise takes a pretty wide range, and discusses with more or less fulness, a great variety of topics, among which are the following:—Jewish Literature, the Teachings of the Talmud, Sayings of the Rabbis, Biblical Studies, the Ten Tribes, Metaphysical Schools, Rabbinical Code of Ethics, the Synagogue, the Day of Atonement, Restoration of Israel, Demons, Traditions and Fables, Poetry, Position in Society, Stumbling-blocks, &c., &c. In some of these chapters will be found valuable information to be had nowhere else, and in others what could be had only by the purchase of costly volumes, the acquisition of difficult languages, and years of laborious research. Nor does it often happen that either German or Hebrew succeeds so well in presenting his thoughts in an English dress. But the learned Doctor, though engaged constantly in preaching to the Germans, has evidently been a close student of our language.

It is customary with some critics, when commending a book, to end by assuring us that "no library is complete without it." As every library, especially every "complete" one, must contain poor books as well as good ones, I will not urge so doubtful a plea, but close by expressing a wish that Dr. Freshman may find a publisher to bring out his work in proper style, and not only the Wesleyan people, but the public at large, may give his literary labors that encouragement to which they are so well entitled.

I am, yours truly,

Victoria College, April 21, 1869.   S. S. NELLES.

RECOMMENDATIONS.

To the Editor of the *Christian Guardian*.

DR. FRESHMAN'S NEW BOOK.

DEAR SIR,—I have lately had an opportunity of examining in manuscript a new work, entitled "Ha-Jehudim," by Dr. Freshman. The work is an exposition of the history, religion, customs, &c., of the Jews from the time of Christ downwards. It is divided into six parts. Part I. treats of the history and customs of the race. Part II. of the religion of the Jews, including a description of many of their principal ceremonies as practised in modern times. Part III. treats very extensively of Jewish literature, setting before us, not only their great writers, but also their schools of philosophy, and an account of the Talmud and Kaballa. Part IV. gives the student much valuable instruction in the study of Hebrew language. Part V. is a kind of Jewish miscellany, varying from grave to gay, dealing with many aspects of their social life, and giving us a strange view of some of the absurdities which men of intellectual culture may believe.

Part VI. is perhaps the most interesting and important of all: "The relation of Judaism and the Jews to Christianity." Here the Doctor deals with Israel's stumbling-blocks, and their means of evading the evidences of the Messiahship of Jesus. He shows also the relation of the Judaism of our Lord's times to His teachings, and the Doctrine of Christianity, and concludes the book with a most eloquent chapter on the restoration of Israel.

We look upon the work as one that will secure the attention of the scholar and critic, as well as the general reading public. It is full of interest. The materials are new to an English public, and the German-English dress, in which the Doctor presents them, adds to their interest. Here, too, the scholar will find many facts bearing upon the greatest question of the age, "What was the form of intellectual and religious life in the midst of which Jesus of Nazareth established the grand system of Christianity?" Everything which tends to elucidate this question, and make the narrative of the Gospels a living picture, set in its true relations to a background of real life, will be acceptable to the Biblical student—and this the work before us can scarcely fail to do.

N. BURWASH,

Cobourg, April, 1869.   Professor.

Dr. Freshman has kindly placed the manuscript of his new work in my hands for a short time. I have read it with care, and feel pleasure in adding my testimony to that of Dr. Nelles, Prof. Burwash, and the *Christian Guardian*, respecting the value of this great work. The subjects handled are of permanent interest to Christian ministers and laymen of all denominations; and are treated with much learning and ability. We have no book that I am aware of in the English language that at all supplies the information contained in this work. It will be the cheapest, fullest, and most accurate cyclopedia on Jewish matters within the reach of the public. From personal acquaintance with Dr. F., and from the frequent conversations with him on subjects of Old and New Testament criticism, and Hebrew literature, I had reason to expect such a work as he now presents to the Christian public.

An unusual interest has been felt in the recent controversy concerning Christ and the Talmud; and in this new work by Dr. F. the whole matter is discussed with great fulness, in the light of a thorough acquaintance with the Talmud, and also of a clear scriptural knowledge of Christianity. This, together with his discussion of the Metaphysical systems, and Ethical Codes of the Rabbies, will prove a valuable acquisition to the libraries of all readers, and of ministers in particular. In short it would require a lengthy review to present fully the merits and claims of this valuable work. I hope it may speedily find its way into the library of every family in the land.

Nor does this work exhaust Dr. Freshman's purpose of service in the cause of Christian authorship. He has in a state of forwardness, a commentary on difficult passages of the Old and New Testament, which, when published, will enrich our libraries with a new, and standard work, in this department of Biblical literature.

GEORGE COCHRAN.

Toronto, June 5th, 1869.

CONTENTS.

	PAGE.
PREFACE	v
INTRODUCTION	vii
RECOMMENDATIONS	xiv

PART FIRST.

CHAPTER I.

THE JEWS—Persecution defeats itself; the Jews an example—Their influence in Commerce—Poetry—Philosophy—Literature—Religion.. 1
JEWS IN ROME—Persecutions... 4
THE SAMARITANS—Their origin—Belief—Animosities—United with Judea against Rome... 4
JEWS IN SPAIN AND FRANCE—Early settlement—Sufferings................... 7
JEWS IN INDIA—Emigration to Malabar—Immunities—Persecution—Relief—Intercourse with Holland—Occupation—Dr. Buchanan's account.. 8
JEWS IN CHINA—Degraded Condition—Belief and Customs—Inscriptions in their Synagogue... 10
THE SECT OF THE CHASIDIM, IN THE NORTH OF EUROPE................... 12
JEWS IN HUNGARY—Fugitives from oppression—Numbers—Occupations—Education—Religion.. 15
ESSENEES—Habits—Doctrines—Extinction.. 17
HELLENISTS—Rise—Kabbalism—Superstitions...................................... 17
PHARISEE—Ceremonies—Name—Talmudical account of Classes.............. 19
SADDUCEES—Origin—Hetrodoxy—Customs.. 20
THE DIVISION AND DISTINCTION OF THE LEARNED OF THE NATION..... 21
THE CARAITES—Extreme Legalism—Morality—Nazaritism—Funeral Rites—Metempsychosis... 24
CHRISTIAN JEWISH SECTS IN RUSSIA.. 27
JEHUD CHEBER—Jethro—Rechabites—Physique—Antipathies—Jewish Customs—Government... 28
FREEMASONRY AMONG THE JEWS—Curious Traditions—Synagogue in Prague—"Maranos"—Traces of Freemasonry—Alt-Neu.............. 31

CHAPTER II.

THE NAMES OF A JEW—Hebrew—Israelites—Jew—Origin and Import of these Names defined.. 35

CHAPTER III.

HEBREW WOMEN—Polygamy, though practiced, was discouraged—High position assigned to Woman—Betrothal—Marriage—Divorce—Mutual duties of Husband and Wife—Love of Hebrew Women for their Kindred 36

CHAPTER IV.

POSITION THE JEWS WERE AND ARE STILL OCCUPYING IN SOCIETY 41

PART SECOND.

CHAPTER I.

JUDAISM—Interest of the subject—No people more spoken of—Command the attention of the world—Present great varieties of character and social status—The *Times* quoted—The little rill issuing in the mighty river—Ceremonies and customs: 1st, those of the written law, containing 613 commandments; 2nd, those of the oral law—the Talmud; 3rd, those customs which have arisen in course of time—All agree in the 1st and 2nd, but there is much difference in the 3rd particular—Classes according to nationality—Modern Caraites—Few Jews converse in the Hebrew—Origin of the MISHNA and TALMUD—Superstitious regard for dreams—Justice in dealing enjoined—Cooking food—Eating—Killing animal food—Phylacteries—Duties of women—Thirteen articles of Jewish belief—Manner of making proselytes—Cabalistic magic—Jewish Eschatology 43

CHAPTER II.

CONFESSION—Traditions and authority of the Rabbies—Unable now to keep the Law of Moses—The birth of a son—Circumcision—Birth of a daughter—Redeeming the first-born—Genealogy lost—Teaching of children—Courtship—Marriage—Divorce—Sabbath and its observances... 55

CHAPTER III.

MODERN CELEBRATION OF THE PASSOVER—The Feast of Weeks—The New-year—The Day of Atonement—Its ceremonies—The Feast of Tabernacles—The Feast of Dedication—Feast of Purim—Feast of the destruction of the two Temples—Ceremonies for the sick, dying and dead—Burial rites 65

CONTENTS. xix

CHAPTER IV.

SYNAGOGUES—Origin of Synagogues—A Lawful Assembly................. 72
A CARAITE Prayer... 72

CHAPTER V.

TUNES, MUSIC, AND MELODY—Music of the Temple which survives—
Obscurity of the subject—Nature of Hebrew notation—Character of
Hebrew Melodies—Christian Chants adopted from Temple Melodies—Specimens reduced to modern notation........................... 74

CHAPTER VI.

ADORATION AND PRAYER—A Prayer of Adoration and Supplication..... 76
COMMENCEMENT OF MORNING PRAYER... 81
SPECIAL PRAYER FOR MONDAYS AND THURSDAYS............................ 82
PRAYER AND CONFESSION ON THE DAY OF ATONEMENT..................... 85
CLOSING PRAYER ON DAY OF ATONEMENT....................................... 90

CHAPTER VII.

CONFIRMATION CEREMONY AS PRACTISED AMONG THE REFORMED JEWS. 92

CHAPTER VIII.

DAY OF ATONEMENT—Preparation—Repentance—Confession—Humiliation... 94
ATONEMENT—Interpretation of Psalms cx., and Isaiah ix. 6............. 97
INTERPRETATION OF THE 110TH PSALM BY THE JEWS....................... 98
TRANSLATION OF ISAIAH ix. 6, BY THE JEWS.................................. 98

CHAPTER IX.

THE JEWISH CALENDAR—Tishri—*September*—Day of Atonement—Feast
of Tabernacles—Marchesnen—*October*—Kisley—*November*—Feast
of Dedication—Tevetto—*December*—Shebat—*January*—Adar—*February*—Feast of Purim—Nisan—*March*—Passover—Eyor—*April*—
Sivon—*May*—Feast of Weeks—Tamus—*June*—Great Fast—Ab—
July—Great Fast Day for Destruction of Jerusalem—Elul—*August*—Blowing of Trumpets... 99

CHAPTER X.

COMPUTATION OF TIMES AND FESTIVALS—Celebration of the New Moon
—Difficulties of Jews residing out of Palestine—Present order of
reckoning... 119

CHAPTER XI.
A SERMON ON THE CREATION.. 123

CHAPTER XII.
DEDICATORY SERMON.. 129

CHAPTER XIII.
A SERMON ON SACRIFICES.. 143

CHARTER XIV.
A SERMON ON MARRIAGE.. 149

CHAPTER XV.
A FUNERAL SERMON... 155

PART THIRD.

CHAPTER I.
JEWISH LITERATURE—Ingnorance on this subject............................. 159

CHAPTER II.
LITERARY MEN AMONG THE HEBREWS—Standard works in German and French, but not in English—Misrepresentations resulting from this—Contributions of Jewish Scholars, of twelfth to the sixteenth century, to Biblical Literature—The Rabbinical Language—Its formation and richness—Mistaken idea that the Jews are ignorant, or that their learning is a mere collection of fables—Like estimating English Literature from the story of Jack the Giant Killer—Rabbinical translations of Aristotle, Plato, Euclid, &c.—Original treaties on Grammar, Logic Metaphysics, and the various branches of Mathemathics—The Jews for four-and-a-half centuries the most learned men in Europe—Illustrious examples....................................... 161

CHAPTER III.
THE TALMUD—Use made of the Talmud in modern literary investigations—A universal endeavor to gather useful thought from every source, and a disposition to appreciate what is good in every ancient work—In this spirit study the Talmud—Second-hand knowledge of, and reference to the Talmud—Ignorance and misrepresentation of the work—Lack of a good "Introduction" to the work—The censor at Baslo—A critical edition never completed—The Editio Princeps—

CONTENTS. xxi

PAGE

Interdictions, burnings, &c., of the book—Anecdote of Clement V.
—The confiscation instigated by Pfeffer Korn—Reuchlin comes in to
the rescue—The contest which ensued — Reuchlin's friends—It
results in the printing of the first complete edition of the work at
Venice, A.D. 1520.. 165

WHAT IS THE TALMUD ?—Its wide extent—The topics proposed to be
treated—A body of law—It can be best judged by comparison with
other bodies of law, especially with the Justinian code—The Talmud
originates with the return from the Babylonish captivity—Change
which took place during the captivity—Love of the Scriptures
which sprung up—Its exposition "Midrash"—Four methods—
P R D S—The literal, the suggestive, the homiletic, the
mystical—An allegory—The Talmud not a systematic code—Rather
the result of intermingled currents of thought—One logical, the
other imaginative—Logic more prominent in study of the Law—Imagination in that of the other portions of the Bible—"Halacha" and
"Haggada"—Mishna and Gemara—The development of the Oral
Law—Its deductions from the written—The Scribes—Three periods
—The Sanhedrin and schools of the second period—The teachers
and their method—The rise of Christianity—The Pharisees—The
Mishna—Hillel—Akiba—Jehuda—The contents of the Mishna—
Character of its laws—Their administration—Capital punishment—
The Gemaras of Jerusalem and Babylon—Size of the Babylonian
Talmud—Cause of the authority and popularity of the Talmud—
The language of the the Talmud—The Haggadah—Its use to the
Eastern mind—Account of the creation—Angels—God's name—The
soul—Resurrection and immortality—No eternal punishment—
Prophets.. 173

SAYINGS OF THE TALMUD—Synoptical history of the Talmud, Mishna,
and Gemara—Account of the authors of the Bible 204

CHAPTER IV.

TEACHINGS OF THE RABBIES—Consisting of various proverbs or moral
sayings selected from the teachings of the most celebrated Rabbies of
all ages... 215

CHAPTER V.

RABBINICAL CODE OF ETHICS—Conscience—The highest maxim of moral
law—God's command and not our happiness the motive to virtue—
Self love not entirely excluded—The internal motive—Time of its
appearance—Moral perfection finite and capable of increase—Duty
of advancement—Freewill—Degrees of virtue—There are no small
sins—No insuperable barrier to repentance—Degrees in sin—No
man perfect—Demons—Merit not transferable—Moral judgment of

ourselves—Classification of duties—Man should do by himself as God commands—Collision of duties—How decided—Justice precedes mercy—One's own dues those of others ; and the good of the whole that of a part.. 247

CHAPTER VI.

EXTRACTS FROM RABBINICAL WRITINGS—The Spiritual Body—The Israelites at Sinai—Joshua—Enoch—R. Ribbi and Antonius......... 250

CHAPTER VII.

KABALA AND KABALISTS—Term defined—Two classes of the Mystical School—Philo and the Kabalists—Age of the latter system—Its dialect—Divisions of the Science—Standard works—Axioms—Pantheism—The Jetsira and Tohar... 253

CHAPTER VIII.

THE METAPHYSICAL SCHOOLS OF THE JEWS, ANCIENT AND MODERN—
  Sec. I.—*Preceding Maimonides* : The Bible not metaphysical—Origin of evil—Free-will—The Talmud—Mercaba—Allegorical characters of Rabbinical literature—The Caraites—Progress of metaphysics among the Rabbinites—Saadia ben Joseph—The Book of Creeds—The school at Cordova—Solomon ben Gabriel—The Fons Vitæ—Bahya ben Joseph—Juda ha Levi and book Khozari—Differences between theology and philosophy, and attempts at reconciliation—Maimonides—More Nevochim—Prohibition and burning of his work... 254
  SEC. II.—*Subsequent to Maimonides* : Fabulous accounts of the Kabala—Yetsira and Zohar—Date of the Zohar—Contents of the books—Theories of the origin of evil—Cabalistic theory—The manifestation of God—Theories of emanation—Remarks on this system and comparison with other systems of philosophy—Neoplatonists and Gnostics—The Cabala and Christianity—Shem Job—Judaia Penini—Joseph Ibn Caspi—Marter Leon—Moses ben Joseph—Ahron ben Elias, the Caraite—Decay of Peripateteism—Joseph Albo—Abraham Bibago—Joseph ben Shem Job—Elias del Medigo—Expulsion of the Jews from Spain—Abraham and his son Leo—The Dialogues of Love—Close of the history of Jewish metaphysics with the sixteenth century—Modern philosophers not peculiarly Hebrew. 267

CHAPTER IX.

WORKS OF MAIMONIDES.—TALMUDICAL : Perush, Hamishurah—Mishna Torah—Sepher Hamtisroth—Maamar Techyath Hamethim—Commentary on the Gemara—Questions and answers......................... 288

PHILOSOPHICAL—Moreh Nebuchim—Epistle to the Learned—Maamar Hayichud—Miloth Higeyon.. 290
MEDICAL: Canon of Avicenna—Hanhagoth Habyryuth—Sepher Harephnoth, &c.. 291
MISCELLANEOUS: Iggereth Teman—Iggereth Lehamarr Hagadol, &c.... 292

CHAPTER X.

MAIMONIDES ON REPENTANCE—Explanation of Passages seeming to deny free-will to some men—Power of Repentance taken away judicially—God's foreknowledge not consistent with individual free-will. 294

CAAPTER XI.

THE RESURRECTION OF THE DEAD PROVED FROM THE OLD TESTAMENT SCRIPTURES—Rabbi Johannan—Rabbi Simoi—Rabbi Jismael—Rabbi Joshua—Rabbi Mair—Analogies of the Resurrection........... 297

CHAPTER XII.

HEBREW POETRY—Poetry characteristic of the Hebrews—Selections—Selections from the later Hebrew Poetry. 300

PART FOURTH.

CHAPTER I.

THE HEBREW BIBLE—Study of the text—Historical evidence of the accuracy of the Textus receptus.. 319

CHAPTER II.

BIBLICAL STUDIES—The Poetry of Youth and Old Age—Application of the principle to the Jewish nation and history—Gentile Historians—A history and literature more ancient than political institutions—Jewish nationality—Four epochs in Jewish history........................... 321

CHAPTER III.

HEBREW ORTHŒPY, OR POINTS AND ACCENTS—Invented by the Masorites—Necessary when the language ceased to be spoken—Accents—Four uses—Works on the subject—Pointed manuscripts and a standard text—The name "Sopherim"—The labours of the Masorites—Note on the subdivision of the books................................ 327

CHAPTER IV.

THE STATE OF THE HEBREW LANGUAGE IN OUR DAY—Revival of Hebrew as a living tongue—Books, periodicals and newspapers—Comparison of Hebrew with classics—Objections by persons deficient in knowledge of Hebrew—Modern works in pure Biblical Hebrew on general and secular subjects. 330

CHAPTER V.

A NEW METHOD OF LEARNING TO READ HEBREW—Hebrew Reading.. 334

CHAPTER VI.

JEWISH TEACHERS OF CHRISTIAN STUDENTS—Celebrated theologians and scholars who were instructed by Jewish teachers—Professors in Schools and Universities, and Learned men of the present day—Prejudice against the Jews.. 336

PART FIFTH.

CHAPTER I.

MISCELLANEOUS ADDENDA—General Remarks upon Sundry practices and beliefs of the Jews... 339
MENTION OF CHRIST'S NAME IN A BLASPHEMOUS MANNER IN THE TALMUD AND RABBINICAL WRITINGS.................................... 344

CHAPTER II.

CERTAIN PECULIARITIES OF THE JEWISH RACE—The Jews are found in all lands—Are imperfectly understood—Aaronic descent, how ascertained—Statistics of Jewish population—Language and Literature—Physical peculiarities.. 345
COMPARATIVE TABLE OF MORTALITY AMONG JEWS AND GENTILES....... 351

CHAPTER III.

TEMPLE AND HALF SHEKEL—Loyalty of the Jews to the Temple at Jerusalem—The Half Shekel—The Falashas of Abyssinia............ 353

CHAPTER IV.

JEWISH MONEY.. 359

CHAPTER V.

THE GOLDEN VESSELS OF THE TEMPLE—Where they are.................... 360

CHAPTER VI.

THE HIGH PRIESTS—Imperfection of the Genealogical Registers—Lists of Names so far as ascertained.. 362

CHAPTER VII.

DOCTORS OF DIVINITY—Diplomas—Status and Powers of Rabbis in different ages... 364

CHAPTER VIII.

SCHOOLS—Jewish zeal in the promotion of learning—Vernacular of the people in the time of Christ—Greek prohibited for sacred purposes—Strictures on Lightfoot.. 366

CHAPTER IX.

MEDICINE AND CHIRURGERY—Physicians amongst the Hebrews—Modes of treating the sick—Diseases mentioned in Scripture.................... 368

CHAPTER X.

THE LOST TEN TRIBES—Conflicting Opinions—Curious Stories by Dervishes and Travellers—Deportations from Israel—Fate of the Exiled Israelites—Localities of the Captives of Judah—Their fate—Account of the Ten Tribes in Esdras—Indians of America supposed to be part of the Lost Ten Tribes—Other Conjectures........................... 375

CHAPTER XI.

DEMONS AND EVIL SPIRITS—Opinions of the heathen on Evil Spirits—Views held by the Reformed Jews—Doctrines taught by orthodox Jews.. 389

CHAPTER XII.

TRADITION OF THE JEWS—The unwritten Law—The Mode of its Transmission—"Making a Hedge for the Law"—Divisions of the Law... 393

CHAPTER XIII.

ABSURD LEGENDS AND STORIES... 395

CHAPTER XIV.

JUDAISM NOT BORROWED FROM THE EGYPTIANS............................... 397

CHAPTER XV.

THE PRAYER "ALENU.".. 399

PART SIXTH.

CHAPTER I.

FALSE CHRISTS—Accounts of false Christs who have arisen, A. D. 114 to A. D. 1862—Involves the principle of the ceaseless expectation of Messiah—General remarks...... 401

CHAPTER II.

OFFICES AND TITLES OF THE MESSIAH AS TAUGHT IN RABBINICAL WRITINGS...... 408

CHAPTER III.

HOW THE FIFTY-THIRD CHAPTER OF ISAIAH IS EXPLAINED AMONG THE JEWS...... 409
DESCRIPTION OF THE SUFFERINGS OF ISRAEL BY THE KINGS: ISAIAH liii..... 412
THE CAUSE OF THE SUFFERINGS AS THE KINGS WILL CONCEIVE IT...... 412
THE PROPHET'S DEFENCE OF THE JUSTICE OF PROVIDENCE...... 414

CHAPTER IV.

DID CHRIST BORROW FROM THE RABBIES?—Use of the Rabbinical writings in explaining the New Testament—Several illustrative examples—Note on Christ's relation to truth, old and new...... 415

CHAPTER V.

TESTIMONY CONCERNING JESUS FROM A REFORMED RABBI...... 426

CHAPTER VI.

ISRAEL'S STUMBLING-BLOCKS...... 427

CHAPTER VII.

SUFFERINGS OF THE JEWS—Sufferings in the olden time—In Britain—On the Continent of Europe—From the wickedness of their own people—On account of false Messiahs—Accounted for from the WORD OF GOD—Dawn of a better day—Notes on persecutions by Christians...... 436

CHAPTER VIII.

THE RESTORATION OF ISRAEL...... 453
CONCLUSION...... 455

HA-JEHUDIM AND MIKVEH ISRAEL.

PART FIRST.

THE JEWISH PEOPLE AND THEIR CUSTOMS.

CHAPTER I.—THE JEWS.

PERSECUTION defeats itself; the Jews an example—Their influence in Commerce,—Poetry—Philosophy—Literature—Religion. JEWS IN ROME—Persecutions. SAMARITANS—Their origin—Belief—Animosities—United with Judea against Rome. JEWS IN SPAIN AND FRANCE—Early settlement—Sufferings. JEWS IN INDIA—Emigration to Malabar—Immunities—Persecution—Relief—Intercourse with Holland—Occupation—Dr. Buchanan's account. JEWS IN CHINA—Degraded Condition—Belief and Customs—Inscriptions in their Synagogue. JEWS IN HUNGARY—Fugitives from oppression—Numbers—Occupations—Education—Religion. ESSENEES—Habits—Doctrines—Extinction. HELLENISTS—Rise—Kabbalism—Superstitions. PHARISEES—Ceremonies—Name—Talmudical account of Classes. SADDUCEES—Origin—Hetrodoxy—Customs. SCRIBES—Oral Law—Its succession—The Sanhedrim—Fencing the Law—Prayers. CARAITES—Extreme Legalism—Morality—Nazaritism—Funeral Rites—Metempsychosis. HISTORY OF CHRISTIAN JEWISH SECTS IN RUSSIA. JEHUD CHEBER—Jethro—Rechabites—Physique—Antipathies—Jewish Customs—Government. FREEMASONRY—Curious Traditions—Synagogue in Prague—"Maranos"—Traces of Freemasonry—Alt-Neu.

THE JEWS.

In looking over the history of the human race for the last eighteen hundred years, we have invariably found that persecution and oppression have recoiled upon themselves. When the Catholics employed fire and sword to root out Protestantism, were not some of the first men the world ever produced the Protestant martyrs? Again, when Protestanism gained the upper hand, and fiercely persecuted Catholicism, were not the cleverest and most learned men that faith has ever brought forth the martyrs? Where is there a race or body of men who have been so perseveringly pursued to destruction as the Israelites? For eighteen centuries, in all parts of the world, an Israelite has been looked upon as a criminal—as something unclean—as a thing to be trampled on, robbed, kicked and despised. Yet, when did that race stand higher than at present? When did we ever before find as many of the brightest ornaments of the financial, the mercantile, the literary, the musical, and the dramatic world to be Israelites?

The world to-day worships Mammon as zealously and as entirely as it ought to worship God, and the very high-priest of this religion, the financier of the world, who holds peace and war in his hands, at whose frown emperors quake, kings tremble, and republics maintain peace, is an Israelite. In literature, the Hebrew element is still more prominent. The D'Israels—the elder immortal through his "Curiosities of Literature," and the younger, a novelist of the first class, and the leader of the protectionist party of the British Commons, are alone sufficient example. In the musical and dramatic world—Rachel, the queen of tragedy; Juliana, the matchless cantatrice; Mario, the great tenor; Rossini, Mendelssohn and Meyerbeer, the composers, and Henry Heine, the critic, poet and philosopher, are but a portion of the illustrious Hebrew list.

Verily, the Israelite is outliving persecution and the world's scorn. Hunted up and down the earth these many centuries past, and held good prey for the Christian in all the civilized world, he is at length redeeming his status in the human family, and entering into the councils and consideration of nations. In England, where two centuries ago, it was hardly a misdemeanor to plunder him; he is now a member of the House of Commons, and was Lord Mayor of London. In Paris, St. Petersburg, London, Hamburg, and Madrid, he is the monarch of the exchange. We do not shrink from contact with him, as of old. In spite of his iron creed, he Christianizes, or at least humanizes, under the genial influences of a tolerant age.

The Israelites always have been a religious people, and whatever they profited in science and art, was transplanted by them into the province of religion. So, when the first harp of Israel resounded upon foreign soil, first after the last psalmist touched the cords of Judah's divine lyre, hymns sublime and sacred flow from the lips of Gabriel, Abitur, Judah Hallevi, the prince of poetry, and a hundred minor poets, who sang the praise of their Maker in inspired lays, the mission and sufferings of Israel, the greatness and holiness of God's sacred words, and a hundred other themes, in either the Arabic or Hebrew tongue.

Poesy is the morning dawn; the juvenile epoch of philosophy and criticism, their jovial companion, and their last and longest re-echo. So it was, also, among their ancestors, in the Arabic Empires. Poesy, philosophy and criticism were rivetted by diamond ties, and the brilliant stars on the horizon of poetry are also the great luminaries in the temple of philosophy and criticism. As in poesy, so in science, the Israelites proved to be a religious people. Their ancient scholars directed their attention principally to their religious literature. While one class of scholars was engaged in Hebrew grammar, lexicography and philology, another class studied the Bible with the results of the former, by the double light of national traditions and the predominating systems of philosophy, and left to posterity their immortal commentaries. Another class of their scholars were engaged in the same way, with investigations into the Talmud, and the rest of our national literature, and labored with the same happy result. While again one class was busy to abstract the moral and religious theories of the Bible, and their national literature, and shape them systematically, according to the then state of philosophy; another class compared these results with the dogmas of Grecian philosophy, and attempted to harmonize them both.

These faint outlines of the mental and literary activity of our ancestors in the Arabic empires, and chiefly in Spain, will enable you to form a correct judgment of their literary productions. Comparing them to Hebrew scholars in Christian Empires, it must be admitted, while the former has two guides—tradition and philosophy—the latter had but one tradition; hence, the former labored for Israel and mankind at large, while the latter worked almost exclusively for their people, being excluded from the rest of men by unjust mandates. But these two classes of scholars did not remain long separate from each other. The Hebrew merchant brought not only the products of one country to the other; he was also the vehicle to the exchange of the Illeas manuscripts, and, finally, also, the books of different lands and climes, and the scholars of either land were benefitted by the labors of those of other countries, and the Israelite was always inclined to learn.

The Hebrew scholars wrote in Hebrew, and this was a sacred language to which the prejudices of the priests had no objection, and which was more accessible to them than any other language except their own, and so another prophesy was fulfilled: "And the nations will go to thy light, and the kings to the lustre of thy sun;" and also this: "I, God, have called thee in justice, and have taken thee by the hand, and have formed thee, and set thee to a covenant of the people, to a light of the nations; to open the eyes of the blind; to bring out the captive from the dungeon, and those who sit in darkness, from the house of prison." Notwithstanding the vigilance and severity of Rome's servants, the new literature of the Hebrews was studied, and Latin translations were furnished at an early date by the unterrified friends of science, in the cloisters and outside of them; and the religious views of the age underwent a revolution, to which Hebrew literature had given the impulse and the substance, the books and the teachers. If any credit is due to the Reformation in the history of religion, a large amount of it may justly be claimed by the Hebrew scholars, for most every great man of that age had Hebrew teachers; and Schudt, this great enemy of Israel, tells us that Martin Luther himself had several Hebrew teachers. The translation of the Bible by Martin Luther, gives abundant evidence that the Reformation was a consequence, and the Hebrew literature of the Mediæval ages was the cause thereof.

THE JEWS IN ROME.

The Christian Clergy in the Roman States tried unceasingly to convert the Jews to Christianity, and, as they could not get hold of their souls in spite of all their troubles, they took revenge on their poor bodies. Theodorich, King of the East Goths, who took possession of all Italy after the death of Odoaker, showed great wisdom in sustaining his power in matters of the Church. Above all, he disliked the changing of religion. His successor, Theodat, was, also, very tolerant. The Jews acknowledged this fully, and proved their fidelity to him at the time when Justinian warred against the East Goths. They had taken possession of the upper part of the City of Naples. When Belisarius, the General of Justinian, with his soldiers, had stormed the lower part of the City, and held it, the Jews kept their own till they succumbed to superiority of numbers. Belisarius admired such fidelity, and recommended his soldiers to treat them leniently, but only after great labor was he able to put a stop to the carnage of his troops. Quite different was Justinian. He oppressed and persecuted them—treated them as heretics—and robbed them of their acquired rights and possessions. Thus, he commanded them to keep the Passover on the day of the Christian Easter. He declared that no Jew could be a witness against any Christian—pronounced their testaments of no value—and forbade the African Jews the exercise of their religion, and the other Israelites to educate their little children in the faith of their forefathers. But, as usual, all those decrees for the extinction of the Hebrew religion missed their aim.

THE SAMARITANS.

Justinian's severe treatment of the Israelites was the cause of a general rising of them in Cæsarea. The Samaritans united with them, but with what luck, we have to pass over for the moment, in order to give some explanation about the rise of that sect.

When Salmanasser destroyed the Kingdom of Israel, he transferred, in accordance with the tyrannical custom of his age, the ten conquered tribes of Israel into Assyria, and from thence to the most distant countries of Asia, from whence they never returned, but got partly mixed up with other nations; losing their identity, partly as believers in the Mosaic law, but as members of other States, and partly as a separate nation, under their own rulers and separate government, are found there to this day. In the orphan's land of the ten tribes, and especially in the neighborhood of the capital, Schomron (Samaria), the King of Assyria transplanted other conquered tribes, called Chutaei, after a city in Persia, wherein they formerly dwelt, and, latterly, Samaritans, after the name of their new capital. Soon after settling, they suffered the consequences of the desolation of the land, as a herd of hungry lions drove terror and dismay among the new inhabitants, who considered those accidents as a punishment from heaven for omitting to worship the deity of the land. They reported, straight-off, the unlucky news to the Cyprian king, asking for an Israelite priest, who might teach them the worship of the God of this country, which request was readily granted. Thus the Chutaei got, in their opinion, a knowledge of the God of the Israelites, without renouncing their old Gods; stopping between heathenism and Judaism, they formed a ridiculous hybrid, and the Israelites gave them the nickname of the " Lion Converts."

This half-way heathenism of the Samaritans opposed a union of them with the Israelites. But the more they were initiated in the Bible, the quicker they had to acknowledge that the Hebrew God, as the God of the Universe, can not suffer another one besides him. Yet, the division between both parties continued, spiritually, but the cause of it was not any longer their heathenism, but rather the way and manner in which they understood the Hebrew religion.

A full century separated and cut off from all intercourse with the Israelites, they studied their Hebrew religion exclusively from the Pentateuch. Neither knowing, nor caring to know, about the progress and the advancement of the Mosaic law, they returned to the state of Judaism as it was a thousand years ago, and remained there firm, when all this time the religious life of the Israelites renovated itself, in the course of time, through priests and prophets— a life which is itself creating and forming—yea, altering and adopting itself to the difference of circumstances. Thus the Judaism of the Chutæi was, for itself, the cause, and the Judaism of the real Israelites could not amalgamate with differences.

This fight between Samaritans and Israelites rose to the highest pitch of animosity, when the latter showed their zeal to take part, with all their strength, in the re-building of the second temple at Jerusalem, but were decidedly and strenuously refused by the Samaritans. In consequence thereof, a certain Manasse, son-in-law of Sambelat, a captain of the Chutæi, and very hostile to the Israelites, built for the Chutæi another temple, similar to that of Jerusalem, on Mount Gerisim, not far from the city of Schechem (Nablus), to which town, then, the most of the Samaritans emigrated, and this sealed the separation for all eternity.

The Samaritans now live entirely to themselves, and thus misjudgments and scandalizing had full play from both parties. The Israelties not only denounced the religion of the Samaritans as a counterfeit one, but raised against them the cry of idolatry. Some would have seen that there was put up on Mount Gerisim an image, in the form of a dove, to which they paid divine homage; the Israelites had raised and promulgated the maxim, that the Chutæi should be treated in all points like idolaters, although even the Talmud had to acknowledge that the Samaritans kept those laws, which they had adopted from the Israelites; more strictly and more conscientiously than the Israelites themselves. Notwithstanding this, the Samaritans never ceased to acknowledge themselves the pure Israelites, and to accuse the Israelites of having falsified the Bible. They affirmed that the pure worship was only in the Temple on Mount Gerisim, whose altar was built from stones out of the river Jordan, but not in Jerusalem, and cited as proof Deut. 27 c. 4 v. Hatred rose from day to day, and from mere spite the Israelites excluded Samaria from the Holy Land. Sirach said, "Two kinds of people I dislike from all my heart, but the third I hate as none else, the Samaritans, the Philistines, and the crazy mot of Shechem." Hyrkan conquered them, to amalgamate them with the Israelites, took Schechem and destroyed their temple. Hyrkan's ideas were not fulfilled, but animosity and division increased. Both parties evaded each other like plague ridden, and troubled one another in all possible manners, even after Herodes had their city rebuilt, the memory of their lost temple, which never rose again, filled their hearts with bitterness and rage.

But a change came under the further dominion of Rome. During the many wars of Rome against Judea, who never passed through the land of the Samaritans without inflicting a great deal of injury, the heart of the Samaritans left the Roman side and inclined to the Israelites. In the Hebrew-Roman war they made common cause with the Israelites, and fought bravely and heroically. Henceforth they had to share the fate of the Israelites; yea, often they fared worse. At the time of the Emperor Antonin the Pious, the Israelites received from time to time certain favors, but to the Samaritans even the rite of circumcision was forbidden. Under the Emperor Yeno, A. D. 490, they laid claim to several Christian churches, but they had to pay for it with the loss of their mountain, where a Christian church was erected, which was destroyed again under Anastasius, by some Samaritan women. The guilty ones were severely punished by the governor of Nablos.

When the Israelites were severely treated under Justinian, the Samaritans made common cause with them, murdered a great many Christians under the head of their own King Julianus, devastated the land, and killed the governor in his own palace. As soon as the Emperor Justinian got news of this rebellion, measures were taken to suppress it. The chief rebels were killed, the other Samaritans had either to quit the country, or, in order to save their property, embrace Christianity, which a great many did. Thus ends their history about the year 575.

THE JEWS IN SPAIN AND FRANCE.

Even in the first centuries after Christ, the Jews in Spain were already so numerous and powerful, that the Christian clergy feared, the whole country would turn Jew. According to doubtful memorials, there were Jews already in Spain at the time of King Solomon, but it is more probable, that they immigrated about 100 years A. C. from Africa to the Pyrenic peninsula, where they soon grew in numbers and importance. But this well-to-doism begat envy and hatred, and thus it came, that already the Synod of Eliberis, an old Spanish city (A.D. 300 to 313), issued the edict that henceforth no Christian farmer may employ Jews as husbandmen. They also forbade clergy and laity keeping company, or to intermarry with the Jews; as there is no doubt that at that time a great many Christians leaned towards Judaism. A few centuries later, in the year 582, the third council found it necessary to renew the decree against the intermarriages with Jews; and as the Spanish Jews were the chief traders in the slave market, the Synod interdicted that trade, and promised freedom to their slaves. Even the old West Gothic of Spain already made efforts to convert the Jews by force to Christianity, and it is therefore easily explained, that, under such circumstances, the Jews were pleased with the invasion of the Saracens in Spain.

Jews must have settled very early in France, for Childebert I. (540), already ordered that no Jew shall be seen on the streets of Paris from Ash Thursday to Easter Sunday, and at Orleans a similar decree was passed by a society of ecclesiastics.

The Jews were in such bad favour that Bishop Ceriol, who treated them kindly, was dismissed from his office. King Childerich (560), and King Dagober (628), treated the Jews with the utmost severity. Incited by King Heraclius, Dagobert desired to banish the Jews, but the Abbot Damianus and the courts of Toulon resisted it with all their power, and for justice's and humanity's sake even assisted them by force of arms. King Wamba then ordered his favorite, the Count Paul, to punish the rebels, but he united with the Jews, took Narbon; yet he had to succumb to the power of the king. He and his associates were condemned, and the Jews banished. In spite of these unfavorable times, the Jews did not neglect their studies, and their cities were celebrated for their Talmudical schools.

THE JEWS IN INDIA.

"After the destruction of the second Temple in the 3828th year of the creation, 3168th of tribulation, and 68th of the Christian era, about 10,000 Jews and Jewesses came to Malabar, and settled themselves at Cananganore, Paloor, Tahdam, and Porlootto. In the year 4139 B. C., and A. D. 379, Cheruman Perumul, Erari Verma, emperor of Malabar, granted to the Jews the honor and privileges which they were to exercise; and which grant was engraved on copperplate, called Champeada, in Malayalim; and thereby appointed Joseph Rabbaan the head of the Jews."

In the deed it is stated, that the sovereign of Malabar, while wielding the sceptre of royalty in a hundred thousand places, granted to the Jews the privileges of using day lamps, of wearing long apparel, of making use of palanquins, umbrellas, copper vessels, trumpets and drums, garlands for the person, and garlands to be suspended over the roads; and relinquished all taxes for these, as well as for houses and synagogues.

The Malabar Jews resided at Cananganore until the arrival of the Portuguese in that quarter; but as that nation inflicted great oppression upon them, they removed to Cochin in the year 1565 of the Christian era, and were hospitably received by the rajah of that place. He granted them permission to build their synagogue and houses next the palace, in order to protect them better; but hither they were followed by the Portuguese, who again treated them with the utmost cruelty and injustice. The arrival of the Dutch, who took possession of Cochin in 1663, relieved them from their sufferings, and since that time they have lived in peace.

In the year 1686, they were visited by four Hebrew merchants from Amsterdam, who rejoiced to find them enjoying a state of prosperity, and agreed to live with them. They wrote an account of their reception to their brethren at Amsterdam, who sent out to them a supply of books of the Law and the Prophets, that were much wanted. Since that time an intimate correspondence has been maintained between the Jews of Cochin and those of Holland. At Amsterdam, a liturgy has been printed expressly for the Israelites of Malabar.

The White Jews never intermarried with their black brethren, and look upon them as an inferior race. The latter have none of the Cohen or Levi family (Priests or Levites) among them, but their rites and ceremonies in a great measure resemble those of the white Jews. Their number has been greatly reduced by various causes, and is stated to be somewhat over 1000. Some time ago, several of the white Jews of Cochin addressed a statement of their condition to a gentleman named Baber, of the Bombay Civil Service, in which they defend themselves from various charges made against them by a recent traveller, and among other things, give the following account of their occupations:

"As for the industry of the Jews, they earn a good livelihood as handicraftsmen, being in general sawyers, fishermen, blacksmiths, bricklayers, tailors, bookbinders, and other artificers, of which number many for want of employment at or about Cochin, travel up the Malabar coast to Bombay to get a subsistence; three-fourths of the Black Jews are vendors of household necessaries."

When Dr. Buchanan, the author of "Christian Researches," visited this interesting people in 1806, he made investigations into the character of the Hebrew manuscripts which they possessed. He discovered, among other remarkable writings a curious version of the New Testament. We shall give an account of it in his own words :—

"I heard that there were one or two translations of the New Testament in their possession, but they were studiously kept out of my sight for a considerable time. At last, however, they were produced by individuals in a private manner. One of them is written in the small rabbinical or Jerusalem character, the other in a large square letter. the history of the former is very interesting. The translator, a very learned Rabbi, conceived the deisign of making an accurate version of the New Testament, for the express purpose of confuting it. His style is copious and elegant, like that of a master in the language, and the translation is in general faithful.* It does not, indeed, appear that he wished to pervert the meaning of a single sentence, but depending on his own abilities and renown as a scholar, he hoped to be able to controvert its doctrines, and to triumph over it by fair contest, in the presence of the world. The translation is complete, and written with greater freedom and ease towards the end, than at the beginning. How astonishing it is that an enemy should have done this! That he should have persevered resolutely to the end of his work; not always, indeed, calmly, for there is sometimes a note of execration on the Sacred Person, who is the subject of it, as if to unburden his mind, and ease the conflict of his laboring soul. At the close of the gospels, as if afraid of the converting power of his own version, he calls heaven to witness that he had undertaken the work with the professed design of opposing Epicureans, by which term he contemptuously designates the Christians." Dr. Buchanan says that in almost every house he found Hebrew books, printed or manuscript, particularly among the White Jews.

THE JEWS IN CHINA.

In all probability this sect took refuge here about the third century of the present era, but not later—coming from India across the northwestern boundary of China. At first they numbered seventy clans, but at present not more than one-tenth of this number exists. They are chiefly located in the centre of Kaifung city and in the vicinity of their Synagogue. A few are shop-keepers, some are peasants; but the majority are sunk in poverty and misery, almost destitute of raiment and shelter—so poor, indeed, that some of the materials of the Synagogue premises have been sold by the professors to supply the wants of their families. Still they retain their distinctness from the surrounding masses of Mohammedans and Pagans, although by the mere name of their religion. Originally they were called followers of the Tienchuh religion, that is "the Indian religion"—Tienchuh being the Chinese name for India—from which country the sect is reported to have come. But, instead of that appellation, they now go by the name T'ian-Kin Kian

—"cutting the sinew sect"—because everything the Jews eat, mutton, fowl or beef, must have the sinews taken out.

The rite of circumcision is still practised on males within one month after birth. Of festivals, one is "for perambulating round the Scriptures;" this is the twenty-fourth of the eight month. Their Sabbath is the European, or our Saturday. They intermarry only among themselves, not with Pagans nor Mohammedans. Nor is it permitted to marry two wives. They are forbidden to eat pork. In the observance of Divine service they have to wash their bodies before entering the Synagogue; and, for this purpose, on each side of the holy place ("as they term it") there is a bath. During service they face the west, in the direction of Jerusalem, or, rather as near that direction as they know. In the performance of sacred worship, the priest at one time used to wear a blue head-dress and blue shoes—hence the name by which Jews have gone in China, "the blue bonnet Moslems." The people are not permitted to enter the temple with their shoes on their feet, nor the women with napkins on their heads, the common head-dress among the Chinese females of Honan province. However, the expectation of the Messiah seems to have been entirely lost. There seems none able to decipher Hebrew writings. Indeed they have begun recently to amalgamate themselves with the myriad Pagans and Mohammedans in the vast population of Kaifung, which must amount to at least one million.

Although the Jews must have entered China so early in the Christian era, it appears that their Synagogue was not built before the close of the twelfth century, or nearly 1,000 years after their entrance. Jewish professors used to call this building, "the temple of Yihsze-lo-hi-uieh," in which, possibly, there was an attempt at expressing the name Israel phonetically; but the inscription over the door at present is "the true and pure temple." According to the accounts brought by the Chinese investigators, the Synagogue itself stands within a third enclosure. Here there is one large hall eighty feet deep and forty feet wide, the roof of which is covered with green tiles. In this stands a seat—"Moses' seat"— about a foot above a wooden floor, where, on grand festive seasons, the Rabbi took his seat under a large red, satin umbrella, held over his head, which is still preserved in the building. Here, too, was a cell for depositing "the twelve tubes containing Heaven's records." During their researches these messengers copied many inscriptions within the Synagogue, and on its various pillars, some in Chinese and a few in Hebrew characters. We transcribe one or two of the latter from their journal, exactly as they are given by themselves, without vouching for their accuracy or making any correction.

Over a tablet in Chinese, similar to what is found in Mohammedan mosques or Budhist temples, with the customary formula—

"May his imperial majesty live forever," &c., there is this inscription: "Hear, O Israel! Jehovah our God is one Jehovah,—Blessed be the name of his glorious kingdom forever and ever." These sentences are repeated in another part. Close to the cell for containing the Scriptures we have this sentence: "Ineffable is his name, for Jehovah is the God of Gods."

Of the Chinese inscriptions, which are very numerous, the following couplet is singular: "The sacred Scriptures consist of fifty-three sections; these we recite by mouth and meditate on, praying that the imperial sway may be firmly established. The letters of the sacred alphabet are twenty-seven; these are taught in our households, in hope that the interests of our country may prosper."

From two long Chinese tablets outside the gateway of the Synagogue, the following extracts were made by the same: "From the beginning of the world our first father Adam handed down the doctrine to Abraham; Abraham handed it down to Isaac; Isaac handed it down to Jacob; Jacob handed it down to the twelve patriarchs; and the twelve patriarchs handed it down to Moses; Moses handed it down to Aaron; Aaron handed it down to Joshua; and Joshua handed it down to Ezra, by whom the doctrines of the holy religion were first sent abroad, and the letters of the Jewish religion first made plain." The founder of this religion is Abraham, who is considered the first teacher of it. Then came Moses, who established the law and handed down the sacred writings. After his time, during the Han dynasty, this religion entered China."

THE SECT OF THE CHASIDIM, IN THE NORTH OF EUROPE.

The Khasidim, or "The Righteous," are widely spread in several parts of Russia and Poland. The principal Rabbi then was called Rabbi Bar, a son of the great Rabbi Solomon, of Laddi, whose fame had spread throughout Russia. Their mode of worship differs from that of all other Jews. The Chasidim being very strict in their discipline, call other Jews Oulamshe, or worldly men, otherwise Mithnagdim, or Protestors, who look upon the Chasidim with the same contempt as they do upon baptized Jews. They are very careful to prevent their children coming under the instruction of the Chasidim; and if a son of theirs goes secretly over to them, he will not be received again by his father when he returns. Great division often arise in families on this account; divorces between man and wife occur. The opposite parties carry their animosity so far that neither will eat of butcher's meat killed by the other—nor would a Chasid be allowed to be interred in the burial ground of the other party. But, now, being more spread and better known, their animosity has subsided, and they are not so much disliked, and other Jews do intermarry with them. They neglect much the study of the Talmud. The books which they study most are the "Zohar Hakadosh," *i. e.*, the holy Zohar (shining light), written by the great Rabbi Shimoun ben Yachai, and by his son, Rabbi Elizer; and other cabalistical books; also sermons, or lectures, by the modern Rabbis of the Chasidim. They have small places of worship, called Bethhamidrashs. The Chasidim, in their worship, are very noisy, and fond of singing, clapping hands and jumping, in order to banish wordly thoughts. The more pious of them continue their prayers from six in the morning to three in the afternoon, when they take both breakfast and dinner at once, for no Jew will taste anything before his morning prayers, except, when delicate in health, a single cup of tea or coffee. They return to afternoon and evening prayers, in which they are engaged till midnight. Before morning prayer, they go to the Mikvah, or well of purification, both in summer and winter; and some also attend to their ablution, before their afternoon prayers.

Previous to prayer, they employ half an hour or an hour in meditation; some walk about in silent thought; some are singing in an undertone; others are smoking their pipes while thus engaged. When the reader feels prepared in his mind, he begins prayer, and is joined by that part of the congregation that may be in readiness to enter upon their devotions. Some, for the sake of greater privacy, retire to a private room, called the "Meditation Room," for they say they would rather not pray at all than come hastily before the Lord, not perceiving clearly in their minds whom they are about to address, and for what they are about to ask. They say, prayer without the mind is like the body without the soul. And, indeed, this is a great rule laid down by the Rabbis; and you find in every Synagogue the following inscription on the front of the reading desk, in bold letters, "Know before whom thou standest."

The grand principle of their system is unity and brotherly love. They address each other in familiar language, like the Friends, except when speaking to the Rabbi. Their chief aim is to abolish self, which they call "bitul hayesh," so that none should think of himself, or use the phrase "I am" of himself, but to know that Jehovah only is the great "I am."

They do not speak to, or look upon, strange women, and as little as possible to their own wives. They avoid females in the road; and should their way be intercepted by a crowd of women, they wait for their dispersion. They carefully banish melancholy, because, they say it comes from the "evil one," and in cabalistic language is called "sitera ochra," the opposite part.

They are very liberal, constantly go about to do good; and visit the fatherless and widows. They come from a great distance to hear the Rabbis, who lecture every evening. They take a text out of the Scriptures, which they explain in a cabalistical manner, and give the spiritual meaning of it.

When the Rabbi has gone up to the pulpit, he sits in a posture of meditation, his head leaning upon his hand; he beckons to the people to commence singing, when instantly the whole congregation join in singing a hymn, in which two or three thousand voices often unite. They continue to sing, some with and some without words, until the spirit of the Rabbi is revived, when a sign is given by him, and they stop in deep silence and close attention. The sermon frequently lasts two or three hours. As soon as the Rabbi leaves the pulpit, the whole congregation is broken up in small companies of fifteen or twenty in each group. Clever young men are appointed to repeat the sermon to these companies, while others write down the whole.

In every small town or village where the Chasidim are, there is a *mechozir*, or "repeater," who is sent twice a year to the Rabbi to be further instructed in the doctrines of the Chasidim. Every Chasid is bound to visit the Rabbi at least once in three years, and to take advice from him in spiritual matters, the Chasid's real motive for going to the Rabbi, is to have the benefit of his counsel amidst the difficulties and obstacles that he may meet in his spiritual course, and learn how to overcome any besetting sin. The Rabbi questions him as to his mode of life, habits and bodily constitution, and then tells how many days he should fast, and the nights he should watch and pray, and points out suitable Psalms. There are certain hours appointed for communicating with the Rabbi, when each person enters his room, and has a private interview. They, however, do not confess as the Papists do to their priests.

THE JEWS IN HUNGARY.

During the reign of that ultra-popish, priest-ridden empress, Maria Theresa, on the Austrian throne, Hungary became—to use an expression of the Jews, the "city of refuge" to the Jewish inhabitants of the provinces of that empire. Very few, therefore, of the present Jewish citizens in the land of the Magyars can trace their Hungarian origin higher up than to the fourth generation. Though the Jews were very much oppressed and despised in Hungary till recently, and particularly in cities where the German element prevailed; and, though they were subjected to many restrictions and wrongs, as, for instance, if a nobleman killed a Jew, his penalty was to pay a fine of thirty florins—about $5—still, their condition might be considered a princely life, if compared with that of their brethren in the rest of the Austrian Empire.

The Jewish population in Hungary, therefore, is a conglomeration of German, Bohemian, Moravian, and Polish fugitives, who there found shelter from the thievish officials of the wicked government, and are, with the exception of those features and peculiarities common to the Jewish race wherever it is, different in character and in degree of civilization. There are highly educated men among the Jews in Hungary, distinguished as physicians, merchants, mechanics and agriculturists, and there would have been others in many other branches had they been permitted to practise them. They are in general a hospitable, kind-hearted and liberal people; a missionary, therefore, may not only fearlessly travel through the length and breadth of the land, but may be sure of a friendly reception on the part of the Jews.

Number.—The number of Jews in Hungary is estimated at 500,000, and we think it is not exaggerated. Countrymen, recently arrived, state that, in the city of Pesth alone, there are nearly thirty thousand souls of the Jewish persuasion. Next to Pesth, in respect to numbers, are Old-Buda and Presburg.

Occupation.—Most of the Hungarian Jews are engaged in mercantile business, some branches of which are exclusively in their hands. In other branches, as, for instance, the retailing of dry goods and small wares, they have but few and feeble competitors, in the Greeks, and Armenians, who are gradually disappearing, as they are not as skilful as their Jewish neighbors. About thirty years ago the retail business of Pesth was exclusively in the hands of the Greeks, the Jews not being permitted to open a store of that kind. The Greeks, proud of their privileges of monopoly, took such high percentage, that their customers rather waited for a Jewish pedlar, or for the weekly fair, when the Jews were allowed to sell their goods in little booths or tents. It has always been the policy of the Jews to sell at very low profits, thus exchanging their capital ten times and oftener before the proud Greek merchant could once. After the Jews obtained the privilege to open retail stores in the city of Pesth, the Greeks waned gradually away, so that, at present, there are very few, if any at all. Since 1836 a goodly number have engaged in mechanical trades of various kinds; particularly as tailors, shoemakers, turners, fringe-makers, silver, gold, and tin smiths, watch and clock makers, &c., and a few in agriculture. There are no Jewish paupers in Hungary, and very few, and these in the greater congregations only, who need the support of their wealthier brethren.

Education.—Till within a few years, the Jewish schools in Hungary were in a deplorable condition. The cheder system was the general one, and regular normal schools were the exceptions, and only found in Pesth and a few other prominent places. The literal meaning of the word "cheder" is "a room," but, in the Jewish jargon, it was understood to mean "a school-room." Imagine a small, low and damp room, with such a floor as mother earth gives it; two boards, nailed upon four poles, which are rammed in the ground, for tables; some benches of the same material as seats, and a wooden chair for the "Rabbi," or teacher, and you have the faithful picture of a "cheder." Then imagine a man, with unkempt hair and beard, holding a large rod constantly in his hand; some ragged books, and a dozen or two ragged, barefooted children around the table, and you have the picture of a cheder, when in operation. The more surprising, therefore, is it that so many great men, great in the literary world, were, at least in their early days, pupils of such teachers, attendants of such cheders. M. Saphir, the celebrated humorist in Vienna, and his brother, A. Saphir, the distinguished superintendent of schools in Pesth, both of them received their early education in a cheder; and the former not seldom amused emperors and kings, with anecdotes and experiences from the cheder. To the honor of the present Emperor of Austria we must say, that after he took possession of Hungary as an Austrian province, normal and high schools were everywhere established, and put under government supervision, and are now in a flourishing condition.

Religion.—The great bulk of the Hungarian Jews are orthodox, or of the Rabbinic school, but by far more moderate in their own practice, and more liberal towards other religionists, than their neighbors in Poland and Moravia.

THE ESSENEES.

They resided for the most part on the borders of the Dead Sea, and were a kind of Jewish monks, who led a quiet life, almost monastic and ascetic. They hated luxury, and so abhorred covetousness and selfishness, that they introduced community of property. Their principal religious doctrines were: Unity of God, immortality of the soul, purification after death, and eternal reward or punishment. Their principal moral doctrine was, Love; love to God, to our fellowmen and to virtue. They advocated celibacy, and were allowed to take an oath only when initiated into the society. The novice received an axe, an apron and a white dress—emblems of industry and cleanliness. The society was organized into three different degrees. Into as many classes they divided their schools and their officers. This sect, composed only of men who abhorred all worldly enjoyment, numbered a great many members, not only in Judea, but in other countries, especially in Egypt. It is true, their doctrines were excellent; but their scrupulous abstinence, their strict seclusion, their philosophy on the creation, their mystical doctrines of the spirits, and the communion those latter hold with men, led them to an arrogant self-admiration, and the less gifted members to believe in miracles. Enjoying the reputation of performing wonders, they exercised the most pernicious influence over the superstitious people. When the Academy of Tiberias was destroyed in 360, this sect became extinct.

THE HELLENISTS,

That means, Jews speaking the Greek language. So were called the Jews living out of Palestine who had adopted the language and manners of the Greeks, and the doctrines of oriental philosophy, as far as regards the ideas of God and creation. The founder of this class was Onias, son of Onias III. Disappointed in his pretensions of being elected as High Priest—which office had been given to Alcymus—he went into Egypt. The King appointed him and another youth, Dositheus, commanders-in-chief of the Egyptian army. After the pattern of the temple in Jerusalem, only in a reduced scale, Onias then built a temple in Leontopolis, where, without resigning his command, he officiated as High Priest. His followers were Hellenists, who differed in many a religious point from the Jews in Palestine. They thought little of traditional Judaism; they read the Bible, but in the Greek language, explaining it in an allegorical manner. The dry study of the ceremonial law could not satisfy mind and heart; political oppression directed the hope of the people to a transcendental and happier order of affairs; and hence originated, at this time, the cultivation of the *Kabbalah*. This science was, in the beginning, a system of mystic ideas, involving the highest questions of transcendental philosophy, founded on the most arbitrary reading of the Bible. This exegesis degraded the Kabbalah to a superstitious mixture of explanations, computations, and mysterious use of signs, certain words and letters, by virtue of which hidden powers or problems could be discovered and made subservient to the will of man. There exists a great analogy between the doctrines of the Kabbalah and those of some religious sects in Persia—a great resemblance on the part of the former to the Zend-Aresta, the Persian Bible—for, since the Babylonian captivity, the Jews had remained in continual intercourse with their old masters. Hence, it may be inferred that the Kabbalah originated with the religion of the Persians, which was changed so far as to adapt it to the mind of the Jewish people, and that many Jewish customs, introduced by the Kabbalah, were of Persian origin. So, for instance, the custom of looking at the point of the fingers on the evening of the Sabbath. The Persian dare not leave his bed in the morning, nor walk four steps, without having put on the holy girdle, the Kosti, believing that during the night he had been defiled by the touch of some evil spirit; he dare not touch any part of his body without washing his face and hands three times in succession. We find such regulations in the Rabbinical law, founded upon similar suppositions.

We find in the Persian Liturgy, prayers to be recited before and after casing nature, &c., &c.; such prayers are found also in the Jewish prayer-book. But, more clearly still can we ascribe to the Persian influence all the vestiges of superstition and fear of evil spirits in which the Kabbalah and the Talmud abound. The Kabbalah assigns to the evil spirits the power of injuring man's soul and body. Man is scarcely born before these monsters await already on the cradle to snatch them away from God and his mother. They surround man with all kinds of dangers, frighten him with the most hideous apparitions, and trouble him even in the hour of death. Has he escaped them in this fatal hour, by virtue of his moral excellence, then ensues the trial in the grave. They will break the sinner's bones, and torture him in the most agonizing manner. This belief of some old Rabbins in the power of evil spirits, is of Persian origin. The Bible strictly forbids it, and common sense ridicules it.

PHARISEES.

They distinguished themselves by their holiness, by a scrupulous practice of a host of ceremonies, and by a life full of resignation. They adhered strictly to the Bible and oral traditions, which they believed were also given to Moses on Mount Sinai. They cared less for the letter of the Bible than for its spirit; and tried, by means of lectures, adapted to the mind of the people, to make it the common property of all. They adopted the most liberal views of those doctrines of the Bible which clashed with the requirements of the time; softened the rigor of criminal proceedings, and asserted that every sublime thought found in literature was borrowed from the Bible.

They advocated a sober, reasoning and unprejudiced faith. They were in favor of all the foreign customs which the people, in course of time, had become accustomed to; and as the members of the supreme court were of their party, they exercised an immense influence over the divine service and the hearts of the people; the more so as their religious life commanded universal regard, and they themselves willingly submitted to what they ordered the masses to do.

Some of them who, pursuing selfish interests, secretly led a life of vice and lust, were exposed and sharply criticised by the Pharisees themselves. They mention six different classes of such hypocrites: 1st, פרוש שכמי, those who make a great ado about the observance of the law; 2nd, פרוש נקפי, the sycophants; 3rd, פרוש קיזאי, those who atone for the sin of to-day by repentance to-morrow; 4th, פרוש מדוכיא the hypocritical devotees; 5th, מדוש מה חובתי ואעשנה those who make but a pretence of fulfilling their duties; and 6th, פרוש מיראה, those who perform the divine commands from mere fear of punishment.

As the Sadducees on the one hand, made nothing of traditions at all, so the Pharisees, on the other hand, did make exceedingly too much, separating and singling themselves in a more strict course of ceremonious devotion, from other people. The Jews write their name, ' Pharish' and 'Parushim' with a in the second syllable. But the Greek of the New Testament and Josephus, as also the Syriac and Arabic, read it with i ' Pharish'; suitable to the Chaldee and Syriac language, which was then spoken.

The Talmud nameth seven kinds of Pharisees:—1. The Shechemite Pharisee, that doeth like the Shechemites, who circumcised themselves, not for the commandments sake, but for advantage. 2. The dashing or stumbling Pharisee, that avoids thrusting upon men in the way; and dashes his feet against the stones; "he went along at such a demure and grave pace, that he would not lift up his feet from the ground, but dashed and stumbled against every stone that lay in his way." 3. The Phlebotomizing Pharisee; he, as he went, would thrust up to the wall, lest he trouble the passengers that went and came; "so hard, that he would dash his face against the wall and draw blood." 4. The Pestle Pharisee, that wrapped his coat about his hand and kept off himself from touching any man lest he should be defiled, using his hand muffled in his clothes, as it were a pestal to drive off men from him. 5. The Supererogation Pharisee, that said, "What is my duty, and I will do it, and to spare? show me my transgression, and I will amend it," as meaning that there is no man that can show wherein ever I have transgressed. 6. Another dashing Pharisee, that went bending double in show of humility; and winked as he went, and dashed his feet against stones, but his heart was naught. He drew blood by dashing against walls, seeming to be very humble; and for the abundance of his humility, he would not look about him as he went, but dashed his arms and shoulders against walls, and drew blood; and all this, not in the fear of God, but to deceive men. 7. The Pharisee of love; that became a Pharisee for the love of men, or for the love of God.

THE SADDUCEES.

The chief of this sect was *Zadak*, who, with Boethus, were pupils of Antigonus, the president of the Supreme Court. They did not understand the sublime saying of their teacher: "Be not like servants who serve their master for the sake of their wages" (reward)—but misconstrued this maxim by teaching that there was neither a reward nor punishment hereafter, nor any future life at all. They adhered *but* to the written law, rejected every ordinance that was not contained therein; differed from the Perashim in the practice of the religious ceremonies—and asserted that besides God there were neither spirits, nor angels, nor devils; neither a resurrection, nor an immortality, or future reward. They maintained that good ought to be done on account of its intrinsic value, and the bad repudiated for its vileness. Therefore, they administered the law with rigid cruelty, and passed sentences of death without any hesitation: as for the rest, they advocated the enjoyment of life in all its pleasures. They were few, but still ranked amongst the most wealthy of the Israelites. At first they formed but a political party, with the intention of opposing the government of the Pharisees; but they soon became their religious antagonists, and the authors of civil wars and other national calamities.

The Sadducees were addicted to a ceremonious religion, as well as the Pharisees, though in all things they did not go so far, and in some things they went not always alike.

They used phylacteries as well as the Pharisees, but they did not wear them after the same fashion. Sometimes one of the priests administered the service at the Temple, after the way of the Sadducees, different from the ordinary way; but such (as the Jerusalem Talmud relates) died strange deaths. They would own none of the ceremonies they used as derived from tradition, but (as they pretended) deduced in all points from Moses' text. For they acknowledged nothing but what was written; they joined in many things with the traditional ceremonies, but scorned to receive them from tradition, but would try to find grounds for them in the text.

THE DIVISION AND DISTINCTION OF THE LEARNED OF THE NATION.

The first and general division of the nation into learned and unlearned, men bred up in the study of the law, and men that were not, took place long before the Christian era. The learned of the nation, which were called "the wise" and "the scholars," or "diciples of the wise," were parted, and even crumbled, into many sub-divisions: Scribes, Pharisees, Sadducees, Herodians, mentioned in Scripture—and Essences, Chasidim, Jechidim, Zelobä, in Jewish writers. Now, the reason of this their division, was in regard of some of them holding to, and others of them warping from, the national and state religion; some more, some less, some one way, some another. For if their own authors did not tell, reason itself and common sense would do it. The national and state religion of the Jews in the times of Christ, was a religion, however much pretexted to the Scriptures for their rule, yet lay, in a manner, all in traditions, which they not only valued above the Scriptures, but, by them, they made the Scriptures of no effect at all. Their traditions were twofold; either those that they called and accounted הלכה למשה מסיני "an unwritten law given to Moses at Sinai," and handed by tradition from generation to generation; or the practical glosses and canons, which were made upon that unwritten and traditional law, in the several generations as they passed; both these were called the traditions of the fathers and of the elders. The deliverers of the unwritten law (which they say, came directly from Moses) they will name you, as directly from generation to generation, as the Papists will name you popes successively from Peter. "Moses (say they) received this traditional law from Sinai, and delivered it to Joshua, Joshua to the elders, the elders to the prophets, and the prophets to Ezra's great Synagogue." After the return of the captivity, they derive its pedigree thus: "Simeon the Just received it from Ezra; Antigonus of Soco, from Simeon; Jodes, the son of Joezer of Zeredah, and Joseph the son of Johanan of Jerusalem, received it from Antigonus; Joshua, the son of Perekiah, and Mittai, the Arbelite, received it from them; Judah, the son of Tabbia, and Simeon, the son of Shetah, received it from Joshua and Mittai; Shemiah and Abtalion received it from Judah and Simeon; Hillel and Shammai from them; Rabban Simeon, the son of Hillel, and Rabban Jochanan Ben Zaccai received it from Hillel and Shammai; Rabban Gamaliel, called the Old (Paul's master) received it from Rabban Simeon, his father; Rabban Simeon, the son of Gamaliel, received it from Gamaliel (he was slain at the destruction of the temple); after him was his son Rabban Gamaliel, of Jabneh, who received it from his father; and after him was Rabban Jochanan Ben Zaccai, who had received it from Hillel and Shammai, &c.

This is the tradition concerning the descent and conveyance of the traditional law, of which persons, and of which law, these two things are to be taken notice of:—1st. That all those, that are named single in this succession, were the heads or presidents of the Sanhedrins, and where they are named double, or (זוגות) "pairs," the first-named of the two was "Nasi," or president, and the second named was "Ab beth din," or vice-president. 2nd. That this cabala, or traditional law, whose conveyance they thus pretended from Moses, might not be disputed, as concerning the truth or certainty of it, though it received in every generation some illustration and practical gloss for the laying out of its latitude and extent.

They that fixed these positive practical senses upon it, were the elders of the great Sanhedrim, concluding thereupon in the council, and commenting this traditional law into particular laws and ordinances, as rules to the nation whereby to walk; and the Sanhedrim of every generation was adding something in this kind or other. And so they held, "That the great Sanhedrim at Jerusalem was the foundation of the traditional law, and pillars of instruction, and from them decrees and judgments went out unto all Israel; and whosoever believed Moses, and his law, was bound to rest and lean upon them for the matters of the law.

Now, the way or manner of their legislative determining upon this unwritten law, was thus:—1. The general rule by which they went to work, was עשה כיג לתורה to make a hedge to the law, that men should not break in upon it, to transgress it. And this was a special ground and rise, and a specious color, for all their traditions; for they, pretending to make constitutions to fence the law from violation, and to raise the observance of it the higher, they brought in inventions and fancies of their own brains for laws; and so made the law, indeed, nothing worth. Take a pattern of one or two of their hedges, that they made to this purpose. The written law forbade "Thou shalt not seethe the kid in her mother's milk." Now, to make sure, as they pretended, that this should not be broken in upon, they fenced it with this tradition, " Thou shalt not seethe any flesh whatsoever in any milk whatsoever." All things that were appointed to be eaten the same day, the command taught till the dawn of the next morning; if so, why do the wise men say but till midnight? Namely, to keep men far enough from transgressing.

And such another hedge they made to the times, in that story that is mentioned by Tanchumah: "A man, in the time of the persecution, in the days of the Greeks, rode upon a horse upon a Sabbath-day; and they brought him before the Sanhedrim, and they stoned him, not because it was fit to do so, but, because of the times, it was necessary to do so."

2. This then, being the ground upon which they went to work (with an aim to this hedge, as they pretended in all their constitutions), they hammered their cabala, or unwritten law, into these three parts, or forms: הנהגות גזירות תכנות constitutions, decrees and customs, or practices. They were (in a few words) laws, which they hewed out of their cabala, enjoining some things to be done, or forbidding others, or prescribing the manner of doing. We shall take up one example or two to this purpose: " It is a command to pray every day, as it said, Ye shall serve the Lord your God. They learned by tradition, that this service is prayer, because it is said, Ye shall serve him with all your heart. The wise men say, What service is that, that is with the heart? It is prayer. Now there is no number of prayers appointed by the law, nor no fixed time for prayer set down in the law;" that is, no mention of persons tied to it.

Therefore, the Sanhedrim, in several generations, made canons and constitutions to decide and determine upon all these particulars, as their own reason and emergencies did lead them and give occasion. As in one generation they prescribed such and such times for morning and evening prayer. In process of time, they found these times allotted to be too straight; therefore, the Sanhedrim of another generation did give enlargement as they thought good. And so concerning the number of prayers to be said daily, one Sanhedrim appointed so many. But time and experience found afterward, that these did not answer such or such an occasion, as, it seems, was not observed when they were appointed; therefore the Sanhedrim of another generation thought good to add more and more still, as occasions, unobserved before, did emerge; and so the number of their daily prayers grew at last to be eighteen. And in the days of Rabban Gamaliel, heretics increased in Israel (meaning those that, from Judaism, turned to Christianity), and they vexed Israel and persuaded them to turn from their religion. He, seeing this to be a matter of more import than anything else, stood up, he and his Sanhedrim, and appointed another prayer, in which there was a petition to God to destroy those heretics; and this he set among the prayers, and ordained it to be in every one's mouth; and so all the daily prayers were nineteen.

Thus was the state religion of the Jews, and thus stated and settled. The ground-work was pretended traditions from Moses, expounding the written law, delivered from hand to hand in the Sanhedrims of several congregations; the superstructure was legislative, and practical senses made hereupon, and determined for the use of the people by the Sanhedrim. Now, they that had to deal in these determinations, were called "the Scribes;" and those were divided into four ranks:—

1. The "Nasi," and "Ab beth din," that is "President" and "Vice-President," who were the special treasurers of the Cabala; which, they pretended, did descend from Moses.

2. The whole Sanhedrim itself, which made their canons and constitutions out of this Cabala, and did impose them upon the people.

3. Those men of the Sanhedrim or others that kept divinity schools, and read public lectures in explication of these traditions, as Hillel, Shammai, Gamaliel, Tyrannus, or Turnus; and

4. Those that expounded these laws, as the public preachers in their synagogues.

THE CARAITES.

The Caraites are such strict observers of the law which prohibits the manufacture of any image for worship, that they do not, even in their houses, tolerate any statue, or any other figure in relief. During prayer in the Synagogue, they are wrapped in their praying scarfs, but have repudiated altogether the use of phylacteries. This appears very inconsistent, for the praying scarf, as at present used by the Rabbinical Jews, are clearly a Rabbinical institution, whilst the use of the phylacteries is enjoined in the Pentateuch. In their prayers they are exceedingly devout, always turning their faces towards Jerusalem. In their devotions they kneel down, an attitude which the Rabbinites have discarded, except on solemn holidays, ever since the destruction of the Temple, as only befitting that glorious sanctuary, to which alone a symbol of the divine presence—the shekinah—was vouchsafed. The Caraites also unscrupulously pronounce the ineffable name of God.

His name they also spell somewhat different from the other Jews; their writing it with two jods and a var. Their Sabbath prayers are exceedingly long, and they stay, therefore, in synagogue till four o'clock in the afternoon.

Their festivals coincide with those of the other Jews; but they are celebrated by the Caraites in a different manner. Thus, for instance, formerly no Caraite was seen on holidays in the streets. They shut themselves up in their homes, which they did not quit, except for religious purposes. They thus literally kept the commandment, "Ye shall not go forth from your place on the Sabbath day." The Sabbath eve they spent in an extraordinary manner. Interpreting the law literally, not a light was seen in the house of the Caraites on the Sabbath. The Sabbath eves they passed in darkness. They walked about in their homes, groping along like the blind. In winter they shivered the whole day, but not a spark of fire was seen in their dwellings. However, those who resided in Poland and Lithuania were, at least in this respect, compelled by necessity to yield, and to adopt the Rabbinical interpretation of the law. So intense is the cold in the winter in these regions, that the absence of fire for twenty-four hours is dangerous to life. Nor are the Caraites quite consistent in their literal interpretation of the law. Thus, the command of blowing the cornet on the new year is distinct enough, yet the Caraites do not observe it, stating that it was only to be complied with whilst the Jews were in possession of their own land. By a similar mode of interpretation, the citron and palm branch are not, on the Feast of Tabernacles, carried to the synagogue, but placed in the tabernacles. They do not celebrate the feast of *chanuka*, as not being mentioned in the Bible.

Their morals are exceedingly pure, (their strict integrity gained them the respect of the government under which they lived. This fact, as also discarding a legion of Rabbinical notions, which rendered the Rabbinate obnoxious to the Barbaro-Christian population around them, secured the Caraites from those persecutions which their brethren, the Rabbinate, had to suffer elsewhere.)

In marriage laws they go beyond the text of the Bible, applying to them an interpretation of their own, whereby the circle of matrimonial choice becomes very restricted indeed. The young Caraite has often to go to a very distant place to find a bride not coming within the degree of prohibited affinity. A strange custom among the Caraites is the occasional dedication by parents of their children, as *Nazarites*, to the Lord. The hair of such children is not cut, nor are these permitted to drink any wine, or, in fact, to transgress any of the laws prescribed for the observance of the *Nazarites*. In this state such children are kept for seven years. On the anniversary of the eighth, they are taken to the synagogue, and there, for the first time in their lives, the hair of their head falls under the operation of the scissors, and a cup of wine is given to them to drink. They now are like every other Caraite, and all their deprivations cease. There are some, however, who submit the whole of their lives to the abstinence of a Nazarite.

As many of the animals declared to be unlawful to be eaten, are only known from Rabbinical tradition, rejected by the Caraites, they abstain from eating the flesh of several, especially birds; they are partaken of by Rabbinical Jews. For the same reason they carefully avoid eating the blood of fish, from which a Rabbinical Jew does not abstain. They are, however, divided in reference to the lawfulness of eating flesh boiled in or with milk. Some, like the Rabbinical Jews, consider it forbidden, while others are of a contrary opinion.

A melancholy spectacle is presented by their funeral processions. They adhere to the letter of the Bible, which declares a dead body impure; the body of the beloved departed is carried to the last resting place by paid persons of another creed. Around, and by the side of the coffin, walk the family and friends of the deceased, but they are scrupulously careful not to draw nigh. The touching of a corpse would, in their belief, render them unclean, and contaminate them. What is strange is, that these deniers of all tradition should scrupulously observe the laws referring to the killing of animals slain, to be eaten by Israelites, as the Rabbinical Jews themselves, although most of their rites rest only on Rabbinical traditions. In these rites there is to be discovered a trace of the belief of some, at least, of their doctors in the transmigration of the soul. For one of these doctors teaches, that the killer, whilst performing his functions, should pray in his heart that the Lord should grant the animal a happy transmigration, in recompense for the sufferings undergone.

CHRISTIAN JEWISH SECTS IN RUSSIA.

Towards the close of the 18th century, the so-called Jewish sect produced a great stir in the Russian Church. Its origin is ascribed to a Jew named Zacharias, who is described as an astrologer and necromancer, and who came from Poland to Novgorod, about the year 1470. He began to teach secretly that the only divine law was that of Moses; that the Messiah was still to come; and that the worship of images was a sin. He made his first converts among clergymen and their families, who became so zealous in their new persuasion that they desired to receive circumcision. But Zacharias persuaded them not to discover by such an act their real sentiments, and to conform outwardly to the Christian religion. The clergymen strictly followed this prudent advice. The number of proselytes considerably increased, chiefly among the clergy and some principal families of the town. These sectarians covered their real opinions with such a display of zeal in the rigid observance of the precepts of the Church, that they acquired a great reputation for sanctity. Two of them, Alexis and Dionysius, were accordingly transferred to Moscow, in 1480, by the Grand Duke, Ivan Vaalorich, as priests to two of the principal churches of the capital. Alexis advanced high in the favor of that monarch, to whom he had free access, which was a rare distinction. This circumstance gave him great facilities for propagating his opinions, and he made many proselytes; the principal of them were the secretary of the Grand Duke, Theodore Kuritzin, who was employed on several diplomatic missions, and Zosimas, the Archimandarite of the convent of St. Simon, whom the Grand-Duke, on the recommendation of the same Alexis, raised to the dignity of Metropolitan of Moscow.

Alexis died in 1489, and it was only after his death that his opinions became known. The Grand Duke then declared that he remembered some very strange mysterious words of Alexis. It is also said that he confessed that his daughter-in-law, Helena, daughter of Stephen the Great, Prince of Wallachia, was seduced to the Jewish sect by a disciple of Alexis. The existence of this sect was discovered by Gennadius, Archbishop of Novgorod, who sent to Moscow several priests accused of having insulted the cross and the images of the saints, of having blasphemed against Christ and the Virgin, and denied the resurrection of the dead. A synod was assembled at Moscow, in 1490, in order to try these heretics. The Metropolitan, Zosimus, presided, whose participation in their tenets was not then discovered. The accused denied the charge, but sufficient evidence was brought forward to prove the fact. The bishops wished to punish the heretics severely, but the Grand Duke opposed them, and declared that they should only be anathematized and imprisoned.

Theodore Kuritzin, and other adherents of the sect, continued to propagate its doctrines, and to increase the number of its followers, particularly in teaching astrology.

This began to spread a spirit of doubt and inquiry among many people—the clergy and laymen were constantly disputing about the dogmas of religion. The sectarians were protected by the Metropolitan, Zosimus, who is accused of having persecuted the orthodox clergy.

The details about this sect are contained in a work by Joseph, Legumenos, or Abbot, of the Convent Volokolainsk, who died in 1516, and who was the most zealous adversary of this sect. Zosimus resigned his dignity in 1494, and retired into a convent. The persecution ceased for some time in Moscow, but the Archbishop of Novgorod continued it in his district, whence many sectarians fled to Poland and Germany. In 1503, the representatives of the clergy who were supported by this Joseph, induced the Grand Duke to issue an order for the trial of these heretics. They were tried before an ecclesiastical court, of which Joseph was a member and the chief accuser. The heretics acknowledged their opinions, and maintained them to be true. They were condemned, and some of them publicly burnt, others had their tongues cut off, and many were shut up in prisons and convents. Nothing more has been heard of the sect since the date of 1503, but there now exists among the Roskolniks of Russia a sect which observes the Mosaic rites, and it is very probable that it is derived from the sect which we have described.

In several parts of Poland, Turkey, and in the Russian government of Tula, there are followers of Jelesnewshcheena. The origin of this appellation is unknown, and it is probably derived from the name of their founder, or some leading member. Although Russians by origin and language, they strictly observe the Mosaic law, perform circumcision, keep the Sabbath on Saturdays, and abuse the Christian religion. It may be that they are the descendants of that Jewish sect which appeared at Novgorod and Moscow at the close of the fifteenth century.

JEHUD CHEBER.

The Jehud Cheber are the descendants of Jethro, or Cheber, the Kenite, the father-in-law of Moses, the servant of God. In 1 Chron. ii,

55, and in Jer. xxxv, 58, 59, they are called the "sons of Rechab," or Rechabites, who according to the command of their father, abstained from wine and strong drink, from dwelling in permanent houses, and from tilling the ground. This tribe is still in existence, although they live isolated, anxiously avoiding to be known as Jehuds, and particularly disliking to hold intercourse with Jews.

The bulk of that powerful tribe live in Arabia, near the eastern shores of the Red Sea, and engaged in no other business but that of raising cattle. In the district of Junbua, a seaport on the eastern shore of the Red Sea, there are some of them engaged as blacksmiths and traders with other Arabs; that is, to exchange their produce for other articles. The other Arab tribes call the Jehud Cheber "Arab Sab'th," which signifies, Arabs who keep the Sabbath holy, and are not only estimated as very honest people, but feared also as strong and almost giant-like men. They speak, it is said, the Arabic and Hebrew languages, but will have nothing to do with Jews; and if they are ever met by such and recognized, they deny their origin, and say that they are only Arabs. In their intercourse with the latter, they are very careful not to touch them; they keep, therefore, always at a distance from them, and never eat anything offered by them. They always appear on horse-back and armed to the teeth.

Persons who have had opportunities to observe them, say that they have seen zitzith (fringes) on their garments.

During the reign of Ibrahim Pascha, when it was quite safe to travel in those wild regions, two Jewish tinsmiths undertook a journey among the Arabs to find work. They left Safet with their working tools, and passed the Jordan in a south-east direction towards the Hauran. They found plenty of work, and being strictly orthodox, lived on bread, milk and honey, having their table at some distance from that of the Arabs.

After several weeks, some Arabs from the south came to the place where these two Jews labored at their business. At dinner, they asked the host who these men were who sat separately? They were told that they were "Jehuds." The strangers laughed heartily at this information. "What!" they cried "these dwarfs Jehuds?" We know many of them; they are a powerful giant-like tribe." It was, however, explained to them that there were other Jehuds besides the "Jehud Seb'th."

From time to time some Jehud Cheber made their appearance in Palestine, and even in Jerusalem; but they always anxiously avoid publicity and recognition. The reason for their doing so remains as yet inexplicable. It is certain, however, that they live according to the law of Moses, and are not entirely unacquainted with the heroes of the Rabbinical school. Some years ago, two German Jews from Jerusalem went down to Tiberiah, to visit the sepulchre of R. Akiba. After they had performed their devotional exercises, and stepped outside of the cave, two stately Arabs on horseback passed by, and asked "What Tzaddick (pious or righteous) rests in this cave?" The Jews answered, "Rabbi Akiba." The men immediately alighted and went into the cave; and after a while the Jews heard them to their great astonishment, pray in pure Hebrew. They waited until they finished and came out, and then asked the men, whom they supposed to be Arabs, who they were? They received in reply, "We are Jehud Cheber; but we conjure you by the name of the God of Israel to speak to no man about us, until we are beyond reach." They then disappeared, on their swift animals.

It is known, however, that this tribe lives under the government of a chief, whom they call Melek-King. This became known by the following circumstances:—About thirty years ago, the Sultan of Zannah intended to fulfil the duty of a pilgrimage to the holy city Mecca. Being afraid to go by sea, as usual, he made up his mind to cross the desert. Well provided with all possible necessaries, and a sufficient number of armed men, he started on his journey; but their guides soon lost their way, and after wandering about for several days, they began to suffer for want of provisions, and particularly water. After another day or two, almost dying of thirst and exhaustion, the travelers discovered a fine oasis, and a large city of white tents on its shores. Not doubting one moment to find there a tribe of Arabs, they rushed forward to a large and beautiful tent, and cried out, "Water, brethern, water, or else we die." At this strange noise, a tall and stout Arab stepped out from the tent, and cried, "Keleb! (dog) who dares to make such a noise in the hour of prayer?" The pilgrims told, in a few words, who they were, and how they came there, and that they were exhausted to death, and repeated their supplications for water. The Arab told them that the tent was that of their Melek-King, and that they were just congregated to perform the evening prayer. They were permitted to look into the tent, and saw a large congregation of stately men, engaged in silent devotion. The pilgrims were immediately provided with water and food, and some tents to rest in; and after they had recovered from fatigue, they were well provided with everything they needed, and brought upon the right track towards Mecca, where they safely landed, after two weeks. To the enquiry of the pilgrims who their benefactors were, they received in reply, "We are Jehud Cheber," and from that time the Sultan of Zannah became exceedingly friendly to the Jews.

FREEMASONRY AMONG THE JEWS.

It is a historical fact, that the Jews in Spain and Portugal were the standard-bearers of philosophy, astronomy, philology, pharmacology, and other sciences and arts, in those countries, during the reign of the Moors, and even further down, to the end of the fourteenth century; but, whether they were also the guardians of geometry, and especially of architecture, is a matter which remains to be ascertained, and which, we think, would open a wide field for the student of ancient history, in all its branches. We maintain that they were also the masters of the latter sciences; and, as strange as this idea may appear, it is not a mere phantom, but rather founded on the basis of some historical, or, at least, traditional facts.

It is a wide-spread tradition among the Spanish Jews (now generally known under the name of "Portuguese Jews,") that Israelites who were dissatisfied with the reign of King Solomon (who, according to 2 Kings, xii., 4, put a heavy yoke upon the people), migrated to Tarshish, which, it is supposed, is Spain, in the ships which Solomon sent out, and settled there. When, after Solomon's death, his son and successor, Rehoboam, lost ten parts of his kingdom by the imprudent answer which he gave to the people when they appealed for relief from the heavy taxes; he sent, notwithstanding, his collector, Adoram, into the provinces to enforce payment, and also to the newly planted colonies of Spain. There, however, the people—who, it is supposed, were not of the tribe of Judah—stoned him to death. It is a fact, that there are numerous tombstones, with old Hebrew or Samaritan inscriptions, in Seville or Toledo—we cannot positively say in which of these two places—and among them is one which bears the name of Adoram, the collector of Solomon and his son Rehoboam.

Another tradition, and probably nearer the truth than the former, is that Jews emigrated to Spain in Phoenician ships, at the time when the land of Israel was groaning under the tyrannical yoke of the successors of Alexander the Great. This seems to be confirmed by a great many coins which were recently dug from some ruins in the city of Tarragona; and, also, by another very important circumstance, namely, that, in the days of Herod and Pontius Pilate, the Jewish community in Toledo wrote a letter to the High Priest, Eliezer, and the High Council, or Sanhedrin, to the effect, to beware of condemning Jesus of Nazareth to the penalty of death. How much truth may be in any of these statements it would be very hard, or, perhaps, altogether impossible, to ascertain; this much, however, is certain, that Jews were the founders and builders of most of the ancient cities of Spain, as Toledo, Seville, Barcelona, and others; and that Jews were the inhabitants of those places at the time when the Ostrogoths invaded the Peninsula, and planted, with the cross, oppression, persecution and cruelty, against all who would not bow their knees to it, and especially the Jews.

Before we go further in the history of the Spanish and Portuguese Jews, which induced us to think that there are traces of Freemasonry having existed among them, we must mention another tradition which lives in the mouth of almost every Jew in Bohemia, and particularly in Prague, the capital of that country. There is scarcely a traveller who goes to see the world, and to study the different customs and habits of the nations, and see the rarities of their cities, who, on stopping a few days in Prague, would not also go to see the antiquities in the Jews' quarter, and particularly the "Al-Tenai"* synagogue. It is a remarkable building, and peculiar in its structure, which is neither altogether the Greek style nor the Gothic. No visitor ever crossed the threshold of this building without feeling, as it were, an ice-cold stream running through his veins, and an involuntary veneration for a temple with which so many wonderful events are connected. The most ancient chronicle of Bohemia says, that this building was found there, when the founder of the city of Prague laid the first corner-stone of it, and that he felt such a veneration for that strange edifice, that he suffered not his people to use it for any purpose. Soon after this, Jews came to settle there, and claimed that building as a synagogue, which had been erected by their ancestors for a house of worship. The tradition of the origin of this synagogue is this:—There were Jewish colonies—and perhaps also Israelitish, from the ten tribes—in several parts of the then inhabited parts of Europe, especially in Spain and France, known as "Sephorod," and "Tserophoth," during the second temple. They were numerous and wealthy, and often made pilgrimages to Jerusalem, in obedience to the command of God. Here, in the pleasant valley on the shores of the beautiful river Moldau, at that time the extreme point of habitation, they chose to be a place appointed, where they waited until all were gathered who intended to go, and then pursued their way eastward in a large body, without fear of the savage hordes who made those regions unsafe. As they had often to tarry for weeks and even months, they agreed to build a substantial building, which should serve them not only for a house of worship, but also for a fort, in which a thousand people

---

* "Al-Tenai" means *on condition*; that is, that the building was erected to be not exclusively a house of worship, but for other purposes also.

could be protected, should the savages of the forest dare at any time to attack them.

There is no doubt a great deal of truth in this tradition, inasmuch as it is partly confirmed by the Bohemian Chronicles. This, however, is evident, that Jews erected that building, and that they did it without the assistance of other hands than their own. If this was the case, there must have been indeed skilful masters in the art of architecture among them, who formed an association like those of other nations.

We now return to the Jews in Spain and Portugal. After the downfall of the Ostro-Gothic Empire, under the reign of the Onajades, or Moors, the Jews regained their former position in those countries; they enjoyed perfect liberty, and had time, means and opportunity, to extend their knowledge and wisdom in all branches of science and art. We find them in the highest stations at the courts, as well as in the institutes of learning. Even after the golden age of Spain had passed away; after the expulsion of the Moors by popish kings, the Jews, though oppressed and often persecuted, again enjoyed high stations at the different courts of the Spanish monarchs, for nearly a hundred years. In the middle of the fourteenth century, however, the sufferings of the despised race became intolerable; and tens of thousands professed publicly a religion which, in their hearts, they hated and abhorred to the uttermost. They were called "Noros Christianos," or new Christians; or, together with the new converts from the Moors, "Maranos;"* and this latter name was more common among the people than the first.

It is a well-known fact, that the Maranos, who were Jews in their hearts, held secret meetings on certain days and at certain places, to worship God according to their own conviction. To these meetings none could obtain admission except members of a similar association, and this only after a strict examination. Generally they met in public houses, as taverns, hotels, &c., kept by one of their own people, in order that their coming and going might not excite the attention and suspicion of their enemies, the spies of the devil's tribunal, the Inquisition. The room where they met had two entrances, one for the brethren of the same congregation, which was never known to a visitor, although he gave satisfactory evidences that he was a member of the brotherhood, and in consequence of which he obtained admission. The other door was for the entrance of visitors. They appeared in a peculiar dress, mostly in

---

* The name "Maranos" they received from the circumstances that they were often frightened by the cry: Maran atha! "The Master comes," when assembled together for prayer.

4

monks' cowls; and the last rule of precaution which they employed among them, was, that whenever visitors from other communities were introduced, they appeared all masked, while the visitors were obliged to show their faces. In examining visitors who were not known to them personally, they used, like Freemasons, certain signs, grips, and passwords, which together with the facts of their being skilled in geometry and architecture, makes it most probable that these communities practised a kind of Freemasonry among themselves. But there are other circumstances which confirm us in that idea. The history of that persecuted race, thousands of which ended in "*Auto de fès*," records of innumerable cases where brethren were delivered when in great distress, from the most cruel death, even from the foot of the scaffold; and once a party of several hundred persons, men, women and children, who were already sentenced to be burnt alive on the next morning, were carried out from the prison of the Inquisition in Lisbon, brought on board of two vessels which were waiting for them, and safely landed at Amsterdam.

One fact more we will mention. There were often traitors in spite of all the means of precaution which they employed; but scarcely one of them escaped the avenging dagger. It found the treacherous heart in the inner chamber of the king's palace, as well as the foot of the altar in the cathedral; his life was forfeited; there was no spot on this globe where he could flee to, and no cave where he could hide himself; the invisible arm of "vengeance" reached him everywhere.

CHAPTER II.

THE NAMES OF A JEW.

HEBREW— ISRAELITES—JEW—Origin and Import of these Names defined.

THE NAMES OF A JEW.

In regard of the name of this nation, they are known from times of old, till our day, under three different names. They are called *Hebrews*, *Israelites*, and also *Jews*. We will give a reason for this variety.

The name *Hebrew*, or, more correctly, *Ebri*, is decidedly the oldest, as we find yet in Genesis xiv., 13, is that the ancestor of this nation was called by the Gentiles *Abraham, the Ebri*, because he was from the other side of the Euphrates, for the Hebrew root *avar*, from which the English word *over* is derived, signifies to transgress over a sea or river. The word *Hebrew*, or *Ebri*, is, therefore, only an *appellation* to the descendants of Abraham, who crossed the Euphrates. Quite different from this is the name *Israelite*, for this is a *patrommic* name, derived from the patriarch Jacob, who was surnamed by God: *Israel*, which signifies, according to some, "a prince of God," and according to others, "a warrior of God." This name is almost exclusively used in the Bible.

The name *Jew*, or rather *Jehudi*, is about eleven hundred years younger than the former, and was attributed to that nation when, after the death of King Solomon, the Israelitish Empire became divided into two kingdoms, namely, that of *Israel*, under Jeroboam, and that of *Judah*, under Rehaboam, the sons of Solomon and the latter was, therefore, called the Empire of Jehudah, as it consisted only of the two tribes of Jehudah and Benjamin, of which empire Jehudah formed the majority; as also in honor of the kingly dynasty, which descended from the tribe of Jehudah. So only a small part of Israel was called at that time Jehudah; but when, at a later period, the Israelites, namely, the people of the ten tribes, were carried into captivity by the Assyrian king Salamanasser, which was transacted 134 years before Nebuchadnezzar, king of Babylon, destroyed Jerusalem, and as the ten tribes were dispersed by that tyrannical emperor into a mountainous region in the interior of Asia, so that until this time history is silent in regard to the fate of those lost ten tribes; all the surviving Israelites were called from that time *Jehudim*, or *Jews*—though the name Israelite is the more correct one; for every Jehudi or Jew is, of course, an Israelite, but not every Israelite a Jew, or Jehudi.

CHAPTER III.

HEBREW WOMEN.

Polygamy, though practiced, was discouraged—High position assigned to Woman—Betrothal—Marriage—Divorce—Mutual duties of Husband and Wife—Love of Hebrew Women for their Kindred.

HEBREW WOMEN.

The position assigned by the Hebrews to the female sex, has been frequently misunderstood. From the permission of polygamy, from its supposed general practice, and from isolated expressions by some Rabbins, it has been hastily inferred to have been low. To arrive at correct views on this subject, we ought to compare the position of the Hebrew female, not only with the elevated place which Christianity, in acknowledgment of her real vocation, has assigned her, but chiefly with that which she then occupied, and, even at the present time, holds among other eastern nations. The readers of the New Testament cannot but feel that the relations there indicated proceed upon the assumption that monogamy was the rule, and polygamy the exception. The permission of polygamy—the comparative facility of obtaining a divorce—and the practice of keeping concubines (especially at an earlier period), may seem to militate against the fundamental idea of the marriage relation. But, against these drawbacks, we have to put the two indubitable facts, that, generally, men were only united in wedlock to one wife, and that Jewish females occupied not only a comparatively, but an absolutely high position. The law throughout recognized and protected the rights of a woman, and discouraged the practice of polygamy. An impartial reader cannot rise from the perusal, not of a few isolated passages, but of the sections, of the *Mishna* bearing upon this subject, without being impressed with this conviction. To the age of twelve years and one day, females were reckoned minors (boys, to thirteen years and one day), during which period they were absolutely in the power of their father, who might betroth or give them in marriage, and who derived the benefit of what they might earn by their personal exertions.

Marriage was preceded by a betrothal, which, in the Province of Judea, was celebrated by a feast. The conditions of the marriage were then very precisely fixed, the dowry brought by the wife, and the sum of money to be paid to her in case of divorce or of widowhood, settled.

Only a *bona fide* breach of these engagements was deemed a valid ground for dissolving the bond thus formed. From the moment of this formal betrothal, the couple were looked upon as married, and the relation could only be dissolved by divorce. A betrothal might be entered into by the parties personally, or by delegates, but in order to be valid it was necessary for the bridegroom to hand to the bride, either in money or otherwise, the value of at least a perutah. From the period of the betrothal, twelve months were allowed to either party (if the bride was maid, and thirty days if a widow) to prepare for the marriage. In cases of longer delay, the bridegroom was bound to maintain his betrothed. If the bride was divorced before marriage, she received the sum settled at the betrothal, which, in the case of a maid, was by statute not less than 200, and in that of a widow, 100 dinars, but might be augmented to any extent, according to previous agreement. But it is doubtful whether, in case of divorce before marriage, the bride could sue for any very considerable increase of the statutory sum. On the marriage day, the bridegroom, with his friends, went to bring home his espoused wife, who was accompanied by her companions.

Festivities, lasting for some time, inaugurated the happy event. Maidens were generally married on the fourth day of the week (Wednesday), to allow three free days to prepare for the marriage, and to enable the bridegroom, without delay, to bring any complaint as to the past chastity of his bride, before the tribunals, which met every Thursday. Widows were generally married on the fifth day of the week. At their marriage, maidens wore garlands of myrtles, or a peculiar kind of veil covering the eyes; sometimes their hair hung loosely down. It was a common practice to distribute among the company dried seeds, and in some parts of the country, to carry before the newly-married couple a pair of fowls, probably to indicate a wish for their fruitfulness. Legally speaking, marriage was concluded by the handling of money, by a written contract, or by co-habitation; and it was again dissolved by a divorce, or by the death of either parties. While the law, no doubt, afforded considerable facilities for obtaining a divorce, it also protected the rights of women, and generally gave a preference to their testimony in cases of dispute. On the legitimate grounds of divorce, the two theological schools differed materially. The Shammaites restricted them to the commission of an iniquitous action by the wife (probably adultery); the Hillelites going to an opposite extreme, and playing upon the original of the text (Deut. xxiv. 1), quoted by Shammai, inferred that a divorce was warranted even when the wife had only spoiled her husband's dinner.

Rabbi Akiba endeavoured, in the same manner, to prove that a man might lawfully dismiss his wife, if he found another more attractive. Passing over such exceptional extravagances, it was held lawful to dismiss a wife without paying her the legally secured portion, if she transgressed the law of Moses and of Judah, which was applied not only to sin, but to acts of impropriety, such as going about with loose hair, spinning in the street, familiarly talking with men, ill-treating her husband's parents in his presence, and brawling, *i. e.*, speaking with her husband so loudly that her neighbors could hear her voice in the adjoining houses; a general bad reputation in the place, or the discovery of damaging circumstances which had been concealed before marriage. On the other hand, the wife could insist on being divorced from her husband if he was a leper—if he was affected with polypus (cancer?) —or if his trade obliged him to perform either dirty or disagreeable manipulations, as in the case of tanners and coppersmiths. To discourage a plurality of wives, it was enjoined, that, in her claims, the first married wife should always take precedence of the second, the second of the third, &c. The ordinances with reference to divorce by absent husband, were, as all legislation on this subject, very punctilious.

The law specified the mutual duties and rights. The husband was bound to love and cherish his wife, comfortably to support her, to redeem her if she had been sold into slavery, and to bury her. On these occasions, the poorest Israelite was bound to provide, at least, two mourning fifes and one mourning woman. On the other hand, the wife was to grind the meal, to bake, to wash, to cook, to suckle her children, to make her husband's bed, and to work in wool. These regulations were modified if she was wealthy. If she had brought with her one slave, she was not required to grind the meal, to bake, or to wash; if two slaves, she was also free from cooking and suckling the children; if three slaves, she was not required to make the bed, or to work in wool; if four slaves (it is added), she might sit in her easy chair. However, this indulgence was limited, and, under all circumstances, the wife expected, at least, to work in wool.

If, by a rash vow, a husband had forsworn himself not to allow his wife to work, he was bound immediately to divorce her, as it was thought that idleness induced insanity. The whole of the personal property of, or the income derived by, the wife, belonged to her husband. On the other hand, he was bound to make over to her one-half more than her dowry if it consisted of ready money, and one-fifth less if it consisted in any property. Besides, the bridegroom was to allow his wife one-tenth of her dowry for pin-money. If a father gave away his daughter without making any distinct statement about her dowry, he was bound to allow her, at least, fifty *sus*; if it had expressly been provided that the bride was to receive no dowry, it was delicately enjoined that the bridegroom should furnish her, before her marriage, with the necessary outfit. Even an orphan, who was given away by her natural guardians, the parochial authorities, was to receive, from the common funds, at least, fifty *sus* as dowry. Any real property which a bride might have acquired, either before her bethrothal, or between her bethrothal and her marriage, (in the latter case only if unknown to the bridegroom,) might again be disposed of by her, either by sale or gift. A husband could not oblige his wife to leave the Holy Land or the City of Jerusalem, or to exchange a country for a town residence, and *vice versa;* or a good for a bad house, and *vice versa*. A widow might insist on being maintained in her husband's house, or if the surviving relations, and she herself were young, in her father's house. If she had bred in her father's house, she was at all times at liberty to claim her legal portion, but if she had spent twenty-five years with the heirs of her late husband, her money was forfeited, as it was considered that during that period she must have spent in charity a sum equal to that to which she was legally entitled.

From this curious provision, it would appear that the calculated annual expenditure for purely charitable purposes, was at least one-eighth of one's income. We only add that priests were bound to enquire very particularly into the purity of the family with which they allied themselves in marriage, lest they might enter into connection with heathens or with bastards. Children begotten in ordinary wedlock, were ordinarily reckoned as belonging to the family of the father, but if the mother alone was a Jewess, her offspring were also considered Jews. The same privilege was also extended to the children of those who had forsaken Judaism. Of the first, we have an instance in the circumcision of Titus by Paul; of the second, in the claims put forward by the daughters of the apostate Acher. The period of suckling is variously stated. The Mishna fixes it at two years, or, at least, eighteen months. The education of daughters was almost entirely confided to their mother, and even in that of sons she sustained an important part. Besides their peculiar domestic duties, daughters were to be taught the written, but not the oral law, as such studies might lead to undue familiarity with the other sex. Daughters were, whilst minors, so absolutely in the power of their father, that he might even sell them into slavery. If a person died, leaving sons and daughters, the former were sole heirs, but were obliged to support their sisters, and that although the property were only sufficient for the latter purpose. As mothers should admonish their sons to apply themselves to study, so wives were to encourage their husbands to the same.

The Hebrew woman in her love for her kindred, soars above her Christian sisters. The tender devotion which the daughters of Israel bestow upon their parents, especially upon their father, is full of beauty and pathos. In the dark alleys of the world's Ghetti, when the old Hebrew man toddles home from his daily strife, with prejudice and lucre, a wondrous change transforms his face as he crosses the threshold of his weather-beaten house. The furtive glance expands, the crooked gait is made straight, the many wrinkles of his brow are made smooth, the crouching form of the peddler disappears, and the old man stands erect, as if he were worthy of better things; the smile loses its sinister grin, and is clothed with genial beauty. Rebecca has kissed away the ugliness of the money-changer, and to see him sit down at his table, after having sent up to Jehovah a prayer for good luck, and plenty of gain, for the coming day, and chat with his daughter, who delights in humoring his jokes, is a treat for an artist in search of the picturesque, or for the poet in quest of the romantic. Rebeccas abound, not only in the regions of the Ghetti, but in the middle and highest order of Hebrew abodes. Here we find the daughter, as a class, watching, with Argus eyes, father's and mother's happiness and comfort. Here, on the domestic shrine, all the fires of love and affection are burning so vigorously, that, unwittingly, even the sympathies are consumed which are wanted to kindle the great flames round the sacred altar of common humanity. Unless this drawback is constantly kept in view, our description of the Hebrew daughter's love for her parents, would be calculated to surround the feelings with a too angelic atmosphere.

CHAPTER IV.

POSITION THE JEWS WERE AND ARE STILL OCCUPYING IN SOCIETY.

In France there are Jews in the highest political, professional, and military positions.

Mr. Anspach, member of the Imperial Court of Paris. Mr. Bedarride, president of the Imperial Court, Aix. Mr. J. Bedarride, chairman of the Bar at the Imperial Court of Montpellier.

Messrs. A. Fould, Cremieux, Cerfbeer, members of the Royal Parliament under Louis Philippe.

Messrs. Goodcheaux, Alean, Ennery, Konigswarter, members of the Legislative Assembly in 1848.

Messrs. L. Saval, Konigswarter, members of the present Chamber of Deputies.

Mr. Cremieux, Minister of Justice, and Goodcheaux, Minister of Finance.

Mr. Achelle Fould, Secretary of State, and Minister of the Imperial Household.

Mr. Maurice Meyer, Inspector of Primary Schools.

Mr. A. Widal, Professor of Philosophy at Douai.

Mr. Isidore Cohen, Professor of Philosophy at Napoleon Vendee.

Mr. Alean, Professor at the Conservatory in Paris.

Mr. S. Munk, member of the "Institute."

Mr. F. Halevy, member of the "Institute," and perpetual Secretary of the Section of Fine Arts.

Mr. Ad Frank, member of the "Institute," of the Imperial Council of Public Instruction, and Professor at the "College de France."

Mr. Germain Lee, director of the Hospitals of Paris.

Mr. Michel Levy, director of the Military School of Val-de-grace.

In the Province of Music, are distinguished, Halevy, Cohen, Alkan, Emils, Jones, Offenbach, Seligman.

In Printing and Sculpture.—Messrs. Lehman, Adam, Solomon, Ullman.

In Journalism, Lettres and Sciences.—Messrs. Leon, Coglan, Weil, Ratisbonne, Horn, Cohen, Cohen, Black, D'Enary, Gerson, Levy, Wigue, Albert Cohen, Salvador, Terquem, Stauben.

In Medicine.—Germain, in Paris; Hartz, Professor in Strasburg; Toro, Professor in Paris.

It was formerly generally asserted, that the Jews were unfit for military service; but the statistical facts of France proves this assertion to be a mere calumny. Out of the 4,000 scholars, who since 1830 were admitted in the "Ecole Polytechnique," over 100 belong to the Jewish religion, and thus, while the Jewish population forms hardly the 400th part of the French population, they are represented in the military schools, in the proportion of one 40th. Again, when leaving these schools, these young Israelites do not prefer an employment in the civil services, but join the army, and engage in military service. Thence, during the campaign in Italy, there were 140 Jewish officers in the army, viz.: 35 captains, 3 chiefs of cavalry companies, 1 commander of engineers, 2 colonels, 2 majors, 1 lieutenant-colonel; of these 29 were Knights of the Legion of Honor, 5 officers and 5 commanders of the same order.—*Dr. Gallavardin of Lyons.*

PART SECOND.

THE RELIGION OF THE JEWS.

CHAPTER I.—JUDAISM.

Interest of the subject—No people more spoken of—Command the attention of the world—Present great varieties of character and social status—The *Times* quoted—The little rill issuing in the mighty river—Ceremonies and customs: 1st, those of the written law, containing 613 commandments; 2nd, those of the oral law—the Talmud; 3rd, those customs which have arisen in course of time—All agree in the 1st and 2nd, but there is much difference in the 3rd particular—Classes according to nationality—Modern Caraites—Few Jews converse in the Hebrew—Origin of the MISHNA and TALMUD—Superstitious regard for dreams—Justice in dealing enjoined—Cooking food—Eating—Killing animal food—Phylacteries—Duties of women—Thirteen articles of Jewish belief—Manner of making proselytes—Cabalistic magic—Jewish Eschatology—Confession—Traditions and authority of the Rabbies—Unable now to keep the Law of Moses—The birth of a son—Circumcision—Birth of a daughter—Redeeming the first-born—Genealogy lost—Teaching of children—Courtship—Marriage—Divorce—Sabbath and its observances—Modern celebration of the Passover—The Feast of Weeks—The New-year—The Day of Atonement—Its ceremonies—The Feast of Tabernacles—Feast of Dedication—Feast of Purim—Feast of the destruction of the two Temples—Ceremonies for the sick, dying and dead—Burial rites.

JUDAISM.

This subject has an interest not alone to the Christian, but also, to all persons of intelligence. Since the existence of the Hebrew people is well calculated to arrest the attention of all who are inclined to trace great effects to some well-defined causes.

Perhaps not any people have ever been more spoken about than the Israelites; the religionist has constantly to refer to them when expounding his own peculiar views, and one is not far wrong to asssert, that scarcely a public religious meeting takes place, in which the Jews are not either mentioned by name, or at least alluded to in some manner. Those, however, who do not pay any deference to the popular ideas in religion, are also not indifferent spectators on the presence of the Hebrew race, and either praise them for their sturdy common sense, when it suits them to denounce or revile other persuasions, or, if their object be to reject all positive religion, they not rarely cast ridicule on the Israelites, for what they fancifully style their superstition. And, with all this constant attention directed towards this people, we are, on the other hand, fully warranted in asserting that no class of men is so much misunderstood, or possibly so unknown, as are these self-same Jews. Perhaps they are a mystery to themselves: they are at once yielding and obstinate, submissive and unbending; shrewd, yet simple; covetous, yet generous; living in every land, yet peculiar in all; assuming the manners and languages of all nations, and yet distinguishable at first sight as a separate people; and all this, not because they desire to be singular, but because they cannot help it; for they are as they are, from what may be termed a natural conformation, from an indelible, unalterable impression, which they received in their very origin, and which they have carried with them down the path of the world's history, until this very moment. A writer to the *Evangelical Review*, says, "This miraculous people still command the attention of the world, even in their fallen state; and the intellectual or moral advancement of mankind, with all the gigantic march of events, does not preclude the certainty of God's express arrangements for Israel. While the infidel sneers at them as the Pariahs of the globe, or the more friendly Christian, in reverting to their long past history, and looking for their promised spiritual regeneration, as well as the national return to their own land, designates them the aristocracy of the world; as yet the Hebrew walks on in his self-conceited stubbornness; empires become extinct, tribes and languages become amalgamated, but these remain an indestructible race; they are dealt with by an unparalleled discipline, and an unparalleled result will hereafter redound to the glory of God." An able writer in the *Times* says, "The character of this race is, in the main, everywhere the same, but in each country there is a different variety, and the Jews of Turkey are not the least interesting. The English species we know well. The showily dressed gentleman, with rings and breast-pin, bushy, black whiskers, and a mouth full of glittering teeth, who keeps a gig, and is connected with a theatre, is one variety. Then there is the flaxen-haired type, generally poor and shabby, serving in cheap tailors' marts, and bidding against each other at picture auctions. The German Jew is, intellectually, superior. He is more of the type which Rembrandt loved to paint—small, with dark, dry features, acute, but with a mind by no means always set on sordid gains and low enjoyments. His researches are often as laborious as those of the Teutonic professors among whom he lives; his logic is as sound, his critical powers as keen, his imagination as brilliant. As a philosopher, he adds another system to the metaphysical universe; as a theologian, he gives a deeper meaning to the dogmatic teachings of John and Paul. The Jew of Eastern Europe is, physically, the finest of his race. The bearded old Hebrew, who comes from Poland, with a wallet at his back, is often caught by admiring artists, and made to sit for portraits of Abraham, or Eli. These Constantinople Jews are mostly relics of the tribes who fled from the fires of the Inquisition in Western Europe, and their thick Shemitic Spanish is still heard in the close alleys where congregate outcasts lower than the lowest, and beings on whom the meanest Rayah may inflict in turn the insults which he receives from his Turkish master. They are a quiet race, slender and stooping, with something weak and idiotic in their features, which are far more delicate than those of their English countrymen. Occasionally there is one whose countenance might have been intelligent, if a better fortune had ever allowed any noble or elevating thoughts to be presented to the dormant mind, or the sun of hope had ever broken through the chill mist of contempt and poverty which must encircle the journey of his life. Though they are what they are, one can still imagine that in the schools of Cordova and Toledo, their forefathers were great in philosophy and medicine; they were the physicians of emperors and kings, and even gave many a bishop to the church which persecuted them. However, the descendants are poor and miserable, earning a scanty meal by the sale of stationery and petty wares, and there they stand, at the entrance of the bazaar, whispering confidentially to each Englishman that passes, and offering their services, with that mysterious air of secrecy which characterises their race."

Far down in the valley of time, we see a little stream making its way between shelving rocks and trickling overhanging branches; we behold a little rill just escaped from its flinty birth-place, gradually urging its way to reach the broad plain where other and broader streams pursue their course. But ever and anon its progress is checked by obstacles which the nature of its bed presents to it at every turn; yet the very narrowness and depth of the channel, which it has to follow, preserves its waters from being wasted and dried up by summer's heat; and, constantly refilled from the icy source whence it springs, it rushes onward, though at times unseen, till it emerges with irrepressible power, a mighty river in the presence of the Lord, before its waters finally mingle with the vast ocean, to which it furnishes an unmistakable accession of strength, far away in its briny floods.

Such a stream, in the history of the human race, is the family of Israel, which, never very numerous, is still one of the weakest of mankind, if importance is to be considered as ascribable only to millions and material power. It was in Chaldea, the ancient seat of learning and early civilization, that *one* man, rising above the superstitions of his friends, neighbors, and relatives, rejected the idols, the works of human hands, and proclaimed aloud his belief and trust in One, eternal and invisible God, whom he designated and adored as the Possessor of Heaven and earth, comprehending, under the last term, the globe on which we live, and by the other, the whole structure of the universe, in comparison with which our earth is but like an atom, that dances before our eyes, in the bright sunbeams of a glorious summer's day. Their customs, manners, habits and religion, are surely worthy of an inquiry, and deserving the serious consideration of every one feeling an interest in that people, from which were the chief sources of revelation—or in other words, of whom the prophets and our blessed Redeemer was born.

The ceremonies and customs of the present Jews, are not all of equal authority, neither are they observed by all the Jews alike, for which reason the ceremonies are divided into three classes. The first includes the injunctions of the written law, viz.: those contained in the five books of Moses. These injunctions consist of two hundred and forty-eight affirmatives, and three hundred and sixty-five negatives, which, in all, amount to six hundred and thirteen, and are called *Mezvoth Hatorah* (commandments of the law.) These six hundred and thirteen commandments are contained, as they conceive, in the Hebrew word *Torah*, which signifies the law. The letters in this word, if considered as numbers, make up six hundred and eleven; the better to account for the two remaining precepts, they insist that God himself gave the first, which relates to his unity, and to the prohibition of paying divine adoration to any images or state.

The most learned of the Rabbis are of opinion that the two hundred and forty-eight affirmatives, answer to the same number of members which are found in the human body; and, forasmuch as it is written in Ecclesiastes, "That to keep God's commandments is the whole duty of man," they add, that all the members of a man are supported and maintained by these commandments—as if each limb answered some particular one; and, as for the three hundred and sixty-five negatives, the Rabbis imagine that they denote the days of a year.

The second class relates to the oral law, or that which was delivered by word of mouth—and this denomination is given to those comments or annotations which the Rabbis and Doctors have made in their days upon the Pentateuch, and to an infinite variety of ordinances and laws, which they call *Mezwath Rabanin* (commandments of the Rabbis) and which were collected into one large volume, called the Talmud.

The third class includes such things as custom has given a sanction to, in different times and places, or which have been but lately introduced, and, therefore, they call them *Minhagim*, or customs. Of these three classes, then, the first and second, which comprise the written law by Moses, and the oral law, transmitted from their Rabbis by tradition, are received by all the Jews in general, wherever scattered and dispersed, without any considerable variation among them in that respect, as appears from the Talmud. But, as for the third, which has relation to their customs only, they differ very much from one another, because, the Jews, dispersed into divers parts of the world, have fallen into the manners of those countries. They differ from each other, then, in the third class only, and principally the Eastern, German and Italian Jews. In the Eastern, we may comprise those of Greece and Barbary. Under the name of German Jews, we may include those of Bohemia, Moravia, Hungary, Poland, and others. The Jews in America are divided into four classes, viz.: English, Germans, Poles and Spanish. These, therefore, also differ very much from one another in their customs and religious ceremonies.

There is a certain sect of Jews, who call themselves Caraims, or Caraits, a word derived from the Hebrew word *Mikra*, which signifies "The pure text of the Bible," for they rely wholly on the Pentateuch, and practice it in its literal sense, without paying the least regard to the precepts of the Rabbis. The Caraits are looked upon by the other Jews as heretics, notwithstanding they observe the Law of Moses.

There are some of this sect at the present day in Constantinople, Cario, and other parts of the East. There they live according to their own manner; they have their own synagogues, and observe such ceremonies and customs as are peculiar to themselves, though, at the same time, they insist that they only are the true Jews and observers of the Mosaic Law. Such Jews as deviate from their persuasion, they call *Rabbanim*, or disciples of the Rabbis; but the latter have a natural aversion to the Cariats, and will make no alliances, nor have any conversation with them; they call them *Mamzerim*, or bastards, because they keep none of the precepts of the Rabbis; but their theology is in no way different from that of the other Jews, except, perhaps, in its being more pure, and less superstitious, for they pay no regard to the explications of the Cabalists or their allegories, which in reality, have no foundation. They believe in the immortality of the soul, and in a future state—their basis on this point being, "Let us make man in our own image." The spirit of man, they say, owes its rise and its origin to things above, and his body to those below, for, they add, their soul is of an Angelic nature, and immediately after the creation, the future state was made for the soul of man.

Among our modern Jews, there are but comparatively few who are able to discourse in the Holy Tongue, or, as they call it, *Lashan Hakodesh;* they are as much at a loss with respect to the Chaldaic or the Targum, although they spoke these languages whilst they enjoyed their privileges, and were in their own country. Thus, the Jews of Italy and Germany, talk Italian, Dutch and German; those of the East and Barbary, Turkish and the Moscow tongues; they made these foreign languages so absolutely their own, that many of those Jews, who went from Russia to Poland and Hungary, carried the languages with them into those countries, and transmitted them to their posterity. Those, also, who were forced out of Spain, and fled for refuge to the East, also carried their language with them into those parts. The Jews, however, mingle many corrupt Hebrew words in their every-day conversation. But few of them, as has already been mentioned, understand the Scriptures thoroughly, much less (except some of their Rabbis) can they converse freely in the Holy Tongue.

About one hundred and twenty years after the destruction of the second Temple, Rabbi Judah, who at that time was called Rabenuh Hakadosh, or, our holy master—on account of his exemplary life and uncommon virtues—this Rabbi, who was a gentleman of fortune, and a favorite of the Emperor Antonius Pius, taking notice that the dispersion of the Jews made them negligent, and forgetful of the oral law, took therefore, and wrote down the ordinances and traditions of all the Rabbis up to his time. This compendium of his, which is called *Mishna*, is divided into six parts. The first treats of agriculture and seeds—the second of festivals—the third, of marriages, and everything relating to women—the fourth, of fables and disputes—the fifth, of sacrifices—and the sixth, of things clean and unclean. But this book created abundance of disputes, which, as they daily increased, obliged two Rabbis of Babylon, one named Ravina, and the other Ravasha, to collect all the interpretations, controversies, and additions which had been written down in the *Mishna*, together with a supplement of short histories, maxims and memorable sayings, and place them together, out of which they then composed the book called the *Talmud*. It is divided into sixty parts; and upon this book the Jews lay a great stress, some of them even consider it equal to the five books of Moses.

Orthodox Jews are great believers in dreams, so much so, that if any of them are made uneasy by a frightful dream, particularly when relating to those kinds explained by Rabbis, they fast all the next day, that is, abstain from both eating and drinking; and, in short, nothing but a dream can place a Jew under obligations to fast on their Sabbath day, or any other festival. On the evening following the fast, the person who has dreamed, and fasted accordingly, sends for three of his friends before he presumes to eat, to whom he says seven times, "May my dream be fortunate," to which they answer each time "Amen, God grant it so." After this ceremony, they add some passages of the Prophets, and then, that the dreamer himself may have some omen, they repeat to him the words of Ecclesiastes, "Go thy way, eat thy bread with joy," after which he who had fasted sits down to his supper.

Every Jew is obliged, both by their written and oral law, to be true to his word; not to over-reach or defraud any person whatever— Jew or Gentile; and, in all their dealings, to comply with the rules of commerce, prescribed in several places in Scripture, particularly in the 19th chapter of Leviticus, from the 33rd verse to the end.

They make use of different sets of utensils, both for kitchen and table use, for some of them are appropriated to meat only, others for milk, but never mixed, for, when they eat meat, they must wait six full hours before tasting either milk or butter. They have, also, particular dishes, &c., set apart for the Feast of the Passover. When they purchase such vessels as are made use of in the kitchen, they are immediately taken and plunged into the river, or into any large quantity of water, before made use of.

The Jews are not permitted to taste the flesh of any four-footed beast, unless its hoof is parted, and chews it cud. They never eat rabbits or swine, neither do they eat those fish that have no scales, nor birds of prey, or reptiles. Whatever they eat must be dressed by Jews, and even the utensils must belong to their own people, for fear of their pollution by any forbidden meats; some of the Jews are so scrupulous, as not to make use of another man's knife.

Neither are they permitted to eat the fat of beef, lamb or kid, nor the hind-quarter of any animal, because very few are able to draw out the veins and sinews in a proper manner. They never eat the blood of a four-footed beast, or of a bird, not even an egg, if it contains the least drop of blood.

The person who is appointed to slay any beasts for the use of the Jews, must be a pious and religious man. He must study that profession for a certain time, and undergo an examination by the chief Rabbi. This office is generally in connection with the duties of the minister. Only in large congregations, where they are able to support well, do they engage one to teach and preach, and another to read the prayers and prepare their meat; but here, in America, it is necessary for most ministers, or the so-called Rabbis, to perform this office for their congregations. There are several particulars to be observed on this occasion. The knife must be very sharp, and without any notches—the throat of the animal must be cut at once, and the blood must flow out as fast as possible, without any interruption. When fowl are killed, their blood must be immediately covered with ashes. They must not kill a cow and her calf on the same day; neither dare they eat it. If any such beast or bird as they are permitted to eat, happens to die of itself, or if killed in any other manner than the above, they must not taste it. They are also obliged to leave their meat remain in salt for an hour before using it, in order that the blood may come out thoroughly. They are not allowed to eat, at the same time, meal of both meat and milk, or cheese, because it is written, "Thou shalt not seethe a kid in his mother's milk."

According to the opinions of the ancient Rabbis, the Jews are forbidden to drink any wine that has been made, tasted, or even touched, by any one beside their own people. The Russian, as well as German Jews, are very scrupulous on this point. Before the Jews sit down to eat at table, they must first wash their hands as clean as possible. The Rabbis and ancient Jews were very particular about this, as well as about washing their hands when they rose in the morning. As soon as they are seated at table, they repeat the twenty-third Psalm, "The Lord is my shepherd, I shall not want," &c., after which the master of the family takes a loaf of bread, blesses, breaks it, and gives a piece of the size of an olive to each member of his household. After this ceremony, they may eat as much as they please. They are also obliged to say grace before drinking water.

Every Jew is obliged to fasten to every door through which he daily passes, a *Mesusa*, or piece of parchment, having the words "Hear O Israel, the Lord our God is one God," etc., written on it, which is enclosed in a piece of tin. The portion of Scripture written on the parchment is to be found in Deut. vi. 4, 10 and xi. 13, 22. He is also obliged, during the time of his morning devotions, to put on *Tephilin*, commonly called frontlets or phylacteries.[*] Both of these last mentioned ceremonies

---

[*] Two Phylacteries, one on the head, the other on the left arm. In the one that goes on the head, the following four passages, on four different pieces of parchment, are written viz. :—1. Exod. xiii. 1, 11. 2. Exod. xiii. 11, 17. 3. Deut. vi. 4, 10. 4. Deut. xi. 3, 22. In the one that is on the arm, there is but one piece of parchment, and all the former-mentioned passages are written on it.

were instituted by the Rabbis, and founded upon the words in Deut. vi. 8, 9 : "And thou shalt bind them for a sign upon thine hand, and they shall be as frontlets between thine eyes. And thou shalt write them upon the posts of thy house, and on thy gates." St. Jerome speaks of these phylacteries almost in terms of contempt; for in his exposition on the words of the Gospel, where the phylacteries are mentioned, he says, "The Pharisees, by a false construction of this passage, wrote the ten commandments of Moses on parchment, which they rolled up and tied on their forehead, making a kind of crown round their heads, that they might have them always before their eyes." The Caraite Jews have nothing to do with these ceremonies, for they believe it is only a figurative mode of expression, and that when God directed the Jews to write them down upon the posts of their houses, it was only with the intention that they should have their minds continually upon them.

When the Jews pray, they are always covered with a *Talith*, or large white shawl. Their head must also be covered, and according to their Rabbis, if a Jew eats or drinks anything, walks or even sits down, with an uncovered head, the same is considered as sacrilege among them; and he is looked upon as a non-Jew. He is obliged to wear a little garment, having fringes at its four corners. This he must wear continually, yes, and without which he is not even permitted to walk four yards.

A woman is exempt from all these customs. She is under obligations to refrain from all which men are enjoined to refrain, but the Rabbis have agreed that no woman should be forced to observe such ceremonies or customs, as require any length of time for their performances, with the exception of the three following precepts : First,—To observe the law of purification. Second,—After kneading her bread, to make a small cake of part of the same and throw it into the fire; and Third,— To light the lamp every Friday evening, in preparation for their Sabbath Eve. There are, however, some amongst them who are even more zealous and warm-hearted in their religious devotions than their husbands, who not only care to train up their children in the way they should go, but use their utmost endeavors to reclaim their husbands from a vicious course of life. A lad who is a day and thirteen years old, is henceforth looked upon as a man, and is obliged to observe all the commandments of the Law, for which reason he is called "Barmitzvah," which signifies "A son under the commandments." As to girls, they are considered women at the age of twelve years and a-half. Jewish children feel themselves strictly bound to honor and implicitly obey their parents, for their Rabbis early expound to them the command, "Honour thy father and thy mother," &c., and their obligations to their parents while alive. They have also duties to fulfil to their deceased parents, but we shall treat more fully on this subject hereafter.

The Jews have thirteen fundamental articles of belief, which they term their creed, and are as follows:

1st. That there is but one God, the Creator and first principle of all things, who is self-sufficient and independent, and without whom no created being can subsist.

2nd. That God is one and indivisible, but of a unity peculiar to Himself alone.

3rd. That God is an incorporal being, having no bodily quality of any kind whatever, and cannot be imagined.

4th. That God is eternal, and that all beings, except Himself, had once a beginning.

5th. That none other but God is the object of divine adoration, and that no created being ought to be worshipped as a mediator or intercessor.

6th. That there have been, and may still be, prophets duly qualified to receive the inspirations of the Supreme Being.

7th. That Moses was a prophet, superior to all other prophets, and that God Almighty honoured him with a peculiar gift of prophecy, which was never granted to any other.

8th. That the law which was left them by Moses, was the pure dictation of God Himself, and that nothing contained therein related in the least to Moses, consequently the explications of those commandments, which were handed down to them by tradition, came directly from the mouth of God, who delivered it to Moses.

9th. That this law is unchangeable, *i.e.*, that nothing can either be added to or taken from it.

10th. That God knows and governs all the actions of mankind.

11th. That God rewards those who strictly observe His law, and severely punishes those who are guilty of its least violation; that eternal life is the best and greatest reward, and damnation of the soul the most severe punishment.

12th. That a Messiah should come, more deserving than all the kings that have ever lived; and that, although He (the Messiah) delays His coming, no one ought on that account to question the truth of it, or set an appointed time for it, much less produce Scripture in proof of the time of His coming.

13th. That God shall raise the dead at an appointed time.

These thirteen articles were instituted by Maimonides, a distinguished Doctor of the thirteenth century.

When a stranger has any inclination to become a Jew, three Rabbis, or others of authority and reputation, are obliged to examine him very strictly, and, if possible, find out the true cause and motive of his resolution. If they observe that it be for his own interest, and not religion, that he has resolved to become a Jew, he is at once discharged, representing to him, at the same time, the severity of the Mosaic law—that its followers are at present in an abject and deplorable condition—and that it would be more to his advantage to continue as a member of his former church. If, however, after this exhortation, the man still requests to be admitted among them, they circumcise him, and, when he is healed, wash and sprinkle his body in the presence of the Rabbis who first examined him. After the performance of this ceremony, he is looked upon by them as one of themselves, viz.,—a Jew.

As to their theology, the ancient Jews have generally had recourse to fables and illusions, with which they so embellished their books, that there is even to be found in some of them a sort of mythology, not differing widely from that of the pagans. Some of them applied themselves to the Platonic philosophy, which they blended with their own idle chimeras, from whence their cabalistic learning proceeded.

The several ways of expression which frequently occur in their old allegorical writings, are much the same as those made use of by the Christians in explaining the mystery of the Trinity.

Their cabala is divided into two parts, the speculative and the practical. They make use of the latter in the operation of their imaginary miracles, which they profess to accomplish by the pronunciation of some particular names of God and of angels, or some verses of the Psalmist most applicable to their purpose. The Jews, particularly those of Russia and Poland, are, in this respect, so superstitious, that, in case one of them is accidentally condemned to death, or put in prison, he immediately has recourse to his practical cabala to effect his escape. But we do not find it to have proved of any advantage to them; yet their historical books contain accounts of miracles performed by cabalistic means. And, although this practical cabala is very erroneous, yet those who profess the art, boldly assert that they have frequently experienced the truth of it, taking delight and pleasure in deluding those who are inclined to believe them. They also pretend, through this agency which they have in their books, to cure sick persons, by writing down mysterious words on a piece of paper, which is afterwards burned, and the ashes thereof given in a glass of water to the sick, who is then, as they declare, healed. The speculative cabala relates to the influence of the stars, the magic power of their characters, and many other things of a like nature, which have no other foundation than the extravagant whims of the cabalistic doctors. The idle results of magic, which we find in Agrippa, and some others, are generally extracted from the Jewish cabala, to which other fabulous amusements have been added.

The Jews believe that there is a paradise, which they call Gan Eden, signifying the Garden of Eden, and that such souls as are in that happy state enjoy the beautiful vision. As for hell, they imagine that the souls of such as are wicked are burned there in raging flames, and also endure other torments; that some of them have no hopes of mercy, and suffer those pains forever, whilst others are only doomed to remain there for a certain period. Such Jews that have not offended against the commandments of the Rabbis, are, they believe, discharged from purgatory, within the space of a year, and these, they imagine, make up the greatest number. Some Jews are of the opinion that souls transmigrate from one body to that of another, which they call *Gilgal*, and produce several passages of Scripture, extracted principally from Job and Ecclesiastes, for the confirmation of it. We shall mention two of these passages. The first is the 15th verse of the 4th chapter of Ecclesiastes, which reads as follows, "I considered all the living which walk under the sun with the second child that shall stand up in his stead." The second passage is the 14th verse of the 14th chapter of Job, which runs thus, "If a man die, shall he live again? All the days of my appointed time will I wait till my change come." The Jews also acknowledge the resurrection of the dead, which is included in one of their articles of belief; that at the last day God would pronounce a universal judgment upon all mankind, both in body and soul, according to Daniel xii. 2, "And many of them that sleep in the dust of the earth shall awake, some to everlasting life, and some to shame and everlasting contempt." In short, the Jews believe in a paradise, a purgatory, and a hell; and, although it would be difficult to prove these beliefs by any formal quotations from the law of Moses, yet no one presumes to deny them.

It would be needless to make any reflections here upon the affinity that exists between the belief of the Jews and that of the Christians, relating to some of the articles already mentioned; for, doubtless, the Christian religion took its rise from that of the Jews, which must be accounted its basis and foundation. St. Austin says, "That in reality, they are but one and the same religion;" for which reason, also, our blessed Saviour assures us that he did not come to destroy the religion of the Jews, but to complete and perfect it.

CHAPTER II.

The Jews have no other form of confession than that which they make to God himself in their prayers; they most commonly have one prayer, composed alphabetically, which they call *vidu*, or confession. Mondays and Thursdays are the stated days set apart for making these solemn confessions. They are likewise repeated on every fast day, as also in private, on the feast of expiation. The days appointed for penance, commence on the first of the month, *Ellul*, (September), and are held till the day of expiation. Yet all times are equally proper for those whose minds are uneasy, and whose consciences accuse them.

Such as have not a sufficient capacity to discharge this duty aright of themselves, consult some Rabbi, and beg his assistance, or, if they have learning enough, they apply themselves to books written upon the subject of penance, where they are informed what penance is most suited to their peculiar sins—whether abstinence or fasting, or scourging, or benefaction to the poor, or prayers and good works, is most proper to make an atonement for the sins they have from time to time committed.

The Jews also acknowledge other precepts besides those contained in the law of Moses and in the Talmud, which they call the injunction of the *Hachamim*, (sages), whom they indulged with the same liberty of making new laws or statutes, as Moses himself had. This privilege, they say, is founded on the words of God himself, who directed them to consult the Elders of the Sanhedrim, or judges, for the solution of such controversies, or debates, as might arise from the law. For this reason, the Jews imagine that they are under as great obligations to obey the ordinances of the Rabbis, as the commandments of the Law. And, though these constitutions are inferior to those received of Moses, yet they pretend that these Elders were under the immediate influence of God, and, consequently, infalliable in their decisions.

The whole body of Jewish tradition is comprised in that collection, entitled, the Talmud. Those Rabbis who lived immediately after the Talmud was written, were distinguished by the name of *mechakrim*, or speculative Rabbis.

It must be acknowledged that the traditions now composed in the Talmud, or at least a portion of them, are very ancient, for the primitive fathers of the Church not only spoke of them in general, but also quoted some of them precisely as they are found at the present day in the books of the Jews. For our better satisfaction, we need only search the writings of Origen, St. Epiphanius and St. Jerome, more especially the latter, who quotes a vast number of them in his annotations, chiefly on the Prophets. The Jews, in all probability, invented most of these traditions, when they had no settled oracles to consult, and that, soon after their return from Babylon to Jerusalem. Their Rabbis, fond of gaining applause by their new interpretations of the law, and hence arose all those fables and idle allegories which are now found in the books of the Talmud. The followers of these teachings, especially the Pharisees, became, at last, the most prevailing sect among the Jews.

There were, however, a few Rabbis who were opposed to these traditions, and were impatient to see such a number of idle chimeras stand in competition with the text of the law. These, then, who are opposed to the traditions of the Rabbis, were designated by the name of Caraites, a sect that has already been noticed.

Although the Jews pretend that their traditions would never have appeared in writing, had it not been for the misfortunes of the times; yet we cannot conceive how they could have avoided it, for they were so numerous, that even though they are written, yet through carelessness, or otherwise, they lost some of their principal traditions; among others, those relating to their sacrifices, for they are perfect strangers to the names of several animals their law prohibits them from eating. Notwithstanding their ignorance, they still take the liberty to assert, that they have observed the Law of Moses in all its purity and perfection, as he received it from the mouth of God upon Mount Sinai.

We would here just mention a single fact, by which will be seen, that the Jews were not able, from the time of the destruction of their Second Temple, to observe the law of Moses. What answer can they give, or what excuse have they to offer, for not going thrice every year to visit the City of Jerusalem, at the great feasts of Passover, Pentecost, and Tabernacles, which is a direct commandment in their law, and for which negligence no excuse can be made, for in that very law is it not written : " Cursed is every one that continueth not in all things that are written in the books of the law to do them," and still, though not able to keep Judaism, refuse to receive Christ.

On the birth of a son, the father is congratulated by all his relatives and friends, in the following manner, Mazol Tove, מזל טוב which signifies good luck, or "I give you joy." The Jews write the names of Adam and Eve upon small slips of paper, and lay them in each corner of the mother's bedroom, or nail them on doors and windows.

Some write the words "Lilet be gone," who was, according to Jewish tales, Adam's first wife; but being disobedient, and an eternal scold, left him and flew up into the air, where she is considered as a nocturnal fury, and an enemy to new-born babes. But most of them write down the hundred and twenty-first Psalm, with the name Shadai, שדי "Almighty," and the names of the patriarchs, and three guardian angels, as a charm to secure the child from all hurt, or any impious incantations. They are in no wise enjoined or obliged to observe these ceremonies; yet this is only the effect of their superstition, and a tender regard for the infant's welfare. The father is under an indespensable obligation to have his son circumcised on the eighth day, in obedience to the command which runs thus: "He that is eight days old shall be circumcised among you, every manchild in your generation." But in case the child be sick, or infirm, the rite may be deferred until he is perfectly recovered. The night before the day appointed for the circumcision of the child, is called the "watch night," because the whole family sit up to take care of the infant, for they imagine that on this particular night, the child is in danger, to be snatched away by one of those nocturnal furies; and, indeed, in some places in Germany, the Jews are so superstitious on this point, that they place the knife, with which the child is to be circumcised, under his head; believing that the knife possesses the power over such incantations. They choose a godfather to stand by the child at the time of its circumcision, and a godmother to carry it to the synagogue and back home.

Every Jew is allowed to perform the ceremony of circumcision, provided he understand the operation. One who understands this art thoroughly, is looked upon amongst the Jews as an ingenious and valuable man, and often the infant's father performs the operation himself.

The chair upon which the child is placed on that occasion, is called "The chair of the prophet Elijah," whom they imagine to be present, though invisible.

The articles which are used, are, a razor or knife, which is made for the purpose, a kind of powder, a small piece of linen and some oil. The child is usually well in about twenty-four hours.

The operator, before he commences the operation, pronounces a blessing in the following terms: "Blessed be Thy name, O Lord, who hast instituted for us the circumcision." After the operation is completed, he takes a cup of wine and repeats a benediction for the child, and at the same time gives him a name of which his father best approves. On the same day as the child is circumcised, the father of it entertains his relations and friends in as handsome a manner as his circumstances will allow. After the entertainment benedictions and prayers are added for the infant, and they beg of God to bless him with health and prosperity, and give him grace to live in the faith and fear of God. Some of the Jews spend such days in playing cards, and other like amusements.

Every one who performs the operation of circumcision, has a memorandum book into which he chronicles the names of those he has circumcised. This book is placed in his coffin with him when he is buried, for they imagine that if the number in their memorandum book corresponds to the numbers contained in their own name, they are discharged from purgatory. For instance, if the name of the circumciser is David, which name is equal to 14, and if he have circumcised 14 children, he feels certain that he is entitled to the glories of heaven.

There are no ceremonies when the new-born child is a girl, excepting that as soon as the mother is fully recovered, the father informs the Rabbi, and he repeats a short blessing for the child and the mother, and at the same time the Rabbi gives the child a name, such as her father has designated. If a male child should happen to die uncircumcised, they circumcise him before he is buried.

If the first-born child be a boy, it is customary, as soon as he be 30 days old, to send for one of the descendants of Aaron, whom they call a priest, and unto whom all the first-born, if they are males, belong, to redeem; it is in compliance with the injunction: "Sanctify unto me all the first-born, all the first-born of man amongst thy children shalt thou redeem." This ceremony is performed in the following manner: the appointed, so-called priest, several friends and relations, being assembled in the house, the father brings a considerable sum of gold and silver in one dish or basin, and the child in another, to deliver him into the hands of the priest, who, turning to the mother, says with a loud voice, "Madam, is this boy yours?" to which she replies "Yes." "Had you no child before this, either male or female?" To this she replies "No." Then adds the priest, "The child being your first-born, it is my right and property." Turning to the father, he says, "If you are inclined to have this child again you must redeem it." "This gold and silver," replies the father, "was brought for that purpose." The priest then turning towards the assembly, says loudly, "This child is a first-born, and is my property according as it is written, Numb. xviii. 16, 'And those that are to be redeemed shalt thou redeem for the money of five shekels,' instead of which I content myself with this," taking one or two of the golden or silver pieces, and returns the child to his parents. This day is also one of great joy among them.

In case the father or mother are descendants of priests or Levites, they are not obliged to redeem their first-born.

This observance is called פדיון הבן "Pidyon Haben."

We should here mention, that these so-called Priests, who claim to be descendants of Aaron, are honoured by the rest of the Jews, and are permitted on their festival days to repeat the benediction of Aaron in their synagogues. But, since the genealogy of the Jews was lost, from the time of our blessed Saviour, no Jew in our days can particularize or discriminate his tribe; and, consequently, those assuming such titles are much mistaken as to their rights to them. Many have called themselves descendants of Aaron who emigrated to a strange country, but have often afterwards proved themselves to be imposters.

The first Scripture lesson taught to a child*, as soon as it is able to speak, and which every father and mother in Israel tries to engrave upon the hearts of their children, is as follows: "Hear, O Israel: The Lord our God is one Lord: and thou shalt love the Lord thy God with all thine heart, and with all thy soul, and with all thy might." Deut. vi., 4, 5. At the same time, the child is taught the ceremony of the *Fringes*. This consists in putting upon it a little garment having four fringes, one at each corner, which, from thenceforth, he must wear continually; and, as often as he repeats the above mentioned prayer, he must kiss these fringes. According to the Rabbis, the father of the child is held responsible for it in all matters till it reaches the age of thirteen, and, when the boy attains that age, he becomes a *Bar-mitzvah*. After this all responsibility is taken away from his parents, and he becomes responsible for himself. From this time forth the boy is obliged† to wear phylacteries during the time of morning prayer, and make use of the ceremony of the "Fringes," on which occasion he pronounces the following blessing: "Blessed be Thou, Jehovah, our God, who hast sanctified us and commanded us to observe the ordinance of Fringes."

---

* Females are exempt from observing the ceremony of fringes and phylacteries.
† Sabbath and festival days excepted.

According to the Talmud, every orthodox Jew is under obligations to marry at the age of eighteen, and he who remains single after this time, is considered as living in the actual commission of sin. According to the law of Moses, a Jew is permitted to marry as many wives as he chooses, but, at the present day, they do not marry more than one. They are allowed to marry their brother's or sister's daughters, or their first cousins, but a Jew dare not marry his aunt. He may, however, in case of his wife's decease, marry her sister. A widow, or a woman divorced from her husband, cannot marry again until ninety days after the death of the one, or the separation of the other, in order that it may be known whether she be pregnant or no.

If a man die, and his widow have still an unweaned babe, she cannot marry again before the child be two years old.

When the parents of an intended couple have come to an agreement with regard to money, the marriage articles are signed by the future husband and relatives of the wife, after which, the former pays a formal visit to his intended bride, and are solemnly engaged for six or twelve months, sometimes even for two years, according to the agreement made between the parties. During this time, the young lover pays frequent visits to his future mistress, and uses the utmost familiarity consistent with decency in her company.

When the marriage day is appointed, which, if she be a maiden, is on a Wednesday or Friday; or if a widow, on a Thursday. It is insisted that the intended couple should fast on the day of the marriage, until the blessing is pronounced upon them. The nuptial solemnities are performed in the following manner: The young husband takes a gold ring, and in the presence of the Rabbi, places it upon the third finger of his bride, and says: "Be thou sanctified to me with this ring." After which the Rabbis reads the marriage contract, and gives them the benediction. During this solemn ceremony, the young husband is obliged to keep his head covered with a silk cap, made for that purpose, and presented him by his bride. When all is over, there is sometimes a short address delivered to those present.

If a husband die, and leave no issue, his brother (if he have one living) has full authority over the widow, and may either marry her himself, or permit her to marry again, as she chooses. This custom is founded on the precept contained in the law of Moses, which reads as follows: "If brethren dwell together, and one of them die, and have no child, the wife of the dead shall not marry without unto a stranger;

her husband's brother shall go in unto her, and take her to him to be his wife, and perform the duty of an husband's brother unto her."

Modern Jews, however, generally allow the widows their own free choice. This permission is called חליץ הנעל: or the "Loosing of the shoe," found in the Law of Moses: "Then shall his brother's wife come unto him, in the presence of the elders, and loose his shoe from off his foot, and spit in his face, and shall answer and say, 'So shall it be done unto that man, that will not build up his brother's house.'"

This ceremony is a very curious one, and is performed in the following manner: the brother of the deceased husband, in the presence of Rabbis and witnesses, puts on a shoe which is larger than his usual one, made expressly for the purpose. Then the widow repeats the following verse, "My husband's brother refuseth to raise up unto his brother a name in Israel, he will not perform the duty of my husband's brother." The brother-in-law immediately answers the following: "I like not to take her," upon which declaration the widow looses his shoe with her thumbs and fourth fingers, and throws it upon the ground with resentment and disdain, at the same time spitting upon him, and saying in Hebrew, "So shall it be done unto that man that will not build up his brother's house," which sentence she repeats three times. As soon as this is over, the Rabbi informs her that she is now at perfect liberty to marry whom she pleases.

A husband can obtain a divorce from his wife for the least cause whatever, and is founded on Deut. xxiv. 1, "When a man hath taken a wife, and married her, and it comes to pass that she find no favor in his eyes, because he hath found some uncleanness in her, then let him write her a bill of divorcement, and give it in her hand, and send her out of his house."

But the Rabbis refuse to give letters of divorcement, unless well-founded reasons are given for the act of separating. The form of the bill of divorce given to the wife is called גט "Gett," and must be written upon parchment by a Jewish notary, in the presence of one or more of their learned Rabbis or ministers. It must contain no more than twelve lines, and written in square characters, with a number of other trivial punctilious. Moreover, neither the notary, nor the Rabbis or witnesses, must in any way be related to the party wishing to be divorced. This is the purport of the bills of divorce, headed with the date of year, month, day, and name of place, &c.: "I A. B., do voluntary and freely divorce thee, and put thee away, and discharge thee,

C. D., who hast formerly been my wife, and I do hereby give thee full and free permission to marry whom thou pleasest." There are ten persons present at the signing of the bill, besides the two who sign it. After this the ceremony commences. The Rabbi bids the woman to hold open her hands in order that she may receive the bill, and close them tightly again not to drop it, for if it happens, that in her confusion she let it drop, another bill has to be written, and the time postponed. The husband then gives her the bill, saying, "This is thy divorce; I put thee away from me, and give thee full liberty to marry whomsoever thou wilt." The woman takes the bill and delivers it to the Rabbi, who reads it over again, and then she is divorced; but the Rabbi exhorts her not to marry till after three months from the time of divorcement.

There is no festival day for which Jews have such a veneration as their Sabbath-day*—that is, such who keep strictly to their religion, for a great number publicly violate this day, especially in America. The ancient Rabbis reduced all those things which God had forbidden to be done on the Sabbath-day, to thirty-nine articles, whereof each had its particular circumstance and dependencies, namely, not to plow, sow, or reap, to bottle or tie up, to wash, or bake, or card, or spin, or break anything into pieces, or build, or demolish, or beat with a hammer, or hunt, or fish, or ride on horseback, or write, or kindle, or extinguish, or kill, or slay, or carry anything out of doors into the street, &c., &c., &c.

They are strictly forbidden to talk of worldly affairs, or make any bargains with respect to buying and selling. An orthodox Jew adheres to this very firmly, and will forbear from conversation of any kind, except it be of a religious character. No Jew is allowed to walk over two thousand cubits outside of any city, town, or village, wherein he resides, on the Sabbath-day; neither dare they touch any money on that day; neither are they permitted to play on any musical instrument. On Sabbath-eve, they put on clean linen, wash their faces and hands, take their prayer-books, and go to their synagogues. It is necessary to remark here that no orthodox Jew uses a razor to his face; but, instead, either a pair of scissors, or a sort of powder boiled together with lime, which causes the hair to burn away. A woman must light the lamp on Friday evening, before she goes to the synagogue, and, from the moment that she has pronounced the benediction over the lighted lamp, the Sabbath begins.

---

* The Jewish Sabbath is Saturday.

The usual hymn sung first in the synagogue on Sabbath eve, commences thus: "Come, my beloved, to meet the bride; the presence of the Sabbath let us receive," &c. The following in the same hymn is remarkable: "Shake off the dust; arise, O my people, and adorn thyself with thy beautiful attire; for by the hand of Jesse, the Bethlemite, redemption draweth nigh to my soul."

After the ninety-second Psalm has been chanted, the Sabbath begins everywhere.

After this meeting, the usual salutations are exchanged, not with a "Good evening," or "Good night," but "A Good Sabbath to you." As soon as the parents return home, they bless their children, and sing a song to welcome the angels who, they believe, visit them in their houses on the Sabbath. The father then takes a glass of wine in his hand, and repeats the first three verses of the second chapter of Genesis, after which he returns thanks to God for having instituted the Sabbath, and blesses the wine, of which he then drinks a part himself, and gives a small quantity to those who sit at table with him. After this he blesses the bread and distributes it to all, who then eat, and spend the Sabbath in a joyful and happy manner.

Some Jews believe that they possess an additional soul, which enters into them on Friday evening, and departs from them on Saturday night; therefore, they say, their appetites become stronger, and, hence, must eat twice as much on those days as on others.

They go to the synagogue on Saturday morning, where they repeat several psalms and prayers in commendation of the Sabbath, which are intermixed with their common prayers. The five books of Moses, which are written on parchment, and neatly arrayed, are then taken out from the ark, and seven persons called up to the altar to hear the Minister read the allotted section for that day, for the law of Moses is divided into fifty-two portions, a portion for every Sabbath in the year.

After the reading of the section, the Minister reads a solemn benediction for the Sovereign under whose government they live, wherein he beseeches Almighty God to keep him or her in joy and peace; that all his or her undertakings may prosper; that his or her dominion may be increased; and that he or she may love their people. At the conclusion of this prayer, he sometimes repeats a prayer for the departed souls, and then the law is carried back to the ark. If the Minister is qualified enough, he delivers a short address, in which he commends virtue, discourages vice, &c., illustrating his ideas by passages taken out of the Talmud. Most of the Jewish Ministers, however, preach only monthly, or quarterly, and also on their festival occasions. When this is over, an additional service is held, instead of sacrifices, in which they repeat the order of the sacrifices, and pray that God might restore them their Temple, and enable them all once more to bring their sacrifices into that holy place. This ends the morning service. In the afternoon, there is another short service in the synagogue; but, as soon as evening approaches, and they can discover three stars of any considerable magnitude, their Sabbath is over, and they are permitted to work, as on any other day. Yet, they always prolong the Sabbath as much as possible; for they have a superstitious opinion among them that the souls of the damned, as well as those in purgatory, endure no pain or torments on this day. At the close of the Sabbath, they sing hymns to welcome Elijah, the prophet, who, they imagine, visits their houses every Sabbath evening, and whom they expect to come with their long-expected Messiah. They then salute each other again with a "God grant you a lucky week."

CHAPTER III.

When the Sanhedrim, that is to say, the judges of Jerusalem, bore sway and exercised their authority, two men were appointed by them, specially, to give notice of the first appearance of the moon, and upon their report to the Sanhedrim, public notice was given, that the month began from that day, and thereby they fixed their holidays, with relation to the times prescribed for their festival days. But since the Temple was destroyed, they settle it by computation, and print a calendar every year, which shows them the times of the new and the full moon, the seasons of the year, and their festivals. They also set down the festival days of the Christians, in order to know what days are most suitable to trade with them.

The fifteenth day of the month *Nisan*, answering to our April, is the first day of their feast of the Passover, which they call "*Pasech*," in commemoration of the Jews' departure from Egypt. It continues a whole week, during which time they must eat unleavened bread; they dare not even have leavened bread in their houses. The bread they eat is called *Matzoth*.

The eve on which the Passover commences, the table-cloth being laid as usual, three plates are placed thereon; in one, is put three Passover cakes, in another, the shank bone of the shoulder of lamb, and an egg, both roasted on the coals; in the third, some lettuce and celery, or chervil and parsley; and a cup of vinegar, or salt water; likewise, a compound formed of almonds, apples, &c., worked up to the consistence of lime.

The table being thus formed, every one at table has a glass or cup of wine placed before him; for on these nights every person is obliged to drink four glasses or cups of wine, called ארבע כוסות. The four cups, which are in commemoration of the four different expressions in connection with the redemption of the Jews from Egypt. The whole family then take hold of the dish which contains the unleavened bread, and say the following: "Lo! this is as the bread of affliction, which our ancestors ate in the land of Egypt: let all those who are hungry enter and eat thereof; and all who are necessitous come and celebrate the Passover. At present we celebrate it here, but the next year we hope to celebrate it in the land of Israel. This year we are servants here, but next year we hope to be freemen in the land of

Israel." Thus is initiated the service of the Passover. In preparation for this feast they must change all their kitchen utensils, and are not allowed to taste any beer, brandy, or anything that has leaven in it.

From the day after the Passover is completed to the thirty-third day following, they spend the time in a sort of mourning, neither marrying, nor cutting their hair, nor shaving themselves, nor even dressing themselves in any new clothes, or showing any public demonstration of joy, for they say that, during this time, there was a great mortality among the pupils of a most celebrated Rabbi, ten thousand of whom perished in one day.

Seven weeks after the first day of the Passover they celebrate the "Feast of Weeks." This feast is likewise called in Scripture "The day of first fruits;" because the first fruits of the year were offered in the Temple upon that day. But the Rabbis give another reason for this festival. They say, that, on this day, the law was given to Moses on Mount Sinai, and hence, many Jews are accustomed to spend the whole night of that festival in reading the whole law.

The Talmudists do not agree as to the time when the world came into existence. Some insist that it was in the Spring, and others again that in was in Autumn. The latter notion has so far prevailed, that they begin to count the months of the year from Autumn, and though it is written in Scripture of the month of "*Nisan*" (April), "This month shall be unto you the beginning of months." Yet they, notwithstanding, commence to count the year from the month *Tishri*, (September.)

The Jews hold from tradition, that particularly on the first day of their first month, God Almighty judges the actions committed through the past year, and orders those things to happen in the coming year. This day being, as it were, the very point of time of the world's birth, they imagine that God thereon carefully reviews all the occurrences of the preceding year. This day they call the Feast of the New Year, and is kept very solemnly by almost all Jews. On this day they promise repentance, and sound the trumpet or horn in the synagogue. Some orthodox Jews believe that every sound which proceeds from the trumpet, in some mysterious way sends forth some angels, who afterwards fight with Satan, or some other evil-spirit, who occupies the door of Heaven, to prevent prayers from reaching the throne of God. They also call upon certain angels by name, and beseech them to carry their prayers Heavenward. On the same day, after evening service, they go to a river, and cast small crumbs of bread, or any other particles they may have in their pockets, into the water, at the same time repeating the words of Micah:

"Who is a God like unto Thee, that pardoneth iniquity, and passeth by the transgressions of the remnant of His heritage? He retaineth not His anger for ever, because He delighted in mercy. He will turn again; He will have compassion upon us; He will subdue our iniquities; and thou wilt cast all their sins into the depths of the sea." After this ceremony, they imagine all their sins are cast into the deep, to be remembered no more against them. At this feast, they usually eat their bread with honey, which signifies "to have a sweet year." Their salutation on this occasion is, "may a good year be written down for thee."

The tenth day of the same month, they celebrate the day of expiation, which is also called the day of atonement. They keep this day very strictly, for they believe that on this day all their sins and crimes are blotted out, according to Leviticus xxiii, 27 : "Also on the tenth day of this seventh month there shall be a day of atonement : it shall be an holy convocation unto you ;" &c.

On the day before this festival, they practice a very curious ceremony. Every Jew takes a living fowl, and swings it thrice around his head, at each time repeating, "Let this be sacrificed in my stead." This custom is called *Caparoth*, and though it is not actually commanded, and is a groundless and idle superstition, yet almost every Jew performs this ceremony. These fowls are afterwards killed and eaten; for the Jews indulge themselves in eating much more on this day, on account of their having to fast the whole of the next day. On the eve before the day of atonement, many of them receive thirty-nine stripes with a leather strap, which is done as follows :—A certain man, who must be a pious Jew, and appointed for that office, stands at the door of the synagogue and asks each one, as he passes in, if he wishes to receive the thirty-nine stripes? If the answer be "Yes," he prostrates himself on the floor, and receives them from the executioner.

In former times, the ceremony was performed under the rule of the Sanhedrim, and persons who committed crimes were condemned to receive these thirty-nine stripes.

On this day, they ask pardon of those whom they have injured, and forgive those who have injured them. They also give alms, and show all the demonstrations of a sincere repentance. Many put on their grave clothes, (in which every Jew is married, and wears them once every year, which is on this day of atonement), and are obliged to stand shoeless in their synagogues, when the whole day is spent in prayer and weeping. Some even remain their over night and sing psalms. They also read the account of the sacrifices, and relate the celebrated ceremony of the

High Priest, who was never permitted but on this day, to enter into the holy of holies, there to burn frankincense, and cast lots upon the two goats; one of which was for the Lord and the other for *Asasel*.

They confess their crimes and sins on this day ten times, and so loud that all may hear them; in doing which they strike their breasts, and weep bitterly, some even as loud as their strength permits.

Children who are over twelve years old, are also obliged to fast on this day. As evening approaches, and the three stars are visible, they sound the horn, which denotes that the feast is ended. Then they return home from the synagogue, and wish each other long life, with its blessings, in a very cordial manner. Parents also bless their children, and then sit down to a hearty meal.

On the fifteenth day of the same month, is celebrated again the feast of tents, or tabernacles, which they call *Sukath*, in commemoration of encampment in the wilderness, when they departed out of Egypt, and is founded on the institution which is written in the xxiii ch. 42 v. of Leviticus—"Ye shall dwell in booths seven days," &c. Every family, therefore, makes a tent in some open place near the house, which is then covered with leaves, and adorned inside in the best manner possible, with fruit and beautiful flowers. The Jews eat and drink in these tents, and some even stay there over night. This feast is celebrated a whole week. On this feast they secure themselves with a branch of the palm tree, and three small twigs of the willow perfect and complete, according to Scripture,—"And ye shall take you on the first day the boughs of goodly trees, branches of palm trees, and the boughs of thick trees, and willows of the brook."

During the repetition of several psalms in their synagogues, they hold these branches in their right hand, and a citron in their left, and shake them towards the four quarters of the earth. In singing some particular hymns, they move in solemn order round the altar, once a day; but on the seventh day of this feast, they take willow branches, and move in solemn order seven times round the altar, which is erected in the synagogue, singing "Hosannah," which word occurs in the New Testament, and was sung when our blessed Redeemer entered into the City of Jerusalem. The word "Hosannah," is a Hebrew word, and signifies, "Help! O Lord!" or as commonly translated, "Save! O Lord!"

On the eighth day of this feast, they finish the reading of the five books of Moses, and spend the remainder of the day in amusements of various kinds.

They have also a feast of Dedication on the the twenty-fifth of the month *Kislef* (December), in commemoration of the victory which the Maccabees obtained over the Greeks. This feast is simply celebrated by reading an additional portion of prayers, and every Jew is obliged to light eight lamps every evening, in celebration of a great miracle, which, they believe, happened with a bottle of oil in the temple.

On the fourteenth of the month *Adar* (March), is the feast of "Purim," observed throughout the world, by all the Jews, in honor of Esther, the Queen, who, upon that day, preserved the people of Israel from the conspiracy of a wicked Haman. This feast is celebrated by reading over the history of Esther twice, after which the whole day is spent in pleasure and amusement.

The ninth day of the month *Ab* (August), they keep as a fast day, in commemoration of the destruction of their two temples, for on this day they were both destroyed. They meet in their Synagogues on this day, put off their shoes, sit on the floor, and repeat the Lamentations of Jeremiah, and mourning hymns composed by their Rabbies. Here, it must be observed, that the Jews on their fast days are not permitted to taste anything from the eve of one day till the eve of the next day.

The Jews consider themselves in duty bound, and as a very laudable action, to visit the sick, and assist them in time of distress.

When any one is apprehensive that his life is in apparent danger, he sends for several persons. One at least, if possible, must be a Rabbi, or a pious Jew. In their presence, the sick man repeats in a solemn manner the general confession, and then humbly begs of God, if it is his blessed will, to restore him to his former state of health; but if not granted, he recommends his soul to Almighty God, and prays that his death may be accepted as an expiation for his sins. After this is over, he begs pardon of all whom he may at any time have offended, and likewise forgives those who had done him wrong, even his most inveterate enemies. In case he have children, or domestics, he calls them to his bedside and gives them his benediction. If his own father or mother be present, he receives their blessing; and if he desires to make his will, and dispose of the worldly estate with which God was pleased to bless him, he is at perfect liberty to do it as he pleases.

There are some who, when dangerously ill, give charity to the poor, contribute towards the synagogue, and ask a public prayer to be offered up in their behalf, at which time the Rabbi gives him an additional name. This is called פדיון נפש *(Pidyon Nefesh)*, which, they believe, will effect a change for the better.

When the person sick is in immediate danger of death, they never leave his bedside, but watch over him both day and night, in order to be present at the separation of the soul from the body. The person who is present when the dying man expires, rends some part of his clothes, and it is customary among them to throw out into the streets all the water there is in the house, or that can be found in the neighborhood, which denotes that some one lies dead not far from the place.

The dead body is wrapped in a sheet, and laid upon the floor, with the face covered. A lighted candle is placed at its head. After the corpse is thoroughly washed with warm water, he is dressed in his grave clothes, of which has already been spoken, and is covered with his *Talith*. Thus dressed, the body is placed in a coffin made specially for it, with a linen cloth over it, and another beneath. A small bag of earth is placed under the head, and then the coffin is covered with black and carried out of the house. All the people attending crowd around it, and as it is considered very meritorious, as many as can, carry it upon their shoulders to the grave. In some places the mourners follow the coffin with lighted flambeaux in their hands, and sing mournful hymns as they march along. The nearest relatives of the deceased must also rend a small part in one of their garments. When this is over, the coffin, nailed up, is lowered into the grave, and each of the friends throw a handfull of earth upon it, until the grave is filled up. On their departure from the grave, each one tears up two or three handsful of grass, or something else, and throws it behind him, at the same time repeating the seventy-second psalm. Then they wash their hands, and return to their respective abodes, for no Jew is allowed to enter a house before he has washed his hands. When the corpse is conveyed away to the grave, a lighted lamp is placed at the head of the bed, which burns for seven days without interruption. Some Jews will even have it burning for thirty days. They also place a glassful of water, and a towel, with the lamp, for they believe that the soul of the departed comes to wash there every night.

The nearest relatives of the deceased party, after returning home from the burial service, immediately sit down upon the floor, and having taken off their shoes, are served with bread, wine, and hard eggs, with which they refresh themselves. Those who are the nearest relatives reside in the house for seven days, during which time they sit and eat upon the floor, except on the Sabbath day, when they, with a select company, go to the synagogue. During these seven days, they are not permitted to do any manner of business. The husband must separate himself from his wife, and every morning and evening ten persons go into the house of mourning to pray with them, and offer up an additional prayer for the soul of the departed one, on which great stress is laid. The Jews dress in such mourning clothes as is customary, according to the country in which they live, for no divine directions are given concerning this matter.

After the expiration of the seven days, they leave the house and go to the synagogue, where they order lamps to be lighted, procure prayers to be read, and promise charitable contributions for the soul of the departed. This is repeated at the close of each month.

If there be a son of the deceased, he generally goes daily to the synagogue, both morning and evening, and there repeats a prayer called *Ka-dish*, for the soul of his departed parent, for eleven months. Children are obliged to visit the graves of their parents every year, and pray there. The daily prayers for a departed soul cease at the close of the eleven months, for so long, they believe, the soul suffers in Purgatory.

In some places, they set a monument over the grave, and cut not only the name of the deceased upon it, but also an index to his character, so that a man is able to discover, from the description on the tombstone, what sort of a person the buried was, and judge of his moral and religious character.

CHAPTER IV.

SYNAGOGUES.

Origin of Synagogues—A Lawful Assembly—A Caraite's Prayers.

SYNAGOGUES.

Although the word "Synagogue" is rarely found in the Old Testament, spelled with so many letters in our English Bibles, yet both reason, and equivalent expressions used there, do more than, probably, persuade us, that such conventions and meeting places were no strangers to Israel in those days.*

R. Phinehas, in the name of R. Hoshaia, saith :—There were four hundred and sixty synagogues in Jerusalem : every one of which had a house of the book and a house of doctrine, that is, where the Scripture might be read, and a house of doctrine for traditions, that is, the Beth Midrash. Their preciseness in not commencing public worship before having the number of ten adult male members present, arose from this—because they held that not to be a lawful congregation, nor pleasing to God, in which there were not ten persons, "And they read not in the law, nor in the prophets, or in the synagogue, nor lifted up their hands (Priests), unless there were ten persons present." For they thought not that God was present there, if there were not so many present. "The Divine Majesty dwelleth not among less than ten. When the holy, blessed God, cometh into the synagogue, and findeth not ten there, he is presently angry: as it is said, Wherefore came I, and there was no man!"

A CARAITE PRAYER.

Cantor—On account of the palace which is laid waste:
People—We sit down alone and weep.
Cantor—On account of the temple which is destroyed:
People—We sit down alone and weep.
Cantor—On account of the wall which is pulled down:

---

* Synagogues must have been in existence before the first restoration. Commonly they were called Batch Knesioth (בית הכנסת) Sing.

People—We sit down alone and weep.
Cantor—On account of our majesty which is gone:
People—We sit down alone and weep.
Cantor—On account of the precious stones which are burned:
People—We sit down alone and weep.
Cantor—On account of the priests which have stumbled:
People—We sit down alone and weep.
Cantor—On account of our kings who have despised Him:
People—We sit down alone and weep.

Another.

Cantor—We beseech thee have mercy upon Zion:
People—Gather the children of Jerusalem.
Cantor—Make haste, Redeemer of Zion:
People—Speak to the heart of Jerusalem.
Cantor—May beauty and majesty surround Zion:
People—And turn with thy mercy to Jerusalem.
Cantor—Remember the shame of Zion:
People—Make new again the ruins of Jerusalem.
Cantor—May the royal government shine again over Zion:
People—Comfort those who mourn at Jerusalem.
Cantor—May joy and gladness be found at Zion:
People—A branch shall spring forth at Jerusalem.

CHAPTER V.

TUNES, MUSIC, AND MELODY.

Music of the Temple, which survives—Obscurity of the subject—Nature of Hebrew notation—Character of Hebrew Melodies—Christian Chants adopted from Temple Melodies—Specimens reduced to modern notation.

TUNES, MUSIC, MELODY.

After the destruction of the Temple by the Romans, under Titus, the voice and harp of both Levites and people became mute, and the sufferings the Israelitish nation underwent during the first years of their captivity and dispersion, left them no leisure for the cultivation of music, devotional or otherwise; but as soon as public worship could be again re-established, and "The utterance of the lips" had replaced the former "offerings of bulls," the ancient well-remembered, and traditionally preserved temple melodies, were also re-introduced, and the selection of Psalms, which then and since have formed an integral part of their prayers, were sung to them. It is scarcely to be doubted, that the acknowledged efficacy of music, as a handmaid to devotion, and the general inclination and aptitude of the Israelite nation for that sublime art, led them, even during that period of captivity and distress, to repeat in their services, at least vocally, the ancient, traditional, and venerated tones and sacred melodies, which they naturally then valued and cherished, more as the sole remains of the former temple service, as consolatory tones in their distress, and as the sweet reminiscences of better times of national glory.

That most of these melodies were forgotten and lost in the course of time, is a result which will not surprise any one acquainted with the unparalleled sufferings and dispersions the Israelites had to endure, during the many ages of their subsequent history, especially when it is also considered, that the most strenuous exertions of the learned have hitherto failed to elucidate the music of the Greeks, the Romans, and of other ancient nations more powerful and prosperous than the Israelites, and that the art of musical notation was not invented till the fourteenth century. Still some, though very few, of these melodies exist, of which there is reason to suppose, that owing to their having been traditionally preserved, and transmitted from one generation to another, with religious care and veneration, have reached our times.

The reading of the sacred Scriptures, was from the earliest times, always accompanied by the observance of certain signs or accents intended to determine the sense, and as musical notes, which, although they have a distinct form and figure, do not, nevertheless, present a determinate sound like our present musical notes, but their soul is dependent on oral instruction, since the same signs vary in sound in the various scriptural books, and are modulated according to the tenor and contents of them.

In considering the structure and character of the ancient melodies, traditionally and orally descended to us, we find that either as original compositions, or as adaptations, they are eminently calculated to fulfil their intended purpose; for though simple in character, yet they are sufficiently melodeous to please the ear, and attract the multitude. They have the further merit of adaptability to the use of a great mass, and of whole congregations, who might, perhaps, be without the aid of instrumental music to guide and direct them.

Hence the cause of their simplicity, in order to enable them to be acquired and executed by most voices, and also the reason of their shortness, which, though it proves monotonous, especially in long pieces, by the too frequent repetition of the same melody, is an inconvenience overlooked by them, for they feel themselves amply compensated by the more important advantage of their being easily acquired and executed by a mixed congregation, and as easily transmitted, by constant practice, to following generations.

It has also been clearly proved, that the chants of the early Christians are derived from the temple melodies, and are adopted by them from the Jews.

CHAPTER VI.

ADORATION AND PRAYER.

A Prayer of Adoration and Supplication—A Morning Prayer—A Special Prayer for Mondays and Thursdays—Confession and Prayer for Day of Atonement.

ADORATION AND PRAYER.

The breath of all living bless Thy name, O Lord, our God! The spirit of all flesh, continually glorify and extol Thy memorial, O our King! Thou art God from eternity to eternity; besides Thee, we acknowledge neither King, Redeemer or Saviour; Thou redeemest, deliverest, maintainest, and hast compassion over us, in all times of trouble and distress; we have no king but Thee. Thou art God of the first, and God of the last, the God of all creatures; the Lord of all productions; Thou art adored with all manner of praise; who governeth the universe with tenderness, and Thy creatures with mercy. Lo! the Lord neither slumbereth nor sleepeth, but rouseth those who sleep, awakeneth those who slumber; causeth the dumb to speak; looseth those that are bound; supporteth the fallen; and raiseth up those who droop; and therefore, Thee alone do we worship. Although our mouths were filled with melodious songs, as the drops of the sea; our tongues with shouting, as the roaring billows thereof; our lips with praise, like the wide-extended firmament; our eyes with sparkling brightness, like the sun and moon; our hands extended like the towering eagles; and our feet as the hinds for swiftness; we, nevertheless, are incapable of rendering sufficient thanks unto Thee, O Lord, our God! and the God of our fathers; or to bless Thy name, for one of the innumerable benefits which Thou hast conferred on us and our ancestors. For Thou, O Lord, our God, didst redeem us from Egypt, and release us from the house of bondage; in time of famine didst Thou sustain us; and in plenty didst Thou nourish us. Thou didst deliver us from the sword; saved us from pestilence; and from many sore and heavy diseases, hast thou withdrawn us. Hitherto Thy tender mercies have supported us, and Thy kindness hath not forsaken us. O Lord, our God! forsake us not in future. Therefore the members of which Thou hast formed us, the spirit and soul which Thou hast breathed into us, and the tongue Thou hast placed in our mouths; lo! they shall worship, bless, praise, glorify, extol, reverence, sanctify and ascribe sovereign power unto Thy name, our

King! every mouth shall adore Thee, and every tongue shall swear unto Thee; unto Thee every knee shall bend; every rational being shall worship Thee; every heart shall revere Thee; the inward part and reins shall sing praise unto Thy name; as it is written—all my bones shall say, O Lord! who is like unto Thee? who delivered the weak from him that is too strong for him; the poor and needy from their oppressors; who is like unto Thee? who is equal unto Thee; who can be compared unto Thee? great, mighty, and tremendous God! most high God! possessor of Heaven and earth! We will praise, adore, glorify, and bless Thy name; so saith David—Bless the Lord, O my soul! and all that is within me, bless His holy name. O God! who art mighty in Thy strength! who art great by Thy glorious name! mighty for ever, tremendous by Thy fearful acts. The King! who sitteth on the high and exalted throne, inhabiting eternity, most exalted and holy is Thy name; and it is written, rejoice in the Lord, O ye righteous, for to the just, praise is comely. With the mouth of the upright shalt Thou be praised; blessed with the lips of the righteous; extolled with the tongue of the pious; by a choir of saints shalt Thou be sanctified.

And in the congregation of many thousands of Thy people, the house of Israel shall Thy name, our King! be glorified in song throughout all generations; for such is the duty of every created being towards Thee, O Lord, our God! and the God of our fathers, to render thanks, to praise, extol, glorify, exalt, ascribe glory, bless, magnify, and adore Thee with all the songs and praises of Thy servant David, the son of Jesse, thine anointed. May Thy name be praised for ever, our King, the Almighty, the King; the great and holy in heaven and upon earth; for unto Thee appertaineth, O Lord! our God, and the God of our fathers, song and praise, hymns and psalms, might and dominion, victory and power, greatness, adoration, glory, holiness and majesty; blessings and thanksgivings are Thine from henceforth unto everlasting! Blessed art Thou, O Lord! Almighty King, great with praises, Almighty to be adored, Lord of wonders, who hast accepted songs of psalmody. King, Almighty, who livest eternally.

All beings give thanks unto Thee; they all praise Thee, and every one declares that there is none holy like the Lord. They all extol Thee for ever, O Thou who formest all things. O God! who daily openest the portals of the gates of the east, and cleavest the windows of the firmament; bringest forth the sun from its place, and the moon from the place of its residence, and enlightenest the universe, and all its inhabitants, which thou didst create according to Thy attribute of mercy.

Thou who with mercy illuminated the earth and those who dwell therein, and in Thy goodness every day constantly renewest the work of the creation. Thou art the only King to be extolled, praised, glorified, and exalted, ever since the creation. Thou art the everlasting God; in thine abundant mercy have compassion on us; O Lord! Thou art our strength, the rock of our fortress, the shield of our salvation, be Thou our defence. There is none to be compared with Thee; nor is there any besides Thee; there is no other save Thee, and who is like unto Thee? There is none to be compared with Thee, O Lord our God, in this world; nor is there any beside Thee, O our King! in a future state. There is no other save Thee, O our Redeemer! in the days of the Messiah; and who will be like Thee, O our Saviour! at the resurrection of the dead?

God is the Lord of all productions; he is praised and adored by the mouth of every soul breathing; his power and goodness fill the universe. Knowledge and understanding encircle him, who exalted himself above the angels, and is adorned with glory on his heavenly seat. Purity and rectitude are before His throne; kindness and mercy complete his glory. The luminaries which our God created are good; for He formed them with knowledge, understanding, and wisdom; He hath endued them with power and might, to bear rule in the world. They are filled with splendor and radiate brightness; their splendor is graceful throughout the world. They rejoice when going forth, and are glad at their return; and with reverential awe perform the will of their Creator; they ascribe glory and majesty to His name, joy and song to the commemoration of His kingdom. He called the sun, and it rose in resplendent light; and at His look the moon assumed its varying form. The whole heavenly host ascribe praise unto Him; the seraphim ophanim, and holy angels, ascribe glory and majesty.

Who is like unto Thee, O Lord! among the mighty? Who is like unto Thee, O Lord! among the mighty? Who is like unto Thee, glorious in holiness, tremendous in praises, working miracles?

Thou strong rock of Israel, rise in assistance unto Israel, and relieve according to Thy promise, Judah and Israel. As for our Redeemer, the Lord of Hosts is His name, the holy one of Israel. Blessed art Thou, O Lord! the Redeemer of Israel.

PRAYER.

O Lord! open Thou my lips, and my mouth shall declare Thy praise.

Blessed art Thou, O Lord, our God, and the God of our fathers, the God of Abraham, the God of Isaac, and the God of Jacob; the great God! powerful and tremendous; the most high God! bountifully dispensing benefits, the Creator of all things, who, remembering the piety of the fathers, will send a Redeemer to their posterity, for His name's sake, in love. O King! Thou art our supporter, Saviour and protector. Blessed art Thou, O Lord! the shield of Abraham. Thou, O Lord, art forever powerful; Thou restorest life to the dead, and art mighty to save. Sustaining by Thy benevolence, the living, and by Thine abundant mercy animating the dead; supporting those that fall; healing the sick; setting at liberty those that are in bonds; and performeth Thy faithful words unto those that sleep in the dust. Who is like unto Thee, O Lord! most mighty? or who may be compared with Thee! the King who killeth and again restoreth life, and causeth salvation to flourish. Who is like unto Thee, most merciful Father; who remembereth His creatures in life. Thou art also faithful to revive the dead. Blessed art Thou, O Lord! who revivest the dead. Thou art holy, and holy is Thy name, and the saints praise Thee daily—Selah. Blessed art Thou, O Lord! holy God!

Return us, O our Father! to the observance of Thy law, and draw us near, O our King! to thy service; and convert us to Thee, by perfect repentance. Blessed art Thou, O Lord! who vouchsafest repentance.

Forgive us, we beseech thee, O our Father! for we have sinned! pardon us, O our King! for we have transgressed; for Thou art ready to pardon and to forgive. Blessed art thou, O Lord, who art gracious, and ready to pardon. O look upon our afflictions, we beseech Thee, and plead our cause; and redeem us speedily for the sake of thy name; for Thou art a mighty Redeemer. Blessed art thou, O Lord; who redeemest Israel. Heal us, O Lord! and we shall be healed; save us, and we shall be saved! for Thou art our praise. O grant us a perfect cure for all our wounds; for Thou art an omnipotent King! a merciful and faithful Physician. Blessed art Thou, O Lord! who healeth the diseases of His people Israel. O Lord, our God! bless this year for us, as also every species of its fruits for our benefit; and bestow dew and rain for a blessing upon the face of the earth. O satisfy us with Thy goodness, and bless this year as other good and fruitful years. Blessed art thou, O Lord! who blesseth the years. O sound the great cornet as a signal for our freedom; hoist the banner to collect our captives, so that we may all be gathered together from the four corners of the earth. Blessed art thou, O Lord! who gather together the outcasts of his people Israel.

O restore our judges as aforetime, and our counsellors as at the beginning; remove from us sorrow and sighing. O Lord! reign Thou alone over us in kindness and mercy; and justify us in judgment. Blessed art Thou, O Lord! the King who loveth righteousness and justice. O let the slanderers have no hope; all the wicked be annihilated speedily, and all the tyrants be cut off quickly; humble Thou them quickly in our days. Blessed art Thou, O Lord! who destroyest enemies, and humblest tyrants. O Lord our God! may Thy tender mercy be moved toward the just, the pious and the elders of Thy people, the house of Israel; the remnant of their scribes, the virtuous strangers, as also towards us; and bestow a good reward unto all those who faithfully put their trust in Thy name; and grant that our portion may ever be with them. Blessed art Thou, O Lord! who art the support and confidence of the just. O be mercifully pleased to return to Jerusalem, Thy City; and dwell therein, as Thou hast promised. O rebuild it shortly, even in our days a structure of everlasting fame, and speedily establish the throne of David thereon. Blessed art Thou, O Lord! who rebuildest Jerusalem. O cause the offspring of Thy servant, David, speedily to flourish, and let his horn be exalted in Thy salvation; for we daily hope for Thy salvation. Blessed art thou, O Lord, who causest the horn of salvation to bud. Hear our voice O Lord, our God! O have compassion and mercy upon us, and accept our prayers with mercy and favor; for Thou art Omnipotent. Thou harkenest to prayers and supplications, and from Thy presence, O our King! dismiss us not empty; for Thou hearest the prayers of Thy people Israel in mercy. Blessed art Thou, O Lord, who harkenest the prayers. Graciously accept, O Lord, our God! Thy people Israel, and have regard unto their prayers. Restore the service to the inner part of Thine house, and accept of the burnt offering of Israel, and their prayers with love and favor. And may the service of Israel, Thy people, be ever pleasing to Thee. Our God and the God of our fathers, shall cause our prayers to ascend, and come, approach, be seen, accepted, heard, and be thought on; and be remembered in remembrance of us, and in remembrance of our fathers; in remembrance of Thine anointed Messiah, the son of David, Thy servant, and in remembrance of Jerusalem, Thy holy city, and in commemmoration of Thy people, the house of Israel, before Thee, to a good issue: With favor, with grace, and with mercy, to life and peace. O Lord, our God! remember us thereon for good; visit us with a blessing, and save us to enjoy life; and with the word of salvation and mercy, have compassion, and be gracious unto us. O have mercy upon us, and save us, for our eyes are continually towards

COMMENCEMENT OF MORNING PRAYER.

Thee, for Thou, O God! art a merciful and gracious King. O that our eyes may behold Thy return to Zion with mercy. Blessed art Thou, O Lord, who restoreth His Divine presence unto Zion.

We reverentially acknowledge that Thou art the Lord our God, and the God of our fathers, the God of all creatures; our Former, the former of the beginning; let blessing and thanksgiving be ascribed unto Thy great and holy name, for Thou hast preserved us alive and supported us; even so grant us life, be gracious and assemble our captives at the courts of Thy sanctuary, and to perform Thy holy will with an upright heart, for with gratitude we confess thee. Blessed be God, to whom appertaineth all grateful praises.

We adore Thee for the miracles, the redemption, mighty deeds, salvation and triumph which Thou didst bestow upon our ancestors in former time. O grant peace, happiness and blessing of race, favor and mercy, unto us, and all Thy people Israel; bless us, even all of us together, our Father! with the light of Thy countenance; for by the light of Thy counntenance hast thou given us, O Lord, our God, the law of life, benevolent love, righteousness, blessing, mercy, life and peace; and may it please Thee to bless Thy people Israel, at all times, with Thy peace.

O, my God, be pleased to guard my tongue from evil, and my lips from uttering deceit. And be Thou silent, O my soul, to those who curse me, and grant that my soul may be humble as the dust to every one. Open my heart to receive Thy law, that my soul may pursue Thy commandments. Speedily, I beseech Thee, frustrate the devices and destroy the imaginations of all those who think evil against me. O grant it for Thy name; grant it for Thy right hand; grant it for Thy holiness; grant it for Thy law; that Thy beloved may be delivered. O save me with Thy right hand, and answer me. May the words of my mouth, and the meditations of my heart, be acceptable in Thy presence May He who maketh peace in His high heavens, grant peace unto us and all Israel.

Let it be acceptable before Thee, O Lord, our God! and the God of our fathers, that the Holy Temple may speedily be re-built in our days, and let our portion be in Thy law.

COMMENCEMENT OF MORNING PRAYER.

Blessed is He who said, "and the world existed;" blessed is He; blessed is the Creator of the beginning; blessed is He that sayeth and accomplished; blessed is He who decreeth and establisheth; blessed is He who hath compassion on all creatures; blessed is He who compensateth good reward to those who fear him; blessed is He who liveth for ever and existeth everlasting; blessed is He who redeemeth and preserveth; blessed is His name; blessed art Thou O Lord, our God! King of the Universe! the Almighty, merciful Father! who is praised with the mouth of His people; extolled and glorified with the tongue of His saints and servants; therefore with the psalms of David, Thy servant, we will praise Thee, O Lord, our God! and with songs and praises we will magnify, praise and extol Thee; yea, we will remember Thy name, and proclaim Thee our King! our God! the only one who liveth eternally. The King, praised and glorified be His great name for ever. Blessed art Thou, O Lord! a King magnified with praises.

SPECIAL PRAYER FOR MONDAYS AND THURSDAYS.

He, the most merciful! forgiveth iniquity and destroyeth not; yea, He frequently turneth His anger away, and awakeneth not all His wrath. O Lord! withhold not Thy mercies from us; let Thy benignity and truth preserve us continually. Save us, O Lord, our God! and gather us from among the nations, that we may give thanks unto Thy holy name, and glory in Thy praise. If Thou wilt mark our iniquities, O Lord! who will be able to exist? But forgiveness is with Thee, that thou mayest be revered. O deal not with us according to our sins, nor reward us according to our iniquities. Although our iniquities testify against us, O Lord! yet grant our request, for Thy name's sake. O Lord, remember Thy mercy and benevolence; for they are everlasting. The Lord will answer us in the day of trouble; the name of the God of Jacob shall be our refuge. Save us, O Lord! The heavenly King shall answer us on the day when we call. Our Father, and our King! be gracious unto us, and regard us, for we are destitute of good works; act therefore charitably by us, for Thy name's sake. O Lord, our God! hear the voice of our supplications, remember the covenant with our ancestors, and help us for Thy name's sake. O Lord our God! who has brought forth Thy people out of the land of Egypt with a mighty hand, and didst acquire a glorious name; we acknowledge that we have sinned, we have done wickedly. O Lord! according to all Thy righteousness, we beseech Thee, to let Thy anger and Thy wrath be turned away from Jerusalem, Thy City, and Thy holy mountain; for on account of our sins, and the ini-

SPECIAL PRAYER FOR MONDAYS AND THURSDAYS. 83

quities of our ancestors, Jerusalem, and thy people, are become a reproach to all who surround them. Now, therefore, O our God! hear the prayer of Thy servant, and his supplication, and cause Thy countenance to shine upon Thy sanctuary, which is desolate, for Thy sake, O Lord!

O my God! incline Thine ear, and hear; open Thine eyes, and behold our desolations, and the desolation of Thy City, which is called by Thy name; for we do not presume to present our supplication before Thee, for our righteousness, but for Thy great mercy. O Lord, hear. O Lord, forgive. O Lord, be graciously attentive, and grant our request; delay not, for Thine own name sake. O my God! for Thy City and Thy people are called by Thy name. Our Father, who art a merciful Father, show us a good token, and gather our dispersions from the four corners of the earth. Then shall nations know, and acknowledge that Thou, O Lord, art our God. And now, our Lord, Thou art our Father, and we are but as clay, yet hast Thou formed us, and we are the work of Thy hands. O Save us, for Thy name's sake, our Creator, for Thou art our King and Redeemer. O Lord, have compassion on Thy people, and deliver not thine heritage to reproach, suffering the nations to rule over them; for wherefore should they say among the people, where is their God? We know we have sinned, and there is none to intercede for us; but Thy great name, we hope will support us in time of trouble. We know we are destitute of good works, act therefore charitably by us, for Thy name's sake. As a father hath compassion on his, so have Thou compassion on us, O Lord, and save us, for Thy name's sake. O have pity on Thy people, and be merciful to thine heritage; spare us we beseech Thee, according to thine abundant mercy. O be gracious unto us, and answer us; for righteousness is thine, O Lord! Thou performest wonders at all times.

We beseech Thee to look kindly, and compassionate Thy people speedily, for Thy name sake; and through Thine abundant mercy, O Lord, our God! be merciful to spare, and save the sheep of Thy pasture; and suffer not Thine anger to prevail against us, for our eyes look in suspense towards Thee. O save us, for Thy name's sake. Have mercy upon us, and answer us in time of trouble, for salvation is thine, O Lord, and our hope is in Thee. Thou art the God of forgiveness. O pardon us, we beseech Thee, for Thou, O God! art good and ready to forgive, and Thou, O God! art a most gracious and merciful King.

O most merciful and gracious King! we beseech Thee to remember, and have respect to the covenant made between the parts, and let the binding of the holy child (Isaac) be continually seen before Thee, for the sake of Israel. Our Father and our King! O be gracious unto us, and answer us, for we are called by Thy great name. O Thou who workest wonders continually, act by us according to Thy tender mercy. O Thou who art gracious and merciful; have respect to us and answer us in time of trouble; for unto Thee, O Lord! belongeth salvation. Our Father, and our King, who art our shield, we beseech Thee, not to do unto us according to our evil doings. O Lord, remember Thy mercy and tender kindness, and save us according to Thine abundant goodness; and have compassion on us, for we acknowledge no other God besides Thee. O Lord our God, our Creator, forsake us not; neither be Thou far from us; for our soul is oppressed. O deliver us from the sword, captivity, pestilence, plague and all manner of trouble and sorrow, for we hope in Thee; put us not therefore to shame, O Lord, our God; but cause Thy countenance to shine on us, and remember unto us the covenant of our ancestors, and save us, for Thy name's sake. O behold our afflictions, and hear the voice of prayers, for Thou hearest the prayer of every mouth. O most merciful and gracious God, have compassion upon us, and on all Thy works, for there is none like unto Thee. O Lord, our God! our Father, King, Creator, and Redeemer, we beseech Thee now to pardon our transgressions. Thou art The living and ever existing God, mighty in power, gracious and beneficent to all Thy works; for Thou art the Lord our God. O God, who art long-suffering and full of compassion, deal by us according to Thine abundant mercy, and save us, for Thy name's sake. Hear our prayers, O our King! and deliver us from all trouble and sorrow. Thou art our Father and our King, and we are called by Thy name; deal therefore kindly by us, for Thy name's sake. O desert us not, nor forsake us, our former; for Thou, O God! art a most gracious and merciful King.

O Lord, our God! there is none like unto Thee, gracious and merciful. O Omnipotent! there is none like unto Thee, long-suffering and abundant in mercy and truth: save and deliverer us, O Omnipotent, from storms and earthquakes. Remember Thy servants, Abraham, Isaac and Jacob: look not unto our stubbornness, nor to our wickedness, nor to our sins. Turn from thy fierce wrath, and alter the decree concerning the evil against Thy people; and remove from us the stroke of death, for Thou art merciful: for such is Thy divine attribute, to shew mercy gratuitously throughout every generation. Have compassion on Thy people, O Lord! and shield us from Thy wrath; and remove from us the afflictive plagues, and every evil degree, for Thou art the guardian of Israel. Righteousness, O Lord! is Thine! but unto us, confusion of face. Wherefore should we complain? for what can we say? What can we declare? or how shall we justify ourselves? Let us search and examine our ways, and return unto Thee, for Thy right hand is stretched out to receive the penitent. O Lord! save us now, we beseech Thee. O Lord! prosper us now, we beseech Thee. O Lord! we beseech Thee, answer us when we call. Unto Thee, O Lord! we look: in Thee, O Lord, we confide. O be not silent; afflict us not, for the heathens say, their hope is lost; but unto Thee alone shall every knee bend, and those of high stature bow down.

O Thou, who art ready to receive penitent sinners and transgressors, forget us not for ever; for our increasing troubles disturb our souls. Our Father and our King! although we be destitute of righteousness and good works, yet remember unto us the covenant made with our ancestors, and our testimony which we bear daily, that Thou, O Lord! art a UNITY. O have respect to our afflictions; for the troubles of our heart, and our pains, are abundant. Have compassion on us, O Lord! in the land of our captivity, and pour not Thy fierce anger upon us, for we are Thy people, the children of Thy covenant. O Omnipotent! have respect to our diminished glory among the nations, and our abhorred state: which is equal to the defilement of a woman during the time of her severation. How long shall Thy strength remain in captivity, and Thy glory in the power of the enemy? Awaken Thy might and Thy jealousy against Thine enemies, so that they may be put to shame, and be dismayed at the loss of their power; but suffer not our weariness to seem light in Thy presence. O cause Thy mercy to precede the day of our trouble; and though not for our sake, yet do it for Thine own sake, and destroy not the memorial of our residue, but be gracious unto a people who, with fervent love, twice daily proclaim the unity of Thy name; saying, hear O Israel, the Lord is our God, the Lord is a UNITY.

PRAYER AND CONFESSIONS ON THE DAY OF ATONEMENT.

Thou dost put forth Thy hand to transgressors, and Thy right hand is stretched out to receive the penitent; and thou hast taught us, O Lord, our God! to make confession in Thy presence of all our iniquities, that we may restrain our hands from fraud; for thou wilt receive us, when we turn with perfect repentance, as thou didst the burnt-offerings, and sweet savours that were offered in Thy presence, for the sake of Thy word which Thou hast spoken ; for there is no end to the burnt offerings of our sins, nor any number to the sweet savour of our trespasses ; Thou knowest also that our end is to be food for the worm and insect ; therefore hast Thou multiplied our means of pardon. What are we ? What is our life ? What is our piety ? What is our righteousness ? What is our salvation ? What is our power ? What is our might ? What shall we say in Thy presence, O Lord, our God ! and the God of our Fathers ! Are not the mightiest heroes as nothing before Thee ? And men of fame as if they had not existed ; wise men, as if they were without knowledge ; and the intelligent, as if void of understanding ; for the majority of our actions is emptiness ; and the days of our life but vanity in Thy presence ; and man's pre-eminence over the beast is nought ; for all is vanity.

Thou didst distinguish man from the beginning, and didst favour him that he might stand in Thy presence ; for who can say unto Thee, what doest Thou ?

And although He be righteous, what can He give unto thee ? But in love hast Thou given us, O Lord, our God ! this day of atonement, a termination, pardon, and forgiveness for all our iniquities, that we may restrain our hands from fraud ; and return to perform the statutes of Thy will with an upright heart. And through Thine abundant mercies, deign Thou to compassionate us ; for Thou dost not delight in the destruction of the world ; as it is said, seek ye the Lord while He may be found ; call ye upon Him while he is near at hand. And it is said, let the wicked forsake his way, and the iniquitious man his thoughts ; and let him return unto the Lord, for He will receive him with compassion ; and unto our God, for He aboundeth in forgiveness. And Thou, God of forgiveness, art gracious and merciful, long-suffering, and abundant in mercy ; diffusing good abundantly. Thou dost also delight in the repentance of the wicked ; and hast no pleasure in their death ; as it is said, say unto them, as I live saith the Lord God, I have no pleasure in the death of the wicked ; but that the wicked turn from His evil way, and live. Turn ye, turn ye from your evil ways ; wherefore will ye die, O house of Israel ? And it is said, have I any pleasure in the death of the wicked, saith the Lord God ; but rather that he turn from his evil ways and live. And it is said, for I have no pleasure in the death of him that dieth, saith the Lord God, therefore turn ye and live. For Thou art the pardoner of Israel, and who grantest remission of sins unto the tribes in Jerusalem, and besides Thee there is none to whom we appeal for pardon and forgiveness.

PRAYER AND CONFESSION ON THE DAY OF ATONEMENT. 87

Our God, and God of our ancestors, may our prayers come before Thee, and withdraw not Thyself from our supplications; for we are not so shameless of face, or hardened as to declare in Thy presence, O Eternal! our God! and the God of our ancestors, that we are righteous, and have not sinned; verily, (we confess) we have sinned.

We have trespassed, we have dealt treacherously, we have stolen, we have spoken slander, we have committed iniquity, and have done wickedly; we have acted presumptuously; we have committed violence; we have framed falsehoods; we have counselled evil; we have uttered lies; we have scorned; we have rebelled; we have blasphemed; we have revolted; we have acted perversely; we have transgressed; we have oppressed; we have been stiff-necked; we have acted wickedly; we have corrupted; we have done abominably; we have gone astray, and caused others to err; we have turned aside from Thy excellent precepts, and institutions, and which hath not profitted us; but Thou art just concerning all that is come upon us; for Thou hast dealt most truly, but we have done wickedly.

O! what shall we say in Thy presence, O, Thou, who dwellest above the Universe? Or, what shall we declare unto Thee, who resideth above the skies? Knowest Thou not all the secret things, as well as the revealed?

Thou knowest all the secrets of the world, and the most hidden transactions of all living. Thou searchest all the inward parts, and examinest the veins and heart; so that there is nothing concealed from Thee, neither is there anything hidden from Thy sight. O may it then be acceptable in Thy presence, O Eternal, our God! and the God of our fathers, to pardon all our sins, and forgive all our iniquities, and grant us remission from all our transgressions. For the sin which we have committed against Thee, either by compulsion or voluntarily. And for the sin which we have committed against Thee, with a stubborn heart.

For the sin which we have committed against Thee, out of ignorance. And for the sin which we have committed against Thee, with the utterance of our lips.

For the sin which we have committed against Thee with incestuous lewdness. And for the sin which we have committed against Thee, either publicly or secretly.

For the sin which we have committed against Thee with deliberate deceit. And for the sin which we have committed against Thee, with speech of the mouth.

For the sin which we have committed against Thee, by oppressing our neighbour. And for the sin which we have committed against Thee, by the evil cogitation of the heart.

For the sin which we have committed against Thee, by assembling to commit fornication. And for the sin which we have committed against Thee, by acknowledging our sins with our mouth, (but do not repent in our heart.)

For the sin which we have committed against Thee, by despising our parents and teachers. And for the sin which we have committed against Thee, either presumptuously or ignorantly.

For the sin which we have committed against Thee, with violence. And for the sin which we have committed against Thee, by the profanation of Thy name.

For the sin which we have committed against Thee, with defiled lips. And for the sin which we have committed against Thee, with foolish expressions.

For the sin which we have committed against Thee, with evil imagination. And for the sin which we have committed against Thee, either knowingly, or without deliberation.

Yet for all of them, O God of forgiveness, forgive us, pardon us, and grant us remission,

For the sin which we have committed against Thee, by denying and lying. And for the sin which we have committed against Thee, by taking or giving a bribe.

For the sin which we have committed against Thee, by scoffing. And for the sin which we have committed against Thee, by calumny.

For the sin which we have committed against Thee, in traffic. And for the sin which we have committed against Thee, in meat and drink.

For the sin which we have committed against Thee, by extortion and usury. And for the sin which we have committed against Thee, by immodest discourse.

For the sin which we have committed against Thee, by chattering. And for the sin which we have committed against Thee, with the twinkling of our eyes.

For the sin which we have committed against Thee, by our haughty looks. And for the sin which we have committed against Thee, with shamelessness.

Yet for all them, O God of forgiveness, forgive us, pardon us, and grant us remission.

For the sin which we have committed against Thee, by shaking off the yoke of thy law. And for the sin which we have committed against Thee, by litigiousness.

For the sin which we have committed against Thee, by treachery to our neighbor. And for the sin which we have committed against Thee, by envy.

For the sin which we have committed against Thee, by levity. And for the sin which we have committed against Thee, by our stubbornness.

For the sin which we have committed against Thee, by running swiftly to do evil. And for the sin which we have committed against Thee, by tale-bearing.

For the sin which we have committed against Thee, by false swearing. And for the sin which we have committed against Thee, by causeless enmity.

For the sin which we have committed against Thee, by embezzlement. And for the sin which we have committed against Thee, by extasy.

Yet for all them, O God of forgiveness, forgive us, pardon us, and grant us remission. Also for the sins for which we were obliged to bring a burnt-offering.

And for the sins, for which we were obliged to bring a sin-offering.

And for the sins, for which we were obliged to bring an offering according to our ability.

And for the sins, for which we were obliged to bring a trespass-offering, either for a certain or doubtful sin.

And for the sins, for which we were obliged to suffer the stripes of contumacy.

And for the sins, for which we were obliged to suffer flagellation.

And for the sins, for which we incurred the penalty of death by the hand of God.

And for the sins, for which we incurred the penalty of extirpation and being childless.

And for our sins, for which we have incurred the penalty of four kinds of death, formerly inflicted by our tribunal of justice, viz. :— Stoning, burning, beheading, and strangling ; for transgressing affimative precepts, or negative precepts ; whether an action be appropriated thereto, or not, as well as those which are known to us, as those which are unknown unto us, we have already made confession of them before Thee, O Lord, our God ! and the God of our fathers.

And those which are unknown to us, are known and evident before Thee, as it is said the secret things belong unto Thee, O Eternal, our God! but the revealed things belong unto us and our posterity for ever, to perform all the words of this law, for Thou art the pardoner of Israel, and who granteth remission of sins unto the tribes of Jeshurun in all ages; and besides Thee, there is none to whom we appeal for pardon and forgiveness.

O my God! before I was formed, I was unworthy; and now that I have been formed, am as though I had not been formed; dust I am at my life-time, and more at my decease. Behold, I stand before Thee as a vessel full of shame and confusion. O may it be acceptable in Thy presence, O Eternal, my God! and the God of my fathers, to assist me, that I sin no more; and the sins which I have already committed against Thee, blot out through Thy mercy, but not by Thy chastisement and malignant sickness.

CLOSING PRAYER ON DAY OF ATONEMENT.

Thou dost put forth Thy hand to transgressors, and Thy right hand is stretched out to receive the penitent; and Thou hast taught us, O Lord, our God! to make confession in thy presence of all our iniquities, that we may restrain our hands from fraud; for Thou wilt receive us, when we turn with perfect repentance, as thou didst the burnt-offerings and sweet savours that were offered in Thy presence, for the sake of Thy word, which Thou hast spoken; for there is no end to the burnt-offerings of our sins, nor any number to the sweet savour of our trespasses; Thou knowest also, that our end is to be food for the worm and insect; therefore, hast Thou multiplied our means of pardon. What are we? What is our life? What is our piety? What is our righteousness? What is our salvation? What is our power? What is our might? What then shall we say in Thy presence, O Lord, our God! and the God of our fathers? Are not the mightest heroes as nothing, before Thee; the men of fame, as if they had not existed; wise men, as if they were without knowledge; and the intelligent, as if void of understanding? For the majority of our actions is emptiness, and the days of our life but vanity in Thy presence; and man's pre-eminence over the beast is nought, for all is vanity.

Thou didst distinguish man from the beginning, and didst favor him, that he might stand in Thy presence; for who can say unto Thee,

What doest Thou? And although he be righteous, what can he give unto Thee? But in love hast Thou given us, O Lord, our God! this day of atonement, a termination, pardon, and forgiveness from all our iniquities, that we may restrain our hands from fraud; and return to perform the statutes of Thy will with an upright heart. And through Thine abundant mercies deign Thou to compassionate us; for Thou dost not delight in the destruction of the world; as it is said, seek ye the Lord while he is near at hand. And it is said, let the wicked forsake his way, and the iniquitious man his thoughts; and let him return unto the Lord, for He will receive him with compassion; and unto our God, for He aboundeth in forgiveness. And Thou, O God of forgiveness, art gracious and merciful, long-suffering, and abundant in mercy; diffusing good abundantly. Thou dost also delight in the repentance of the wicked; and hast no pleasure in their death; as it is said, say unto them, as I live saith the Lord God, I have no pleasure in the death of the wicked; but that the wicked turn from his evil way and live. Turn ye, turn ye from your evil ways; wherefore will ye die, O house of Israel? And it is said, have I any pleasure in the death of the wicked, saith the Lord God, but rather that he turn from his evil ways and live. And it is said, for I have no pleasure in the death of him that dieth saith the Lord God; therefore turn ye and live. For Thou art the pardoner of Israel, and who grantest remission of sins unto the tribes in Jesurun, and besides Thee there is none to whom we appeal for pardon and forgiveness.

CHAPTER VII

CONFIRMATION CEREMONY, AS PRACTISED AMONG THE REFORMED JEWS.

The candidates for this ordinance, if boys, are dressed in black suits, and if girls, in white, (among the Orthodox Jews, girls are never confirmed,) each bear a prayer-book under their arm, and on some occasions a boquet of flowers in the hand. The Rabbi receives the candidates with the words of the Psalmist, "Blessed be he who cometh in the name of the Lord," etc., after which the young recite a prayer suitable to the service. This done, the Rabbi addresses the congregation on the importance of the occasion. At the conclusion of the address, he turns to the young, and questions them on the outlines and principles of their religion. We will quote some of the questions and replies :

What is religion ?

Religion is a system of doctrines, to regulate the conduct of man toward God, toward his fellow-man, and toward himself.

What is Judaism ?

Judaism is the religion revealed by God, taught by Moses, and expounded by the Prophets, and Sages of Israel.

What is the first fundamental doctrine of Judaism ?

There is one God, who is the Creator, Governor and Preserver of the universe, and the only God, Ruler or King, acknowledged by Israel, as Sacred Scriptures teaches : "Hear, Israel, God is our Lord, God is one."

What is our second fundamental doctrine ?

Man was created in the image of God ; he was gifted with a divine nature, capable of the utmost development, and he prefers, if circumstances do not corrupt him, justice to injustice, virtue to vice, and godliness to impiety.

What is the third fundamental doctrine ?

It is the duty of man to worship God, do His will, imitate His perfections, and love Him above all things ; to love his neighbor, the stranger, and his enemy, and to preserve his own life, cultivate the godly sentiments of his heart, develop his mind, strive at perfection, and become holy as God is holy.

What is the fourth fundamental doctrine ?

God delights in justice, virtue and purity, and is displeased by wickedness and impurity. He created man with such a nature, that he is happy only in the practice of justice, virtue and purity; but man frequently errs, and God, in order to restore him to happiness, rewards the good, and punishes the evil doer, here and hereafter, in this world, and in the world to come.

After some further questions, the Decalogue is recited, also the three different duties of man, and the holidays, and their causes.

The candidates for confirmation, then declare their firm will to live and die in the religion of Israel. Next follows the blessing " Every one according to his qualities, he blessed them," in imitation of father Jacob.

During the intervals, the choir sing different parts of Holy Writ, as also several choruses.

CHAPTER VIII.

THE DAY OF ATONEMENT.

Preparation—Repentence—Confession—Humiliation—Atonement—Interpretation of Psalms cx., and Isaiah ix., 6.

THE DAY OF ATONEMENT.

The tenth day of *Tishri* (September) is set apart by Sacred Scripture as the Day of Atonement, in regard to which it is promised, "For on this day he will pardon you, to purify you from all your sins, that you be pure before your God." The last part of this verse is expounded by the ancient doctors, "Sins committed between man and his God are pardoned on the Day of Atonement, but sins committed between man and man, are not pardoned on the Day of Atonement, until satisfaction has been given to the offended neighbor."

Besides the additional sacrifices which the Bible prescribes for this day, and the services of the High Priest, as performed in the Tabernacle, and the Temple, the Jews are commanded in Scripture, "And ye shall also afflict your persons." This command is expounded by the ancient doctors of the law, to have a double signification—a negative and a positive one. The negative command is, to abstain from all carnal pleasures and enjoyments, "From evening to evening," not only as an affliction on our person, but also as a declaration of independence, and sole dominion of the mind over the body and carnel propensities. The negative nature of these afflictions is wisely preferred to the positive, as these latter led men to the most extravagant, cruel, and revolting practices. The sacrifices of human life to appease the gods, the wounds which the false prophets afflicted on each other to the same purpose; the practice of the *Flagellants*, who chastised each other daily for the same reason; the confessions of Catholics, and the different acts of cruelty inflicted by the orders of Popes and Priests on the penitents, are only some of the extravagances which are prevented by this negative exposition of the Scriptural text by the ancient doctors of law.

Besides all this, it must be admitted, that abstaining one day from all carnal pleasures and enjoyments, is an excellent lesson for every man. It teaches him, that his will and his intellect actually have dominion over his person, if he only desires to obey them. It teaches him how little there is necessary to make a man happy; and few necessities are equal in the scale of happiness to extensive wealth. It teaches him, moreover, that all evil inclinations, all carnal propensities, could easily be subdued, and man could be happy, here and hereafter, if he always was "Master over his sins."

The positive signification of this Biblical text, is "Repentance;" to afflict oneself with the consciousness of sin, and the determination not to fall back again in a sinful life. The consciousness of a sinful life, to be ashamed thereof, and to feel that remorse, which is its invariable result, is indeed an affliction of which Cain already exclaimed "My iniquity is too great to bear it." It must also be admitted, that a day set apart for the sole purpose of man's rendering account to himself and his Maker, is a wise and beneficent institution. Man's occupation and aspirations in the storm-tossed ocean of life, are of such a wild nature, that he but seldom awakes from his intoxication; scarcely ever stands still for a moment to reflect on his conduct and his course of life.

He dreams on; and runs on in wild excitement, and frequently loses all his excellencies in the roaring current of mutable life. There comes, however, the day of atonement, the watch-tower erected by Providence, and calls powerfully: "Man stand still and consider." Many do stand still; retire from the excitement of life, with its numerous joys and sorrows, its hopes and disappointments, its treasures and delusions; they spend one day in perfect dominion over their passions, the source of all sins, and spend the day before God, in the House of God, and in the worship of God.

The principle on which the day of atonement is based, is one distinguishing Judaism from all other creeds. They believe repentance and amendment of conduct, is all that is required to obtain God's favor again. Some of the ways of repentance are, that the penitent calls on the Lord with weeping and supplication, practices acts of charity according to his ability; keeps himself far from the places and objects of his sin; changes his name, as much as to say: I am another and not the same individual who committed those sins; changes his actions for the better, and for the way of uprightness, and emigrates from his place, as exile is an expiation of sins, forcing him to humble himself, to be meek and of a modest mind.

They also believe it deserving of great praise to be penitent, to confess publicly, make known his transgressions, uncover his sins committed on his neighbors, and say publicly, "Verily, I have committed a sin on this or that man, I have done him so and so, and this day I do turn and repent."

But whoever is too haughty to acknowledge his faults, and attempts to hide them, has not truly repented them, as it is said, "Who hides his transgressions, will not succeed." This can be said in regard to sins between man and his neighbor; but sins committed between man and his God should not be made public; he only should return and state his sins before God, make in public only a general confession, and it is for his best not to make them public, as it is said, "Blessed be he whose trangression is forgiven, whose sin is hidden."

The Day of Atonement is considered by the Jews as the proper time of repentance for all, for the individual and the congregation; it is the end, forgiveness and expiation of sins to Israel, therefore, all should repent and confess their sins on the Day of Atonement. The command, in this respect, is to begin the confession the evening previous, before eating the last meal; perhaps he might die thereof without confession of sins. Although he has confessed his sins before eating the last, he shall do so again in the evening, morning, additional, afternoon, and concluding prayers. The formula of confession, adopted by all Israel, is, "But we have Sinned," and this is the main confession. Sins confessed once, the Day of Atonement, may be confessed again the other Day of Atonement, even if they are not committed again, as it is said, "For I know ever my transgression, and my sin is always before me."

They firmly believe that neither the Day of Atonement, nor repentance, brings remission of other sins than those between man and his God; sins between man and his neighbor, as wounding, cursing, or robbing his fellowman, and the like, will never be forgiven him, until he gives satisfaction, and pacifies his neighbor. Although a restitution of money be made to the offended neighbor, he must be pacified also, and requested to forgive the offence. If one only offends his neighbor with words, he must attempt to reconcile him and urge him for forgiveness. If his neighbor refuses to forgive him, he must come to him with three men of his friends, urge him, and request his forgiveness. If he still refuses, he must repeat it a second and a third time, and if he then would not forgive the offense, he himself is the sinner, and the offender need do no more. But if the offender is his teacher, he must come to him even a thousand times, until he is reconciled.

If one offended his neighbor, who died before he had asked his pardon, he must go to his grave with ten men, and say in their presence, "I have sinned before Israel's God, and this man; so and so, have I done him." If it was a money matter, he is obliged to make restitution to the heirs of the deceased, and if no heirs are left, let him, with his confession, deposit it at the public court.

ATONEMENT.

Atonement signifies the reconciliation between God and man. Sin separates man from God, and brings him under the dominion of the brutal passions.

There are two kinds of sins: 1st. Not to do our duty, and 2nd, to do what the divine laws prohibit. The first is passive sin, the second is active sin. The passive sin is proof of the absence of the good will. The active sin proves the presence of an evil will in the sinner. The remedy for the passive sinner is the acquirement of a good will, and the remedy for the active sinner, is to obtain dominion over his wicked propensities. The application of this remedy is called "To return to God." "O Israel return to God, thy Lord, if thou hast fallen by thine iniquity; take with you words, and return to God," &c,—(Hosea xiv., 1, 2.) "And thou shalt say unto them: thus saith God Zebaoth, return unto me saith God Zebaoth, and I will return unto you saith God Zebaoth."—(Zechariah i., 3.) "I have blotted out, as a thick cloud, thy transgressions, and as a cloud thy sins: return unto me, for I have redeemed thee."—(Isaiah xliv., 22.)

The act of returning to God from the path of sin, consists of the following elements:

1. The conviction of guilt or ingratitude to God.
2. Penitence, or to feel grieved to have sinned, and to be ashamed thereof, which is the severest penance to man.
3. The resolve on amendment of life.
4. In making good whatever was neglected, restoring whatever was taken unjustly from others, and repairing whatever we spoiled.

Thus man returns, and is reconciled to his God; thus ATONEMENT is made. God's punishment is intended for man's correction only; for God is neither angry nor revengeful. "Thou shalt also consider in thine heart, that as a man chasteneth his son, so God thy Lord chasteneth thee."—(Deut. viii., 5). "My son despise not the chastening of God; neither be weary of his correction: for whom God loveth he correcteth; even as a father the son in whom he delighteth."—(Proverbs iii, 11, 12). "Behold, happy is the man whom God correcteth; therefore despise not thou the chastening of the Almighty."—(Job v., 17).

If man corrects himself and amends his life, punishment will not follow after the repented sin; because it is not necessary, and God is all just, all-wise, and most gracious—(Deut. xxx., 1 to 10; ii. Sam. xii., 13; i. Kings, viii., 46 to 53; 21, 27, 28, 29; ii. Chron., xxxiii., 10 to 13; Psalms, xxxii. and ciii., 2 to 6).

"Let the wicked forsake his way, and the unrighteous man his thoughts: and let him return unto God, and he will have mercy upon him; and to our God, for he will abundantly pardon."—(Isaiah xlv., 7.)

See on this topic.—(Ezekiel iii., 17 to 21; xviii., 21 to 23; and xxxiii., 1 to 20).

INTERPRETATION OF THE 110TH PSALM BY THE JEWS.

Verse 1 is rendered in the authorised version:—"A Psalm of David. The Lord said unto my Lord, sit thou at my right hand until I make thine enemies my footstool." Now this phrase: "The Lord said unto my Lord," if prounced by David, (they say) would indeed be unintelligible. Who can be my Lord to whom David alluded after speaking of God as "the Lord."

Mendelssohn got rid of this passage by attributing the authorship of the Psalm, not to David, but to another, addressed to David, similar to many other psalms, which were addressed to other persons, and evidently *not* composed by David.

TRANSLATION OF ISAIAH ix., 6, BY THE JEWS.

"For a child was born unto us. A son was given unto us. And the government shall be on his shoulders. And His name shall be called Wonderful; a sublime councillor, a councillor of the mighty; a possessor of booty, a prince of peace."

This, our readers will see, is different from what is in our authorised version. Their explanation for this verse is as follows:

"The child, or son, who will govern after Ahaz, shall be a wonderful man. His wisdom shall be his power; he shall be a sublime councillor; a councillor of the mighty, who fight his battles; still he will be the possessor of the booty, made of the defeated. He shall be, not in wars like a prince, but 'a Prince of Peace.' Therefore he shall be called Wonderful, because he will be a sublime councillor, a councillor of the mighty, in time of war, when actually he is 'A Prince of Peace;' still he shall carry the spoil, not by bravery, but by wisdom. He shall make war only to repel invasions, war for the sake of peace; but then he shall be successful."

CHAPTER IX.

THE JEWISH CALENDAR.

TISHRI—*September*—New Year—Day of Atonement—Feast of Tabernacles—MARCHESVEN—*October*—KISLEV—*November*—Feast of Dedication—TEVETTO—*December*—SHEEBAT—*January*—ADAR—*February*—Feast of Purim—NISAU—*March*—Passover—EYOR—*April*—SIVON—*May*—Feast of Weeks—TAMUS—*June*—Great Fast—AB—*July*—Great Fast Day for Destruction of Jerusalem—ELUL—*August*—Blowing of Trumpets.

THE JEWISH CALENDAR.

The first month of the Jewish year, is generally called "Tishri;" the real Hebrew name, however, is "Ethanim." In this month are the most important feasts and fasts, according to the law of Moses, and a good many additions from the Rabbins, "the precepts of men," even in flat contradiction to the Divine ordinances. The Rabbins arbitrarily made the first day of this month New Year's day, while God commanded the month "Nisan," to be the first of the twelve, viz., the New Year. They cannot deny this fact, and therefore they say, that Nisan (April) is indeed the head, or principal, among the rest of the months; but the first of Tishri is the head of days, and therefore New Year's day. According to the law of God, this day is the feast of "trumpets; the Rabbins not only added one day more to the feast, but declared it to be the season when the Heavenly Supreme Court is in session, to judge the world, and particularly the Jews, and to determine everything which shall occur to every individual Jew; life, death, and what kind of death; health, sickness, and even how much one shall gain or lose in business; &c., &c., is minutely appointed. No wonder, then, that these two days put every Jew in a condition of great solemnity and devotion. This is the very best occasion to pray for long life, health, riches and honor.

The Rabbins also teach, that in these days every one's sentence is written; the righteous immediately to life, the wicked to death, and those who are half and half—like luke-warm water—are kept in suspension until the day of atonement; and it depends from their conduct during the interval, whether they be entered in the book of life, or in the black book. The blowing of the "ram's horn" is done in such sounds as express nothing, neither joy nor mourning, and are very strange to every other ear but that of a Jew. Every sound has another name; and angels, with queer, cabalistic names, are appointed to carry these sounds up before the Throne of Glory. He who sits upon it, Jehovah, is said to be so pleased with this music, that He at once turns from the seat of justice to that of mercy, and tears in pieces all the bands of Israel for another year.

On the third day of Tishri, is the Fast of Gedaliah; on that day we are told that the Jewish chief, who was left in the land of Israel as the governor over the few who remained there, of the poorer classes of the people, appointed by the King of Babylon, was slain by the rebels, Ismeal ben Nethaniah, and his gang. (See ii. Kings, xxv., 22 27.)

On the seventh, we are told, was given the sentence of God, that the whole generation who took part in worshipping the golden calf, should die in the wilderness.

The Sabbath, which is between the New Year's day and the day of atonement, is called "the Sabbath of Repentance," and is one of the two Sabbaths on which the Rabbi of the Orthodox Jews preaches, if preaching it can be called. The Rabbi has six months' time to prepare an essay on some point in the Talmud, in which he shows his wit and learning; and well he may prepare, because the learned among his congregation rally around him, and watch closely whether he says anything which does not concur with some Rabbi who lived before him, or make some, according to their opinion, wrong conclusion.

Woe unto him if they catch him in any of these things; a controversy then begins, which to a non-Jew, seems like a violent quarrel among uncivilized people. In former times, it was not a rare thing, that enraged zealots dragged the poor Rabbi down from his pulpit, and pulled his grey beard. But whether the derashah (preaching) ended this way, or peaceably, the unlearned people—the vast majority, therefore—stood in awe, and admired the great wisdom and knowledge which fell from the lips of their Rabbi, although his language was like Chinese to them. They left the synagogue, and said to each other, "He is a great man in Israel; may he live a hundred years."

On the ninth, is the day of preparation for the Day of Atonement. This is a very notable day, because eating and drinking on *that* day are considered as meritorious as fasting on the next. The reason which the Rabbins gave for that not very unpleasant good work—to eat and drink—is this:—Every Jew has, if he observes the regular daily prayers and blessings, to repeat one hundred blessings every day;[*] this day, however, he ought to speak ten times as many, namely, one thousand

---

[*] The word "blessing" is applied to those prayers in which the form "Blessed art Thou, Jehovah our God" occurs; and this is done while taking a drink of water, a bit of bread, or a fruit, &c.

This is also the day on which every pious Jew tries to be released from all his promises, vows and oaths, which he made during the past year. This is done by a court of three men, before whom he stands, and says that he regrets having promised, sworn, or vowed, and wishes to be released. He reads a long story from a book, of which in most cases, neither he nor the Judges understand a word. After he has finished, the three Judges say: "Thou art unloosed," three times, and he is free. Then he sits down as Judge, and one of the three rises in order to get rid of his obligations; and thus the ceremony is repeated until all are free. There are places where they are very pious, and apply to each other the forty stripes, less one, as a kind of atonement for sins, for which they have deserved this punishment, according to the law of Moses. That they take care not to hurt each other is understood; they want only the form of the thing, and not the thing itself, if it is of such a nature as receiving a whipping. In short, everything is done on that day to come off with as little sin as possible, that there remain not much to be forgiven.

On the tenth day is the great Day of Atonement. The description of this "Sabbath of Sabbaths" we may omit, as probably most, or all of our readears, are well acquainted with it. One thing, however, we would mention, which may be new to Christians, viz., after the day has been spent in fasting, weeping and praying in an unknown tongue; and when the sound of the long blowing of the horn has ceased, and the blessing of the moon has been performed, then every one hastens home and breaks his fast. After the gnawing hunger is satisfied, the husband goes out in the yard, selects a place for the tabernacle, and drives one pole at least into the earth; or, in other words, begins to build the tabernacle for the next coming feast. This is done, it is said, to silence Satan, the accuser, who otherwise would come before God, and would say, "Now, see here thy people; what are they doing after thou didst forgive them their sins? They eat and drink, and do not even think of doing some good work." But as they immediately engage in keeping the command of making a tabernacle, the enemy must keep his peace.

On the fifteenth day commences the Feast of Tabernacles. The Rabbins added the sixteenth; and both are kept as Sabbaths, with the exception of preparing food, and smoking a segar, which is allowed. Nobody is allowed to taste anything before he has spoken the blessing over the Lulab, (branch of the palm tree). Again, we meet here with a remarkable Rabbinical law. In the law of Moses, the command reads as follows: "And ye shall take you, on the first day, a nice fruit of a tree, branches of a palm tree, and the boughs of thick trees and willows of the brooks, and ye shall rejoice before the Lord." The Rabbinical law is, to take a fruit from a tree, the wood of which smells just like the fruit; and this has caused the poor Jews, to give sometimes *one hundred dollars* and more for such a fruit, which is not even eatable, because it was brought from Corfu, or some other island in the Mediterranean Sea.

On the twenty-first day, is another self-made feast, called "Hoshannah Rabbah." On this day, it is said, all sentences and decrees which have been pronounced on the days on which the Heavenly Court was in session, are sealed, and every recourse is vain; no appeal being possible.

On the twenty-second day, is the feast of the Solemn Congregation. The Rabbins added the next one, the twenty-third, and called it "The day of rejoicing with the law." In old orthodox Jewish synagogues, there are quite tumultuous proceedings. The scrolls of the law are taken out from the shrine; old and young dance, and sweetmeats, cakes and brandy are distributed freely in the house of worship. This closes the feast in the month of Tishri.

"Marcheshvan," or the month corresponding to our November, is the next month. There are several fast days in it, but they are not observed now-a-days, except three, viz: on the 20th, 23rd and 27th. These are known among the Jews as the second, the fifth, and the second; or Monday, Thursday and next Monday. The origin of these days may be found in the Talmud, Tract Taanith, "On Fasts," where it is said: If the seventeenth day of Marcheshvan has passed by without rain having fallen during the month, they shall fast on the next following Monday, Thursday, and the Monday of next week. The reader will easily perceive that the Jews being deprived of their own land, have not the slightest reason for keeping these fasts, whether rain falls in time in that land or not. But it is written in the Talmud!

On the seventh, it is said, Zedekiah, the King of Judah, was brought before Nebuchadnezzar, who commanded the children of the wretched prisoner to be slaughtered before the eyes of the father, and then to put out his eyes.

The third month is called "Kislev." Before we begin to give an account of the notable days in this month, we shall inform our readers of another Rabbinical ordinance, of considerable antiquity, which has been scrupulously kept, and is by orthodox Jews, still observed to this day. The day before every new-moon, with the exception of that of "Tishri," in which the New Year taking the place of the new moon, the latter is not celebrated, is a fast day, and is called, "The lesser Day of Atonement." The service begins at one o'clock, P.M., connected with the daily evening prayer. Those who have fasted, put on the phylacteries and the talith, which is not customary on other evenings. The scroll of the law is taken from the shrine, and a portion of it read, to which three persons stand up to the al-memra (an elevated platform in the centre of the synagogue, where the desk stands, on which the scroll is unfolded when read). The third person reads the maftir. The portion from the law is in Exodus, 32nd chapter, from v. 11 to 15, and 34th chapter, from v. 1 to 11. The maftir is from Isaiah, from 55 : 6 to 56 : 9. Both passages are very appropriate for this and other similar occasions; for nothing is more adapted to convince self-righteous Israel of their frailty, sinfulness, and inconsistency, than the remembrance of the golden calf which their fathers made and worshipped, a few days after they had heard "I am Jehovah, thy God," from the mouth of the Almighty; and then the condition upon which Jehovah granted them forgiveness. The second passage is, first, an earnest call to repent and to seek the Lord while He is yet to be found, and to call upon Him while He is near; and then it closes with glorious promises and encouragements. Alas, that so very few of those who so solemnly recite these Divine testimonials, and other very excellent prayers composed for such occasions, understand not a word of it, and therefore derive no benefit from the solemn service! The idea of a public day of fasting and humiliation every month, is a good one, and might, we think, be recommended to Christian congregations.

On the first day of this month, it is said, King Jehoiakim burnt the epistle which Baruch, the son of Neriah, wrote from the mouth of the prophet Jeremiah. There are, however, diverse opinions as to the day; some say that it was on the fifth; others on the seventh; others again, on the 25th; all, however, agree that this important act of the wicked king of Judah was committed during the month of Kislev. On the 25th, in the evening, the feast of "Chanukah" begins. The origin of this "feast of dedication" is to be found in the book of "Maccabees." We suppose all our readers to be acquainted with the history of that family of Jewish heroes, the Hasmoneans, who freed their land and their people from the cruel Macedonians, and then became the reigning house over Judah, until the wicked Herod exterminated every branch of that truly great, royal, priestly family. Had this feast been instituted in commemoration of the wonderful deliverance from a mighty and cruel enemy, by means of a family of priests, who gathered a host of half-naked and almost starving fugitives in the mountains, and who finally, by the help of the God of Israel, became the deliverers of their people, it would stand as a monument of gratitude towards God and the noble Hasmoneans. But this is not the case. The principal reason which the Rabbins give for instituting the " Chanukah," is the following miraculous event : When Antiochus, generally called " the wicked," entered the holy temple, he made everything in it unclean by touching it with his unholy hands. The holy oil, also, which was every year prepared for use in the holy candlestick, was all defiled; and the temple was without oil. After the enemy was compelled to flee from the city and the whole land of Judah, the temple and its furniture underwent the lawful purification; but, as to the oil, they were altogether helpless. Finally, they succeeded in finding a small bottle of undefiled oil, which one of the priests had secreted from the grasp of the enemy. This, however, was sufficient for one day only, and there was no prospect of obtaining new oil before eight days. Still, the people praised God with great joy, and the priests filled the holy candlestick and lighted the temple; and behold ! the oil lasted full eight days, when the temple was supplied with new oil. This miracle, then, is the principal foundation of the feast ; it lasts, therefore, eight days. The ceremony observed is simply this : Every *good Jew* is provided with a chanukah-lamp, which has eight small saucers. On the first evening, one of these saucers is filled with pure oil, and lighted; the second evening, two, and so on, till, on the eighth evening, all are lighted, which, altogether, makes thirty-six lights. In the morning services, the " Hallel," " Song of praise," composed of several psalms, is inserted, and another small piece of thanksgiving is inserted in the eighteen benedictions, and in the blessings at the table, which reads as follows :

" We thank Thee for the miracles, the redemption, mighty deeds, salvation and (victories) in wars, which Thou didst to our fathers in those days and in this season."

" In the days of Matthias, son of Jochanan, the high-priest, the Hasmoneans and his sons, the wicked government of Javan (Greece) rose up against Thy people Israel, causing them to forget Thy laws and to pass by Thy statutes; but Thou, in Thine abundant mercies, didst rise up in their behalf, in the time of their trouble. Thou didst fight their battle, judge their cause, and avenged their wrongs. Thou deliverest the mighty into the hands of the weak, great numbers into the hands of a few; the impure into the hands of the pure; the wicked into the hands of the righteous, and the evil-doers into the hands of those engaged in

Thy law. Thou hast made Thy name great and holy in Thy world; and to Thy people Israel Thou hast done great salvation and redemption in that day. Then, Thy children came into Thy house, cleansed Thy temple and purified Thy holy place. They also lighted the lamps in the courts of Thy sanctuary, and appointed these eight days of Chanukah, to thank Thee, and to give praise to Thy great name."

There is no other distinction between these, and other week-days; every man may follow his business and do his work, except in that half hour in which the chanukah light is burning. The evenings are generally spent in visiting neighbors, telling stories, or playing cards.

A most deplorable circumstance is, however, that not five per cent. of all the people who scrupulously keep the chanukah, know anything of those great events, by which it was brought into existence; it is therefore one of the merits of modern Judaism, that they have introduced Israel's history in their schools, by which the children become acquainted with the wonderful dealings of God with their fathers. Would that they would teach their children of the greatest of all events in the history of Israel, when God sent his only begotten Son into the world, to save that which was lost, and first of all the lost sheep of the house of Israel!

The next month is called, in Hebrew, "Tebeth," and takes the place of our January. The first Sabbath in it is somewhat more than the common weekly Sabbaths, because it is combined into the "Feast of Dedication," and is called "Sabbath Chanukah."

The third is the last day of Chanukah, and is particularly celebrated.

On the eighth there is, according to the lunar account, the shortest day and longest night in the year. On the same day the Bible was translated into Greek, in the days of Talmay-Ptolemy, the King; it was therefore made a fast day, on account of the Holy Scriptures having been translated into a profane language.

The ninth is another fast day, though it is not fully known what evil happened to Israel on that day. In the book "Calbo," however, we find written that this is the day in which Ezra, "the Scribe," died, which may be the ground for the fast.

The tenth is one of the four great fast days in the year, with the exception of the scriptural Day of Atonement. On this day Nebuchadnezzar commenced the siege of Jerusalem, which ended with the destruction of the city and temple.

On the twenty-third, is the "Thekuphah," or "Winter Solstice," when the sun enters Capricorn. The real meaning of the Thekuphah, however, is very little known among the Jews. Instead of this, the following fabulous tradition is current among them. They are told, that four times in the year, two Kelipoth—evil angels—meet in the air and fight with each other, until a drop of blood falls to the earth from one of them. Now this drop of blood generally falls into a vessel, which contains fat of any kind, and this fat then is *trephah*, unlawful to be used and poisonous too. The falling of the blood into anyone's provision of fat can be prevented by putting a piece of iron in it. It is therefore customary among the Jews to put an iron nail in the vessel in which they preserve fat of any kind. In addition to this precaution, the shamesh (sexton) goes, a few days before the Thekuphah, from house to house, and writes in large letters on the door: "Beware, for the Thekuphah, which will fall on —— day and —— hour."

The twenty-ninth is the last day of the month; and the day previous is the "lesser day of atonement."

The fifth, in order, of Hebrew months, is called "Shevat," and equal to February in the Christian Almanac.

On the fifteenth, is a day of recreation, particularly for children. This day is one of the four New Year's days according to the Talmud. It is said that on this day trees are filled with fresh sap, and begin to shoot forth new twigs and leaves. We suppose this was the case in Palestine while under the cultivating hand of the Hebrews.

There is no other day of very great importance during this month.

The next month is called "Adar," and takes the place of our March.

On the 7th, died Moses, the servant of God; and it is therefore a fast day. But as this is very little known among the Jewish people at large, a few only keep it.

On the 9th, there is another Rabbinic fast day, on account of the division which took place between the two high schools; that of Shamai and that of Hillel, which it is said, took place on that very day. (This proves that the ancient Jews knew already that *secession* is a great evil; they, therefore, constituted a national fast on that day on which *secession* occurred.)

On the 13th, is the fast of Esther, in commemoration of the fast which that Queen ordered to her people before she went to Ahasuerus, to make petition for the lives of her kinsmen.

On the 14th, is the day of Purim; and the following that of Susan-Purim. Our readers will doubtless know that the name of this national feast, Purim, is derived from Pur, "lot," because Haman cast lot, according to heathen superstition which month and which day was to be most favorable to destroy the Jewish nation. Haman did not understand the counsel of God, and, stirred up by Satan, wanted to destroy that nation of whom, according to the flesh, Messiah, the Saviour of the world, to destroy him, the evil one. It has always been, and still is, the custom to celebrate these days with as good a table as possible, and entertainments of every kind. In my native country, Hungary, it is particularly customary that the wealthy prepare tables heavily laden with good things, and wines of different kinds; and every man, without exception, is at liberty to enter, and to eat and drink what he likes best. In the first night, and on the next following morning, the "Megillah," or manuscript containing the book of Esther, is read in turns peculiar to this subject only. The children, several days before, prepare the "Haman Klopper," that is, an instrument which looks like a door-knocker, with a double hammer beating on a board. This they take along with them into the synagogue; and whenever the name Haman is mentioned, they knock with that instrument, which produces a tremenduous noise. The idea of it was, that they knock down Haman, that arch-enemy of Israel, a descendant of Amalek, who was the first who offended Israel after they had left Egypt; and since then the enmity between Amalek and Israel has continued.

This feast recalls to the Jewish recollection one of those miraculous deliverances with which the history of Israel abounds. If the oral law, or Talmud, simply contented itself with commanding the observance, and prescribed the mode of worship for such an important season, we should have no fault to find: but, as the oral law claims for itself divine origin and authority, we are compelled to examine its pretentions and to scrutinize its features, in order to see whether they really bear the stamp of Divinity. The following law, respecting the meal to be provided on this occasion, did certainly not come from Heaven: "A man's duty with regard to the feast is: that he should eat meat, and prepare a suitable feast, according to his means, *and drink wine, until he be drunk,* and fall asleep in his *drunkenness.*" The Talmud, however, is not satisfied with so indefinite a direction, but lays down, with its usual precision, the exact measure of intoxication required: "A man is bound to get so drunk with wine on Purim as not to know the difference between (the two sentences) Cursed be Haman, and Blessed be Mordecai." (Megillah, fol. 7, 2.) In order, however, to meet the objections of some modern champions of the Talmud, who say that all such things are to be taken figuratively, we need only to refer to the celebrated Rabbins: R. Saloman Jarchi (generally known under the abridged name, Rashi), and

R. Moses Maimonides, who, both of them, understood literal drunkenness, and have named wine as the legitimate liquor. But, not these commentators alone, but the Talmud itself admits no figurative interpretation, for, immediately after that famous precept, it goes on to propose an example, and to furnish an illustration of its meaning, in the following history of the very Rabbi on whose authority this traditional command rests: "Rabba and R. Zeira took their Purim meal together. When Rabba got drunk he arose and killed R. Zeira, by cutting his throat. On the following morning, he, Rabba, prayed for mercy, and restored him, R. Zeira, to life. The following year, Rabba proposed to R. Zeira again to make their Purim meal together, but the latter refused, saying: 'Miracles don't happen every day.'" Are we, therefore, brethren of the house of Israel, not your friends in trying to persuade you to abandon the doctrines of the Talmud, being contradictory to the law of God, and to embrace the doctrines of the New Testament, that are in harmony with God's will and law?

The month corresponding to our April is known among the Jews by the name "Nisan," a name, it is supposed, they brought with them from Babylon. The Hebrew name, however, is "Abib," a ripe ear, as, in that month, the barley began to ripen. This is the "head," or first month in the year; in it the most important events in the wonderful history of Israel took place, the greatest of which were the crucifixion, burial and resurrection of Jesus of Nazareth, our glorious Messiah.

The great feast of unleavened bread, or Passover, is celebrated in this month. Every Jew is careful to provide himself and family with "Matzoth," or unleavened bread, for the week. When a Jew has thus provided himself, he feels as happy as a king; and, as often as he sits down with his wife and children to their meal, he or she will say: "Thank God, we have Matzoth."

Having been relieved from that care, the mistress of the house enters upon her duties of whitewashing, scrubbing, and cleaning every corner, from the top to the bottom; and then changing everything in the kitchen, as well as the table utensils, plates, dishes, knives, forks, spoons, &c., &c. It is most remarkable, that she never gets through with this annual renovation until the very evening of the feast.

On the 12th is the "great Sabbath," on which the Rabbis of the orthodox make a speech in the synagogue, in which they try to show their skill in Rabbinical lore and Talmudic tactics. One would expect that the laws and ordinances, or rites of the approaching feast, would be the subjects of this discourse, but this is seldom the case. The Rabbi chooses some subject—perhaps on matters of matrimony—over which he has brooded all winter, and with this he feeds the hungry congregation, most of whom rally around the pulpit, with mouth wide open, to snatch every word as it falls from the lips of the Tzadick.

On the 14th, the day of preparation, the afternoon is spent by the husband in arranging the table for the "Szeder," while his wife is preparing in the kitchen an extraordinary supper. The dishes are peculiar to this solemn night, and we can assure our readers that these dishes are very tasteful, and particularly so to us, being a "bechor," or first-born, and obliged to fast that day. The principal one is the celebrated never-failing "matzelocksh," a pudding made of ground matzoth. The requisites to the szeder-table are as follows: a large flat tin or silver plate, upon which the matzoth, wrapped in a fine white linen towel, are placed. These three matzoth represent the three orders, Priest, Levite, and Israelite, which are used for certain purposes, which we shall see hereafter. A handful of water-cresses, some parsley, a piece of horse-radish, or the green top of it, a saucer of salt-water, and another with a mixture of apple, almond, cinnamon, and wine, representing the clay of which our fathers in Egypt made the bricks; an egg, and a bone with a little meat on it, representing the Passah (Paschal) lamb; all these things are nicely arranged on the top of the three matzoth. Next comes the bottle with wine—red wine is preferred—and a cup for each person, even the children who are able to sit at the table, and a "Hagadah" which is a little book, containing the ritual, songs, and prayers for that occasion, and the history of the wonderful exodus of our fathers from the "house of servitude."

Everything now ready, the husband goes to the synagogue; and on his return, immediately proceeds to the performance of the ceremonies of the "Szeder." During his absence in the synagogue the wife has prepared the "Hesse-bed," that is, either a sofa, or two chairs put together, and a number of cushions upon it, overspread with white linen, intended to represent a throne. He then puts on the peculiar robe, consisting of a long and wide tunic with wide sleeves, which is made of white linen, trimmed either with lace or gold, according to his means, and a cap of the same material and trimming. Now the whole family, and often one or two strangers, who have been invited to participate in the good things which God has provided for them, take their seats around the table; and the husband, of course, ascends his throne. The cups, which are in perfect harmony with the price of the wine, and the means of the host, either large or small, are now filled; and he, who thinks himself a king this evening, speaks the benediction over it and the feast, upon which every one drinks a little from his cup. To the honor of our countrymen we must here state, that they, being a sober and temperate people, do not obey their Rabbins, who say, that every man must drink at least two-thirds of the contents of his cup, and this, too, four times during the evening; but most of them sip only a very little of the liquor.

After this, the queen—for, of course, if the husband is king his wife is a queen—brings a wash-basin, a pitcher with water, and a towel, and approaches the throne; the king holds his hands over the basin, and the queen pours water over them, and dries them with the towel. The profoundest silence reigns in the room. He then takes the parsley from the plate, cuts as many portions as there are persons at the table, dips them into the salt water, and, giving a portion to each, pronounces the following blessing: "Blessed art Thou, Jehovah, our God, King of the universe, who created the fruit of the earth." Each eats his portion. He then breaks the middle of one of the three matzoth, or the "Levite," in twain, leaves one-half on the plate, and puts the other half wrapped in a white handkerchief, under one of the cushions on his throne. The egg and the bone—the representative of the Passah lamb —are taken from the plate, and all who can reach it lift the plate up, and say the following in the Aramaic language: "Like this poor bread *is that* which our fathers ate in the land of Egypt. Whosoever is hungry, let him come in and eat; whosoever is needy, let him come in and hold Pessah with us. This year we are here *in this land:* but in the year to come, *we hope to be* in the land of Israel; this year we are servants: in the year to come *we hope to be* children of freedom."

The cups are now filled a second time; and if there is such a child present able to read Hebrew, it reads a passage from Hagadah, containing several questions, why this feast is celebrated, and what is the meaning of these ceremonies, and why they eat unleavened bread. Then the history of the Exodus is chanted. After all this, which takes half an hour, half of the Halell, composed of the 113th and 114th Psalms, is read, the cup is blessed, and each drinks a little of it. The whole company then wash their hands, as usual, saying the blessing. The King breaks the matzoth on the top, or the Cohen (Priest), and so many portions are made as there are partakers of the meal. Then he breaks the third, or the "Israelite," making again portions of it, gives a piece of both to each member, and repeats the following blessing: "Blessed art thou, Jehovah, our God, King of the universe, that thou bringest forth bread from the earth." Blessed art thou, &c., &c., who sanctified, and commanded us to eat unleavened bread." After that, he takes a little of the water cress, dips it into the imitated clay, and, giving to each of the company, says : " Blessed art thou, &c., &c., who commanded us to eat bitter herbs."

There remains yet one article to be disposed of—the horse-radish. This is cut into small pieces, put between two pieces of matzoth, and they are eaten together, as, it is said, Hilell the great Rabbi did so. These things are then removed from the table, and the real supper is now taken, spiced with friendly conversation. After supper, the cup is filled the *third* time, and the usual thanksgiving after a meal, with some additions appropriate to the feast, is pronounced, and the cup, over which the blessing was spoken, goes around the table, and each member drinks of it. The szeder-plate is then replaced on the table, the door of the room thrown open, and the following verses are spoken : Psalm 79 : 6 and 7 ; Psalm 69 : 25 ; and Lament. 3 : 66. In referring to those passages, the reader will be startled with the terrible curse they contain ; we must therefore, give them a somewhat long explanation, in order to prevent the Christian reader from thinking that our Jewish brethren, in these days, entertain so strong a hatred against their non-Israelitish fellow-men as to utter against them such a horrible curse ; and secondly, to prevent our Jewish reader from thinking evil of us, as if, in relating this ceremony to the Christian public, we intended to raise ill-feeling towards them. What we desire, is, to show that the great majority of the Jews are ignorant of the meaning of the ceremonies they continue to perform, and induce them to accept of that liberty offered them by Jesus Christ, the real Passah-lamb, slain in Jerusalem, to take away the sins of the world, and of which that in Egypt was but a type or shadow. We desire, furthermore, to induce Christians to more zealous labor, and more earnest prayer, for Israel's deliverance from the bondage of unbelief.

The introduction of this terrible curse, in the midst of praises and thanksgivings of joy, may be traced back to the dark ages of terrible persecutions, which the ancient people of God suffered from the pretended followers of the sweet and lovely Jesus, Messiah. No wonder that, in remembering the miraculous deliverance of their fathers, rose up in frightful colours before their minds and filled their lips with curses upon their persecutors. The history of Israel in those dreadful ages contains innumerable cases in which their enemies lurked at their doors and windows to see whether they used the blood of Christian children at their passover ; and, not seldom, threw dead children into the Ghetto, synagogues, or private dwellings of the persecuted race, in order to have a pretence to fall on them, slaughter and rob their victims. In order, therefore, to be sure that no listening traitor watched behind the door when that curse upon their enemies was uttered, the Rabbins ordered the doors to be thrown open.

This real cause for opening the doors was known to a few chosen only, and not to the masses of the Jewish people, fearing that some, either through ignorance or malice, would carry the password over into the enemy's camp. The Rabbins, therefore, invented the following story, which the more easily found a hearing among the oppressed Jews, as it fully coincided with their hopes and expectations. They said that Elijah, the prophet, goes about, in the two szeder nights, and visits many Jewish families, to see whether they perform the ceremonies of the szeder in due form, and, of course, leaves great blessing upon those whom he finds doing right. Every family, therefore, may expect to see the celebrated prophet enter their room, and they must be prepared for that happy event. An additional cup, filled with wine, stands upon the table, and is called "Elijah's cup," and, before filling the cup the *fourth and last time*, the door is opened to let Elijah come in; and it is this that most of the Jews believe to be the real cause for opening the door. The cup is now filled for the fourth time, and the second part of "Halell," comprising from Psalm 115 to 118, inclusive, is read, and several other songs are chanted. The blessing over the cup is then spoken, and, after each has drank of it, the thanksgiving for the fruit of the wine—or, as it is generally called, *the after-blessing*—is said, after which it is not allowed to drink any more wine that night. The ceremony is concluded with chanting some more songs, in which, and particularly in the last, there is so very little or no sense at all, that the Rabbis were compelled to say, in order to satisfy the people, that it contains a sacred mystery—too sacred to be understood. Finally, the "Song of Songs" is read; but the children and the female part of the party are generally asleep at that time.

The second evening's services contain nearly the same. There is, however, an addition, namely, the counting of the Omer; and we refer our readers to Leviticus xxiii., 10-18, the reading of which will give them the best explanation.

The 22nd of Nisan is the last day of the feast of unleavened bread. They are now so tired of Matzoth—the miserable bread, as they call it—that they look with great impatience for the appearance of the stars, for, then, they are at liberty to eat leavened bread, and there is a general rush to the Gentile bakers, who, knowing this, are well prepared.

The month corresponding to the May of Christian nations, is called "Eyor;" it has 29 days.

In order to make our readers understand the meaning of the word "Omer," we refer them to Levit. 23, 10—13; and by the reading of that passage it is clearly seen, that the first sheaf of the new harvest was brought to the priest, in order to wave it before the Lord. This is the "Omer," and from that day, which was the second of the feast of unleavened bread, fifty days were to be counted; and, on the fiftieth day, two loaves of the new crop were to be brought in as a meat offering. Although it is plainly understood, that this *counting* means nothing else but to appoint, that the interval between the waving of the sheaf and the offering of the two loaves, shall be full seven weeks, the Rabbins made it a special duty of every Jew, even after the destruction of the Temple. when all offerings ceased, to count the days. The formula of this imaginary commandment is this :—

"I am now ready and prepared to fulfil the commandment of counting the Omer. In the name of the union of the Holy One, blessed be He and His Shekinah, because the same is hidden and concealed in the name of all Israel."

"Blessed art Thou, Jehovah our God, King of the universe, who had sanctified us with His commandments, and commanded us to count the Omer."

"This day is the first (second or third, &c.) day of Omer. May it be Thy pleasure before Thee, O Lord our God, and the God of our fathers, that the house of the sanctuary (the Temple) be rebuilt soon, and in our days, and give us our portion in Thy law."

There is, however, another tradition connected with these days of the Omer. It is said that Rabbi Akiba—that famous Rabbi who elevated the Bar Cochba to the Messiahship, 130 years after Christ—had some *eighty thousand disciples*, who were taken away by a certain disease which commenced on the first day of the Omer, and stopped only on the thirty-third of that period, after which it raged again, till the end of the month of Eyor. On account of this sad event, the Rabbins constituted these days as a time of mourning; no marriage or any other entertainment is allowed during that time, and men are prohibited shaving. But the thirty-third day is excepted, and is therefore a little feast day, on which men are permitted to shave themselves, parties join in marriage, and people may amuse themselves in any way they like.

The month "Sivon" comes next, in Bible language is called "Jzor," which means *clearness*, because in this month the atmosphere is pure and clear. It corresponds with the month of June, and has thirty days. This is one of the most important seasons in the year; for, the giving of the law in the old dispensation, and the pouring out of the Holy Spirit in the new, took place in it. On the first is the new moon feast; the third, fourth and fifth are called "the three days of "Hagbalah," which represent those three days on which Moses prepared the people of Israel to receive the law of God. On the sixth, is the " Feast of Weeks," on which day Israel received the Holy Law of God, who himself descended upon Mount Sinai, and said, " I am Jehovah thy God," a solemn scene which no other people was ever honoured with, and which, alas, they forgot but a few days afterwards, pointing to the golden calf, they said, "These are thy God, O Israel."

The feast is also called Mathan Torah, " The giving of the Law," and were it not for the many gross superstitions with which the services of the day abound, it would be a most solemn one. But Rabbinic absurdities worked themselves into the very life-blood of the Jewish people, and defiled even their prayers and praises which they send up to the great Jehovah.

"The Feast of the Weeks," or, as it is called in English, "Pentecost," was also one of the three Feasts on which God commanded Israel that every male should appear before the Lord in the place that He would choose. No wonder, then, that, when on that very day the poor, trembling disciples of Jesus came together to pray, and the promised Comforter, for whom they were so anxiously waiting, suddenly came down upon them, there were Jews from every habitable part of the globe where Jews had settled. They all were at that time at Jerusalem, in obedience to that command, each of them speaking the language of the country in which he lived.

No wonder, then, that they were surprised to hear these illiterate men of Galilee speaking and praising God in the language of each of them.

It is to be wondered at, however, that the brief and plain sermon of Peter resulted in the immediate conversion of *three thousand* persons, while, in our days, with all the light and knowledge we possess, many men sit under ministerial preaching all their life-time without being converted ! On the " Feast of the Weeks," the pious Jews adorn their synagogues and houses with green boughs of the forest and flowers, and strew fresh grass on the floors, thus representing Mount Sinai in its beautiful spring dress. Of all the feasts of the year, this is, undoubtedly, the most pleasant, as the season is most desirable. May the Lord hasten the time when the true and general Pentecost shall dawn upon all children of Israel, and the prophecy of Joel be fulfilled to its greatest extent!

"Tamus" is the next month. This name is foreign to the Hebrew, and must have been brought up from Chaldea or Assyria. It must have been the name of some idol, because it is mentioned in Ezek. viii., 14: "Then he brought me to the door of the gate of the Lord's house, which was toward the north, and, behold, there sat a woman weeping for the 'Tamus.'" Some writers maintain that it was the name of an idol representing the sun, identical with the Adonis in Greece and the Osiris in Egypt. This month corresponds with our July.

On the 17th, is one of the four great fast days in the year, besides the Day of Atonement. The women in Israel wept and mourned for the imaginary death of an imaginary god, not even dreaming that their descendants would have to weep and mourn, in the same season, over bitter realities. This fast day, as also the remaining three, had already been during the second temple, as we find them mentioned by the prophet Zachariah viii., 19, where he, in the name of Jehovah Zebaoth, prophesied, that, in a future age, these fasts should be turned into "days of joy and gladness, and good seasons." It is a fact, that, in this month, the walls of Jerusalem were first broken down by the besieging forces of the Chaldeans.

According to the record of the Bible, this took place on the ninth day of the fourth month (Tamus). "On that day the city of Jerusalem was broken up, and all the princes of Babylon entered; Zedekiah was captured in his flight, and his eyes were put out."—Jeremiah xxxiv., 2, 8. The question, why the fast day is now kept on the 17th instead of the 9th, is answered by Baba, that the Chaldeans broke up the city on the 9th, and the Romans, 500 years afterwards, broke it up on the 17th. The Rabbins, however, were not satisfied with this Biblical, and, therefore, true historical fact, which alone is sufficient to make a nation, once great and glorious, mourn over their loss, but, as usual, brought some traditions into account. The following is the passage in the Talmud, Tract Taanith, fol. 27, 1: "Five things (evils) have happened to our fathers on the 17th day of Tamus, and five evils on the 9th of Ab. On the 17th of Tamus, it happened that,—1st. Moses broke the two tables of stone, on which the laws of God were written with his own finger. 2nd. The daily sacrifices were suspended. 3rd. The city of Jerusalem was broken twice. 4th. Apostomus, the wicked, burnt the law; and, 5th. The abominations placed in the most holy place." The Talmud then continues to calculate, in some way or another, that these facts (and facts they are) all took place on that very day.

This month has but 29 days.

The next month is called "Ab," and this name, too, is of foreign birth. It corresponds with the month of August.

On the 9th day of "Ab" is the great fast in commemoration of the destruction of the city of Jerusalem, and the house of God, in which His glory dwelt.

The services of this fast are touching and soul-stirring for every beholder who has a heart to feel and sympathize with the woes of others. On the eve of the 8th, the people congregate in the synagogue, which is but dimly lighted. The daily evening prayer is conducted in a low, almost whispering, tone. After prayer, the "reader" chants the whole book of Lamentations, in doleful, heartrending tunes, while the congregation listen in profound silence, interrupted only by groaning, sighing and weeping, which might soften a heart of stone. Having finished the chanting of Lamentations, several other hymns of the same character are sung, and the congregation is dismissed.

We will here mention an anecdote which, it is said, comes from Frederick the Great, King of Prussia. The story runs thus: the king, who lived on good terms with Moses Mendelssohn, the celebrated Jewish philosopher, came once from Potsdam, his residence, to the city of Berlin, and halted at the house of Moses, wishing him to come out to his carriage and have a talk with him. The king was told that Mr. M. was not in. "Where is he," inquired the king. "He is in the synagogue," was the reply. A few minutes afterwards, the royal carriage stopped at the door of the synagogue. The king silently entered, and stood leaning on his thick cane looking on, and listening to the heart-rending chanting, sighing and weeping. At a pause he stepped forward, raised his cane as a sign that he would speak, and then said: "O ye foolish Jews, why are you sitting here on the floor crying like little children who have not got what they wished to have? By weeping, groaning, fasting and chanting, you will never regain your holy temple, your lost country, or rebuild Jerusalem your city. That will not do; get up from the floor, take up arms, you have money, and I will give you soldiers and generals. Go up to Palestine, conquer it, drive out the ugly Turks, and then build your city and your temple." The old king was right: it is exactly so.

From the 17th of Tamus to the 10th of Ab men are not allowed to shave; none are permitted to put on a new dress, no marriage, or any other kind of entertainment, is admitted. From the 1st to the 10th day of Ab, there is a kind of Lent; the Jews are restricted from eating meat, except on the Sabbath day.

On the 13th, is another Sabbath, which is known by a particular name; it is called "Sabbath Nachamu," and is derived from the portion of Scripture which commences with the word "Nachamu." The reader will find it in Isaiah xl. 1-28: "Comfort, comfort ye my people."

The last month is called "Ellul," and corresponds to our September.

The following practice is recommended during this month. Giving alms to the poor, and donations for congregational expenses, more than during the rest of the year. To attend synagogue more frequently than heretofore. To pray more diligently. To avoid committing sins unheeded during the whole year (this means *little* sins); and finally, to fast frequently, make confession of sins, and immerse himself, if possible, every day, or at least on those days on which he fasts. In this immersion, the sinner undresses himself entirely, goes down into the water, which must reach up to the breast, speak a formula of confession, and then plunges under the water.

The following Psalms are particularly recommended to be recited at least once a day. The 27th Psalm is among the foremost, and is therefore spoken in the synagogue wherever Rabbinical Jews exist. But the Psalms 77, 88, 115, and 124, are only spoken by the pious, who believe they contain a mysterious virtue, for the purification and sanctification of body and soul; to cut off all defects and plagues, their own as well as others—as far as they may concern themselves, to keep away all unclean powers in the world, and to deprive the evil of all power over them. Moreover, the recital of these four Psalms will protect those who repeat them from evil thoughts and delusive dreams, and enable them to come before God without sin at the great Day of Atonement.

On Repentance, says Rabbi Jonah, the pious :—" The Holy One has sent us His message through His servants the prophets; and through the prophet Ezekiel He said : "Then saith the Lord God, return, turn from all your transgressions, whereby you have transgressed, and make to yourselves a new heart and a new spirit; for why will ye die, O house of Israel ?" (18-31.) Now if there is any man who has transgressed the law of God, and desires to seek shelter under the wings of Shechinah, and to enter upon the road of repentance, let him come; I will give him understanding, and give him a light to make his way sure. Let him not be frightened by his own imaginations; let him not be falsely ashamed to return. Let no man say: How can I be so brazen-faced, as to come forward before God, after I have transgressed His holy law innumerable times, and have rebelled against Him continually? Am I not like a thief apprehended in the deed? How can I set my foot in His courts? No, let him not think so. The evil seducer sits like a fly in the avenue of the human heart; is every day renewed; is lurking and watching to avail himself of every opportunity to throw stumbling blocks in the way, and stir up the heart to evil thoughts. Let every man consider that it is the attribute of the Creator; blessed be He to extend His hand to repenting sinners; let every man, therefore come forward and repent."

CHAPTER X.

COMPUTATION OF TIMES AND FESTIVALS.

Celebration of the new moon—Difficulties of Jews residing out of Palestine—Present order of reckoning.

COMPUTATION OF TIME AND FESTIVALS.

The celebration of the New Moon (*i. e.*, not the so-called astronomical new moon, when the moon is in conjunction with the sun) was not definitely fixed until the crescent (phase) of the moon had been actually observed in the sky; and when this fact was reported by honest, credible witnesses (who had been sent out for the purpose of discovering it, from the high mountains near Jerusalem) to the Supreme Judicial Court in Jerusalem, the president of this body fixed the time of celebration by exclaiming "Hallowed" before the whole assembly. Rosh Hashansh, 11, 1, 7, of 1, 8, 11, 6. All witnesses who were able to announce, with certainty, that they had seen the newly-visible moon, were allowed to travel on the Sabbath even, so that the prescribed services of the Temple might take place "at the appointed time" (Lev. xxiii. 2). After the destruction of the second Temple, the neglect on the part of the witnesses of the Sabbatical ordinance was granted only in the first and seventh months (*Nisan* and *Tishri*), for on the beginning of these months depended the appointing of the festivals, of which notice was to be given throughout the land, as well as the timely dispatching of the messengers, who were to go to Syria on the morning immediately following: Rosh Hash, 1, 4, 5, 11, 4, compare 6, 9. If, now, the moon was not visible till the night of 31st day, the last month of 30 days was called "over full" (*meubar*); if, on the other hand, the moon became visible earlier, it was a "defective" (*chaser*) month of 29 days, the 30th becoming the first of the following month. It often happened, however, that the new moon was visible in the night to the 30th day, while the witnesses who were able to report the same, came too late. In that case it was resolved that their report be accepted, as long as the sun had not set; but not in case no time was left to perform, before the appearance of the stars, the solemn proclamation of the new moon. The next preceding month was in the latter case regarded as "over full," and the 31st as the day of New Moon.

On the 31st day, of course, there was no longer any necessity for the witnesses to report, since no month can have more than 30 days, nor less than 29: Rosh Hash 25 a (10).

Those who lived far away from Jerusalem, could not, in general, receive in due season information in regard to the proclamation of the New Moon.

On this account, both the 30th and 31st were, in doubtful cases, celebrated as the days of the New Moon. In consequence of this, too, those who lived beyond Palestine were in doubt as to the proper day on which the holy days in the relative month occurred, for the messengers who proclaimed the festival could not reach them. From this resulted a two-fold celebration of the festivals—the so-called "second holy of the exiled." Hence the Passover was celebrated eight days; the Pentecost, two; the Feast of Tabernacles, nine days, in order to be sure not to miss the proper day. Though, subsequently, when the knowledge of astronomy was more widely diffused, this doubt was removed, and an infallible computation of the New Moon introduced; it was, nevertheless, thought necessary, in view of possible eventualities, that *those who lived out of Palestine* should, in general, acquiesce in the celebration of the "second holy days." There were, however, some exceptions and extenuations granted in reference to the observances on such days; on the other hand, a certain *Nathan bar Assi* was laid under the ban because he openly profaned a second holy day. A stricter regard, however, was at all times paid to the New Moon, which coincides with the day of Memorial (solemnly observed also at the New Year.) In this instance, no work was permitted even on the 30th day. For the witnesses might possibly announce the appearance of the New Moon seen in the preceding night. If the witnesses actually came on the 30th [in that case, the first of the next following month], the *mincha* sacrifices, which were to be sacrificed before the setting of the sun were yet offered, the ceremonies and hymns of the day introduced, and the day was recognized as actually holy. On one occasion, however, they returned *after* the *mincha* (evening) sacrifices, and there was a doubt in regard to the rites relative to the sacrifices. It was therefore resolved, that, henceforth, no report shall be received on that day, if the witnesses came after the *mincha* sacrifice had been already offered. When, therefore, the witnesses did not appear on the 30th day at all, or when they came too late, the 31st of the sixth month (Ellul) was observed as the day of Memorial (New Year), the 30th being, of course, spent as a day of cessation from all labour. The Rabbins, furthermore, ordain that both these days of the festival of New Year shall be holy; that they shall be solemnly observed even in the land of Israel, and that, on the second day, even though after the first and proper day of the New

Moon has been correctly computed, no mitigation in regard to observances is to take place, except in some special instances, 1. g., in the interment of the dead. If, now, for the sake of consistency, the *Day of Atonement,* also, should have been observed on two days, yet only one day was (and still is) observed, because the Sanhedrin would not lay the people under the too heavy burden of fasting two days in succession.

According to the present regulation of the calender*, the twelve months have, alternately, 29 and 30 days, when the year is regular, thus:—1. Nissan (corresponding very nearly to April), 30; 2. Jjar, 29; 3. Sivan, 30; 4. Thammuz, 29; 5. Ab, 30; 6. Ellul, 29; 7. Tishri, 30; 8. Marcheshvan, 29; 9. Kislev, 30; 10. Tebeth, 29; 11. Shebat, 30; 12. Adar, 29. In case an interculary month is inserted before the twelfth, the former has 30 days. There are, however, cases in which Marcheshvan has 30 days, and, again, cases where Kislev has only 29 days.

In the former instance the year is called (over) " full " Shelemah ; in the latter " defective " Chaserah. There are various circumstances which have an influence on the regulating of the calendar in this respect, such as the due equalization of the lengths of the lunar and solar year, and the prevention of an immediate concurrence of certain festivals with a Sabbath.

The lunar months contain, according to Rosh Hash, 25 to 29 days, $12\frac{3}{4}$ hours and 73 " portions," 1,080 (15) of which are contained in an hour, (there being 24 hours a day.) The lunar year is, therefore, nearly 11 days shorter than the solar year, (reckoning the latter at 365 days, 5 hours, $997\frac{2}{3}$ " portions.") In the course of time, then, it would happen that the calculation of the year, by 12 lunar months, would so widely depart from the solar year, that the festivals of one season would occur in another, or one entirely opposite. To prevent this, 7 months of 30 days respectively are intercalated in the course of every period of 19 years, so that the lunar and solar year from time to time mutually balance to each other. The intercalation of a month, at present, always happens in the years, 3, 6, 8, 11, 14, 17, 19. Such a year has, in that case, after the 12th, another month, both of which are called " Adar " (in the calendar the second is denoted by Ve-Adar). The first, however, is regarded as the intercalary month proper.† In former times, before the computation of the calendar was fixed, it was possible to determine

---

* The Hebrew calendar was established about 300 A. E. C.

†When the year, accordingly, has thirteen months, the feast of Purim, (and every anniversary which occurs in the 12th month) is celebrated in the 13th month.

from the progress of vegetation, whether the new festival year could begin immediately after the 12th month; for according to Scripture, the first month of the year was at the same time to be the month of ripened ears. If the produce of the field had not yet so far matured, it was decreed in the middle of the twelfth month, that a thirteenth shall be added. In dispatching a decree of this kind to the inhabitants of Babylonia and Media, R. Gamaliel mentions, that the doves and lambs (which were required for the paschal sacrifices) were yet too young. There was still another sign: The full moon, during which the Passover was celebrated, was not to precede the vernal equinox; in like manner, the feast of Tabernacles was not to precede the autumnal equinox, for according to Exodus, xxxiv., 22, the *tekupha* (turning revolution) of the year must have already taken place when this feast is celebrated. The Rabbins understand by the term *tekupha*, the time when the sun enters one of the four signs of the Zodiac, viz: Aries, (Spring), Cancer, (Summer), Libra, (Autumn), and Capricorn, (Winter), which at that time denoted a change of the seasons. It is well known, however, that now owing to the percession of the equinoix, the signs of the ecliptic no longer coincide with the corresponding constellations. From one *tekupha* to another there elapse 91 days 7 hours, 519 thirty-one ninty-sixth "portions." According to Rosh Hash, it was avoided making the Sabbatical year one of 13 months, that the cultivation of the soil might not be interrupted for too great a length of time. This circumstance could not, of course, be taken into account, in case the season was not yet sufficiently advanced, and the vernal equinox had not yet arrived.

Notice of the celebration of the New Moon, as determined by Synedrium in Jerusalem, was given to the inhabitants of Palestine, and even Babylonia, by means of bundles of flaming combustibles. These were waved to and fro upon the mountain tops. The flaming signals were communicated from height to height; the nearest inhabitants of Babylonia, as soon as the signals reached their view, lit torches on the roofs of all their houses, so that the whole region presented the aspect of being in flames. The malevolent Samaritans, however, by means of false signals, occasioned mistakes in regard to the day of New Moon. On this account it was thenceforth proclaimed through messengers.

CHAPTER XI.

A SERMON ON THE CREATION.

The history of our first parents is the history of all their descendants. *They* first entered into the battle of life, and, since their days, the contest has continued without cessation. Now, it has raged with fierceness, like some struggle between phalanx and legion; now it has subsided into sullen horror, like some midnight massacre of civilization by barbarism; but the fight has gone through thousands of years, and still the combatants are ranged in opposing columns, nor will victory declare itself till one side be utterly exterminated.

The God of Battles himself decreed *this* battle when he animated the perishable "dust of the earth" with the spirit of immortality. He thus placed in antagonism the evanescent and the eternal—the impulses of nature and the restraints of conscience, passion and principle, evil and good. Since then, religion, philosophy, rationalism and infidelity have done their best to complicate the difficulties of the struggle; but, effectually, no change has occurred, because man cannot supersede Providence

Why this battle should have been ordered, is the question which has most agitated mankind. Wherefore humanity should have been so constituted that its elements naturally militate against each other, has been made the lasting problem of the world.

But this is one result of the struggle itself—blind judgment against prescient wisdom. The pages of revelation solve the proposition. It has been said that man is born in sin, and that, but for a vicarious atonement, the millions of earth had been created to everlasting perdition. It has been said that the all-perfect Eternal delegated to frail mortals the right to pardon and to anathematize. It has been said that belief is the privilege of power, and, hence, the sword and stake have claimed their victims; and, in the name of that Being designated the God of Mercy, mercy has all but been annihilated. It has been said that nature is self-existent—that right and wrong have no higher source that man himself—that here is the end of life, for that there is no hereafter; but the words of the Divinity proclaim the worthlessness of these and all other human interpretations, and light us to that knowledge which alone can lead to the victory that shall terminate the battle.

"We will make man in our image," was the behest which called man into existence; "and, he said, have dominion over the fish of the sea, over the fowl of the heaven, and over the beasts, and over all the earth," was the fiat which declared him the lord of creation, thus pronounced to be for his service.

The image of God is eternity; the spirit of creation is love. Man, then, must have been designed eternal; love must have been the predominate principle, not only of his being but of that of all things. Let us harmonize this with the words of Holy Writ. There is nothing in the organisation of man which needs to be terminable. We are so accustomed to see helpless infancy progress to vigorous maturity, and then degenerate to worn out old age, to subside in death, that we do not pause to reflect if this be inherent or acquired. And yet in what does the constitution of man differ from that which renders nature permanent? Grant gravitation, inertia, and a projectile force, and the orbs of heaven roll through countless ages: eternal motion in infinite space. Grant a supply of food as the material for animal combustion, and a supply of oxygen as the medium in which that combustion may be carried on, and animal life becomes as endless as "summer and winter," "heat and cold," which cease not. The spirit of creation is love. What but love infinite as the wisdom which the harmony of the universe from the confusion of chaos, could have impressed on matter that reproductiveness which perpetuates without the necessity of a new creation. In everything was "its seed within itself." In everything was displayed the boundless care of boundless love for the preservation of that seed, so that the embryo might become endowed with the necessary vitality. In vegetables and in the inferior animals, nature and instinct stand for this spirit of love. In vegetables, the husk, the bulb, the fleshy fruit, the horny flower cup, and its demonstrations. In animals it is seen in the lair of the carnivora, the nests of birds, the migrations of fish. Man develops it in obedience to the divine command which enjoins marriage, but as he is superior to all other productions, so his development is higher and more conformable to the reason which constitutes his supremacy.

The spirit of creation is love. We trace it in the mutual support which animals and vegetables give to each other; in the adaption of things to the localities in which they are placed; in the universality of man destined to rule all; in the agencies constantly at work to maintain the equilibrium between the inanimate and the animate, to promote intercommunication through necessity, between the inhabitants of dis-

SERMON ON THE CREATION. 125

tar. climes. But, above all, we trace it in the double nature given to hu ·nity, whereby mankind may merit what it aspires to learn.

If man has been created perfection, error would have been impossible to him; virtue would have been entitled to no reward, because it would have been inherent; there would have been no necessity for any state beyond the one existence, because all that creation demanded would have been fulfilled in its perfection. If man had been made with a preponderant tendency to evil, cruelty, and not love, would have condemned him, to an endless and fruitless wrestle with himself, and would have judged him because he had not succeeded where success was impossible.

If he had been born in sin, and if to it had been given dominion over him, reason, which should bless by its power to raise, would curse by its subservience to what it abhorred; for the function of reason admits of no cavil. It is that portion of the divine within us which renders man improvable by comparison and combination; it enables him to discriminate between that which conduces to the general weal and that which promotes the common woe, and thus it permits him to appreciate good and evil. To give man this guide, to teach him that his happiness depended on a course which it approved, and which it would willingly pursue, but from which it was debarred by an irresistible influence, might be the characteristic of some Indian Mahadeva, or some Roman Atè; impiety only could apply it to the Eternal God, long suffering, abundant of kindness and truth.

Man, then, was not called into existence with any bias, except such as love gave. And, truly, there was the sublimity of eternal love in the idea of creating a being endowed with a double nature, so nicely balanced that the portion which was all perishable could never become utterly corrupt, because the portion which was all heavenly could never entirely lose its purity. To give to this being volition to choose its own career, and thus to secure the merit of its actions, conscience to judge those actions, and thus to be capable of working out its own happiness, was only consistent with that love. There remains only to investigate how this scheme failed.

Causes produce effects. Love in the Divinity was to produce gratitude in man. God was to rule through love; man was to obey through gratitude. Conformable with man's double nature—the immaterial and the material—his gratitude was to have a double development—his religion, which was to be all soul; his actions, which were to be all bodily. The type of his spirituality was the knowledge of God and of his will; the type of his corporeality was obedience to the behest which prohibited the eating of the tree of good and evil. This knowledge of God was to be limited by Divine will; to be satisfied with this restraint was to be happy—to strive to break it was to sin. Man, yielding to the ignoble pleadings of appetite, eat of the forbidden fruit, and thus exhibited his desire for a knowledge which had been declared inconsistent with his being—a knowledge of those inherent consequences of good and evil which had been impressed as mysterious laws on creation.

But the Eternal had said : " On the day thou eatest thereof thou shalt surely become mortal," and man, who had braved this penalty, was now to learn the result of his wantonness. The fruit he found did not confer what he had coveted, but the lightning of reason showed him the crooked way he had chosen, and the thunder of conscience condemned him to fear. He hid himself. Then came to his cowering shame the sentence of his disobedience—not the punishment, but the inevitable consequences of his allowing mortal corruption to prevail in his being. Woman, the original instigator of the wrong, was to become secondary to man. Having been the means of giving death to the world, she was to provide for the continuation of her race as the mother of future generations, and, in her maternity, she was to find alike her danger and her dependence. Man, because he had yielded to be led where he should have sought to guide, was thereafter to assume his legitimate position—lord of created things; by bringing corruption to himself, he had brought it to all below him : " The earth is cursed on thy account." Having been the slave to his desires, he was thereafter to find in labour his servitude and his mastery.

But, the image of God is eternity; the spirit of creation is love. Man had voluntarily deprived himself of his participation in those divine principles; it remained with the All Merciful that they should not, therefore, cease from earth. Then came the great law of compensation, which preserved man to eternity and love to creation. Sin had doomed nature to decay, life to mortality; existence thus became incomplete.

Desire had introduced toil and sorrow; happiness thus became jeopardised. The body was thus to pay the penalty of these evils; the soul was to remain immortal. Through the aire of death the spirit was to pass, but beyond that dread visitation beamed an eternal future. Thus, being was rendered perfect, and eternity was preserved to the world. Woman was to risk her life to perpetuate her race; man was to spend his days in labour, but woman was to become a mother in obedience to her love, and in her maternity she was to find the solace for the danger she had passed, and the affection which rendered her happy even in trouble; man was to learn that in labour consisted his best safeguard against future temptations, and that through it alone could he procure the activity necessary to his well-being. Thus the dependence of woman and the labour of man were hallowed by the spirit of love.

Sin had come into creation. Constant enmity had been pronounced between it and society: "He shall bruise thy head, and thou shalt bruise his heel." Antagonism has been instituted between the body, which has become corrupt and perishable, and the soul, which was to remain capable of perfection and immortality. The design of creation, human happiness, was compromised by this battle of life; thus voluntarily engaged in by man.

Moreover, as man had fallen from good to evil, and, as in the struggle between his contending natures (it is so in all struggles) bad passions were to be excited, and, therefore, further evil was to ensue, it became necessary that Divine wisdom should provide means for regenerations. Again, the spirit of love spoke through the mouth of the Eternal. On Adam and Eve was bestowed one compensation, to Cain was imparted another. He had taken away a life, unconsciously, but still, wickedly, because he had yielded to the influence of evil thoughts. When the stern voice of God announced to him the magnitude of his crime and the consequences which conscience would entail: "A fugitive and a wanderer wilt thou be on earth"—he trembled before the terrible future he had evoked, and, in the bitterness of his prostration, he exclaimed: "My iniquity is greater than I can bear." Then, said Mercy: "Atonement lieth at the door, and to thee is its desire; and through it thou shalt rule." And when the guilty one, thus told that the road to heaven still lay open before him, was awakened to the new fear that some act of violence similar to his own might prevent his treading that through the gates of repentance, "But it may come to pass, that anyone meeting me may slay me." God gave him "an assurance" of safety, and so confirmed the fiat that expiation is the antidote for vice.*

Since that time, the dawn of the world, human life has resembled an April day. Now sunshine, now shower; now the bright light of spring, now the sombre darkness of winter; but amid all, the glorious daystar remained resplendent, although temporarily obscured, and the coming summer loomed in the future as the realisation of hope. Since that time the battle of life has continued without intermission. Now virtue has prevailed, now vice has ruled; now men have yielded to the divine influence of spirit, now they have succumbed to the debasing control of matter; but around all, atonement shone the great Mediator, and still before us glittered the prospect of human regeneration and human happiness, as essential to the merciful design of creation.

Since that time, self love, which in mortal minds usurps the place of genuine love, has invented a thousand excuses for excesses in the cause of zeal, for shortcomings in the path of duty; but ever the character of man, in the aggregate, has continued the same. Power has abused its privileges, crime has used its opportunities; philanthropy has ministered on the one hand to the satisfaction of conscience, on the other hand to the gratification of vanity; religion, in its purity, has taught the highest virtue, in its impurity, has inculcated the lowest vice; it has preached charity and practised atrocities; it has spoken peace and acted war. Progress has been made to mean the advancement of the mass, and the advantage of the individual; either merit has led the van, or it has ceded its place to nepotism; public service has been confined to the worthy, or it has been abandoned to favoritism; it has been wielded for the emergencies of the times, or it has rusted in the fetters of routine. Confidence in heavenly mercy has led martyrs to the grave, and has consecrated them in it; confidence in mortal resources has conducted criminals to the abysses of sin, and has there deserted them. Good has risen to the very type of the Godhead; evil has descended to the depths of perdition; but amid all, no man has been found pure, no man has been found so corrupt that atonement has not, at the last, proved his redeemer.

Since that time, mortal cunning has devised a thousand means for deceiving itself or others, and in every way man seemed to have exerted himself to render void the decrees of Providence, founded on its own inalienable law. But ever the great principles deducible from the history before us have remained permanent. In appearing to shape their individual courses, men have only contributed to one harmonized whole. Right has always prevailed, even though wrong may have been supported by prejudice and maintained by power.

Volition, while most unrestrained, is most subservient to a superior, though unseen, will; responsibility strives in vain to shake off its yoke because it is obedient to judgment beyond its control. And above all, no human efforts have been able to banish from earth the compensation (through a future state) or even for death, or that given for labour through atonement and regeneration; for the image of God is eternity, the spirit of creation is love.

CHAPTER XII.

DEDICATORY SERMON.

"Bless, O my soul, the Lord; and all that is within me, bless His holy name!" Yes, every aspiration of my mind, every chord and every impulse of my heart; all my feelings and thought, my whole being—all unite in one exulting shout of joy, rising to God, my Creator. For this is man's true greatness, that Thou, O Lord, hast created him in Thy resemblance and in Thy image, and in Thy infinite mercy. Thou hast brought this truth to our knowledge and to our living consciousness. Therefore bless the Lord, O my soul, thou daughter of heaven, and never forget this, His great mercy! Yes, this is the dignity of man, that He alone of all beings, feels and knows his origin. Born of dust, walking upon graves, he reaches with his mind, with his soul, into Heaven itself. Thus rises now my soul upon the wings of devotion to Thee, fountain of my existence, and fervently I pray to Thee, O God! Thou who hast guided me, Thy humble servant, from the beginning of my existence to the present day; Thou who hast called me to this holy office of spiritual guide; Thou who hast placed me at the head of this congregation of Israel, that I may guide and lead it as a faithful shepherd; Thou who hast deemed me worthy to speak in this new, magnificent Temple, the first word of consecration and of instruction, bless the words of my mouth, that I may worthily proclaim Thy glory and Thy praise.

As Moses once, timid and full of hesitation, answered Thy call, O my Lord, I am not eloquent, for I am slow of speech, and of a slow tongue, so I tremble and hesitate; for that which lives in my heart and inspires my soul; that which I feel so deeply and so devoutly; that which I would infuse into the minds of my audience, and especially of its younger members, with the holy fire of the deepest inspiration, I am compelled to say to them in a foreign tongue, in a language which I have never spoken, in which I am not versed, and which is not the language of my childhood. Therefore, bless O Lord the words of my mouth, as Thou once didst Moses; open my lips, that I may worthily proclaim Thy praise.—Amen.

In the name of the Eternal One, I bless and greet you, my brethren, who have gathered exulting, and beaming with joy, in this new house, which was built in honor and in praise of Him who was, who is, and who will be to all eternity. I greet you on this day of jubilee and of joy;

you who have come kneeling to the steps of this sanctuary to do homage to the King of Glory. Yes, with just pride, with God-inspired joy, amidst the organ's roar, with songs of rejoicing and alternate choruses, with timbrel and harp, we have assembled here at our first entrance into these halls of devotion and consecration. For O thou band of Israel, a house, a house of God, has risen in our midst, giving evidence of thy piety, of thy fidelity and thy devotion to thy God. Yes, the words of Holy Writ, "How beautiful are thy tents, O Jacob, thy tabernacles, O Israel," which greet in golden splendour the visitor upon his entrance, they find an immediate living echo in the breast of each and every one who comes to this magnificent house of God. Lovely and fair, holy and majestic is this temple, and proudly and worthily may it take its place among the high and sublime houses of God, that have been consecrated to the King of Glory, here in the New, or yonder in the Old World. But what signifies all the external magnificence and beauty of this edifice? What all the dazzling splendour that charms the eye, and that satisfies the æsthetic feeling, in comparison with the inner beauty and satisfaction which it offers to the fervent and devoted believer?

For these walls are dead; these stones and columns are without feeling; these external forms, the proudly elevated domes, are mute and motionless, and even that sublime instrument, whose lofty melodies warm the heart and cause devotion to soar on high, is itself cold and insensible. True beauty is imparted to this temple only, when a living echo is aroused in the heart of the prayerful by the inspired word of the pious Psalmist: "How amiable are Thy tabernacles, O Lord of Hosts! My soul longeth, yea even fainteth for the courts of the Lord; my heart and my flesh crieth out for the living God." We feel the full truth of these words that meet our eye there, above, that Thy tents, Thy temple, O Israel, are eternally, unchangeably beautiful only; when the whole congregation, in profound devotion, in living enthusiasm, in holy harmony, bring heart and mind to the living God. True beauty is imparted only to this temple, when we learn to consider all that are here assembled, whatever may be their faith, their rank or station, as brethren, as children of one Father; when we learn to understand here, and to obey beyond the walls of the temple, the admonishing words of the prophet: Have we not all one Father? Hath not one God created us? Why do we deal treacherously, every man against his brother, by profaning the covenant of our fathers? Yes, we may rightfully exclaim: "Beautiful is thy temple, O Israel!" Only when the words of truth and wisdom, the words of religion which are proclaimed here before the assembled congregation from this pulpit, when these words of salvation sound into the chaos of your souls, as the words inscribed here over the holy ark, "Let there be light," sounded once into the chaos of the material world; when your mind is enlightened, your heart warmed, your soul aroused; when the word of God incites you to noble deeds of piety; to divinely inspired works of love and justice, of gentleness and mercy; when precept and practice agree and harmonize, and just because we are so thoroughly and completely convinced, not only of the external, but more especially of the internal beauty of our temple, this day is to be a day of feasting and joy.

For this our song of jubilee and rejoicing is so fully justified, for this we all join in the sublime hallelujah of the Psalmist: "Oh praise the Lord all ye nations; praise him all ye people; for his merciful kindness is great toward us, and the truth of the Lord endureth forever." Praise ye the Lord! Yet, here the question is forced upon us: Do all the people join us in this great hallelujah? Do all the nations sympathize fully and cordially with us in our celebration? Are there not millions upon millions opposed to the band of Israel, who call to us, though perhaps only in the stillness of their heart: Moderate your exultation; restrain your joy; for the way in which you seek the Lord will never bring you near to Him. Your path toward God is not the true one; your road is not the straight and even road. The Israelite who has clearly resigned his higher mission; who comprehends his relation to his God, will not be confused by this language. But as the minority, we owe to the world at large, to the millions who differ from us in their faith, an explanation of our jubilee of victory, at this time when we consecrate this magnificent Temple of the Eternal One; and we will not hesitate frankly and freely to give this explanation, by submitting three points to a close discussion and examination. We maintain:—

I. Our Temple is an unchangeable monument of the fidelity and devotion of Israel to the Eternal One.

II. Our Temple is a monument of the fidelity of Israel to itself.

III. The Israelitish Temple is a monument of the fidelity of Israel to mankind.

1st. Our Temple is a monument of the fidelity of Israel to the Eternal One. Yes, thou most faithful, my people, in the dark and gloomy centuries of suffering and oppression; mayest thou prove the same fidelity in the mild sunbeams of happiness and freedom. He who is acquainted with the sad history of our people during the past eighteen centuries—a history penned with blood, replete with persecution and oppression; He who knows how Israel was scoffed and scorned, humbled, and persecuted. How it was restricted and confined in its civil life; how its industrial and intellectual activity and development were crippled; how numberless funeral piles were kindled for its annihilation; how it was accused of all imaginary crimes; how this unfortunate race was held responsible for every public calamity, and all these cruel persecutions; these false accusations for the sake of its faith, for the sake of its religion; he who considers and examines these things calmly and deliberately, must surely grant to Israel the honorable testimony of fidelity and devotion to the Eternal One; he must surely admire the power of sacrifice displayed by the Israelite, who sacrificed all earthly enjoyment, honor, riches, rank and station to his religion; to his faith in the Eternal One. In the time of suffering, when the sky of its fortune was veiled with gloomy clouds, Israel did not abandon its hope of a better state, of the time of the Messiah. But was Israel the only sufferer in this general misery? No. Those nations of the Old World, that had put Israel in chains, groaned themselves under the heavy yoke of tyranny and despotism. Nay, even the enlightened knights of mind, who had recognized the failings of their time, and who ventured upon the holy struggle for light, for truth, for liberty, and for humanity, generally fell victims to the fanaticism of their period. Constantly the sword of Damocles was suspended over the head even of glorious Luther, to whose memory, a few weeks ago, grateful Germany dedicated, in the old City of Worms, a magnificent monument—a ceremony honored by the presence of kings and princes. Only gradually and slowly the sunbeams of culture and of civilization dispersed the gloomy shadows of past centuries.

Even now the execrable ghost of despotism, in its ghastly form, prowls about in the Old World. Even now those nations, who once oppressed and cruelly persecuted our innocent people, still groan under the yoke of arbitrary tyrannical princes, who, for selfish purposes, condemn their people to misery, want and wretchedness; to bloody war, with its terrors, to standing armies, and to enormous burdens of taxation. And now how brilliantly shines in this land of liberty and of equality, the sun of true civilization and of true humanity; how constantly do his beams increase in power and in extent. Here one needs but to be a human being in order to enjoy human rights and liberty. Not your faith, but your acts and deeds: the visible fruits of faith, speak and testify for you. Therefore, O Israel, this temple upon the free soil of America is a monument not only of the fidelity to the Eternal One, but also a worthy monument of the perfect liberty of conscience, and of the fraternal equality of all citizens of the land. Therefore, O Israel, sound thy hymns of victory in this new Temple. Glorious, like the sun from beneath dark clouds, thou hast come in triumph out of the dark delusions of past centuries. Those formerly powerful nations, that had sworn thy destruction, have themselves suffered this fate, but thou livest and thrivest, and as a testimony of thy fidelity even in the days of prosperity, thou hast erected to the Eternal One, this Temple of gratitude and of praise. But what shall we say to those who, to-day, yet assert that Israel is only a fallen trunk, incapable of yielding blossoms and fruit ; that Israel can have no hope ; that its faith is not the true faith? Surely an examination of this assertion cannot excite the slightest shadow of a doubt in the mind of a true Israelite.

On the contrary, this subject is calculated to arouse in him a feeling of sacred pride. For supposing the faith of Israel in the Eternal One, the Creator of heaven and earth, the Father of all mankind ; supposing all this were founded on error, what do you think, my friend, I should do, if God were one day to hold me responsible for my error? I should, if a mortal could be permitted to be so presumptuous, I should step before God and remonstrate with Him ; I should dispute with Him ; it would be my turn to come with complaints and reproaches to the steps of His holy throne. I should say to him : Thou, O God, hast revealed Thyself in Thy majesty before the eyes of my whole people, so that even every servant saw Thee prophetically, and doubt was dispersed like mist before the light of the sun. Thou, eternally unchangeable God, hast announced the great word upon Sinai : "I am the Lord thy God; thou shalt have no other God beside me." On numberless occasions, Thou hast punished and chastised my fathers, whenever they left the idea of unity but for a moment. Through Thy servant Moses, in his farewell at the close of his earthly career, Thou hast commanded us : "Only take heed to thyself and keep thy soul diligently, lest thou forget the things which thine eyes have seen, and lest they depart from thy heart all the days of thy life ; but teach them, thy sons, and thy sons' sons. Specially the day that thou stoodest before the Lord thy God!" Through all thy prophets, Thou hast warned Israel not to abandon Thee, the one Lord. Through Thy great prophet Isaiah, Thou hast proclaimed unto us : "Ye are my witnesses," saith the Lord, "and my servant, whom I have chosen, that ye may know and believe Me, and understand that I am He ; before Me there was no God formed, neither shall there be after Me ; I, even I, am the Lord, and beside Me there is no Saviour." And now, in the face of this great revelation upon Sinai; in the face of these lucid teachings of the prophets; in the face of the chastisements and punishments of my people, whenever they abandoned their faith in the one God, can it be possible that dark visions, prophetic sayings, open to the most varied interpretation, should be able to prejudice and to diminish this faith in the strictest oneness of God? "Why," I should continue to argue with my God, "why, if it were Thy intention, O God, to modify this oneness in the least, why didst thou not descend from Thy sublime throne, before the eyes of the whole people, in order to silence all doubt, as Thou didst on Mount Sinai? Can Thy revelation upon Mount Sinai be recalled or modified in any particular, in any way except by a similar revelation? Or should miracles be able to shake my strong belief in the Eternal One, when Moses himself destroys the belief in miracles, in opposition to Thy oneness, O God, when he admonishes us, in the voice of warning, not to trust any prophet or any seer even if they should appear with miraculous deeds before us; if they dare to attack the oneness of God, even in the slightest degree? I ask you, my friends, if a father, having in a most solemn manner given a strict command to his child, warn him that no one may recall this command, would the child not be guilty of the most criminal disobedience if he should listen to the words of even the most faithful servant, if the father himself did not recall or change his will? And should God be less strict than man? No, God is not a man that He should lie; neither the son of man that He should repent. He is no erring being to retouch, amend or improve His works or words. He could not be a perfect, omniscient God, should He revoke, or even modify, the word once solemnly proclaimed. And with proud Israelitish self-consciousness, I should call the defensive language to God an amiable defiance. Therefore, my friends, on this day of Jubilee, join in our hymns of victory, and in our songs of rejoicing, for this Temple is a monument of thy fidelity, O Israel, to the Eternal One, the Creator and Father of all mankind.

2nd. Our Temple is a monument of the fidelity of Israel to itself. But although attempts were often made, in the gloomy past, to tread Israel under foot; although even to-day many are unwilling to acknowledge its historical significance, Israel never despaired of itself, always remembered its dignity, its exalted mission, never forgot the word of God: "Israel is my first-born son: ye shall be a peculiar treasure unto Me above all people, and ye shall be unto Me a kingdom of priests, and a holy nation!" And may you, my people, continue to vindicate this preference, to be proud of this privilege of being a nation of priests, and let it be attested by this magnificient Temple which we have built and consecrated. But how is this? Many a one might reproachfully ask: Would you, in our enlightened age, in this land of liberty and equality, would you attempt to establish antiquated prerogations? Would you stir up pride, self-conceit and presumption? Have not privileges of ONE people, or ONE class, in opposition to OTHERS, brought enough misery into the world? Shall now, even religion serve as a cloak to presumptuous privileges? Let us see, my friends, whether this objection, this charge, is just. Let us draw a comparison between the prerogatives and privileges of Israel, and the prerogatives and privileges of the nobility of the Old World, who also assert that their ancient privileges are sacred and unimpeachable. Let us examine and compare the respective documents, in order to see how far the respective claims are right and justified. The privileges of the nobility of the Old World, destroy the rights of the citizen and of the peasant; they despise the so-called lower classes of their native dignity, and of their independance. In short, these privileges of a few constitute the oppression and subjugation of millions. The code of the old European nobility declares: One law for the nobleman, and another for the citizen and for the peasant, while, on the other side, the old document which exalts us into a privileged people, says: "As ye are, so shall the stranger be before the Lord: *one* law and *one* manner shall be for you, and for the stranger that sojourneth with you." The right of nobility, O Israel, does not allow thee, as with the world's nobility, to take tithes from the peasant, but, on the contrary, thy old charter of nobility admonishes thee: Thou shalt truly tithe all the increase of thy seed that the field bringeth forth, year by year; thou shalt not wholly reap the corners of thy field, neither shalt thou gather the gleaning of thy harvest; thou shalt leave them to the poor and the stranger. Thy charter exclaims to thee: Thou shalt love thy neighbour as thyself; thou shalt not curse the deaf, nor put a stumbling-block before the blind; thou shalt not wrest the judgment of thy poor in his cause, and thou shalt take no bribe, and the stranger thou shalt not oppress; and a hundred similar laws of gentleness and love. Where are here the injured classes to complain of injustice and oppression? Just this, then, O Israel, is thy privilege, thy priestly mission, everywhere to promote the welfare of thy fellow-men, to sow happiness and peace. Therefore, remain faithful, O Israel, to thyself and to thy mission; be proud of thy title of nobility, which no one will dispute so long as thou remainest faithful to it. Thy ancient privileges never can and never will be cancelled by the culture of our period.

For in this consists the superiority of our religion, that it is capable of development and progress, that it bears ever fresh blossoms and fresh fruit. The nucleus of our religion is not made up of dead formalities and empty ceremonies; these belong to perishable time, and share its fate. Therefore, remain faithful, O Israel, to the teachings of Moses, and to the teachings of the prophets, who, though yielding to the requirements of their own age, still taught in Moses' spirit. If you ask me now, what the Judaism of our time requires of us, I answer you, in the voice of the Talmud: Just the same that our religion has required of us thousands of years ago, as the most essential thing. For this we read at the close of the Talmud treatise. Makkot's, 613 commandments and prohibitions, were given by God to Moses, to be obeyed by Israel. David reduced these 613 commandments for his time to eleven, and the prophet Micah, to only three. These eleven commandments of David, we find recorded in the fifteenth Psalm. David begins with the words: "Lord who shall abide in Thy tabernacle; who shall dwell in Thy holy mount?" Is this not the same question, which, to this day, is asked by millions; about which there are discussions and controversies, and which so often with ridiculous self-conceit is answered incorrectly? Who is entitled to stand in the holy mount of the Lord—in the immediate presence of God? Well, my friends, to whom truth is dear, consider the answer well; consider well this ONE point, which cannot be disregarded. The question has reference to God, and the answer to your fellow-men. You strive to raise to God. Direct your looks below to your fellow-men, and in this act you ascend to God. Who shall dwell in the holy presence of God? Hear the answer of the Psalmist: "He that walketh uprightly, and worketh righteousness, and speaketh the truth in his heart; he that slandereth not his neighbor, nor doeth an evil to his neighbor, nor taketh up a reproach against his fellow-man, in whose eyes a vile person is despised; but he honoreth them who fear the Lord. He that sweareth to his own injury and changeth not; he that putteth not out his money upon usury, nor taketh a bribe against the innocent; he that doeth these things shall never fall." These lucid truths, satisfying heart and mind, are unfortunately to-day inaccessible to the great mass of men, who think to find the majesty of God only in the misty and mystic, whereas his glory fills the whole earth. For, ask thousands of men: What doth the Lord require of you, and how can you ascend his holy mountain? and they will answer you: "Certain mystic ceremonies and rites are the means of salvation which surely lead to God." But what are all your offerings; all your ceremonies; all your formalities; your mystic and unintelligible religious rites, compared with one offering; one solemn ceremony, which I shall now name to you, and in whose contemplation you who believe you are bringing to your God the most difficult and acceptable sacrifice, must grow dumb? For, tell me my friends, is there a more sublime, a more solemn ceremony; is there a greater self-denial than when the father and the mother consecrate their greatest born, the joy and happiness of their life; when they devote their flesh and blood, their only child, for immolation to the Lord? Well, the prophet Micah asks the same question which David has previously asked in the 15th Psalm: "Wherewith shall I come before the Lord, and bow myself before the High God? Shall I come before Him with burnt-offerings; with calves of a year old? Will the Lord be pleased with thousands of rams, or with ten thousands of rivers of oil? Shall I give my first-born for my transgressions; the fruit of my body for the sins of my soul?" O how these words move us; how they humiliate and crush us; even this greatest of all sacrifices, our beloved children, seems yet insufficient for sinful man as atonement for his guilt and his misdeeds. With trembling and hesitation, the ears are strained to listen to the continuation of the prophet's sentence. If even the resignation of the beloved child is not a sufficient sacrifice, what then does the Mighty Lord require? And the prophet continues, punishing the stubborn, the hypocritical, and the wicked with reproach, and softly allaying the fear of the faithful, the pious and the Godly; "He hath told thee, O man, what is good, and what the Lord doth require of thee; nothing but to do justice, and to love mercy, and to walk humbly with thy God." Here we have the sacrifice which the God of love requires of you. But have we all reached this high standard? There are many who are, it is true, just in greater things, but in smaller matters they tread justice under foot, without considering that these small acts of injustice develop the most atrocious deeds of injustice; and others again are just in little things, but too weak and wavering to exercise and to promote justice in great things, and have love and mercy, which always tremble on our lips. Has mercy, the second requirement of the prophet, already penetrated all our hearts? Are there no more poor, unhappy and needy, to complain of our hard-heartedness? Alas! as long as gold and jewels, and pearls upon thy neck yield thee more enjoyment than the pearls of grateful tears, glistening in the eyes of the helpless and abandoned, thou art no follower of the laws of mercy and gentleness. And how is it with the third and last requirements of the prophet? Do we all walk in humility and modesty with our God? Do we live and act in God? Do we thank and praise Him always, not in this Temple only, but also at our houses, for all the happiness and all the pleasures that we enjoy? When we arise from the sick bed, do we acknowledge that it is He who sends recovery and life; that it is He who feeds and clothes us? And how much more exalted than your empty formalities and rites is this requirement, this holy commandment, to practice justice, to exercise love and mercy, and to walk humbly before God, in which, according to the Talmud, the whole Mosaic law is concentrated. For your ceremonies can only be performed at certain times, but these sublime commandments can and should be observed every moment of your life, as the Psalmist urges, the words inscribed here: I have set the Lord always before me, therefore remain faithful, O Israel, ever faithful to this sublime doctrine, and let this holy Temple serve as a testimonial and as a monument to thy unchangeable fidelity to thyself, and to thy ever blessed truth.

3rd. Our Temple is, however, in the third place, also a monument of the fidelity of Israel to all mankind. As at the time when the temple at Jerusalem still existed, priests and Levites lived scattered in Palestine, in order to prepare Israel for its high mission to become a nation of priests, so God, the All-wise and All-good, after Israel had been strengthened in the idea of the oneness of God, has scattered His nation of priests over the whole world, in order gradually to educate the whole world into one people of God, into priests, so as to realize the last words of Aaron's priestly blessing: "May He give thee peace!" Or are the expectations and hopes of mankind perhaps already fulfilled? Have we already reached the golden age of general humanity and brotherly love? And especially in our age of culture and enlightenment, when natural science has opened to the aspiring human mind, never anticipated and new, untrodden paths, and imparts to it so bold and sublime a flight; does not cold skepticism undermine, decompose and dissolve all that has been transmitted to us by past centuries, as sacred and unimpeachable? Do not the materialists deem themselves capable of storming Heaven, and of dethroning God? What an alarming state of things; the more the natural sciences gain in depth and scope, the more the human mind, formed in the image of God, unveils the mysteries of nature, so much the more the infidelity and skepticism. Where shall we, in this general corruption, whose threatening waves spread wider and wider, and shake faith more and more, where shall we find a safe anchorage? Though men of mind, materialists, may for a time become the prey of doubt; though with progressing culture, the number of skeptics may increase infinitely, and the small band of believers may dwindle away more and more, this does not diminish the eternal truth of the assertion: Man, powerless, frail, heaven-born man, sustained by a higher power, is a religious being, that cannot do without religion; his soul, though it may go astray for a time, will always long for the higher, the invisible; in one word, religion—that is the relation of man to God—will never, never die in man. But how and where will these men of science; these men of mind culture; where will these men of doubt, who have already renounced all faith, where will they find consolation, tranquility, and satisfaction? Let us pronounce courageously, and without fear, the bold but eternal truth: It is the religion of Israel alone that extends her loving, motherly arms, and that grants to mankind all for which the mind strives, and for which the heart longs. The religion of Israel, most ancient, yet ever young, is destined to become the religion of the world, and therefore we said: This magificent and proud Temple, which is scarcely equalled by another in our city in splendor and beauty, is a monument of the fidelity of Israel to all mankind. If you ask me by what authority I am justified in the bold assertion that a religion which has so often been looked upon as subdued, the religion of Israel, is promised a future so rich in blessings, I answer: Will, indeed, the materialists, the men who have already renounced all faith; will the thousands who waver and are victims of skepticism; will the enlightened world, who consider our age perhaps more fully penetrated by the divine spirit, than was the case with remote antiquity; will all these feel, indeed, inclined to support their faith, with the frail crutch of old, miraculous legends? No, the simpler a religion, the less it fetters the mind; the less it restrains the freedom of thought; the less it disagrees with reason; the less it denies satisfaction to the mind and comfort to the heart; the more prospect has such a religion of becoming a universal religion; the more readily and the more willingly will mankind accept its gentle yoke. And such a religion, simple and sublime, we have in the religion of Israel, and therfore the palm of victory must, and will ultimately, fall to his lot. Not miracles, whose power and influence was destroyed already by Moses, and in his spirit by Maimonides in the 12th, and by Moses Mendelssohn, in the last century, form the support of anchorage of our religion. Its eternal, unimpeachable truth finds its verification and its power of conviction in the harmonious conformity with the truth, written by the finger of God in nature, and in the history of mankind. Great was the one miracle, when the Lord revealed Himself to Israel on Mount Sinai, amidst fire, smoke and lightning, and by this revelation, diffused light, and filled the hearts with salvation and happiness. Greater I call the everlasting and ever-active miracle, when now the Lord speaks to all mankind, and reveals Himself to the whole world in the lightning of the telegraph, and the smoke of the steam vehicles, accomplishing thereby not less, but perhaps more, general brotherhood and union among the children of the whole earth. This wonderful revelation of God, however, which has been made in our time, amidst fire, smoke, and lightening, which gradually will unite the nations of the whole earth in one family, and by which their spiritual, as well as their industrial interests, will be more and more interwoven, is a guarantee to us of the time, which Isaiah and Micah have already prophetically seen and proclaimed, when the nations shall beat their swords into plow-shares, and their spears into pruning-hooks; nation shall not lift up sword against nation, neither shall they learn war any more. And the words of the prophet Isaiah will be fulfilled: "And many people shall go and say, come ye and let us go up to the mountain of the Lord, to the house of the God of Jacob, and he will teach us in his ways, and we will walk in his paths." Then will the prophetic word be realized, with which the Israelite, from time immemorial in his synagogues, hopefully concluded his morning and his evening prayer: "And the Lord shall be king over all the earth; in that day shall there be one Lord and His name One!" If now I assert that the whole world will one day be converted to the religion of Israel, I do not wish to imply that they will follow our present ceremonies with us, and celebrate our feast with us. No, if the edifice is completed, the scaffolding must fall! I only wish to imply as Israel, from time immemorial to the present day, in good and in evil times, has encouraged itself with the words: "Hear, O Israel, the Lord, our God, is one Lord!" So will all the children of men, sooner or later, call unto us: "Hear ye, O Israel, the Lord is also our God, He is one Lord!" And therefore I may exclaim from the depths of my heart with Solomon, who consecrated the first Temple: "But also the stranger, who is not of thy people Israel, when he shall come and pray at this house, mayest Thou listen in Heaven, the place of Thy dwelling, and do according to all that the stranger will call on Thee for, in order that all the nations of the earth may know Thy name, and fear Thee, as do Thy people Israel, and that they may understand that this house, which I have built, is called by Thy name." Yes, these doors are open to all, of whatever belief; to you who are heavily oppressed by the burdens of life, who want consolation and who are sore with suffering.

O, my unfortunate brother, thou who sighest and complainest, heavily oppressed by the burden of earthly existence, whom the chains of poverty and misery hold fettered ; thou who feelest thy bitter woe a thousand fold, because thy misery affects those that are so near thy heart—wife and children. O, suffering brother, who art deficient in all that is so imperatively demanded by the necessities of life ; thou who are wanting bread to still thy hunger, clothing to cover thy nakedness, a safe shelter to rest thy weary head. O thou unfortunate one, who dost not know the compassion of thy brethren, who art not warmed by the gentle breath of love and sympathy on the part of thy fellow-men, who lookest upon thyself as the outcast suffering son of mankind ; dull and hopeless thou often raisest thy tearful eye, and from thy lips escapes the wild cry of anguish : " Whence and when shall help come to me ?" O, thou unfortunate one—even if the whole world were to appear to thee as a hostile camp—come hither to the steps of this sanctuary, and whatever oppresses thy heart ; whatever torments and racks thee, pour it out before God in these silent halls, for He is a gracious and merciful God ; it is He that makes rich and poor, high and low, who gives to the grave and recalls to life ; here thou wilt find comfort in thy sufferings, consolation in thy sorrow.

And thou, too, my unfortunate brother, who art entangled in the mazes of sin, whom vice holds in her poisonous embrace, whom the world despises and forever condemns, if a consciousness of thy better self return to thee ; if repentance seize thy heart ; if thou look back with grief and longing to the lovely fields of pure innocence, come to this sanctuary with a courageous heart, confess thy guilt, thy missdeed, promise improvement and atonement ; for God, the merciful, does not require the destruction of the sinner, but only the return of the sinner from his evil paths in life.

But thou, too, happy one, who baskest in the sunshine of wealth, honor and esteem ; who hast never eaten thy bread in tears ; who art in the full enjoyment of health, and all earthly joys ; upon whom the world beams a smiling spring, O, forget not in the intoxication of thy good fortune, to appear often, very often in this house of God. Here thou shalt learn to bend thy knee before the God of our destinies, remembering that the wheel of fortune may suddenly turn, that no earthly happiness is permanent. Here thy earthly greatness shall be glorified in the light of humility and modesty. Yes, in good and in bad fortune, in joy and in sorrow, in the sunshine of wealth, and in the dark day of poverty, at the house of God, be to us a house of refuge and of comfort. Ye fathers and mothers, when a young blossom of life gladdens your parental heart, when the All-Merciful blesses you with the heavenly boon of a son, of a daughter, then come rejoicing hither to thank the kind Giver, and to intrust in full faith the fate of the tender offspring to His care.

Ye blooming boys and girls, here, before the holy ark, you will appear on the day of your confirmation, in order to vow, in the presence of your parents and of the all-seeing God, fidelity to the religion of your fathers. Here, in this Temple, ye will appear, ye Israelitish sons and daughters, when the vow of eternal love and fidelity is to invite you when you enter the holy bonds of matrimony, so that your houses, like his Temple, may become temples of harmony and peace! And when the sickle of death sweeps away the dear father, the beloved mother, from hence into the realms of eternal peace and blessedness, then, ye sons and daughters, ye will enter this sanctuary and pronounce the great "Kadish,"—the holy prayer—praising God in your sorrow, as ye thank Him in fortune and in joy. Yes, one generation passeth away and another generation cometh. As to-day we have made a pilgrimage to this sanctuary, so we all shall, the one sooner, the other later, make a pilgrimage to the sanctuary above, for our true and permanent home is not here below, but there, above. Our soul, the heaven-born, rises to God, the source of life, whence it sprang, but our bodies will return to dust and ashes. Nay, these halls of stone and wood, they will by far outlast our perishable frame. And then, in later days, yet thou, O! Temple of Israel, wilt stand here, an eloquent monument of our fidelity to the Eternal One, to ourselves, and to all mankind. Amen.

CHAPTER XIII.

A SERMON ON SACRIFICES.

Reference to ceremonies, whose existence has been obliterated, does not afford much interest to the general reader. The inquisitive and curious, may turn with some degree of excitement, to the mysterious recitals connected with the names Eleusis, Isis, or Walhalla; but this excitement depends entirely on the mystery connected with all heathen celebrations, and on the importance to be attached to their interpretations. The simple, unpretending rites, of the Levitical sacrifices; their want of all that can awaken speculation, or leave room for controversy; the utter cessation, not only of such religious expositions, but of everything analagous to them; all contribute to deaden the feelings, and to forbid speculation, and therefore to deprive the portion of the law before us, of much that can make reflection profitable. But something still remains, which may not be wholly uninteresting, and which may resolve itself into the following questions:—Why were sacrifices ordained as exponents of man's duties to Heaven? Did they take the place of that devotion which now exhibits itself in prayer? What was their moral effect?

Why were sacrifices ordained as exponents of man's duty to Heaven? It must not be forgotten, that the Divine legislator adopted into Judaism many of the ceremonies already existing among idolatrous nations. Of all such ceremonies, sacrifices held by far the most universal sway, not only among heathens, but even among those older individuals who bowed to the true God. Already in the earliest years of creation, when Abel and Cain sought to pour out into visible form the expression of their gratitude to Heaven, sacrifice was the method they adopted. When earth, freed from the overwhelming deluge, again bared her maternal bosom to nourish her restored offspring, sacrifice was the type by which Noah displayed his thankfulness for escape from the universal destruction. Abraham, Isaac, and Jacob, all offered sacrifices as proofs of their devotion to the service of God. Nor can we wonder at this development of human feelings. Gratitude is a sentiment that seeks to express itself in deeds, somewhat parallel to the benefits which evoked it. In those times, men were essentially agricultural; their riches consisted in the produce of the earth, and in domestic cattle. But the produce of the earth was either speedily perishable, or was consumed as now, for the ordinary maintenance of life. What we call capital, therefore, the accumulation of past labor, consisted then of cattle. Cattle formed the medium of exchange, afforded a ready means for the investment of superabundant vegetable production, and thus became the general standard by which wealth was estimated. The possession of cattle also rendered necessary the acquisition of grazing land, and the co-operation of numerous shepherds and herdsmen, and thus contributed, not only through numbers, to personal security, but to that system of colonization which was so needed to prevent the nomade habits of living, of idleness, and of pillage, from holding entire dominion.

To cattle, men looked, therefore, as to their highest gifts, through which they became respectable and respected. To cattle they owed many advantages: food, means of draught, clothing, and numerous domestic conveniences were contributed by the quiet ox, the gentle sheep or goat. Can we be surprised, then, that, in seeking to display gratitude to the source of their wealth, men should have chosen for the expression of that gratitude, that which they valued most; or that God, in opening, as it were, relations between himself and mortals, should have deigned to declare himself willing to accept the tribute which the holiest feelings of humanity had already sanctified? Assuredly not; more, if we were now called on to determine what would have been the most appropriate form of devotion, we should certainly pronounce in favour of what seems to have possessed so many claims for that peculiar end. Always at hand, always valuable, always associated with comfort and happiness, cattle were at all times ready for sacrifice. Did some long-continued prosperity determine a man to pour out his gratitude, the marks of that prosperity were the best means for his so doing. Did some escape from sudden accident or momentary temptation, evoke thankfulness, the store of home at once afforded scope for celebrating the escape or the resistance of temptation. If famine threatened, what fitter to propitiate than the food on which, in case of famine, existence depended? If we concede, then, that man is called on by gratitude to Providence, by his sense of Divine protection, and his want of Divine aid, to develop in some way his thankfulness, his dependance, or his penitence, we must, at the same time, allow that no type could have been more appropriate than the one selected.

It returned in some way a portion of His divine blessing, and by enabling man to part with that which was valuable to himself, and rendered him valued in the eyes of others: it prevented selfishness and avarice, and gave play to those warmer feelings of generosity and benevolence which do so much to cement the bonds of society. Fine sentiments, eloquently clothed, may command admiration and excite respect, but they may be little else than glittering externals, covering a worthless character, and may disgrace the utterer as they deceive the hearer. Homely thoughts, simply expressed, may fail to rouse the imagination or awaken the fancy; but, when the convictions they convey are substantially proved by the sacrifice of something valuable or pleasurable, while we may fail to approve, we cannot refuse to appreciate the sincerity and honesty of which they are the emanations. Prayer may be only verbiage; sacrifice must be, to a certain extent, genuine. And this leads to the second question.

Did sacrifices take the place of that devotion which now exhibits itself in prayer? It is strange, that, while modern religion throughout the civilized world has adopted prayer as the medium of its communication with heaven—while Holy Writ contains abundant evidence that all the patriarchs, judges and prophets of old must all have felt the power of prayer, and have used it—while our present liturgy contains passages of antiquity so remote, that no precise date can be given to their introduction, we nowhere find in the Pentateuch any ordination concerning prayer. And this is the more strange, when we consider the minuteness of detail in every respect that can affect human welfare, either through moral, sanatory, social, or ceremonial law.

Even the fashion of the priestly garment is not thought too light for a special ordination. How, then, can we account for the absence of all rules as to prayer; or, are we to suppose that sacrifice superseded the necessity for oral communication with heaven? To us it has always seemed evident that prayer was not ordained, because it was not to consist of any formula prescribed by God, but was left to the free will of man. While it was quite natural that a gracious Providence should point out to men desirous of testifying, by tangible means, their repentance or gratitude, their sorrow or hope, the manner most agreeable to its acceptance, it was equally natural that the expression of sentiments which prompted those testifying, should be left to themselves. The solemn and impressive words of a recognized liturgy may penetrate into the heart, although constant repetition render them somewhat too familiar, but the spontaneous effusions of a soul pouring itself out before the throne of grace, must awaken a responsive echo in the deepest recesses of the mind and body. Besides, the sacrifices being once ordained, some individuals might have imagined that the whole religious duty was involved in the offering, and, that, to propitiate or atone, it was only necessary to bring an ox or a lamb, with the certainty of its being accepted. And, that this could not have been the end of sacrifice, is too apparent to require proof. It seems clear, therefore, that the devotion of our ancestors was to be of a two-fold nature—real and ideal; the real being the visible sacrifice and ceremony, the ideal being the accompanying sentiment which animated the act, with all that rendered it holy, and which expressed itself in the form of spontaneous prayer. There must have been, and, doubtless, there were, certain formula which accompanied periodical sacrifice, such as the two daily offerings, the Sabbath and festival offerings, &c., these formulæ were probably recited by the ministering priests, and, perhaps, repeated by the surrounding worshippers; but, for personal sacrifice, the form of prayer was left to the feelings of the individual; and a standard was thus furnished by man himself for estimating the sincerity of his devotion. But, it may be urged, why, if prayer was to be determined by man, should the offering also be not so decided? The reply will be evident from a consideration of the third point: What was the moral effect of sacrifices?

Sacrifices were principally of two kinds: of atonement for sin, and thus partook of the nature of the punishment, &c.; of thanksgiving for divine mercy, and thus they assumed the character of charity. Now, as has been before observed, one of the primary objects of punishment is to set an example to the culprit of the consequences entailed by misdeeds—to the world, of the evil effects which sin produces. There is also no doubt that the discovery of guilt, and its exposure to the eyes of one's fellow-creatures, produce more shame than the guilt itself; and that, perhaps, the best means to prevent crime would be to compel every criminal to publish his shame. Viewed in this light, the determining of the expiatory sacrifice, by divine command, was alike necessary to prevent the sinner from concealing his guilt, and important to place him in his true character before his fellow-men. And this will be the more readily conceded when it is recollected, that, although an act of sin offend only an individual, it is essentially a wrong against society, and that the sufferer has neither the power nor the right to acquit the culprit, without suitable reparation to the offended majesty of the law.

Hence, to leave the form of an atonement offering to the sinner, would have been to deprive it of one of its most important functions, viz.: its being the medium for exposing the evil-doer, and its consequent tendency to prevent error through shame. Even the most hardened sinner could not, at some time, fail to acknowledge the omniscience of God, and he would thus, also, recognize the necessity for appeasing his anger in the way ordained by his mercy; the hypocrite, also, who, under the cloak of sanctity, violated every principle of morality, would, at some moment of compunction, feel impelled to attempt an expiation. Both, however, while endeavouring to make their peace with their offended Maker, could only do so by allowing their fellow-men to be the witnesses of their contrition and humiliation: and thus the very best safe-guard against recurring criminality, was the abasement to which a public act of penitence compelled submission. And that this idea prevailed with the Divine legislator, may be inferred by the particular sacrifice ordained for the involuntary sin, or for the "sin of ignorance." A broad line of demarcation was thus drawn between crime and error; while the one was held up in all its flagrancy, the other was exposed only as a warning against frailty, and as a caution to acquire that true knowledge of God's law which might prevent the ignorance that had fallen. But, in both cases, the religious nature of the expiation deprived it of all that could render the sinner's humiliation a theme for mockery, or a means for insult. Men may pelt the victim in the stocks, but there is something so solemn and holy in an act of devotion to God, that even scoffers are silenced, and unbelievers can only sneer. A consciousness of the general weakness of human nature may restrain from an acknowledgment of error to one's fellow-man, and may support, even under the obloquy of invective, to which undiscovered evil-doers are too apt to resort, when any opportunity offers for blurring another; but there is no such excuse in confessing frailty before the perfection of heaven, for there is no degradation in divine reproof. In regard to the atonement offerings, therefore, it is evident that the moral effect must have been most impressive; they deprived guilt of all means for subterfuge, and yet awakened no revengeful feelings against human injustice; they compelled exposure of crime, and thus produced shame, but it was a shame which left no sting in the culprit, because he felt that sincere repentance was ennobling, and which afforded no triumph to others, because all knew their own short-comings, and were conscious that it might but too soon be their duty to atone.

The offerings of gratitude—"free will and peace"—were no less beneficial, in a moral sense. They were designed to represent man's thankfulness for heavenly goodness, and to be exponent of his resources in the eyes of the world. But, as has been said, wealth in those times consisted in cattle, and not in money. A man's friends may be over or under estimated by common report, or by appearances, but no mistake could be made in respect to property which was so bulky, and, of necessity, so apparent to the public. If, therefore, parsimony or selfishness prompted to a scanty or inadequate sacrifice, there was no room for pleading a mistaken estimate or the scarcity of available capital. Just as true charity left the "corners of the field" ample, while niggard economy contracted them to the very corners, so a free-will offering represented the exact state of a man's philanthropy, and afforded no excuse which the world could not well appreciate. Laws, however, are made to bind only the dishonourable; true honesty requires no bridle. Real gratitude to heaven, expounded in genuine charity, needed no ordinance to enforce the magnitude of its offering; it was only the pseudo philanthropy which selfishness puts on as a mask, which was exposed by the extent of its sacrifices. And thus, as now, some only give that their names may figure in subscription lists, or become celebrated as patrons, so, in all times, there have been pretenders to philanthropy and traders in charity. Our means of convicting such hypocrites are fallible, but, before God, they are exposed in their true colours; we do not succeed in detecting the fraud, and impunity begets courage to persevere, but divine wisdom is not to be deceived, and conscious dishonesty of purpose dares not prevaricate before its heavenly Judge. And so, here again, the religious nature of the act of charity, its connection with the service of God, was the best security for its genuineness. While the publicity of the sacrifice, and the means thus afforded for comparing its adequacy with the known resources of the giver, were checks against the parsimony of the miser or the niggardliness of the selfish, the sanctity attached to the offering was its safe-guard, alike against the pretensions of hypocrisy, and against the vanity that aims at worldly applause. Bow we, then, to the wisdom which ordained sacrifice to be the preservative of honesty, the exponent of honours, which opened the door to sincere repentance, by graciously showing how its words might be proved by suitable deeds, and which secured man against fraud, and effected sanctimony by reflecting them in acts which he might safely estimate, because they were assayed in the mint of the Lord.

CHAPTER XIV.

A SERMON ON MARRIAGE.

When the merciful Creator impressed upon human nature the principle of love, he provided the best safeguard for the preservation of society. "Wherefore man will leave his father and mother, and cleave to his wife, and they will become one flesh." Obedient to this law, man, through the marriage contract, becomes the means of forming the most hallowed union that is known to earth. Friendship, as sung by poets, or painted by authors, is a beautiful idea ; the reality is too often fair on the surface, but rotten at the core. Self sets up its host of wants and interests, and these, as various as the characters of men, diverge into opposite extremes, instead of converging to a centre. Even the sublime tie that binds parents and children, yields to the link of marriage ; for as parents themselves, sought helps meet for them, so do children, in their turn, build homes elsewhere, and in the new associations, forget the old love. But the bonds of matrimony are permanent ; man assumes them voluntarily, to part with them but with death. Wife and husband, when the union is perfect as it should be, cease to be different individuals. They are essentially the reflex of each other. No image represented in a mirror, resembles more entirely its original, than do husband and wife. His interests are her interests : his success or failure is her success or failure. For her he forgets his sternness : for him, if needs be she lays aside her gentleness. For her he forsakes the most fascinating attractions of worldly pleasure ; for him society presents no alurements of her. This intimate communion benefits both. Man gains therefrom a solace from his labors, a haven of comfort which receives him buffeted by the storms of outer life, a refuge from himself when embittered by the coldness or falsehood of the world. Woman acquires a protection from her weakness, which commands the respect of society ; a shield to defend her from the attacks of malice or violence ; a support which gives to her soft nature strength to endure her share of earth's troubles. But above all, means are provided through marriage, for the proper introduction into life of well qualified members. Man, the highest of created beings, is also the slowest to attain the mature development of his faculties. Inferior animals, requiring only physical powers, may be dismissed from the parents' lair, as soon as their young strength enables them to provide for their wants, and their future career will derive no loss from the dismissal. Man requires mental and moral training; not only must his years of infancy and childhood pass in necessary education; but even his puberty must not be without its cultivation. He needs not only precept but practice; it is not enough that he is taught what is right, he must see it performed; his mind must be fortified by precept, his imitativeness must be guided by example.

And where but in the hallowed precincts of the home of marriage, can children receive this requisite treatment. Contrast the fate of those unfortunate victims to their parents' weakness, who are ushered into life without the pale of matrimony. How many fall a prey to disease, either of mind or morals, and become the pariahs of civilization; how few attain to anything higher than the brute perfection of physical growth.

But in order that marriage may fulfil its legitimate functions, it is necessary that there be entire confidence between husband and wife. Each is the depository of the other's honor, and this is a trust so sacred, that it must be guarded, even at the sacrifice of life itself. Nature and society league in some respect to give immunity to man, which is denied to woman; but no cloud must obscure the brightness of her fidelity. Pure as the unsunned snow that glitters eternal on the mountain top, she lives only in the insolation from all external influence. Yet the weakness of mortality oftentimes operates against her; she may become the object of a suspicion which she does not merit, or she may have violated her duties without being suspected. Grant the latter, and the results must not only be fatal to her own peace of mind, but to her happiness as a wife, to her fulfilment of her charge as a mother. Grant the former, and the consequences are no less hurtful to her. Her husband sees in her affection only a hollow mockery, a hideous skeleton fills the place of a living love in his heart; his children become hateful to him, because he doubts their mother, and instead of seeking his home for comfort and affection, he flees from it as from something too horrible to contemplate. With these obstacles to human happiness before us, can we wonder that Providence, ever so watchful in our behalf, should have deigned to interfere in favor of an institution of its own creation, and which tends so much to promote its design. Now, if the demon jealousy invades a household, with all its train of attendant fiends, peace for ever departs, and there is no chance that any future contingency can restore the calm once broken. In the days of our ancestors, in the land of promise, there was a means sanctified by religion, and dictated by one who, having fashioned the heart of man, knoweth all its imaginations. The offering of jealousy was at once the sure dove of hope, or the certain arrow of destruction, between husband and wife. Say she was innocent, before the evident manifestation of her purity, as ratified by God, even the most inveterate and deeply rooted suspicion vanished. Restored again as she deserved, to her husband's arms and love, she found herself the object of increased attentions and care, that all past sorrows might be obliterated; her soul revived under the invigorating beams of affections, and expanded into all that is beautiful in the wife, all that is tender in the mother; roses again bloomed where once had grown weeds, and harmony gave to life a strain of melody to replace the jarring notes of domestic discord. Say she were guilty; say she were that sinful thing which had crept like a parasite into the bosom of a husband, to tear therefrom all its existence, and to leave the trunk which had supported it sapless and dead; there was no retreating from the punishment that awaited her, there was no concealment of the vengeance of outraged honor. To her God she appealed as the bitter waters passed her lips, and he answered as she deserved. To crime against her husband, she added perjury before heaven, and even as a physical disobedience of our first parents introduced moral corruption into themselves and their descendants, so in her case a moral deflection produced physical disorganization. She became a monument of her own disgrace, and thus, convicted before God and man, she could no longer pollute the home which she had already outraged. And by this means was man defended from the effects of his unfounded suspicion; by this means was woman either preserved to her legitimate and honorable functions, or she was degraded according to her demerits, beyond the opportunity of doing further evil to her husband, or further wrong to her children.

To man belongs only the present, and so fleeting are the moments that pass, even as he endeavors to arrest them, they elude his grasp, till he can scarcely call one his own. Even when he begins to act he knows not if he shall be able to accomplish. He therefore who opens his mouth to say that he will, opens his mouth to folly; he that vows, and thereby attests his folly by God, commits a positive crime. The law of the Eternal, does not coerce man, it seeks to prevent rather than to punish, to restrain, not to force. But, Providence demands respect, and wisely insists that any pledge taken in his name shall be held sacred and inviolable. Hence the regulations affecting the Nazarite. A man who, having arrived at maturity, must have been fully cognizant of his own inherent infirmities, must have felt the constant struggle between the principles and the passions, and must have known the strength requisite to ensure stability of purpose, voluntarily impose on himself obligations which it might even be an impossibility for him to perform. His folly fully deserved that he should suffer, his sin that he should be a warning to others. It was necessary that he should, as much as possible, be sustained in the contest into which he had thrown his nature; it was more necessary that others should be cautioned against involving themselves in struggles which might prove fatal to their happiness.

Hence he was called on to refrain from all intoxicating and stimulating drinks, from all delicate and luxurious viands, so that his appetites not being pampered, his blood might permeate his veins under due control, and not run like liquid fire through his frame, inviting him to passion and excess. He had set himself apart to God, and therefore God set him apart from the world and its temptations, because it was better that he should altogether be deprived of the sensual pleasures, natural to his humanity, than that he should enjoy them at the expense of his honor and truth. Man is framed for social intercourse, but he should rather violate all his propensities as a solitary hermit, than abandon himself to them as a member of society. Besides, the Israelite who took the vow of a Nazarite, probably knew too well the failings which he desired thereby to correct, and it was wiser to exterminate these failings, to prevent them from again leading him astray, than to permit them to exist, even though in a latent but still dangerous state. But it was nevertheless not consistant with right that man, by vowing himself to a certain line of conduct, should arrogate a right over the future. Hence, in the case of the voluntary servant, who preferred his dependant condition to the free lot which is man's birthright, some external distinction was needful to deter others from imitating a bad example. The Nazarite, therefore, was to wear his hair differently from the rest of his brother men, and was thus to hold himself up as a constant warning, first to deter men from assuming votive obligations inconsistant with their condition, and not demanded by religion; and, secondly, to caution them against that insane indulgence in passion which has hurried him unto excesses, to curb which, it was necessary to lean as much beyond the straight line of right as he had before fallen short of it. "The Eternal bless thee and preserve thee; the Eternal cause His countenance to shine upon thee, and be gracious unto thee; the Eternal lift his countenance to thee and grant thee peace."

These were the terms in which the priests were commanded to bless the Israelites. Nor are they improperly placed in close connection with the laws of the Nazarite. Blessings, like vows, belong to the future; they, also, in so far as man is concerned, are empty words, whose accomplishment does not depend upon him who utters them.

God having pointed out, by implication, the unnatural condition to which man might reduce himself, and having placed before mortals a fellow-creature as a warning, immediately points out that other condition of human nature by which man may subserve the claims of nature, and, still, not oppose the demands of heaven. But he especially desires that there be no mistake. In the outset, he prevents us from supposing that his power over the future is to be delegated to frail man. Blessings and curses are of God only; man can only exhort or admonish, and, when he promises, promise in the name of Him who faileth not. Wherefore, having announced the words in which the priests are to address their flock, he distinctly says: "And *they* shall put my name upon the children of Israel; I will bless them." In other words, *they* may recommend to my people the line of conduct necessary to their welfare, but happiness or misery must depend on me alone. And what is the intent of these words? The evil consequences of indulgence having been pointed out, the contrast is at once presented. Man alone is weak and erring; even where his will is strongest, his volition is most weak. In spite of himself and of his independance, he requires that hidden and unapparent support which is of God. This it is which enables him to support the soul against the body, to maintain that in his aspirations, to fortify this in its resistance against attacks. The words of the blessing—only so called because it is a lesson, by the learning of which man's conduct shall prove a source of blessing to him—are, therefore, admonitory, and mean as follows: The eternal bless thee with His unseen and often unappreciated aid; may He preserve thee from those erring tendencies to which men are so prone, and, which once indulged, prove so destructive; may He cause that divine light, which is the reflection of heavenly purity, to shine on thee, and so to illumine thee that thou see the true path in which man should go, and mayest thou proceed in accordance with the road thus placed before thee, so that he can be gracious unto thee; may He turn His countenance to thee, watching over thee and guarding thee from all ill; and may He give thee that peace of conscience which arises from a sense of rectitude, and which is the perfection of all happiness.

Thus in three different ways the portion before us displays providential care for human welfare. But these ways, though so opposite in their direction, are all connected with each other, by leading to the future, after which it is our nature so constantly to aspire. The offering of jealousy is designed to promote the future happiness of the domestic circle, and to secure the affection and harmony necessary to the proper training of another generation. The law of the Nazarite renders him a tablet whereon the past engraves indelible characters for the benefit of the future. The blessing of the priest points out the direct road by which man may gain salvation. The first governs the future by giving man a test whereby to detect his own weakness; the second gives him a warning to caution him against himself; the third shows him the source of his real strength to be dependance on God. And so, again, bow we to the ever-vigilant wisdom which seizes on every phase of life, and renders it available to our virtue and well-being. Again bend we in adoration before the all-watchful mercy which makes our failings subservient to our happiness, by showing us thereby how to avoid sin. And ever as we feel ourselves the objects of this wisdom and this mercy, let us pour out our hearts in gratitude to the Divine Parent of mankind, who has created us for his glory and our own regeneration.

CHAPTER XV.

A FUNERAL SERMON.

MY DEAR FRIENDS, MEN AND WOMEN,—We stand here on the brink of a grave. Death makes all equal, rich and poor, high and low, old and young. The saying is, "Now such a one is also gone,"—what is gone is gone. Now the meaning of this expression does not appear to us quite clear; it is even ambiguous. For it seems to imply that there is no difference between the departure of the pious and virtuous, and that of the ungodly and wicked. The pious, whose life was a continuous exertion of benevolence and godliness, is, at the conclusion of his earthly career, to occupy the same position with the wicked and ungodly, whose life formed one chain of iniquities and abominations. Impossible! Such a view might lead to questioning the ways of Providence. The question might be put: For what purpose does the Almighty concede existence to beings whose life is devoted to mischief, and cannot but raise the incessant anger of the Creator? To this query, however, our sages reply, in the treatise of Aboth, Providence watches over everything, yet to man the choice is left to act according to his free will, as it is written, (Deut. 30, 19) For behold (says God), I have placed before thee life and death, blessing and curse, and thou mayest choose life. Now, therefore, for the very reason because God placed man on earth for his happiness and salvation, he has also endowed him with free-will in his actions; for, had man been created with equal dispositions and aptitudes so that their sphere of activity, either for good or evil, would have been predetermined by their Maker, what merit would there have been in being good and pious, since their proceedings would have been marked out beforehand, and what reward could have been claimed by the virtuous? Hence the struggle of man with evil desires which he has to conquer, if he wishes to be considered as a hero; as our sages observe—"Who is strong?" He that conquers his passions; and even as a monument is erected in honour of a hero who has well deserved of his country, in order to imortalize and transmit his memory to posterity; even so the pious establishes for himself a perpetual monument unto immortality, through his godly actions and benevolent foundations. It is true some people will say: What is the good of rendering oneself immortal? There was many and many a prominent individual in his age who is not even remembered now. And was there not also a tyrant of old, who endeavored to ensure to himself immortality, by inflicting a most irreparable loss on mankind, through burning a most valuable library containing works of Romans and Greeks, which could not be replaced? But let us dispel delusion, my friends; let us examine the object and worth of immortality. Knowing, as we do, that beyond the grave every passion is hushed for ever, what good does it do the wicked that they are remembered after their death? They cannot hear it. It can only serve to awaken once more against them the Divine judgment, to bring over them additional tortures. Their immortality therefore, can only tend towards increasing their sufferings, as it is written: "But the name of the wicked shall rot." It is different with the pious. The remembrance of their names will always recall some benevolent features or other excellencies in their virtuous lives wherein, naturally, every well disposed person will feel his sentiments reflected and whereby he will feel himself stimulated to the like. They thus, even after their death, continue to do good. This is the distinction in the death of the pious. Here it cannot be said: God is gone; but he lives and acts continually. In this sense, my friends, I interpret the words of King Solomon. (Proverbs x., 7). The remembrance of the righteous is for blessing to posterity.

If we now cast a glance at the life and activity of the deceased, we shall see at once the rank occupied by her. Yes, my friends, she practised what was good, not like so many rich, who, revelling in abundance and enjoyments, occasionally drop to the poor a crust or so, deeming thus to have discharged their duty, knowing, as they do, that such is expected from them, and that they ought to give something; no, with her it was quite different. She did good because her kind heartedness impelled her thereto. Her hand was open at all times for those who needed succour, irrespective of race or creed. No doubt she would have done more if the dependant condition consequent upon her sex had not confined her within certain limits. Still more, my dear listeners, she differed, also, in this from other rich persons, that she never laid herself open to the charge of harshness, or other offences, employing charity as a means for washing out stains that might have attached to her, or as an inadequate fine, imposed as a compensation for the breach of the contract entered into with Providence, since the sacrifices made bear no proportion to the wealth accumulated. No; with her it was not thus, for, apart from her charity, she was exceedingly pious and God-fearing. She never missed prayer-time, whether in her own house or at synagogue. As late as the penitential days just passed, she was observed to have been the worshipper early in the morning in the ladies' gallery. She, the septuagenarian, could make it convenient to attend the early morning service, when many younger ones found it more comfortable to stay at home. Pervaded by an equal spirit was her conduct in the domestic circle. How often have I heard her say, "Children, be fair in all your dealings; better to fare on a dry crust, earned honestly, than to enjoy the fat of the land, obtained by injustice. A feature in her character deserving particular notice, was, that, unlike those who, in their dying hour, conscious that they cannot carry their wealth with them, dispense in charity what they cannot enjoy any longer, she, in conjunction with her husband, whilst yet in the prime of life and vigour, had funded as a "Karen Kajemeth" a capital of five hundred dollars, the interest of which was to be laid out for the benefit of the poor in the winter season. This was hitherto kept a secret. But as, now, the benevolent donor is gone, the veil may be lifted. These are monuments which will rescue her name from oblivion, and which will make us feel her loss most painfully. O! how many tears will flow in silence to her blessed memory. But none can feel that loss more deeply than those who, in life, stood nearest to her, who had for everyone a cheering word in store, and who was beloved by every one, because, forsooth, she had love for every one. The happiness she enjoyed in her family circle was corresponding. Here she could give full vent to those gentle feelings of which her whole being consisted. Here she could resolve herself without restraint into those profound sympathies with everything that was good and lovely and holy. The contemplation of all this which we possessed, and now lost, only awakens the most poignant grief in our bosoms. Alas, we have sustained a loss not easily reparable. Our only consolation is the reflection that her sweet slumber now will be followed one day by an awakening, by a blissful resurrection in the regions of light, as Hannah, in her fervent prayer, so truly expressed :—"The Eternal sendeth death and restoreth to life, bringeth down into the grave and raiseth up."

We now bring our remarks to a close, in the words of King Solomon :—" Many daughters have done virtuously, but thou excellest them all. Favour is deceitful, and beauty is vain, but a woman that feareth the Lord, she shall be blessed. Give her of the fruit of her hands, and let her own works praise her in the gates."

PART THIRD.

THE LITERATURE OF THE JEWS.

CHAPTER I.

INTRODUCTORY.

Extent of Jewish Literature—Ignorance on this subject—Standard Works in German and French, but not in English—Misrepresentations resulting from this—Contributions of Jewish Scholars, of twelfth to the sixteenth century, to Biblical Literature—The Rabinical Language—its formation and richness—Mistaken idea that the Jews are ignorant, or that their learning is a mere collection of fables—Like estimating English Literature from the story of Jack the Giant Killer—Rabinical translations of Aristotle, Plato, Euclid, &c.—Original treatises on Grammar, Logic, Metaphysics, and the various branches of Mathematics—The Jews for four-and-a-half centuries the most learned men in Europe—Illustrious examples.

JEWISH LITERATURE.

The Jews have a vast literature besides the Bible and the Talmud. They have had excellent writers in all ages and zones, on all the different topics of human knowledge and genius; but there is not an English book in existence, in which information could be obtained on this point. The world knows, that Halewi, Maimonides, Spinoza, and Mendelssohn were Hebrew philosophers; that Ibn Ezra, Nachmonides, Rallag, and Abarbanel, in Spain; Rashi, Rashbam, Redak, in France; Mendelssohn, Wessely, Dubna, Levy, Eichel, &c., in Germany, were grammarians, lexicographers, exegetics and philologians; but very few know what those men wrote, and still fewer know the vast number of poets, mathematicians, physicians, philosophers, jurists and theologians of the Jewish persuasion, who wrote standard and classical works on their respective branches of science.

They have a history of thirty-five centuries, a most remarkable one, that presents all phases of universal history, in which God's Providence is revealed as clear as sunshine at noonday; a history which is the most ancient monument, inscribed with the hieroglyphic characters of all ages, and variegated with the rainbow colours of all climes and zones, such as no other nation has—a history which records more heroism than that of Rome, more literature and philosophy than that of Greece; more virtue, piety and faithfulness than that of any other nation, ancient or modern; but there is not one standard work in English literature, from which the inquisitive could inform himself on this topic. Germany has its Jost, Herzfeld and Graetz. France has its Basnage and Salvador; but the English literature has not one complete and classical work on this subject. Therefore, ignorance prevails on this subject, and any scribbler can write Jewish history. Therefore, whenever journalists speak of our forefathers, they will invariably misrepresent them. Therefore, none comprehends the Jewish character in its historic totality. Show us the English book that will inform a man of what Israel's philosophers wrote, what they taught, and how they demonstrated it? No such book is in existence; therefore prejudice and ignorance may howl of our money-making disposition; imposters may weep and cry (and cut fantastic tricks before high heaven, to extort a few dimes from credulous men-women), about the wretched and neglected state of the Jewish mind.

CHAPTER II.

LITERARY MEN AMONG THE HEBREWS.

There are found in every department of Literature, Works of Travel and Geography, commencing in the seventh and eighth centuries, when travellers and works of travel were rare—Authors of works on History and Biography—Poetry.

LITERARY MEN AMONG THE HEBREWS.

It is generally supposed that the mental activity of the Jews during the middle ages, was expended solely on theological speculations. This is a great error. There was scarcely a walk of literature, or branch of knowledge cultivated at the time, but it was also successfully treated by the Rabbis. Let us look to a province, supposed to have been altogether deserted by Jews. Few were the travellers during the middle ages, and still fewer the travels published; still, we can enumerate the following works :—

The most prominent authors of travel are: Isaac, a member of the Embassy of Charlemagne to the Khalif Harun er-Raschid (802,) perhaps the first who effected a communication between France and the Babylonian Gaonim; Jacob ———, whose accounts of the east, and the Sultan of Singair, (?) are inserted by the Karaite Jehuda Hedesi, in a work containing some historical and cosmographical information; the celebrated Benjamin of Tudela, of whom different estimates have been formed, and whose travels have been recently, for the first time, critically edited; Petachja of Regensburg (1170–80); Samuel Ben Samson, of France, (1210), apparently the precursor of more than 300 French and English Rabbis who travelled to Palestine, (1211). The following works also belong here: The correspondence of Chisdai, Ben Isaac, with the king of the Chozars, (659); the cosmography of Gerson, Ben, Solomon, Catalno, of Alres, (13th century); the important work of Esthori, (not Isaac), Parchi, (1322), recently re-printed, but miserably incorrect: the Hebrew translation of "*Image du Monde*," (1245); and a part of the pretended letters of Petre (or Petro), Joan to Pope Eugene or Frederick IV., (1442, 1460). At the end of the fifteenth century, Portuguese Jews occupy no unimportant place of geography. That there were never a lack among the Jews of poets, philosophers and mathematicians, even in the darkest period of the middle ages, is generally known; we will therefore not mention them. But who would have thought they also had numerous historians, geographers, and antiquarians? Yet the enumeration of their names, works, and editions, would occupy ten pages. We can only mention a few :

Chronicles, (comprising also the general events of the world), comprehensive historical works, and essays on the biography of learned men, were composed at the end of the preceding period, by Joseph Ben Zadik, at Arvalo, (1467) ; Saadja, Ben, Meimum, Ibn, Danan, in Spain, (1485) ; and Abraham Zacatben Samuel, (1505), whose work was published with arbitrary omissions and additions, by Samuel Shullam, at Constantinople, (1566), and again with notes by Moses Isserls, (ob. 1573). The Spaniard, Jehudah Ibn Verga, wrote a history of the persecutions of the Jews, which was completed by his relative Solomon, and his son Joseph, (1554), and was subsequently translated into Jewish-German, (1591), and in Spanish, (1640), by Meir DeLion. Of Elia Kapsoli's various historical compilations, and interesting narratives, continued to his own times, (1523), there exists a MS. copy in Italy, and an imperfect one has lately been purchased by the British Museum. Joseph Coben wrote a history of France and Turkey, (1554), containing an account of the rebellion of Fiesco, at Genoa, where the author lived, inserted with a German translation, in the Anthology of Zedner, who points out the strange blunders of Bialloblotzky, the English translator of the whole work for the Oriental Translation Fund.

He also gave an account of the persecution of the Jews, (1575), which was continued by an anonymous writer down to the year 1605, and has lately been published with the valuable notes of professor S. D. Luzzato. As. De Rossi investigated ancient history and cronology. On the Jewish learning of the East and South, in the 16th and 17th centuries, the chronological work of David Conforte (1677-1683), is a valuable authority. A profound critical work on the learned men of the Talmud, made use of and plagiarised by many recent authors, was published by Jechiel Heilprin, Rabbi at Minsk (ob. after the year 1728), who also took up and completed, but with less ability and knowledge, the Bibliographical List of Sabbatai Bass (Bassist, subcantor of Prague, 1680.) The Jewish poets in the Spanish language, were celebrated by Dr. L. De Barrios, (1683). A biographical and Bibliographical Lexicon, collected in many and distant journeys (1777-1796), was written by Ch. D. J. Asulai, of Jerusalem, at Leghorn.

LEARNING AND SCIENCE OF THE JEWS.

Among the various influences that have produced the present state of Biblical knowledge throughout Christendom, we are not to overlook the element that has been contributed by the Jewish Rabbis, from the twelfth century, downward to the period of the Reformation. Forming a language of their own, simple but yet comprehensive, severely philosophical and exact, built upon the basis of the Scriptural Hebrew; yet borrowing its nomenclature from the languages of every country of their captivity and exile—from the ruins of Babylon to the wharfs of Amsterdam—the Rabbis, like their ancient fathers, have made themselves possessors of the treasures of the Gentiles, taking and fabricating into a dialect, conformable to the genius of their own venerable tongue, terms of life, and learning, and science and art, from the Arabic, and Chaldee, and Syriac, and the Greek and the Latin, and the Italian, and the German, and the Dutch, and the Spanish, and the Portuguese. They have embodied in those mystic symbols, like so many emblems of victory over Gentile nations, the results of their labors in the criticism and interpretation of those sacred records, which, in many respects, they must be allowed best to understand, as being originally written in their native tongue, of which they were made the earliest depositaries, and in relation to which we may still say they are the librarians of the world.

There is a strong and wide-spread prejudice against the literature and intelligence of the Jews, and even among Christian men, it has been too generally supposed, that leaving out of consideration the inspired productions of the Hebrew Scriptures, wisdom has entirely perished from the sons of Abraham. The conclusion, like other prejudices, has its origin in ignorance. Because they have heard of the fables of the Talmud, how that the ostler of Rabbi Judah, the holy, was more rich than the King of the Persians; or how every member of the great Sanhedrin was skilled in seventy languages; or how Rabbi John Ben Narbai dispatched three hundred calves and three hundred flagons of wine at dinner; or how three hundred asses were scarcely able to carry the keys of the treasure houses of Corahi; or how David, by the flight of a single arrow, killed eight hundred men at once; or how two thousand soldiers in the army of Coziba, were endued with such adroitness that while they rode past, by a simple twitch of their right hand, they could each pluck up a cedar of Lebanon;—such persons, tickled with curious marvels like these, and being at once strangers to the genius of the East, abounding in fiction and allegory, have hastily concluded that all the learning and acquirements of the modern Hebrews, are nothing but a collection of falsehood and infatuation. A judgment as fallacious and unfounded, in regard to Hebrew literature, as if from the "Adventures of Jack the Giant Killer," or the "Exploits of King Arthur and the Knights of the Round Table," a stranger to the comprehensive literature of our country should conclude that the literature of England was utterly unacquainted with rich and intellectual philosophy. The fact is there is no department of philosophy in which the modern Jews have not excelled. They have enriched their language by a translation into their peculiar dialect of the finest works of Greece, Persia and Arabia. Aristotle, Plato, Euclid, Hippocrates, and Galen; Avienna, Averroes, and Sacrobosco, are found clothed with the dignity of a Hebrew dress. Original treatises in grammar, and logic, and metaphysics, and criticism—in arithmetic and algebra, and geometry and astronomy—and the most subtle and learned questions in hermeneutics and theology, start up in the old language of the Rabbi, with an accuracy and a skill, with a precision that may well compare with the works of the acutest schoolmen, or the most accomplished mathematician in any country or in any age.

There can be no question, that from the time of the dispersion of the Hebrews from the College of the Geonim, in Cordova, in 1039, down to their expulsion from Spain in 1492, when, according to Mariana, eight hundred thousand were banished, the Jews were the most learned, scientific and enterprising men in Europe. They filled the chief offices in the court of Spain; adorned the academies of Cordova, and Seville, and Granada; were the chief assistants of Alonzo the Tenth, surnamed the Wise, in making his sideral observations, compiling his astronomical tables, and publishing his Book of Circles in that Chaldean science; they were the instructors of the Moors, and the forerunners of that brilliant course of discovery which, under Henry Duke of Visco and Vasco da Gama, revealed the headlands of Africa, doubled the Cape of Good Hope, and opened up a maritime road to the commerce and riches of India. It was the Jews who carried the astronomy of Chaldea, the dialectics of Greece, and the chemistry of Spain, into the Universities of France and England. They taught in the Universities of Paris and of Oxford, and students from different parts of the world came flocking to the plains of Andalusia.

The works that the Jews have published in Venice, in Thessalonica, in Constantinople, and throughout the towns and cities of Germany, are a sufficient refutation of those who imagine that this branch of literature abounds in few authors. Many thousands of volumes of Rabbinical literature, in every species of excellence, are to be found in the Jewish catalogues. And one may boldly affirm of the multitude of Rabbinical books existing at this day, in every department of art and science, that the Hebrews, even in this respect, may, with perfect facility, be compared with any Gentile nation.

CHAPTER III.

THE TALMUD.

Use made of the Talmud in modern literary investigations—A universal endeavour to gather useful thought from every source, and a disposition to appreciate what is good in every ancient work—In this spirit study the Talmud—Second hand knowledge of, and reference to the Talmud—Ignorance and misrepresentation of the work—Lack of a good "Introduction" to the work—The censor at Basle—A critical edition never completed—The Editio Princeps—Interdictions, burnings, &c., of the book—Anecdote of Clement V.—The confiscation instigated by Pfeffer Korn—Reuchlin comes in to the rescue—The contest which ensued—Reuchlin's friends—It results in the printing of the first complete edition of the work at Venice, A.D. 1520. WHAT IS THE TALMUD?— Its wide extent—The topics proposed to be treated—A body of law—It can be best judged by comparison with other bodies of law, especially with the Justinian code—The Talmud originates with the return from the Babylonish captivity— Change which took place during the captivity—Love of the Scriptures which sprung up—Its exposition "Midrash"—Four methods—P. R. D. S.—The literal, the suggestive, the homiletic, the mystical—An allegory—The Talmud not a systematic code—Rather the result of intermingled currents of thought— One logical, the other imaginative—Logic more prominent in study of the Law —Imagination in that of the other portions of the Bible—"Halacha" and "Haggada"—Mishna and Gemara—The development of the Oral Law—Its deduction from the written—The Scribes—Three periods—The Sanhedrin and schools of the second period—The teachers and their method—The rise of Christianity—The Pharisees—The Mishna—Hillel—Akiba—Jehuda—The contents of the Mishna—Character of its laws—Their administration—Capital punishment—The Gemaras of Jerusalem and Babylon—Size of the Babylonian Talmud—Cause of the authority and popularity of the Talmud—The language of the Talmud—The Haggadah—Its use to the Eastern mind—Account of the creation—Angels—God's name—The soul—Resurrection and immortality—No eternal punishment—Prophets—Select "Sayings" from the Talmud—Synoptical history of the Talmud, Mishna and Gemara—Account of the authors of the Bible.

What is the Talmud? What is the nature of that strange production of which the name, imperceptibly almost, is beginning to take its place among the household words of Europe? Turn where we may in the realms of modern learning, we seem to be haunted by it. We meet it in theology, in science, even in general literature, in their highways and in their byways. There is not a hand-book to all or any of the many departments of biblical lore, sacred geography, history, chronology, numismatics, and the rest, but its pages contain references to the Talmud. The advocates of all religious opinions appeal to its dicta. Nay, not only the scientific investigators of Judaism and Christianity, but those of Mohammedanism and Zoroastrianism, turn to it in their dissections of dogma, and legend and ceremony. If, again, we take up any recent volume of archæological or philological transactions, whether we light on a dissertation on a Phœnician altar, or a cuneiform tablet,

Babylonian weights, or Sassanian coins, we are certain to find this mysterious word. Nor is it merely the restorers of the lost idioms of Canaan and Assyria, of Himyar and Zoroastrian Persia, that appeal to the Talmud for assistance; but the modern schools of Greek and Latin philology are beginning to avail themselves of the classical and post-classical materials that lie scattered through it. Jurisprudence, in its turn, has been roused to the fact that, apart from the bearing of the Talmud on the study of the Pandects and the Institutes, there are also some of those very laws of the "Medes and Persians,"—hitherto but a vague sound—hidden away in its labyrinths. And so, too, with medicine, astronomy, mathematics, and the rest. The history of these sciences, during that period over which the composition of the Talmud ranges— and it ranges over about a thousand years—can no longer be written without some reference to the items preserved, as in a vast buried city, in this cyclopean work. Yet, apart from the facts that belong emphatically to these respective branches, it contains other facts, of larger moment still—facts bearing upon human culture in its widest sense. Day by day there are excavated from these mounds pictures of many countries and many periods, pictures of Hellas and Byzantium, Egypt and Rome, Persia and Palestine, of the temple and the forum, war and peace, joy and mourning, pictures teeming with life, glowing with colour.

These are, indeed, signs of the times. A mighty change has come over us. We children of this latter age are, above all things, utilitarian. We do not read the Koran, the Zend Avesta, the Vedas, with the sole view of refuting them. We look upon all literature, religious, legal, and otherwise, whensoever and wheresoever produced, as a part and parcel of humanity. We, in a manner, feel a kind of responsibility for it. We seek to understand the phase of culture which begot these items of our inheritance, the spirit that moves upon their face. And, while we bury that which is dead in them, we rejoice in that which lives in them. We enrich our stores of knowledge from theirs, we are stirred by their poetry, we are moved to high and holy thoughts when they touch the divine chord in our hearts.

In the same human spirit, we now speak of the Talmud. There is even danger at hand, that this chivalresque feeling—one of the most touching characteristics of our times—which is evermore prompting us to offer holocausts to the manes of those whom former generations are thought to have wronged, may lead to its being extolled somewhat beyond its merit. As these ever new testimonies to its value crowd upon us, we might be led into exaggerating its importance for the history of mankind. Yet an old adage of its own says, "Above all things study, Whether for the sake of learning or for any other reason, study. For, whatever the motives that impel you at first, you will very soon love study for its own sake." And, thus, even exaggerated expectations of the treasure-trove in the Talmud will have their value, if they lead to the study of the work itself.

For, let us say it at once, these tokens of its existence, that appear in many a new publication, are, for the most part, but will-o'-the-wisps. At first sight one would fancy that there never was a book more popular, or that formed more exclusively the mental centre of modern scholars, Orientalists, theologians or jurists. What is the real truth? Paradoxical as it may seem, there never was a book at once more universally neglected and more universally talked of. Well may we forgive Heine, when we read the glowing description of the Talmud contained in his "Romancero," for never having seen, the subject of his panegyrics. Like his countryman Schiller, who pining vainly for one glimpse of the Alps, produced the most glowing and faithful picture of them, so he, with the poet's unerring instinct, gathered truth from hearsay and description. But how many of these ubiquitous learned quotations really flow from the fountain-head? Too often and too palpably it is merely—to use Sampson's agricultural simile—those ancient and well worked heifers, the "Tela ignea, Satanae," the "Abgezogener Schlangenbalg," and all their venomous kindred, which are once more being dragged to the plough by some of the learned. We say learned, for as to the people at large, often as they hear the word now we firmly believe that numbers of them still hold, with that erudite Capucin friar, Henricus Seguensis, that the Talmud is not a book but a man. "Ut narrat Rabbinas Talmud"—"as says Rabbi Talmud"—cries he, and triumphantly clinches his argument!

And of those who know that it is not a Rabbi, how many are there to whom it conveys any but the vaguest of notions? Who wrote it? What is its bulk? Its date? Its contents? Its birth place! A contemporary lately called it a sphinx, towards which all men's eyes are directed at this hour, some with eager curiosity, some with vague anxiety. But why not force open its lips? How much longer are we to live by quotations alone,—quotations a thousand times used, a thousand times abused?

Where, however, are we to look even for primary instruction? Where learn the story of the book, its place in literature, its meaning and purport, and, above all, its relation to ourselves?

If we turn to the time-honoured *authorities*, we shall mostly find that, in their eagerness for some cause, they have torn a few pieces off that gigantic living body; and they have presented to us these ghastly anatomical preparations, twisted and mutilated out of all shape and semblance, saying, "Behold, this is the book!" Or they have done worse. They have not garbled their samples, but have given them exactly as they found them; and then stood aside, pointing at them with jeering countenance. For their samples were ludicrous and grotesque beyond expression. But these wise and pious investigators, unfortunately, mistook the gurgoyles, those grinning stone caricatures that mount their guard over our cathedrals, for the gleaming statues of the saints within; and, holding them up to mockery and derision, they cried, "These be thy gods, O Israel?"

Let us not be misunderstood. When we complain of the lack of guides to the Talmud, we do not wish to be ungrateful to those great and earnest scholars whose names are familiar to every student, and whose labours have been ever present to our mind. For though in the whole realm of learning there is scarcely a single branch of study to be compared, for its difficulty, to the Talmud, yet, if a man had time and patience, and knowledge, there is absolutely no reason why he should not, up and down ancient and modern libraries, gather most excellent hints from essays and treatises, monographs and sketches, in books and periodicals without number, by dint of which, aided by the study of the work itself, he might arrive at some conclusion as to its essence and tendencies, its origin and development. Yet, so far as we know, that work, every step of which, it must be confessed, is beset with fatal pit-falls, has not yet been done for the world at large. It is for a very good reason that we have placed nothing but the name of the Talmud at the head of our article. We have sought, far and near, for some one special book on the subject, which we might make the theme of our observations—a book which should not merely be a garbled translation of a certain twelfth-century "Introduction," interspersed with vituperations, and supplemented with blunders, but which, from the platform of modern culture, should pronounce impartially upon a production which, if for no other reason, claims respect through its age—a book that would lead us through the stupendous labyrinths of fact, and thought, and fancy, of which the Talmud consists; that would rejoice even in hieroglyphical fairy lore, in abstruse propositions and syllogisms; that could forgive wild outbursts of passion, and not judge harshly and hastily of things, the real meaning of which may have had to be hidden under the fools cap and bells.

We have not found such a book, nor anything approaching to it. But closely connected with that circumstance is this other, that we were fain to quote the first editions of this Talmud, though scores have been printed since. Even this first edition was printed in hot haste, and without due care; and every succeeding one, with one or two exceptions, presents a sadder spectacle. In the Basle edition, of 1578—the third in point of time, which has remained the standard edition almost ever since —that amazing creature, the censor, stepped in. In his anxiety to protect the "Faith" from all and every danger—for the Talmud was supposed to hide bitter things against Christianity under the most innocent-looking words and phrases—this official did very wonderful things. When he, for example, found some ancient Roman, in the book, swearing by the Capitol, or by Jupiter " of Rome," his mind instantly misgave him. Surely this Roman must be a Christian, the Capitol the Vatican, Jupiter the Pope. And forthwith he struck out Rome, and substituted any other place he could think of. A favorite spot seems to have been Persia, sometimes it was Aram, or Babel. But, whenever the word " Gentile " occurred, the censor was seized with the most frantic terrors. A "Gentile" could not possibly be aught but a Christian; whether he lived in India or in Athens, in Rome or in Canaan; whether he was a good Gentile—and there are many such in the Talmud—or a wicked one. Instantly he christened him; and christened him as fancy moved him, an " Egyptian," an "Aramathean," an " Amalekite," an " Arab," a " Negro"; sometimes a whole " people ." All this is extant in our very last editions.

Once or twice, attempts were made to clear the text from its foulest blemishes. There was even about three years ago, a beginning made of a " Critical " edition, such as not merely Greek and Roman, Sanscrit and Persian classics, but the veriest trash written in those languages, would have had ever so long ago. And there is—M. Renan's unfortunate remark to the contrary nothwithstanding*—no lack of Talmudical MSS., however fragmentary they be for the most part. There are innumerable variations, additions, and corrections to be gleaned from the Codices at the Bodleian and the Vatican, in the libraries of Odessa, Munich, and Florence, Hamburg and Heidelberg, Paris and Parma. But an evil eye seems to be upon this book. This corrected edition remains a torso, like the two first volumes of translations of the Talmud, commenced at different periods, the second volumes of which never saw

---

* "It is said there is not a single Manuscript of the Talmud left by which to correct the printed editions."—*Les Apotres*, p. 262.

the light. It therefore seemed advisable to refer to the Editio Princeps, as one that is at least free from the blemishes, censorial or typographical, of later ages.

Well does the Talmud supplement the Horatian "Habent sua fate libelli," by the words "even the sacred scrolls in the Tabernacle." We really do not wonder that the good Capucin of whom we spoke, mistook it for a man. Ever since it existed—almost before it existed in a palpable shape—it has been treated like a human being. From Justinian, who as early as 553 A.D. honoured it by a special interdictory Novella, down to Clement VIII. and later—a space of over a thousand years—both the secular and the spiritual powers, kings and emperors, popes and anti-popes, vied with each other in hurling anathemas and bulls, and edicts of wholesale confiscation and conflagration against this luckless book. Thus within a period of less than fifty years—and these forming the latter half of the sixteenth century—it was publicly burnt no less than six different times, and not by single copies, but wholesale by the waggon load. Julius III. issued his proclamation against what he grotesquely calls the "Gemaroth Thalmud" in 1553 and 1555, Paul IV. in 1559, Pius V. in 1566, Clement VIII. in 1592 and 1599. The fear of it was great indeed. Even Pius IV., in giving permission for a new edition, stipulated expressly that it should appear without the name Talmud. It almost seems to have been a kind of Shibboleth, by which every new potentate had to prove the rigour of his faith. And very vigorous it must have been, to judge by the language which even the highest dignitaries of the Church did not disdain to use at times. Thus Honorius IV. writes to the Archbishop of Canterbury, in 1286, anent that "damnable book" (liber damnabilis), admonishing him gravely, and desiring him vehemently to see that it be not read by anybody, since "all other evils flow out of it." Verily these documents are sad reading, only relieved occasionally by some wild blunder that lights up, as with one flash, the abyss of ignorance regarding this object of wrath.

We remember but one sensible exception in this Babel of manifestoes. Clement V., in 1807, before condemning the book, wished to know something of it, and there was no one to tell him. Whereupon he proposed, but in language so obscure that it left the door open for many interpretations, that three chairs be founded, for Hebrew, Chaldee, and Arabic, as the three tongues nearest to the idiom of the Talmud. The spots chosen by him were the Universities of Paris, Salamanca, Bologna, and Oxford. In time he hoped to be able to produce a translation of this mysterious book. Need we say that this consummation never came to pass? The more expeditious process of destruction was resorted to again and again, not merely in the single cities of Italy and France, but throughout the entire Holy Roman Empire.

At length a change took place in Germany. One Pfefferkorn, a miserable creature, began, in the time of the Emperor Maximilian, to agitate for a new decree for the extermination of the Talmud. The Emperor lay, with his hosts, before Paria, when the evil-tongued messenger arrived in the camp, furnished with goodly letters by Kunigunde, the Emperor's beautiful sister. Maximilian, wearied and unsuspecting, renewed that time-honoured decree for a confiscation, to be duly followed by a conflagration, readily enough. The confiscation was conscientiously carried out, for Pfefferkorn knew well enough where his former co-religionists kept their books. But a conflagration of a very different kind ensued. Step by step, hour by hour, the German Reformation was drawing nearer. Reuchlin, the most eminent Hellenist and Hebraist of his time, had been nominated to sit on the committee which was to lend its learned authority to the Emperor's decree. But he did not relish this task. "He did not like the look of Pfefferkorn," he says. Besides which, he was a learned and honest man, and, having been the restorer of classical Greek in Germany, he did not care to participate in the wholesale murder of a book "written by Christ's nearest relations." Perhaps he saw the cunningly-laid trap. He had long been a thorn in the flesh of many of his contemporaries. His Hebrew labours had been looked upon with bitter jealousy, if not fear. Nothing less was contemplated in those days—the theological Faculty of Mayence demanded it openly—that a total "Revision and correction" of the Hebrew Bible, "inasmuch as it differed from the Vulgate." Reuchlin, on his part, never lost an opportunity of proclaiming the high importance of the "Hebrew truth," as he emphatically called it. His enemies thought one of two things would follow. By officially pronouncing upon the Talmud, he was sure either to commit himself dangerously—and then a speedy end would be made of him—or to set at naught, to a certain extent, his own previous judgments in favour of these studies. He declined the proposal, saying, honestly enough, that he knew nothing of the book, and that he was not aware of the existence of many who knew anything of it. Least of all did its detractors know it. But, he continued, even if it should contain attacks on Christianity, would it not be preferable to reply to them? "Burning is but a ruffianly argument." Whereupon a wild outcry was raised against him, as a Jew, a Judaizer, a bribed renegade, and so on. Reuchlin, nothing daunted, set to work on the book, in his patient, hard-working manner. Next he wrote a brilliant defence of it. When the Emperor asked his opinion, he repeated Clement's proposal to found Talmudical chairs. At each German university there should be two professors, specially appointed, for the sole purpose of enabling students to become acquainted with this book. "As to burning it," he continues, in the famous memorial addressed to the Emperor, "if some fool came and said, 'Most mighty Emperor! your majesty should really suppress and burn the books of alchemy, because they contain blasphemous, wicked, and absurd things against our faith', what should his Imperial Majesty reply to such a buffalo or ass, but this? Thou art a ninny, rather to be laughed at than followed. Now, because his feeble head cannot enter into the depths of a science, and cannot conceive it, and does understand things otherwise than they really are, would you deem it fit to burn such books?"

Fiercer and fiercer waxed the howl, and Reuchlin, the peaceful student, from a witness became a delinquent. What he suffered for and through the Talmud, cannot be told here. Far and wide, all over Europe, the contest raged. A whole literature of pamphlets, flying sheets, caricatures, sprang up. University after university was appealed to against him. No less than forty-seven sittings were held by the theological Faculty of Paris, which ended by their formal condemnation of Reuchlin. But he was not left to fight alone. Around him rallied, one by one, Duke Ulrich, of Wurtemburg, the Elector Fredrick of Saxony, Ulrich von Hutten, Frank von Sickingen—he who finally made the Colognians pay their costs in the Reuchlin trial—Erasmus of Rotterdam, and that whole brilliant phalanx of the "Knights of the Holy Ghost," the "Hosts of Pallas Athene," the "*Talmutphili*," as the documents of the period variously style them: they whom we call the Humanists.

And their Palladium and their war-cry was—oh! wondrous ways of History—the Talmud. To stand up for Reuchlin, meant to them, to stand up for "the Law;" to fight for the Talmud was to *fight for the Church*. The rest of the story is written in the "Epistolae Obscurum Virorum," and in the early pages of the German Reformation. The Talmud was not burnt this time. On the contrary, its first complete edition was printed. And in the same year of grace, 1520 A.D., when this first edition went through the press at Venice, Martin Luther burnt the Pope's bull at Wittenberg.

WHAT IS THE TALMUD?

Again the question rises before us in its whole formidable shape,—a question which no one has yet answered satisfactorily. Would it not indeed be mere affectation to presuppose more than the vaguest acquaintance with its language, or even its name, in many of our readers? And while we would fain enlarge upon such points, as a comparison between the law laid down in it, with ours, or with the contemporary Greek, Roman and Persian Laws, or those of Islam, or even with its own fundamental code, the Mosaic; while we would trace a number of its ethical, ceremonial and doctrinal points in Zoroastrianism, in Christianity, in Mohammedanism; a vast deal of its metaphysics and philosophy in Plato, Aristotle, the Pythagoreans, the Neo-Platonists, and the Gnostics —not to mention Spinoza and the Schellings of our own day ; much of its medicine in Hippocrates and Galen, and the Paracelsuces of but a few centuries ago—we shall scarcely be able to do more than to lay a few *disjecta membra* of these things before our readers. We cannot even sketch, in all its bearings, that singular mental movement which caused the best spirits of an entire nation to concentrate, in spite of opposition, all their energies for a thousand years upon the writings, and for another thousand years upon the commenting, of this one book. Omitting all detail, we shall merely tell of its development, of the schools in which it grew, of the tribunals which judged by it, of some of the men that set their seal on it. We shall also introduce a summary of its law, speak of its metaphysics, of its moral philosophy, and quote many of its proverbs and saws—the truest of all gauges of a time.

We shall, perhaps, be obliged occasionally to appeal to some of the extraneous topics just mentioned. The Talmud, like every other phenomenon, in order to become comprehensible, should be considered only in connection with things of a similar kind ; a fact almost entirely overlooked to this day. Being emphatically a corpus juris, an encyclopædia of law, civil and penal, ecclesiastical and international, human and divine, it may best be judged by analogy and comparison with other legal codes, more especially with the Justinian code and its commentaries. What the uninitiated have taken for exceptional Rabbinical subtleties, or in matters relating to the sexes, for gross offences against modern taste, will then cause the Talmud to stand out rather favorably than otherwise. The Pandects and the Institutes, the Novellæ and the Responsa Prudentium, should thus be constantly consulted and compared. No less should our English law, as laid down in Blackstone, wherein we may see how the most varied views of right and wrong have been finally blended and harmonised with the spirit of our times. But the Talmud is more than a Book of Laws. It is a microcosm, embracing, even as does the Bible, heaven and earth. It is as if all the prose and poetry, the science, the faith and speculation of the Old World, were, though only in faint reflections, bound up in it *in nuce*. Comprising the time from the rise to the fall of antiquity, and a good deal of its after-glow, the history and culture of antiquity have to be considered in their various stages. But, above all, it is necessary to transport ourselves, following Goethe's advice, to its birthplace—Palestine and Babylon—the gorgeous East itself, where all things glow in brighter colours, and grow into more fantastic shapes.

The origin of the Talmud is coeval with the return from the Babylonish captivity. One of the most mysterious and momentous periods in the history of humanity, is that brief space of the exile. What were the influences brought to bear upon the captives during that time, we know not. But this we know, that from a reckless, lawless, godless populace, they returned transformed into a band of Puritans. The religion of Zerdursht, though it has left its traces in Judaism, fails to account for that change. Nor does the exile itself account for it. Many and intense as are the reminiscences of its bitterness, and of yearning for home, that have survived in prayer and in song, yet we know that, when the hour of liberty struck, the forced colonists were loth to return to the land of their fathers. Yet the change is there, palpable, unmistakable—a change which we may regard as almost miraculous. Scarcely aware before of the existence of their glorious national literature, the people now began to press around these brands, plucked from the fire—the scanty records of their faith and history—with a fierce and passionate love, a love stronger even than that of wife and child. These same documents, as they were gradually formed into a canon, became the immutable centre of their lives, their actions, their thoughts, their very dreams. From that time forth, with scarcely any intermission, the keenest as well as the most poetical minds of the nation, remained fixed upon them. "Turn it and turn it again," says the Talmud, with regard to the Bible, "for everything is in it." *Search* the Scriptures, is the distinct utterance of the New Testament.

The natural consequence ensued. Gradually, imperceptibly almost, from a mere expounding and investigation, for purposes of edification or instruction on some special point, this activity begot a science—a science that assumed the very widest dimensions. Its technical name is already contained in the book of Chronicles. It is "Midrash" (from *darash*, to study, expound)—a term which the authorised version renders by "story."*

There is scarcely a more fruitful source of misconceptions upon this subject, than the liquid nature, so to speak, of its technical terms. They mean any and everything, at once most general and most special. Nearly all of them signify, in the first instance, simply study. Next, they are used for some one very special branch of this study. Then they indicate, at times, a peculiar method, at others, the works which have grown out of these, either general or special mental labours. Thus Midrash, from the abstract expounding, came to be applied, first to the exposition itself, even as our terms "work," "investigation," "inquiry," imply both process and product; and finally, as a special branch of exposition—the legendary—was more popular than the rest, to this one branch only, and to the books that chiefly represented it.

For there had sprung up almost innumerable modes of "searching the Scriptures." In the quaintly ingenious manner of the times, four of the chief methods were found in the Persian word Paradise, spelt in vowelless Semetic fashion, P R D S. Each one of these mysterious letters was taken mnemonically, as the initial of some technical word that indicated one of those four methods. The one called P(*peshat*) aimed at the simple understanding of words and things, in accordance with the primary exegetical law of the Talmud, "that no verse of the Scripture ever practically travelled beyond its literal meaning—though it might be explained, homiletically and otherwise, in innumerable new ways." The second, R (*remes*), means Hint, *i. e.*, the discovery of the indications contained in certain seemingly superfluous letters and signs in Scripture. These were taken to refer to laws not distinctly mentioned, but either existing traditionally or newly promulgated.

This method, when more generally applied, begot a kind of *memoria technica*, a stenography akin to the "Notarikon" of the Romans. Points and notes were added to the margins of scriptural MSS., and the foundation of the Massorah, or diplomatic preservation of the text, was thus laid. The third D *(derush)*, was homiletic application of that which had been to that which was and would be, of prophetical and historical dicta to the condition of things. It was a peculiar kind of sermon, with all the aids of dialects and poetry, of parable, gnome, proverb, legend, and the rest, exactly as we find it in the New Testament. The fourth, S, stood for *sôd*, secret, mystery. This was the secret science, into which but few were initiated. It was theosophy,

---

* See 2 Chron., xiii., 22 ; also, xxiv., 27.

metaphysics, angelology, a host of wild and glowing visions of things beyond earth. Faint echoes of this science survive in Neo-Platonism, in Gnosticism, in the Kabbalah, in "Hermes Trismegistus." But few were initiated into these things of "the Creation" and of "the chariot," as it was also called, in allusion to Ezekiel's vision. Yet here again the power of the vague and mysterious was so strong, that the word Paradise gradually indicated this last branch, the secret science, only. Later, in Gnosticism, it came to mean the "spiritual Christ."

There is a weird story in the Talmud, which has given rise to the wildest explanations, but which will be intelligible by the foregoing lines. "Four men," it says, "entered *Paradise*. One beheld and died. One beheld and lost his senses. One destroyed the young plants. One only entered in peace and came out in peace." The names of all four are given. They are all exalted masters of the law. The last but one, he who destroyed the young plants, is Elisha ben Abuzah, the Faust of the Talmud, who, while sitting in the academy, at the feet of his teachers, to study the law, kept the "profane books" of "Homeros," to wit, hidden in his garment, and from whose mouth "Greek songs" never ceased to flow. How he, notwithstanding his early scepticism, rapidly rises to eminence in that same law, finally falls away and becomes a traitor and an outcast, and his very name a thing of unutterable horror; how one day (it was the great day of atonement) he passes the ruins of the Temple, and hears a voice within murmuring like a dove, "all men shall be forgiven this day save Elisha ben Abuzah, who knowing me, has betrayed me"—how, after his death, the flames will not cease to hover over his grave, until his one faithful disciple, the "Light of the Law," Meir, throws himself over it, swearing a holy oath that he will not partake of the joys in the world to come without his beloved master, and that he will not move from that spot until his master's soul shall have found grace and salvation before the Throne of Mercy—all this, and a number of other incidents, form one of the most stirring poetical pictures in the whole Talmud. The last of the four is Akiba, the most exalted, most romantic, and most heroic character, perhaps, in that vast gallery of the learned of his time; he who, in the last revolt under Trajan and Hadrian, expiated his patriotic rashness at the hands of the Roman executioners, and—the legend adds—whose soul fled just when, in his last agony, his mouth cried out the last word of the confession of God's unity: "Hear O Israel, the Lord our God is *One*."

The Talmud is the storehouse of the "Midrash" in its widest sense, and in all its branches. What we said of the fluctuation of terms applies emphatically also to this word Talmud. It means, in the first instance, nothing but "study," "learning," from *lamad*, to learn; next, indicating a special method of "learning," or rather arguing, it finally became the name of the great Corpus Juris of Judaism.

When we speak of the Talmud as a legal code, we trust we shall not be understood too literally. It resembles about as much what we generally understand by that name, as a primeval forest resembles a Dutch garden. Nothing, indeed, can equal the state of utter amazement into which the modern investigator finds himself plunged at the first sight of these luxuriant wildernesses. Schooled in the harmonizing, methodising systems of the West—systems that condense, and arrange, and classify, and give everything its fitting place and its fitting position in that place—he feels almost stupefied here. The language, the style, the method, the very sequence of things (a sequence that often appears as logical as our dreams), the amazingly varied nature of these things— everything seems tangled, confused, chaotic. It is only after a time that the student learns to distinguish between two mighty currents in the book—currents that at times flow parallel, at times seem to work upon each other, and to impede each others actions: the one emanating from the brain, the other from the heart—the one prose, the other poetry— the one carrying with it all those mental faculties that manifest themselves in arguing, investigating, comparing, developing, bringing a thousand points to bear upon one, and one upon a thousand; the other springing from the realms of fancy, of imagination, feeling, humour, and, above all, from that precious combination of still, almost sad, pensiveness, with quick catholic sympathies, which in German is called *Gemüth*. These two currents, the Midrash, in its various aspects, had caused to set in the direction of the Bible, and they soon found in it two vast fields for the display of all power and energy. The logical faculties turned to the legal portions in Exodus, Leviticus, Deuteronomy —developing, seeking, and solving a thousand real or apparent difficulties and contradictions, with what, as tradition, had been living in the hearts and mouths of the people from time immemorial. The other, the imaginative faculties, took possession of the prophetical, ethical, historical, and quaintly enough, sometimes even of the legal portions of the Bible, and transformed the whole into one vast series of themes almost musical in their wonderful and capricious variations. The first named, is called "Halacha" *(Rule, Norm)*, a term applied both to the process of evolving legal enactments, and the enactments themselves. The other, "Haggadah" *(Legend, Saga)*, not so much in our modern sense of the word, though a great part of its contents comes under that head, but because it was only a "saying," a thing without authority, a play of fancy, an allegory, a parable, a tale, that pointed a moral and illustrated a question, that smoothed the billows of fierce debate, roused the slumbering attention, and was generally—to use its own phrase—a comfort and a blessing.

The Talmud, which is composed of these two elements, the legal and the legendary, is divided into MISHNAH and GEMARA: two terms again of uncertain, shifting meaning. Originally indicating, like the technical words mentioned already, "study," they both became terms for special studies, and indicated special works. The Mishnah, from *shana* (*tana*), to learn, to repeat, has been of old translated, second law. But this derivation, correct as it seems literally, is incorrect in the first instance. It simply means "Learning," like Gemara, which, besides indicates "complement" to the Mishnah—itself a complement to the Mosaic code,—but in such a manner that, in developing and enlarging, it supersedes it. The Mishnah, on its own part again, forms a kind of text, to which the Gemara is not so much a scholium as a critical expansion. The Pentateuch remains in all cases the back ground and latent source of the Mishnah. But it is the business of the Gemara to examine into the legitimacy and correctness of the Mishnic development in single instances. The Pentateuch remained, under all circumstances, the immutable, divinely given constitution, the *written law*: in contradistinction to it, the Mishnah, together with the Gemara, was called the oral or Unwritten law, not unlike the Roman "Lex Non Scripta," the Sunnah, or the English Common Law.

There are few chapters in the whole history of jurisprudence, more obscure than the origin, development, and completion of this "Oral Law." There must have existed, from the very beginning of the Mosaic law, a number of corollary laws, which explained in detail most of the rules broadly laid down in it. Apart from these, it was but natural that the enactment of that primitive Council of the Desert, the Elders, and their successors in each period, together with the verdicts issued by the later "judges within the gates," to whom the Pentateuch distinctly refers, should have become precedents, and have been handed down as such. Apocryphal writings—notably the fourth book of Ezra—not to mention Philo and the Church Fathers, speak of fabulous numbers of books that had been given to Moses, together with the Pentateuch; thus indicating the common belief in the divine origin of the supplementary laws that had existed among the people from time immemorial. Jewish tradition traces the bulk of the oral injunctions, through a chain of distinctly-named authority, to "Sinai" itself. It mentions in detail, how Moses communicated those minutiæ of his legislation, in which he had been instructed during the mysterious forty days and nights, on the Mount, to the chosen guides of the people, in such a manner that they should for ever remain engraven on the tablets of their hearts.

A long space intervenes between the Mosaic period and that of the Mishnah. The ever-growing wants of the ever-disturbed commonwealth necessitated new laws and regulations at every turn. A difficulty, however, arose, unknown to other legislations. In despotic states, a decree is issued, promulgating the new law. In constitutional states, a bill is brought in. The supreme authority, if it finds it meet and right to make this new law, makes it. The case was different in the Jewish commonwealth of the post-exilian times. Amongst the things that were irredeemably lost with the first temple, were the "Urim and Thummim" of the high priest—the oracle. With Malachi, the last prophet died. Both for the promulgation of a new law, and the abrogation of an old one, a higher sanction was requisite than the mere majority of the legislative council. The new act must be proved, directly or indirectly, from the "Word of God"—proved to have been promulgated by the Supreme King—hidden and bound up, as it were, in its very letters, from the beginning. This was not easy in all cases; especially when a certain number of hermetical rules, not unlike those used in the Roman schools (inferences, conclusions from the minor to the major, and *vice versa*, analogies of ideas or objects, general and special statements, &c.), had come to be laid down.

Apart from the new laws requisite in sudden emergencies, there were many of those old traditional ones, for which the *point d'appui* had to be found, when, as established legal matters, they came before the critical eyes of the schools. And these schools themselves, in their ever restless activity, evolved new laws, according to their logical rules, even when they were not practically wanted, nor likely ever to come into practical use—simply as a matter of science. Hence, there is a double action perceptible in this legal development. Either the scriptural verse forms the terminus *a quo*, or the terminus *ad quem*. It is either the starting-point for a discussion, which ends in the production of some new enactment; or one never before investigated, is traced back to the divine source by an outward hint, however insignificant.

This process of evolving new precepts from old ones, by "signs"—a word curiously enough used also by Blackstone in his "Development" of the law—may, in some instances, have been applied with too much freedom. Yet, while the Talmudical Code practically differs from the Mosaic, as much as our Digest will some day differ from the laws of the time of Canute, and as the Justinian Code differs from the Twelve Tables, it cannot be denied that these fundamental laws have been consulted, carefully and impartially, as to their spirit, their letter being often but the vessel or outward symbol. The often uncompromising severity of the Pentateuch, especially in the province of the penal law, had certainly become much softened down under the milder influences of the culture of later days. Several of its injunctions, which had become impracticable, were circumscribed, or almost constitutionally abrogated, by the introduction of exceptional formalities. Some of its branches also had developed in a direction other than what at first sight seems to have been anticipated. But the power vested in the judge of those days, was in general most sparingly and conscientiously applied. This whole process of the development of the "law" was in the hands of the Scribes, who, according to the New Testament, "sit in the seat of Moses." We shall speak presently of the Pharisees, with whom the word is often coupled. Here, meantime, we must once more distinguish between the different meanings of the word "Scribe" at different periods. For there are three stages in the oral compilation of the Talmudical Code, each of which is named after a special class of doctors.

The task of the first class of these masters—the "Scribes," by way of eminence, whose time ranges from the return from Babylon down to the Greco-Syrian persecutions (220 B. C.)—was above all to preserve the sacred Text, as it had survived after many mishaps. They enumerated not merely the precepts, but the words, the letters, the signs of the Scripture, thereby guarding it from all future interpolations and corruptions. They had further to explain these precepts, in accordance with the collateral tradition of which they were the guardians. They had to instruct the people, to preach in the synagogues, to teach in the schools. They, further, on their own authority, erected certain "Fences," *i. e.* such new injunctions as they deemed necessary, merely for the better keeping of the old precepts. The whole work of these men ("Men of the great synagogue") is well summed up in their adage : "Have a care in legal decisions, send forth many disciples, and make a fence around the law." More pregnant still, is the motto of their last representative—the only one whose name, besides those of Ezra and Nehemiah, the supposed founders of this body, has survived—Simon the Just. "On three things stands the world, on the law, on worship, and on charity."

After the "Scribes" come the "Learners," or "Repeaters," also called Banaim, "Master-builders," from 220 B.C. to 220 A.D. In this period falls the Maccabean Revolution, the birth of Christ, the destruction of the Temple by Titus, the revolt of Bar-Cochba under Hadrian, the final destruction of Jerusalem, and the total expatriation of the Jews. During this time, Palestrina was ruled successively by Persians, Egyptians, Syrians, and Romans. But the legal labours that belong to this period were never successfully interrupted, however dread the event. Schools continued their studies. The masters were martyred time after time; the academies were razed to the ground; the practical and the theoretical occupation with the law was proscribed on pain of death—yet in no instance is the chain of the living tradition broken. With their last breath, the dying masters appointed and ordained their successors; for one academy that was reduced to ashes in Palestine, three sprang up in Babylonia, and the law flowed on, and was perpetuated in the face of a thousand deaths.

The chief bearers and representatives of these divine legal studies, were the President (called Nasi Prince,) and the Vice-president (Ab-Beth Din—father of the house of judgment,) of the highest legal assembly, the Synedrin, Aramaised into *Sanhedrin*. There were three Sanhedrins, one "great Sanhedrin," two "lesser" ones. Whenever the New Testament mentions the "Priests, the Elders, and the Scribes" together, it means the Great Sanhedrin. This constituted the highest ecclesiastical and civil tribunal. It consisted of seventy-one members, chosen from the foremost priests, the heads of tribes and families, and from the "Learned," *i.e.*, the "Scribes" or Lawyers. It was no easy task to be elected a member of this Supreme Council. The candidate had to be a superior man, both mentally and bodily. He was not to be either too young or too old. Above all, he was to be an adept both in the "Law" and in science.

When people read of "Law," "Masters," or "Doctors of the Law," they do not, it seems to us, always fully realize what the word "Law" means in Old, or rather New Testament language. It should be remembered that, as we have already indicated, it stands for all and every knowledge, since all and every knowledge was requisite for the understanding of it. The Mosaic code has injunctions about the sabbatical journey; the distance had to be measured and calculated, and mathematics were called into play. Seeds, plants, and animals had to be studied in connection with the many precepts regarding them, and natural history had to be appealed to. Then there were the purely hygienic paragraphs, which necessitated for their precision a 'knowledge of all the medical science of the time. The "seasons" and the feast-days were regulated by the phases of the moon, and astronomy—if only in its elements—had to be studied. And—as the commonwealth successively came in contact, however much against its will at first, with Greece and Rome—their history, geography and language, came to be added as a matter of instruction to those of Persia and Babylon. It was only a handful of well-meaning, but narrow-minded men, like the Essenes, who would not, for their own part, listen to the repeal of certain temporary "Decrees of Danger." When Hellenic scepticism, in its most seductive form, had, during the Syrian troubles, begun to seek its victims, even in the midst of the "Sacred Vineyard," and threatened to undermine all patriotism and all independance, a curse was pronounced upon Hellenism; much as German patriots, at the beginning of this century, loathed the very sound of the French language; or as not so very long ago, all things "foreign" were regarded with a certain suspicion in England. But, the danger over, the Greek language and culture were restored to their previous high position, in both the school and the house, as indeed the union of Hebrew and Greek, the "Talith and Pallium." "Shem and Japheth," who had been blessed together by Noah, and who would always be blessed in union, was strongly insisted upon. We shall return to the polyglot character of those days, the common language of which was an odd mixture of Greek, Aramaic, Latin, Syriac, Hebrew; but the member of the Sanhedrin had to be a good linguist. He was not to be dependent on the possibly tinged version of an interpreter. But not only was science, in its widest sense, required in him, but even an acquaintance with its fantastic shadows, such as astrology, magic, and the rest, in order that he, as both lawgiver and judge, should be able to enter also into the popular feeling about these wide-spread "arts." Proselytes, eunuchs, freedmen, were rigidly excluded from the Assembly. So were those who could not prove themselves the legitimate offspring of priests, Levites, or Israelites, and so, further, were gamblers, betting men, money lenders, and dealers in illegal produce. To the provision about the age, viz., that the senator should be neither too far advanced in age, "lest his judgment might be enfeebled," nor too young, "lest it might be immature and hasty;" and to the proofs required of his vast theoretical and practical knowledge—for he was only by slow degrees promoted from an obscure judgeship to his native hamlet to the senatorial dignity—there came to be added also that wonderfully fine rule, that he must be a married man, and have children of his own·

Deep miseries of families would be laid before him, and he should bring with him a heart full of sympathy.

Of the practical administration of justice by the Sanhedrin, we have yet to speak, when we come to the corpus juris itself. It now behooves us to pause a moment at those "schools and academies," of which we have repeatedly made mention, and of which the Sanhedrin formed, as it were, the crown and the highest consummation.

Eighty years before Christ, schools flourished throughout the length and the breadth of the land—education had been compulsory. While there is not a single term for "school," to be found before the captivity, there were, by that time, about a dozen in common usage. Here are a few of the innumerable popular sayings of the period, betokening the paramount importance which public instruction had assumed in the life of the nation : " Jerusalem was destroyed because the instrtuction of the young was neglected." "The world is only saved by the breath of the school children." "Even for the re-building of the Temple, the schools must not be interrupted." "Study is more meritorious than sacrifice " "A scholar is greater than a prophet." "You should revere the teacher even more than your father. The latter only brought you into the world, the former indicates the way into the next. But blessed is the son who has learnt from his father : he shall revere him both as his father and his master; and blessed is the father who has instructed his son."

The "High Colleges," or "Kallahs" only met during some months in the year. Three weeks before the term, the Dean prepared the student for the lectures to be delivered by the Rector ; and so arduous became the task, as the number of disciples increased, that in time no less than seven Deans had to be appointed. Yet the mode of teaching was not that of our modern Universities. The professors did not deliver lectures, which the disciples, like the student in "Faust," could "comfortably take home, in black and white." Here all was life, movement, debate ; question was met by counter-question, answers were given wrapped up in allegories or parables, the inquirer was led to deduce the questionable point for himself by analogy—the nearest approach to the Socratic method. The New Testament furnishes many specimens of this contemporary method of instruction.

The highest rank in the estimation of the people, was not reserved for the "Priest," about whose real position some extraordinary notions are still afloat—nor for the "Nobles "—but for these Masters of the Law, the "Wise," the "Disciples of the Wise."

Many of the most eminent "Doctors" were but humble tradesmen. They were tent-makers, sandal-makers, weavers, carpenters, tanners, bakers, cooks. A newly-elected President was found by his predecessor, who had been ignominiously deposed for his overbearing nature, all grimy in the midst of his charcoal mounds. Of all things the most hated, were idleness and asceticism; piety and learning themselves only received their proper estimation, when joined to healthy bodily work. "It is well to add a trade to your studies; you will then be free from sin." "The tradesmen at their work, need not rise before the greatest doctor." "Greater is he who derives his livelihood from work, than he who fears God,"—are some of the most common dicta of the period.

The exalted place thus given to Work, as on the one hand it prevented an abject worship of learning, so on the other hand, it kept all ascetic eccentricities from the body of the people. And there was always some danger of them at hand. When the temple lay in ashes, men would no longer eat meat or drink wine. A Sage remonstrated with them, but they replied weeping: "Once the flesh of sacrifices was burnt upon the altar of God. The altar is thrown down. Once libations of wine were poured out. They are no more." "But you eat bread; there were bread offerings." "You are right, master, we shall eat fruit only." "But the first fruits were offered up." "We shall refrain from them." "But you drink water, and there were libations of water." And they knew not what to reply. Then he comforted them by the assurance that He who had destroyed Jerusalem, had promised to rebuild it, and that proper mourning was right and meet, but that it must not be of a nature to weaken the body for work.

Another most striking story, is that of the Sage who, walking in a market-place crowded with people, suddenly encountered the Prophet Elijah, and asked him who, out of that vast multitude, should be saved. Whereupon the prophet first pointed to a weird-looking creature, a turnkey, "because he was merciful to his prisoners;" and next two common-looking tradesmen, who came walking through the crowd, pleasantly chatting. The Sage instantly rushed towards them, and asked them what were their saving works. But they, much puzzled, replied: "We are but poor workmen, who live by our trade. All that can be said for us is, that we are always of good cheer, and are good-natured. When we meet anybody who seems sad, we join him, and we talk to him, and cheer him so long that he must forget his grief. And if we know of two people who have quarrelled, we talk to them and persuade them, until we have made them friends again. This is our whole life."

Before leaving this period of Mishnic development, we have yet to speak of one or two things. This period is the one in which Christianity arose; and it may be as well to touch here upon the relation between Christianity and the Talmud—a subject much discussed of late. Were not the whole of our general views on the difference between Judaism and Christianity greatly confused, people would certainly not be so very much surprised at the striking parallels of dogma and parable, of allegory and proverb, exhibited by the Gospel and the Talmudical writings. The New Testament, written, as Lightfoot has it, "among Jews, by Jews for Jews," cannot but speak the language of the times, both as to form, and, broadly speaking, as to contents. There are many more vital points of contact between the New Testament and the Talmud, than divines yet seem fully to realize; for such terms as "Redemption," "Baptism," "Grace," "Faith," "Salvation," "Regeneration," "Son of Man," "Son of God," "Kingdom of Heaven," were not, as we are apt to think, invented by Christianity, but were household words of Talmudical Judaism, to which Christianity gave a higher and purer meaning. No less loud and bitter in the Talmud, are the protests against "lip searing," against "making the law a burden to the people," against "laws that hang on hairs," against "Priests and Pharisees." The fundamental mysteries of the new faith, are matters totally apart; but the ethics in both are, in their broad outlines, identical. That grand dictum, "Do unto others as thou wouldst be done by," against which Kant declared himself energetically, from a philosophical point of view, is quoted by Hillel, the President, at whose death, Jesus was ten years of age, not as anything new, but as an old and well-known dictum, "that comprised the whole Law." The most monstrous mistake, has ever been our mixing up, in the first instance, single individuals, or classes, with a whole people, and next our confounding the Judaism at the time of Christ, with that of the time of the Wilderness, of the Judges, or even of Abraham, Isaac and Jacob. The Judaism of the time of Christ (to which that of our days, owing principally to the Talmud, stands very near), and that of the Pentateuch, are as like each other as our England is like that of William Rufus, or our America like that of the Indians. It is the glory of Christianity to have carried those golden germs, hidden in the schools and among the "silent community" of the learned, into the market of humanity. It has communicated that "Kingdom of Heaven," of which the Talmud is full from the first page to the last, to the herd, even to the lepers. The fruits that have sprung from this through the wide world, we need not here consider. But the misconception, as if to a God of Vengeance had suddenly succeeded a God of Love, cannot be too often protested against. "Thou shalt love thy neighbour as thyself," is a precept of the Old Testament, as our Saviour Himself taught His disciples. The "Law," as we have seen and shall further see, was developed to a marvellously, and, perhaps, oppressively minute pitch; but only as a regulator of outward actions. The "faith of the heart"—the dogma prominently dwelt upon by Paul—was a thing that stood much higher with the Pharisees than this outward law. It was a thing, they said, not to be commanded by any ordinance, yet was greater than all. "Everything," is one of their adages, "is in the hands of Heaven, save the fear of Heaven."

"Six hundred and thirteen injunctions," says the Talmud, "was Moses instructed to give the people. David reduced them all to eleven, in the fifteenth Psalm: Lord, who shall abide in thy tabernacle, who shall dwell on thy holy hill? He that walketh uprightly," &c.

"The prophet Isaiah reduced them to six (33, 15): He that walketh righteously," &c.

"The prophet Micah reduced them to three (6, 8): What doth the Lord require of thee but to do justly, and to love mercy, and to walk humbly with thy God?"

"Isaiah once more reduced them to two (56, 1): Keep ye judgment and do justice."

"Amos (5, 4) reduced them all to one: Seek ye me and ye shall live."

"But lest it might be supposed from this that God could not be found in the fulfilment of his whole law only, Habakkuk said (cap. 2 v. 4): The just shall live by his Faith."

Regarding these "Pharisees" or "Separatists," themselves, no greater or more antiquated mistake exists, than that of their being a mere "sect" hated by Christ and the Apostles. They were not a sect—any more than Roman Catholics form a "sect" in Rome, or Protestants a "sect" in England—and they were not hated so indiscriminately by Christ and the Apostles, as would appear at first sight, from some sweeping passages in the New Testament. For the "Pharisees," as such, were at that time —Josephus notwithstanding—simply *the* people, in contradiction to the "leaven of Herod." Those "upper classes" of free-thinking Sadducees, who, in opposition to the Pharisees, insisted on the paramount importance of sacrifices and tithes, of which they were the receivers, but denied the immortality of the soul, are barely mentioned in the New Testament. The wholesale denunciations of "Scribes and Pharisees," have been greatly misunderstood. There can be absolutely no question on this point, that there were among the genuine Pharisees, the most patriotic, the most noble minded, the most advanced leaders of the party of progress. The developement of the law itself was nothing in their hands but a means to keep the spirit as opposed to the word—the outward frame—in full life and flame, and to vindicate for each time its own right to interpret the temporal ordinances, according to its own necessities and acquirements. But that there were many black sheep in the flock—many who traded on the high reputation of the whole body—is matter of reiterated denunciation in the whole contemporary literature. The Talmud inveighs even more bitterly and caustically than the New Testament, against what it calls the "Plague of Pharisaism," "the dyed ones, who do evil deeds like Zimri, and require a goodly reward like Phineas, they who preach beautifully, but do not act beautifully." Parodying their exaggerated logical arrangements, their scrupulous divisions and sub-divisions, the Talmud distinguishes seven classes of Pharisees, one of them only is worthy of the name. We have described them under their respective head, and shall, therefore, but briefly mention them. They are—1. Those who do the will of God from earthly motives. 2. They who make small steps, or say, just wait awhile for me; I have just one more good work to perform. 3. They who knock their heads against walls in avoiding the sight of a woman. 4. Saints in office. 5. They who implore you to mention some more duties which they might perform. 6. They who are pious because they *fear* God. The real and only Pharisee is he "who does the will of his Father who is in Heaven, *because he loves Him.*" Among those chiefly "Pharisaic" masters of the Mishnic period, whose names and fragments of whose life have come down to us, are some of the most illustrious men, men at whose feet the first Christians sat, whose sayings—household words in the mouths of the people—prove them to have been endowed with no common wisdom, piety, kindness, and high and noble courage; a courage and a piety they had often enough occasion to seal with their lives.

From this hasty outline of the mental atmosphere of the time when the Mishnah was gradually built up, we now turn to the Code itself. The bulk of ordinances, injunctions, prohibitions, precepts, the old and new, traditional, derived or enacted on the spur of the moment—had, after about eight hundred years, risen to gigantic proportions—proportions no longer to be mastered in their scattered, and be it remembered, chiefly unwritten form. Thrice, at different periods, the work of reducing them to system and order was undertaken by three eminent masters, the third alone succeeded. First, by Hillel I, under whose presidency Christ was born. This Hillel, also called the second Ezra, was born in Babylon. Thirst for knowledge drove him to Jerusalem. He was so poor, the legend tells us, that once when he had not money enough to fee the porter of the academy, he climbed up the window-sill one bitter winter's evening. As he lay there listening, the cold gradually made him insensible, and the snow covered him up. The darkness of the room first called the attention of those inside to the motionless form without. He was restored to life. Be it observed by the way, that this was on a Sabbath, as, according to the Talmud, danger *always* supersedes the Sabbath. Even for the sake of the tiniest babe, it must be broken without the slightest hesitation, "for the babe will," it is added, " keep many a Sabbath yet, for that one that was broken for it."

And here we cannot refrain from entering an emphatic protest against the vulgar notion of the "Jewish Sabbath" being a thing of grim austerity. It was precisely the contrary, a day of joy and delight, a "feast day," honoured by fine garments, by the best cheer, by wine, lights, spice, and other joys of pre-eminently bodily import; and the highest expression of the feeling of self-reliance and independance is contained in the adage, "Rather live on your Sabbath as you would on a week day, than be dependant on others." But this is only by the way.

About 30 B.C., Hillel became President. Of his meekness, his piety, his benevolence, the Talmudical records are full. A few of his sayings will characterize him better than any sketch of ours could do—"Be a disciple of Aaron, a friend of peace, a promoter of peace, a friend of all men, and draw them near unto the law." "Do not believe in thyself till the day of thy death." "Do not judge thy neighbour until thou hast stood in his place." "Whosoever does not increase in knowledge, decreases." "Whosoever tries to make gain by the crown of learning, perishes." Immediately after his lectures, he used to hurry home. Once asked by his disciples what caused him to hasten away, he replied that he had to look after his guest. When they pressed him for the name of his guest, he said that he only meant his soul, which was here to-day and there to-morrow.

One day a heathen went to Shammai, the head of the rival academy, and asked him mockingly to convert him to the law while he stood on one leg. The irate master turned him from his door. He then went to Hillel, who received him kindly, and gave him this reply, since so widely propagated—"Do not unto another what thou wouldst not have another do unto thee. This is the whole Law, the rest is mere commentary."

Very characteristic is also his answer to one of those "wits" who used to plague him with their silly questions. "How many laws are there?" he asked Hillel. "Two," Hillel replied, "one written and one oral." Whereupon the other said " I believe in the first, but do not believe in the second." "Sit down," Hillel said, and he wrote down the Hebrew alphabet. "What letter is this?" he asked, pointing to the first. "This is an Aleph." "Good: the next?" "Beth." "Good again; but how do you know that this is an Aleph and this a Beth?" "Thus," the other replied, "we have learned from our ancestors." "Well," Hillel said, "as you have accepted this in good faith, accept also the other." To his mind the necessity of arranging and simplifying that monstrous bulk of oral traditions, seems to have presented itself first, with all its force. There were no less than some six hundred vaguely floating sections of it in existence by that time. He tried to reduce them to six. But he died, and the work commenced by him was left untouched for another century. Akiba, the poor shepherd, who fell in love with the daughter of the richest and proudest man in all Jerusalem, and, through his love, from a clown became one of the most eminent doctors of his generation, nay, "a second Moses," came next. But he, too, was unsuccessful. His legal labours were cut short by the Roman executioner. Yet the day of his martyrdom is said to have been the day of the birth of him who, at last, did carry out the work—Jehuda, the Saint, also called " Rabbi," by way of eminence. About 200 A.D., the reduction of the whole unwritten law into a code, though still unwritten, was completed, after immense efforts, not of one school, but of all, not through one, but many methods of collection, comparison and condensation. When the code was drawn up, it was already obsolete in many of its parts. More than a generation before the destruction of the Temple, Rome had taken the penal jurisdiction from the Sanhedrin. The innumerable injunctions regarding the Temple service, the sacrifices and the rest, had but an ideal value. The agrarian laws, for the most part, applied only to Palestine; and but an insignificant part of the people had remained faithful to the desecrated land. Nevertheless, the whole code was eagerly received as their text book, by the many academies, both in Palestine and in Babylonia, not merely as a record of past enactments, but as laws that at some time or other, with the restoration of the commonwealth, would come into full practice, as of yore.

The Mishnah is divided into six sections. These are sub-divided again into 11, 12, 7, 9 (or 10), 11 and 12 chapters respectively, which are further broken up into 524 paragraphs. We shall briefly describe their contents :

Section I., *Seeds*: of Agrarian Laws, commencing with a chapter on prayers. In this section, the various tithes and donations due to the Priests, the Levites, and the poor, from the products of the lands, and further the Sabbatical year, and the prohibited mixtures in plants, animals, and garments, are treated of.

Section II., *Feasts*: of Sabbaths, Feast and Fast days, the work prohibited, the ceremonies ordained, the sacrifices to be offered on them. Special chapters are devoted to the Feast of the Exodus from Egypt to the New Year's Day, to the day of atonement (one of the most impressive parts of the whole book), to the Feast of Tabernacles, and to that of Haman.

Section III., *Women*: of betrothal, marriage, divorce, &c.; also of vows.

Section IV., *Damages*: including a great part of the civil and criminal law. It treats of the law of trover, of buying and selling, and the ordinary monetary transactions. Further, of the greatest crime known to the law, viz., idolatry. Next, of witnesses, of oaths, of legal punishments, and of the Sanhedrin itself. This section concludes with the so-called "Sentences of the Fathers," containing some of the sublimest ethical dicta known in the history of religious philosophy.

Section V., *Sacred things*: of sacrifices, the first born, &c.; also of the measurements of the Temple (Middoth).

Section VI., *Purifications*: of the various Levitical and other hygienic laws, of impure things and persons, their purification, &c.

There is, it cannot be denied, more symmetry and method in the Mishnah than in the Pandects; although we have not found that minute logical sequence in its arrangements, which Maimonides and others, have discovered. In fact, we do not believe that we have it in its original shape. But, as far as the single treaties are concerned, the Mishnah is for the most part free from the blemishes of the Roman Code. There are, unquestionably, fewer contradictory laws, fewer repetitions, fewer interpolations, than in the Digests, which notwithstanding Tribonian's efforts, abound with so-called "Gemiuationes," and so forth; and as regards a certain outspokenness in bodily things, it has at last been acknowledged by all competent authorities, that its language is infinitely purer than that, for instance, of the mediæval casuists.

The regulations contained in these six treatises, are of very different kinds. They are apparently important and unimportant, intended to be permanent or temporary. They are either clear expansions of Scriptural precepts, or independent traditions, linked to Scripture only hermeneutically. They are "decisions," "fences," "injunctions," "ordinances," or simply "Mosaic Halachah from Sinai."

The uniform reverence for all the manifold contents of the Mishnah, is best expressed in the Redactor's own words—the motto to the whole collection,—"Be equally conscientious in small as in great precepts, for ye know not their individual rewards." Compute the earthly loss sustained by the fulfilment of a law, by the heavenly reward derived through it, and the gain derived from a transgression by the punishment that is to follow it. Also contemplate three things, and ye shall not fall into sin; know what is above ye—an eye that seeth, an ear that heareth—and all your works are written in a book.

The tone and tenor of the Mishnah is, except in one special division, devoted to ethics, emphatically practical. It does not concern itself with metaphysics, but aims at being merely a civil code. Yet it never misses an opportunity of inculcating those higher ethetical principles, which lie beyond the strict letter of the law. It looks more to the "intention," in the fulfilment of a precept, than to the fulfilment itself. He who claims certain advantages by the letter of the law, though the spirit of humanity should urge him not to insist upon them, is not "beloved by God and man." On the other hand, he who makes good by his own free will, demands which the law could not have enforced; he, in fact, who does not stop short at the "Gate of Justice," but proceeds within the "Line of Mercy," in him the "Spirit of the wise" has pleasure. Certain duties bring fruits (interest) in this world; but the real reward, the "capital," is paid back in the world to come; such as reverence for father and mother, charity, early application to study, hospitality; doing the last honour to the dead, promoting peace between man and his neighbor. The Mishnah knows nothing of "Hell." For all and any transgressions, there were only the fixed legal punishments, or a mysterious sudden "Visitation of God,"—the scriptural "rooting out." Death atones for all sins. Minor transgressions are redeemed by repentance, charity, sacrifice, and the day of atonement. Sins committed against any man are only forgiven when the injured man has had full amends made, and declares himself reconciled. The highest virtue lies in the study of the law. It is not only the badge of high culture; but there is a special merit bound up in it, that will assist man both in this and in the world to come.

To discuss these laws, their spirit, and their details, in this place we cannot undertake. But this much we may say, that it has always been the unanimous opinion of both friends and foes, that their general character is humane in the extreme; in spite of certain harsh and exceptional laws, issued in times of danger and misery, of revolution and reaction ; laws, moreover, which, for the most part, never were and never could be carried into practice. There is an almost modern liberality of view regarding the "fulfilment of the Law" itself, expressed by such frequent adages, as the Scripture says, " he shall live by them"—that means he shall not *die through them.* " They shall not be made pitfalls or burdens to him, that shall make him hate life." " He who carries out these precepts to the full, is declared to be nothing less than a ' Saint.'" "The law has been given to men, and not to angels."

Respecting the practical administration of justice, a sharp distinctinction is drawn by the Mishnah between the cival and criminal law. In both, the most careful investigation and scrutiny is required ; but while in the former three, judges are competent, a tribunal of less than twenty-three is required for the latter. The first duty of the civil judges is always—however clear the case—to urge an agreement. When, says the Talmud, do justice and good will meet ? When the contending parties are made to agree peaceable. There were both special local magistrates and casual " justices of peace," chosen *ad hoc* by the parties. Payment received for a decision annuls the decision. Loss of time only was allowed to be made good in case of tradesman judges. The plaintiff who was proved to have asked more than his due, with a view of thus obtaining his due more readily, was non-suited. Three partners in an action must not divide themselves into one plaintiff and two witnesses. The judge must see that both parties are pretty equally dressed, *i. e.* not one in fine garments, the other in rags ; and he is further particularly cautioned not to be biassed *in favor of the poor against the rich.* The judge must not hear anything of the case, save in the presence of both parties. Many and striking are also the admonitions regarding the judge. " He who unjustly hands over one man's goods to another, he shall pay God for it with his own soul." " In the hour when the Judge sits in judgment over his own fellow-men, he shall feel, as it were, a sword pointed at his own heart." " Woe unto the Judge who, convinced in his mind of the unrighteousness of a cause, tries to throw the blame on the witnesses. From *him* God will ask an account." "When the parties stand before you, look upon both as guilty ; but when they are dismissed, let them both be innocent in thine eyes, for the decree has gone forth."

It would not be easy to find a more humane, almost refined, penal legislation, from the days of the old world to our own. While in civil cases, whenever larger tribunals (juries) had to be called in, a majority of one is sufficient for either acquittal or condemnation; in criminal cases a majority of one acquits, but a majority of two is requisite for condemnation. All men are accepted in the former as witnesses—always except gamblers (dice-players), betting men (pigeon-flyers), usurers, dealers in illegal (seventh year's) produce, and slaves, who were disqualified from "judging and bearing witness"—either for the plaintiff or the defendant; but it is only for the defence that everybody, indiscriminately, is heard in criminal cases. The cross examination of the witnesses was exceedingly strict. The formula (containing at once a whole breviary for the judge himself,) with which the witnesses were admonished in criminal cases, was of so awful and striking a nature, that "swearing a man's life away" became an almost unheard of occurrence.

"How is one," says the Mishna, "to awe the witnesses who are called to testify in matters of life and death? When they are brought into court they are charged thus: Perchance you would speak from conjecture or rumour, as a witness from another witness—having heard it from "some trustworthy man"—or perchance you are not aware that we shall proceed to search and to try you with close questions and searching scrutiny. Know ye, that not like trials about money, are trials over life and death? In trials of money, a man may redeem his guilt by money, and he may be forgiven. In trials of life, the blood of him who has been falsely condemned, will hang over the false witnesses, and also that of the seed of his seed, even unto the end of the world: for thus we find that when Cain killed his brother, it is said: "The voice of thy brother's blood is crying to me from the ground." The word blood stands there as in the plural number, to indicate to you that the blood of him, together with that of his seed, has been shed. Adam was created alone, to show you that he who destroys one single life in Israel, will be called to account for it, as if he had destroyed a whole world. . . . . But, on the other hand, ye might say to yourselves: What have we to do with this misery here? Remember then, that Holy Writ has said (Lev. v. 1): "If a witness hath seen or known, if he do not utter, he shall bear his iniquity." But perchance ye might say, "Why shall we be guilty of this man's blood?" Remember, then, what is said in Proverbs (5, 1-10): "In the destruction of the wicked there is joy."

The "Lex Talionis" is unknown to the Talmud. Paying "measure for measure," it says, is in God's hand only. Bodily injuries inflicted, are to be redeemed by money; and here again the Pharisees had carried the day against the Sadducees, who insisted upon the literal interpretation of that verse. The extreme punishments, "flagellation" and "death," as ordered in the Mosaic Code, were inflicted in a humane manner, unknown as we have said, not only to the contemporary courts of antiquity, but even to those of Europe, up to within the last generation. Thirty-nine was the utmost number of strokes to be inflicted; but—the "loving one's neighbor like oneself" being constantly urged by the penal code itself, even with regard to criminals—if the life of the culprit was in the least degree endangered, this number was at once reduced. However numerous the delinquent's transgressions, but one punishment could be decreed for them all. Not even a fine and flagellation could be pronounced upon the same occasion.

The care of human life was extreme indeed. The Judges of capital offences had to fast all day, nor was the sentence executed on the day of the verdict, but it was once more subjected to scrutiny by the Sanhedrin the next day. Even to the last, some favorable circumstance that might turn the scale in the prisoner's favor, was looked for.

The place of execution was at some distance from the Court, in order that time might be given to a witness, or the accused himself, for naming any fact fresh in his favor. A man was stationed at the entrance to the Court with a flag in his hand, at some distance another man, on horseback, was stationed, in order to stop the execution instantly, if any favorable circumstance should still come to light. The culprit himself was allowed to stop four or five times, and to be brought back before the judges, if he had still anything to urge in his defence. Before him marched a herald, crying, "The man M. M., son of N. M., is being led to execution, for having committed such and such a crime; such and such are the witnesses against him; whosoever knows aught to his favor, let him come and proclaim it." Ten yards from the place of execution, they said to him, "Confess thy sins; everyone who confesses his part in the world to come; for thus it is written of Achan, to whom Joshua said, My son, give now glory to the God of Israel." If he "could not" offer any formal confession, he need only say, "May my death be a redemption for all my sins." To the last the culprit was supported by marks of profound and awful sympathy. The ladies of Jerusalem formed a society, which provided a beverage of mixed myrrh and vinegar, that, like an opiate, benumbed the man when he was being carried to execution.

There were four kinds of capital punishment—stoning, burning, slaying with the sword, and strangling. Crucifixion is utterly unknown to the Jewish law. "The house of stoning" was two stories high, "stoning" in the Mishnah, being merely a term for breaking the culprit's neck. It was the part of the chief witness to precipitate the criminal with his own hand. If he fell on his breast, he was turned on his back; if the fall had not killed him on the spot, the second witness had to cast a stone on his heart; if he still survived, then, and then only, the whole people hastened his death by casting stones upon him. The modes of strangling and burning were almost identical; in both cases the culprit was buried to his waist in soft mud, and two men by tightening a cord *wrapped in soft cloth*, round his neck, caused instantaneous death. In the "burning," a lighted wick was thrown down his throat, when he opened his mouth at his last breath. The corpse was buried in a special place appropriated to criminals. After a time, however, the bones were gathered together and transferred to the burial place of the culprit's kin. The relations then visited the Judges and witnesses, as much as to say, "We bear no malice against you, for a righteous judgment have ye judged." The ordinary ceremonies of outer mourning were not observed in such cases, but lamentation was not prohibited during the first period of grief —"for sorrow is from the heart." There was no confiscation of the culprit's goods.

Practically, capital punishment was abrogated even before the Romans had taken it out of the hands of the Sanhedrin. Here, again, the humanising influences of the "Traditions" had been at work, commuting the severe Mosaic Code. The examination of witnesses had been made so rigorous, that a sentence of capital punishment became almost impossible. When the guilt had, notwithstanding all these difficulties, been absolutely brought home, some formal flaw was sure to be found, and the sentence was commuted to imprisonment for life. The doctors of a later period, notably Akiba, who in the midst of his revolutionary dreams of a new independence, kept his eye steadily on a reform of the whole jurisdiction, did not hesitate to pronounce openly for the abolition of capital punishment. A court which had pronounced one sentence of death in seven or seventy years, received the name of "Court of murderers."

So far the Mishnah, that brief abstract of about eight hundred years legal production. Jehudah the "Redactor," had excluded all but the best authenticated traditions, as well as all discussion and exegesis, unless where particularly necessary. The vast mass of these materials was now also collected, as a sort of apocryphal oral code. We have, dating from a few generations after the redaction of the official Mishnah, a so-called external Mishnah, (Boraita); further, the discussions and additions belonging by rights to the Mishnah, called "Tosefta," (Supplement); and, finally, the exegesis and methodology of the Halacha (Sifri, Sifra, Mechilta), much of which was afterwards embodied in the Talmud.

The Mishnah, being formed into a code, became in its turn what the Scripture had been, a basis of development and discussion. It had to be linked to the Bible, it became impregnated with and obscured by speculations; new traditions sprang up, new methods were invented, casuistry assumed its sway—as it did in the legal schools that flourished at that period at Rome, at Alexandria, at Berytus—and the Gemara ensued. A double Gemara: one the expression of the schools in Palestine, called that of Jerusalem, redacted at Tiberias, (not at Jerusalem), about A.D. 390, and written in what may be called "East Aramæan;" the other, redacted at Syria in Babylonia, edited by R. Ashe (A.D. 365-427). This final close of this codex, however, the collecting and sifting of which took just sixty years, is due to the school of the "Saboraim," at the end of the fifth century, A.D. The Babylonian Gemara is the expression of the academies of Syra, Nehardea, Pum-Veditha, Mahusa, and other places, during six or seven generations of continuous development. This "Babylonian" Talmud is couched in "Western Aramæan."

Neither of the two codes were written down at first, and neither has survived in its completeness. Whether there ever was a double Gemara to all the six, or even the first five divisions of the Mishnah, (the sixth having early fallen into disuse), is at least very doubtful. Much, however, that existed has been lost. The Babylonian Talmud is about four times as large as that of Jerusalem. Its thirty-six treatises now cover, in our editions, printed with the most prominent commentaries (Rashi and Tosafoth), exactly 2,947 folio leaves, in twelve folio volumes, the pagination of which is kept uniform in almost all editions. If, however, the extraneous portions are substracted, it is only about ten or eleven times as large as the Mishnah, which was redacted just as many generations before the Talmud.

How the Talmud itself became by degrees what the Mishnah had been to the Gemara, and what the Scripture had been to the early Scribes, viz: A Text; how the "Saboraim" and "Gaonim," those Epigoni of the "Scribes," made it the centre of their activity for centuries; what endless commentaries, dissertations, expositions, responses, novellæ, abstracts, &c., grew out of it, we cannot here tell. Only this much, we will add, that the Talmud, as such, was never formally accepted by the nation, by either General or Special Council. Its legal decisions, as derived from the highest authorities, certainly formed the basis of the religious law, the norm of all future decisions: as undoubtedly the Talmud is the most trustworthy canon of Jewish tradition. But its popularity is much more due to an extraneous cause. During the prosecutions against the Jews in the Persian Empire, under Jesdegerd II., Firuz, and Kobad, the schools were closed for about eighty years. The living development of this law being stopped, the book obtained a supreme authority, such as had probably never been dreamt of by its authors. Need we add, that what authority was silently vested in it, belonged exclusively to its legal portions? The other, the "haggadistic," or legendary portion, was "poetry," a thing beloved by women and children, and by those still pensive minds which delight in flowers and in the song of wild birds. The "authorities" themselves often enough set their faces against it, repudiated it, and explained it away. But the people clung to it, and, in course of time, it gave to it, and it alone, the encyclopædic name of "Midrash."

We have now to say a few words respecting the language in which these documents are couched, as furnishing an additional key to the mode of life and thoughts of the period. The language of the Mishnah is as pure a Hebrew as can be expected in those days. The people themselves spoke, as we mentioned above, a corrupt Chaldea, or Aramaic mixed with Greek and Latin. Many prayers of the period, the Targums, the Gemaras, are conceived in that idiom. Even the Mishnah itself could not exclude those all-pervading foreign elements. Many legal terms, many names of products, of heathen feasts, of household furniture, of meat and drink, of fruit and garment, are borrowed from the classical languages. Here is a curious addition to the curious history of words! The bread which the Semites had cast upon the waters, in the archaic Phœnician times, came back to them after many days. If they had given to the early Greeks the names for weights and measures, for spice and aromas, every one of which is Hebrew; if they had imported the "sapphire, paper, emerald," the fine materials for garments, and the garments themselves, if the musical instruments, the plants, vessels, writing materials, and last, not least, the alphabet itself, came from the Semites; the Greek and Latin idioms repaid them, in the Talmudical period, with full interest, to the great distress of the later scoliasts and lexicographers. The Aramaic itself was, as we said, the language of the people. It was, itself, a most pellucid and picturesque idiom, lending itself admirably, not only to the epigrammatic terseness of the Gemara, but also to those profoundly poetical conceptions of a daily phenomena, which had penetrated even into the cry of the watchmen, the passward of the temple guards, and the routine-formula of the critical functionary. Unfortunately, it was too poetical at times. Matters of a purely metaphysical nature, which afterwards grew into dogmas through its vague phraseology, assumed very monstrous shapes indeed. But it had become, in the hands of the people, a mongrel idiom; and, though gifted with a fine feeling for the distinguished characters of each of the languages then in common use; ("Aramaic lends itself best to elegies, Greek to hymns, Hebrew to prayer, Roman to martial composition," as a common saying has it), they got mixed up, all of them, somewhat in the manner of the Pennsylvanians of to-day. After all, it was but the faithful reflex of those who made this idiom an enduring language. These "Masters of the Law" formed the most mixed assembly in the world. There were not only natives of all the parts of the world-wide Roman Empire among them, but also denizens of Arabia and India; a fact which accounts for many phenomena in the Talmud. But there is hardly anything of domestic or public purport, which was not called either by its Greek or Latin name, or by both, and generally in so questionable a shape, and in such obsolete forms, that both classical and Semitic scholars, have often need to go through a whole course of archæology and antiquities, before unravelling it. Save only one province, that of agriculture. This alone, together with some other trades, had retained the old homely Semitic words: thereby indicating, not, as ignorance might be led to conclude, that the nation was averse to it, but exactly the contrary; that from the early days of Joshua they had never ceased to cherish the thought of sitting under their own vine and fig-tree.

The Talmud does, indeed, offer us a perfect picture of the cosmopolitanism and luxury of those final days of Rome, such as but few classical or post classical writings contain. We find mention made of Spanish fish, of Cretan apples, Bithynian cheese, Egyptian lentils and beans, Greek and Egyptian pumpkins, Italian wine, Median beer; garments were imported from Pelusium and India, shirts from Cilicia, and veils from Arabia. To the Arabic, Persian, and Indian materials contained, in addition to these, in the Gemara, a bare allusion may suffice.

We had long pondered over the best way of illustrating to our readers the extraordinary manner in which the "Haggadah," that second current in the Talmud, suddenly interrupts the course of the "Halacha," —when we bethought ourselves of the device of an old master. It was a hot Easter afternoon, and while he was expounding some intricate subtlety of the law, his hearers quietly fell away in drowsy slumbers. All of a sudden, he burst out : " There was once a woman, in Egypt, who brought forth, at one birth, six hundred thousand men !" And our readers may fancy how his audience started up at this remarkable tale of the prolific Egyptian woman. Her name, the master calmly proceeded, was Jochebed, and she was the mother of Moses, who was worth as much as all those six hundred thousand armed men together, who went up from Egypt. The professor, then, after a brief legendary digression, proceeded with his legal intricacies, and his hearers slept no more that afternoon. An eastern mind seems peculiarly constituted. Its passionate love for things wise and witty, for stories and tales, for parables and apologues, does not leave it even in its severe studies. They are constantly needed, it would appear, to keep the currents of its thoughts in motion : they are the playthings of the grown-up children of the Orient. The Haggadah, too, has an exegesis, a system, a method of its own. They are the peculiar, fantastic things. We would rather not follow too closely its learned divisions, into homiletical, ethical, historical, general and special Haggadah.

The Haggadah, in general, transforms Scripture into a thousand themes for its variations. Everything being bound up in the Bible—the beginning and the end ; there must be an answer in it to all questions. Find the key, and all the riddles in it are solved. The persons of the Bible —the kings and the patriarchs, the heroes and the prophets, the women and the children, what they did and what they suffered, their happiness and their doom, their words and their lives—became, apart from their presupposed historical reality, a symbol and an alegory. And what the narrative had omitted, the Haggadah supplied in many variations. It filled up these gaps, as a prophet looking into the past might do ; it explained the motives ; it enlarged the story ; it found connections between the remotest countries, ages, and people, often with a startling realism ; it drew sublime morals from the most commonplace facts. Yet it did this by quick and sudden motions, to us most foreign ; and hence the frequent misunderstanding of its strange and wayward moods.

Those who look with an eye of disfavor upon all these extraneous matters as represented by the Haggadah in the Talmud—the fairy tales, and the jests, the stories and the parables, and all that strange agglomeration of foreign things chrystalized around the legal kernal—should remember, above all, one fact. As this tangled mass lies before us, it represents at best a series of photographic slides half broken, mutilated and faded; though what remains of them is startlingly faithful to the original.

We shall devote a brief space to this Haggadah. And for a general picture of it, we shall refer to Bunyan, who, speaking of his own book, which is very Haggadistic, unknowingly describes the Haggadah as accurately as can be:—

> . . . Wouldst thou divert thyself from melancholy?
> Wouldst thou be pleasant yet be far from folly?
> Wouldst thou read riddles and their explanation?
> Or else be drowned in thy contemplation?
> Dost thou love picking meat? Or wouldst thou see
> A man i' the clouds, and hear him speak to thee?
> Wouldst thou be in a dream, and yet not sleep?
> Or, wouldst thou in a moment laugh and weep?
> Wouldst lose thyself, and catch no harm?
> And find thyself again without a charm?
> Wouldst read thyself, and read— thou knowest not what?
> And yet know whether thou art blessed or not
> By reading the same lines? O then come hither,
> And lay this book, thy head and heart together.

We would not reproach those who, often with the best intentions in the world, have brought almost the entire Haggadistic province into dispute. We really do not wonder that the so-called "Rabbinical stories," that have from time to time been brought before the public, have not met with the most flattering reception. The Talmud, which has a drastic word for every occasion, says, "They dived into an ocean, and brought up potsherd." First of all, these stories form only a small part in the vast mass of allegories, parables and the like, that make up the Haggadah, and they were partly ill-chosen, partly badly rendered, and partly did not belong to the Talmud, but to some recent Jewish story-book. It seems of more moment to call attention to an entirely new branch of investigation, namely, talmudical metaphysics and ethics, such as may be gleaned from the Haggadah, of which we shall not take a glance.

Beginning with the Creation; we find the gradual development of the Cosmos fully recognized by the Talmud. It assumes destruction after destruction, stage after stage. And in their quaintly ingenious manner, the Masters refer to the verse in Genesis, "And God saw all that he had made, and behold it was very good," and to that other in Eccles. III, 11, " God created everything in its proper season," and argue " He created worlds upon worlds, and destroyed them one after another, until he created this world. He then said, 'This pleases me, the others did not ;'—' in its proper season '—it was not meet to create *this* world until now."

The Talmud assumes some original substance, itself created by God, out of which the universe was shaped. There is a perceptible leaning to the early Greek schools. "One or three things were before this world: Water, Fire, and Wind: Water begat the Darkness, Fire the Light, and Wind begat the Spirit of Wisdom." The *How* of the Creation was not even matter of speculation. The co-operation of angels, whose existence was warranted by Scripture, and a whole hierarchy of whom had been built up under Persian influences, was distinctly denied. In a discussion about the day of their creation, it is agreed, on all hands, that there were no angels at first, "lest men might say, "Michael spanned out the firmament on the south, and Gabriel on the north." There is a distinct foreshadowing of the Gnostic Demiurgos—that antique link between the Divine Spirit and the world of matter—to be found in the Talmud. The angels—whose names, according to the Talmud itself, the Jews brought back from Babylon—play, after the exile, a very different part from those before the exile.

Much as the Talmudical authorities inveigh against those "heathen ways," sympathetic cures, the exorcism of demons, the charms, and the rest, the working of miracles, very much in vogue in those days, yet, they themselves were drawn into larger concessions to angels and demons. Besides the seven Angel Princes, there are hosts of ministering angels, whose functions, besides that of being messengers, are two-fold ; to praise God, and to be guardians of man. In their first capacity they are daily created by God's breath, out of a stream of fire that rolls its waves under the divine throne. As guardian angels, two of them accompany every man, and, for every good deed, man acquires a new guardian angel, who always watches over his steps. When the righteous dies, three hosts of angels meet him. One says, (in the words of Scripture,) "He shall go in peace," the second takes up the strain, and says, "Who has walked in righteousness," and the third concludes, "Let him come in peace, and rest upon his bed." If the wicked leaves this world, three hosts of wicked angels come to meet him.

"Every nation," says the Talmud, "has its special guardian angel, its horoscopes, its ruling planets and stars. But there is no planet for Israel. Israel shall look but to Him. There is no mediation between those who are called His children, and their Father which is in heaven." The Jerusalem Talmud, written under the direct influence of Roman manners and customs, has the following parable : "A man has a patron.

If some evil happens to him, he does not enter suddenly into the presence of this patron, but he goes and stands at the door of his house. He does not ask for the patron, but for his favorite slave, or his son, who then goes and tells the master inside. The man, N. N., is standing at the gate of the hall—shall he come in or not? Not so the Holy, praised be He. If misfortune comes upon a man, let him not cry to Michael, and not to Gabriel, but unto Me let him cry, and *I* will answer him right speedily—as it is said, every one who shall call upon the name of the Lord shall be saved."

The end and aim of creation is man, who, therefore, was created last, "when everything was ready for his reception." When he has reached the perfection of virtue, "he is higher than the angels themselves."

Miracles are considered by the Talmud—much as Leibnitz regards all the movements of every limb of our body—as only possible through a sort of prestabilited harmony; *i. e.*, the course of creation was not disturbed by them, but they were all primerally "existing," "preordained." They were created at the end of all other things, in the gloaming of the sixth day. Among them, however, was—and this will interest our palagraphers—also the art of writing: an invention considered beyond all arts: nothing short of a miracle. Creation, together with these so-called exceptions, once established, nothing could be altered in it. The laws of nature went by their own immutable force. however much evil might spring therefrom, "These wicked ones not only vulgarize my coin," says the Haggadah, with reference to the propagation of the evil-doers and their kin, bearing the human face divine, " but they actually make me impress base coin with my own stamp."

God's real name is ineffable; but there are many designations indicative of his qualities, such as the merciful (Rachman, a name of frequent occurence both in the Talmud and Koran), the Holy One, the Place, the Heavens, the Word, Our Father which is in Heaven, the Almighty, the Shechinah, or Sacred Presence.

The doctrine of the soul, bears more the impress of the Platonic than of the Aristotelian school. It is held to be pre-existing. All souls that are ever to be united to bodies, have been created once for all, and are hidden away from the first noment of creation. They being creatures of the highest realms, are cognizant of all things, but at the hour of their birth in a human body, an angel touches the mouth of the child, which causes it to forget all that has been. Very striking is the comparison between the soul and God, a comparison which has an almost partheistic look. "As God fills the whole universe," says the Haggadah, "so the soul fills the whole body; as God sees and is not seen ; as God nourishes the whole universe, so the soul nourishes the whole body ; as God is pure, so the soul is pure." This purity is specially dwelt upon in contradistinction to the theory of hereditary sin, which is denied. "There is no death without individual sin, no pain without individual transgression. That same spirit that dictated in the Pentateuch, "and parents shall not die for their children, nor the children for their parents," has ordained that no one should be punished for another's transgressions. In the judgment on sin, the *animus* is taken into consideration. The desire to commit the vice is held to be more wicked than the vice itself.

The fear of God, or a virtuous life, the whole aim and end of a man's existence, is entirely in man's hand. "Everything is in God's hand save the fear of God." But one hour of repentance is better than the whole world to come. The fullest liberty is granted in this respect to every human being, though the help of God is necessary for carrying it out.

The dogma of the resurrection and of immortality, vaguely indicated in the various parts of the Old Testament, has been fixed by the Talmud, and traced to several Biblical passages. Various are the similes by which the relation of this world to the world to come is indicated. This world is like unto a "Prosdora" to the next : "Prepare thyself in the hall, that thou mayest be admitted into the Palace," or "This world is like a road-side inn (hospitium), but the world to come is like a real home." The righteous are represented as perfecting themselves and developing all their highest faculties, even in the next world : "For the righteous there is no rest, neither in this world nor in the next, for they go," say the Scriptures, "from host to host, from striving to striving ; they will see God in Zion." How all its deeds, and the hour when they were committed, are unfolded to the sight of the departed soul, the terrors of the grave, the rolling back to Jerusalem on the day of the great trumpet, we need not here tell in detail. These half-metaphysical, half-mystical speculations are throughout, in the manner of the more poetical early church fathers of old, and of Bunyan of our own times. The Resurrection is to take place by the mystic power of the "Dew of Life" in Jerusalem—on Mount Olivet and the Targums.

There is no everlasting damnation, according to the Talmud. There is only a temporary punishment, even for the worst sinners. "Generations upon generations" shall last the damnation of idolaters, apostates, and traitors. But there is a space of only two fingers' breadth between Hell and Heaven; the sinner has but to repent sincerely, and the gates to everlasting bliss will spring open. No human being is excluded from the world to come. Every man of whatever creed or nation, provided he be of the righteous, shall be admitted into it. The punishment of the wicked is not specified, as indeed all the descriptions of the next world are left vague; yet, with regard to Paradise, the idea of something inconceivably glorious, is conveyed at every step. The passage, "Eye has not seen nor has ear heard," is applied to its unspeakable bliss. "In the next world there will be no eating, no drinking, no love and no labour, no envy, no hatred, no contest. The righteous will sit with crowns on their heads, glorying in the splendor of God's majesty."

The essence of prophecy gives rise to some speculation. One decisive Talmudical dictum is: That God does not cause his spirit to rest upon any one but a strong, wise, rich and humble man. Strong and rich are explained in the Mishnah, in this wise: "Who is strong? He who subdues his passion. Who is rich? He who is satisfied with his lot." There are degrees among prophets. Moses saw everything clearly; the other prophets, as in dark mirrors. Ezekiel and Isaiah say the same thing; but Ezekiel, like a town-bred man, Isaiah like a villager.

The "philosophy of religion" will be best comprehended by some of those "small coins," the popular and pithy sayings, gnomes, proverbs, and the rest, which, even better than street songs, characterise a time. With these we shall conclude this article. We have thought it preferable to give them at random, as we found them, instead of building up from them a system of "ethetics" or "Duties of the heart." We have naturally preferred the better and more characteristic ones that come in our way.

SAYINGS OF THE TALMUD.

"Be thou cursed, not he who curses. Be of them that are persecuted, not of them that persecute. Look at Scripture; there is not a single bird more persecuted than the dove, yet God hath chosen her to be offered on his altar. The bull is hunted by the lion, the sheep by the wolf, the goat by the tiger. And God said, 'Bring me a sacrifice, not from them that persecute, but from them that are persecuted.' We read, (Ex. xvii. 2,) that while, in the contest with Amalek, Moses lifted up his arms, Israel prevailed. Did Moses' hands make war, or break war? But this is to tell you, that as long as Israel are looking upwards, and humbling their hearts before their Father which is in heaven, they prevail; if not they fall. In the same way you find, (Num. xxi. 9,) 'And Moses made a serpent of brass, and put it upon a pole: and it came to pass, that if a serpent had bitten any man, when he beheld the serpent of brass, he lived.' Dost think that a serpent killeth, or giveth life? But as long as Israel are looking upwards to their Father which is in heaven, they will live; if not, they will die. 'Has God pleasure in the meat and blood of sacrifices?' asks the prophet. No; he has not so much ordained as permitted them. It is for yourselves, he says, not for me, that you offer. Like a king, who sees his son carousing daily with all manner of evil companions: You shall henceforth eat and drink entirely at your will at my own table, he says. They offered sacrifices to demons and devils, for they loved sacrificing, and could not do without it. And the Lord said, 'Bring your offerings to me; you shall then, at least, offer to the true God. Scripture ordains that the Hebrew slave who 'loves' his bondage, shall have his ear pierced against the door-post. Why? because it is that ear which heard on Sinai. 'They are My servants, they shall not be sold as bondsmen.' They are *My* servants, not servants' servants. And this man voluntarily throws away his precious freedom. 'Pierce his ear.' 'He who sacrifices a whole offering, shall be rewarded for a whole offering; he who offers a burnt-offering, shall have the reward of a burnt-offering; but he who offers humility unto God and man, shall be rewarded with a reward as if he had offered all the sacrifices in the world.' The child loves its mother more than its father. It fears its father more than its mother. See how the Scripture makes the father precede the mother in injunction. 'Thou shalt love thy father and thy mother;' and the mother, when it says, 'Honour thy mother and thy father.' Bless God for the good as well as for the evil. When you hear of a death, say, 'Blessed is the righteous judge.' Even when the gates of prayer are shut in heaven, those of tears are open. Prayer is Israel's only weapon, a weapon inherited from its fathers, a weapon tried in a thousand battles. When the righteous dies it is the earth he loses. The lost jewel will always be a jewel, but the possessor who has it—well may he weep. Life is a passing shadow, says the Scripture. Is it the shadow of a tower, of a tree? A shadow that prevails for a while? No, it is the shadow of a bird in his flight—away flies the bird, and there is neither bird nor shadow. Repent one day before thy death. There was a king who bade all his servants to a great repast, but he did not indicate the hour: some went home, and put on their best garments, and stood at the door of the palace; others said,

There is ample time, the king will let us know beforehand. But the king summoned them of a sudden; and those that were in their best garments were well received, but the foolish ones, who came in their slovenliness, were turned away in disgrace. Repent to-day, lest to-morrow ye might be summoned. The aim and end of all wisdom are repentance and good works. Even the most righteous shall not attain to so high a place in heaven as the truly repentant. The reward of good works is like dates: sweet, and ripening late. The dying benediction of a sage to his disciples was: I pray for you, that the fear of heaven may be as strong upon you as the fear of man. You avoid sin before the face of the latter: avoid it before the face of the All-seeing. 'If your God hates idolatry, why does he not destroy it?' a heathen asked. And they answered him; Behold, they worship the sun, the moon, the stars; would you have him destroy this beautiful world for the sake of the foolish? If your God is a 'friend of the poor,' asked another, why does he not support them? Their case, a sage answered, is left in our hands, that we may thereby acquire merits and forgiveness of sin. But what a merit it is! the other replied; suppose I am angry with one of my slaves, and forbid him food and drink, and some one gives it him, furitively, shall I be much pleased? Not so, the other replied: suppose you are wroth with your only son, and imprison him without food, and some good man has pity on the child, and saves him from the pangs of hunger, would you be so very angry with the man? And we, if we are called servants of God, are also called his children. He who has more learning than good works, is like a tree with many branches, but few roots, which the first wind throws on its face; whilst he whose works are greater than his knowledge, is like a tree with many roots and fewer branches, but which all the winds of heaven cannot uproot.

"Love your wife like yourself, honour her more than yourself. Whosoever lives unmarried, lives without joy, without comfort, without blessing. Descend a step in choosing a wife. If thy wife is small, bend down to her and whisper into her ear. He who forsakes the love of his youth, God's altar weeps for him. He who sees his wife die before him, has, as it were, been present at the destruction of the sanctuary itself—around him the world grows dark. It is woman alone through whom God's blessings are vouchsafed to a house. She teaches the children, speeds the husband to the place of worship and instruction, welcomes him when he returns, keeps the house godly and pure, and God's blessings rest upon all these things. He who marries for money, his children shall be a curse to him. The house that does not open to the poor shall open to the physician. The birds in the air, even, despise the miser. He who gives charity in secret is greater than Moses himself. Honour the sons of the poor, it is they who bring science into splendor. Let the honour of thy neighbour be to thee like thine own. Rather be thrown into a fiery furnace than bring anyone to public shame. Hospitality is the most important part of divine worship. There are three crowns: of the law, the priesthood, the kingship; but the crown of a good name is greater than them all. Iron breaks the stone, fire melts the iron, water extinguishes fire, the clouds drink up the water, a storm drives away the clouds, man withstands the storm, fear unmans man, wine dispels fear, sleep drives away wine, and death sweeps all away— even sleep. But Solomon the wise says: Charity saves from death. How can you escape sin? Think of three things: whence thou comest, whither thou goest, and to whom thou wilt have to account for all thy deeds: even to the King of kings, the all-holy, praised be He. Four shall not enter Paradise: the scoffer, the liar, the hypocrite, and the slanderer. To slander is to murder. The cock and the owl both await the daylight. The light, says the cock, brings delight to me, but what are you waiting for? When the thief has no opportunity for stealing, he considers himself an honest man. If thy friends agree in calling thee an ass, go and get an halter around thee. Thy friend has a friend, and thy friend's friend has a friend: be discreet. The dog sticks to you on account of the crumbs in your pocket. He in whose family there has been one hanged, should not say to his neighbour, Pray hang this little fish up for me. The camel wanted to have horns, and they took away his ears. The soldiers fight and the kings are the heroes. The thief invokes God when he breaks into the house. The woman of sixty will run after music like one of six. After the thief runs the theft, after the beggar, poverty. While the foot is shod, smash the thorn. Descend a step in choosing a wife, mount a step in choosing a friend. If there be anything bad about you, say it yourself. Luck makes rich, luck makes wise. Beat the gods, and the priests will tremble. Were it not for the existence of passions, no one would build a house, marry a wife, beget children, or do any work. The sun will go down all by himself, without your assistance. The world could not well get on without perfumers and without tanners; but woe to the tanner, and well to the perfumer! Fools are no proof. No man is to be made responsible for words which he utters in his grief. One eats, another says grace. He who is ashamed will not easily commit sin. There is a great difference between him who is ashamed before his own self, and him who is only ashamed before others.

It is a good sign in man to be capable of being ashamed. One contrition in man's heart is better than many flagellations. If our ancestors were like angels, we are like men; if our ancestors were like men, we are like asses. Do not live near a pious fool. If you wish to hang yourself, choose a big tree. Rather eat onions and sit in the shadow, and do not eat geese and poultry if it makes thy heart uneasy within thee. A small stater (coin) in a large jar makes a big noise. A myrtle even in the desert remains a myrtle. When the pitcher falls upon the stone, woe unto the pitcher; when the stone falls upon the pitcher, woe unto the pitcher; whatever befalls, woe unto the pitcher. Even if the bull have his head deep in his trough, hasten upon the roof and drag the ladder after you. Get your living by skinning carcasses in the street, if you cannot do otherwise, and do not say, I am a priest, I am a great man; this work would not befit my dignity. Youth is a garland of roses, age is a crown of thorns. Use a noble vase even for one day—let it break to morrow. The last thief is hanged first. Teach thy tongue to say, I do not know. The heart of our first ancestors was as large as the largest gate of the temple, that of the later ones like that of the next large one; ours is like the eye of a needle. Drink not, and you will not sin. Not what you say about yourself, but what others say. Not the place honours the man, but the man the place. The cat and the rat make peace over a carcase. A dog away from his native kennel dare not bark for seven years. He who walks daily over his estates finds a little coin each time. He who humiliates himself will be lifted up; he who raises himself will be humiliated. Whosoever runs after greatness, greatness runs away from him; he who runs from greatness, greatness follows him. He who curbs his wrath, his sins will be forgiven. Whosoever does not persecute them that persecute him, whosoever takes an offence in silence, he who does good because of love, he who is cheerful under his sufferings—they are the friends of God, and of them the Scripture says, And they shall shine forth as does the sun at noonday. Pride is like idolatry. Commit a sin twice, and you will think it perfectly allowable. When the end of a man is come, everybody lords it over him. While our love was strong, we lay on the edge of a sword; now it is no longer strong, a sixty-yard wide bed is too narrow for us. A Galilean said: When the shepherd is angry with his flock, he appoints to it a blind bell-wether. The day is short, and the work is great, but the labourers are idle, though the reward be great, and the master of the work presses. It is not incumbent upon thee to complete the work, but thou must not therefore cease from it. If thou hast worked much, great shall be thy reward, for the master who employed thee is faithful in his payment. But know that the true reward is not of this world. . . . . "—*Quarterly Review.*

THE TALMUD.

The Talmud is a commentary on the *Mishnah*, as the Mishnah is upon the *Law*. It is remarked by Dean Prideaux, that on the first publication of the *Mishnah*, several of the learned Jews began to employ themselves in writing commentaries on it; and from these were formed the two principal *Talmuds*; that written by the Jews of Jerusalem, about A.D. 300, called the *Jerusalem Talmud*, and that by the Jews of Babylon, about two hundred years after, called the *Babylonish Talmud*. The word Talmud is used to signify both itself, which is the *Comment*, and the *Mishnah*, which is the *Text* on which it is written.

Neither the Mishnah nor Talmud has been translated into English; but tracts, selections, and extracts have been made by different writers, for the purpose of illustrating the phraseology of the Scriptures, to which, in the hands of Lightfoot and others, they have been successfully applied.

The Talmud of Jerusalem was compiled by R. Jochanan. The Jews deeply engage themselves to stand by the Talmud and Mishnah. The Talmud of Babylon is their standard for rule and religion to this day. The Talmud has two parts, the Mishnah and Gemara. This is the Jews, Council of Trent—the foundation and ground-work of their religion. Rabbi Tanchum, the son of Hamlai, saith: "Let a man always part his life into three parts; a third for the Scriptures, a third for the Mishnah, and a third for the Gemara." Two for one—two parts for the Talmud, and one for the Scriptures. So highly do they, Papist-like, prize the vain traditions of men.

The word "Talmud" is the same in Hebrew, that "doctrine" is in Latin, and "doctrinal," in our usual speech. It is, (say the Jews), a commentary upon the written law of God. And both the law and this (say they), God gave to Moses; the law by day, in writing—and this, by night and by word of mouth. "Moses, they say, received the law from Sinai, and delivered it to Joshua, Joshua to the elders, the elders to the prophets, and the prophets of the great synagogue." And thus like a snow-ball, it grew bigger with going. Thus do they father their fooleries upon Moses, and elders, and prophets, who (good men) never thought of such fancies. Against this their traditional law, our Saviour makes part of his sermon on the Mount—Matt. 5. But he touched the Jews' freehold, when he touched their Talmud, for greater treasure in their conceits, they had none; like Cleopatra in Plutarch, making much of the viper that destroyed them.

The chief end of both Talmuds, the Jerusalem and Babylon, they say, is to explain the old Testament. We shall give an instance or two:— Judges ix, 13, it is said by the vine, " Shall I leave my wine, which cheereth God and man? How doth wine cheer God?" Rabbi Akiba saith : " Because men give God thanks for it." There they also question or controvert, " Whether a man should give thanks, or say grace, for his meat and drink, before he taste it?" And otherwise; " Whether a man may bless God for the sweet smell of incense, which he smells offered to idols?" " Whether a man may light a candle at another candle, that burns in a candlestick that hath images on it?" " Whether a man, at his devotions, if a serpent come and bite him by the heel, may turn and stoop to shake her off, or no?" Which question Rabbi Tanchum answers very profoundly, that " they must not so much as shake the foot to get a serpent off;" and gives a strong reason : " For (saith he) such a one was praying, and a serpent comes and catcheth him by the heel; he holds on his devotion and stirs not ; and presently the snake falls away stark dead, and the man not hurt."

For their allusions, take a piece out of the book Mincha.—" Our Rabbins teach, Israel is beloved because God hath favored them with phylacteries upon their heads and upon their arms, fringes upon their garments, and marks upon their doors. And concerning them, David saith, " Seven times a day do I praise thee, because of thy righteous judgments." At the time that David went into the bath, and saw himself naked, he said : " Woe is me, that I stand naked without the commandment, (or without my phylacteries)." But when he remembered the circumcision in his flesh, his mind was at quiet. Afterward, when he went out, he made a song of it, as it is said: " To him that excelleth upon Sheminith (or an eight) a Psalm of David;" because of the circumcision, that was given on the eighth day. Rabbi Eliezer, the son of Jacob, saith : " Whosoever hath phylacteries upon his head, and phylacteries upon his arm, and fringes upon his garments, and a mark on his door— all this will keep him from sinning ; as it is written, 'a threefold cord is not easily broken,' and he saith, the angel of the Lord pitcheth round about those that fear him, to deliver them."

The Talmud, has, alas ! shared the same fate, under which, even now, the Jewish nation suffers in most empires, in the Old World. It is well known that when one Israelite commits any wrong or crime, it is not said that X or Y has perpetrated an evil act, but what great rogues the Jews have proved themselves, or what a low and cunning people are the Jews!

The same misfortune befel the Talmud. If one or the other Rabbi has misspent his life with useless studies and sophisms, and in establishing paradoxical opinions, it is not said that this Rabbi was a sophist, but what a set of deceivers and fools have the Rabbi's been, or what a nonsense is the ancient Judaism.

Should one or the other superstitious view be found in the Gemara,—for instance, witchcraft and demons,—and should even one or the other injurious opinion have been expressed, they must, nevertheless, be regarded as nothing else except what they are in reality, namely, the errors of a few individuals, aberrations of the intellect, sprung from a few fanatics, from whom no religious sect is altogether free.

For instance, Christian theologians of the fifteenth century, busied themselves with the inquiry, whether God could commit a sin if He would; whether it would be possible for God to assume a human nature, and especially that of a woman. A very distinguished French theologian has shown the derivation of the word "Diabolus," in this way—"Dia" means "two," "bolus" "a bite," hence, "diabolus" two bites, because the devil makes only two bites when he would swallow us. The first is the body, the second is the soul. Again, there was a dispute by Christian theologians nearly three hundred years, whether in a certain prayer, if said in the German language, a pronoun must be said before or after the noun.

Unjust as it would be to conclude from this, that all Christian theologians of the fifteenth century whiled away their life in so foolish a manner; just so absurd would it be to reject, at the present day, the ancient Judaism, as represented in the Talmud, as sophistry, because some few Rabbi's were sophists.

It is true, it reads, *Sanhedrin*, p. 59—" Rabbi Johanan said: A Samaritan who studies the law, is guilty of death. Resh Lakish said: "A Samaritan who keeps the Sabbath, is guilty of death." But these strange statements of these two Rabbis, are contradicted by a most ancient passage: Rabbi Mair taught that a Gentile who studies the law of Moses should be as highly appreciated as the High Priest—(Sanhedrin 59, Baba Kamma, 58, &c.) Again it reads—Treat. Sabbath, 118: "Rabbi Chiza, son of Abba, taught, in the name of Rabbi Jochanan: "Whosoever keeps the Sabbath day holy, according to law, although he worshipped idols, like the generation of Enoch, his sins will be forgiven." Again, we read, Prikta Rabati, chapter 25 : "The Sabbath was commanded to Gentiles, in the first ten commandments, and to the Israelites, in the latter." Again, Treatise Chullin, 94, it reads : "Samuel taught, we dare not deceive anybody, not even an idolatrous person." Again, to the passage, Genesis xxii., 12 : "For now I know that thou fearest God," the Midrash Rabbah adds, "because our patriarch Abraham, of blessed memory, opened his house to all the heathens, and gave them food."

THE MISHNAH AND GEMARAH.

Rabbi Jehudah immortalized himself, by collecting and arranging, into systemmatic order, all the Rabbinical laws and explanations, as well as the remarks and expositions given in the various academies, during previous centuries. The ritual, ceremonial and judicial ordinances, had not heretofore been written down, but according to the custom of the time, they were orally handed over from one generation to the other. Rabbi Jehudah assumed the great work of reducing them to writing, for which purpose he used some works, prepared by Hillel, Rabbi Akiba, and by others. The innovation was decried by many a fanatic as heresy. They considered this Rabbinical collection an unlawful undertaking, and injurious to the Mosaic law. But Rabbi Jehudah, with undaunted courage, carried his views, maintaining that the tradition would be forgotten in the gloomy days of exile, unless collected in a written form. For the scattered remnants of the Jews were continuing to emigrate into the most distant countries; had to strain every nerve to earn a scanty living, and were thus prevented from frequenting the academies, and applying themselves to the study of law. Hence he preferred to reduce the tradition to writing, than to expose the whole to the risk of being misunderstood or forgotten. He finished his book about 180 A. D., called it the Mishnah (repetition of the law), divided it into six principal parts, *Sedarim*, each of these again into single books, called "Masechet." The collection of the Mishnah concludes the period of the Thanaim, (this was the collective name of all the Rabbis, from the days of Simon the Just, down to the times of Rabbi Jehudah.) The Rabbis and chiefs of Academies henceforth are called *Amoraim*, "commentators." The text of the Mishnah, however, was too vague, and did not provide for all emergencies, the letter of this new code was again subject to conflicting explanations. Unfavorable political circumstances prevented the correct study thereof, and soon many parts of it became subjects of spirited controversy to the following generations. The newly established academies did not take firm root. In the dark times of impending danger, youth found no time to study, and amidst the many alarming calamities, the civilization of the Jews could neither prosper nor advance. All the circumstances combined, contributed to render the Mishnah unintelligible, and new commentaries developing its contents, were called for. Rabbis of fame and distinction added to the Mishnah new remarks, called *Gemarah*, and both parts, Mishnah and Gemarah, constitute the Talmud. The contents of the Gemarah are the further deductions and explanations of the text of the Mishnah, corollaries of law and justice, ordinances against the trespass of the Mosaic law; customs and new institutions required by the emergencies of the time; debates on definition of the law; different opinions given in final decisions; historical tales, remarks, anecdotes and biographical notices. The Talmud is a kind of record of all that the Rabbis said and practised in the circle of their friends and families, as well as what they publicly taught in the academies.

There are two different Gemaras in existence, the *Hierosolomyton*, and the *Babylonian*. Rabbi Jochanan—about the year 370—a pupil of Rabbi Jehudah, collected the explanations on the Mishnah, and the new decisions, given by Rabbis of later times, into one work, called the Hierosolomyton Gemarah. The decisions, given by the other academies than that of Tiberias, are collected in the Babylonian Gemarah.

Rabbi Ashe, chief of the Babylonian academy of Sura, and his pupil, *Abina*, are said to have passed sixty years in the compilation of the Babylonian Gemarah, which gigantic work is divided into sixty books, according to the order of the books of the Mishnah. By and by several copies of this book were disseminated, among the various congregations, and as the continuous wars of the different nations interrupted, for a long time, the independent study and cultivation of the law, the Talmud, in course of time, assumed the importance of a canon.

Henceforth, the study of the Talmud was the chief and almost exclusive occupation of the Rabbis; it is universally regarded as the groundwork of the law, the compilation of all the sciences, and the source from which emanated the deepest researches, into all matters pertaining to the religious and civil ordinances of the Jewish people.

TALMUDICAL ITEMS.

The Authors of the Bible—(Old Testament.)

According to Treatise Baba Bathra, page 14, are the following: "Moses wrote his book, the chapter of Zilcam and Job; Joshua: his book, and *the last eight verses of the Pentateuch;* Samuel: his book, Judges and Ruth; David: the Psalms, (but assisted by others;) Jeremiah: his book, the Book of Kings, and the Lamentations; Hezekiah and his contemporaries collected: Isaiah, Proverbs, Canticles and Ecclesiastes; the Men of the Great Synagogue: Ezekiel, the Twelve Minor Prophets, Daniel and Esther; Ezra: his book, and the Chronicles."

CHAPTER IV.

TEACHINGS OF THE RABBIES.

Consisting of various proverbs or moral sayings selected from the teachings of the most celebrated Rabbies of all ages.

TEACHINGS OF THE RABBIES.

Moses received the law from Sinai, and delivered it to Joshua; and Joshua to the elders, and the elders to the prophets; and the prophets to the men of the great Synagogue. They said three things: "be deliberate in judgment; train up many disciples, and make a fence for the law."

Simon the Just was the last of the men of the great synagogue. He used to say, that the world existed by virtue of three things, viz.: the law, the temple service, and acts of beneficence.

Antigonous of Socho, received the *oral law* from Simon the Just. He used to say, be not like servants who serve their master for the sake of receiving a reward; but be like servants who serve their master without a view of receiving a reward; and let the fear of heaven be upon you.

Jose Ben Jozer, of Tseredah, and Jose Ben Jochanan, of Jerusalem, received the *oral law* from them. Jose Ben Joezer, of Tseredah, said: Let thy house be the house of assembly for the wise men; and dust thyself with the dust of their feet; and drink their words in thirstiness. Jose Ben Jochanan, of Jerusalem, said: Let thy house be wide open; and let the poor be thy domestic servants; and be not prone to much discourse with women-kind; not even with thy wife, much less with thy neighbour's wife; hence the wise men say, whoever converses much with women, bringeth evil on himself, and thus neglects the study of the law, and at last will inherit hell. Joshua Ben Perechiah, and Natai, the Arbelite, received it from them. Joshua Ben Perechiah said: Procure thyself a master, and obtain an associate; and judge all mankind favourably. Natai, the Artelite, said: Withdraw from an evil neighbour, and associate not with the wicked; neither flatter thyself to escape punishment. Judah Ben Tabai said: Consider not thyself as the arranger of the law, and when the parties are before thee in judgment, consider them as guilty; but, when they have departed from thee, consider them as innocent, when they have acquiesced in the sentence. Simeon Ben Shetach said: Be extremely careful in the examination of the witnesses, and be cautious in thy words, least they from thence should learn to utter a falsehood. Shemaiah and Abtalyon received it from them; Shemaiah said: Love thy business, and hate dominion; and thus make thyself not known to government. Abtalyon said: Yes, sages, be cautious of your words, least ye be doomed to captivity, and carried captive to a place of infected waters, and the disciples who follow you should drink of them, by which means the name of God may be profaned. Hillel and Shamai received it from them; Hillel said: Be of the disciples of Aaron, who loved peace, and pursued peace; so that thou love mankind, and allure them to the study of the law; he used to say, whoever is ambitious of agrandizing his name, destroys his name, and who doth not increase in the knowledge of the law shall be cut off; and who doth not study the law, is deserving of death; and he who serves himself with the crown of the law, will be consumed. He also said, if I perform not good works myself, who can do them for me? and when I fully consider myself, what am I? and if not now, when shall I? Shamai said: Let thy study of the law be fixed; say little, and do much; and receive all men with an open, respectable countenance. Rabban Gamliel said: Procure thyself an instructor, that thou mayest not be in doubt; and accustom not thyself to give tythes by conjecture. Simeon, his son, said: I have all my life been brought up among the wise men, and never found anything so salutary to the well-being of the body as silence; neither is the study of the law the principal, but the practice thereof: and whoever is profuse of words causeth sin. Rabban Simeon Ben Gamliel said: The duration of the world depends on three things: viz., justice, truth, and peace; as it is said, truth, and the judgment of peace, shall be in your gates.

Rabbi Chananya Ben Akashya said: Thy blessed God was pleased to render Israel meritorious; he therefore multiplied the law and the precepts, as it is said, the Lord was pleased for his righteousness sake, to magnify the law and adorn it.

Rabbi saith: Which is the most eligible path for man to make choice of? all such as are an ornament to those who tread therein; and procureth them honour from mankind. Be also careful of the observance of a light precept, as a weighty one; because thou knowest not the due reward of the precepts; and balance the loss sustained by the non-performance of a precept against its recompense; and the reward of sin against its loss of happiness. Consider also three things, and thou wilt not commit sin. Understand what is above thee; an all-seeing eye, and a hearing ear, and that all thine actions are written in a book. Rabban Gamliel, the son of Natti Judah Hanase, said: That the study of the law, and the commerce of the world, are commendable together; as the conjunction of those two annihilates sin; and all study of the law, that is not supported by business, will become of non-effect, and will be the cause of sin; and whoever is engaged in the service of the congregation, ought to act for God's sake; then will the merit of their ancestors support them, and their charitable deeds exist to eternity, and I shall account ye deserving of a great recompense, as if ye had actually done it. Be ye warned of following princes (or courtiers), as they do not bestow favours on men but for their own interest; they shew themselves as friends, while they are useful to them; but will not support a man in the time of need. He used to say, do his will, as if it was thine own will; that may accomplish thy will, is, as if it was his will. Hillel said: Seperate not thyself from the congregation; nor have confidence in thyself until the death. Judge not thy neighbour till thou art in his situation; neither utter a sentence, as if it was incomprehensible, that afterwards may be comprehended; nor say when I shall have leisure I will study, lest thou shouldest not have leisure. He also said, a poor cannot be a fearful sin, nor can a rustic be a saint; the bashful will not become learned, nor the passionate a teacher; neither will he who is much engaged in traffic become wise; and where there are no instructing men, strive thou to be a man. He having also seen a skull floating on the water, said, because thou didst make others float, have they floated thee! and the end of those who made thee float, will be that they will also float. He also said, he who increaseth his flesh, multiplieth food for worms; he who augmenteth riches, multiplieth care; he who multiplieth wives, increaseth witchcraft; he who multiplieth female servants, increaseth lewdness; he who multiplieth men servants, increaseth robbery; but he who augmenteth his knowledge of the law, augmenteth life; he who augmenteth his study in College, increaseth wisdom; he who multiplieth counsel, increaseth prudence; he who augmenteth justice, multiplieth peace; if he had thus acquired a good name, he hath acquired it for himself; if he hath acquired a pure doctrine of the law, he hath obtained for himself immortal life in a future state. Rabbi Jochanan Ben Zacchai, received it from Hillel and Shamai; he frequently said: If thou hast spent much time in the study of the law, yet pride not thyself therein; for, for that only wast thou created. Rabbi Jochanan Ben Zacchia had five disciples; and these are they: Rabbi Eleazar Ben

Hyrcanus, Rabbi Joshua Ben Chananya, Rabbi Jose, the Priest, Rabbi Simeon Ben Nathaneal, Rabbi Eleazar Ben Arach. He used thus to appreciate their merit, viz., Eleazer Ben Hyrcanus is a well plastered pit, which loseth not a drop; Joshua Ben Chananya, happy are they who begat him; Jose, the Priest, is a saint; Simeon Ben Nathaneal feareth sin; Eleazar Ben Arach is a powerful spring. He used to say: If all the sages of Israel were in one scale of the balance, and Rabbi Eleazer Ben Hyrcanus in the other, he would overbalance them all. Abba Saul said, in his name, if all the sages of Israel were in one scale, and even Rabbi Eleazer Ben Hyrcanus with them, and Rabbi Eleazer Ben Arach in the other, he would overbalance them all. He also said to them: Go forth, and consider which is the good path for man to adhere to; to this Rabbi Eleazer answered, a good eye; Rabbi Joshua said, a worthy associate; Rabbi Jose said, a good neighbour; Rabbi Simeon said, he who forsees the consequences of an undertaking; Rabbi Eleazer said, a benevolent heart. He then said unto them: I prefer the sentiment of Rabbi Eleazer Ben Arach above yours, as his words include the whole of yours. He also said unto them: Go forth, and consider which is the evil way that man should shun; to which Rabbi Eleazer said, an evil eye; Rabbi Joshua said, an evil associate; Rabbi Jose said, an evil neighbour; Rabbi Simeon said, he who borroweth, and payeth not; for when one borroweth of man it is equal as if he borrowed from God; as it is said: The wicked borroweth, and payeth not again; but the righteous sheweth kindness and giveth. Rabbi Eleazer said, an evil heart. He then said unto them: I prefer the sentiment of Rabbi Eleazer Ben Arach above yours, as his words include the whole of yours. They also said three things: Rabbi Eleazer said: Let the honour of thy associate be as dear to thee as thine own; and be not easily moved to anger; and repent one day preceding thy decease; and warm thyself by the fire of the sages; but be careful that their bite is as the bite of a fox, and their sting as the sting of a scorpion, and their burn as the burn of a fiery serpent; and all their words as fiery coals. Rabbi Joshua said: An evil eye, an evil imagination, and misanthropy, cause the death of man. Rabbi Jose said: Let thy associate's property be as dear to thee as thine own, prepare thyself to study the law, as it cometh not to thee by inheritance; and let all thine actions be in the name of God. Rabbi Simeon said: Be careful of reading the Shemang, and the other prayers; and when thou art praying, consider not thy prayer as ordinary, but as supplicating mercy in the presence of the Supreme; as it is said, for he is merciful and gracious, long suffering, and of abundant kindness, and repenteth of the evil; and depreciate not thyself in thine own mind. Rabbi Eleazer said: Be expeditious to study the law, that thou mayest know how to confute the epicurean; consider also, in whose presence thou art labouring, and in whose service thou art employed, who will pay thee the reward of thy labour. Rabbi Tarphon said: The day is short, but the labour is much, and the labourers slothful; though the reward is great, and the master of the house presseth for dispatch. He used to say, it is not incumbent on thee to complete the work, neither art thou at liberty to abstain wholly from it; if thou hast diligently studied the law, thou wilt receive great reward; for the master who employed thee, is faithful to pay thee the reward of thy labour, but know that the payment of the reward of the righteous is in a future state. Akdbea Ben Mahalallel said: Ponder on three things, and thou wilt not be led to the commission of sin; consider from whence thou comest, and whither thou goest, and in whose presence thou must in futurity render an account in judgment. From whence comest thou? from a fœtid drop; and whither art thou going? to a place of dust, worms, and reptiles; and in whose presence art thou in futurity to render an account in judgment? even before the Holy Supreme King of Kings, blessed is he. Rabbi Chaneena, a priest of the second order, said: Pray for the peace of the kingdom, for were it not in deference thereof, men would swallow each other alive. Two who are sitting together, and have no discourse concerning the law, are accounted to an assembly of scorners; as is said: In the seat of the scorners do not sit. But two who sit together, and discourse of the law, the Divine Presence may be said to rest on them; as is said: Then they who feared the Lord spake every one to his neighbour, and the Lord gave ear and heard; and a book of remembrance was written before him, for them who feared the Lord, and for them who thought on His name. This refers to two; but whence can we infer, that if but one sits engaged in the study of the law, that the holy, blessed God will appoint him a reward. Because it is said: Let him sit alone and be silent, because he has laid it upon him. Rabbi Simeon saith: Three who have eaten at one table, and have not discoursed on the subject of the law, are to be considered as if they had eaten of the sacrifices of idols; for it is said: For all their tables are full of vomit and filthiness, so that no place is free. But three who have eaten at one table, and have discoursed on the subject of the law, are considered as if they had eaten at God's table; as it is said: And he said unto me, this is the table which is before the Lord. Rabbi Nechunya Ben Hakana said: Whoever lays on himself the yoke of the law, shall be relieved from the yoke of the kingdom, and the custom of the world; but, whoever divests himself of the yoke of the law, shall be burdened with the yoke of the kingdom, and the custom of the world. Rabbi Chaneena Ben Chacheenai said: he who walketh in (or all) the night, travelleth in the road alone, and turneth his heart to vanity, is guilty of his own soul. Rabbi Chalaphta, an inhabitant of the village of Chananya, said: Ten who are assembled together, and engaged in the study of the law, the Shechina presideth among them; as it is said: God standeth in the congregation of the mighty; and hence it is inferred, that it is also with fire; because it is said, and hath founded his troop on (or above) the earth. And hence it is said, that it is likewise so with three; because it is said, he judgeth among judges; and hence it is inferred, that it is also with two; because it is said: They who feared the Lord, spake every one to his neighbour; and the Lord gave ear and heard; and hence it is inferred that it is likewise so with one; because it is said: In every place where I record my name, I will come unto thee, and I will bless thee. Rabbi Eleazer, an inhabitant of Bartotha, said: Give unto Him (God) of His own; for thou, and all thou possessest, are His. And thus said David, for all things are from thee; and from the gift of thine hands have we given unto Thee. Rabbi Jacob said: He who journeyeth on the road, meditating on the law, and ceaseth therefrom, in order to admire this beautiful tree, or that handsome village, is considered in scripture, as endangering his life. Rabbi Dorsethai, the son of Jonai, in the name of Myer, said: Whoever forgetteth anything of what he had obtained by study, is considered in scripture as having endangered his life; as is said: Only take heed to thyself, and guard thy soul dilligently, lest thou forget the things which thine eyes have seen. Perhaps you may imagine, that even his study has been too powerful for him. No, because it is said, and lest they be put away from thy heart all the days of thy life. Hence, he endangers not his life, till he deliberately removes them from his heart. Rabbi Chaneena Den Dose, said: Whosoever's fear of sin hath precedency of his wisdom, his wisdom will be permanent; but whosoever's wisdom hath precedency of his fear of sin, his wisdom will not be permanent. He also used to say, whosoever's good deeds exceed his wisdom, his wisdom will be permanent; but he whose wisdom exceedeth his good works, his wisdom will not be permanent. He also used to say, with whomsoever the spirit of mankind is gratified, the spirit of the Supreme is also gratified; but with whomsoever the spirit of mankind is not gratified, the spirit of the Supreme is not gratified. Rabbi Dose Ben Harchenas said: That the morning sleep, wine at noon, the conversation of youth, and the assembly of the ignorant, take men out of the world. Rabbi Eleazer Hamodai said; He who profaneth the holy offerings, despiseth the solemn feasts, puts his neighbor to shame in public, maketh void the covenant of our father Abraham, and explaineth the law contrary to its true sense. Although he be well learned in the law, and possessed of good deeds, yet hath he no share in the future state. Rabbi Ishmael said: Be humble to thy superior, and affable to thy inferior, and receive all mankind with joy. Rabbi Akeeba said: Laughter and levity accustom mankind to lewdness; tradition is a fence to the law; tithes are a fence to riches; vows are a fence to absence; the fence to wisdom is silence. He used to say: Man is beloved, as he was created in the image of God; but an additional love was shown to him, in that he was created in the image of God; as is said, in the image of God he made man. Beloved are Israel, in that they are called the children of God; but an additional love was shown to them, in that they are actually called the children of God; as is said: Ye are the children of the Lord your God. Beloved are Israel, to whom was given the desirable vessel, wherewith the world was created; as is said: for I give you good doctrine, therefore forsake ye not my law. Everything is seen by Providence, though of choice is given to man; the world is judged in goodness, though all is according to the multiplicity of the deed. He used to say, everything is given to man on security, and a net is spread over every living creature; the shop is open, the merchant credits; the book is open, and the hand records; and whoever chooses to borrow—for the collectors are continually going round daily, and obtain payment of man, whether with his consent, or without it—as they have good authority to support them, and the judgment is true justice, and all are prepared for the feast. Rabbi Eleazer Ben Azarya said: If there is no knowledge of the law, there can be no good manners; and if no manners, there certainly is no law; if there is no wisdom, there is no fear of God; and if there is no fear, there is no wisdom; if there is no understanding, there is no knowledge; and if there is no knowledge there is no understanding; if there is no meal, there can be no study of the law, and if there is no law there will be no meal. He used to say: To what may he be likened, whose wisdom exceedeth his good deeds? To a tree whose branches are multiplicious, and its roots scanty, so that the wind cometh, and plucketh it up and overturneth it, as said: For he shall be like a blasted tree upon the waste, which is not sensible when good cometh, but is continually exposed to scorching heats in the desert, a barren land, and uninhabitable. But to what is he like, whose good deeds exceed his wisdom? To a tree whose branches are few and its roots multifarious, so that if the most violent tempest discharges its fury against it, it will not be able to move it from its place; as is said: For he shall be like a tree planted by the water side, which, by the side of the stream, sendeth forth its roots, and is not sensible when heat cometh, but its leaf is green, and in a year of drought, it is without concern, nor doth it decline bearing fruit. Rabbi Eleazer Ben Chisma said: The laws of the sacrifices of the doves, and the commencement of the menses, are important constitutions; astronomy and geometry are the ornaments of wisdom.

Ben Zoma said: Who is wise? he who is willing to receive instruction from all men; as is said: Of all my teachers I gathered understanding. Who is mighty? he who endureth his evil imagination; as is said: He who is slow to anger is better than the mighty, and who ruleth his spirit than he who taketh a city. Who is rich? he who rejoiceth with his lot; as it is said: For thou shalt eat the labour of thy hands; then happy shalt thou be, and it shall be well with thee; happy shalt thou be in this world; and it shall be well with thee in the future one. Who is honourable? he who honoureth mankind; as it is said: for they who honour me, I will honour; and they who despise me shall be lightly esteemed. Ben Azai said: Run to the performance of the slightest precept, and flee from the commission of sin; for the performance of a precept causeth another, and the commission of a sin causeth another sin; as the reward of a commandment is another precept, and the reward of a sin is another sin. He used to say: Despise not all men, nor oppose all things; for there is no man who hath not his hour, neither is there a thing that hath not its place. Rabbi Lesee Tas, an inhabitant of Jabna, said: Be exceedingly humble of spirit, as all the hope of man is to be food for worms. Rabbi Jonannan Ben Beroka said: Whosoever profaneth God's name in secret, will be punished publicly; whether it be done ignorantly or presumptiously, it is all one in the profanation of God's name. Rabbi Ishmael said: He who learneth, that he may be able to teach others, will be enabled to study and to teach others; but he who studieth in order to perform the precepts, will be enabled to study, teach, observe, and do the commandments. Rabbi Zadoc said: Make not the study of the law subservient to thy aggrandizement; neither make a hatchet therefore, to hew therewith. And thus said Kullel: Whosoever receiveth any profit (or emolument) from the words of the law, depriveth himself of life. Rabbi Jose said:

He who honoureth the law shall be personally honoured by mankind; but whosoever profaneth the law shall be personally despised by mankind. Rabbi Ishmael said. He who avoids being a judge, delivereth himself from enmity, robbery, and false swearing; but he who is arrogant in judging, is a proud, wicked fool. He used to say: Judge not singly by thyself, for none ought to judge but ONE; neither say authoritatively: Receive ye my opinion, for they are at liberty to accept it, but thou canst not compel them. Rabbi Jonathan said: Whosoever performeth the law in poverty, shall in the end perform it in riches; but he who neglects the law on account of riches, will, in the end, neglect it on account of poverty. Rabbi Hyer said: Diminish your worldly affairs, and engage in the study of the law, and be humble spirited in the presence of all men; and if thou neglect the law, there are many hindrances to oppose thee; but if thou hast laboured in the study of the law, there is much recompense to be given thee. Rabbi Eliezer, the son of Jacob, said: He who performeth but one precept, obtaineth for himself an advocate; and he who commits a single sin, procures himself an accuser; repentance and good deeds are a shield before the divine punishment. Rabbi Johanan, the shoemaker, said: Every assembly that is formed for God's sake, will be permanent, but those which are not for God's sake, will not be durable. Rabbi Eleazer Ben Shammang said: Let the honour of thy disciple be as dear to thee as thine own, and the honour of thy companion as the fear of thy master, and the fear of thy master as the fear of thy God. Rabbi Judah said: Be careful in the study of the law, for the error of it is accounted as presumptious sin. Rabbi Simeon said: There are three crowns; the crown of the law, the crown of the priesthood, and the crown of the monarchy, but the crown of a good name is superior to all of them. Rabbi Neporay said: Flee to a place where the law is studied, and do not say that it will follow thee; for thy associates will establish it for thee; and depend not on thine own understanding. Rabbi Yanai said: we experience not the prosperity of the enriched, nor the chastisements of the righteous. Rabbi Mathyta Ben Charash said: Be forward to greet all men; and be rather at the tail of the lion than the head of the foxes. Rabbi Jacob said: This world may be likened to a court-yard, in comparison with the future world; therefore, prepare thyself in the ante-chamber, that thou mayest enter into the dining-room. He used to say: One hour employed in repentance and good deeds in this world, is preferable to the whole life in the future one; and one hour's refreshment of spirit in the future one, is preferable to the entire life of this. Rabbi

Simeon Ben Eleazer said: Attempt not to pacify your neighbour in the moment of his anger; and do not console him while his dead lieth before him; enquire not of him in the moment of his vowing; nor be desirous of seeing him in the time of his calamity. The meek Saul used to say, rejoice not when thine enemy falleth, and let not thine heart be glad when he stumbleth; lest the Lord should see it, and it be evil in his sight, and he turn his wrath from him. Elisha Ben Abuya said: He who teaches a child, is like to one who writes on clean paper; but he who teaches old people, is like to one who writes on blotted paper. Rabbi Jose, the son of Judah, an inhabitant of a village near Babylon, said. To what may he who learneth the law from little children, be likened? To one who eateth sour grapes, and drinketh new wine; but he who learneth from the old man, may be compared to one who eats ripe grapes, and drinks old wine. Rabbi Myer said: Look not at the flask, but that which is therein; for there are new flasks full of old wine, and old flasks which have not even new wine in them. Rabbi Eleazer Hakkapar said: Envy, lust, and ambition, take men out of the world. He used to say, those who are born, are doomed to die, the dead to live, and they who are risen from the dead, to be judged; to make us know, understand and be informed, that he is God; he is the Former, Creator, intelligent *being*, Judge, witness, and suing party; and who will judge thee hereafter; for in His presence there is no unrighteousness, forgetfulness, respect of persons, nor acceptance of a bribe; for everything is His. Know, also, that everything is done according to the account: and let not thine evil imagination persuade thee, that the grave is a place of refuge for thee; for against thy will wast thou formed, and against thy will wast thou born; and against thy will dost thou live; and against thy will must thou hereafter render an account, and receive judgment, in the presence of the supreme King of kings, the holy God, blessed is he.

With ten expressions the world was created; but wherefore is this predicted, for verily God could have created it with one expression? but this was to punish the wicked, who destroy the world, that was created with ten expressions. There were ten generations from Adam to Noah, to make us know that God is long-suffering, as all those generations provoked him before he brought the deluge upon them. There were ten generations from Noah to Abraham, to shew us that God is long-suffering; as all those succeeding generations provoked him, until Abraham appeared and received the reward of all. Our father Abraham was proved with ten proofs, and in all of them he stood firm; and which shows how great the love of our father Abraham was towards God. Ten miracles were wrought for our ancestors in Egypt, and ten at the Red Sea. Ten plagues did the blessed God inflict on the Egyptians in Egypt, and ten at the Red Sea. Ten times did our ancestors tempt the blessed God, in the Wilderness, as is said: And have tempted Me now these ten times, and have not hearkened unto My voice. Ten miracles were wrought for our ancestors in the holy temple, viz: no woman miscarried from the scent of the flesh of the sacrifices, neither did the flesh of the sacrifices ever stink; nor was a fly ever seen in the slaughter house; nor did an unclean accident happen to the high priest on the Day of Atonement, neither did the rain extinguish the fire of wood arranged on the altar, nor did the wind prevent the straight ascension of the pillar of smoke; neither was there any defect found in the omer, the two loaves, and the shew bread. And although the people stood close pressed together, yet, when they worshipped there was room sufficient, neither did a serpent or scorpion injure a person in Jerusalem; nor did a man say to his neighbor, I have not room to lodge in Jerusalem. Ten things were created on the eve of the Sabbath in the twilight, and these are they; the mouth of the earth, the mouth of the ass, the mouth of the spring, the rainbow, the manna, the rod of Moses, the Shameer, the characters, writing and the tables. And some say, also, the demons, and the grave of our legislator Moses, and the ram of our father Abraham, and also the prepared instrument of a tongs.

Seven things are to be met with in a rude person, and seven in a wise man. The wise man will not speak before one who exceeds him in wisdom and years, nor will he interrupt his neighbour in his discourse; neither is he in haste to answer. He enquireth according to the subject, and answereth according to the constitution; and will answer the first proposition first, and the latter last; and what he hath not heard he will acknowledge he hath not heard, and confesseth the truth; and the reverse of these are to be met in a rude person. Seven sorts of punishment are brought on the world for seven important sins! For when a part of the people give tithes, and the other doth not, a scarcity and dearth ensues, so that some are filled, and others suffer hunger; but when the whole agree not to give tithes, a famine of dearth and confusion ensues. If they offer not up the cake, a confusion and fire ensues. Pestilence cometh into the world, for the commission of sins said to be punishable with death in the law, but are not cognizable by our judges; and, for not observing the law concerning the fruits of the seventh year. The sword entereth the world on account of the delay of justice, and the perversion thereof; and on account of those who explain the law contrary to the true sense thereof. Evil devouring beasts come into the world on account of false swearing, and the profanation of God's name. Captivity entereth the world on account of idolatry, whoredom, bloodshed, and not suffering the land to rest on the Sabbatical Year. At four seasons the pestilence is prevalent; in the fourth year, the seventh, and the end of the seventh, and the end of the feast of tabernacles in every year. In the fourth year, for not giving the poor's tithe of the third year; in the seventh, for withholding the poor's tithe of the sixth year, and at the end of the seventh, on account of the fruits of the seventh year; and at the end of the feast of tabernacles yearly, on account of robbing the poor of the gifts due to them.

Four qualities are to be met with among mankind, he who saith: That which is mine is mine, and that which is thine is thine, is a passable custom; and some say this was the custom of Sodom. He who saith: What is thine is mine, and what is mine is thine, is the behaviour of the vulgar. He who saith: What is mine is thine, and what is thine is also thine, is the custom of the pious. He who saith: What is mine is mine, and what is thine is mine also, is the custom of the wicked. There are four different forms in the passions of mankind. He who is easily provoked, and easily pacified, loses more than he gains; he whom it is difficult to provoke, and difficult to pacify, gains more than he loses; he whom it is difficult to provoke, and easy to pacify, is pious; but he who is easily provoked and with difficulty pacified, acts wickedly.

There are four qualities perceivable in disciples, viz.: he who is quick to apprehend and quick to forget, looses more than he gains: he who with difficulty forgets, gains more than he looses; he who apprehends quickly, and with difficulty forgets, hath a good portion; he who with difficulty apprehends, and quickly forgets, hath an evil portion. There are four qualities perceivable in those who bestow charity. He who is willing to give, but does not wish that others should give, hath an envious eye towards others; he who likes to see others give, but will not give, hath an evil eye towards himself; he who is willing to give, and that others should also give, acts piously; he who will not give, and likes not that others should give, acts wickedly. Four qualities are perceivable in those who go to college. He who goeth, but doth not study, can but claim the reward of going; he who studieth and doth not go, is entitled to the reward of action; he who goeth and studieth, is pious; he who neither goeth nor studieth, is a wicked man. There are four qualities to be met with in those who attend to hear the instruction of the sages, viz.: those who act as a sponge, a funnel, a strainer, and a sieve: as a sponge, which sucketh all up; as a funnel, which receiveth at one end and dischargeth at the other; as a strainer, which letteth the wine pass, but retaineth the lees; and as a sieve, which dischargeth the bran, but retaineth the fine flour. Every affection that depends on some sensual, worldly cause, if that cause ceaseth, the affection ceaseth; but that which doth not depend on such cause, will never cease. Where do we meet with an affection dependent on a sensual cause? Such was the love of Ammon to Tamar; but that which doth not depend on such a cause, was the love of David and Jonathan. Every dispute that is instituted for God's sake, will be in the end established; but that which is not for God's sake, will not be established. What may be considered as a dispute for God's sake? Such as the disputes of Hillel and Shamai; but which is not for God's sake, was the dissension of Korah and his assembly. He who justifieth the public, no sin will be caused through his means; and whosoever causeth the public to sin, is not suffered to repent. Moses acted meritoriously, and caused the public to obtain merit; the merit of the public was attributed to him, as is said: He executed the justice of the Lord, and his judgments with Israel. Jeroboam, the son of Nebat, sinned, and caused Israel to sin. The sin of the public was attributed to him, as is said, because of the sins of Jeroboam which he sinned, and which he made Israel sin. He who possesseth those three virtues, is of the disciples of our father Abraham; and he who is possessed of the three opposites, is of the disciples of the wicked Balaam. The disciples of our father Abraham possess a benevolent eye, a humility of spirit; and a humble, contented mind. The disciples of Balaam have an evil eye, a haughty spirit, and a narrow mind. What is the difference between the disciples of our father Abraham, and the disciples of the wicked Balaam? The disciples of our father Abraham eat the fruit of their good works in this world, and inherit the future one; for it is said: That I may cause those that love me, to inherit subsistence, and I will fill their treasures. But the disciples of the wicked Balaam inherit Gehinnam, and the infernal regions, as is said: But Thou, O God, shalt bring them down into the pit of destruction: bloody and deceitful men shall not live out half their day, but I will trust in Thee.

Judah Ben Tamai said: Be bold as a leopard, light as an eagle, swift as a roe, and strong as a lion, to do the will of thy Father, who is in heaven. He used to say, the impudent are for Gehinnam; and the modest for Paradise. May it be acceptable in thy presence, O Lord, our God, and the God of our fathers, that the holy temple may speedily be rebuilt in our days, and let our portion be in Thy law. He also said, at five years a child should study the Bible; at ten, the Mishnah; at thirteen, to observe the precepts; at fifteen, to study Gemarah; at eighteen, to enter into wedlock; at twenty, to pursue the study of the law, and the observance of the precepts; at thirty, he is arrived at full strength; at forty, he is arrived at all understanding; at fifty, to give counsel; at sixty, he is accounted aged; at seventy, he is called grey; at eighty, he may be accounted strong; at ninety, only fit to discourse of the law; at a hundred, as if already dead, and forgotten from the world. Ben Bag Bag said: Ponder and ponder again on the law, for all things are contained therein; contemplate it perpetually, and depart not therefrom; for there is no quality preferable to it. Ben Hea Hea said: According to the affliction which thou wilt endure, so shall be thy recompense.

The sages learned in the language of the Mishnah; blessed is he who made the choice of them and their learning. Rabbi Myer said: He who is engaged in the study of the law for its own sake, meriteth many things; and not only that, but the whole world is under the greatest obligation to him. He is called a dear friend; dear to God, and dear to mankind, he rejoiceth God, and rejoiceth his creatures; it clotheth him with meekness and the fear of God; and directeth him to become just, pious, righteous, and faithful; it removeth him from sin, and bringeth him nearer to merit; and the world is benefitted by his counsel, sound wisdom, understanding, and strength; as is said: Counsel is mine, and sound wisdom; I am understanding, I have strength. It also bestoweth on him empire, dominion, and ratiocination; the hidden secrets of the law are revealed to him; and he shall be as an increasing fountain, and a never-failing river; and it will cause him to be modest, slow to anger, and ready to pardon an injury done to him; thus will it magnify and exalt him above all things. Rabbi Joshua Ben Levi said: Every day, a Bath-kol proceedeth from Mount Horeb, which proclaimeth and saith, woe be those who contemn the law, for whoever is not engaged in the study of the law, may be considered as under excommunication; as is said: As a jewel of gold in a swine's snout, so is a fair woman, who is without discretion. And it is said: And the tables were the work of God, and the writing the writing of God, graven upon the tables. Read not graven, but freedom; for none are accounted free, but those engaged in the study of the law; and whoever is engaged in the study of the law, is exalted; as mentioned: And from Mattanah to Nachliel, &c. He who learneth from his associate one chapter, sentence, verse, or expression, ought to behave toward him with respect; for thus we find by David, King of Israel, who having learned only two things from Ahithopel, called him his teacher, preceptor, and friend; as is said: But it was thou, a man, mine equal, my guide, and my friend. Hence it may be deduced, that if David, King of Israel, who learned but two things of Ahithopel, called him his rabbi, preceptor, and friend, how much more ought he who learneth from his fellow, a single chapter, sentence, verse, or expression, to show him the utmost respect? But this honour is naught, but the knowledge of the law; as is said: The wise shall inherit glory, and the perfect shall inherit the good, but nothing is really good, but the law; as is said: For I give you good doctrine, forsake you not my law. Thus is the law to be observed: Thou shalt eat bread and salt, and water by measure shalt thou drink; on the earth shalt thou sleep, and a life of trouble shalt thou live, and shalt labour in the study of the law. If thou actest thus, thou shalt be happy, and it shall be well with thee; thou shalt be happy in this world, and it shall be well with thee in the future one. Seek not grandeur to thyself, neither covet more honor than thy learning meriteth; perform the precepts, and crave not after the tables of kings; for thy table is greater than theirs, and thy crown is greater than their crown, and the master who employeth thee, is faithful to pay thee the reward of thy labour. The law is more excellent than the priesthood and royalty; for royalty is acquired by thirty properties, and the priesthood by twenty-four; but the law is acquired by forty-eight things, and these are they, viz: With study, attention, eloquence, an understanding heart, an intelligent heart, with dread and meekness, fear, and joy; with attendance on the sages, the acuteness of associates, and disputations of the disciples; with sedateness, the study of the Bible, and the Mishnah; in purity, in taking little sleep, in using little discourse, in being little engaged in traffic, in taking little sport, in enjoying little delight, and little worldly manner, in being slow to anger, in having a good heart, in having faith in the sages, and in bearing chastisements; in being sensible of his situation, and to rejoice in his portion; in being circumspect in his language, in not pretending to pre-eminence, in sincerely loving God, and loving his creatures; in loving admonition, and that which is right; in avoiding honour, and not priding himself on his acquired knowledge, nor rejoicing in pronouncing sentence; in bearing the burden equally with his neighbour, and inclining him to merit, and confirming him in truth, and in peace is sedate in his study, enquireth according to the subject, and answereth according to the constitution;

is attentive to study, and attendeth it; learneth it with a view to the teaching of others, and also with a view to perform the precepts; increaseth his preceptor's knowledge, and is attentive to his instruction; and reporteth everything in the name of the person who predicted it; hence it is inferred that whoever reports anything in the name of the person who affirmed it, procureth redemption for the world; as is said: And Esther certified the king thereof in Mordecai's name. Great is the law, which bestoweth life on the observers thereof, both in this world and in the future one; as is said: For they are life unto those who find them, and health unto all their flesh. And it is said: It shall be health to thy navel and marrow of thy bones. And it is said: It is a tree of life to those who lay hold on it, and the supporters thereof are happy. And it is said: For they shall be an ornament of grace to thine head, and chains about thy neck. And it is said: She shall give an ornament of grace to thine head; a crown of glory shall she deliver to thee. And it is said: Length of days are in her right hand, and in its left are riches and honour. And it is said: For length of days and long life, and peace shall they add to thee. Rabbi Simeon Ben Judah, in the name of Rabbi Simeon Ben Jocai, said: Beauty, strength, riches, honour, wisdom, age, hoariness, and many children, are suitable to the righteous, and agreeable to the world. As is said: The hoary head is a crown of glory, if it be found in the way of righteousness. And it is said: The glory of young men is their strength; and the beauty of old men is the grey head. And it is said: And the moon shall be confounded, and the sun shall be ashamed; for the Lord of Hosts shall reign on Mount Zion, and in Jerusalem, and before his ancients shall be glory. Rabbi Simeon Ben Menasya said: Those seven qualities which the sages enumerate as proper for the righteous, were all accomplished in the person of the Rabbi and his children. Rabbi Jose Ben Kishma said: I was once travelling on the road, and met a certain person who saluted me with peace, and I returned his salutation; he then said unto me, Rabbi, whence art thou? I answered him, from a great city, abounding in sages and scribes. Said he unto me, If thou art willing to dwell with us, in our city, then I will give thee a thousand thousand golden deenars; to this I answered him, If thou wouldest give me all the gold and silver in the universe, I would not dwell but in a place where the law is studied, because, at the time of a man's departure from this world, he is not accompanied either with silver or gold, but with the law and good deeds only; as is said: When thou goest, it shall lead thee; when thou sleepest, it shall keep thee; and when thou awakest, it shall talk with thee; when thou goest, it shall lead thee, that is, in this world; when thou sleepest, it shall watch over thee in the grave; and when thou awakest, it shall talk with thee in the future world. And thus it is written in the book of Psalms, by the hand of David, king of Israel: The law of Thy mouth is better to me than thousands of gold and silver. And it is said: The silver is mine, and the gold is mine, saith the Lord of Hosts. Five possessions hath the holy, blessed God purchased in this world; and these are they, viz.: the law is one possession; heaven and earth another; Abraham another; Israel another, and the holy temple another. Now, whence is it to be proved that the law is one possession? Because it is written, the Lord possessed me in the beginning of his way, before his works of old. And whence is it proved that heaven and earth is another possession? Because it is said, thus said the Lord; the heavens are My throne, and the earth is My footstool; where is the house that ye can build for me? and where is the place of my rest? And it is said: How manifold are Thy works, O Lord! in wisdom hast Thou made them all; the earth is full of Thy possession. Whence is it proved that Abraham is one possession? Because it is written, and he blessed him, and said, blessed be Abraham of the most high God, possessor of heaven and earth. Whence is it proved that Israel is one possession? Because it is written, until Thy people pass over, O Lord, till Thy people pass over, which Thou hast purchased. And it is said: But the saints that are in the earth, and to the excellent, in whom is all my delight. Whence can it be proved, that the holy temple is one possession? Because it is said, the sanctuary, O Lord! which Thy hands have established. And it is said: And he brought them to the border of his sanctuary, even to this mountain, which His right hand hath purchased. Everything which God created, He created but for His glory; as is said: Every one that is called by my name; for I have created him for My glory. I have formed him; yea, I have made him.

CHAPTER V.

RABBINICAL CODE OF ETHICS.

Conscience—The highest maxim of moral law—God's command and not our happiness the motive to virtue—Self love not entirely excluded—The internal motive—Time of its appearance—Moral perfection finite and capable of increase—Duty of advancement—Freewill—Degrees of virtue—There are no small sins—No insuperable barrier to repentance—Degrees in sin—No man perfect—Demons—Merit not transferable—Moral judgment of ourselves—Classification of duties—Man should do by himself as God commands—Collision of duties—How decided—Justice precedes mercy—One's own dues those of others; and the good of the whole that of a part.

RABBINICAL CODE OF ETHICS.

SECTION I.—The consciousness of good and evil, being the original foundation of virtue and morality, is the voice of God in the heart of man.

REMARKS.—It is an undeniable fact, that certain actions arouse an approving and others a disapproving sensation in our heart. We denominate this sensation conscience, and invest it with a warning voice, by which the sinner is called back from his evil ways. According to the Talmud, we may call this "the voice of God within the heart of man." "And the Lord seized him by his garments and said, Amend!" (Sanhedrin, 102, a.) Though conscience is the voice of God, it does not impart to us a knowledge of the real good and the true evil; man must be taught by the will of God, revealed externally to himself, what is good and what is evil, that he may understand rightly the voice of conscience.

The ancient idolaters, if honest in the profession of their so-called religion, and no intentional, but only deceived deceivers, were uneasy in their conscience when their altars lacked human sacrifices. Therefore, a certain preparation is necessary, that we may perceive the voice of God within us; that is, that we may understand it correctly, even as a certain qualification was necessary for the perception of the voice of God revealed externally to us, and correctly to understand its meaning.

SECTION II.—The highest maxim of the code of ethics: Act in such a manner, that your actions may be agreeable to God and to men.

REMARKS.—"How may you concentrate the law into one sentence? In all your actions remember the Lord!" (Barachoth, 63 a.) "Let not mercy and truth forsake thee; so shalt thou find favor in the eyes of God and men." (Prov. iii, 4.) "Which is the the straight way that man should choose? That which will be beneficial for him—the observation of the duties towards himself— and which honors him in the eyes of his fellow-men," that is, which is also useful to others. That by this is not meant the way of law and justice merely, but the way of fairness and kindness also, is proved by the question itself. Why ask it at all, since we possess the Pentateuch, in which the precise way of the law is pointed out? This is further proved by the expression "ornament," (tifereth.) For not the actions of justice, nor those of simple virtue, but the actions of kindness and genuine virtue, will make man an ornament of his race. "He whose actions find favor with man, finds also favor with the Lord, and he whose actions are displeasing to men, is also displeasing to the Lord." (Ds. iii, 10.)

The establishment of a highest maxim of moral law, has troubled philosophers much. Live according to nature—act reasonably—endeavor to approach perfection—obey the commands of God; and others have been established by philosophers as the highest maxims. But according to my opinion, the importance of the Talmudical maxim is far greater than the importance of these. Religion without morality degenerates into superstition; and morality, torn away from the root of religion, is fragile, and may be easily shattered by desire and selfishness. According to this principle, God cannot want us to do that which is injurious to mankind. But if the execution of that which I believe to be the will of God, is injurious to none, then no one has a right to feel evil disposed towards me, because, I do that which cannot hurt him. "He whose works find no favor in the eyes of men, finds no favor in the eyes of God," can only be understood: "He whose works are justly displeasing to men." For superstition and religious hatred have often influenced men to be displeased with the actions of such as have in reality lived to please God and mankind. When it will have become a truism everywhere, that different religions cause different usages and ordinances, but not different rights and duties, then men will be able to make their actions agreeable to God and mankind.

SECTION III.—The code of ethics is no empirical principle, but pure one; that is, man should not be virtuous because happiness is acquired by virtue; but because God has commanded him to be so. "Be not like servants that serve their master with a view of reward." (Oboth, 1, 3.)

REMARKS.—The doctrines of Eudemonology are taken into favor by many philosophers; as for example, a moral philosopher of France says: "Les hommes n'ont qu'un penchant decide c'est l'interest." In another passage, "L'amour propre, bien entendu." This seems designed to express, if self-love does not degenerate into base interest,—" Et la source de vertus, morales et premier bien de la societe."—(Duclos.) Even the Talmudists do not reject them wholly. " Who gives to the poor with the intention of acquiring salvation thereby, or that his son may live—that is, that he may be kept alive by the Lord, is still called a pious man."—(Pessachim 8, a.) The objections of the philosophers to Eudemanology, namely: That morality would be brought into the sphere of sensuality, and that the only virtue established by such a code of morals would consist in wisdom; that everything necessary to make one virtuous would then be a wise calculation of each circumstance, in its consequences, of the advantages and disadvantages which would be the result of our actions, or, as a French philosopher has aptly expressed it: " Un interet quelcouque, est un motif et non pas une sanction. Une sanction est invariable et imprescriptible, la meme en tout temps en pour tous; en lieuqu'un interet et un motif variant a l'infine suivant les character, les affections, les circumstances, les lumieres," etc.—(La Harpe.) These objections are overruled by the Talmud; first, by making a distinction between noble and ignoble interest. " Man should do good, even if he be moved by interest; for by doing good with an end in view, he will be led to do good with pure intentions."—(Pessachim, 50 b.) While in another place this passage occurs: " Who does good from interested motives merely, it had been better for him if he had never been born."—(Barachoth 17, a.) And the commentaries explain this contradiction, by saying that a good action can only be recommended by noble intentions."—(Tossephoth.) In the second place, these objections are set aside by the Talmud, since to it the code of ethics is a command of God, and not as to the philosophers, a product of reason.

To the Talmud, its ethics are something already established, and not a thing to be obtained; you must be virtuous, not because reason, but because God recommends you to be so; thus, self-interest may incite, but can never compel man to do things prohibited by the code of ethics. The distinction consists in the different views with which the commands of God are obeyed. And for that reason, as we have already stated, the Talmud does not wholly reflect the opinions of Eudemonology. Still the Talmud acknowledges the principle of virtue as a pure one, and a virtue excited through positive motive—as an expectation of reward—as well as one called forth by negative motives, as fear of punishment, is a virtue of an inferior degree. " The convicted sins are turned into merits, if repentance is caused by love for virtue; but if caused by the fear of punishment, they are turned into errors."—(Yoma, 86 b.) "Man should not be virtuous for the sake of the blessings with which the Lord has promised to reward virtue, but because he loves God, who has commanded him to be so."—Maimon H. Teshuba 10, 1.) The following passage is characteristic: "One hour of this life, devoted to penitence and good deeds, is preferable to the whole future existence; and one hour of the divine joy of future, is preferable to a whole life on earth."— (Aboth 4, 17.) The Talmud acknowledges here that a single hour of future is preferable to a whole life spent on earth. But since the highest aim of man, consists not of future celestial joys, but of good deeds performed for the sake of virtue alone, one hour devoted to good deeds, may be preferable to all the joys of the future.

SECTION IV.—The code of ethics is the objective motive of his actions to man, but to make his actions correspond to the law, not alone externally, a subjective motive is necessary, an internal propensity must exist, and this is called "the good propensity."

REMARKS.—The code of ethics should be followed for the sake of compensation and profit: therefore, another incentive must be present in man. This is called, by the philosophers, "respect for the law;" the Talmud calls it "the good propensity," (Jetzer Hatob.) According to the Talmud, man possesses good and evil propensities, (Jetzer Horah.) The latter is the natural propensity, which has its own peculiar sphere of action, and inquires not whether an action is right or wrong, good or evil, but whether it is agreeable, or disagreeable, beneficial or injurious, and is, therefore, not ruled by ethics, but by physical laws. The good propensity is the delight of the soul in the value of virtue, as Kant, (*Criticisms of Practical Reason*,) says: "Two things fill the soul with ever new and increased admiration and awe, the more frequently and the longer the mind dwells thereon, the starry skies above me, and the moral law within me." Kant says, further: "Virtue enters the soul, even against the will, and wins from bad men, also, respect, though not always obedience." The Talmud coincides with this: "The wicked are despised even by those who derive profit from their wickedness." (Sanhedrin, 29 a). The good and evil propensities are for ever at war with each other, the virtuous victory will become more and more easy; he continues to find more and more pleasure and joy in being virtuous. "One good deed makes way for another." (Aboth, iv. 2.) Because man gets more and more used to being good and virtuous, and, therefore, the struggle is less difficult. But the strife between good and evil propensities never cease entirely during life. "Trust not to yourself till the day of your death." (Ds. ii., 4.)

Krug says the same: "Man cannot feel pure love, as long as he is a sensual being. If any maintain the contrary opinion, they either speak about the mere ideal, or believe that state to be acquirable through self-deception, or are boasting heroes of virtue." To this struggle may be applied Young's beautiful words, (*Night Thoughts,*)—"Body and soul, like peevish man and wife, united jar, and yet are loth to part."

"The Talmud makes, very appropriately, the evil propensities appear at the birth of the child, while the good propensities make their appearance on the arrival of man at his religious majority; for sensual desire exists already in the child, but respect for moral laws and ethics are only possessed by reasonable man.

SECTION V.—Man is a finite being, and, therefore, his moral perfection can be but finite, that is, limited, and is always capable of increase. Therefore, man can never be virtuous enough, but must always strive to become still more virtuous.

REMARKS.—"Ye shall be holy, for I, the Lord your God, am holy." (Lev. xix, 2.) This passage commands us to endeavour to become holy, even as the Lord is holy. But holiness can only be thought of in the Lord, because his moral perfection is not capable of any increase; man, on the contrary, may always become holier, that is, more perfect; but can never acquire holiness, that is, absolute perfection. Sufficiency in virtue is, for this reason, a vice; Whoever does not advance, recedes; a pause in human perfection, is impossible. "It has not been granted to you to finish the work, therefore, you are never released, and may not withdraw." (Aboth. ii. 16.) The Talmud pictures even future life, not as a quiet contemplative, but also as a progressing existence. "The pious have no rest—that is, they remain not quiet in a certain degree—not in this world, nor in the next." (Barachoth, 64, *a.*)

The endeavor for perfection is the task of man himself. The principle of the influence of divine power in this respect, that is, a predetermination of human actions, is rejected with great emphasis by the Talmud. Put no faith in what the other nations say, that God influences man to become pious or to remain wicked; every man may become as pious as Moses, and as wicked as Jeroboam. He is controlled by no one, no one has pre-determined anything in this respect; man has an unlimited free-will; this is a high principle, and the pedestal of ethics; so it is written: Lo, I have put before ye life and death (Maimon. H. Teshuba, 5, 2 and 3). Though another passage speaks thus: "If the Lord would not assist man, he would submit to his evil propensity (Sukoth 52)." Yet this may only be understood, if no revealed religion existed; man, assisted only by reason, could not remain victor in the struggle of life. And since religion was given to us by God, it is God who gives us assistance to oppose the evil propensity and remain pure.

Hillel, who lived in times when many theologians began to teach man could not be virtuous by himself, but virtue in man is effected by the Lord, and that to receive grace man must see the proffered means of grace, and so forth, according to which opinions, no natural, but merely a supernatural virtue existed, said, in contradiction: "If I do nothing for myself, who else will do anything for me." (Aboth 1, 14)

SECTION VI.—Virtue itself is perfect and absolute, but the virtue of men is capable of being divided into degrees; but since the greater or lesser virtue consists in the intentions, a precise classification of, and decision about it, is uncertain.

REMARKS.—"Judge not your fellow-man, if you were not placed in the same position." (Aboth, 4.) But it is impossible to be wholly in the position of another, or to arrive ever there. To be able precisely to determine the degree of virtue attained, we must take into consideration, firstly, the extent of the action. Though it is said: "To accomplish much or little, is the same to God, but the intention must be a heavenly one," (Menachath, 110 a) yet therewith is meant, if he who does little cannot do more; as the example of the poor man's sacrifice illustrates. But, if it is possible to do more, the little cannot be valued equal to much. Secondly, the obstacles which had to be surmounted. "*That* virtue, which is mentioned as praiseworthy by the Lord himself, is when the virtuous had to withstand great temptations, and to surmount serious obstacles. (Pessachim, 113, a b). Thirdly, the sentiments, that is, the internal motives, which have co-operated.

The duration of virtuous conduct which the philosophers also specify as defining the degree of virtue, has a few advocates in the Talmud; according to it, "man may acquire his future world in one hour." (Rosh Hashanah, 17 b.) Now, what man can know and measure these circumstances? Therefore, none but the Omniscient Being can pronounce a completely certain judgment concerning the degree of human virtue. "There exists but *one* who can judge." (Aboth, 4, 8.)

SECTION VII.—The code of ethics contains no trifles, no so-called smaller, unimportant sins, since, where duty is spoken of, everything is of importance. Again, no absolutely great vice is mentioned therein, since nothing can resist repentance and amendment.

REMARKS.—" Be careful in observing the least, as well as the most important command." (Aboth. 2, 1.) "You should observe the least

commands, even those which you think may be trodden under foot."
(Midrash Jalkot Ekeb.) The Talmudical code of ethics further distinguishes itself from the philosophical, in this respect, that it pronounces mistaken actions, which, though not immoral, yet are unlawful, that is, in cases where the action has been committed, objectively against the law, and yet no want of respect for the law has occurred, sins needing pardon, and if the same error is repeated several times, styles it carelessness. Then, again, there is no vice which cannot be expiated by repentance and amendment. "The man who, having been virtuous throughout his whole previous life, towards the end of it becomes vicious, loses the whole of his merit, and is called an evil man. He who, having been vicious throughout his whole previous life, becomes virtuous at last, his sins will not be remembered, and he is called a virtuous man." (Kidushin, 40, b.) "No sin can resist repentance and penance." (Maimon H. Teshuba, iii. 14, and Aboda Sera 7 b.) That is, no sin is so great and so persevering, that the sinner could not amend, and which could not be expiated, through sincere repentance.

It is true, that some passages of Scripture have the appearance as if they intended to convey the idea that there are some sinners who are irretrievably lost, but it is well known that Scripture uses phrases and expressions as figurative as those of man.—(Chulin 90 b.) It is, therefore, rather hasty of Maimonides, (H. Teshuba, 6, 19), from such passages to conclude that the Lord prevents the amendment of some great sinners, that they may perish in their wickedness. Repentance expiates for all sins, only the Lord prevents amendment; this is a hypothesis not derived from the Talmud, and which is contradictory to the spirit of Judaism. "We agreed in this opinion, that no external punishment was to be feared, for the Lord cannot make any of His creatures so infinitely miserable. Neither can any creature deserve by his actions the punishment of being miserable for ever." "It is sin itself which I have to fear. Has it been once committed, then divine punishment is a benefit, and I am sure, whenever it ceases to be a benefit, it will be released." If the Talmud says: "He will not be able to expiate who leads a community to sin," then this is first a psychological truth, since a false shame generally prevents the founder of a sect from acknowledging his error; secondly, it is a consequence of the sin itself which can hardly be amended. For, though man may amend his own conduct and repent, yet how can he amend those whom he has led astray? The Talmud expresses itself figuratively: "The returned founder of a sect would then be in the Garden of Eden, and those by him seduced, scholars in

Gehinom.—(Yoma 7, a.) We must remark here, that though it is said in Abath "He will *not* be able to amend," in Yoma it is expressed: "He will *scarce* be able to amend," &c.

The same doctrines are applicable in respect to the definition of the degrees of vice, as in the definition of the degrees of virtue, (Sec. 8,) and in respect to the struggle with the evil propensities, quite the contrary to what is said of the virtuous may be applied. For vice makes the victory of the good over the evil propensity, the victory of the active moral state over the passive, more and more difficult. "One sin makes way for another."—(Aboth 4, 2.) "Woe unto these that draw iniquity with the cords of falsehood, and as with waggon ropes, sinfulness."—(Jesaiah 5, 18.)

SECTION VIII.—Immoral actions may be committed intentionally, or through neglect; they may further be either sins of commission or omission. The highest degree of immorality is to sin from love to the evil. In judging another, the most palliating view must be taken.

REMARKS.—Erring actions cannot be called immoral. But the action may be committed with a knowledge of its unlawfulness, or from unmindfulness, inconsiderateness, or precipitation. A sin from negligence is denominated in the Talmud, "Sadan," an intentional sin. "Pesha." On immorality from love for the evil, Kant expresses himself thus: "Wickedness, *thought* of in a highest degree, consists of a direct inclination, which, without temptations of any kind, finds pleasure in evil, and which leads to the commission of evil deeds, without any consideration in regard to profit or enjoyment." But still both Kant and Krug doubts, and doubts justly, whether any man be capable of such wickedness. The Talmud denominates such a villian: "A sinner out of spite —that he may offend."—(Mummar Chachis); in contradiction to "a sinner out of sensuality.—(Mummac Lethenbon.) It seems that the reason of this may be found in the circumstance that the Talmud identifies the ceremonial and the moral law; and in ceremonial law, such a degree may be thought of.

Concerning the judgment of others, it is written: "Judge each man according to the mildest view."—(Aboth 1, 6.) But this is thereby a moral and not a civil principle. The Judge may and can act in most cases according to this principle. "As long as the contending parties are before you, look upon them as guilty, but when they are destroyed, and you cease to be the judge of the parties, and are again man to man, look upon both as though none were guilty."—(Aboth 1, 18.)

SECTION IX.—Since moral perfection is capable of being constantly increased, human virtue may always be viewed as imperfect, and man is, therefore, never without fault. The more serious and sincere are the endeavors of man to reach moral perfection, the stronger and more vivid will be the consciousness of his own imperfections, and he will, therefore, never over-value his merit.

REMARKS.—"For there is not a just man upon earth, that does good and sinneth not."—(Eccles. 7, 20.) The relations of the Talmud respecting four Biblical characters, who are said to have never sinned, is a fable, and cannot be applied here. The natural deduction from the foregoing will be, that no man can be proud of his merits.

The qualities of the scholars of Abraham are: A kind look, a modest soul, and a humble mind.—(Aboth, 5, 19.) "Always be very humble."—(Ds. 4, 6.) This paragraph may also be taken in an opposite way: No man lives who does not possess some merit. "Therefore, despise no man."—(Ds. 4. s.) "Never account yourself a reprobate."—(Ds. 2, 18.) That your moral strength and power to amend might never be weakened. A reasonable being without any merit at all, is the ideal of evil, a devil and not a man. We must notice here, that the Talmudists were not free from faith in the existence of Satan and demons; but they are not described in the Talmud as reasonable beings, possessed of an absolutely evil will. Krug says: "If we do not accept according to Dualism, the theory of two infinite beings, conceived in the eternal struggle between good and evil, then the devils must be imagined as finite beings." And the Talmud corroborates the proposition: "The Shedim (evil spirits) eat like men, multiply like men, and die like men."—(Chagiga 16, a.) The Talmud relates, even of a very kind natured demon called "Joseph Sheda." The king of demons is not called Satan, but Ashmodai, and described as "a jovial fellow." And, besides, the Talmudical faith in demons, influences neither a religious opinion, nor a religious faith; it is simply a play of the imagination. The only Satan, as an accepted accuser, has entered the sphere of prayers and usages through the agency of Cabbala, as for instance, the intermission of sounding the cornet on the day before Rosh Hashanah, therewith to confuse Satan; this is of no import, but to prove that the views of these times have somewhat influenced the Talmudists.

Krug cites a Hamburg correspondent of November 4, 1817, who announces the following: "The devil in the form of a black pig, was formally killed, hanged, and burned in England, October 14, 1817."

Is it then astonishing that the Talmudists of 1800 years ago believed in demons? And so innocent was this faith of theirs, that they even permitted the conjuration of demons—not for the purpose of delivering those possessed, but merely to talk with them. Because their conception of the devil was a different one from that of later times, and their Satan was capable of manifesting good intentions, in regard to Israel, in his actions.—(Beth Bathra, xvi. a.) R. Lakish there expresses the correct opinion: "The evil propensity is both Satan and the angel of death." Consequently no Satan exists externally to ourselves, but within our own heart; he also causes men to die through excess of sensuality. R. Lakish seems to have entertained enlightened views throughout—he says: "The future world contains no hell; but the Lord will take from their bodies the sun of enlightenment, which is concealed and darkened by the frame of the body during this life; the pious will be cured thereby, and live joyously in the happy consciousness of having done good deeds; the wicked will be judged thereby, and feel uneasy in the fully acquired consciousness of committed sin."

SECTION X.—Merits and faults, in a moral respect, are not transferable, therefore, neither merits nor faults can be put to another man's account.

REMARKS.—The fathers shall not be put to death for the children, neither shall the children be put to death for the father; every man shall be put to death for his own sin.—(Deut. xxiv, 16). In a judicial sense, this is a matter of course, since the action can be imputed only to him who has committed it; but in practical life, the children of virtuous parents enjoy a preference, confidence, &c. Since we pre-suppose that they are well educated, and saw good examples in the house of their parents. The preference and confidence given to them, is owing in part to an acknowledgment of the merits of their parents. And on the contrary, the children of wicked parents are neglected and avoided, because of a suspicion in regard to their education, and the bad examples they might have had in their parental home. Therefore Scripture says: "God visits the iniquity of the fathers upon the children."—(Exod. xx., 5.) Though this occurs in every-day life, yet it is contradictory to the code of ethics, since what jurisprudence decrees about imputation, is also acknowledged by the code of ethics. It seems that the Mosaic decision is not well founded. The Talmud remarks, in one place, with remarkable boldness: "Four decrees were issued by Moses, that have been abolished by other prophets." Moses said: "God visits the iniquities of the parent upon the children." But Ezekiel has contradicted him: "The soul that sinneth, it shall die! The son shall not bear the iniquity of the father, neither shall the father bear the iniquity of the son. The righteousness of the righteous shall be upon him."—(Ezekiel xviii, 20; Makoth xxiv. a.) In another passage the Talmud says: "Moses means, should the children commit the same sins as the parents."—(Sanhedrin 27, b.). That is, the children of wicked parents suffer for their own misdeeds. But since they hardly would have acted so, had they not seen their parents' example, they suffer for the wickedness of their parents nevertheless.

A tale of the Midrash says, "Zebulon made a contract with Isachar that one should study and the other earn a living, and then divide the gain with the one; in compensation, Zebulon would receive one-half of the Divine reward for the merits of Isachar." On another occasion the Talmud relates: "Hillel was poor; but, in spite of his poverty, he educated himself to be a great teacher; his brother went into business and acquired wealth; then the latter said: 'I will give you half of my wealth, if for it you will give me half of your earned reward.' A Divine voice then spake: 'Though man were to offer his whole fortune, he cannot buy love.'" These two passages give rise to the following conclusion: A contract can be made for one's support from another, to be able to devote one's self to study without check by the considerations of life; in compensation of which, half of the Divine reward may be made over to our supporter; but has one already occupied himself with study, the already earned reward cannot be sold. If, instead of "Divine reward," the words "moral merit" are inserted, and in point of fact the expressions are identical, the above conclusion is quite apposite and correct. The one man aids the other in the practice of good actions; without the one's co-operation, the other could not have practised them at all, or, at least, so completely; therefore, it is quite natural, and but just, that he share the moral merit. But if a good deed is once done, and another wants to buy the moral merit, then comes into play the principle: "Neither moral merit nor moral wrong can be made over."

SECTION XI.—The moral judgment of man should be frequently applied to judge his own actions. Man should always act with a consciousness of being seen by a higher judge. Still, both of these moral means cannot be looked upon as infallible.

REMARKS.—"It would be better for man had he never been born; but since he exists, he ought frequently to investigate his actions." (Eruben 13, b.) "Every night, man should investigate the actions of the previous day. The more frequently man listens to his conscience, that is, makes use of his power of judgment, the greater expertness he acquires in the judgment of himself, and consequently in the practice of good and the avoidance of evil. Frequent self-judgment also serves the purpose of keeping man always prepared to appear before his heavenly judge. "His disciples inquired of R. Eliezer: What is the meaning of the sentence, repent one day before your death? How is it possible for man to know the day of his death?" The Rabbi replied, "The more necessary is it for him to repent every day, since he may die the next." Maimonides writes, therefore: Man should always look upon himself as if his last hour were present, and for this reason, repent *always* (H. Teshuba 78.) But before what law may the moral power of judgment arraign those actions depending on the will, that it may decide whether they agree therewith or not? Philosophers say: before that law established by practical reason. But to the Talmud the Lord alone is legislator, and at the same time eternal judge. And this judge should be always present to man. "Fear the Lord, even as ye fear men," said R. Johanna to his disciples. "And not more?" was their question. The Rabbi replied, "Are ye not afraid to do evil in the presence of other men? Therefore, feel awe in the presence of the Lord," (Berachoth 28 b.) The later Rabbis say "I have set the Lord always before me," (Psalm xvi. 8.) This principle ought to be taken into the heart, and bound to the soul. Man's behaviour, his movements and his actions, if he is alone, at home, are not like his motions and actions in the presence of a great king; his conversations with the family and the relations, is not like what it would be if a great king were present. If man reflects, therefore, that above him thrones the highest king, the Holy One, blessed be his name, whose splendor fills the earth, and sees his actions, then awe and meekness must make him ashamed to sin. Take to heart three things, and you will never fall into sinfulness. Know what is above thee; an all-seeing eye, an all-hearing ear, and a precise account of your actions.

But neither of these means is infallible. Many a one may attribute as a merit to himself what in reality is a wrong; to persecute persons of a different opinion, and convert them through the exercise of power, for the purpose of making one's self agreeable to the Lord. The ability of judging correctly whether actions agree with the law, or rather the ability of acting according to the law, presupposes a correct knowledge of that law; therefore, such a high, yea, even the highest value is put, by the Talmud, upon a precise and minute investigation of the law. "The study of the law bears a higher value than all the previously mentioned commands." (Peath i, 1.) The Talmud acknowledges, it is true, that the study of the law constitutes merely the means, but does not constitute the aim. "Not the study but the practice, is the chief thing." (Aboth. i, 17.) Nevertheless, the study is more important, since only this can lead to the practice, that is, the correct practice. The philosophers, too, are compelled to acknowledge, that if man does not understand the laws established by practical reason, his conscience cannot pronounce a correct judgment. And to him who neglects his mind, that is, does not perfect it, reason will establish no law, or at least not a correct one.

SECTION XII.—The Talmudical code of ethics has various duties: 1. To one's self. 2. To other living men. 3. To deceased men. 4. To animate beings. 5. To inanimate things.

REMARKS.—It is true, the Talmud contains duties to God also, or rather to the Talmud, all duties are duties to God; for God is the highest legislator, and judge of all finite moral beings. But since this is no religious code, those duties touching God alone cannot be enumerated here.

But in a strict sense, our actions cannot touch God. If thou sinnest, what dost thou against him, and if thy vices accumulate, what dost thou unto him? If thou art just, what dost thou give him, or what receiveth He from thy hand? The Talmud also acknowledges that the laws are useful to man, and not to the Lord. Well known is a reply of Rabbi Akiba: A prince asked him, to wit: "If the foreskin is such an abomination to the Lord, why are not men born circumcised?" "Because," he replied, "the laws are merely given to purify man." The ceremonial laws discussed here, are not the ultimate aim, but merely the means to purify and perfect man, and, therefore, they are no duties to the Lord, but to one's self.

SECTION XIII.—Since man is the property of God, he has no other rights over himself, but those granted to him by God, and has to observe these duties to himself, which God commands.

REMARKS.—If some one says: "Deprive me of sight; cut off my hand; break my foot, and you shall be free from all blame;" then the other, if he does it, is still guilty, because the body, or rather man, is not his own property. "For unto me the children of Israel are servants, they are my servants."—(Lev. xxv., 55.) On which passage the Talmud observes: " but not the servants of servants."

Duties pre-supposes rights. I have duties to myself, but who possesses the rights? I have no right over my foot, over my hand, &c., other men have still less right over them; now who possesses these rights ? The Talmud would not adopt the abstraction and separation of the physical from the moral man, would not elevate itself to this philosophical subtility and say : Man has rights over man, and man has also duties to man. The Talmud says : God is the proprietor of man, and his right of possession God does not cancel, as long as he lets life dwell in man. "Only when man is dead, he is liberated from the commands of the Lord." And this solves the question judicially. Whoever hires out his strength to another man, is not permitted to do anything that will diminish his strength. As for instance, a hired man is not permitted to fast. Since my strength and all I possess belong to God, it is a matter of course, that I have duties to preserve the Lord's property for him. But, just for this reason, I must devote life and all to higher aims, since by that sacrifice I serve the Lord. In a philosophical view, man can never be looked upon as the property of the Lord, and the Talmud makes use of this conceded right of possession, merely as a figurative expression. For it is repeated several times, "You are no servants, but children to the Lord, your God." This conceded right of property expresses, therefore, nothing else ; but that man is absolutely bound in duty to observe the Lord's will. Moreover, God desires man to observe the duties to himself, consequently he is bound to their observation.

SECTION XIV.—Since the code of ethics has various laws, cases of collision between some of them are inevitable, in which cases generally is applied the rule : The unimportant duties must make way for the more important ones. But what duty must be placed in the more important position, cannot be determined precisely in all cases. The following axioms may serve as indications :

1. Duties of justice are more important than duties of kindness.

2. In equal circumstances, duties to one's self are more important than those to others.

3. Duties to the whole are more important than duties to single parts.

REMARKS.—You may think, it is true, justice is on the side of the wealthy, but since he is obliged to sustain the poor, I will decide in favor of the poor ; therefore it is written : "Favor not the poor." (Not as it is told of Crispin—he stole leather from the rich, to make shoes for the poor. For according to the Talmudical civil laws, the bench of judges may force the wealthy to contribute towards the sustenance of the poor, even by pawning his goods, and this is the moral view of communism.) To force the wealthy to be charitable to the poor, is a duty of kindness, but to decide a case justly, is a duty of justice, and, therefore, the other must make way for this.

But not merely duties of justice, such as are commanded by the laws of justice, or so-called compulsory duties, but also duties resulting from the code of ethics, are more important than the duties of kindness. For instance, it is a moral duty of kindness to be obliging to man, but is a moral duty of justice, to be obliging to him, because you have promised to do so, or out of gratitude?

2. "Whatever belongs to thee is to be preferred to things which belong to another man." "If his own life, and that of another one is in danger, man may save himself, before saving the other one." The circumstances in these cases are equal, life against life, property against property, and the duties to one's self are more important than those to others.

"One should suffer torture, and not betray the innocently persecuted to his pursuer." In this case the circumstances are not alike—life of another one against the pains of thy own body—and in this case the duties to one's self are not more important. That the whole fortune should be sacrificed, rather than betray the pursued to his pursuer, is a matter of course in the Talmudical code of ethics. Treachery is a trespass of the code of ethics; but to avoid committing trespasses, man should sacrifice his whole fortune. But whether man is also obliged to sacrifice his fortune, if, therewith, he can save the life of another, since the abstaining from saving the other's life is merely a sin of omission, the Talmudical code of ethics does not decide. It is true, one passage expresses this opinion: "Man is obliged to *hire* men, that they may save the life of another." But the hire of the saviour cannot comprise the whole fortune. The Talmudical law forbids man to save his own life at the sacrifice of another's life, though the other one must lose life at the same time. If assassins say to a number of men, "Give us one of you that we may kill him; if you do not we will kill ye all, ye shall all suffer death, and not sacrifice one," but if the delivering up of a certain person is demanded, amongst the threats of killing all, in case of refusal, they need not suffer death for his sake, since man is not obliged to sacrifice, for the life of another, his own life. "If one man is desired to kill another, or to suffer death, he must submit to being killed." In this case he does not sacrifice himself for another one, but for the sake of not committing the greatest injustice—murder. For a less important injustice, man is obliged to sacrifice life. But on the contrary, man may not save his own life, by transgressing a law of justice. "No one may save himself through the money of another."

Concerning defence, the Talmudical code of ethics teaches the same laws as the philosophical. "If any one comes to murder you, get up and kill him;" that is, we may defend ourselves against a murderous attack, even by the death of the assailant. The thief discovered committing theft, is declared to be free by holy writ. The defence, by the death of the assailant, is permitted, even in cases where the assailant is responsible for his actions, and even, where the pursuer has a certain right to pursue the pursuer.

3. If an epidemic prevails in a city, man is obliged to leave it, because no one may expose himself to danger of life. When the community is suffering, no one may absent himself; but the single man must suffer with the community. The contradiction between these two passages is cancelled by the explanation. He may not expose himself to danger, if his presence can be of no use to the community; but does his presence benefit the community, he is not permitted to separate himself, but must also suffer and expose his life to danger like the rest. Man is part of a community, and the duties to the whole community are more important than those to a single part, as well as those to one's self. So Jonathan boasted of David: "For he did put his life in his hand, and slew the Philistines."—(1. Samuel xix., 6.) He has exposed his life for the benefit of the nation.

It is true, we have seen that a number may not save themselves with the life of a single one, but a number is not a whole, but merely several parts of a whole.

CHAPTER VI.

EXTRACTS FROM RABBINICAL WRITINGS.

The Spiritual Body—The Israelites at Sinai—Joshua—Enoch—R. Ribbi and Antoninus.

EXTRACTS FROM RABBINICAL WRITINGS.

Before man is born, his soul is clothed in a spiritual body, similar to that which shall afterwards be of flesh. The following story is related in Sohar 71, 1 : When Rabbi Perachjah approached the door of Paradise, the entrance of heaven was opened to him, and a voice was heard saying : "Take off from him his clothes, for the earthly body cannot enter the kingdom of heaven." The cloth of flesh was taken from him, and he was enveloped in the air of the Garden of Eden, (in a spiritual body.) He then delighted in the intuition of the outer heaven and its angelic host. When he was compelled to return to earth again,—as his time was not up,—his soul received again her fleshly body. Another passage in Sohar says, (49, 4) : When the Israelites stood at the foot of Mount Sinai to receive the most holy law, they were dressed in pure and holy clothes—spiritual bodies—but when they defiled themselves, with the worship of the golden calf, they were deprived of that glory. As it is written, (Exod. xxxiii., 6) : "And the children of Israel were stripped of their ornaments by the Mount Horeb." * Again, Sohar, on Zachar, 3, 3 : " Now Joshua was clothed with filthy garments, and stood before the angel." The filthy garments must be understood to mean the body with which the spirit is clothed when it is commanded to live upon earth, because the flesh is defiled by sin in disobedience to God. Jalkat Rubeni says : "By their garments the children of men will be known at the last and great day, whether they lived, when on earth, a virtuous or wicked life. The actions of every man retain their impressions, even upon that spiritual body with which the soul is clothed at the resurrection.

R. Tanchum taught : The garment with which the soul is clothed in the life which is to come, is woven of the rays which are emitted from the throne of God, Therefore the Psalmist says : " Light is for the righteous, and gladness for the upright in heart." At the time when

---

* In the English version it is translated : "stripped themselves ;" but the original says : "they were stripped," as if this was done by others.

Enoch was taken up to heaven, everything which is kept secret from man, was now opened to him. He wrote all that he saw and heard in a book and gave it to his son, but it is now lost. At that time Enoch was clothed in pure light, and all those who denied God, their maker, became confounded. Further: when the righteous dies, the angel of death clothed him with a worthier apparel than that which he had in this earthly life, by which he is enabled to enter the paradise and behold Divine things. (Sohar Syn. 137.) There is a parable in the Talmud, Tract Sanhedrin, fol. 91, page 1, which we quote:

"The Emperor Antoninus, in his conversation with R. Ribbi, asked the Rabbi: How can God—according to thy religion—punish a sinner after death? If he summons the soul or spirit of man after it has abandoned the body, now dead, will it not say: 'My Lord, thou knowest that I came pure out of thine hand, and that I am not able to sin, as there is no earthly lust in my substance. It is the body, the flesh and blood that transgressed thy holy law.' The body, if summond, will say, 'Lord thou knowest I am nothing but a lump of earth; not I but the soul which thou hast given me, induced me to all that I have done. Now since that spirit left me, I have not done anything, neither good nor bad! Which of both will God punish? The Rabbi answered:—

"I will tell thee a parable, O Caesar, by which thou shalt understand the judgment of God. There was once a king, who possessed a garden of wonderful beauty, and in which the fruits ripened earlier than anywhere else. The king had great trouble with his own servants, the keepers and watchmen of the garden; they could not resist the temptation to eat of the precious fruits; they were, therefore, punished and dismissed. At last he put a blind man and a lame man in the garden, to watch and keep it. When the precious fruits ripened, the lame keeper said to the blind: 'O couldest thou see with mine eyes, or could I walk with thy legs! How beautiful are these fruits, and how profusely are they placed upon these trees, and how sweet must they be to eat!' After a long consultation they agreed upon the following plan: The blind man, who had sound legs, took the lame with sound eyes, upon his shoulder, and directed him how to reach the fruit; and thus satisfied both their lusts. Next day the king visited his garden, and observed that many of the precious fruits were stolen He summoned the keepers before him, and said: Which of you has stolen my fruit? The lame man answered: 'O my king, thou knowest that I cannot use my legs; and were the fruits even of precious gold, I could not reach them.' The blind man said: 'O my king, I am blind; I cannot see either the tree or its fruit;

it was, therefore not I who stole them.' But the king was convinced that none else but the keepers could have taken the fruits of his garden; he commanded, therefore, the lame to be put upon the shoulders of the blind, and then punished them together, as they had committed the crime together. At the day of judgment, God will unite again soul and body; there will be again a living man; and then he will receive the reward for what he has done while in this life."

CHAPTER VII.

KABALA AND KABALISTS.

Term defined—Two classes of the Mystical School—Philo and the Kabalists—Age of the latter system—Its dialect—Divisions of the Science—Standard works—Axioms—Pantheism—The Jetsira and Tohar.

KABALA AND KABALISTS.

The term *Kabala*, is a correlative with *Masora*. *Kabal* signifies "to receive;" *Masora*, "to hand down or communicate." The Kabalists believe that God has expressly committed His mysteries to certain chosen persons, and that they themselves have received those mysteries in trust, still further to hand them down to worthy recipients.

There has been always for the last two thousand years, a mystical school, more or less numerous, who have treated the written word as the symbolic vehicle of an esoteric doctrine. This school may be said to consist of two classes: 1. Those with whom that interior spiritual signification shapes itself into a philosophical system, which they nevertheless hold either from or in connexion with, a foreign or Gentile teaching, such as Platonism. Their representative is Philo. They blend the Mosaic law with the Gentile monotheism. 2. The other class are the *Kabalists*, properly so called, who, from the impulse of the mind after a deep and satisfying knowledge of the inmost mysteries of being, have given themselves up too much to the tutelage of the imagination, and constructed a system which combines, at once, the sublime and the despicable.

To become acquainted with the Kabala in its real character, the student will find that he must ascend to the consideration of its primitive metaphysical principles, as laid down in the earliest documents of the science, because in latter times the professors of the Kabala have mixed it with many doctrines taken from the Greek and Arabian philosophies. Those of them, too, who, from superstition, kept themselves aloof from the general culture of their times, abandoned by degrees, the profound speculations of which the Kabala was the result, and preserved merely the grosser types, which had been used by the earlier masters only, as the drapery of the truth which they veiled.

The system itself is undoubtedly of very great age. Without spending a moment on the obvious exaggerations which refer it to Moses, to Abraham, and even to Adam in Paradise, we must admit that, so far back as the *Tanaim*, there are evident traces of its existence. The numerous allusions to it in the Mishna and Gemara abundantly show that, under the *Tanaim*, a certain philosophy, or religious metaphysic, was secretly taught, and that this system of esoteric teaching related especially to the creation and the Godhead, *Bereshith* and *Merava*. So early as A.D. 189, the time of the Mishna reduction, it was thus recognized as an established theosophy, the privilege of select disciples. We may, therefore, safely believe in its operation in the second century. The style is not Talmudic, nor past-Talmudic, so neither is it the pure Hebrew of the Biblical Scriptures, but the dialect which was used by the learned Jews at the time of the opening of the Christian era. In a word, it belongs to the period of the first Mishnaists; that is, between a century before, and about eighty years after, the birth of Christ. The work itself might even have been a collection of fragments of various earlier times.

The Kabala, considered as a constructed science is, 1st, theoretical; 2nd, practical. The practical department comprises a symbolical apparatus, and rules for the use of it. The theoretical part consists of two branches: the cosmogonic, as relating to the visible universe. The second is theogonic and pneumatological, as relating more directly to the spiritual world, and to the perfections of the Divine nature. The technical name of this part is *maasé merkava*, alluding to the *merkava*, or chariot throne, with its attendant angels, in the vision of Providence, described in the first chapter of Ezekiel.

In the books *Jetsira* and *Zohar*, the Kabala is thought; in them we get the sure principles of the science laid down and explained by the great masters themselves. The student will master both the *Jetsira* and the *Zohar* with greater facility, if he bring with him to the task a premonition on some axioms which the Kabalists consider to be fundamental, such as are the following:—1. From nothing, nothing can proceed. 2. Therefore, no substance that now exists has been produced from nothing. 3. All existing substances are emanations from one eternal substance. In the act of what is commonly called "creation," the Eternal Being drew from Himself. 4. Consequently there is no such thing as matter; strictly speaking, that which we call "matter" is only a form or species under which spirit gives itself a manifestation. 5. So that the universe is a revelation of the Infinite; an eminent effect of his ever active power and presence. 6. But though all existence thus flowed from the Divinity, yet is the world different from the Godhead, as the effect is different from the cause. Nevertheless, as not separate from, but abiding eminently in Him, it is evermore the manifestation of Himself. It is the mantle with which He clothes Himself; or rather it is a revelation of the Godhead, not in His hidden essence, but in His visible glory. 7. In giving existence to the universe, the first act of the Almighty was the production of a power or principle intimately, and especially, relating to Himself, to which are given the names of "His Holy Spirit," "His personal Word," and "His First-begotten Son," and which the Kabalists personify as the Adam Kadmon; who, in his turn, caused to proceed by emanation from Himself, all the lower forms of actual existence in their several descending gradations. The principles of the Kabala may be summed up in one; and that one—*Pantheism*. This character of the system appears partially in the *Jetsira*, and more fully in the *Zohar*.

The Jetsira opens its instructions with something of the tone and manner of the Bible, and announces that the universe bears upon itself the imprint of the name of God; so that, by the means of the great panorama of the world, the mind may acquire a conception of the Deity; and from the unity which reigns in the Creation, it may learn the oneness of the Creator. So far, the way of thinking is in agreement with the common one. But now, instead of tracing in the universe the laws which govern it, so as to ascertain from those laws the thoughts of the Lawgiver, it is sought rather to arrive at the same end by finding some tangible analogy between the things which exist, and the signs of thought, or the means which thought and knowledge are principally communicated and interpreted among men; and recourse is had for this purpose to the twenty-two letters of the Hebrew alphabet, and to the first ten numbers. (According to the Kabalsts, God is the author of the letters. Speech is a revelation of thought, and the form in which intellect pronounces itself most distinctly.)

The *Zohar*, the sequel to the *Jetsira*, is held, from the greater amplitude of its doctrine, as the standard and code of the Kabalistic system. The title of this book in full is, "The Book of Splendour on the Law, by the very holy and venerable man of God, the Tana Rabbi Shemun C. Yochai, of blessed memory." The body of the work takes the form of a commentary, extending over the five books of Moses, of a highly mystic and allegorical character. But the Zohar is not considered complete without the addition of certain appendices, attributed either to the same author, or to some of his personal or successional disciples.

When we say that the *Zohar* is a commentary on the Pentateuch, it must be understood that the principle of interpretation is Kabalistic. The authors consider the literal sense of the words as a covering to a truer meaning. According to them the real doctrine is a living body, of which the literal text is only the vestment.

It is here that they develop their most solemn theology, the true knowledge of the only true God.—*Hebrew Literature*.

CHAPTER VIII.

THE METAPHYSICAL SCHOOLS OF THE JEWS, ANCIENT AND MODERN.

SECT. I.—PRECEDING MAIMONIDES—The Bible not metaphysical—Origin of evil—Free will—The Talmud—Mercabâ—Allegorical characters of Rabbinical literature—The Caraites—Progress of metaphysics among the Rabbinites—Saadia ben Joseph—The Book of Creeds—The school at Cordova—Solomon ben Gabriel—The Fons Vitæ—Bahya ben Joseph—Juda ha Levi and the book Khozari—Differences between theology and philosophy, and attempts at reconciliation—Maimonides—More Nevochim—Prohibition and burning of his works.

SECT. II.—SUBSEQUENT TO MAIMONIDES—Fabulous accounts of the Kabala—Yetsira and Zohar—Date of the Zohar—Contents of the books—Theories of the origin of evil—Cabalistic theory—The manifestation of God—Theory of emanation—Remarks on this system and comparison with other systems of philosophy—Neoplatonists and Gnostics—The Cabala and Christianity—Shem Job—Judaia Penini—Joseph Ibn Caspi—Marter Leon—Moses ben Joseph—Ahron ben Elias, the Caraite—Decay of Peripateticism—Joseph Albo—Abraham Bibago—Joseph ben Shem Job—Elias del Medigo—Expulsion of the Jews from Spain—Abraham and his son Leo—The Dialogues of Love—Close of the history of Jewish metaphysics with the sixteenth century—Modern philosophers not peculiarly Hebrew.

METAPHYSICAL SCHOOLS AMONGST THE JEWS, DOWN TO THE TIMES OF MOSES MAIMONIDES.

The part of M. Munk's work which treats of Jewish philosophy, is necessarily shorter than that which refers to the Arabs. If we except Ibn-Gebirol, Moses Maimonides, Leo Habræus, and a few others, all the mediæval writers of Hebrew origin were mere Biblical commentators, or else they excercised their ingenuity in illustrating the mysteries of Rabbinical literature. Still, however, the question we are now approaching deserves to be thoroughly examined.

The books of the Old Testament present to us no system of philosophy in the generally received sense of the word; no trace can be found there of those speculations in which both the Greeks and the Hindoos so freely indulged; the Hebrews, as M. Munk remarks, did not seek to penetrate into the secret of *being;* the existence of God, the spirituality of the soul, the knowledge of good and evil, were with them a matter of *faith,* not the result of a series of syllogisms. And yet to every thinking mind, the existence of evil in a world created by Him who is the Supreme God, must have always been a most puzzling problem. How can it be admitted without seeming to impose limits upon that Being from whom no evil can proceed? And how can these limits be acknowledged without thereby denying the unity of the absolute God—

without falling into Dualism? The answer given to these questions by the Mosaic doctrine, may be summed up as follows:—

"Evil has no real existence: it has no place in creation; which, being the work of God, cannot at the same time be the abode of evil. At each period of creation, God *saw that it was good*. Evil enters this world only when intellect makes its appearance; that is to say, at the moment when man, having become an intellectual and moral being, is destined to struggle against matter. A collision then takes place between the intellectual principle and the material one—and from this collision evil results; for man, gifted as he is with moral perception, and enjoying the freedom of his movements, should endeavour to make his actions harmonize with the supreme good; and if he allows himself to be conquered by matter, he reduces himself to become the artizan of evil. This theory of evil, contained in the third chapter of Genesis, is intimately connected with that of the freedom of will, which is one of the fundamental doctrines of Mosaism; man enjoys the absolute liberty in the use of faculties; 'life and good, death and evil, are set before him.' (Deut. 30, 15, 19.) It is important to bring out here, in all its force, this doctrine, in subordination to which the Jews have always placed the various metaphysical speculations of foreign origin, which they embraced at different epochs. The development of this theory, in its connection with Divine Providence, and with the will of God, considered as the sole cause of creation, has ever been deemed, by Jewish teachers, one of the most important topics for their meditation."

We do not think it necessary to give any details respecting the state of Jewish theology during the golden age of that nation. The observations we might make on the various books of the Old Testament, or on the sects of the Pharisees, Sadducees, and Essenes, would be mere repetitions, or *résumés*, of the able disquisitions published in modern cyclopædias. We shall, therefore, go on at once to the first centuries of the Christian era, and consider the Jews as they stood immediately after the appearance of the promised Messiah. The circumstances amidst which they were thrown, told most unfortunately upon intellectual culture; in the first place, the nation was absorbed by the political struggles which followed the terrible catastrophe of Jerusalem; and when, after the unfortunate attempt of Barcochebas, the doctors who succeeded in escaping from the vengeance of the Romans, became convinced that Jerusalem could no longer be the centre of their worship, and the head quarters of the Jewish community, their first care was to strengthen the bonds which could link together as a religious society the children of

Abraham, throughout all the civilized world. The system of the Pharisees embraced, by the majority, did not allow of merely confirming the authority which belonged to the sacred books; it was necessary that an equal weight should be attached to traditional interpretations and developments, which had till then only been inculcated by oral teaching, for the few partial written reproductions of the commentaries could not aspire to the honours of canonicity.

Such was the origin of the *Mishna*, which appeared during the first quarter of the third century, and which it took three hundred years to annotate, to discuss, and to amplify. At the same time, an immense critical undertaking was begun, for the purpose of fixing irrevocably the text of the sacred books, from a collection of the most authentic MSS; and, in their desire for accuracy, the Rabbins went so far as to count the letters contained in each book. Throughout the voluminous compilations which remain to us, and which were made during the first five or six centuries of the Christian era in the *Talmud*, as well as in the allegorical interpretations of the Scriptures, there are only few traces of metaphysical speculations. If we often find there, reminiscences of Kabbalistic doctrines, they bear almost exclusively upon angelology, and exoteric points; the existence of the speculative part of the Kabbala, is revealed to us merely by the mention of the mysteries contained in the *Bereschith*, or the first chapter of Genesis, and in the Mercaba, or visions of Ezekiel.

A complete account of the Talmud, its history and its literature, would require a separate article; but to give our reader an idea of what may be called the esoteric doctrines of Rabbinism, we shall put together a few passages relating to the Mercaba, just mentioned. After discoursing of the angels and other spiritual intelligencies which occupy an intermediate place between God and man, Maimonides says :—

"That which we have said in these two chapters on this subject, is as a drop of the ocean in comparison with what ought to be explained under this head. Moreover, the explanation of all the radical principles, contained in these two chapters, is called *the matter of the chariot*. The sages of old have directed that no one shall lecture upon these subjects except to a single person, who also must be wise and intelligent by his own knowledge, and, even then, we may only point out the passages to him, and inform him very little of the matter; and he being intelligent by his own knowledge, may become acquainted with the end and depth of the matter. Now these things are exceedingly profound, and not every intellect is capable of sustaining them; wherefore Solomon in his wisdom says respecting them, by way of parable, '*The Lambs are for thy clothing.*'—(Prov. 27, 26.) So the sages say as an explanation to this parable: "*The things which are the mystery of the universe, let them be as a garment to thee;* meaning: Let them be kept to thyself alone, and do not discuss them before many people. Thus also he (Solomon) says respecting them : 'Let them be only thine own, *and not strangers with thee*' (Prov. 5, 17.) Again, with respect to them he says: '*Honey and milk (are) under thy tongue*' (Song of Songs, iv. 11), which the sages of old explain in this manner: '*The things which are like honey and milk ought to be under thy tongue.*'"

That the *matter of the chariot* refers to the first chapter of Ezekiel, is apparent, from the following quotation :—

"How far (*i.e.*, to which verse of the chapter) is (it called) the *matter of the chariot*? The Rabbi says: 'Even to (the words) *and I saw as the color of Hashmal*,' recorded last (*i.e.*, in the twenty-seventh verse of the chapter, and not merely to the *Hashmal* mentioned in the fourth verse.)

"Rabbi Isaac says: 'To (the word) *Hashmal;* as far as the word ואראּ, *and I saw*, we may point out the passages (to every learner), but thence further, if he (the learner) be wise and intelligent by his own understanding, we may, and if not, we may not."

We are led to conclude, first, that the *matter of the chariot* was an allegorical and mystical commentary on the first chapter of Ezekiel. Second, that those persons who were allowed to study the *matter of the chariot*, were previously made acquainted with a similar exposition of the first chapter of Genesis, designated as *the matter of creation*. Third, that both these speculations were of a strictly esoteric character, and reserved for a limited number of duly qualified students.

Before we pass on to examine the intellectual condition of the Jews at the time of Mahomet, we would say a few words on the use of Rabbinical literature. There is no doubt that the undue prominence given to allegory, coupled with a servile attachment to legal and ritual traditions, have too often filled the Talmud with the most extraordinary puerilities ; but it would be wrong, on the other hand, to denounce the study of Hebrew theological writings as unprofitable and worthless.

The intellectual development of the Arabs under Mahomet, was felt most strongly by the synagogue. Controversies arose, of a nature totally different from those to which the Rabbis had been hitherto accustomed ; and it became evident that the weapons supplied by the Talmud would no longer prove sufficient. During the reign of Abu-

Dja'-far al-Mancur, second Khalif of the Abbaside dynasty, 'Anan ben David, one of the chief Jewish doctors of the Academy of Babylon, placed himself at the head of a party whose purpose it was to throw off the Rabbinical hierarchy, and the yoke of tradition. 'Anan proclaimed the rights of reason and the principle of free inquiry; acknowledging, however, that traditions, by allowing more flexibility to the sacred text, enabled Judaism to become progressively perfect, he did not, like the old Sadducees, discard the necessity of interpretation of every kind of tradition; but he wanted both always to be in perfect harmony with reason as well as with the text of the Holy Scriptures; and he contested the compulsory observation of a number of laws inserted in the *Mishna*. The members of this sect assumed the name of Karaim (textuaries or upholders of the text), and they are known amongst modern authors as Caraites. It has been objected that for want of fixed principles, and on account of their acknowledging no other authority than the individual opinions of their doctors, the Caraites ended by building up a mass of contradictions and fine-drawn arguments, much more difficult to clear up than the Talmudical discussions; but, on the other hand, no one can doubt that Caraism, at least in its earliest manifestations, had the result of giving to Hebrew doctors a salutary impulse, by employing the weapons of reason to attack Rabbinism, and by compelling the Rabbis to have recourse to the same arms in self-defence. The *Caraites*, besides, were alone fit to found a true system of Biblical exegesis by an alliance between theology and metaphysical speculations. In this respect they were no doubt very much influenced by the example of the Arab *Motecallemin*; for their doctrines, and their position as schismatics, gave them many features in common with the *Motazales*, who had originated amongst the Mahometans the science of the *Calam*. The Caraite divines adopted themselves the designation of *Motecallemin*; and Maimonides tells us positively that they borrowed their arguments from the Mussulman *Motecallemin*. These arguments had for their object the establishment of the fundamental doctrines of Judaism on a metaphysical basis. The theologians, both Mahometans and Jews, were much indebted to the dialectics of Aristotle, which were then beginning to be known amongst the Arabs, although they made use of these newly acquired weapons for the purpose of attacking the philosophical theories of the Stagyrite.

The principal positions maintained in the works of the Caraites, are the following. 1st. Original matter has not always existed; 2nd. The world is created, and consequently it has a Creator; 3rd. The Creator, who is God, has neither beginning nor end; 4th. He is a purely spiritual being, and is not enclosed within the limits of space; 5th. His science embraces all things; 6th. His life consists in intelligence, and is, itself, pure intelligence; 7th. He acts with free will, and his will is in conformity with his omniscience.

None of the works of the most ancient Caraite doctors have come down to us, and we know them only through a few scanty quotations to be found in recent writers. One of the most celebrated amongst them, is David ben-Marânal-Mokammec, of Racca in Arâk-Arabia, who flourished during the ninth century. His work is quoted by some Rabbinites, such as Ba'hya and Jedaia Penini, who do not seem to have been aware that he was a schismatic. We are thus brought to the conclusion that ben-Mervânal only discussed fundamental doctrines admitted by both sects, and that his works had not a polemical character. We are informed by Jépheth ben'-Ali (tenth century) that he maintained, amongst other points, the pre-eminence of man above the angels, as being the *microcosm*.

The Rabbinites, or followers of the Talmud, speedily profited by the example which the Caraite doctors had set them; and they endeavoured to strengthen their own religious edifice through the help of arguments borrowed from the metaphysical teaching of the day. The first man who made this experiment with some measure of success, and whose doctrines obtained some authority amongst the Jews, was Saadia ben-Joseph al-Fayyoumi, celebrated as an exegetical writer, a divine and a Talmudist, and at the same time one of the most powerful opponents of Caraism. Amongst his numerous works, the one which interests us chiefly, is his book of *Creeds and Opinions,* which he composed in Arabic (934); it was translated into Hebrew in the twelfth century by Jehouda Ibn-Tibbon, went through several editions, and has lately been clothed in a German dress by M. Furst. Together with the authority of Scripture and tradition, Saadia acknowledges that of reason; he asserts not only the right but the duty of examining religious belief; for, says he, our faith must be an intelligent one in order that it may be both strengthened, and capable of defending itself against attacks from without. Reason teaches the same truths as revelation; but through the help of the latter, we arrive more speedily at the knowledge of those highest verities which, by the assistance of the former, we could obtain only with much labour and difficulty. The topics discussed by Saadia are, in general, those to which we have already alluded in speaking of the Caraites: the unity of God, His attributes, creation, the revelation of the law, the nature of the human soul, etc. A few points of a secondary nature, beyond the cognizance of reason, such as the resurrection of the dead, are admitted by him, and he merely shows that they are not repugnant to reason. He qualifies as absurd and utterly rejects other doctrines which had then become popular amongst the Jews; for instance, the transmigration of souls (lib. 6, cap. 7). In his commentary of the book of Job, Saadia denies the existence of Satan, and asserts—opinion extremely bold, considering the time in which he lived—that Satan, as well as the sons of God, mentioned in the beginning of the book, were nothing but men.

Polemics occupy a large space in the *Book of Creeds;* and they are interesting to us, because they bring before us, the opinions which were then current in the domains of religion and of philosophy. We thus learn that the Jewish metaphysicians had adopted, like the *Metecallemin*, the doctrine of atoms, which they deemed eternal; others, unable to resist the consequences of rationalism, rejected all the miracles, endeavoring to explain them by natural causes. Philosophy, we should add, occupies in Saadia's works only a subordinate place; it is the handmaid of religion, and used merely as a weapon to defend the articles of the Jewish faith.

Pateticism had at that time only made small progress amongst the Arabs; it was just beginning to establish and strengthen itself through the labors of Al-Farâbi. The only points of the Peripatetic metaphysics which Saadia discusses, are the categories, and he proves at some length that they cannot be applied to God (lib. 2 cap. 8.) His theory of the creation of matter, is an attack against the philosophers of antiquity in general. Amongst the Jewish authors whose names have been handed down to us, Saadia is the first who taught systematically the doctrine of creation *ex nihilo*, which had been undoubtedly professed before him by the Caraite divines. Saadia demonstrates it especially in an indirect manner, by a lengthened refutation of all the systems contrary to it (lib. 1, cap. 4); the will of God is the only principle which he introduces as the cause of creation. Another point fully developed by Saadia, is that of the freedom of the will, founded upon the four-fold evidence of the senses, of reason, of Scripture, and of tradition (lib. 4, cap. 23). The great merit of Saadia, is that of having taught his contemporaries not to fear the light of reason, but, on the contrary to believe that religion finds in reason a firm support. He thereby prepared the introduction of real philosophical studies amongst his fellow-religionists, and inaugurated the glorious epoch of the Jews of Spain and of Provence.

Shortly after Saadia's death, the metaphysical writings of the Eastern Arabs began to spread themselves throughout Spain. At the same time the Spanish Jews threw off, as a troublesome burden, the religious authority of the academy of Sora, founded a rival school at Cordova, and under the impulse of an eminent physician, Hasdai-ben-Isaac-ben-Schafrout, then high in credit at the court of the Khalifs, became distinguished in all the branches of sacred and profane literature. It is commonly thought that the Mussulman philosophers of Spain were the teachers of Jews in the pursuit of Metaphysical researches; as far as Maimonides and his successors are concerned, the assertion is true; but the example of Ibn-Gabriel (Aricebron), whom we must now consider, proves that the Spanish Jews cultivated philosophy with the greatest success, before that science had found amongst the Mahomedans a worthy representative.

Few names have been so popular amongst the Jews as that of Solomon Ben Gabriel; a great number of his hymns are even now preserved in the Hebrew liturgy of all countries. Yet all that we know, with certainty, about his life is, that he was born at Malaga and educated at Saragossa, where he composed, in 1045, a treatise on ethics. We know neither the date of his birth or that of his death. According to the chronicle of Abraham Zacuto, he died at Valentia in 1070; but this indication has been questioned. One of the poems ascribed to him bears date, Hegira, 461, (1069.) We know that he composed an elegy on Hâya Gayon, chief of the Jewish academies of the East, and who died in 1038; we have also another elegy by him on a certain Jekouthiel, killed in 1040; and as it is probable that these poems were composed shortly after the death of the two individuals who were the subject of them, we must assign 1025 as the latest year that can be named, with any probability, for Ibn Gabriel's birth. From the various evidences brought together, it is clear that our poet-controversialist began to make himself known as a philosopher, about the middle of the eleventh century. His works are numerous; but the only one which we shall consider here, is the "Fons Vitæ," a Latin translation of which was discovered some years ago, amongst the MSS. of the Paris Imperial Library. The three principal points of Ibn Gabriel's system, refer to, 1st: The theory of form and matter; 2nd. The Oriental, or rather Alexandrine view of emanation, carefully restricted within the limits of the universe; 3rd. The attempt made by the author to place a Pantheistic system of cosmology, an intelligent and all-powerful will, a free and powerful God, thus preventing, if we may so say, the fatal current of emanations from ascending as high as the Divine essence.

Metaphysical science, which ought to be preceded by logic and psychology, has for its object three things: 1st. The knowledge of matter and of form; 2nd. That of the Divine will, or of the *creative word*; 3rd. That of the primary substance, or of God. This last point can be seized by man only in a very imperfect manner, and is beyond the range of metaphysical speculation alone. The will, first efficient cause, and whose essence contains the form of all things, holds the middle between God and the world. It is not from the Divine *intellect*, but from the *will* that the creation emanates; that is to say, creation is not a necessity but a free act of God. God gives freely to the world the perfection he chooses, and what the inferior world receives from the will, is very little compared with what remains in the will itself.

The Divine will manifests itself gradually through different hypostases, and proceeds successively from the simple to the compound.

The first and direct emanations of the Divine will are matter and form in their highest universality; universal matter embraces at the same time the spiritual and the bodily world; this *power* or *faculty* of being exists in everything, that is, with the exception of God, who is the Absolute Being, always acting. Matter receives from the will, existence, unity and substantiality, which constitute together the most universal form.

The universal soul is the second hypostasis; it manifests itself in three different manners in the universe (macrocosm) as well as in man (microcosm). Being in itself the principle of life, through the rational soul, it is connected with the intellect; whilst by means of the nutritive faculty, it is connected with *nature*. Nature is a simple substance, distinct from the world of corporeity, bodily substances; it is a superior force, which governs this world, and especially imparts to it movement. This force being more directly in relation with the sensible world, than are the superior substances of the soul and of the intellect, we might designate it as *natura naturans*, by opposition to the *world of corporeity*, which would be the *natura naturata*; but we must bear in mind that Ibn-Gabriel does not, like Giordano Bruno and Spinosa, identify the *natura naturans* with God; on the contrary, for him it is only one of the inferior hypostases of the Divinity, and is under the dependance of the superior hypostases which act in connection with it.

The substance of nature, which is the last of simple substances, forms the limit between the spiritual and the sensible worlds; from it emanates the world of corporeity, in which we likewise distinguish various degrees, in passing always from the simple to the more compound. Here begin time and space; space is an accident which manifests itself at the inferior extremity of form. It is, first, the imperishable heaven with its various spheres, and, then, the sublunary world, or that of birth and of destruction.

With this system of emanation is connected what the author says respecting the different manifestations of matter. In the various gradations of being established by Ibn-Gabriel, we can distinguish four different *matters* (if we can make use of such an expression), placed within one another, and particularizing themselves more and more as we proceed downwards. 1. The absolute universal matter, or that which embraces at the same time the spiritual and the bodily worlds. It is generally *substratum* of all that *is*, except God. 2. The bodily universal matter, or that which serves as a substratum to the forms of corporeity and of quantity, and which embraces together the celestial spheres and the sublunary world. 3. The matter common to all celestial spheres. 4. The universal matter of the sublunary world, or that of the elements, seat of contingency, and which our author designates as *natural general matter*. To each of these four *matters*, corresponds a universal form, and these *forms*, in the same way as their respective *matters*, particularize and condense themselves more and more, in proportion as we descend the scale of beings.

Forms in general are of two kinds : the one, constituting the essence of all things, in common to all that proceeds from the Divine will ; the other, limiting being more and more, varies at each degree of the scale of beings. The former of these kinds is anterior to the latter ; for matter has, first, the *faculty of being* in general, and it is only when it assumes the forms of *existence* and of *substance*, that it becomes such and such a thing in particular.

As the whole universe is one single individual, the superior part of it is the prototype of the inferior, and from a consideration of the latter, we can judge of the former, and penetrate its mysteries. The higher we ascend, the more insufficient is our knowledge. The will is impenetrable to our unassisted mind, and we can become acquainted with it only through a kind of ecstasy which places us in the sphere of the Deity. In accordance with this proposition, Ibn Gabriel here and there attempts to prove the existence of the Supreme will, not by rigorous demonstrations, but by mere inductions. The primary substance is inaccessible to us, and if we know it, it is only through the actions which emanate from it by the medium of the will.

Such are the principal features of Ibn Gabriel's system. The reader acquainted with the history of metaphysics, cannot fail to recognize in it the traces of a three-fold influence, viz : That of the Jewish traditions, that of Aristotle, and especially that of Alexandrine Neo-Platonists. One of the most essential points in Ibn Gabriel's doctrine is, that he acknowledges the existence of the material principle in being of a purely intelligible nature; now on this point he is entirely in agreement with Plotinus, and it is erroneously that he has been considered as the first, who ascribed a material principle to the soul and to the other simple substances.

We need scarcely say that Ibn Gabriel's theory about ecstacy is identical with that both of the Neo-Platonists, and of the sceptics of every school, both ancient and modern.

The Jewish theologians could not fail to notice the dangers which threatened religion, in consequence of the rapid strides made by philosophy. Ba'hya Ben Joseph, (close of the eleventh century), tried for the first time, in his treatice on the *Duties of the Heart*, to present a complete and systematic theory of the ethics of Judaism. He began by an essay on the "Unity of God," a work in which he manifested an evident predilection for Saadia's method, although he gave proofs of an intimate acquaintance with all the different parts of the Peripatetic system. The superiority which he assigns to practical ethics over mere speculation, renders him similar to Al-Gazali, whose contemporary he was.

A more direct reaction was manifested in the book *Cosri*, or, better, *Khozari*, composed about 1140 by the celebrated poet, Judah ha Levi. This *Khozari* probably helped to revise the study of the Kabbala.

The efforts of Juda Ha-Levi were not powerful enough to deal a decisive blow at the study of philosophy, which had just then been taking a fresh start, in consequence of the brilliant labours of Ibn-Badja. But the reactionary movement embodied in the *Khozari* created an extraordinary amount of fermentation. The doubts and questionings of even the most enlightened and independent thinkers of that epoch, are faithfully portrayed in the Biblical commentaries of the celebrated Abraham Ebn-Ezra, where we see a singular mixture of rational criticism, and of puerilities borrowed from the Kabbala, of ideas sound and worthy of a philosopher, and of astrological superstitions.

Abraham ben-David, of Toledo, tried, in his book entitled the *Sublime Faith*, to reconcile the Jewish theologians with Aristotelic philosophy, but this attempt did not much succeed. In order to bring about, if possible, an *entente cordiale* between Judaism and metaphysics, it was necessary that a man should come forward thoroughly acquainted with them both, joining calmness and lucidity with energy and depth, capable by extensive learning and searching criticism, of lighting up the whole domain of religion with the torch of science, and of determining precisely the respective limits of reason and of faith. This man was Moses ben-Maimon, more commonly called Moses Maimonides.

Moses ben Maimon was born at Cordova, according to the most authentic documents, March 30, 1135. His father, a distinguished Talmudist, and author of a commentary on Alfarghani's *Compendium of Astronomy*, initiated him from his earliest years to the study of theology and of other sciences. He frequented also the Arab schools, where, as he informs us, he had for a master a pupil of Ibn-Badja, and for a fellow-student a son of the celebrated astronomer, Geber, or Djaber ben-Aflah, of Seville. He had scarcely reached his thirteenth year, when the fanatic Khalif, founder of the Almohade dynasty, took the city of Cordova, and both Jews and Christians were compelled to choose between the adoption of Islamism and exile. A great many families, unwilling to leave Spain, outwardly conformed to the faith of the conquerors, whilst others, rather than incur the heinous guilt of hypocrisy, "travelled about," as Maimonides himself tells us, " by land and by sea," without finding a resting place for the sole of their foot. In 1159-60 we find Moses with his parents at Fez, where they were obliged, at the imminent peril of their lives, to make a profession of Islamism. The Jews of that city still relate about him curious legends, which are connected with the residence he made amongst their forefathers. After having spent some years in that part of Africa, Maimonides could finally withdraw from the oppression which had been weighing down upon him, and he embarked for St. Jean d'Acre, where he arrived with all his family, May 16, 1165. He only stopped there five months, and in company with his father and a few friends, he started on a pilgrimage to Jerusalem, notwithstanding the severe laws which at that time prohibited the Jews from visiting the holy city. Finally, he went to Egypt, and selected as his residence Fostat, the port of Cairo. Then began for Maimonides a period of prosperity. Whilst maintaining himself by the commerce of precious stones, he delivered public lectures, which procured for him, as a philosopher, a theologian, and especially a physician, the greatest reputation. An important political event, of which his adopted country was then the theatre, further increased his prosperity, and added new lustre to his reputation. The famous Saladin, after having overthrown the Khalifate of the Fatimites, had caused his own authority to be recognized throughout Egypt. The friend and minister of that prince, the Kadhi Al-Fadhel, had enjoyed the opportunity of becoming acquainted with Maimonides, and of appreciating his eminent qualities; he took him under his protection, afforded him the means of giving up his industry for the purpose of devoting himself exclusively to science, and procured him the appointment of court physician. So high a state of favour necessarily excited the jealousy of our philosopher's enemies, and they tried to bring about his ruin. However, through the constant protection of Al-Fadhel, Maimonides remained undisturbed in the enjoyment of his well-earned repose until his death, which happened December 12, 1204. On that sad event the Jews and Mahometans of Fostat had public mourning for three days, the Jews of Jerusalem proclaimed a day of extraordinary humiliation, reading publicly the threatnings of the law (Deut. 28), and the history of the capture of the ark by the Philistines (1 Sam. 4, etc.); for they regarded Maimonides as the ark containing the law. His remains were conveyed to Tiberias; and the reverence which the Jewish nation still cherish for his memory, is expressed by the well-known saying, "From Moses, the law-giver, to Moses (Maimonides) no one hath arisen like Moses," in allusion to Deut. 34, 10.

We shall not give a bibliographical list of the numerous works composed by Maimonides. His great work, the *More Nevochim*, is the one which affords the completest insight into his metaphysical views, and to a brief examination of it we shall confine ourselves. It is divided into three parts, very clearly marked out by the author himself:—The object of the first is to lay down the basis of the system of interpretation which should be applied to the Scriptures, and to refute certain opinions incompatible with philosophy and sound faith. 2. The second, consecrated to an exposition of theodicy and cosmology, such as Maimonides understood them, is terminated by a singular theory of prophecy. 3. The third is more particularly moral and exegetical: it treats of evil, of liberty, of providence, and shows that there is nothing in the law which does not find its justification either in person or in history. Instead of proceeding at random as Philo, or having recourse to arbitrary assertions, like the Kabbalists, Maimonides seeks, in the very language of the Scriptures, the foundation of all his allegorical interpretations. Taking one by one all the expressions which the Scripture makes use of in speaking of God, and by which it ascribes to Him our infirmities and our passions, he analyzes them, compares them together, shows that they are susceptible of various significations, and always succeeds in eliciting from the text a spiritual or figurative sense. Thus to see, to look, to hear, to walk, to go up, to come down, are expressions which apply not only to the body, but to the mind; thus, the image after which we have been created, according to the passage in Genesis, signifies, not a material image, but that intellectual form which constitutes the imperishable substance of our soul. This part of our philosopher's work is a real dictionary of the Old Testament, a dictionary of synonyms composed for the use of spiritualism, and no one can imagine what an amount of patience, erudition, and ingenuity, such a labour must have cost. By means of this magical key, a refined mind can discover in the Scriptures, and even in the Rabbinical writings, whatever it thinks proper to assume, nor does anything remain there that can shock our reason.

Maimonides is not satisfied with protesting against material anthropomorphism; he also endeavors to refute that error from a moral or intellectual point of view, and in order to strike at the root of the evil, he maintains that a true conception of God is inconsistant with the ascription to Him of any positive attributes.

Before the time of Maimonides, the Jewish Divines, principally those of Spain, had already established, as an essential proposition, that we can declare not what God *is*, but what He *is not*, and that the attributes generally ascribed to Him, far from expressing an affirmation, only indicate the exclusion of their contraries; thus when we say that God is one, we only mean that He is not multiple, and when we say that He is eternal, we mean that He is not created, etc. The Arab philosophers adopt the same view, and some Mussulman sects, particularly the *Dhirariyya*, make the negative attributes an essential point in their doctrine. The Caraite, Ahron Ben-Elias, in his "*Tree of Life*," (Cap. 71), refutes the upholders of the negative attributes. These Metaphysicians believed they were countenanced, in their teachings, by Aristotle, whom Ba'hya quotes in the following manner: "Therefore," Aristotle says, "the negative attributes of the Creator are more true than the affirmative ones; for all the attributes that might be ascribed to Him affirmatively, could only be those of substance or of accident; now the Creator both of substance and of accident, cannot have in his essence any of their attributes. But the attributes which are removed from Him, (*i. e.*, the attributes expressed negatively), are undoubtedly true." The above passage, quoted likewise by Ibn-Talaquéro is evidently a spurious one. It is a fact that Aristotle, whilst speaking of the *original motor*, very often makes use of negative terms; but he never excludes affirmative terms, and the absolute assertions of the Arab philosophers, in this respect, seem taken from Neo-Platonist commentators, and may be referred to the doctrines of Plotinus.

We then see that if Maimonides was much indebted to Aristotle for some of the doctrines taught in the *More Nevochim*, he made, on the other hand, the Stagyrite responsible for a number of theories which are of a quite different origin.

After having defended the immateriality of God against a false religion, servilely attached to the letter of Scriptures; after having, as he supposed, defended his unity against a false philosophy, which distinguished the Divine attributes from God Himself, Maimonides undertakes to combat the Arab *Motecallemin*, who occupying a middle position between the theologians and the metaphysicians, were equally disowned by both sides, and failed to defend both reason and faith. But, whilst he criticises the doctrines upheld by that sect, he makes us acquainted with them through a very accurate and extensive exposition, and this portion of his work (part 1, cap. 71, 73-76) is of the highest importance as a contribution to the history of philosophy.

If the views of the *Motecallemin* are erroneous, it is necessary that we should establish, upon a more solid basis, the fundamental truths of philosophy and religion. This Maimonides undertakes to do in the second part of the *More Nevochim*. By way of introduction, the author lays down twenty-five demonstrable proprositions, and one hypothetic, serving as premises for the Peripatetics to prove the existence, the unity and the immateriality of God. He then explains the peripatetic demonstrations, and shews that they preserve all their worth, even if we reject the theories of the eternity of movement and of time. The idea of intermediate beings between God and the universe, is unfolded according to the teachings of Arabianism; Aristotle and the author endeavors to shew that these doctrines are consonant both with Scripture and with tradition. We now come to the *vexata quæstio* of the origin of the world. Religion teaches us that the world was created from absolute nothingness, by the free-will of God, and that it has, therefore, had a beginning. If, on the contrary, we believe Aristotle, the universe has always existed, as the necessary effect of a motive cause perpetually acting. Maimonides quotes, as an intermediate opinion, that of Plato, who admits the eternity of chaotic matter, but denies that both of movement and of time. This hypothesis may agree with religious belief, but as it is based upon no demonstration, it can also be rejected. The Peripatetics have alleged in favor of their views, a certain number of demonstrative proofs; the author, however, shews that Aristotle did not deceive himself in this respect, and that he never made the pretention of being able to prove rigorously the eternity of the world. Maimonides then takes a step in advance; the creation *ex nihilo* is not, he says, susceptible of demonstration any more than the eternity of matter, but it has the advantage of being less improbable. The movement of the heavenly bodies offer the greatest difficulties, if we assume that everything in the universe follows an eternal and immutable law. All the theories of successive emanations applied to heavenly intelligences and spheres, cannot account for the multiplicity and diversity which exist in the world; whereas these problems vanish as soon as we acknowledge the action of a free will, manifesting itself *designedly* and not *by necessity*. The hypothesis imagined by astronomical science, have not in themselves much probability; they are, besides, little in agreement with physical laws, and with the principles of movement as laid down by Aristotle. In conclusion, all Aristotle's theories on the nature of the sublunary world, are unquestionably true; but with respect to what exists above, he has been unable to state any proposition capable of proof; and what he has said in reference to this point resembles mere conjectures, which cannot impair the doctrine of creation. This doctrine, besides, is a postulate of religion; if we deny it, we are necessarily led to deny likewise prophetic inspiration and the whole scheme of miracles. However, because we admit creation *ex nihilo*, it does not follow that we are compelled to believe in the ultimate destruction of the universe. Maimonides thinks on the contrary, that the world will never cease to exist such as it is; and he proves that all the passages in the Old Testament, supposed to allude to a final dissolution, must be taken in a figurative sense. Miracles are only momentary interruptions of the laws of nature; they are exceptions to these laws, restrictions placed upon them when they are first established by God. Maimonides then explains according to the directions given in the Talmud, certain particulars of the narrative of creation, proving that everything there said respecting sublunary things, agrees with the peripatetic theories. The whole discussion terminates with a few observations on the institution of the Sabbath, which symbolizes the doctrine of creation.

The opinions respecting the Providence of God, were reduced to five: 1st. Epicurus and his followers deny it absolutely, and admit in the universe, nothing but the empire of *chance*. 2nd. Aristotle, as interpreted by Alexander Aphrodiseus, says that the action of Divine Providence is only exercised throughout the heavenly spheres, and is limited by the orb of the moon. Under this class we may head the view of the Peripatetics, who admit a providence for universal things, for genera and species, but deny it for individuals. 3rd. The *Ascharites*, placing themselves at a point of view directly contrary to that of the

Peripatetics, do not believe in general laws, and acknowledge in God nothing but special purpose, fixed from all eternity, and which determine, in its most trifling details, the life of every individual. 4th. According to the *Matazales*, both God's providence and His remunerative justice, are extended indifferently to all beings, even those who have no liberty, and are therefore irresponsible. No creature, they say, from the smallest insect, up to man, suffers without being entitled to compensation in the next world; none enjoys without having deserved that enjoyment. Thus the innocent mouse, which falls under the cat's tooth, will be adequately remunerated in after life. 5th. Finally, we may suppose that Divine Providence applies to individuals, only so far as they are responsible moral agents. In all other cases, its action is limited to genera and species, whilst individuals are abandoned to the immutable laws of nature. Maimonides examines successively these five different theories, he shows that the first four give no adequate solution of the problem, and he adopts the fifth as satisfying the demands both of reason and of faith.

Whether the providence of God applies to man or to nature, it extends, of course, to the future, and includes foreknowledge. But how can foreknowledge reconcile itself with the fact of human liberty? This momentous difficulty, which has occupied the attention of metaphysicians and divines in all ages, is answered by Maimonides in the only manner consistent with good sense. We know, says he, that freedom is the principle of our actions, and the condition of our responsibility; on the other hand, we have no clear idea of God's foreknowledge, of the manner in which things are present to his thoughts, and submitted to his decree; therefore, we cannot maintain that the two terms of the problem are incompatible with each other.

It would take us too long to explain here the way in which Maimonides undertakes to harmonize the authority of the Scriptures with that of reason. Suffice it to say, that for the purpose of breaking down the barrier which separates religion from rationalism, he calls to his assistance all the resources of his erudition; natural history, medicine, metaphysics, and history are pressed into the service, and whilst marshalling his array of evidences, the author of the *Moré Nevochim* gives us the most curious details on the religion of the ancient Sabæans.

The Jewish theologians attached to their faith, clearly understood the true meaning of the works of Maimonides, and particularly of the Moré. However, it was only after the death of that illustrious thinker, that his opponents gave utterance to the feelings which possessed them.

The Hebrew communities of Languedoc and Provence anathematized all the metaphysical writings of Maimonides, and consigned them to the flames. In their turn, the champions of rationalism hurled sentences of excommunication against the orthodox divines, and a violent schism broke out, which lasted for a century. The victory, nevertheless, finally remained to Maimonides. Whilst his theological treatises preserved all their authority in the estimation of the Talmudists, his *Moré Nevochim* gave the impulse to the free thinkers who appeared in Judaism, from Spinosa to Moses Mendelssohn.

METAPHYSICAL SCHOOLS AMONGST THE JEWS SINCE THE TIMES OF MOSES MAIMONIDES.

The Cabala, as a speculative work, had since the thirteenth century, obtained the greatest popularity. What was its origin? How can it be accounted for? Its enthusiastic admirers tell us that the doctrines with which it is identified were brought down from heaven by angels, for the purpose of teaching to fallen man the way of recovering his original dignity and happiness; others have imagined that Moses received it from God himself during the forty days which he spent on Mount Sinai. He then communicated it to the seventy elders, who in their turn transmitted to others, and thus the Cabalistic tradition was handed down, until Esdras received the order of committing it to writing at the same time as the law.

It is towards the third century before the Christian era, that we perceive the earliest manifestation of certain ideas which afterwards were fully developed in the Cabala; but if we wish to study Cabalistic literature, properly so called, we must come to the two books, *Yecira* and *Zohar*, which represent it in its most complete shape. Respecting the former, we may say briefly, that its author is unknown, but that it was composed at the time when the first doctors of the Mishna flourished. It contains a system, not of natural philosophy, but of cosmology, such as might be expected in an age and locality where physical phenomena were explained by an immediate reference to the primary cause of all things. As a necessary result, the spirit of observation would be destroyed, and certain general and superficial relations perceived in the exterior world, would be deemed to constitute the science of nature.

The *Yecira* is marked throughout with this stamp, and we shall presently endeavour to show, by a brief review of its contents, how mysticism is blended in it with ideas and teachings derived from the Old Testament Scriptures.

The question of the authorship of the book *Zohar*, is beset with great difficulties; various opinions have been proposed as to the date which can be ascribed to it, and the persons who have had any share in compiling it. The problem cannot yet be considered as solved, and we shall here quote M. Munk's remarks on the subject:—

"Whatever may be the antiquity of certain doctrines developed in the *Zohar*, it appears to us beyond a doubt, that the *ensemble* of the work, such as we possess it now, is a compilation, not anterior to the thirteenth century, and the authors of which lived in Spain. As early as the beginning of the seventeenth century, the authenticity of this work was seriously compromised by the critical observations of Jean Morin; and in our own days, the opinion of the celebrated Oratorian has been strengthened by a number of remarks, bearing upon points of detail, which had escaped his erudition and his sagacity. On the other hand, it is impossible for us to admit that the *Zohar* was only a trick and a work of fancy. It seems, indeed, evident to us that the compiler made use of ancient documents, and particularly of certain *Midraschim*, or collections of traditions and Biblical expositions which are no longer extant. We believe also, and we shall shew presently, that striking analogies can be noticed between the *Sephiroth* and the doctrines of some of the Gnostic philosophers, especially Basilides and Valentinian. But several hundreds of passages protest against the opinion, by virtue of which it is supposed that the traditions collected in the book *Zohar*, are spread over a period beginning with first, and ending about the seventh century of the Christian era. We must confess that the arguments alleged against the antiquity of the *Zohar*, in its *ensemble*, are at least as strong as those which have been brought forward as support of that antiquity; hence it naturally follows that we have to deal with a compilation of relatively modern date, in the preparation of which, use has been made of documents belonging to several periods. This question is too complicated for us to discuss here."

If we now attempt to give an idea of the principal contents, both of the *Yecira* and of the *Zohar*, we may observe, in the first place, that the standpoint at which the authors of these works have placed themselves, is a system of allegory, or of mystical interpretation most arbitrary in its character, and which allows the commentator to discover, under the text of Scriptures, anything that suits his fancy.

Returning now to the *Yecira*, we find in it the numbers (Sephiroth) and the letters of the alphabet, as elements of the Divine word, represented as the principles of all things, and considered as the general forms of *being*; they compose together the thirty-two *marvellous paths of wisdom*, at the origin of which is the unity, or God, the *princepium et fons*, the common source of all creatures. The *Sepher Yecira*, that is to say, the *Book of Creation*, is a kind of soliloquy, placed in the mouth of Abraham, and where we learn how the father of the Jews had to understand nature, before he could be converted to faith in the true God. This singular composition, consists only of a few pages, written in a style enigmatical and sententious, like that of oracles; but through its studied obscurity, and the veil of allegory, it allows us to perceive the fundamental idea of the Cabala. It shows us all created beings, both spiritual and corporeal, the angels as well as the brute elements of nature, emerging gradually from the incomprehensible unity, which is the beginning and the end of existence. To these degrees, which are ever the same, despite the infinite variety of creatures, to these inimitable forms of being, *Sepher Yecira* gives the name *Sephiroth*. They are ten in number. The first is the spirit of the living God, or eternal wisdom, identical with the word. The second is the *afflatus* which proceeds from the spirit, or the material sign of the thought and the word; to speak more clearly, it is the air in which, according to the figurative expression of the text, have been engraved and carved the letters of the alphabet. The third is water produced by air, just as air is produced by the voice or the word; water thickened and condensed, produces the earth, clay, darkness, and the grossest elements of this world. The fourth, *Sephira*, is fire,—the subtle and transparent part of water, as earth, is its coarse and opaque part. With fire, God has created the throne of his glory, the heavenly wheels, that is to say, the globes scattered throughout space, the seraphim and the angels. With all these elements combined, He has built His palace and His temple, which is nothing else than the universe. Finally, the four cardinal points and the two poles represent the six last *Sephiroth*. The world, according to the *Sepher Yecira*, is not separated from its principle, and the last degrees of creation constitute one whole with the first. "The end of the *Sephiroth*," says the work, " is connected with their beginning like the flame with the burning wood; for the Lord is One, and there is none other besides Him. Now, in the presence of the One, what is the use of numbers and of words?"

The doctrine of emanation, which is the fundamental principle of the *Sepher Yecira*, presents itself under a new form in the *Zohar*, where, as we shall see, the *Sephiroth* have been symbolized in a different manner. Leaving altogether unnoticed the positive or dogmatic part of the Cabala, which belongs rather to the domains of faith than to those of speculation, we shall limit ourselves here to a consideration of its metaphysical teaching, such as it was gradually developed since the apparition of monotheism, and the dogma of creation, with the great axiom or ancient philosophy: *ex nihilo nihil fit*.

The non-materialist philosophers admitted two fundamental principles—mind and matter; but in this dualism the two principles are limited, the one by the other; the Spirit or the Deity is not free to act, and cannot manifest itself according to its will. On the other hand, this system had the advantage of explaining the existence of evil, both moral and physical, which are ascribed to the intervention of matter; whereas, by admitting only one principle endowed with absolute perfection, the presence of evil could not be accounted for. In the doctrine of Zoroaster the problem is not solved, but merely shifted; for, although, if we admit that scheme, the principle of evil (Ahriman) is *subordinate* to that of good (Ormuzd); still, we ask how evil originated in the world presided over by Ormuzd? In order to clear away the difficulty, the doctrine of *emanation* was suggested. The whole of creation, it was said, has gradually *emanated* from the Divine light; in proportion as it is removed from its origin it approaches darkness, and that portion of matter which is at the farthest extremity is the seat of evil. This doctrine, which introduces us into a fresh puzzle, was popular amongst the philosophers of the Alexandrine school; and of that school the speculative Cabala formed one of the ramifications. We shall give now a *résumé* of the system taught by the Cabalists.

No substance has sprung from absolute nothingness; everything that is, has derived its origin from the source of eternal light, which is God. God is comprehensible to us only through his manifestations; a God non-manifested would be for us a mere abstraction. "Before God was manifested," says the book *Zohar*, "when all things were still concealed in Him, He was the least known among all the unknown." Viewed in this state, He has no other name except that which expresses interrogation. He began by forming an imperceptible point; this was His own thought; then with His thought He constructed a mysterious and holy form; this form He finally clothed with a rich and shining vestment, we mean the universe, the name of which enters necessarily in the name of God.

Another quotation will further illustrate this view of God's manifestation : "The Ancient of Ancients is at the same time the Unknown of Unknown ; He separates Himself from all without being really separated; for everything unites itself to Him, as He likewise unites Himself to everything ; there is nothing which does not exist in Him. He has a form, and yet we can say that He has none. By assuming a form He has given birth to everything that is; in the first place He has produced ten lights which shine in consequence of the form which they have received from Him, and which diffuse on all sides a dazzling splendour ; thus a lighthouse sends forth on all sides its luminous rays. The Ancient of Ancients, the Unknown of Unknown, is an elevated lighthouse, which we know merely by the lights which shine forth before our eyes with so much lustre and abundance. What we call His holy name is nothing else than these lights."

God exists from all eternity, and as such, He is also called nothingness, (*Ayin*) ; thus it is that the world created by him is also said to have sprung from nothingness. This nothingness is unique ; it is the indivisible and infinite ; hence its other name, *En-Soph*, (without end.) The *En-Soph* is limited and determined by nothing, for it is all, and nothing exists out of it ; it manifests itself freely, and by its wisdom, thus becomes the primary cause—the cause of causes. The primitive light of the God-nothingness filled the whole space ; it is space itself. Everything was virtually in it ; but in order to manifest itself it must create, that is to say : be developed by emanation. Through a kind of contradiction, it produced a void, which it afterwards filled gradually by a temperate light, ever more and more imperfect. This concentration or contraction of the light of the *En-Soph*, is called in Cabalistic language, *eimcoum*. By means of such a theory, grounded upon purely material phenomena—the way, that is, of considering the physical effects of the rays of light, the Cabalists fancied they saved the infinite character of Divine light ; for in the other systems identified with emanation, the light appeared limited from the fact of being ultimately lost in darkness. After this concentration, the *En-Soph* manifested itself first in an original principle, the prototype of creation, or *macrocosm*, which is called the Son of God, or the primitive man, (*Adam Kadmon*). It is the human figure which hovers above the symbolic creatures in the prophecy of Ezekiel. From the *Adam Kadmon*, creation emanated in four degrees, forming four worlds, which the Cabalists call *Acila, Beria, Yecira, Asiyya*. The world *Acila*, represents the operating qualities of the *Adam Kadmon*; they are powers or intelligencies emanating from him, and forming at the same time his essential qualities, and the powers by which he operates. These qualities are reduced to ten, and constitute the holy decade of the *Sephiroth*, which is composed of the two sacred numbers *three* and *seven*; the three first *Sephiroth* are essentially intelligences, whilst the seven others are mere attributes. They emanate from each other in the following order: 1. Kether, (crown); 2. Hokma, (wisdom); 3. Bina, (intelligence); 4. Hesed, (grace), or Guedulla, (greatness); 5. Gueboora, (force); 6. Tiphereth, (beauty); 7. Neca'h (triumph); 8. Hod, (glory or majesty); 9. Yesod, (foundation); Malkouth, (reign).

From this first world of emanation, proceeded successively in the same manner, the three other worlds, the last of which, '*Asiyya*, is in same sort the refuse of creation and the seat of evil.

Man, by his nature, participates in the three created worlds, and for this reason he is called the *microcosm*, (*'olum Katan*); for man contains in reality whatever the *Adam Kadmon*, or the *micrososm* contains virtually. By his soul, which is the vital principle, he belongs to the world, '*Assiyya*; by his spirit (rational soul), he forms part of the *Yecira*; and by his intellect, he belongs to the world, *Beria*; this last element in man, is part of the toeity, and has the gift of pre-existence. With a view to express this triplicity, the Hebrew language has three words which signify soul, viz: *Nephesh*, (breath); *Rua'h*, (spirit); *Neshama*, (soul); Isaiah alludes to this division when he says, (chap. xliii., 7.): " I have created him (*berathin*) for my glory; I have formed him, (*Yecarthin*); yea, I have made him (*Afasithin*); Man, then, is composed of two principles, the one good, and the other bad: it depends upon him to make the one prevail over the other; and after his death he is rewarded according to his works, for the *neshama* is immortal.

Such, in substance, is the system of the Cabala. Difficulties, far from being solved by it, are only eluded; the transition from spirit to matter, from absolute good to evil, remains clothed in an impenetrable veil. Through its results, Cabalism completely wanders away from the Mosaic doctrine, and ends in Pantheism; instead of a free God, creating by the action of His will, we find nothing in this system of emanation, but deified nature carrying out fatally its plans of organization. It was not in accordance with M. Monk's views, to institute in his learned work, a parallel between the doctrines of the Cabala and those of the other metaphysical schools of antiquity; we cannot, however, allow this subject to pass entirely unnoticed, and we shall briefly as we can touch upon the principal points of resemblance. If we examine the readings of the

Neo-Platonists, we find, in the first place, the following ideas prominently brought forward: 1st. God is essentially the immanent cause, and the substantial origin of all things. Everything emanates from Him, and unto Him everything returns. He is everywhere and nowhere; everywhere, for all beings are in Him; nowhere, for He is contained neither in any particular being, nor in the sum of all beings. 2nd. God can be conceived only under the form of a Trinity. We have at first a general Trinity, consisting of the three following terms borrowed from Plato: The unity, or the good, the intellect, and the soul of the world, or the Demiourgos. Each of these three terms, produces in its turn, an inferior Trinity. 3rd. The intellect is the essence itself of being. Existence and intellect are absolutely identical in the unity; hence it follows that all the existences of which the universe is composed, and all the aspects under which these existences can be considered, are nothing but the development of the absolute thought; they are a kind of creative system of dialectics, which, in the infinite sphere of its action, produces at the same time, light, reality and life. These three propositions, for the full illustration of which, we must refer the reader to M. Franck's volume, are sufficient to shew, that between the system of the Cabala, and that of Neo-Platonism, there is a similarity which cannot be accounted for on the ground, as our author aptly remarks, of "the identity of the human faculties, or of the general laws of thought."

Passing over the works of Philo, where the Cabalistic views have left deep traces, we come to the founders of the various Gnostic schools. Here points of resemblance are both numerous and extremely striking. To mention only the *Codex Nazarens*, which M. Franck calls the Bible of Gnosticism, when we read it we can fancy we are studying some fragments of the book *Zohar*. Thus God is always called the king and the master of light. He is Himself the purest splendour, the eternal and infinite light. He is also beauty, life, justice and mercy. From Him emanate all the forms, which we perceive in this world; He is their Creator and their Maker; but as for His own wisdom and His own essence, no one knows them. All creatures ask one another what His name is, and they are obliged to answer that He has none. The king of light, the infinite light, having no name that can be invoked, no nature that one can know, the only way to arrive at Him is by a pure heart, an upright soul, and a faith full of love. The gradation by which the doctrine contained in the *Codex Nazarens* descends from the Sovereign Being to the last limits of creation, is exactly the same as the one given by the book *Zohar*.

It is curious to see what influence the Cabala has had upon Christianity itself. A great number of Cabalists became converts to the true faith; we may name, amongst others, Paul Ricci, Conrad, Otto, Rittangel, and the son of the celebrated Abrabanel, Leo Hebræus, author of the *Dialogues of Love*. At a more recent period, towards the end of last century, another Cabalist, the Pole, Jacob Frank, after having founded the sect of the *Zoharites*, embraced Roman Catholicism, with several thousands of his disciples. The Jewish Rabbis discovered long ago the danger which arose from the indiscriminate study of the Cabala. Some denounced it altogether, whilst others endeavored to keep away the profane from it, as from the entrance to the holiest of holies. Leo of Modena, who wrote against the authenticity of the book *Zohar*, a work recently discovered and published in Germany, does not entertain much hope of the salvation of those who publish the principal Cabalistic treatises. On the contrary, the Christians who have been busy on thesame subject, for instance, Knorr Von Rosenroth, Reuchlin and Rittangel, after his conversion, have seen in the Cabala the most efficacious means of throwing down the barrier, which separates the synagogue from the church.

The most profound and learned Jewish philosopher of the thirteenth century, is unquestionably Shem-Tob, son of Joseph Ibn-Falquera, who was translator of the *Fons Vitaé*, and who composed several very remarkable works. Let us also name Jedaia Penini, surnamed Bedersi, because he was a native of Bedersia. He lived about the close of that century, and took a conspicuous part as a promoter of metaphysical studies. His *Be'hinath 'olam* (survey of the world), is an ethical book on sublunary vanities; the elegant style in which it is written, procured to the author the qualification of *eloquent*. Several Christian *savants* have noticed, and Philip d'Aquin, published the text, together with a French translation, (8vo. Paris, 1629). Jedaia proves that man's happiness consists in the practice of religion and of science, and he ends by advising the reader to take for his guide the works of Moses ben-Maimon, the greatest doctor belonging to the synagogue. In an apologetic letter addressed to Solomon ben Adrath, Jedaia defends warmly metaphysical studies against the anathemas hurled by the Rabbis of Barcelona. We have also from the pen of Jedaia, a paraphrase of Al-Farabi's treatise, *De Intellectu et Intellecto*, and several other writings of the same kind.

Joseph ibn-Caspi may likewise be named amongst the philosophers who flourished during that epoch. Born at l'Argentiere, in Languedoc, he composed numerous works, such as two commentaries on the *Ductor*

Perplexorum, and an analysis of Aristotle's *Organon*. Isaac Albalag, celebrated for his bold opinions, and for his version of Al-Gazali's *Makicid*, deserves not to be forgotten. But the man who, as a metaphysician and a critic, surpassed all his contemporaries, was Levi ben-Gerson, of Bagnols, better known by the name of *Master Leon*, who was undoubtedly one of the most eminent Peripatetics of the fourteenth century, and the boldest of all the Jewish philosophers. His works have had immense success amongst his fellow religionists, almost all of them are in print, and several have even gone through many editions. This amount of popularity is the more surprising, because the author acknowledges Aristotle's teaching as being absolute truth; and without adopting the precautionary qualification which Maimonides had deemed necessary, he wrests both the Old Testament, and the articles of the Jewish faith, in order to make them fit his peripatetic notions. It would seem that his merits, as an exegetical writer, made people overlook his errors, in the path of theology and of philosophy, or, perhaps, it was that at an epoch when metaphysical studies had fallen into decay, and when disputes had ceased, the numerous works of Levi, so attractive by the beauty of the style, and the variety of the questions discussed, were read by persons who scarcely understood their complete bearing. Ben-Gerson composed extensive Biblical Commentaries, in which he allowed the lion's share to metaphysical interpretation. His philosophical works, properly so-called, are: 1st. Commentaries—not on Aristotle, as it is erroneously stated in most manuals of Rabbinical lexicography, but on some of the paraphrases or explantions of Ibn Roshd. Many of these are to be found amongst the MSS. of the Paris Imperial Library. Those referring to Porphyry's *Isagoge*, to the *Iategories*, and to the treatise *De Interpretatione*, have been translated into Latin by Jacob Mantino, and printed in the first volume of the two later editions of Aristotle's works, containing the commentaries of Averroes.

2nd. *Milhamoth Adonai*, (the wars of the Lord), a treatise of philosophy and of theology. Here the author develops his metaphysical system, which is in general pure peripatetism, such as we find it in the Arab doctors. He endeavors to show, that with this scheme, the teachings of Judaism are in exact agreement. The *Milhamoth*, finished on the eighth of January, 1329, is divided into six books, which treat of the nature and the immortality of the soul, the knowledge of futurity, and the prophetic spirit, the knowledge which God has of particular or accidental things, of Divine Providence, of the heavenly bodies, and of creation. In the addition published at Riva di Trento, in 1560, the first part of the fifth book has been suppressed; it forms a very extensive treatise of astronomy, and contains calculations peculiar to the author. Amongst the Jewish philosophers of the middle ages, whose works have been handed down to us, Levi ben-Gerson is the first who ventures openly to combat the doctrines of creation, *ex nihilo*. After having proved at some length, that the world can have been produced, neither from absolute nothingness, nor from determined matter, he concludes that it has originated at the same time from nothing and from something. That *something* is original matter which, being destitute of form, is at the same time nothing. By analogous reasonings, Levi, on many other questions, seeks to harmonize philosophy with received dogmas. Such bold opinions, although, as we have said, they did not excite universal distrust, were criticized very severely by the orthodox Rabbis. Isaac Abrabanel, in several of his writings, especially in his commentary on Joshua, mourns over the errors of the Jewish philosophers, who admitting primary matter, deny the action of Divine Providence, with respect to individuals, and see in the immortality of the soul, nothing but its union with the active intellect, which they substitute in the place of God. He blames particularly Levi ben-Gerson, who, says he, has not even thought it necessary to disguise his theories, but on the contrary, explains them with the greatest clearness, broaches on primary matter, the soul, prophecy, and miracles,—discources such that it is a sin to listen to them, much more to believe them. Before Abrabanel, Isaac ben-Shesheth had expressed himself in like manner, but more respectfully towards Levi ben-Gerson, whom he calls a distinguished Talmudist; although, he adds, philosophy has turned him aside from the paths of truth, and he has given utterance to doctrines of which it is not allowable to take cognizance. Moses of Narbonne did not leave so many works as Ben-Gerson, but he equalled him in depth of thought, and his compositions are more interesting for the student of the history of metaphysics, than those of the Rabbi whom we have just considered. Moses ben-Joshua, or *Maitre Bidal*, as he was often called, belonged to a family originally settled in Narbonne but which, had afterwards taken up its residence at Perpignan. It was in this last named place that he pursued his studies under his father's direction. We do not know the date of his birth, but it may be assigned with something like probability, either to the last years of the thirteenth century, or to the beginning of the fourteenth. As for his death, it must have taken place very shortly after the year 1362. His commentaries on the principal Arab philosophers, contain a number of useful particulars, and are extremely instructive. He has elucidated or explained Al-Gazali's *Makacid*, the treaties of the Ibn-Rosh on the "Hylic Intellect, and the possibility of Conjunction," (1344). The physical disquisitions of the same author, and especially his treaties, "De-Substantia Orbis," (1349). The "Hayy Ibn-Yakdhan," of Ibn-Tofail, (1349). The "Ductor Perplexorum," of Maimonides, (1355-1362). All these commentaries exist in several MSS., at the Imperial Library, as well as a treaties by our author on the soul and its faculties. He quotes, besides, an exposition which he had written of the *Physics*, (probably on Ibn-Roshd's intermediate commentary). The style of Moses of Narbonne, is concise, and often obscure; his opinions are not less bold than those of Levi ben-Gerson, but he does not state them with the same clearness, and the same frankness.

At the epoch we are now alluding to, our attention is again drawn towards the east, by a member of the sect of the Caraits, which we had lost sight of since the tenth century. Abron ben-Elias, of Nicomedia, probably settled at Cario, finished in 1346, under the title of the *Tree of Life*, a work of religious philosophy, which can be placed side by side with the *More Nevochim*. Ben-Elias has evidently taken Maimonides as his model, and he has borrowed largely from him.

If the fifteenth century can boast of some remarkable scholastic doctors belonging to the Jewish persuasion, we must at the same time note the gradual decay of peripatetism, and a return to teaching more in harmony with the tenets of Judaism. In 1425, Joseph Abbo, of Soria, in Castille, rendered himself celebrated by his *Sepher Ikarim*, (book of the fundamental principles of the Jewish faith); he there reduces the thirteen articles of faith, which Maimonides had enumerated, to three cardinal principles: the existence of God, revelation, the immortality of the soul. His work marks an epoch in the history of Hebrew theology, but as a contribution to that of metaphysical philosophy, it is of little value. Abraham Bibago composed, in 1446, at Huesca, in Aragon, a commentary on the latter Analytics; some time after, about the year 1470, he was established in Saragosa, where he acquired much reputation as a theologian, by a work entitled the *Road to Faith*. Joseph ben-Shem-Tob, whose father had written against philosophers, and even against Maimonides, obtained the greatest popularity through several theological and metaphysical works, amongst which we notice a very detailed commentary on the Nicomachean ethics, (written in 1455, at Segovia,) and another one in the Ibn-Roshd's treatise on the Hylic intellect. At the same epoch, Italy could boast of a celebrated Hebrew philosopher, in the person of Elias del-Medigo, who taught metaphysics at Padua, and had for his pupil the well-known Picus Mirandulensis, on whose behalf he composed several erudite treatises, and amongst others a work *on the Intellect and on Prophecy* (1482), and a commentary on the disquisition *De Substantia Orbis*, by Ibu-Roshd (1485). His questions on various metaphysical subjects have been published in Latin. In a small Hebrew work, entitled *Enquiry into Religion*, composed in 1491, he endeavoured to shew that the study of philosophy cannot have the effect of destroying religious principles, provided one knows thoroughly to distinguish the questions which belong to the sphere of reason, from those which are accessible only to faith.

Towards the end of the fifteenth century (in 1492), the expulsion of the Jews from the whole of the Spanish Empire, destroyed the focus of Hebrew civilization. Then, the downfall of scholasticism contributed to strike a blow at metaphysical studies amongst the persecuted children of Israel, who crushed down everywhere under a terrible system of oppression, were prevented from taking a part in the revival of intellectual life, now dawning throughout Europe. Judaöo-Spanish civilization disappeared, and for a long time nothing took its place. Isaac Abrabanel, and his illustrious son, were the two solitary exceptions to the general decay; they may be termed the last torches of Jewish philosophy during the middle ages.

The eldest son of Isaac Abrabanel, by name Leo of Judah, and more usually known under the designation of *Leo Hebroëus*, has left a reputation even greater than that of his father. In 1502 he finished the work which has immortalized his name, and which he composed in Italian, under the title *Dialoghi di-Amoræ*. The date of his birth was, probably, between 1460 and 1470, but that of his death is unknown.

Some authors have maintained that Leo Hebraeus embraced Christianity, but this fact has not the slightest foundation. It is true, that in a passage of the first dialogue, St. John the Evangelist is introduced with Enoch and with the Prophet Elijah, who are represented as immortal in body and in soul; and it is precisely from this passage, that persons imperfectly acquainted with the *Dialoghi*, have assumed the hypothesis of our author's Christianity. Not to insist upon the improbable character of the philosopher's conversion whilst his father was living (Isaac Abrabanel died in 1509), we may notice the number of passages contained in the *Dialoghi*, which prove that the author professed Judaism; several times, speaking of Maimonides, he calls him "*il nostro* rabbi Moise;' in the same way, alluding to Aricebron, he says, "*Il nostro* Abbenzubron nel suo libro *de Fonte vitäe.*" When he fixes the epoch of the creation, he makes use of the Hebrew computation, which he calls "*the Hebrew truth ;*" finally, in another passage, the author states as plainly as possible what his religion is: "Noi tutti che chrediamo la sacra legge Mosaica," etc. Nothing more is wanted to show that the author of the *Dialoghi* had remained faithful to the Jewish religion.

Leo Hebraeus is the sole representative amongst the Jews, of that Neo-Platonism which, introduced into Italy by the Byzantine Gemistus Pletho, and by his disciple Cardinal Bessarion, was propagated with enthusiasm under the auspices of Marcilius Ficinus, and combined by Picus Mirandulensis with the mysticism of the Jewish Cabala. The *Dialoghi* have for their subject, love, in the widest and highest acceptation of the term ; love considered under its different aspects, in God and in the universe, in mankind and in the vilest creatures, in the intellect and in the senses ; around this centre are grouped the most varied considerations and doctrines, interpretations of the Biblical traditions and of the Greek fables, between which the author makes ingenious parallels.

The work consists of three dialogues between Philo and his mistress Sophia. The first dialogue treats of the *essence of love ;* Philo having said to Sophia that the acquaintance he had of her excited in him love and desire, Sophia maintains that these two sentiments are incompatible with each other ; and thus the author is led to examine them and define them separately, enumerating the particulars in which they differ. With this view, he studies them from three stand-points, distinguishing their various objects according to the principles of : 1st. Usefulness ; 2nd. Agreeableness ; and 3rd. Honesty. He goes through the different things which deserve to be loved and desired ; the love of what is honest is the highest of all ; the love of God, consequently, transcends everything else in sublimity, for God is the beginning, the middle and the end of all honest or moral actions. But God can be known by our mind and loved by our will only in a very imperfect manner. Seeking, then, what constitutes man's true felicity, the author refutes several opinions proposed on the subject, and concludes that our real happiness is brought about by the union of *our* intellect with the *active intellect, i. e.,* God. This union is the result of combinations, and can only be incompletely realized in this life, but it will be perfect and everlasting in the life which is to come. Then our author passes on to an appreciation of sensual love, which he reproves, as producing nothing but satiety and disgust. True love is essentially intellectual by nature ; it is the father of desire ; and the offspring of reason and knowledge.

The second dialogue treats of the universality of love. There are five causes of love, which are common to man and to the other animals : 1st. the desire of generation ; 2nd. The relations between parents and children ; 3rd. Benefits or gratitude ; 4th. Similarity of species ; 5th. Habitual intercourse. The intellect renders these five causes in man either stronger or weaker ; in him love is more perfect and more noble. Besides, man has two causes of love, which the other members of the animal creation do not enjoy in common with him, viz : 1st. The conformity of natural disposition and of temper in two individuals, and 2nd. The moral and intellectual qualities, by which man gains the affection of his fellow-men. Philo next treats of inanimate beings, which have certain natural inclinations susceptible of being, also called Love, in the inanimate creation, is only a species of attraction ; in animals, it is both natural and sensible ; in man, it is natural, sensible, and rational. This new classification affords Philo the opportunity of surveying the whole domain of natural philosophy, and of cosmology ; and he represents man as a *microcosm*, or the image of the universe. When discussing the loves of the heathen gods, he explains several allegories connected with a great number of Greek myths, and characterizes, *en passant*, the respective methods of Plato and Aristotle, the former of whom, whilst discarding the fetters of rhyme, and writing in prose, has nevertheless enlivened his works by all the graces of poetry and of fiction, whilst the latter has preferred a severe and purely scientific style. Finally, Leo Hebraeus treats of love as considered in the pure intelligences, the celestial spheres. The reason why these intelligences move in their respective spheres, is to be found in God, the object of this love. To conclude, the quickening spirit which penetrates the world, and the bond which keeps the universe together, is love, without which, there would be neither happiness nor existence.

The third dialogue is devoted to the origin of love : and here the author grapples with the abstrusest metaphysical questions. After a preliminary discussion on *ecstasy*, and on the power which the soul possesses of throwing off the influence of our bodily organs ; he examines, successively, the five following questions : whether love exists at all ; and, if so, when, how, from whom, and why does it exist ? In the first place, as a consequence of what has just been said, it results that love exists ; it is the desire which attaches us to what is pleasing. Examining the definition of love, given by Plato and by Aristotle ; the author develops the notion of the beautiful, and that of the good ; and he shews that Aristotle's definition, more general, and more complete, includes divine as well as human love. Love evidently proceeds from something else; it is the product of the object loved, and of the person who loves; the former is the agent, or *father*, the latter may be viewed as the passive matter, or the *mother*. The beautiful, the divine, does not reside in him who loves, but in the object loved, which consequently is superior to the other. Indeed, it happens often, that what is superior loves some inferior thing, but then the superior always lacks a certain perfection which exists in the inferior; and this has in this respect a certain superiority. In God alone, who is absolute perfection, love cannot suppose any defect; and in point of fact the love which God has for created beings, is nothing else than the will He has of increasing their perfection and their happiness. In order to establish when love began to exist, our author explains the three principal systems adduced, to account for the origin of all things. 1st. Aristotle maintains the eternity of the world. 2nd. Plato believes in an eternal chaos, but thinks at the same time that the world has had a beginning. 3rd. The faithful admit the creation *ex nihilo*. Plato's opinions agree with those of the Cabalists, who say that the world lasts only a certain time, after which it returns into chaos and is re-created. The inferior world always exists for six thousand years, and as the duration of chaos is one thousand years more, it follows that after every seven thousand years a new creation takes place. The superior world, or heaven, lasts for seven periods of the inferior world, or forty-nine thousand years; it is likewise subject to a chaotic period of a thousand years, therefore it is renewed at intervals of fifty thousand years. After this cosmological digression, the author, returning to his subject, studies what may be called the *amor princeps*, which is the love that God has for himself, the love of God, knowing and willing towards God, considered as supreme beauty and supreme goodness. This first love is as eternal as God himself. God is the unity of love, of the loving and of the loved; or as the Peripateticians state it, of the intellect, the intelligent, and the intelligible. The second manifestation of love, is that which God has for the universe. Here three kinds of love meet together: 1st. The love of God for the father and mother of the world created by God, and which are identified with the first intellect and the chaos, respectively. 2nd. The reciprocal love of these parents of the world; and, 3rd. The mutual love of all the parts of the universe. According to the opinion of Aristotle, these three loves are eternal; if we believe Plato, the first alone is eternal, whilst the two others at the beginning of time, when creation took place; believers—and the author classes himself amongst them—assert that these three loves were born successively at the beginning of creation. The question of knowing *where* love originated, is thus reduced to the third of the manifestations just alluded to, or to the mutual love of the parts which constitute the universe; and Philo proves to Sophia that this love was first produced in the sphere of the angels, or the pure intelligences. There is to be found the most perfect knowledge of the Divine beauty; from thence it communicated itself to the celestial world, and afterwards to the sublunary one. At this place, the author gives a statement of the doctrine of emanation, as it had obtained amongst the Arabs; he shows how Averrhoes differed from the other philosophers of that nation, and explains by what succession the Divine beauty communicates itself to the various degrees of creation, till it reaches the human intellect. The fourth question, that of knowing from whom love originated, leads Leo Hebræus to interpret the various fables of the ancient poets, on the birth of Eros, or Cupid. Finally, the author comes to the conclusion that the beautiful and knowledge, are the father and mother of love. Whilst considering the beautiful, from every point of view, he speaks of Plato's ideas; he shows that between Plato and Aristotle, there is a complete harmony, and that both philosophers express the same notions under different forms. The fifth and last question relates to the final end of love; this end is the pleasure which he who loves discovers in the loved object. Pleasure is considered with reference to the good and the beautiful, to moral and intellectual virtues; and the author shows that the true end of the love of the universe, is the union of created beings with God, who is the sovereign beauty.

So imperfect an analysis can only give a very feeble idea of the suggestive character of the thoughts developed in the *Dialoghi di Amore*, and of the depth with which the most varied notions are there discussed. The defects of Leo Hebraeus, are those of his time and of the school to which he belonged. His work is not without importance for the history of philosopy, because it is, perhaps, the most perfect representative of that Italian school of metaphysics, which endeavored to reconcile Plato and Aristotle, under the auspices of Cabala, and of Neo-Platonism. Italy rendered full justice to the merits of the Dialoghi; and these merits were great enough to atone for verbal defects, excusable, besides, in a foreigner. The best proof of the sensation produced during the whole of the sixteenth century, by Leo's dialogues, is to be found in the number of editions and translations that were published of them.

Another Leo Hebraeus or Judah, sometimes called Messer Leone, of Mantua, made himself known during the fifteenth century, by several works on philosophy. We have, by him, commentaries on certain portions of Aristotle's *Organon*, and a treatise of logic under the title *Mikhlal Yophi*, finished in 1455. These works are to be found amongst the Hebrew MSS. of the Imperial Library, Paris.

We have now come to the last days of metaphysical speculations, in connection with Judaism. By trying to harmonize Arabic philosophy with their religion, the descendants of Abraham had given to Peripatetism a special character, which made of it, so to say, their national philosophy. If since the sixteenth century, metaphysicians have appeared amongst the Jews, they belong to the history of civilization in general, and had, as thinkers, no special influence over their fellow-religionists. Spinosa was rejected by the Jews; he had wounded, without any consideration, the religious feelings of a community, formed in great majority of Spanish and Portuguese refugees, victims of the Inquisition. Moses Mendelssohn himself, who took up so nobly the cause of his brethren, and who can be regarded as the founder for them of modern civilization—Mendelssohn never would, or could, open a new metaphysical era.

To conclude, the Jews, as a nation, or as a religious society, play only a secondary part in the history of philosophy; that was not their mission. However, they certainly share with the Arabs, the merit of having preserved and propagated metaphysical science during ages of barbarism, and for a certain time they exercised over the European world, a mental influence, which cannot be questioned.

CHAPTER IX.

WORKS OF MAIMONIDES.

TALMUDICAL.—Perush, Hamishurah—Mishna Torah—Sepher Hamtisroth—Maamar Techyath Hamethim—Commentary on the Gemara—Questions and Answers. PHILOSOPHICAL—Moreh Nebuchim—Epistle to the Learned—Maamar Hayichud—Miloth Higeyon. MEDICAL—Canon of Aricenna—Hanhagoth Habryuth—Sepher Harephnoth, &c. MISCELLANEOUS—Iggereth Teman—Iggereth Lehamart Hagadol, &c.

WORKS OF MAIMONIDES.

We shall divide his works into the following classes : 1st. Talmudical; 2nd. Philosophical; 3rd. Mathematical; 4th. Medical; 5th. Miscellaneous.

TALMUDICAL.

1st. Perush Hamishurah (Commentary on the Mishna). This, according to his own testimony, was commenced in Spain in his twenty-third year, and finished in Egypt in his thirtieth. He wrote it originally in Arabic, his native tongue, under the title "Ketob Al Serag," which was translated into Hebrew. Sepher Hamaor, (book of light), and manuscripts of it in the original language, are still extant in various libraries among others in the Bodleian. Parts of it were at different times translated into Hebrew. This commentary of the Mishna, however, was not his first work, for in the preface to this book, he says that he had commented on three divisions of the Gemara.

2nd. Mishna Torah, (Repetition of the Law), also called Yad Chasakah, (strong hand). This work is written in pure Hebrew, and is a methodically arranged digest of all Talmudical decisions; the references to the Talmudical sources, however, being omitted. It is divided into fourteen books. The first is called "Sepher Hamada," (the book of knowledge), in which the author treats of the principles of the Law, of Idolatry and Repentance. The soundness of the doctrines, the sublimity of the precepts, and the correctness of the views therein detailed, have at all times attracted the attention of the scholar, and portions of it have been translated into various languages, amongst others, into English by Ralph Skinner. Maimonides prefixed to this book a preface, in which he declares his motives for writing the work, states his views on the Oral Law, and enumerates the 613 precepts contained in the Pentateuch.

The second book, is called "Sepher Ahabah," (the Book of Love.) It treats of various devotional rites and ceremonies, such as the reading to the Shema Israel, of the wearing of the phylacteries, the fringes, &c. Various portions of the book have been translated into Latin.

The third book, "Semanin" (Seasons), treats of the Sabbath and Festivals, and the rites and ceremonies connected therewith.

The fourth book, called "Nashim" (Women), treats of Marriage, Divorce, and all relations connected with or growing out of the state of marriage.

The fifth book, "Sepher Kedushah" (Book of Holiness), treats of acts derogatory to the dignity of the Israelite, as the partaking of prohibited food, &c. A portion of this book has been translated by Prideaux, and was published at Oxford in 1649.

The sixth is "Sepher Haplaah," (Book of Uncommon Things); it treats of oaths, vows, and the like. A portion of this book is translated into Latin.

The seventh book treats of "Scraim" (Seeds), produce of the soil, and the various laws connected therewith. Portions of it are translated into Latin.

The eighth book is the "Sepher Abodah" (Book of Service). It treats of the Temple and its Vessels, the Divine Service, the Daily and Additional Sacrifices, and every other circumstance connected with these matters.

The ninth book treats of "Korbanoth" (Sacrifices), viz., of those brought on occasions, other than those mentioned in the foregoing book. The whole of this one is translated into Latin.

The tenth book is the "Sepher Tahorah" (Book of Purification). It treats of things, contact with which renders unclean, and also of a mode of purification.

The eleventh book treats of "Nesikin" (Damages), and their compensation.

The twelfth book is the "Sepher Kinian" (Book of Property), and treats of the mode of conveying property, of partnership, and of other circumstances growing out of these relations.

The thirteenth book, the "Sepher Mishpatim" (Book of Judgments), treats of all kinds of trusts, loans, &c.

The last book, "Shoftim" (Judges), treats of the Sanhedrin, witnesses, rebels, kings, wars, and other relations connected with these subjects. Nearly the whole of this most remarkable book exists in Latin translations.

3rd. "Sepher Hamitsroth" (The Book of Precepts). This is an exposition of the 613 precepts, enumerated in the preface to the Mishna Torah. It was originally written in Arabic.

4th. "Maamar Techyath Hamethim," (Epistle on the resurrection of the Dead.)

5th. Commentary to the "Gemara," viz: To the three parts Moed, Nashim, and Nisikim, as also to the treatise of Cholin. This work seems not to have been preserved to our age.

6th. Questions and answers treating on various rites, on which his opinion was asked by certain French and Spansih Scholars.

PHILOSOPHICAL.

1st. Moreh Nebuchim, (Teacher of the Perplexed). This work was originally written in Arabic; copies of it in that language are still extant; four being in the Bodleian. It was translated into Hebrew during the life of the author. The Moreh Nebuchim has been commented upon by several scholars, and in modern times, by the ingenious Solomon ben Maimon. Portions of it have been translated into various modern languages: Townley translated into English that portion which treats of the "Reasons for the Commandments." There exists a German translation of the whole, by Dr. Scheyer, on which criticism has pronounced a favorable verdict. As, however, the Hebrew from which all these translations have been made, is in many places obscure, it is to be regretted that all the modern versions should have been made from this copy. This, probably, induced the celebrated Orientalist, Mons. Munk, of Paris, to prepare a new French version from the original Arabic. This work is divided into three parts; the first contains 76 chapters, and treats of the various synonymes, homonymes, metaphors, allegories, and similies, found in Scripture, and, moreover, comments on prophecy—heaven, the universe and angels. The second part discourses, in forty-eight chapters, on God, on the celestial bodies and their influence, and on the Law. The third divided into eight-four chapters, treats on the vision of Ezekiel, Providence, and the reasons for the Divine commandments.

2nd. Epistle to the learned of Marseilles, written in 1194. This, in an answer to questions put to him concerning certain persons who, believing in astrology, wished to explain everything by means of that pretended science, and concerning a certain Jew who boasted to be the Messiah. It has been translated into Latin.

3rd. Maamar Hayichud, (a treatise on the unity), was originally written in Arabic, and thence translated into Hebrew by R. Isaac ben Nathan. It was written after the Moreh, and is a digest of what the author stated on this dogma in his Yad Chasakah.

4th. Miloth Higeyon, (terms used in the art of thinking). This is a treatise on logic, originally written in Arabic, and translated into the Hebrew. It has also been commented upon by Mendelssohn.

MEDICAL.

1st. Compendium of the Canon of Avicenna,—a beautiful MSS. of this work is preserved at the Dominican Convent at Bologna. It is said that Ferdinand I., offered in vain two hundred gold pieces for this copy.

2nd. Hanhagoth Habryuth, (on the Preservation of Health). It is an epistle addressed to the King of Egypt.

3rd. Sepher Harepuoth, (the Book of Cures). According to Sabtai, the MSS. is in the Imperial Library of Vienna.

4th. Commentary on the Aphorisms of Hippocrates, according to the doctrines of Galenus, in seven Chapters. The Hebrew MSS. under the title of "Book on Medicine," is in the Library of the Vatican.

5th. Garden of Health. This work treats of the animal and mineral productions of nature.

6th. Sepher Hanimsah, (The Book of Existence). This is a medical and moral treatise.

7th. Aphorisms of medicine. It consists of 25 chapters. This work must have been written prior to 1190, the Moreh being quoted in it.

8th. Compendium from 21 books, viz., 16 from Galen, and five from works of other authors.

9th. Treatise on the Hemorrhoides and their treatment, translated into the Hebrew; manuscripts of both are preserved in the Royal Library of Paris.

10th. A Treatise on Poisons and Medicines which may cause death; a Hebrew version is preserved in the above-named place.

11th. Consultation on the snoring of the nose and throat. A copy also in the Paris Royal Library.

12th. A Treatise on Coitus.

13th. A Treatise on Asthma and the remedies for curing it.

14th. Exposition of Drugs.

15th. Consultation of Medicine, composed for a prince of his century.

16th. Method of curing those who have been bitten by venomous beasts, or have been poisoned.

17th. Treatise on the causes of maladies.

18th. Compendium of the medicine of Galen.

19th. On the Podagra.

MISCELLANEOUS.

1st. Iggereth Teman (Epistle to the South). This epistle, written in 1174, was addressed to the Jews inhabiting the countries of the South, in order to strengthen them in their faith, and to caution them against the imposition of a pretended Messiah, then endeavouring to mislead the Jews. The occurrence which called forth the epistle, is thus related by Maimonides in this document:

"A man arose, twenty-two years back, in the south country, who stated that he was a messenger, sent to prepare the way for the coming of the Messiah. He further said that the King Messiah would reveal himself in the south country. Upon this, many people, both Jews and Arabs, assembled, and he wandered about in the mountains, leading them astray, and calling out, 'come with me, and let us go out to meet Messiah, for he sent me to you, to make even the path for him.' And our brethren in the south country wrote me a long letter, informing me of his manners and habits, and of the innovations introduced by him into the prayers, and of what he told them. They further stated that they witnessed such and such of his miracles, and they asked my opinion of him. I inferred from the letter, that this unfortunate man was insane, without any learning, but still fearing God, and that what he said he had done was all a lie. Fearing for the Jews there, I wrote an explicit epistle of Messiah, his characteristics, and the signs of the times in which he is to appear, and warned them to caution the pretender, lest he perish, and the congregations with him. After a year he was taken prisoner, and all his adherents fled from him. One of the kings of Arabia, who took him prisoner, said to him, 'What hast thou done?' upon which he replied, 'My lord, or king, I speak the truth, for I have acted at the command of the Lord.' The king said, 'what proof hast thou?' He replied, 'cut off my head, and I shall be restored to life, and be as before.' The king said, 'there is no stronger proof than this, and if it be so, I and the whole world will believe in thee.' At the command of the king, his head was cut off, and the Jews of many places were heavily fined. There are still, however, many silly persons who say, he will be restored to life, and rise from his grave.

2nd. Iggaroth Lehamaor Hagadol (Epistles to the Great Light). This is a collection of letters on various subjects, addressed to Maimonides, by Spanish and French Scholars, together with his replies.

3rd. Sepher Hanephesh (Book of the Soul).

4th. A book on the Calendar, in Hebrew, still preserved in the Royal Library, at Paris.

5th. Two chapters on happiness.

6th. Treatise on the Sanctification of the Name of God.

7th. Arabic poems of Maimonides.

8th. Iggaroth Harambam (Letters of Rambam). This is a most interesting collection of letters. It appeared in Hebrew in Constantinople. This work is of great importance, containing, as it does, literary notices, and very interesting information as to the author, his contemporaries, and the views and movements of the age.

CHAPTER X.

MAIMONIDES ON REPENTANCE.

Explanation of Passages seeming to deny free-will to some men—Power of Repentance taken away judicially—God's Foreknowledge not inconsistent with individual free-will.

MAIMONIDES ON REPENTANCE.

There are several passages in the Pentateuch, and in the words of the Prophets, which appear to contradict this doctrine (of man's moral liberty.) Many are led to the false conclusions by these passages, that God decrees every man to do good or evil, and man's mind is not in his power to incline to whatever side he chooses. I will lay down one principle which will explain all those verses. If one man, or the people of a whole country, commit a sin, from his or their free choice, God will invariably punish him or them, and God knows how to punish. There are certain sins which supreme justice punishes in the life of man, on his body, his wealth, or on his little children, (for little children who have no knowledge yet, and can keep no Divine commandments yet, are actually the wealth of their parents,—When Scripture says, "Every man dies in his own sin," it only speaks of man and not of children; then there are other sins which Divine Justice punishes in the future life of man, and no harm on their account befals him here; furthermore, there are sins for which man is punished in this life and in the life hereafter. All this, however, takes place only, if man returns not to God in true repentance; but if he returns to God, repentance is a sure defence against all evil, as well as a man may sin with his own knowledge and free-will. It is possible, however, that man commits such grievious crimes, or he is guilty of so many sins, that Divine justice, in order to punish him as he deserves on account of his crimes or manifold sins, which he has committed with his knowledge and free-will, decrees that such sinner lose his free-will, and can return no more in true repentance to God, that he die and perish in his sins. Therefore, God said to Isaiah, "The heart of this people is hardened," &c., and it is said in another passage, "And they have scorned the messengers of the Lord, and despised his priests, and led astray his prophets, until the wrath of the Lord will be spent on His people healed no more;" that is: They have sinned with their free-will, and have transgressed so seriously, that justice declares repentance should be made impossible unto them, which is the healing of the sinner. Therefore, it says in the Pentateuch: "And I will harden the heart of Pharaoh,"—he having sinned with his own free will, and oppressed Israel, who sojourned in his land, as it says: "Go let us deal wisely with them." Divine justice decreed that the power of repentance should be taken from him until he is sufficiently punished—therefore, God hardened his heart. But, if so, why did God send Moses to Pharaoh to admonish him to repentance, when He said beforehand that Pharaoh's heart is heardened? Only to teach coming generations, if the crimes have become too great, the sinner can return no more to God in true repentance, before he has received his punishment, or he dies in his sins, which he committed with his free-will. The same was the case with Sihon; his sins were so great that he could return no more to God in true repentance; therefore it says: "For God, thy Lord, hath hardened his mind, and made obstinate his heart;" the same is the case with the Canaanites, on account of their unutterable abominations, they were deprived of their free-will to repent of their sins, and they made war upon Israel, as it says: "For it was from God to harden their hearts, to go to war with Israel, that they (the Canaanites) be destroyed."

The same was the case with Israel in the time of the prophet Elijah, because their transgressions were numerous; those who sinned were prevented from repentance, as it says, "and thou hast turned their hearts backward," *i.e.*, they were prevented from repentance. Therefore we say: God decreed not over Pharoah to maltreat Israel; or over Sihon to commit sins in his land; or over the Cananites to commit crimes; or over Israel to rebel against God; all of them committed sin with their own free-will, until justice demanded that they be deprived of their free-will to return in true repentance to God. In the same sense, the pious men and the prophets, prayed to God to help them upon the path of truth, as David prayed: "Teach me Thy ways, O God," *i.e.*, let my sins not be the cause of my erring from the path of truth, by which I know Thy ways, and the Oneness of Thy name. In the same sense he prayed: "And let the spirit of goodness support me, *i.e.*, let my mind be free to do Thy will, that my sins prevent me not always to return to Thee, if I err, until I again comprehend and know the way of truth;" so all similar passages must be expounded. When David says: "Good and straight is God, therefore he taught sinners the way;" this signifies, that God sends prophets to admonish the mortal to return to God in true repentance; furthermore, it signifies that God grants to man the capacities to learn and comprehend. This is every man's quality, and walks in the path of wisdom and justice; they are endeared to him, and he longs after them. Therefore our sages said: "Whoever cometh to become pure, he will be helped to it, *i.e.*, he will find in himself resources to support him on the path of purity."

But, it might be asked, is it not stated in the Pentateuch concerning Israel in Egypt: "And they will serve them (the Egyptians)." Did not God decree over the Egyptians to enslave Israel? Then it says, concerning Israel: "And this people will rise and go astray after other Gods;" was it not decreed over Israel to worship idols? How then could they be punished for it? But God decreed not that *this man* of Israel should worship idols, or that particular man, or Egyptians should enslave the Israelites. God only made known the course of the nation in this respect, and not of the individual, who has his free choice not to yield to the corruption of his people or age. This is more as if God had said: there will be pious men, and also wicked ones among this nation; this compels none individually to be pious or wicked. Could not the wicked man, with the same justice say, it is not my fault that I am wicked, for Moses already predicted that there should be wicked men among Israel; hence I am compelled to be wicked. The same was the case with Egypt. Every Egyptian was at liberty to do good or harm to the Israelites; for God decreed not that this Egyptian should do harm to Israel. He only said, that Abraham's seed will be reduced to servitude in a foreign land. In all these matters, it must not be forgotten what we have already said, man has power to know *how* God knows future events.

Maimonides means to say, that man's nature is thus constructed, that if he sinks deep enough in the mire of crime, if he loses free-will, and becomes the slave of his brutal passions and enormities, from which either affliction or death only can save him. This is not the result of speculation, but of solid facts, which one can observe almost daily; in theology such men are called lost sinners; in profane language, we call them stubborn and incurable criminals, who must be rendered harmless to society, or must be brought to their senses by misery and affliction.

CHAPTER XI.

THE RESURRECTION OF THE DEAD PROVED FROM THE OLD TESTAMENT SCRIPTURES.

Rabbi Johannan—Rabbi Simoi—Rabbi Jismael—Rabbi Joshua—Rabbi Elizer—Rabbi Mair—Analogies of the Ressurrection.

THE RESURRECTION OF THE DEAD PROVED FROM THE OLD TESTAMENT SCRIPTURES.*

1. Saith Rabbi Johannan: how can ye prove the resurrection of the dead from the Torah? † It is written: "Thus ye also shall offer a heave offering unto the Lord, of all your tithes which ye received of the children of Israel; and ye shall give thereof the Lord's heave offering to Aaron the priest." Deut. xviii., 28. Now, how could Aaron receive the heave offering, knowing that he died before they entered the promised land? But, the truth is, that Aaron shall rise from the dead; and in the age to come, he will receive the heave offering.

2. Rabbi Simoi says: it is written, "And I have also established my covenant with them, to give them the land of Canaan, the land of their pilgrimage, wherein they were strangers." Exod. vi., 4. Here, then, God made a covenant with Abraham, Isaac, and Jacob, and promised *to them* the land of Canaan; but they have never possessed it; how can God fulfil his promise? This proves that, in the age to come, the dead will rise, and our fathers will inherit the promised land. The Sadducees asked Rabbi Jismeal: "How can it be proved that God will raise the dead?" He answered, "This can be proved from the Torah, the Prophets, and the Haggiographa; but neither of the proofs was accepted by the Sadducees. He said? From the Torah, for it is written, "Behold thou shalt sleep with thy fathers, and rise." . . . But they answered: Why dost thou not continue the verse? God did not say that he, Moses, will rise; but that this people shall rise, after thy death, and go a whoring after strange Gods. Rabbi Ismeal then continued: From the prophets we learn the resurrection thus, it is written: "Thy dead shall live; they shall rise together with my body; awake and shout, ye that dwell in the dust, for thy dew is the dew of lights, (some translate it 'herbs,') and the earth shall cast out the dead." Isaiah

---

* Talmud, Tract Sanhedrin, folio 90, page 2.

† By the word *Torah* is always understood the Pentateuch, or the Law of Moses.

xxvi., 19. But they answered: Perhaps the prophet here predicts the resurrection of the dry bones, performed afterwards through the prophet Ezekiel? Rabbi Ismeal continued: It can also be proved from the Kethabim; (Haggiographs;) for it is written: "And the roof of thy mouth is like good wine, which tastes sweetly to my beloved, and causes the lips of the sleeper to speak." Song of Songs, vii., 6. This, he said, shows that the lips of the dead will yet speak. But they answered: Perhaps it means only living sleepers, who sometimes speak after they have taken wine; or the dead will move with their lips, but not rise; as, also, Rabbi Jochanan said: Any explanation of the law which is recorded, and the name of the author, his (the author's) lips move in the grave, for it is written: "Causes the lips of the sleeper to speak." The Sadducees could not, therefore, be convinced that the resurrection can be proved from the Torah, until the Rabbi quoted the passage in Exod. vi., 4. Now, what can this mean? To say that they who are now standing around him are alive, is nothing, because it is understood by all, that any one who stands upon his feet, and listeneth to a speaker, is alive; but it meant this: Even in that day, when all the world (the inhabitants of it) shall be dead, you who cleave to the Lord shall be alive; that is, shall arise from the dead, and take their reward. The Romans once asked Rabbi Joshua: How can you prove that God will raise the dead, and that God knows all future things? He answered: This I can prove with one verse; and he recited the verse from Deut. xxxi., 16, but they were not satisfied, just as the Sadducees were not. The Rabbi then said: Well, if I had not answered both your questions, I have at least answered the latter, that is, God foreknew that Israel would go astray after the death of Moses. Rabbi Elizer said: In the following manner I repudiated the scriptures of the Cathizem (Samaritans). They say that the resurrection of the dead cannot be proved from the Torah; and I answered them, saying: You set at naught your own scriptures; they are, therefore, of no benefit to you; for is it not written: "Because he has despised the Word of Jehovah, and has broken his commandment, that soul shall be utterly cut off, his iniquity shall remain upon him?" Numb. xv., 31. Now, when the sinner is utterly cut off, how can his iniquity still be upon him? But the meaning is, he shall be cut off from this life, and the sin shall remain upon him until the age to come, when he will rise from the dead, and receive his punishment. Rabbi Akiba remarks: the latter part of the verse has a double meaning; if the iniquity remains upon him, that is, if he continues to sin, then he will receive punishment at the resurrection; but if he repents, and forsakes his evil ways, he shall find mercy at that day.

Cleopatra, the Queen, once asked Rabbi Mair: We know that the dead will be quickened again, for it is written: "And they of the city shall spring up, like the grass of the earth," Psalms 72, 16, which certainly means, that men will grow out from the earth, rise from the dead; but how will they rise, clothed or naked? Rabbi Mair answered: Take an example from the wheat grain, which is buried naked and rises clothed; how much more shall our bodies rise clothed! Cæsar once said to Rabbi Gamaliel: You maintain that the dead will rise; how can this be? Are they not dust? And how can dust become alive again? The daughter of Cæsar, who was present, turned to the Rabbi and said: Be quiet and let me answer my father. She then replied: Suppose there were two creators in our city; one who creates something from water, and the other from clay; which of them is greater? Certainly he who creates something from water, replied Cæsar. Well then, said his daughter; a master who is able to form something of water, should he not be able to make something from clay? Rabbi Ismael said: Take a glass bottle as an example; a glass bottle is made by the breath of men; and when broken, it can be used again (by being pulverized and melted) and made a bottle again; how much more men, who were created by the breath of God, when they are broken, (dead), will be raised again?

A Min* asked Rabbi Ami: How can dust become alive again? He answered: I shall explain it to you in a parable. It is like to a king, who commanded his servants to build him a palace on such a place, where there was neither water nor clay, (which means, where they could not make mortar; still they went on, and performed the work. After several years, that palace was crumbled into dust; and the king then said to the same servants: Now go and build me another palace at such a place, where water and clay are in abundance; and they answered: We cannot. What! cried the king, you could erect a building without those necessary materials; and now, when you have them you say you cannot! Another Min said to Gabiah-ben-Pessisa: Woe unto you sinners, who say that the dead shall live; those who are already living shall die, how shall those who are dead live again? Gabiah answered: Woe unto you, ye sinners, who say that the dead shall not become alive again; those who never were in existence before, are called into existence and life by Almighty God; how much more can those who have already had existence and life, be called into existence and life again by the will of God?

---

* A Gentile or any one who was not a Jew.

CHAPTER XII.

HEBREW POETRY.

Poetry characteristic of the Hebrews—Selections from the later Hebrew Poetry.

HEBREW POETRY.

It may be truly said, that poetry is a grand element in the character of the Hebrew people. Their history is a sublime epic of Providence; their very laws are brightly tinged with poetic beauty; their sacred oracles reveal the future of our common race in magnificent poetic forms; their inspired lyrics furnish the language for the worship of successive generations; they afford a solace in the afflictive cares of life; they hover on the lips of the dying; they are destined to be sung by nations yet unborn; and to be the hymn book of a regenerated world.

This, of course, is to be understood entirely of the songs of the Hebrew Bible. Excellent as are many of the later productions of the Jewish pen in this department, there is an impassable line between them and the compositions of the prophetic writers. The first great distinction between these two classes of poetry, arises from the fact that the Biblical songs were not the products of mere human genius, but a theophany in words, an embodiment of Divine inspiration. They are different also in their forms. The later Hebrew poetry fashions itself in the artistic numbers of prosody; that of the Bible is metrical:

HEBREW POEM.

1.

Before Thy heavenly Word revealed the wonders of Thy will;
Before the earth and heavens came forth from chaos deep and still;
E'en then Thou reignest Lord supreme, as Thou wilt ever reign,
And moved Thy Holy Spirit o'er the dark, unfathomed main.

But when through all the space Thy mighty voice was heard,
The darkness fled, and heavenly light came beaming at Thy word;
All nature then proclaimed Thee King, most blessed and adored!
The great Creator! God alone! the universal Lord!

And when this vast created world returns to endless night,
When heaven and earth shall fade away at Thy dread word of might;
Still Thou in majesty wilt rule, Almighty One alone,
Great God, with mercy infinite, on Thy exalted throne.

Immortal power! eternal One! with Thee what can compare!
Thy glory shines in heaven and earth, and fills the ambient air;
All time, all space, by Thee illumed, grows bright and brighter still,
Obedient to Thy high behest and to Thy heavenly will.

To Thee dominion, sole belongs, and 'tis to Thee alone,
My Father, Saviour, living God! I make my sorrows known.
Thy love, celestial and divine, descends upon my heart,
Inspiring courage, hope, and joy, and bidding grief depart.

Protected by Thy boundless love, my body sinks to rest,
My soul, within Thy heavenly arm, reposes calm and blest,
Lord of my life! in darkest night I sleep and have no fear,
And in the early dawn of day, I wake, and find Thee near.

II.

Eternal! Thou hast thrown us down,
    And scattered us like rain;
No longer can we bear Thy frown,
    O, turn to us again.

Earth hast Thou made to tremble all,
    Her rocks Thine anger breaks;
Lord! close her fissures lest we fall,
    While her centre shakes.

This people, whom Thou callest Thine,
    With hardship, hast Thou bent,—
Thy servants made to drink the wine
    Of deep astonishment.

To those, who fear Thee in the world,
    A banner hast Thou given,
Which, for the truth, must be unfurled,
    In face of earth and heaven.

That Thy beloved and faithful band,
  May be upheld from fear,
Deliver by Thy mighty hand,
  And to Thy prayer give ear.

In holiness the Eternal swears—
  My joy shall be complete,
Shechem will I divide in shares,
  And Succoth's valley mete.

Gilead is mine—Manassah mine,
  While Ephraim, round my head,
Shall strength with beauty wreathed entwine,
  My law shall Judah spread.

In Moab will I bathe my hands,
  O'er Edom cast my shoe,
Philistia! Thy delightful lands
  Shall grace my triumph too.

But who will help me to invade,
  That citidal of strengh?
Who show me Edom prostrate laid,
  And give me rest at length!

Will not the God, whose hand appeared
  From our support withdrawn—
Even Thou, O God! whose aid we feared,
  Had from our armies gone?

Help Lord! for human help is vain;
  Our enemies oppose;
Thro' God fresh triumphs shall we gain,
  For He will crush our foes.

III.

Let us send our voice imploring,
  To Jehovah's starry seat;
To our God this song be soaring,
  Which will mercy for us plead,
    On this happy, happy day,
    For Jehovah hears us pray.

Here united are we meeting,
  In Thy house this Sabbath day ;
Let Thy presence give us greeting,
  As we chant this simple lay.
    O, descend to dwell among
    Thine own people's joyous throng.

We now consecrate this temple,
  To high heaven's noble Lord ;
Full with joy we now assemble,
  And to pious themes resort.
    O, Forgive the sins of all,
    Who have sought this sacred wall.

Give us light, while we are steering,
  In this dark, too dark a path ;
Dwell among us and be cheering,
  The poor victims of Thy wrath ;
    We'll obey Thy dread commands,
    Though we live in foreign lands.

For Messiah are we waiting,
  Who will take us to our home ;
May our glory not be fading,
  From great Judah's sons that roam,
    In all lands to chant a lay,
    On this joyous Sabbath day.
                —Moos.

IV.

On Thee my rock, Eternal! will I call ;
  Not silently do thou attend ;
Lest, Thou remaining silent, I should fall,
  Like those who to the pit descend.
To my imploring voice Thine ear apply,
    When I for mercy cry—
While on Thy holy shrine I gaze,
And to Thine oracle my hands adoring raise.

With vile transgressors draw me not away—
　With those who practice wicked arts—
Who, " Peace be with you," to their neighbors say,
　While hatred works within their hearts.
Thou wilt, according to their evil done,
　　　Reward them every one—
Their practices malevolent,
According to the guilt of their malign intent.

After the wicked deeds their hands have wrought,
　Their recompense wilt Thou assign—
Returning on themselves their evil thought,
　As the desert of their design.
Because to the Eternal's just commands,
　　　And working of His hands,
A due respect they never yield,
He shall destroy them all, and their work never build.

Blest be the Eternal, a gracious ear
　Has to my prayerful voice inclined :
The Eternal is my buckler ever near ;
　In Him all needful strength I find.
In Him my heart confided and believed,
　　　And succor I received ;
My heart is therefore filled with joy,
And to exalt his praise, I will my song employ.

———

V.

Why mourneth Zion's daughter now,
　Her head with ashes strewed ?
She weeps for Judah's broken vow,
　Her spirit is subdued.

Queen of the nations ! thou art reft,
　Of temple, crown and throne ;
Thy music hath no echo left
　But sorrow's plaintive tone.

The glory of the earth wert thou,
    Thy beauty is no more;
For dust defiles thy royal brow,
    Thy garments trail in gore.

Like harts that can no pasture find,
    Thy trembling princes fly;
Mute doves to foreign hands consigned,
    Thy captive daughters sigh.

The arrow in thy breast is sheathed,
    The net thy feet ensnares;
The yoke around thy neck is wreathed,
    Thy portion is but tears.

Can Gilead, then, no balm bestow
    To heal my people's wound?
Oh, God! let hope from Heaven flow,
    And mercy's balm be found!

                —ADAH MENKEN.

VI.

Morn breaks upon Moriah's height!
    A father and his only son,
There bow toward the rising light,
    And humbly say, God's will be done!

With trembling hand, but faithful heart,
    The sire binds his sinless boy:
Prepared with that sweet pledge to part,
    Which he who lent would now destroy.

On Sarah most his thoughts were bent,
    When she no more should meet her child;
But mourn within her lonely tent,
    For him, the pure, the undefiled.

Yet firmly Abraham grasps the blade;
    But ere the fatal stroke descends,
A beam hath round the victim played,
    An angel o'er the altar bends!

Forbear! the test of faith is o'er:
    Unbind the sacrificial cord!
You heaven provided ram secure,
    To bleed and burn before the Lord.

Blow, blow the trumps of gladness now!
    God's clemency and love confess!
Who hath fulfilled His solemn vow,
    In Isaac's seed the earth to bless!

—*The Sacrifice.*   A. J. M.

VII.

Lord of the Universe. He reigned
    Before creation's teeming birth;
Erst, when His fiat all ordained,
    Acknowledged King supreme on earth.

Yet, when these worlds shall pass away,
    He still shall govern, sole, sublime,
Who was, who is, and will be aye,
    All glorious to the end of time.

One only God, with none beside
    To equal Him, or share His throne;
Beyond the reach of time and tide,
    Pow'r and dominion His alone.

Without compare or parallel,
    Ne'r knowing variance or change,
No pow'r can lessen, increase, swell
    His mighty empire, boundless range.

My God and my Redeemer lives,
    A sheltering rock, when woes befal;
My banner He a refuge gives,
    A cup of solace when I call.

To Him my spirit I resign,
    Asleep, or waking, to His care
I yield this mortal frame of mine,
    Nor fear—God's with me everywhere.

אדון עולם

VIII.

When Faith too young for a sublimer creed,
    Her sample text from nature's volume taught,
She 'wakened melody, whose shell and reed—
    Though rude, upon her spirit gently wrought.
But soon from sylvan altars she took wing,
    And music followed still the angel's flight;
Savage no more, she touched a golden string,
    And sung of God, in revelation's light!
Lend, lend your chords ye seraph-pair,
    The soul of Jesse's Son;
That we may in harmonious prayer,
    Exalt the Holy One!

Girt in His lightning-robe, God gave the law,
    From trembling Sinai, to His eldest born;
Tables, that time from memory could not draw,
    A talisman in Judah's bosom worn,
His Spirit before thousands past,
    So one alone revealed;
And mid the thunder's awful blast,
    Faith's covenant was sealed!

Him first, Him last, Him ever let us sing,
    Whose promise yet the Hebrew pilgrim cheers;
Who shall his wandering people once more bring,
    Back to the glory of departed years.
Bright Pillar of our dessert path,
    Through shame and scorn adored;
Chastened in spirit and in word,
    Still, still let our soul-harmony,
Ascend before Thy throne;
    While echoing seraphim reply,
The Lord our God is one!

                      ADAH.

IX.

PSALM III.

Lord, see my foes—the vast array,
    Against me come abroad;
While, of my soul, full many say—
    "No help for him in God."

But Thou, Eternal, art my shield,
    My glory, and my praise;
By thee, mine every wound is healed,
    My head Thy mercies raise.

Eternal, I, for quick'ning grace,
    Besought with earnest voice;
He heard me from His Holy place,
    And caused me to rejoice.

I laid me down, nor dreaded harm,
    I slept from trouble free;
Fresh I awoke, for with His arm
    The Lord God shielded me.

I will not, therefore, be afraid
    Of tens of thousand strong,
Who, round me compassing have laid,
    Foul plots to do me wrong.

Arise, Eternal! save me, God!
    For Thou has smitten those,
Mine enemies; Thy powerful rod
    Has crushed my wicked foes.

Salvation with the Lord God rests;
    Yes, Thou alone Divine;
Thy blessing savingly invests
    All who are truly thine.

X.

SINAI.

On that appalling morn when Israel woke,
    To hear her Lord's omniscient decree;
When, as though Heaven's loud thunder broke,
    The very air grew rife with mystery;
When Sinai's Mount, involved in fire and smoke,
    Outswelled the aspiring eager of the sea;
This be my theme, presuming task! to sing
The praise of Israel's God, her everlasting king!

Oh, for a seraph's tongue or prophet's pen,
    My glorious song, enraptur'd to exalt!
Oh, to have heard Him, "With an angel's ken,"
    From yon triumphal wonder-paven vault,
Come clothed in wisdom to commune with men,
    And bid so near their tents His hierarchs halt!
O'er sapphire floods, the burning escort rolled
Through clouds of roseate fire and molten gold.

Soon from the hill's crest, fearful sounds began
    To radiate slowly to its hallowed base;
Through all the mustering tribes one impulse ran,
    A thrill of joy and fear; o'er shivering space
Pealed the celestial trump, and awe-struck men,
    With suppliant eyes, beheld the wondrous place,
Where eddying mist and lightnings livid stream,
Confest the Lord of Hosts—the Invisible Supreme!

Pillars of smoke, thick-falling caught the eye;
    Dense but a moment; for the reddening blaze
Gushed forth in plunging volleys to the sky,
    Fierce thunders roared and meteors flashed amaze;
The unfathomed empyrean gleamed on high,
    With hues of amber, dazzling to the gaze,
And peal on peal, with wild tumultuous din,
Rolled on, far echoing o'er the wilderness of sin.

In awful glory shone the firmament,
    Save where the vapor stained its glowing form;

Grey Sinai, with mighty earthquake rent,
  Upheaved its surging breast as in a storm,
Shapeless, from side to side, the waves were sent,
  Toss'd by the power of an Almighty arm;
And Israel knelt with hands and eyes upraised,
While down the dusky hills, Jehovah's lightning blazed.

Then lo! the archangel's summons, loud and shrill,
  Shot terror and dismay through all their bands,
And, waxing longer, louder, louder still,
  Reverberating o'er the desert sands,
Bidding God's seer ascend the flaming hill
  From which He issued His divine commands,
And gave them statutes for the promised Home,
And lighted Heaven with love through the etherial dome!

Affectionately inscribed to brother Jacob, by A. J. M.

XI.

PSALM XX.

The Eternal hear thee, in the day,
  When threatening dangers lower;
The God of Israel be thy stay—
  His name thy lofty tower.

O! may He from His temple send,
  To help thee by His grace—
From Holy Zion succour lend,
  Thine arm with vigor brace.

Thine offerings in remembrance bear,
  Thy sacrifice receive—
Fulfil thy heart's unuttered prayer,
  And thy designs achieve.

To us Thy safety shall afford
  A theme of joyful praise,
And in the name of God, the Lord,
  Our banners will we raise.

Now we know that the Lord from harm,
    Will His anointed shield :
Hear Him from Heaven, and His right arm
    With saving vigor wield.

To praise of chariots some declaim,
    For horses some declare ;
But we in mem'ry will the name
    Of God, the eternal, bear.

And thus, while they descending fall,
    We rising shall ascend ;
Eternal ! save us ; when we call
    Do Thou, our King, attend.

—*Jewish Chronicle.*

XII.

It is the holy Sabbath day,
    Let praise to God ascend !
In holiness thy soul array,
    And worldly thoughts suspend.

Come forth, ye weary sons of care,
    Toil-worn and grief-oppressed ;
To heaven send a grateful prayer,
    For those calm hours of rest.

Let not the poorest of ye ask,
    Of Providence long tried,
" If I forego my daily task,
    Whose hand shall bread provide."

Remember that celestial food,
    To Israel ordained,
When mercy *double* portions strewed,
    Lest Sabbath be profaned.

With tenfold gifts will God repay,
    The transient loss incurred ;
But tremble ye who disobey,
    The mandate of the Lord.

With rapture then behold the light
   Of this returning day ;
Direct, O God, our steps aright,
   Nor from Thee let us stray !

XIII.

HYMN FOR THE DAY OF ATONEMENT.

Almighty God! Thy sovereign power
   To us is manifest;
Sustain us in this trying hour,
   And calm the anxious breast.

Give peace to every contrite heart,
   The wounded spirit heal,
Subdue our fears, glad hope impart,
   Thy love divine reveal.

With ever gracious eye behold,
   The penitential tear,
We feel our sins are manifold ;
   Our guilt to us is clear.

Thy unity we will proclaim—
   One God alone adore ;
And glorify Thy holy name,
   Both now and evermore.

C. LINDO.

XIV.

HYMN FOR THE RECEPTION OF THE SABBATH.

Come, my beloved, to meet the bride ;
The presence of the Sabbath let us receive.
   Come, my beloved, &c.

Keep and remember the Sabbath, both words did,
The one peculiar God caused to hear, with an expression ;
The Eternal is unity, and His name is Unity ;
To Him appertaineth renown, glory, and praise.
   Come, my beloved, &c.

Come, let us go meet the Sabbath day,
For it is the fountain of blessing;
In the beginning of old was it appointed;
For though last in creation;
Yet it was first in the design of God.
      Come, my beloved, &c.

O thou sanctuary of the King! O royal city!
Arise and come forth, from Thy subversion;
Thou hast dwelt long enough in the abode of calamity,
For He will now pity thee with kindness.
      Come, my beloved, &c.

Shake off the dust; arise, O my people;
And adorn thyself with thy beautiful attire;
For by the *hand of Jesse*, the *Bethlemite*,
Redemption draweth nigh to my soul.
      Come my beloved, &c.

Rouse thyself; rouse thyself; arise, shine;
For thy light is come; awake, awake; utter, utter a song;
For the glory of the Lord is revealed upon thee.
      Come, my beloved, &c.

O be not ashamed, neither be thou confounded.
O Jerusalem, why art thou cast down?
Why art thou disquieted? For thee, the poor
Of my people shall take refuge,
And the city shall be built on her own heap.
      Come my beloved, &c.

They who spoil thee, shall become a spoil;
And they that swallow thee up, shall be removed far away;
Thy God will rejoice in thee,
As the bridegroom rejoiceth in his bride.
      Come my beloved, &c.

On the right and on the left wilt thou
Be extended, and the Eternal wilt thou revere;
Through the means of a man, the descendant of Pharez,
Will we rejoice and be glad.
      Come, my beloved, &c.

O come in peace, thou crown of
Thy husband; also with joy and mirth,
In the midst of the faithful and beloved people.
Enter, O bride! Enter, O bride!
Come, my beloved, &c.

XV.

VOICE OF ISRAEL.

With feelings wild as the wind;
With a soul no earth-fetters can bind.

Haunting my soul's young life;
   Sighs are gasping,
   Wings are clasping,
In ceaseless meaning strife;
   Baffling control,
   Binding my soul—
This soaring soul to life!
To list a voice from the down-trod grave,
Ever calling this frail soul to save
   From dust, a nation—
   God's generation!

Through crowded streets I hear
   That mournful sound,
   Along the ground,
Creeping to my startled ear—
   In forests lone,
   I hear the tone;
Restless wings beating near;
Folding and unfolding, a spirit band;
Bearing a voice from the silent land—
   Voice of the lowly dead,
   Israel's lonely dead.

Now in the sweetest singing,
   'Tis soft and low,
   Its numbers flow;
Through my dreams 'tis winging,

Like light at morn,
  Israel-born !
With a God-breath flinging.
Thoughts of a glory down this life of mine—
O, this struggling life for light divine !
  Israel's golden light,
  From God's power and might.

O, this voice of mystery,
  Winding slowly,
  Sighing lowly,
Through my soul's life history ;
  Shrieking and sighing,
  Pleading and crying,
A nation's wrongs, the story ;
Wrongs that wail from o'er a sea of blood,
And from o'er Charon's deep mystic flood ;
  " Save God's own nation,
  " Soul's generation."

Lift to my lips the purple wine—
  The wine of life,
  With a glory rife,
To free from this soul of mine,
  The gathered dust,
  And deeper rust,
That I may see the light divine,
To gird on the armor of power and might ;
To battle for Israel, God and our right !
  For the God-crowned nation ;
  Eternal generation.

BY THE ABOVE.

XVI.

O for a glance of heavenly day
To take this stubborn stone away,
And melt with beams of love divine
This heart, this frozen heart of mine !

The rocks can rend, the earth can quake,
The sea can roar, the mountain shake ;
Of feeling all things show some sign,
But this unfeeling heart of mine.

To hear the sorrows Jews have felt,
Dear Lord, an adamant would melt ;
Then grant, O Lord, the Christian grace
To feel in heart for Israel's race.

Eternal Spirit, mighty God !
The Jews, like us, are flesh and blood ;
Then why should we to them alone,
Exhibit but a heart of stone.

Grant then, O Lord, each Christian nation—
To Jews indebted for salvation—
Israel's claim may freely own
And softened have the heart of stone.

C.

XVII.

TO ISRAEL.

Hail ! all hail, mysterious nation,
  "Lot of God's inheritance !"
Sad, though long, thy situation,
  See a brighter day advance !

Clouds and storms have overspread thee ;
  Toss'd thy bark, dishevelled, torn ;
But the hand that chastened, lead thee—
  Sink thou could'st not, by it borne.

Did God's vengeance overtake thee,
  'Twas in *sorrow*, not in hate :
Still the purposes to make thee,
  Above all other nations great.

Hark ! the promise—Israel ! hear it ;
  Hear the voice of Jacob's Rock ;

" I, who scattered thee, will gather,
  " As a shepherd doth his flock.

" In the dark and cloudy day,
  " I will seek my wandering sheep ;
" Gently lead them in the way,
  " From all danger safely keep.

" In the land upon the mountains,
  " Judah, Israel one shall be ;
" Pastures green, and living fountains,
  " I, thy God, will give to thee.

" With my rod and staff I'll guide thee,
  " Safe into the promised land ;
" From all evil will I guide thee
  " In the hollow of my hand."

Israel ! see the day approaches,
  Joyful lift thy voice on high !
Now, no more shall wrongs, reproaches,
  Be thy portion—God is nigh.

Cease to mourn then, favoured nation !
  Trust thy God !—He loves thee still ;
His right arm will bring salvation ;
  He, the promise will fulfil.

R. S.

PART FOURTH.

THE STUDY OF HEBREW.

CHAPTER I.

THE HEBREW BIBLE.

STUDY of the text—Historical evidence of the accuracy of the Textus receptus.

THE HEBREW BIBLE.

Much light might be thrown on the Hebrew Scriptures, by a greater attention to a critical study of the text. I do not, however, think that even the soundest criticism could produce a text different in any material point from that in existence, so as essentially to affect any historical or doctrinal point. The Hebrew Scriptures are now, upon the whole, in the same state in which Ezra left them. It is known that a copy of the Scriptures had been in the Temple. Possible that Ezra's original, or at least a copy thereof, preserved in the temple, was destroyed in the time of Antiochus Epiphanes. But as the interval between this calamity and the restoration of the public worship by the Maccabees, was too short to have obliterated the memory of this copy; as, moreover, copies of the Scriptures were then already too widely disseminated to be destroyed in so short an interval; as, besides, many scribes, under Antiochus, must, also, have witnessed the triumph of the Maccabees, it cannot be doubted but that a *fac simile* of the Temple scrolls was soon executed, and again deposited in the Temple. By this authentic copy, the Scribes, no doubt, revised and corrected their transcripts, which, even before the destruction of the Temple, were carried to Babylon, and to the other Jewish settlements then existing. At the destruction of the Temple, many such corrected copies must have existed all over the world. This authentic copy was not destroyed by Titus, for it was among the trophies carried to Rome, and, more than one-hundred and fifty years after the destruction of the Temple, Rabbi Simeon ben Yochai, a celebrated Mishnaic doctor, declared to have seen it at Rome, preserved with the other trophies carried away from Jerusalem. The peace which the Jews enjoyed under the successors of Hadrian, and especially the high favour in which the compiler of the Mishna, Rabbi Ye'iudah, the prince, stood with some of the

Antonines, make it highly probable that the Jews, if they wished it, could obtain access to this authentic scroll of the law, whilst their deep interest in the matter, it may be assumed, must have impelled them, in cases of doubt, to consult its contents. Long before these trophies were carried away, by the Vandals, to Africa, the work of the Massorah had commenced, in Tiberias, and the present system of vocalisation, if not then invented, was, at least, perfected. Ever since that time, a Massoretic and Biblical literature had sprung up, guarding the text with a scrupulousness which prevented any error from creeping in. Indeed, the controversy of the two critical schools, known respectively by the name of the sons of Ascher, and of Naphtalee, referred only to most unimportant points, and this very controversy shows how universally the text must have spread, which now forms the *textus receptus*. There would be no difficulty whatever in showing that the celebrated Maimonides had access to a copy of the Bible, critically revised by one of the founders of the schools mentioned, and that he corrected by it a copy of the law written by himself. Nor would it be difficult to show that the copy of Maimonides was preserved long after his death, and that, owing to the intimate literary intercourse which existed, during the middle ages, between the Jewish scholars of the East and West, transcripts of this copy could have found their way into Europe. There is no occasion for extending the chain of evidence farther down, as nobody would maintain that any change in the Hebrew text could have been made after that period.

CHAPTER II.

BIBLICAL STUDIES.

The Poetry of Youth and Old Age—Application of the principle to the Jewish nation and history—Gentile Historians—A history and literature more ancient than political institutions—Jewish nationality—Four epochs in Jewish history.

BIBLICAL STUDIES.

Men are apt to ask themselves in their serious moments, why it is that in the ripe years of manhood or old age, a retrospective glance at their childhood or youth offers so poetic a charm—and why, on the other hand, the boy longs to be a youth, and the youth yearns for the ripe age of manhood ; both appearing so poetically colored, that the aged wish to retrace, and the young to anticipate their career ; while the boy, the youth, the man, and the aged, in all those phases of real life, but too often miss such poetry.

It is not difficult to answer this question. Remembrance and hope may be compared to those high mountains, the summit of which command views of the far stretching landscapes, with their different groups combining into one beautiful panorama, while those objects which would tend to disturb the harmony of the whole are lost in the distance, or rendered imperceptible by the overwhelming majority of conspicuous beauties ; but on wandering through all these landscapes and single groups, we shall be led into valleys and glens, through swamps and by rivers which will check our progress, depriving us of the general view, and forcing on us the sight of details, detaining us in uncomfortable places longer than we think desirable, and on lovely spots longer than profitable. Thus we everywhere behold but fragments promiscuously scattered about, without in the least suspecting the grand and beautiful effect which the whole affords.

Such charming Alpine valleys of life, but also such swamps and rocks of time, the history of the human race in general, and that of the Jews in particular, presents to every person undertaking a journey through them, without calling to his aid science and poetry, from the summits of which he would be enabled to obtain a general view of it. The works of such historical wanderers, even if they fill many volumes, would not form a history, but only so many books of excursions, which, unless written in a particularly scientific, or better æsthetically attractive manner, would neither offer anything useful nor agreeable. Such defects are mostly betrayed by writers of the Jewish nation, who compose their works with a certain degree of prejudice, either in favor or against particular tendencies.

In contrast to these writers, the non-Israelite narrators of Biblical history are apt to take their stand as if on the top of a spire, towering into the clouds, and speculating on certain doctrines flattering to the spirit of the age, in order to view the scenery spread before them through the medium of hyperrationalism, through the mist of a cold, material atmosphere—a proceeding certainly, by which, if their artificial telescopes be somewhat dimmed, the lights' shades, and the signs of life on the single portions of the landscapes under their observation, must be lost to them, in consequence of which they deny the existence of whatever they do not procure, and declare everything obscure that appears so to themselves. Historians of this description can only tell their readers of the outward forms, not of the inward life, suffering, and exertions of the people of which they know too little.

The history of the Jews, as compared with that of all other nations, is indeed peculiar. Every other people on the face of the earth is older than its history; obscurity and fable dim the origin of all; the literature of none extends as far back as the first centuries of their existence. The history of Israel, on the contrary, is contemporaneous with its very existence; older even than the Israelites as a nation; for we see the primitive family of Jacob, aye, of his distinguished ancestor, Abraham, taking root, and overshadowing the whole land of Israel. Its literature is more ancient than its political existence; and then, what a literature! Furnished neither by fable nor disfigured myth; but founded from its very outset upon a piously pure tradition, and divinely exalted word. The natural development of every other national history may be compared to a stream rising from some insignificant source or contemptible marsh, small at first, but increasing in dimensions, until swelled by the reception of many tributary streams, it divides into several branches, which lose themselves in the ocean.

The history of Israel, on the contrary, resembles a mighty lake upon some lofty mountain top, flowing down by Divine election as a spiritual Niagara, and branching off into smaller rivers, it passes onward in cataracts, through other streams and seas, yet always sustained by that Divine spring, it does not disappear even on its passage through oceans; so that the vitality of this people may be recognized amidst the floods of banishment and wanderings over the whole earth, even as the waters of the Rhone traverse without mingling with those of the Leman. Again, it emerges from the ocean floods which threatened to absorb it; irrigates fields and valleys; unites itself to other streams by means of ditches and canals; becomes navigable; is turned to industrial purposes, infinitely distributed, used and abused.

The Jewish nation has surpassed the most ancient nations in intellectual culture, and in its later age, has out-lived even the youngest of them. The Israelitish ambassador of God vanquished and subdued Egypt. The Lord's chastened children of twice destroyed Jerusalem have survived Babylon, Rome, Antioch, and the Spanish Inquisition. The mightiest empires, the most flourishing trading cities have perished—Assyria, Persia, Tyre, and Carthage, are no more; and on their sites we see the learned antiquary, Israel's Bible in his hand, absorbed in profound study, standing over their ruins, long overgrown by the moss and grass of ages.

And yet, in spite of all this, they are unable satisfactorily to answer the question, whether the Jews are a national corporation or not? Do they form one people now? We must doubt it. Where is their nationality to be found? Everywhere and nowhere. What bond then unites them? A miracle! The hand of God evidently rules the destinies of their tribe, because neither independence nor language; neither character, knowledge, or manners; neither countenance nor social life, form the common tie of the Hebrew nation. Their state is dissolved; they speak the languages of the peoples among whom they live scattered and isolated. Their Aben-Ezra condemns the cabalist as idolatrous; the cabalist accuses the disciples of Aben-Ezra of heresy. Meyerbeer and the hawker Jew; the Portuguese in the west, and the Chazar Jew in the east of Europe; the Jewish lady in England, and the hawking woman in Lithuania; polygamy in Asia; and strict conjugal ties in civilized lands, are more widely different from each other than perhaps Lutheran and Catholic, lordling and bondman ever were. Yet all of them profess one faith, have one history, and bear one name! And does not all this constitute a miracle? Their history, therefore, is more than a simple science, more than a continuous thread of knowledge; it is a guiding star, a source of consolation and hope, a Divine hint to his chastised but not entirely condemned children.

The chief importance of their history is, that if they place in juxtaposition all the events contained in the many thousand years of Israel's existence, and arrange them into epochs, they find it to be contemporaneous and closely bound up with the history of the Bible. In the first period we find the people great and elevated by the invigorating influence of the Law. We presume human pride never ventured seriously to assert that it was not the Bible which created the people, but that the people created the Bible. All that has been adduced by later rationalists and would-be critics, against the antiquity, eloquence, value and authenticity of Holy Writ, forms part of the latest general history of attacks upon Judaism, just as, on the other hand, the original introduction of the Law could not be effected without resistance on the part of the nation itself. This resistance against the first acceptance of the law, may at the same time serve as a refutation to the latest unbeliever, and cannot interfere with our interpretation of history.

Israel was to identify itself with Holy Writ, and thus become a blessing to all mankind. But the people soon departed from the Law, and consequently ceased to be a spiritual nation, in consequence of which they were overpowered by their neighbors, who were superior to them in physical strength, and whom they ought to have converted by their religious ascendancy. Then it was that the word of God was preserved for the people by men who owed their exalted mental condition to its influence, and for a short time the nation, by their moral power, was kept faithful to it, and in proportion as Israel was firm in its allegiance to its heavenly father, the nationality was preserved. A temple was built to maintain the integrity of Holy Scripture, and King Solomon was to effect by peace what Joshua and Saul could not accomplish by war. But imagining that his reign would be prosperous through his wisdom, without the help of the Law, he was neither happy himself, nor in a condition to render others so. God and the Law were abandoned, the nation was divided and torn piecemeal, till at last the Assyrian and Babylonian captivities, by destroying the temple and dissolving the Kingdom, threatened to devour both nation and Bible, which were narowly saved by the intervention of some men of great genius. Their old philosophers tell them "The Thorah was forgotten, but Ezra restored it."

In the second period, we find a remnant of Jacob's children clinging to what was left them of holy Scripture, for only a portion of the Jews returned from captivity to their own land, and to the young generation only a part of the old Scriptures was preserved; the "Wars of the Land," "The Book of the Just," and the works of many prophets and historians we know only by name. The very entrance to the Book of the Law was shut, the key to the miracles of the Eternal had disappeared, for the Divine Tablets given on Mount Sinai, the pot of manna, the whole history of the prolonged wanderings in the desert, and the doctrines of Moses, had become a mystery, and the human mind was now to accomplish what the Divine blessing no longer effected. The remnant, consisting only of three tribes, took upon themselves to do all that the twelve had originally been bound to execute. The history of the second temple until the dissolution of the patriarchate in Palestine, really represents a gigantic struggle of the human mind, a contest deeply affecting to every spectator. With one hand the people are dragging the stones to rebuild the temple, with the other brandishing the sword against the enemy : here the heart bleeds in its martyrdom, there the soul beams forth on the tribunal of justice ; at times it seems as though God, by a miracle, would again take compassion on his people, and forget their past guilt. But that active human spirit, great in its kind, endeavors to extricate itself by its own exertions ; physical nature and the Law appeared to it sufficient for the accomplishment of the national mission, in respect to a sublime morality, and for securing the spiritual existence of the world Everything was done according to law and justice ; mercy and humanity were to cease, " The Heaven is Heaven for God, but the earth was given by Him to the children of men." This was the device of those who taught the Law, and " we do not meddle with mysteries," was the sentence of the Sanhedrim. Did they forget that both Law and nature contain mysteries which remain unsolved to the present day ? No ; but they proudly hoped to unravel both by bringing their own virtues and studies to bear on them. Unfortunately, virtue, by such proceedings, assumed the form of resigned asceticism, science itself became a mystery, and thus both ceased to be the common property of the people, because their representatives had, with considerable loss of time, to qualify themselves before they were admitted to the school. Excluded from the latter, the people without being aware of it, became factious, which led to internal dissension. Such is the history of Sadduceeism, Pharisaism, and Essaism. The idea was humanly great and humanly exalted : yet God could not obtrude a display of his miracles where none sought for them. The battle was fought with heroism, but time was lost. As young and subtle Greek philosophers gained their influence over mankind by astute disputations, so Israel would have been enabled peacefully to conquer the world by the word of God. But Israel had not thought of peace in the animosity of the contest, and, as during the first period, its idolatrous alliance with the heathens, so during the second period its hatred to, and separation from them, inflicted the first dangerous wound upon its sacred mission. This has been proved by the struggles with the Samaritans and the first Christians. Chivalrously and bravely did the Jews defend their sanctuaries and their rights; yet they fought but a natural, a rational battle, and the world, meanwhile, pursued its own way.

The prophecy that Israel should be a blessing to all the nations of the earth, is delayed to a future period, and the people, even more lamentable than before, are dispersed all over the globe. In the third period, we see the Jews in a state of mind such as that which animates a little band of heroes, who, without the slightest hope of obtaining a victory, prepare themselves to do their duty, and to die in battle. Without obstinacy and without provoking their enemies, they are resolved to encounter death where they stand. Every object within their reach, serves to construct ramparts and bulwarks; they even entrench themselves, to prevent as much as they can, the assaults of the enemy, although by such a proceeding they put their own advance beyond the reach of possibility. For we cannot consider the volumes of the Midrashim, Agadoth, and the later Cabbala, in any other light than as a wall of defence, raised in the hurry and exigency of the moment, from bricks, wood, earth, and even rubbish; the discontinuance of all philosophical studies at that time, though not legally prophibited, is also to be considered only as a defensive moat against unbelief.

The fourth and last period, beginning with the present century, will, it is hoped, be one of happy reconciliation, both of men with one another, and of men with God. Thus much of the Jewish history in general; and now we shall explain how those four epochs were formed by the peculiar events of the time.

1st Epoch—People and Bible ; neglect of the latter by the people ; struggle and fall of the nation ; occupying the period from Abraham till the destruction of the first temple, viz : 1560 years.

2nd Epoch.—Animosity of foreigners against the Bible and the people, from Jeremiah till the end of the patriarchate in Palestine. 1050 years.

3rd Epoch.—Sufferings of the people and mutilation of the Bible. Inferior consciousness and infinite patience. From the fall of the patriarchate in Palestine till the Sanhedrim in France, a period of 1376 years.

4th Epoch.—From the calling of the Sanhedrim, in France, till our own time. Renewed life, renewed hope of saving the people and the Bible. (Israelite.)

CHAPTER III.

HEBREW ORTHŒPY, OR POINTS AND ACCENTS.

Invented by the Masorites—Necessary when the language ceased to be spoken. ACCENTS—Four uses—Works on the subject—Pointed manuscripts and a standard text—The name "Sopherim"—The labours of the Masorites—Note on the subdivision of the books.

HEBREW ORTHŒPY, OR POINTS AND ACCENTS.

That the Masorites were the authors of this system, there can be no reasonable doubt; for, though there might have been some one or two diacritical points in use in preceding times, we have no convincing evidence that anything like the present apparatus was known among the Jews till their day. In the monuments of Biblical Hebrew preserved by Origen, we see no trace of it; nor, judging from St. Jerome's notices of the Hebrew language in his time, was there anything of the kind then in practice. And so the more ancient Kabalists, who made so much of the letters of the alphabet as vehicles, or rather veils of mystery, never attempted the interpretation of Scripture by points; nor, in the exposition of Bible texts in the Talmud, have we, so far as I know, any reference to such a system; all significant evidences that, as yet, it had no existence, or that it was in too nascent a state to possess the weight of authority. But, without going into the controversy which has been waged upon this question, the details of which would require a monograph for themselves, we may observe that the system of points was the necessity only of a language which had ceased to be a currently spoken tongue. To imagine that it was used in times when Hebrew was vernacular in Palestine, is as absurd as to suppose that a people with the natural use of their limbs should have recourse to the crutches of the lame.

The Masoretic school fabricated that admirable system of points and accents, which has given a mathematical precision to the pronunciation of the language. In this way, too, they became the benefactors of posterity, in handing down to all following ages, what they knew to be the true and traditional modes of the language as a spoken tongue.

But though thus comparatively modern as a technical apparatus, the vowel points are exponents of traditional facts in Hebrew pronunciation, as ancient, probably, as the language itself; and no one who wishes to become a master of the language, should fail to make himself thoroughly and practically acquainted with them.

The Accents (distinguish the accents from the vowel points,) appear to have been fabricated by the Masorists to answer four purposes. 1st. Hermeneutic, to certify the meaning of words. 2nd. Grammatical, to indicate the tone of syllables. 3rd. Musical, to regulate the cantilation of Scripture in Synagogue or other reading; and, 4th. Rhetorical, to show the emphasis of an expression, and, like the points or stops in our printed books, to mark the divisions and subdivisions of paragraphs and sentences.

There is a multitude of works on the Hebrew accents, the earliest of which is the *Horaith ha Keri,* " the Doctrine of reading," of an anonymous author who wrote in Arabic prior to the eleventh century, and was translated into Hebrew by Manachem-ben-Nathanial. It exists in manuscript in the Vatican. Next in age may be the treatise of Aaron-ben-Moshe-be-Asher, in the eleventh century; fragments of which are given in the first edition of the Venetian Hebrew Bible, by Bomberg. Since then a host of writers have labored in this apparently uninviting department.

The learned Jews who removed into Europe in the eleventh century brought with them *pointed* manuscripts; and, in the two following sentences, copies were executed with the most rigid care. The exemplers, also, from which these transcripts were accomplished, were those the most highly esteemed for their correctness and suitability for the creation of a standard text.

Some Jewish authors affirm that the destructive name of Soferim, or " Enumerators," originated in the practice they had adopted of numbering the words and letters of the inspired books. If this were so, they must be regarded as the founders of the Masoretic system; but the truth is, the name *Sofer* is much earlier than that day, and had been always used to denote a scribe, or recorder.

The labours of the Masorites, properly so-called, had a two-fold object—the exhibition of a perfect orthoëpic standard of the Hebrew language, and the establishment of a correct and inviolable text of the Hebrew Scriptures. It is evident from the Jerusalem Talmud, that so early as the second century of the Christian era, considerable attention had been drawn to the diversities occasionally detected in the Biblical manuscripts. Hence, as the result, the Jthur Soferim, the "collation of the Scribes," a specification of five instances in which the letter *vaw* was to be overlooked or rejected; and the Tikkun Soferim, 'Restoration of the Scribes," in some sixteen places where wrong readings had been ascertained. To this period also are traceable the *points* which appear over some or all of the letters in some manuscripts, and the first attempt at the *Keri* and *Ketib* with their circular index.* H. L.

---

* The Pentateuch had long before been divided into *sidras*, for Sabbath readings, and that, as some think, almost as far back as the time of Moses, (Berakoth 12). When Antiochus Epiphanes prohibited the reading of the law, they selected fifty-four portions from the other books, which were called *Haftaroth*, and are still in use. In Palestine, the number of sections required three years for the public readings of the Pentateuch throughout. But in Babylonia it was so arranged as to be done in one year. We find *Rao* and *Samuel* engaged in a new arrangement of the sections. The Masorites of Tiberas, therefore, only carried out this mode of partitioning the other books of the old Testament, and superaded the more minute analysis of the text in the manner peculiar to themselves. The division also into verses was very ancient.—(Megilla 22.)

CHAPTER IV.

THE STATE OF THE HEBREW LANGUAGE IN OUR DAY.

Revival of Hebrew as a living tongue—Books, periodicals and newspapers—Comparison of Hebrew with the classics—Objections by persons deficient in knowledge of Hebrew—Modern works in pure Biblical Hebrew on general and secular subjects.

THE STATE OF THE HEBREW LANGUAGE IN OUR DAY.

The Hebrew language revives. It appears once more in all its glory. Proclaim it among the nations, lest tongues profane imagine that they have utterly expelled the sacred tongue. It has, in truth, been commonly supposed that, in consequence of the zeal with which the Israelites have lately prosecuted the study of other languages, their own would be pushed into the back ground. For our part, we are convinced that the reverse of this is the truth, and that just as the rod of Moses swallowed up the others, so the Hebrew language has only to show itself that it may absorb the languages which have sought to supplant it in the affections of its own sons. In Austria, Prussia, Hungary, Galicia, Russia and Poland, this is already the case. In these countries, it is only since the Jews began to study the living tongues, it is only since they began to perceive the beauties of poetry and the power of language in general, that the scientific and earnest study of Hebrew commenced. Having become thoroughly acquainted with the resources of the Hebrew language, they have never since ceased year, by year, to publish in that language the most beautiful productions, both in prose and poetry. Especially within the last ten years the fertile field of Hebrew literature has yielded an extraordinary profusion of the choicest blossoms, fragrant as though proceeding from the garden of Eden. In the countries just mentioned, a large number of periodicals, as well as books on an immense variety of subjects, are incessantly issuing from the press. But the most important proof which has yet been given of the progress of the sacred tongue is, that newspapers have appeared in the Hebrew language.

If the Hebrew language, as such, affords the highest delight to every scholar, be he Jew or not, and is regarded as the sublimest and most incomparable of tongues, what an exquisite pleasure it must give the true Israelite, and how infinitely grand must it appear to him. That it is so regarded by scholars, not Jewish, will be at once admitted.

The great Herder, for instance, expressed himself thus :—" An Ovid, a Virgil and a Claudian compared with a Moses, and Isaiah, and a David, are as a drop of water compared with the ocean ; and it is a shame to confine ourselves to the drop when we have before us the ocean full of greatness and majesty."—(Herder's Fragm, 2, p. 65.)

The Hebrew tongue is the only monument of Jewish antiquity ; it is the language of our Bible, which now almost governs the world ; it alone is the religious bond which keeps all Israel together. From east to west, from north to south, the Jew travels, and everywhere recognises in the synagogue his brethren in faith. The magic of that Hebrew tongue, in which they everywhere pray, touches his heart. He joins in the prayer and feels himself no longer a stranger.

An objection which has been made on the part of many Jews who manifest an indifference to Hebrew, is this—that the language is deficient, and that one cannot employ Hebrew on a subject not Biblical. Those who speak of the deficiencies of the Hebrew language are generally, those who experienced the difficulties of acquiring it, and either had not the ability or the patience to overcome them. In order that their own personal importance may not be lessened by their deficiency in this knowledge, these persons must needs decry the importance of Hebrew, and exclaim with the fox in the fable, " The grapes are sour." But as to the boundless resources of the Hebrew tongue, we have innumerable works both of ancient and modern times, written on subjects by no means Biblical, and yet in the purest Biblical style.

We shall adduce, by way of example, a few of the many books not treating of Scriptural topics, and yet deserving to be called masterpieces in respect of their pure Hebrew style.

Most of the following works have been published within the last 20 years : תלדות הארץ, " A history of Nature," by T. Scheinhak ; תלדות השמים, "The Science of Astronomy," S. Slonimski ; רופא הילדים a medical work on the treatment of children by M. Studenski ; ארחות חיים, a work on longevity, by the same ; גלגול נפש, a satire by Doctor Erter, which if it had been written in a modern language, would have created a great sensation, and which must be regared as the *ne plus ultra* of a pure Biblical style ; אהבת ציון, by J. Mapho, a tale—a perfect tale, and yet in the most beautiful Hebrew, so that in reading it, you cannot but call out, " Hebrew yet lives." In like manner the appearance of a Hebrew newspaper, which of course must treat political subjects, proves the power of this language. Poetical works, morever, in abundance, have appeared within the last few years. We cannot refrain from mentioning two in particular, which, though not on Biblical subjects, are in the best Hebrew style. The one is הקרב, a didactic poem on the game of chess, by T. Eichenbaum, which must be considered the only poem of this kind in good Hebrew; the other is הריסות טויא, the destruction of Troy, translated from Virgil, by M. Lebensohn. If we compare this poem with the German translation of Schiller, it will undoubtedly carry away the palm; and although the subject is peculiar, it is yet as far as its Hebrew style is concerned, most excellent.

CHAPTER V.

A NEW METHOD OF LEARNING TO READ HEBREW.

A NEW METHOD OF LEARNING

HEBREW LETTERS

LETTERS.			VOWELS.				
Name.	Form.	Soft.	Sound	Form.	Name.	Pronounce.	Long Vowels.	Short Vowels.

#	Name	Form	Soft	#	Sound	Form	Name	Pronounce	Long Vowels	Short Vowels
1	Aleph	א	(Veth ב)	1	א	ָ	Komatz	As O in Omen.	תְּנוּעוֹת גְּדוֹלוֹת	תְּנוּעוֹת קְטַנּוֹת
2	Beth	ב		2	אָ	ַ	Patach	" a in Hand.		
3	Gimel	ג		3	אִי		Chirik Gadol	" ee in Greece.	א	א
4	Daleth	ד		4	אִ		Chirik Katon	" i in Him.	Komatz.	Patach.
5	Heh	ה		5	אֵ		Tzerai	" ai in Fainting.	א	א
6	Vau	ו		6	אֶ		Segol	" e in Memory.	Tserai.	Segol.
7	Zain	ז		7	אוּ	וּ	Shuruk Gadol or Mlupum.	" u in Municipal.		
8	Chaith	ח		8	אֻ		Shuruk Katon or Kubutz.	" u in Numerical	אִי Great Chirik.	א Little Chirik.
9	Teth	ט	(Chaph כ)							
10	Yod	י		9	אֹ		Cholem	" ou in Vouch.		א
11	Kaph	כ		10	אֳ		Komatz Chatof	" o in Woman.	אוֹ Shuruk Gadol	Shuruk katon
12	Lamed	ל		11	אְ		Shevo	* See note.		
13	Mem	מ		12	אֳ		Chatof Komatz	like komatz chatof	אֹי Cholem.	א komatz chatof
14	Nun	נ		13	אֲ		Chatof Patach	As a in Happy.		
15	Samech	ס	(Feh פ)	14	אֱ		Chatof Segol	" No. 6, but short'r		
16	Ain	ע								
17	Peh	פ								
18	Tzaddi	צ								
19	Koph	ק								
20	Resch	ר	(Seen שׁ / Sov. שׂ)							
21	Sheen	ש								
22	Tau	ת								

	Finals	Form	Soft
1	Kaph	ך	ך
2	Mem	ם	
3	Nun	ן	
4	Peh	ף	ף
5	Tzadie	ץ	

REMARKS.

‡ 1. Hebrew is read from the right hand to the left.

2. Of the letters, those five א ה ו י ע are vowels; all the rest are consonants.

3. Cholem is often without Vav.

4. There is also a Patach Genubah—which is always inserted under, and read before a final ח ה or ע preceded by any long vowel, but Komatz, as רוּח read *Ruach* not *Rucha*.

5. Dagesh is a period which is inserted in the middle of a *letter*, and thus doubles it except Gutterals and Resh; but in the beginning of a word, and in the middle of one, after a consonant that is pronounced as a mute Schvo, it only hardens the letters, בּגּדּכּפּתּ and causes it to be pronounced with force.

6. Mapik is a period in final ה.

* Schvo is sometimes mute, that is, not pronounced, sometimes it adheres to the preceding, and is accented after a long vowel, before another Schvo, and at the end of a word; it is never pronounced after a short vowel.

Macciph—Joins words, and sometimes vowels, as :— עַל־בֵּן.

Always pronounce written vowels strong, the supplied ones, short and quick.

TO READ HEBREW.
AND READING.

			PRONUNCIATION.						SPELLING.
אָ Oh....	אַ Ah....	אִי Ee...	אַי Ai ...	אֶ Eh...	אוּ U...	אֻ U.....	אוֹ Ou	אֲ "	אָב —Ob.
בָּ Boh...	בַּ Bah...	בִּי Be...	בַּי Bai...	בֶּ Beh...	בּוּ "	בֻּ Bu	בּוֹ "	בְּ "	אַב —Ab.
בָ Voh...	בַ Vah..	בִי Ve....	בַי Vai...	בֶ Veh...	בוּ "	בֻ Vu	בוֹ "	בְ "	אָג —Og.
גָּ Goh...	גַּ Gah...	גִּי Ge...	גַּי Gai...	גֶּ Geh...	גּוּ "	גֻּ Gu	גּוֹ "	גְּ "	אַג —Ag.
דָּ Doh..	דַּ Dah..	דִּי De...	דַּי Dai...	דֶּ Deh...	דּוּ "	דֻּ Du	דּוֹ "	דְּ "	בַּד —Bad.
הָ Hoh...	הַ Hah...	הִי He...	הַי Hai...	הֶ Heh...	הוּ "	הֻ Hu	הוֹ "	הְ "	בֹּשׁ —Bosh.
וָ Woh...	וַ Wah...	וִי We....	וַי Vai...	וֶ Veh...	וּ "	וֻ Vu	וֹ "	וְ "	גֹד —God.
זָ Zoh...	זַ Zah ...	זִי Ze....	זַי Zai ...	זֶ Zeh...	זוּ "	זֻ Zu	זוֹ "	זְ "	זִ — Zi.
חָ Choh...	חַ Chah.	חִי Che..	חַי Chai..	חֶ Cheh...	חוּ "	חֻ Chu	חוֹ "	חְ "	טוֹב —Tob.
טָ Toh ..	טַ Tah...	טִי Te ...	טַי Tai ...	טֶ Teh...	טוּ "	טֻ Tu	טוֹ "	טְ "	
יָ Yoh...	יַ Yah ...	יִי Yo...	יַי Jai ...	יֶ Jeh...	יוּ "	יֻ Ju.....	יוֹ "	יְ "	
כָּ Koh...	כַּ Kah...	כִּי Ke ...	כַּי Kai ...	כֶּ Keh...	כּוּ "	כֻּ Ku	כּוֹ "	כְּ "	
כָ Choh..	כַ Chah..	כִי Che..	כַי Chai..	כֶ Cheh...	כוּ "	כֻ Chu	כוֹ "	כְ "	
לָ Loh...	לַ Lah...	לִי Le ...	לַי Lai ...	לֶ Leh...	לוּ "	לֻ Lu	לוֹ "	לְ "	
מָ Moh...	מַ Mah...	מִי Me ...	מַי Mai...	מֶ Meh...	מוּ "	מֻ Mu	מוֹ "	מְ "	
נָ Noh...	נַ Nah...	נִי Ne...	נַי Nai ...	נֶ Neh...	נוּ "	נֻ Nu	נוֹ "	נְ "	
סָ Soh...	סַ Sah...	סִי Se...	סַי Sai...	סֶ Seh...	סוּ "	סֻ Su	סוֹ "	סְ "	
עָ O......	עַ Oh....	עִי Eh...	עַי Ai ...	עֶ Eh...	עוּ "	עֻ U.....	עוֹ "	עְ "	
פָּ Poh...	פַּ Pah...	פִּי Pe ...	פַּי Pai ...	פֶּ Peh...	פּוּ "	פֻּ Pu	פּוֹ "	פְּ "	
פָ Foh...	פַ Fah...	פִי Fe...	פַי Fai ...	פֶ Feh...	פוּ "	פֻ Fu	פוֹ "	פְ "	
צָ Zoh...	צַ Zah...	צִי Tzee..	צַי Zai ...	צֶ Zeh...	צוּ "	צֻ Zu	צוֹ "	צְ "	
קָ Koh..	קַ Kah...	קִי Ke ...	קַי Kai ...	קֶ Keh...	קוּ "	קֻ Ku	קוֹ "	קְ "	
רָ Roh...	רַ Rah...	רִי Re ...	רַי Rai ...	רֶ Reh...	רוּ "	רֻ Ru	רוֹ "	רְ "	
שָׁ Sho...	שַׁ Schah	שִׁי Sche.	שַׁי Schai.	שֶׁ Scheh...	שׁוּ "	שֻׁ Schu..	שׁוֹ "	שְׁ "	
שָׂ Soh ..	שַׂ Sah...	שִׂי See..	שַׂי Sai ..	שֶׂ Seh...	שׂוּ "	שֻׂ Su.....	שׂוֹ "	שְׂ "	
תָּ Toh...	תַּ Tah...	תִּי Tee..	תַּי Tai ...	תֶּ Teh...	תּוּ "	תֻּ Tu	תּוֹ "	תְּ "	
תָ Soh...	תַ Sah...	תִי The...	תַי Sai ...	תֶ Seh...	תוּ "	תֻ Su	תוֹ "	תְ "	

THE LORD'S PRAYER.

אבינו אשר בשמים יקדש שמך: תבא מלכותך: יהי רצונך כאשר בשמים כן גם בארץ: לחם חקנו תן לנו היום: וסלח לנו את חבתינו כאשר אנחנו סלחים לבעלי חובינו: ואל תביאנו למסה׳ כי אם הצילנו מן הרע: כי לך הממלכה והגבורה והתפארת לעולמים אמן:

ק פרעטטמאן.

CHAPTER VI.

JEWISH TEACHERS OF CHRISTIAN STUDENTS.

Celebrated theologians and scholars who were instructed by Jewish teachers—Professors in Schools and Universities, and Learned men of the present day—Prejudice against the Jews.

JEWISH TEACHERS OF CHRISTIAN STUDENTS.

For centuries, the Biblical scholars and students of modern Hebrew literature, from Reuchlin to the professors Delitzsch and Ewald, were, like Jerome, directly or indirectly, pupils of Israelites. But theologians expressed their gratitude principally in attempts at conversion, or applied for instruction rather to those who understood Judaism in a Christian sense, and made it an object of attack. Baptized Israelites taught Hebrew to the founders of classical studies, as Poggius, not to mention the revivers of Hebrew studies, Reuchlin, Seb, Munster, and others.

A former controversialist against Christianity taught Agricola (1443–1485), and Matthew Adrian was (about 1513) the teacher of W. Capito (ob. 1541), and, perhaps, also (A. D. 1518) of Trotzendorf (ob. 1556). In latter times, Christian de Pomis was tutor of Wulfer (ob. 1714); Ezra Edzard of Franke, the German founder of the mission; and Baptist Lona, of Safet, (ob. 1668,) was the guide of Bartolocci. Among the Israelites important for literary celebrity, who were faithful to their creed, Jochanan Allemano was teacher and friend of Pico del a Mirandolar (ob. 1494).

Widmanstadt (1532) the pupil of Reuchlin, and friend of Ægidius de Viterbo, speaks with respect of his teachers, David Ibn Jajah ben Joseph, of Lisbon, at Naples (born A.D. 1465, ob. at Imola 1543) and Baruch of Beneventum. Through the instrumentality of Ægidius, who was the pupil of the well-known Elia Levita, the above-mentioned Baruch first introduced the book Zohar among Christians; and Reuchlin himself was a pupil of Jacob Jechiel Loanaz, physician in ordinary to the Emperor Linz, (1412,) and of Obadja Sforno, at Rome, (1498).

To Jacob-ben-Isaac Romano, teacher of Harlai de Sanci, at Constantinople (ob. 1650, at Jerusalem), Buxtorf is indebted for the valuable supplement to his " Bibliotheca Rabbinica." Hottinger, whose "Promptuarium" owes much to Menasse Ben Israel's materials for a Bibliotheca Rabbinica, was induced to study Oriental literature by the linguist

Saadja-ben Levi Asankot, (1644). Unger's correspondence with Jacob Abroad at Venice, (1,727). Isaac Cantarini at Padua, and others, assisted Woolf in his "Bibliotheca Hebraica," &c. Scaliger, a pupil of Philip Ferdinand, confesses the Israelites were the only teachers of Hebrew; and Ockley asserts that no one can understand the New Testament so well as an Israelite.

Even public educational establishments were obliged to seek Hebrew teachers, the number of whom is considerable, e. g., the physician, Paul Ricci, at Paris (1529), *protege* of Erasmus; Paul Canossa, of Venice, at Paris, (1530), Peter Flugel, of Strasburg, (ob. 1564), Philip D'Aquino, at Paris since, (1610); and many others. In the Vatican, Hebrew converts, for example, Io, Paul Enstatkins, probably the same as Elia de Nola Ben Menahem, (1552), and others, were employed as copyists; but they were not always well selected, as is shown by their mistakes, some of which are pointed out by Assemani.

We do not intend to give the large number of Israelites who at present are Professors and members of academies. We will mention but a few, who, in the last few years, have been elected to the most important academies of Europe.

Dr. Munk, the celebrated Orientalist, is a member of the Academy of Moral Sciences and Politics in Paris, and Dr. Frank, President of that learned body. Dr. Stem, the mathematician of Gottingen, is member of the Royal Academy of Munich. D. D. Reiss and Pringsheim of that of Berlin; Dr. Coben, of Breslaw, of the Imperial Academy of St. Petersburg; Mr. Halery, Perpetual Secretary of the Academy of Fine Arts in Paris; Mr. Bendeman, Director of the Academy of Fine Arts in Dusseldorf, &c., &c., &c.

The Jews have done their duty, and in a very short time have risen to a very prominent position in science and arts. The prejudice entertained against them has been silenced by their superior merits. When Moses Mendelssohn, the philosopher and father of Jewish reform, was elected member of the Academy of Berlin, even Frederic the Great refused to ratify the election. Humboldt tried to excuse him, by stating, that he was influenced in this decision by the fact that the Empress Catharine, of Prussia, was an honorary member of the Academy, and that he was afraid she would dislike it, to sit on one and the same bench with a Jew.

The philosopher took the matter easy, and remarked only, when informed of the royal refusal, that he prefers by far to be elected by the Academy, and to be rejected by the King, than to be proposed for election as a member by the King and to be rejected by the Academy.

PART FIFTH.

MISCELLANEOUS ADDENDA.

CHAPTER I.

General Remarks upon Sundry practices and beliefs of the Jews—Mention made of our Lord Jesus Christ in the Talmud, &c.

Charity is at present the great hope of the Jews. At the burials of their deceased, a contribution box is passed around to all present, who then put in their offerings. Before the Day of Atonement they also give away a great deal for charitable purposes. "Zedakah tazil mimaweth," is the motto of every Jew.—Prov. x. 4., and xi. 4. The word "Zedakah," (righteousness), they translate "Charity."

When a Jew embraces Christianity, he is designated a "Meshumed," (to be destroyed), but whether he was honest and pious while with them or no, he is not believed to be sincere, when once he departs from his first faith. His very best friends now turn his enemies. He must consider himself as severed from his nearest relatives for ever, who feel anything but a friendly feeling towards him. But is this to be wondered at, when we find that even those who style themselves Christians, look down with disdain upon one who, for the sake of that master whom they too *pretend* to worship, has left home, friends and all?

If a young woman happens to become dissipated or a profligate, which is very seldom the case, she is despised by all, and her chance to get a husband, of any repute, is very small. She remains a cast-out from society as long as she lives. We might state here, that there are no people on the face of the earth, who observe the laws of chastity and purity more strictly than do the Jews, especially the women.

A Jew never pronounces the name Jehovah as we do. Whenever this name occurs in their Bible or Prayer-book, they use the name "Adonai" instead, which means "My Lord." They consider the name Jehovah, to have something mysterious connected with it, and that none but the High priest, and a few especially favored individuals, were intrusted with the right and full pronunciation of this mysterious and very sacred name.

The Jews, on different occasions, practice immersion. They immerse hemselves in water before the Day of Atonement. Some pious Jews do it not only every Sabbath (Saturday) morning, but every morning, in order that they may be more pure and clean when they attend to their prayers. Women also have to observe this on special occasions, as well as observe the law of purification, as commanded in Leviticus xii.

They are not a war-loving people, and a Jew, to save himself from being enlisted in an army of soldiers, will often pay a great sum of money. Especially the orthodox Jews, for fear that they would be obliged to eat Gentile food, which they call "Trefeth," and not be permitted to observe their religious duties aright.

The Jews have no Missionaries to propagate their religion, for they believe that their religion requires no human instrumentality, and that the time will come when the whole world will embrace their own faith, and God alone will be worshipped as Divine Sovereign.

The difference between the Orthodox and the Reform Jew is, that the former believes in the teachings of the Talmud, almost as much as those of the Bible, and still prays for the coming of a Messiah, and expects His coming daily; while the latter has given up the coming of the Messiah altogether. He believes God never promised a personal Messiah, and that where mention is made of a Redeemer in Scripture, it has sole reference to the people of Israel; therefore, they, as a nation, have to suffer for the iniquities of all other nations, and finally will become the Messiah of the world. Neither do the Reform Jews observe so many ceremonies, as the Orthodox, nor lay such stress upon the writings of the Talmud, taken as a whole.

Though the Jews believe that the Messiah, whom they expect will be superhuman; yet most of them deny that His redemption will be a spiritual one. But they firmly believe in the temporal restoration of all their former glory, which, of course, the Reform Jews disbelieve.

The present number of Jews throughout the inhabited world, number from eight to nine millions, who, as we know, are the descendants of two tribes. Now the question presents itself, if the descendants of these two tribes, who have suffered so greatly, have been persecuted, and were forced to embrace the Christian faith; yea, even hundreds and thousands of them slaughtered, for there is scarcely a spot in the world where Jewish blood crieth not forth from the ground. Now if these two tribes have suffered so severely during eighteen centuries, and still number from eight to nine millions, how much greater must the number of the other ten tribes be, who suffered no persecutions, and whose descendants are perhaps living in some part of the world now in peace. Where then are these lost tribes? They must number millions of millions; but this vast number of Jews can be found no where; yet they must exist some where. I, therefore, say that these lost ten tribes are mixed or swallowed up among the other nations of the world. In especial, I would take a certain class of Germans, whose features and customs are not far varied from those of the Jews. Next, the Irish, whose social life and habits correspond well with the Jews. But my special reason for them is, that they cannot trace back their history or origin to any extent, and the very idols which were found some years ago under their soil, are identical with those worshipped by the Jews at the time that they were led captive. Why not believe that a ship in which, perhaps, one or more of these tribes were led away captive, was shipwrecked on the "Green Isle," and there lived for a time, and served their idols, until St. Patrick induced them to turn to Christianity. I also believe that the English people may be the descendants of the ten tribes; but firmly so that the American Indians are really the remainder of these lost tribes.

No divine service, or any public worship, can be commenced in the Synagogue unless ten grown-up persons be present. These must be over thirteen years old, and males, for females cannot be counted. In orthodox Synagogues, the women are separated from the men, and usually sit in galleries; but in more modern places of worship, they are beginning to abolish this custom. In the old established orthodox Synagogues, there is a perpetual light burning, which is kept so by voluntary contribution. The sexton, or whoever happens to open the door of the synagogue, gives it three raps with the key, which is a sort of superstitious habit amongst them. The Rabbis among the Jews are highly respected, and are often better paid than ministers among the Christians. Besides, the Rabbi, a "Chazan," that is a reader, is employed, who has to read the prayers, and chant the portion of Scripture on the Sabbath day, as well as on festivals, and also a small portion of the Pentateuch to be chanted on Mondays and Thursdays in the Synagogue. A great many congregations are without a Rabbi, and only employ a Chazan, who performs the duties of "Schatz Matz,'' which means everything necessary to serve a Jewish congregation, such as to prepare their meat, read and chant in the Synagogue, circumcise, marry, preach, &c., &c. In some places, they have in connection with their Synagogues, *Beth Medrashim*, or "House of Learning," into which free access is given to any one who wishes to study the Talmud, and a great many other books kept there for those entering. Some Jewish congregations employ ten persons, whom they call *Asara Bathlanim*, or ten idlers, who can always be found about the *Beth Hamedrash*. They study a little, quarrel a little, and squander most of their time in idleness; but must always be ready to do anything in connection with Synagogical services. Also, if any one in the congregation becomes ill with a catching disease, and there be no one to watch over him, these ten are employed for such purposes.

The Jews have been accused by Jesuits and other enemies, for using Christian blood on the "Passover," and have often had to suffer greatly in consequence of this atrocious accusation. The red wine which they prefer to any other when they celebrate the feast of Passover, no doubt gave rise to this inhuman accusation. There is not a nation on the face of the earth, who feel more repugnance or abhorrance for using blood, either in eating or drinking, than the Jews. This is only one of the many lies which the devil uttered through the mouthpiece of Jesuits.

As no Jew is allowed to retain anything in the house, which is leaven, during the feast of the "Passover," they sell everything which has become in any wise contaminated with leaven, to some Gentiles, perhaps a servant or some one else who keeps them for eight days, after which they buy the things back again, as though this would cover their hypocrisy.

Every Jew in rising in the morning will wash his hands, and say grace, thus: "I thank Thee Thou living and everlasting King, that Thou hast restored unto me my soul, with Thy great mercy in Thy truth." He must again repeat grace and wash his hands, if he be about to partake of bread, even though it be as small as an egg. Over every drop of water that he drinks, he must also say grace, also over every piece of fruit that he eats. They also repeat two blessings when it thunders and lightnings.

Schalem Alechem, which means "Peace with you," is the common welcome to every stranger, to which is answered, *Alechem Schalem*, "With you be peace." When a Jew enters his neighbor's house, the *Barnch Haba*, "Blessed be he who came," is again the welcome, and the person visiting answers *Barnch Memza*, "Blessed be he who is found here." The Jews are a very hospitable people, and are called *Beney Rach Manim*, "Merciful children."

There is not a nation under the sun, whose bonds of matrimony are considered so sacred, and kept so undefiled as those of the Jews. It is much to be deplored, that a people who live without the light of the gospel, should be, as far as morality is concerned, so much in advance of those who live under the very sound of the gospel.

When an orthodox woman marries, she has her hair cut short, and is strictly forbidden to appear with an uncovered head. A great many wear false hair, but even to this, some have objections. Most of the pious women wear nothing but a black silken band, which is worn on the forehead, in order that the hair might not be seen. But this law is now giving way among the Reform Jews, and even among a great number of the Orthodox Jews.

Dancing is considered no sin among the Jews; yet you will seldom find a pious Jew frequenting the ball-room, or any other public place, except when some of his friends are married, at which dancing is customary. And to their credit, it must be said, that there is neither as much fighting, drinking, nor other vulgar things in vogue among them as among other people.

After every accident of importance, or escape from any danger, a Jew will publicly acknowledge the mercy of God towards him, and distribute charity.

There are, of course, no sacrifices at present among the Jews; instead of which they have nothing but *Repentance, Charity and Prayer.*

Bath Kol, or the so-called "daughter voice," of the Jews, claimed to have been heard in years long past, is now no more in existence; so that at the present time, they have neither oracles, nor prophesies, and no voice from heaven favors them again with the announcement of some great event, as the *Bath Kol* did in former times.

Most of the Jews consider Jesus Christ as an imposter; and there are comparatively few who even think respectfully of our Lord and Saviour.

The modern Reformers say: "We have nothing to do with the supposed fall of Adam and Eve; for the Bible says of God, 'He visits the iniquity of the parents on the children and children's children, to the third and fourth generation of those who hate him.' We have no Redeemer except a virtuous and pious life. We say in our daily prayers the words of Isaiah, 'Our Redeemer is the Lord Zabaoth, the Most Holy of Israel is His name.'"

The restoration of Israel to Palestine is prophesied by Moses; but this belief, or the prayer in this respect, cannot prevent one from being a good citizen of the country where he lives; for we are nowhere told that all Israelites must return to Palestine. Those who wish to stay where they are, may pray to see others restored to the land of their wish. The prayer for the restoration of a kingdom, and a personal king of whatever dynasty, is sinful and un-Jewish.

The custom of cutting the nails: In the *Send-a Vesta Yestho Sadies,* xl. 7, the following passage occurs: "If one cuts his nails, he takes first the ring finger, then the fourth, (from the thumb), next the smallest, the longest, and finally the thumb. An extra knife is necessary for it, by which every nail is cut in two, and at every nail is said the prayer, 'Such it is the pleasure of Ormuzd,' &c. All the nails cut off must be buried in a dry and uncultivated land, or laid upon a hard stone, (wrapped in paper), or they are thrown into a hole," &c.

The Jerusalem Talmud says: There were five things missing from the second temple that were in the first, viz: The Fire from Heaven, the Ark, the Urim, and Thummim, the Oil of Anointing, and the Holy Spirit or the Spirit of prophecy.

The Babalonish Talmud mentions these five: The Ark, Urim, and Thummim, the Fire from Heaven, the Divine presence, or cloud of Glory, and the Holy Ghost, or the Spirit of Prophecy and Miracles.

MENTION OF CHRIST'S NAME IN A BLASPHEMOUS MANNER IN THE TALMUD AND RABBINICAL WRITINGS.

"A disciple corrupting his food as did Jesus of Nazareth."

The Talmudists, being taught by their fathers, do give out, horribly blaspheming, "that Jesus of Nazareth, our Lord, was a magician, a broacher of strange and wicked worship; and one that did miracles by the power of the devil, to beget his worship the greater belief and honour."

"Ben Salda brought magic out of Egypt, by cuttings which he had made in his flesh." By Ben Salda they understand Jesus of Nazareth. "Satda," or "Stada," sounds as much as an "adulterous wife," which the Gemara shows, "She went aside from her husband." They feign that Jesus travelled with Joshua ben Perachia into Egypt, and that he brought thence magical witchcrafts with him; but under the cuttings of his flesh, that he might not be taken by the Egyptian magicians, who strictly examined all that went out of that land, that none should transport their magic art into another land. They add "Jesus practised magic, and deceived and drove Israel to idolatry."

In Talm. Babyl. Sanh. Gem. 431, it is delivered as a tradition: "That Jesus was hanged upon a cross the day before the Passover, because he had enchanted, seduced, and drawn away the people; that it being proclaimed three days for some person to appear in his behalf, to testify his innocence, there was none found to do it."

CHAPTER II.

CERTAIN PECULIARITIES OF THE JEWISH RACE.

The Jews are found in all lands—Are imperfectly understood—Aaronic descent, how ascertained—Statistics of Jewish population—Language and Literature—Physical peculiarities—Comparative Longevity.

The Jew—where do we meet him? From the coldest regions of the north to the interior of Africa; from the centres of civilization in Europe to Tartary, Bokhara, and China, he is everywhere domiciled, yet nowhere at home! In flowing robes, in Kaftan or courtly dress; speaking Arabic, Jewish, or some western language; muleteer, pedlar, or statesman—still they are all like each other, and unlike any one else. They constitute, indeed, a unique phenomenon among the races of the world, for which neither their eastern descent, nor their past history, nor their peculiarity of creed, can sufficiently account. In all countries they seem to commingle with the ordinary population, adopting their language and manners, and entering into [their modes of thinking and political aspirations. Yet, not only in their features and physical conformation, but in their inmost being they continue separate from those among whom they have settled for centuries. Whatever language they may speak, there is a Jewish peculiarity and mode of expression about their dialect; their mental and moral idiosyncrasy remains unchanged, whatever kind of intellectual training they may have received, and, though found in every rank and class of society, they are really of none. You know them immediately. Wheresoever and howsoever they may be, they are still Jews. There was deep truth in the remark made by one of the deputies to the German Parliament, in 1848, however objectionable his motive may have been: That everywhere the Jewish population floated like a drop of oil on the surface of the waters.

And then their history—such interest cannot attach to that of any other nation! From earliest childhood we have heard of patriarchs, priests and warriors, kings and prophets, till every other interest was absorbed in that attaching to the land of Palestine. All our religious hopes are derived from them; the progress of civilization, and the history of the world, are identified with the belief derived from Judea, with the hope in One, who, according to the flesh, was a Jew, and with the knowledge originally spread by those who were Jews. Then, when the rejection of the Saviour led to their dispersion, how varied their fortunes, how tragic their fate! For many centuries has persecution and statecraft sought to destroy their separate national existence; yet, to this day, they flourish as vigorously as ever, unchanged and unchanging. Whatever objection we may be tempted to offer to the *logic* of Frederick the Great's parson, we all intuitively feel the force of his argument, when to that monarch's demand for a brief summary of the evidences in favor of Christianity, he replied in these words: "The Jews, your majesty."

With such interest attaching to them, and so abundant means of observation at command, we may wonder at the ignorance prevailing about their history, opinions, and characteristics. Very little progress has been made in this direction. We know not much more of Jewish theology and life than did the fathers. Certainly, we know less of Rabbinnical literature than many during the past,—Reformation period—much less than the Buxtorffs, the Vitringas, the Seldens, and a host of less distinguished men.

At one time, we reject the whole eighteen centuries of Jewish literature, as a mass of meaningless rubbish; next we oscillate, with the same ignorance of the real state of the case, to the very opposite extreme. A few pages of isolated quotations extracted for a particular purpose, out of so many thousand folio pages, are deemed sufficient to convince that the Jewish Talmud contains all the spiritual elements of the New Testament, and the quintessence of modern civilization; and this, without even enquiring into the general contents, the tendency, and the spirit of that immense work, or into the manifestation of its influence, as apparent in the Talmudical Synagogue.

The "dispersion," so far as at present known, consists chiefly of the descendants of the tribe of Judah. Among them are scattered a number of Levites, and some who trace their descent through the priesthood to Aaron himself. This is ascertained not by genealogical tables, but by certain laws, duties, and privileges, applying to the family of Aaron. Thus the first-born of males are redeemed from them; they are not allowed to remain in the same house with a dead body, &c. The Gentile who visits a Jewish cemetery, will notice on some of the moss-covered stones a rude graving of two hands, lifted up in a strange manner. These are the priestly hands, extended in the atitude of Jewish blessing, and the stone marks the resting-place of one descended in unbroken succession from the great Jewish High Priest. To make the device complete, the hands ought probably to be surmounted by a mitre, with the inscription, "Holiness unto the Lord." Through this, and other means, their Aaronic descent is communicated from father to son, being fixed on the memory from earliest age, by rites and ceremonies which can never be forgotten.

It has been popularly but erroneously supposed, that the Jewish population is, in a great measure stationary. its number little, if at all, exceeding that at the time of the final dispersion. But the ordinary computation at about five millions, and even that of distinguished writers on statistics, such as Kolb, at about seven millions, is far too low. It is extremely difficult to arrive at correctness of numbers, not only from the shifting character of the Jewish population, but from the fact that the countries in which the Jews most numerously reside, are precisely those from which no reliable statistics can be obtained. According to Dr. Pressell, the Jews in Poland amount to 571,678, while a recent Polish writer computes their number at 1,400,000. Again, Pressel reckons the Jewish population of Moldavia and Wallachia at 37,000, while recent careful investigations have shown that it amounts to more than three times that number, or to 115,840 souls. The British Jews must be also more numerous than is supposed, since good authority states them at from 40,000 to 50,000 in London alone. Lastly, while Dr. Pressel calculates the Jewish population of European Turkey at 70,000, there are authorities who claim not less than 90,000 Jewish inhabitants for Constantinople itself. We shall, therefore, not be in danger of exaggerating if we simply reproduce, with certain alterations and remarks, Dr. Pressel's statistical table:—

Country.	Gentile Pop.	Jews.
United States (in 1850)	23,351,207	120,000 (chiefly Germans.)
Great Britain	29,040,000	50,000 (at least.)
France	35,000,000	74,000 (20,000 in Paris.)
Spain	15,300,000	A few here and there.
Portugal	3,500,000	A few under great restrict'n
Italy (including Roman States)	25,492,561	43,620.
The Roman States	....	9,273.
Switzerland	2,390,116	3,146.
Belgium	4,623,089	1,500. [in Amsterdam.]
Holland (with Luxemburg and Limburg).	3,543,775	68,669 (more than 20,000
Austria	32,573,002	1,121,448.
Hungary (including Transylvania, Croatia and the Military Boundary)	....	412,702.
Germany	34,976,674	430,096.
Denmark	2,435,000	4,736.
Sweden	3,639,332	1,100.
Norway	1,490,786	None.
Greece and the Ionian Islands	1,301,339	1,500 (Spanish Jews.)
Russia	71,243,616	Over 2,000,000.*
Turkey in Europe	15,700,000	70,000.†
Turkey in Asia	16,000,000	80,000.‡
African Dependencies, Egypt, Nubia, Tripoli and Tunis	6,200,000	At least 600,000 (chiefly Spanish Jews.)

* This computation is far too low.

† This is obviously far short of the actual number, the Danubian principalities alone, having 115,840 Jews, and Constantinople probably about 60,000, most of them Spanish Jews.

‡ Also too low, Palestine alone numbering between 15,000 and 16,000 Jews.

It will be noticed, that while in this table many countries are unrepresented, in others, the computation comes far short of the real numbers. The classification into German, Polish and Spanish Jewish, is well founded, and depends, not only on geographical and historical grounds, but marks mental and even physical differences. Dr. Pressel arranges "The Scattered Nation" into three classes, according to the countries over which it is dispersed. The first class, inhabiting the interior of Africa, Arabia, India, China, Turkestan, and Bokhara, occupies the lowest stage of civilization. Though generally greatly superior to their Gentile neighbours, these Jews are almost semi-barbarous, and ignorant of their own literature. The second and most numerous class is found in Northern Africa, Egypt, Palestine, Syria, Mesopotamia, Persia, Asia Minor, European Turkey, Poland, Russia, and parts of Austria. It embraces the bigoted, strictly orthodox, and Talmudical Jews, including the sect of the *Kasidim*, or "pious," to the number of about one million, and the interesting but small party of the Karaites, who reject all Rabbinnical traditions. The third class is represented by the Jews of Central and Western Europe, and of the United States. These mingle with their Gentile neighbours, and, indeed, are in many respects their superiors. Religiously, they belong in general to the party known as "Reforming," which attempts to eliminate the old Talmudical element from their religion, and to adapt it to western civilization. Western Judaism is rapidly drifting into Unitarianism or Deism.

It will have been observed, that numerically the Jews are very unequally distributed over the various countries. This, no doubt, is in great part owing to their past history. Still it remains a striking fact, that by far the largest proportion of Jews is found in the latitude of Jerusalem. From some lands they are conspicuously absent, partly from legal restrictions, and partly, perhaps, owing to the character of the Gentile population. Scotland numbers very few Jews; from Spain and Portugal they are virtually excluded; nor are their Jews in Norway, (population, 1,490,786); in some parts of Germany, (Lichenstein population, 7,150; Schaumberg population, 30,144); and in some Provinces of Austria, (Salzberg population, 146,769; Carinthia population, 332,456; Carniola population, 451,941). In other parts of the Austrian Empire, the Jewish population is disproportionately small. Thus Upper Austria, with a population of 707,450, numbers only four Jews; Styria, with 1,056,773, has only six Jews; the Tyrol, with 851,016 inhabitants, has 548 Jews; and the military boundary, with 1,046,922, only 404 Jews. Yet, despite constant persecutions, the Israelites have proved very faithful to the House of Hapsburg; at this time the Austrian army contains not less than 9,850 Jewish soldiers.

On the other hand, there are countries and towns in which the Jewish population abounds quite beyond the proportion which might have been anticipated, from their past history in those districts; or, till quite recently, from their political position.

The subjoined table may assist the reader in forming an adequate idea of the relative proportions of Jews and Gentiles.

In round numbers we reckon:

Throughout the World.........	1 Jew.........	in 1,500	inhabitants.
In Belgium......................	1 Jew.........	in 3,000	"
In Greece	1 Jew.........	in 900	"
In Britain	1 Jew.........	in 700	"
In Italy.........................	1 Jew.........	in 700	"
In France.......................	1 Jew.........	in 500	"
In Prussia......................	1 Jew.........	in 90	"
In Holland.....................	1 Jew.........	in 52	"
In Turkey	1 Jew.........	in 53	"
In Austria	1 Jew.........	in 32	"
In Algiers and North Africa...	1 Jew.........	in 10	"
In Hamburg	1 Jew.........	in 32	"
In Frankfort	1 Jew.........	in 17	"
In Amsterdam	1 Jew.........	in 12	"
In Warsaw (about)..........	1 Jew.........	in 3	"
In Jerusalem	1 Jew.........	in 2	"

Jerusalem has about 9,000 Jews; Safed, 3,000; Tiberias, 1,500; Hebron, 500; Joppa, 200, &c.. the total in the Holy Land amounting, as before stated, to between 15,000 and 16,000.

Besides the Hebrew, of which, however, a very large proportion know little more than the rudiments, or than is sufficient to follow, not to understand the liturgy, the Jews, though scattered over the face of the world, cultivate chiefly three languages. These are the Arabic, Spanish and German. Perhaps we ought to add, as very largely known, a fourth, or rather a patois,—the Jewish,—which consists of a selection from all dialects, the basis being a corrupt German, with frequent intermixture of Hebrew and Aramaic words and phrases. This patois adapts itself to many uses, social, sacred, and gay, being also specially suited to the innumerable, and often clever stories, anecdotes, and witticisms, in which the pent-up popular mind delights, but which it would be well-nigh impossible to translate into Gentile language. It has also a printed literature of its own, which consists chiefly of absurd legends, and tales for the religious edification of women, and of the "ignorant and unlearned." To this debasing literature, there has, however, of late been added a number of Christian tracts, and if we mistake not, even a translation of the Scriptures. It is scarcely necessary to say that writings like those to which we have just alluded, must be carefully distinguished from the magnificent displays of genius and learning, only too little known, with which the Jews have, in all ages and countries, enriched almost every department of literature and branch of science.

It may seem strange that the Jews, being mere units among the thousands of Gentiles around, should have preserved alike their mental and physical peculiarities. The absence of crime among them, and the marked presence of so many social and private virtues—as kindness, charity, reverence, affectionateness and sobriety—are well known. So are that quickness and clearness, that adaptation and perseverance, that endurance and diligence, which have constituted no inconsiderable elements to their success. These are characteristics common to the race.

Scientific observers have noted certain physical peculiarities in the structure of the body, among the Jews. According to the well-known anatomist, Schultz, of St. Petersburg, they differ from all other races inhabiting the Russian empire. A comparison has shown, that whereas the average height of the other races amounts to between 66.46 and 68.16 inches, that of the Jews is only 64.46 inches. Again, while in general the width of the body, when the arms are fully stretched out, exceeds its height by about eight inches, the opposite is the case with the Jews, where the width often falls to one inch below the height. In the negro races the trunk constitutes 32 per cent. of the height of the whole body, in other races, 34 per cent., in the Jews 36 per cent. Lastly, while ordinarily the *perinæum* is about the middle of the body, in the Jewish race it occupies a lower position, being about 5 per cent. beneath its place in other races.

Some interesting *pathological* observations have also been made. It appears that the Jews suffer comparatively rarely from diseases of the respiratory organs, and that they are in a remarkable degree, capable of accommodating themselves to vicissitudes of climate and temperature. From certain diseases they enjoy almost complete immunity. Among infantile disorders of this class, we reckon hydrocephalus and croup; among those affecting all ages, typhus and the pestilence. It has been observed that Jewish communities, however poor, crowded and contravening our modern hygienic rules, suffer comparatively little from cholera and other epidemics. On the other hand, there are disorders of a lighter kind to which the Jews seem peculiarly liable, such as cutaneous diseases, hypochondriasis, hysterical and nervous affections, and obstructions of the portal system. Of late, mania has become more common, especially in certain localities, owing, it is supposed, to frequent intermarriages.

The last, but perhaps the most remarkable physical peculiarity, to which we shall call attention, is the comparatively large ratio of increase and the longevity of the Jewish race. Assuming its present numbers to amount in round figures, to close upon nine millions, their rate of increase has indeed fallen far short of what it had been in Biblical, and even in post-Biblical times. We subjoin the following table, drawn up by Neufrille, and derived from the official registers of the city of Frankfort, between the years 1846 and 1848, in reference to the comparative mortality of the Jews and Gentiles :—

COMPARATIVE TABLE OF MORTALITY AMONG JEWS AND GENTILES.

Age.	Gentiles.	Jews.
1— 4 years	24·1 per cent.	12·9 per cent.
5— 9 "	2·3 "	0·4 "
10— 14 "	1·1 "	1·5 "
15— 19 "	3·4 "	3·0 "
20— 24 "	6·2 "	4·2 "
25— 29 "	6·2 "	4·6 "
30— 34 "	4·8 "	3·4 "
35— 39 "	5·8 "	6·1 "
40— 44 "	5·4 "	4·6 "
45— 49 "	5·6 "	5·3 "
50— 54 "	4·6 "	3·8 "
55— 59 "	5·7 "	6·1 "
60— 64 "	5·4 "	9·5 "
65— 69 "	6·0 "	7·2 "
70— 74 "	5·4 "	11·4 "
75— 79 "	4·3 "	9·1 "
80— 84 "	2·6 "	5·0 "
85— 89 "	0·9 "	1·5 "
90— 94 "	0·16 "	0·4 "
95—100 "	0·04 "	

From this table it appears that the balance of general longevity, is largely in favor of the Jews. In infancy, the death-rate among the Gentiles is more than double that among the Jews. Among adults, the largest proportion of deaths occur among the Gentiles at the ages of from 20 to 29, being 6·2 per cent., among the Jews at from 70 to 74, the rate being 11·4 per cent. Then we have the next largest death-rate among Gentiles, at the ages of from 65 to 69, the proportion being 6 per cent., while among Jews, the per centage for old age is much larger. These comparisons might be easily multiplied. The total result may be expressed as follows:

There died.	Of Gentiles.	Of Jews.
The *fourth* part.......	At 6 years 11 months...	At 28 years 3 months.
The *half*...	" 36 " 6 "	... " 53 " 1 "
The *fourth*............	" 59 " 10 "	... " 71 "

Lastly, the learned French physician, Dr. M. Levy, has recently computed that the average duration of life, among the Gentiles, is 20 years, and among the Jews, 37 years.

ALFRED EDERSHEIM,

CHAPTER III.

TEMPLE AND HALF SHEKEL.

Loyalty of the Jews to the Temple at Jerusalem—The Half Shekel—The Falashas of Abyssinia.

The Temple at Jerusalem was the central station for all Jews, however distant their settlements, however complicated their wanderings and changes of residence. This metropolitan rank was inseparable from that hallowed spot on which a visible sign of the Divine presence had been manifested; and even when the pride of Anius had erected a rival structure in Egypt, every Jew throughout the world still repeated, with the Psalmist—" If I forget thee, O Jerusalem, may my right hand forget—"*

The fixing of the Neominæ was the exclusive prerogative of the Great Assembly or Sanhedrin, which had its seat in Jerusalem—a prerogative the more important, as the appointment and days of celebration of all the Jewish festivals throughout the year, was by that means vested in the Sanhedrin; for each of these festivals was, in the law of Moses, directed to be kept holy on the *so manyeth* day of the month. But the first day of the month was not to be determined by computation only, but by parol evidence of at least two witnesses, who had seen the new moon, and made a declaration to that effect before the Sanhedrin. It was the duty of this council rigidly to cross question these witnesses, and when their declaration was recognised as true, to publish the new moon to the people, first at Jerusalem, and then, by means of lighted beacons from the hill-tops, to the rest of Judea and to the whole *Gola*, " dispersion;" a word by which the Jews of Babylonia, Mesopotamia, Asia Minor, and Upper Asia were designated.

The extreme limit of these beacon-signals the Mishna (tr. Rosh. Hashnah, ii. 3) fixes at *Bet Biltin*, one of the highest peaks of the *Defazayat* or *Brelimmah* chain, near the Euphrates. Ritter (Geography, vol. xi. 736) assumes the mountain *Abul-rs* to have been the Bet-Biltin

---

* The English authorised version of the Bible completes the sentence, by adding the words *her cunning*, (Ps. cxxxvii. 5), whereas in the original Hebrew, the sentence is left incomplete, and terminates abruptly, as if the poet, in the fervor of his agitation, had been carried along without ever perceiving that he had left something unsaid. But this very abruptness, especially where the invocation is so solemn, gives to the Hebrew a force and impressiveness of which the English rendering preserves but a faint idea.

of the Mishna. Whichever of these mountain peaks may have been that extreme limit, it is certain that it was situated not far from the Euphrates, and in a region where great numbers of Jews resided, and from whence the news was rapidly conveyed to the remotest Jewish congregation north and north-east of Judea, who thus were enabled to celebrate the festivals, as nearly as possible, simultaneously with Jerusalem, which otherwise could not have been done. It is from this arrangement that the *Yom Tob sheni shel goliyoth*, "the second holiday of the dispersion," dates its origin.

The tribute or tax of half a shekel, toward defraying the expense of the daily and other sacrifices and public services in the temple, had been annually paid by every Jew before the Babylonish captivity. According to tradition, it was originally levied by the Law of Moses (Ex. xxx. 12, 13), not only as a temporary contribution, but as a permanent tax; and as such we find it recognised by the kings and people of Judah (2 Chron. xxiv. 6). On the return from the Babylonish captivity, and the rebuilding of the temple, the contribution, which had been in abeyance while the Temple laid in ruins, again became obligatory. But as the Jewish shekel or currency had been superseded by the Babylonian, which was as heavy again as the Jewish, and as, moreover, the people were very poor, and could ill afford the doubling of their annual payment to the Temple—which must have been the case if the contribution of half a shekel of actual currency had been insisted on—Ezra and Nehemiah decreed that the annual payment should be reduced to one-third of a shekel currency; and as the Jewish colonists who remained in Babylonia and other provinces of the vast Persian Empire, were desirous of proving their veneration for the Temple of Jerusalem, they voluntarily took upon themselves to contribute annually, toward the support of the offerings and services, the same amount that was paid for the same purpose by the residents of Judea. The Jews are not only a law-abiding people, but also strict observers of precedent. Once introduced, these annual payments became a rule with every Jewish colony and congregation, however remote from the mother country. It appears that in process of time, when the people could better afford it, and the influence of the *Sopherim* (scribes or teachers), everywhere enforced the literal observance of the Law of Moses, the contribution of the half shekel was, notwithstanding the increased value of the coin, everywhere adopted; and when subsequently the Greek currency, which was even heavier than the Babylonian, became general throughout Judea, and its standard was adopted by Simon the Maccabee, the half shekel still continued to be paid; though this amount, similar in name only, was in fact more than three times as large as the tax levied by Moses.

Thus their veneration for the Holy Temple, their dependence on the great national council at Jerusalem, and the share or portion every one of them had in the public sacrifices and services of the sacred metropolis, connected all the Jews throughout the vast *diaspora* all over Asia with the mother-country.

To the south-west and south of Judea, the Jews were spread almost as widely and as numerously as they were in Upper Asia. The Jews in the Egypto-Grecian Empire, were brought in under Alexander the Great and Ptolemy I. They increased and multiplied until their chief seat and metropolis, Alexandria, with its immense Jewish population, magnificent synagogue, and great wealth, became the admiration of their Eastern brethren. Under the Ptolemies the Jews in Egypt rose to high honors and great power. The language spoken by the Jews in that country was a dialect of the Greek.

The Jews in Alexandria had their own Sanhedrin, or seventy elders, and at their head stood an officer recognized by the Government. The etymology of his title or designation, *Alabarch*, is one of great difficulty to philologists; but his functions appear to have been similar to those subsequently exercised by the *Reishi Galratha*, "chiefs of the dispersion," in Upper Asia. The decision of the chief tribunals in Alexandria, are spoken of with respect by the Talmud, (tr. Keluboth, 25 B.); and there is reason to believe that the fixing of the Neominæ for the Egypto-Grecian Jews, was a prerogative exercised by the Sanhedrin at Alexandria. It is certain that the communication, by means of beacon-signals, was not kept up with Egypt; although this may perhaps have been owing to the want of localities proper for the raising of beacons. In other respects the Jews of Alexandria kept up their connection with Judea; for notwithstanding the temple which Onias erected and Philometor patronized, it was the time-honored house of God at Jerusalem, that held the first rank in the estimation of the Hellenists; and to its support the vast majority of them contributed the annual half-shekel, like all their various brethren throughout Asia. From Egypt proper, various branches of the Jewish dispersion extended over the eastern isles, and the southern shores of the Mediterranean Sea. The island of Cyprus, so long dependant on the empire of the Ptolmies, contained a very great number of Jews, and so did the island of Kos.

The Jewish population in the city and territory of Cyrene, on the north coast of Africa, was both numerous and powerful. Another large Jewish congregation resided at Berenicia, the site of the present city of Tripolis, in Barbary, where a column of Parian marble has lately been dug up, bearing an inscription in honor of Marcus Tertius Æmilius, Roman proconsul, (about 44 B.C.E.), by the *Archonts*, (elders), and community of Jews at Beranicia. The attachment of all these Jewish settlements to the metropolis of Jerusalem, and its temple, is frequently noticed by Josephus, (Antiq. lib. xiv. passim.) A striking proof of the deep interest they took in the fortunes of Judea, we still possess in the so-called second book of Maccabees. This is the epitome of a history in five books, by Jason, a Jew of Cyrene, who wrote for the sole purpose of perpetuating the deliverance of Judea, and the glory of the Maccabean brothers. This history has perished, but the epitome has found room among the Apocrypha, and by that means been preserved to us.

Another branch of the *diaspora* of Egyptian Jews, spread over the interior of Eastern Africa, where we find its remains in the *Falashas*, a people of Jews at one time so powerful as to have acquired dominion over the great kingdom of Abyssinia; and who, though subsequently much reduced, are still in existence. There is reason to believe that the first Jewish settlers in these remote regions, were refugees who had fled from persecution by Physcon, in Egypt; but that these Abyssinian Jews did not keep any intercourse or connection either with Alexandria, or with Jerusalem.

Within the last couple of years, much interesting intelligence respecting the Falashas and their religion, has been obtained by means of Monsieur A. d'Abbatie. This gentleman, a French traveller, visited Abyssinia in 1845, and returned to that country in 1848. He had on the occasion of the second journey, been furnished with a list of questions by the youthful but highly gifted Philoxene Luzzato, of the *Collegia Rabbinica* in Padua, who, however, did not live to receive the full and satisfactory answers M. d'Abbatie brought back from the Falashas, and which were published at Paris in the *Univers Israelite*, April to July, 1851. These answers place it beyond a doubt that the Falashas, or Abyssinian Jews, originated from Alexandria or Egypt, but they never had, or very early renounced, connection with that country and with Judea. Among their fast days, totally different from, and far more numerous than those observed by the Jewish nation in every part of the world, they have none to commemorate the destruction of Jerusalem and its Temple, nor yet that of Heliopolis in Egypt—a fact which proves that the severance of their intercourse with Jerusalem, and Alexandria, must have been anterior to these two events, so greatly affecting the public services of the Jewish religion, but of which the Falashas remained ignorant.

It seems, however, that these Abyssinian Jews carried their religion across the Red Sea and established it in Yemen, the south-western portion of the great Arabian peninsula, known to the ancient geographers as *Arabia Felix*. The fact that a Jewish kingdom existed in those rich and fruitful regions, and that it maintained itself during several centuries, is indisputable, and confirmed by several independent historical authorities, though the time when the Jewish religion was first introduced into Yemen, and the circumstances under which it became dominant, are very uncertain, and only known by means of legends equally vague and marvellous.

In the *Kitab Aldjumen* (a Mohammedan chronicle), it is related that a prince of Yemen, named Assad, collected a large army for the purpose of making conquests, not only within the Arabian peninsula, but also beyond its boundaries. He was an idolater, as was indeed the entire population of Arabia in those days, with the exception of a few Jews who had fled from Jerusalem at the time of the conquest of *Bokhtnasar* (Nebuchadnezzar), and had settled in the vicinity of Medina. In the course of his campaigns, Assad took the city of Medina, where he installed one of his sons as ruler. But after his departure with his army, the citizens rose against the young prince and slew him. The tidings of this crime soon reached the father, and so exasperated him, that he sat down before rebellious Medina, with the avowed determination to exterminate the inhabitants and utterly to destroy the city.

The siege proved a long one, when two Jewish sages came to Assad, and said to him, "If it be thy determination, O King, to destroy this city, thou wilt not succeed; for a prophet will arise, Mohammed by name, who, when expelled from Mecca, is to take up his abode at Medina; and this we find in our Torah, therefore it must be true." Assad inquired, "Who or what is this Torah?" to which they replied, "The book of the law which God hath given unto Moses," and they then proceeded to acquaint him with the precepts of the book.

Assad was so pleased with the doctrine he had heard, that he, with his whole army, became converted, and embraced the religion of these sages. He then raised the siege, having granted a pardon to the guilty citizens, because of the future merits of their descendants; and returned to Yemen, accompanied by his two teachers, who worked many wonders, and converted the entire population of the country to their own religion, which was that of Abraham.

Thus far the legend : That, however, fails to tell us which of the many princes of the Tobba named Assad is the hero of our tale. Accordingly, much difference of opinion prevails respecting the date of this conversion. Some place it some centuries before the destruction of Jerusalem, while others assume the third century of the Christian era as the probable date.

After the Jewish Kingdom in Southern Arabia had been subverted by the Christians of Abyssinia, in the fifth century of the Christian era, and the Jewish religion had almost disappeared from that portion of the peninsula, the fact that a system of Judaism, different from that which prevailed in his own days, had at one time been general throughout Yemen, enabled Mohammed to charge the Jews, as he does in his Koran, with having perverted the doctrines of the law, and falsified the Scriptures in which his mission and advent were announced.

CHAPTER IV.

JEWISH MONEY.

The chief money of the Jews was the *shekel* of unmixed silver. Many have thought that they had two sorts of weights—one sacred, or of the sanctuary, and the other royal or profane; but this distinction is grounded upon no passage in the Bible.

The Jewish weights were of stone; from this is the royal weight named (1 Kings) "the stone of justice."

It does not appear that the Jews had coined pieces of gold; but foreign money, either gold, silver or copper, was current among them.

The form of their shekel was the same as our common English penny; on one side there was stamped a vase with flowers, and the words "Shekel Israel" around it; and on the reverse an olive branch with the words "Shekel Hadodesh."

It was the same value as the English half crown, and the half shekel was half as much. They had their shekel either in one piece or in four to make it up.

These four pieces were called in the Greek language, drachms; in the Hebrew, zuzees; in the Latin, pennies.

The shekel was of the weight of three hundred and twenty barley corns; but the wise men added to its weight, and made it the weight of three hundred and eighty-four barley corns.

This was equal to one selaa; the selaa is four denarii; the denarii is six meaks; this is that which, in Moses' time, was called gerah; the meah was two pondions; the pondion two issarim; and a mite the eighth part of an assar. The weight of a mite was half a barley corn.

The Jerusalem money was the eighth part of the Tyrian. On it were stamped the following: David and Solomon on one side; and on the reverse, Jerusalem the holy city.

Upon Abraham's money were stamped on one side, an old man and an old woman; on the other, a young man and a young maid. On Joshua's money, on one side, an ox; on the other, a monoceros. On David's money, on one side, a staff and a scrip; on the other, a tower. On Mardochai's money, on one side, sackloth and ashes; on the other a crown.

CHAPTER V.

THE GOLDEN VESSELS OF THE TEMPLE—WHERE THEY ARE.

The vessels of pure gold which were in the house of our God were very precious, not only of their precious materials, or the wonderful and artificial workmanship on them; but more because they were used in the service of Jehovah, and therefore holy. This is also the reason why the Scriptures give such a detailed description of their forms, and the weight of gold of which they were made. Where is the man, who feels in his heart the great loss of glory and beauty, who would not long to know what became of those holy vessels, after the house of God was destroyed by Titus?

We shall mention some of the possessors of these vessels:

The Emperor Titus brought them, with a great many other costly things, from Jerusalem to Rome: the candlestick, the table, etc.; and according to the custom of the age, that a conqueror of other nations made his entry into the metropolis in triumph, leading behind him a long train of chained prisoners, while slaves carried the best of the spoil; so also Titus commanded the holy vessels to be carried and shown to the people, as the emblems of his conquest. After that they were exhibited in a great Temple, which they called the Temple of Peace. There they remained for many years; probably to the middle of the fifth century.

In the year 450, A.D., there came Gensericus, the King of the Vandals, from Africa to Rome, besieged and conquered it, and made an immense spoil. Among the most precious things he took, were the holy vessels. He carried all in ships to Africa; and they remained there in the King's treasury for 70 years. In the year 520, came Belisarius, the general of the Emperor Justinian, to war against the Vandals. He succeeded in subduing them and made a tremendous spoil; and the holy vessels fell also into his hand. He brought them to Constantina; and also commanded, like Titus, that they should be carried in triumph through the streets of the city.

When these remnants of Israel's glory were thus carried about in the streets of Constantina, a Jew met one of his acquaintences in the King's household, and said to him, "The King does not well to exhibit these sacred vessels in the streets, and then keep them here in his palace. According to my knowledge, there is no other place for them than Jerusalem, the Holy City, where they came from, and where they have been used in the service of God. The incidents also which occurred in connection with them, show that they brought destruction upon those who kept them, and boasted of their possession. Thus Gensericus was permitted to conquer Rome. But as the Africans kept in their hands these holy things, God punished them, by permitting Belisarius to become their conqueror, and spoil them." The King's servant hastily repaired to Justinian, and related to him all that the Jew had told him; and the Emperor trembled for fear, and suffered not the vessels to be brought to his palace; but commanded them to be carried to Jerusalem, and there to be deposited in one of the churches of the Christians.

Thus writes the historian Procopius. This, however, is the last information we have been able to get on this, for us, very important subject.

CHAPTER VI.

THE HIGH PRIESTS.

Imperfection of the Genealogical Registers—Lists of names so far as ascertained.

To give a correct list of the names of the High Priests from Aaron, the brother of Moses, down to the destruction of the first Temple, is a task that has puzzled many a scholar. The newest and best commentators of the Bible have failed in giving a list, answering all the objections heretofore raised.

Josephus, (in his Antiquities, xx., 10), gives the number of the High Priests from Aaron up to the building of the Temple by Schelomah (Solomon), as *thirteen*, and from thence down to the destruction of the Temple by Nebuchadnezzar, as *eighteen*; a number confirmed also by the Talmud.

It is true, the Biblical registers of the High Priests do not entirely correspond with his sketch. But they seem to be given more to a genealogical purpose, than to a historical one, and are, besides, so defective that they can give no reliable decision. The register in Ezra, vii., 1–5, has but fifteen names between Aaron and Ezra, by far too few for a period of 1,000 years.

The second register in I. Chronicles, v., 30-41, contains twenty-two names, instead of the fifteen in Ezra; but it is also incomplete, the names of many a High Priest mentioned in the books of Samuel, Kings, and Chronicles, being openly omitted.

Josephus tells us, as above stated, that from Aaron down to the building of the Temple, there were *thirteen* High Priests. We record them in the following manner:

1. Eleazar.
2. Phinehas.—(Judges xx., 28.)
3. Abishua.
4. Buki.
5. Usi.
6. Secharjah.
7. Merajoth.
8. Amarjah.

} According to I. Chronicles, v., 31–33.

The register then omits the names of Eli and his descendants, very probably on account of their services being rejected by the Lord.—

(I. Samuel iii., 11-14.) He seems, however, to mention one of them, Achitub, who, according to I. Sam. iii., 14, had succeeded Eli in the office of High Priest. If therefore, we insert the historical names of

9. Eli.
10. Achitub.
11. Achijah.—(I. Samuel, iii., 14.)
12. Abimelech, who was slain by Saul.—(I. Samuel, xxii.)—and
13. Ebjatar, who was discharged from the office by Shelomoh,—(I. Kings, ii. 27.) We have from Aaron down to Shelomoh, thirteen High Priests, a number fully corresponding with Josephus, and in a period of about 470 years, giving an average of 35 years of office to each of them, fully in proportion with the life-time of those by-gone days.

From the building until the destruction of the Temple, Josephus gives the number of High Priests as 18. Following the register in Chronicles we find:

1. Zadock, who first officiated in the temple.
2. Achimaaz.
3. Asarjah.
4. Jochanan.
5. Asarjah.
7. Amarjah, (under King Jehoshaphat.)
7. Achitub.
  Here the register omits the names of—
8. Jehajadah, (under King Joash.)
9. Secharjah, (under the same King.)
10. Asarjah, (under King Uzziah.)
11. Urias, (under King Achas.)
12. Asarjah, (under King Jecheskiahu.)
  Then the Biblical record resumes again with—
13. Zadok. }
14. Shalum. } (under the Kings Menasheh and Amon.)
15. Chelkijah, (under King Josiah.)
16. Asarjah.
17. Serajah, (under King Jojachin.)
18. Jehozadak, (who was carried away into the captivity of Babylon.)

This list, giving us exactly eighteen names, corresponds entirely with Josephus and the Talmud. The period from Shelomoh until the destruction of the Temple, comprehending about 420 years, gives an average of 24 years to every High Priest, for the term of his office.

CHAPTER VII.

DOCTORS OF DIVINITY.

Diplomas—Status and Powers of Rabbis in different ages.

The Hebrew or Rabbinical student, it must be well known to many, receives a diploma, which is called by different names, such as מורינו רבינו חבר In possession of such a diploma the student is authorized to officiate as Rabbi. *Semichah*—Laying on of hands. When Joshua was appointed successor in office to Moses (Numb. xxvii., 18 to 23; Deut. xxxiv., 9) Moses laid his hands upon Joshua. The verb to express this act is *Samach*, and the noun *Semichah*. Therefore the act of appointing one to succeed in office was called *Semichah*, except King and High Priest who were annointed, and were therefore called *Messiah*, which signifies " the annointed one." In the Biblical passages quoted above, some expressions must be noticed particularly: "A man in whom there is spirit." "Thou shalt confer upon him from Thy glory." "There was upon him the spirit of wisdom, for Moses had laid his hands upon him."

These passages teach us what was to be conferred upon the appointed successor. 1. From the glory, authority or distinction of the one who appointed; and 2, the spirit of wisdom, knowledge, learning, &c.

This act of Semichah was retained till long after the destruction of the second temple of Jerusalem, to authorize students as Rabbis or Judges, which rendered them eligible to these offices. The title of Rabbi or dozen (Judge) was not introduced in Israel until ten or twenty years before the vulgar era. Simon, the son of Hillel 1, is the first who had this title. Hillel was appointed Nassi, thirty years B. C., and he is yet the plain Hillel, without the title of Rabbi.

In former times, the distinguished scholars were *Hachamim*, (sages), *Soferim*, (scribes), and in a still more ancient time they were called *Sekenim*, (elders.)

In the time of Hadrian's persecution, one of the prohibitions was to teach the law or promote students by the *Semichah*, because thus the national laws of Israel were surely to be abrogated, as in a short time there would have been none in Israel qualified by law to be a judge in penal and other matters. After Hadrian's death, they re-organized the Sanhedrin, and continued the practice of the national laws.

When the title Rabbi became more general, the Nassi was called *Rabbon*.

As long as there was a patriarch in Tiberias and a Sanhedrin, this *Semichah* law was binding, and with a few exceptions none would assume the title or function of Rabbi, without the *Semicha* of the Nassi or Patriarch.

About 450 B. C., the Sanhedrin and patriarch's office ceased, and with them also the *Semichah*, of Palestine; but it was continued in the Babylonian schools, by the highest officer called there *Resh Gelutha*. It was understood in all countries, that none could be a Rabbi unless he had a diploma of the *Resh Galutha*, in Babylon.

With the conclusion of the Talmud, the *Semichah* ceased. In Italy, the form of the *Semichah* was retained for a long time, so that the students were promoted to the Rabbinical office by an assembly of Rabbis only. and in a solemn manner.

The *Morenu* was no more than the title of doctor. It authorized none to the Rabbinical office; to this end he had to pass another examination, and obtain the *Hatorath Haroah*, "The permission to render decisions."

This diploma gave him the Rabbinial authority, if a congregation elected him. The congregations up to this day in Europe, Asia, and Africa, elect none to the Rabbinical office who is not in possession of those diplomas from competent authorities.

Thus the matter stood everywhere in Israel, until, in this country, the *Hazanim*, without any of the above diplomas, examination or ordination, assumed the title and function of Rabbi, or styled themselves reverends, a title entirely strange to the Jews.

The following are recognized Jewish titles:

1. *Rabbi* or *Haham*, authorized by a competent authority, with the *Hatorath Haroah*, and elected by a congregation.

2. *Dayan*, assistant Rabbi, and *Moreh Zedek*, proxy, with the above ordination.

3. *Morenu*, or Doctor of Divinity, more strictly Doctor of the Law.

4. *Hazan*, the officer who conducts the singing, and reading part of Divine service in the synagogue.

CHAPTER VIII.

SCHOOLS.

Jewish zeal in the promotion of learning—Vernacular of the people in the time of Christ—Greek prohibited for sacred purposes—Strictures on Lightfoot.

The Rabbis say there were five hundred schools in Palestine, and in each five hundred pupils. Rabbi Akibah had alone twenty-four thousand disciples who frequented his schools; and in every town where no school existed, the men thereof stood excommunicated till a school was erected.

Besides, the places where the Sanhedrin had their seats, there were great schools to be found, copiously furnished with great men, both in Galilee and Judea; and after the compiling of the Talmud, the University of Babylonia became renowned; and out of that University sprung again colleges, which, to this day, have their existence in all parts of the world where there are large Jewish congrgations. We must not neglect to give them their due credit for the zeal which they exhibit in supporting the various institutions of education among themselves. Even those families who are deprived of sending their children to public or private schools, will keep a tutor or instructress for them at home; and no matter how poor they may be, yet they will never neglect the education of their children, so that seldom, if ever, you are able to find a Jew who is not at least able to read and write.

It was the Hebrew, Syriac, Chaldaic, and Aramean languages, which were taught in their schools, and which were the vernacular tongues of the people, during the time of the existence of the second Temple. It is true that the Greek language was used by the Hellenists, Jews dispersed among the Greeks; but with this exception, the Greek language was neither to be found in their literature nor prayers, and was even considered a crime to be taught. They laid an effectual bar against the learning of the Greek language, and only allowed the family of Rabbi Gamaliel the Greek learning, because they were allied to the Royal blood. This, however, they did not grant freely to others. Here is the decree itself: "Let no man be allowed to teach his children Greek."

It is, therefore, an erroneous idea for anyone to suppose that the Jews, at the time of the coming of our Saviour, used the Greek as their vernacular, especially when we know the following facts: First, *Jonathan*

Ben Uzziel translated the Prophets out of Hebrew into *Chaldaic* (not into Greek) a short period before the coming of Christ; and *Onkeles* did the same with the Law a little time after. Both of these did so, for with this language the Jews were most conversant. Secondly, In the Temple, synagogue, and other places of public worship, the Greek was never used. No debate took place, no ceremony was performed, no Rabbi ever wrote, and no book among the many (especially the Talmud) was written and published in any other but the above-mentioned Hebrew, Syriac, Chaldaic, and Aramean languages, during this period. It is true, that after the Babylonish captivity, there was an alteration of things; that the Hebrew tongue became the Chaldaic tongue, or better to say, the Syriac-Chaldaic. This is plain from those several words, "Bethsaida," "Golgotha," "Akeldama," which are said to be so called in the Hebrew tongue; and yet everyone knows the words to be mere Chaldaic. And this Syriac Chaldaic was *the* language of the Jews at that time. Last, but not least, the many expressions made by our Saviour, will prove that it was the Hebraic Syriac Chaldaic, and *not* the Greek, which was the language of the Jews, and the language in which he spoke to them. As for instance, "Eli, Eli, Lama Sabachthani?" "Eloi, Eloi, Lama Sabachthani?" "Belial." "Belzebub." "Talitha Cumi." "Maranatha." "Rabbi." "Rabbony." "Immanuel." "Jot." "Korban." "Racca." "Abba."

How much mistaken is then Mr. Lightfoot's idea, when he says, "Let those that hold the opinion we are confuting (*i.e.*, that the New Testament was originally published in the Greek, and was the common language used by the Jews, and hence also by Christ,) consider but seriously that Christ called himself by the name of the two Greek letters *Alpha* and *Omega*." How weak does his argument appear, when we know that almost every version of this text uses its own peculiar language. No revelation, nor prophecies were ever made in Greek, and surely Christ the Lord would have preferred to call himself in letters out of a holy tongue, in which Patriarchs, Prophets, and God the Holy Ghost spoke, rather than those of a language which was not only hated by the Jews, but was to the majority an unknown tongue.

CHAPTER IX.

MEDICINE AND CHIRURGERY.

Physicians amongst the Hebrews—Modes of treating the sick—Diseases mentioned in Scripture.

The theory of physic seems never to have made any considerable advances among the Hebrews. Physicians (*rephaim*) are first mentioned in Gen 1. 2; Ex. xxi. 19; Job xiii. 4. Some acquaintance with chirurgical operations is implied in the rite of circumcision; and there is ample evidence that the Israelites had some acquaintance with the internal structure of the human system, although it does not appear that dissections of the human body, for medical purposes, were made till as late as the time of Ptolemy. That physicians sometimes undertook to exercise their skill in removing diseases of an internal nature, is evident, from the circumstance of David playing upon the harp, to cure the malady of Saul, 1 Sam. xvi. 16. The art of healing was committed, among the Hebrews, as well as among the Egyptians, to the priests; who, indeed, were obliged, by a law of the state, to take cognizance of leprosies: Lev. xiii. 1-14, 57; Deut. xxiv. 8, 9. Reference is made to physicians who were not priests, and to instances of sickness, disease, healing, &c., in the following passages: 1 Sam. xvi. 16; 1 Kings, i. 2-4, xv. 23; 2 Kings, viii. 29, ix. 15; Is. i. 6; Jer. viii. 22; Ez. xxx. 21; Pr. iii. 18, xi. 30, xii. 18, xvi. 15, xxix. 1. The probable reason of King Asa not seeking help from God, but from physicians, as mentioned in 2 Chron. xvi. 12, was, that they had not at that period recourse to the simple medicines which nature offered, but to certain superstitious rites and incantations; and this, no doubt, was the ground of the reflection that was cast upon him. About the time of Christ, the Hebrew physicians made advancements in science, and increased in numbers. See Mark v. 26; Luke iv. 23, v. 31, viii. 43; Joseph. Ant. xvii. 6, 5.

It appears from the Talmud, that the Hebrew physicians were accustomed to salute the sick by saying, "Arise from your disease," a salutation adopted by our Lord.—Mark v., 41. According to the Jerusalem Talmud, a sick man was judged to be in a way of recovery when he began to take his usual food. Compare Mark v., 43.

With regard to the treatment of the sick and indisposed, and the expedients they employed to assuage or expel disease, the Hebrews appear to have proceeded by an invariable system, and uniformly to have practised certain rules and methods of cure, which had nothing to recommend them but the sacred prescription and sanction of antiquity. They seem to have regarded *oil* as a more effective remedy, than any other discovery for mitigating or extirpating the various diorders of the human frame. The sick, whatever the distemper might be, they appear to have anointed with oil, as the most powerful preservative they knew from the further progress of the disease, and the most effectual remedy for the recovery and re-establishment of health. We have one of the medical prescriptions, which is in this form :

"He who is affected with pains in his head, or eruptions on his body, let him anoint himself with *oil* ;" and this was deemed of such supreme effect, that one of the Rabbins gave his dispensation for anointing the sick, even on the Sabbath. To this common custom of treating sick persons, reference is made in Mark vi., 13, and James v., 14. Not that this unction, either in the former or latter case, contributed anything to the miraculous cure, which the immediate power of God alone could effect ; it served only as a striking external sign to sick persons, and to every spectator, to raise and engage the attention, and to impress the mind with the deepest conviction, that the miracle was wrought to attest the Divine authority and truth of the gospel. The balm of Gilead was celebrated as a medicine—(Jer. viii., 22 ; xlvi., 11 ; li., 8.)—And mineral baths were deemed worthy of notice, as appears from Gen. xxxvi.. 24. The Hebrews, like other nations of the ancients, attribute the origin of diseases, particularly of those whose natural cause they did not understand, to the immediate interference of God. The ancient Greeks called them *mastiges*,—the *scourges of God*,—a word which is employed in the New Testament, by the physician Luke himself, (vii. 21), and also by Mark v. 29, 34.

In the primitive ages of the world, diseases, in consequence of the great simplicity in the mode of living, were but few in number. At a subsequent period, the number was increased, by the accession of diseases that had been previously unknown. Epidemics also—diseases somewhat peculiar in their character, and still more fearful in their consequence— soon made their appearance; some infesting one period of life, and some another; some limiting their ravages to one country, and some to another. The propriety of this statement, in regard to the original extent and subsequent increase of diseases in general, and to epidemics, will recommend itself to every mind that makes even but small pretensions to attainments in knowledge.

Every region, and every age of the world, has been in the habit of attributing certain diseases to certain causes, and of assigning names to those diseases, derived from the supposed origin or cause, whether it was a real or only an imaginary one. The names thus given have been in many instances retained, both by the vulgar and men of medical science, after different causes had been developed and assigned to the disease in question. In respect to this subject, we know that there are certain words of very ancient standing, which are used to express diseases of some kind or other; it will, therefore, be a prominent inquiry with us to learn what the diseases are that were designed to be expressed by those words.

(1.) *The disease of the Philistines*, which is mentioned in Is. v, 6, 12, vi., 18, is denominated in the Hebrew ophelim. This word occurs likewise in De. xxviii, 27, and the authors of the reading in the *Keri* appear to have asserted to the opinion of Josephus, expressed in Artq. vi., 1, 1!; and to have understood by this word the *dysentery*. But the probable supposition is, that *solpugas* (spiders, like *mice*) were at this time multiplied among the Philistines by the special providence of God, and that, being very venomous, they were the means of destroying many individuals.

(2.) *The disease of King Jehoram*, II. Ch. xxi., 12, 15, 18, 19. This disease, beyond all doubt, was the dysentery; and though its continuance so long a time was very uncommon, it is by no means unheard of. The intestines in time become ulcerated, and are emitted or fall out, which is sufficient to account for the expressions used.

(3.) *False conception* does not appear to have been so unfrequent among the Hebrew women as among those of Europe. If it had been so, it probably would not have made its appearance on the pages of Hebrew writers in the shape of a figure of speech. Is. xiii, 8, 26, 17; II. K. xix., 3; Jer. iv., 31, xiii., 21, xxii., 23, xxx., 6; Mi. iv., 9, 10; Jn. xvi., 21, 22; Is. xxvi., 18; Ps. vii, 14.

(4.) The *leprosy* prevails in Egypt, in the Southern part of Upper Asia, and, in fact, may be considered as a disease epidemic in warm climates generally. Accordingly, it is not at all surprising, if many of the Hebrews, when they left Egypt, were infected with it; but the assertion of Wanetho, that they were *all* thus infected, and were, in consequence of this infection, driven out by force, in which he is precipitately and carelessly followed by Strabo, by Tacitus, by Justin Trogus, and by others more recent, is a mere dream, without any adequate foundation.

We have reason to believe that it is concealed in the internal parts of the system *a number of years*; till at last, it gives the fearful indications on the *skin* of having already gained a deep-rooted and permanent existence. A person who is leprous from his nativity, may live 50 years: one who in after-life is infected with it, may live 20 years; but they will be such years of dreadful misery as rarely falls to the lot of man in any other situation. The appearance of the disease externally is not always the same. The spot is commonly small, resembling in its appearance the small red spot, that would be the consequence of a puncture from a needle, or the pistulæ of a ringworm. The spots, for the most part, make their appearance very suddenly, especially if the infected person, at the period when the disease shows itself externally, happens to be in great fear, or to be intoxicated with anger. Nu. xii., 10; II. Ch. xxvi, 19. They commonly exhibit themselves, in the first instance, on the face, about the nose and eyes, till they become, as respects the extent of surface which they embrace on the skin, as large as a *pea or bean*.

The white spot, or pistulæ, (*morphea alba*) and also, the dark spot, (*morphea nigra*) are indications of the existence of the real leprosy. Le. xiii., 2, 39, xiv., 56. From these it is necessary to distinguish the spot, which, whatever resemblance there may be in form, is so different in its effects, called *Bohak*, and also the harmless sort of scab. Le. xiii. 6, 8, 29. Moses, in Le. ch. xiii, lays down very explicit rules for the purpose of distinguishing between those spots which are proofs of the actual existence of the leprosy, and those spots which are harmless and result from some other cause. Those spots which are the genuine effects, and marks of the leprosy, gradually dilate themselves, till at length they cover the whole body. Not only the skin is subject to a total destruction, but the whole body is affected in every part. The pain, it is true, is not very great, but there is a great debility of the system, and great uneasiness and grief, so much so as to almost drive the victim of the disease to self-destruction. Job vii, 15.

There are four kinds of the real leprosy. The first kind is of so virulent and powerful a nature, that it separates the joints and limbs, and mutilates the body in the most awful manner. The second is the *white leprosy*. The third is the *black leprosy*, or *Psora*: Deut. xxviii. 27, 35; Lev. xxi. 20-22. The fourth description of leprosy is the *alopecia*, or red leprosy. The person who is infected with the leprosy, however long the disease may be in passing through its several stages, is at last taken away suddenly, and for the most part unexpectedly. But the evils which fall upon the living leper are not terminated by the event of his death. The disease is to a certain extent hereditary, and is transmitted down to the third and fourth generations; to this fact there seems an allusion in Ex. xx. 4, 6, iii. 7; Deut. v. 9, xxiv. 8, 9. If anyone should undertake to say, that in the fourth generation it is not the real leprosy, still it will not be denied that there is something which bears no little resemblance to it in the shape of defective teeth, fetid breath, and a diseased hue. Leprous persons, notwithstanding the deformities and mutilations of their bodies, give no special evidence of a liberation from the strength of the sensual passions, and cannot be influenced to abstain from the procreation of children, when at the same time they clearly foresee the misery, of which their offspring will be the inheritors.

The disease of leprosy is communicated not only by transmission from the parents to the children, and not only by cohabitation, but also by much intercourse with a leprous person whatever. Moses acted the part of a wise legislator in making those laws, that have come down to us, concerning the inspection and separation of persons (that the race might not degenerate). The objects of these laws will appear peculiarly worthy, when it is considered that they were designed, not wantonly to fix the charge of being a leper upon an innocent person, and thus to impose upon him those restraints and inconveniences which the truth of such a charge naturally implies; but to ascertain in the fairest and most satisfactory manner, and to separate those, and those only, who were truly and really leprous. As this was the prominent object of his laws that have come down to us on this subject, viz: to secure a fair and impartial decision on a question of this kind, he has not mentioned any of those signs of leprosy, which admitted of no doubt, but those only which might be the subject of contention; and left it to the priests, who also fulfilled the office of physician, to distinguish between the really leprous, and those who had only the appearance of being so. In the opinion of Hensler, Moses, in the laws to which we have alluded, discovers a great knowledge of the disease. Every species of leprosy is not equally malignant; the most virulent species defies the skill and power of physicians. That which is less so, if taken at its commencement, can be healed. But in the latter case also, if the disease has been of long continuance, there is no remedy.

(5.) *The Pestilence*, in its effects, is equally terrible with the leprosy, and is much more rapid in its progress; for it terminates the existence of those who are infected with it, almost immediately, and, at the farthest, within three or four days. The Gentiles were in the habit of referring back the pestilence to the agency and interference of that Being, whatever it be, whether idol or spirit, whom they regarded as the Divinity.

The Hebrews also everywhere attributed it to the agency, either of God Himself, or of that legate or angel whom they denominate *metach*. We are not, however, to suppose that the Hebrews, in using these expressions, mean to attribute the pestilence to the *immediate* agency of God; nor would they permit us to understand by *the messenger* who, they assure us, is the agent in business of so disastrous a nature, the true and appropriate angel or legate of Jehovah. It is true, they tell us, that God sends forth the pestilence, and that the angel goes with it and smites the people with its power; but let it not be forgotten that every angel is the creature of God, and that, in a certain sense, God is the author of all things and all events, whether prosperous or afflictive, whether good or evil. When they make God the author of the pestilence, it is clear they do not mean to say, that He is the immediate author of such evil. In a somewhat recent period of their history, it cannot be denied, that instead of making God the author of evil, they attribute it to a malignant spirit of high origin, viz: Satan; but still they were aware of the origin of this Being, that He was the creature of God, and acted beneath His superintendence. God, in a certain sense, is the author of all things. This is true. But the ancient Hebrews do not appear to have distinguished with sufficient accuracy that liberty, or permission which is given us, in the course of Divine Providence, to do or not to do, good or evil, from the direct agency of God Himself: Deut. iv. 19; Jos. xi. 20; II. Sam. xvi. 10; xxiv. 1. Compare I. Ch. xxi. 1; II. Kings xvii. 14; Psalms lxxviii. 49-51. In consequence of this disposition to identify the agency of God with the actions of his creatures, and to confound the original with second and subsidary causes, we find by consulting the Scriptures, that they sometimes represent men, and sometimes animals, or inanimate existences, as *the messengers or the angels of God*; and this is not only in poetry, but likewise in prose,—Ps. xxxiv. 7; civ. 4; Heb. ii. 2; Acts vii. 53; xii. 23; Gal. iii. 19. Compare Josephus Antiq. xv. 3-5. This mode of speech was so common, that the Sadducees of a more recent age, who, although they received the Scriptures with veneration, denied the existence of any spirits, interpreted passages, where mention is made of angels of other existences, which were employed by God, as instruments, and, as they supposed, were from that circumstance, *merely* denominated the messengers or angels of God. It may be remarked that no one ever recovered from the pestilence, unless the bile of the pestilence came out upon him; and even then he could not always be cured.—II. Kings xx. 7; Is. xxxviii. 21.

(6.) *The disease of Saul and of Nebuchadnezzar.*—A person who understands the extent and the proper bearing of the principle defended in the preceding paragraph, will see that *the Spirit of God*, which departed from Saul, was no other than an upright and a generous tendency of mind; and that *the evil spirit from the Lord*, which beset and filled him with terror, (I. S. xvi., 14, 15; xviii., 10; xix., 9), was a sort of madness, which had the effect of deceiving him into the idea that he was a prophet; for it seems that he prophesied, and in all probability, predicted the loss of his own kingdom. The Targum of Jonothan accordingly renders the word *ithneba*, *he was mad* or *insane*. The evil spirit, in a word, was not more a spirit or messenger from God than the evil spirit, which in Jud. ix., 23, is said to have been sent by Him among the Shechemites; and which certainly, as was evident even to the ancient interpreters, and has been since to everybody else, was nothing more than the spirit of strife and dissension. In the same way *the spirit of fornication*, in Ho. iv., 12, is mere *lust*. Comp. I. S. xi. 6; xvi. 14; Jud. iii., 10, 6; xxxiv., 11, 29; xiv., 6; Ps. li., 11; Ez. xi., 19; xviii., 31. This representation, more than any other, is suitable to the fact that Saul was benefitted by music; for the charms of music, however great its efficacy in any other case, would have been very incompetent to the task of subduing the untractable spirit of a real demon. This mode of speaking did not originate, as some have supposed, in the time of the captivity, from the doctrine held by the Mehastani, although it undoubtedly at that time became more common, and was used with greater latitude than at any previous period. For agreeably to this mode of speech, and to the belief on which it was founded, viz.: the subordinate agency of angels, we find mention made in Da. x., 14, 20, of *star-matchers*. The designs, or the decrees, of these holy matchers, as they are termed, which are made known to Nebuchadnezzar in his vision, and are stated in the verses above mentioned, are referred by Daniel, in 5, 28, of the same ch., to the immediate agency of God Himself; a circumstance which is altogether conformable to what has been already stated, in this and the preceding section, on the subject. *The disease of Nebuchadnezzar*, mentioned in this chapter, was that of insanity or madness. His mind was in such a state, his reasoning powers were so perverted and deranged, that it appeared to him as if he heard a voice from heaven, declaring his expulsion from the kingdom; and he imagined that he was really transformed into a beast. Accordingly, he acknowledges iv., 31, 33, that he had again received the use of his reason; which is an indication that he understood the disease from which he had recovered to be *insanity*.

CHAPTER X.

THE LOST TEN TRIBES.

Conflicting Opinions—Curious Stories by Dervishes and Travellers—Deportations from Israel—Fate of the Exiled Israelites—Localities of the Captives of Judah—Their Fate—Account of the Ten Tribes in ESDRAS—Indians of America supposed to be part of the Lost Tribes—Other Conjectures.

The opinion that the Afghans are of the so-called ten lost tribes of Israel, finds a new basis occasionally. A British officer wrote from India (in January, 1859,) that the Eusyphzic tribe call themselves Hebrews from the tribe of Joseph. They found also an Isaac tribe; but the name Ishmael is too frequent among them not to point to Mohammedan traditions. A certain Mr. H. V. —— sent an abstract of a manuscript found by him called "A fram't Afaghinah," the secret of the Afghans. The original, he says, is in the Pushto language, according to which, the Afghans, or this tribe of them maintain to be descendants of King Saul, who, according to some, was of the tribe of Judah, and according to others, he was of the tribe of Benjamin. That manuscript mentions the war of the Israelites with the Amalekites, the capture of the Ark of the Covenant, the respect shown to it by the idols, and its final return, drawn by a cow, so that the story of Eli's sons is visible in it. Since that, two Hebrew manuscripts were found written on parchment and red-goat skin. A small scroll contained the book of Esther. A large scroll contained the History of the Jews. A large scroll contains the history of the Jews of Cochin and Malebar, from the time of the Babylonian captivity, to the first settlement of Portuguese Jews in Hindostan. De Wise says :

Not being in possession of the manuscripts, we have no means to judge of its correctness. Still we find in this discovery, a confirmation of our opinion that the lost ten tribes must be sought especially in the countries bordering on the Caspian Sea, in Tartary, Afghanistan, Bellochistan and India. Many of them are in Arabia, and the interior of Africa; but the bulk of them must be found there. Not that all those inhabiting these countries are Israelites, but the Israelites must be found among them in large numbers.

The following stories about the ten tribes of Israel, of whom history has lost sight of for more than two thousand years, are current among the older Jewish population in the Holy Land. We will give our readers as much information respecting them as we have been able to gather, without, however, warranting the truth of any part of it.

About twenty-five years ago, there came a Dervish from the east of Asia to Damascus, who carried a sum of money with him, consisting of gold coin, which he wanted to exchange for current money. On one side of the coin was the following inscription, in square Hebrew characters: "Under the reign of our Lord, King Isaac." Upon interrogation as to how he came in possession of the coins, he relates the following: "In my pilgrimage from Adshem, Persia, toward the south-east, I came to a great country; and after many day's journey, reached a great and populous city. My beggar-like dress aroused the attention of the people, who soon followed me in crowds. Finally some persons took hold of me, and brought me into a magnificent mansion, before a majestic-looking person sitting upon a throne-like seat. This man addressed me in the Persian language, asking me where I came from, what my business was, and many other things. After I had given him all the information I could he asked, were there any Jehudim (Jews) in my country? I said, Yes there are; but they are a miserable set of rogues. (The foolish Dervish did not perceive he was in the presence of a Hebrew king.) Upon this I observed that the king was very much displeased; I, therefore, skillfully explained my words: adding, that this is only the way in which the common people look upon them; but the better classes look upon them as the most intelligent, the most liberal, and the most honest people. The king, thereupon, was so pleased that he commanded to give me three hundred pieces of this gold coin."

This Dervish was so illiterate and ignorant in everything, that it was impossible to get any more information about the country and its people from him.

Three years ago, I saw a fine-looking Dervish walking in the street; I approached and entered into a conversation with him. I found him to be a very intelligent and truthful man; I therefore invited him to my house, entertained him, and listened to his interesting conversation on his long travels in the utmost parts of Asia. Among other things, he related also the existence of an immense Jewish empire, lying in the north-east direction, and about four months' journey from Cashmire, a well-known city in Persia. The capital of that Jewish kingdom is called "Adjulun." Almost the whole of the vast empire is surrounded with huge mountains, thus forming a natural fortification, which leaves but one passage where entrance can be effected, and which however, is garrisoned by a strong force of Hebrew soldiers. The Hebrew inhabitants stand in a commercial relation with the surrounding nations: but a stranger is very seldom permitted entrance. His friend, however, also a Dervish, lived several years in Adjulun unmolested, and was afterwards inexhaustible in speaking of the grandeur of the city, and magnificence of the palaces and synagogues, which are almost fairy like. All the inhabitants are Hebrews, except the servants, who are from the neighboring states.

About fifty years ago, there lived a Jew in Calcutta, who, some years before, immigrated from Bagdad, and earned a very poor livelihood. He at once concluded to try his fortune in some remote countries, purchased a small lot of merchandise, and started on a journey toward the east, to reach Ara, in the Burman empire. After he had travelled several months, he arrived at a considerable city, not far distant from the Burman boundary. There, however, he was not allowed to enter, but was informed that strangers, who have goods for sale, must exhibit them outside the gates, where the people of the city are accustomed to come and make their purchases. The Jew hired a stand, and put out his merchandise on shelves; and soon the city people, who consisted of Burmans and Hindoos, flocked to his place, and purchased of his goods. But his business was at once interrupted by the following accident: There came a man to his stand, who took almost every article into his hand, asked the price of each, but bought nothing, and finally put, by stealth, several articles into his pocket. The Jew, in struggling with the thief for his property, gave him a blow on his head, of which he fell down dead. The rage of the people was terrible; but the police guarded the Jew against Judge Lynch, and carried him, fettered hand and foot, into the city, before a tribunal, which was held on a public square, in front of a magnificent palace. There he was tried, condemned, and immediately divested of his clothes, to be beheaded.

The poor trembling Jew stood on a platform, the executioner a drawn sword in his hand, waiting only for a signal from the king, in the opposite palace. But, lo! instead of that death-bringing signal, the king opened the window, and exclaimed with a loud voice: "Hold, sheriff, touch not that man, but rather take care of him, and do thy best, that he may leave our country with friendly feelings." This sudden change not only surprised the Jew, but encouraged him to ask the favor of being brought into the king's presence. His application was granted. The king, a venerable, hoary man, received him very kindly, and condescended to relate to him the following history:

"Know, my son, that this my kingdom is, for many years past, under the protection of, and tributary to, a mighty king, of whom and his people we know nothing, except that every year, at a certain season, a number of exceedingly strong, giant-like men, come to take the annual tribute. About twenty-five years ago, my people and my counsellors urged me to refuse the payment of the annual tribute; when, therefore, those terrible looking messengers came, they were sent away emptyhanded. They left the city seemingly without much feelings of disappointment, and we thought that all was right, and rejoiced in our independent position. Five months after that affair, we received information that a host of giants were on their way towards the city; and we soon perceived that it was the mighty king, who came to avenge the wrong done to him by refusing the due tribute. Before we could make any preparations for defence, the mighty host stood at the very gates of the city. Seeing that there was no hope of escaping from the evil by resistence, I concluded to humble myself before the mighty emperor, and so, to save my people and my land from the consequences of our foolish rebellion, myself, and all the princes and nobles of my people, went out into the camp, clothed in sackcloth; and throwing ourselves at the feet of the king, solicited forgiveness, and promised to remain thenceforth faithful tributaries, paying regularly our debts. And, indeed, I was not mistaken, that the people and their king are as generous as they are powerful; we were forgiven, and they departed in peace without doing any injury or offence in the least. When thou, my son, was divested of thy clothes, I observed a certain piece with fringes on it, exactly like those which that mighty king, and all the men with him wore—although theirs were larger, and worn over all their garments— I thought that thou wast one of them, and that thy death would bring vengeance upon us. This saved thy life."

The most interesting story, however, is the following: Nineteen years ago, the Jewish congregation at Zephath, (Safet), sent a messenger to Yeman, in order to take up collections for the poor in the Holy Land. He stopped for some time in Zanah, where he, of course, attended synagogue regularly. Here he saw a man distinguished in his appearance from the rest of the Jews in that place. On inquiring about that man, he was told that he arrived at Zanah a few days ago, stating that he was an Israelite of the tribe of Dan. This aroused the curiosity of the messenger, who requested the Danite either to call on him, or else to accept a visit from him. The Danite complied with the messenger's wish and called on him. He was a tall and stoutly-built man, with large beaming eyes, long beard and long black hair, which hung down in curls, covering his neck and shoulders. His dress was the same as that of all the Orientals; but he wore a girdle around his waist, upon which the following verse in Hebrew, with square characters, was embroidered: "Dan shall be a serpent by the way, an adder in the path, and a broad-sword on his side." His language was pure Hebrew; but he was very reserved, cautious in his expressions, very temperate, eating almost nothing but bread, drank exclusively water, and devoted a few hours only to sleep. It seemed as if the man spake to a spirit within himself, and listened to his answers; but he observed many ablutions, and his whole character brought to mind that of the Essenes of old. He inquired of the messenger about the state of the Holy Land, the city of Jerusalem, Zion, and the brethren; and when he had heard of their miserable condition, how desolate the land, and how poor and oppressed the few Jews were, he cast himself upon the ground, and hiding his face in the dust, wept bitterly. He lay thus half an hour before he could speak again. He then spoke of his people, the Danites. He said that their tribe was unmixed with any other; have their own land, independent of any king, and are governed by their own chosen Nassi, (prince), who is always the most valiant and the most pious among them; two things which alone qualify the man for that high office. Concerning the objects of his journey, he said he was despatched by the Nassi to inquire into the condition of the brethren in the west, their religious, moral and social state., &c.

The messenger asked him whether he would be willing to take him to the happy land of the Danites, in order that he might be able to bring great tidings to his brethren in Safet and Jerusalem? "With great pleasure," replied the Danite; "and not this alone, but I will, with the help of God, bring you back to this place after a few months." The messenger seems, however, to have been irresolute, from lack of courage, or of faith, and delayed his departure from one day to another, until the Danite lost patience, and suddenly disappeared. The most remarkable circumstance is, that a single man, on foot, dared to undertake such a long and dangerous journey, through a wilderness which abounds with serpents.

In Safet and Jerusalem, the narrative of the messenger concerning the Danites, their land, independent and patriarchal government, and general prosperity, caused a considerable excitement and interest, so that they concluded to send a special mission to them. The man, however, who would undertake that mission was not so easily found, until a certain Rabbi, Baruch Moses, an emigrant from Russia, a physician and a man of great courage and experience, offered himself to execute the plan. After he had been provided with everything necessary for such a journey, he set out by the way of Alexandria and Cairo, to Zanah. Here he engaged an aged Jew to accompany him through the desert. The old man, however, told him that he would go with him as long as either of them would not be hurt by a serpent; but as soon as that should take place, he would consider it as a bad omen, and immediately return.

They went on and nothing happened during the first six days. On the seventh, however, the old man was bitten by a serpent; and although R. Baruch healed him immediately, he refused obstinately to go any further; and thus R. Baruch, who could not pursue his way alone, returned to Zanah; and the idea of visiting the Danites was given up entirely.

The first deportations on record from the kingdom of Israel, is from the two tribes and a half (Reuben, Gad, and half of Manasseh) who had their homes east of Jordan river, in the province, called afterwards Perea. The second deportation from the kingdom of Israel took place during the reign of Pekah, king of Israel (760 to 740 B. C.). The third and largest deportation from the territory of Israel was immediately previous and shortly after the fall of Samaria (721 B. C.)

If Josephus had not informed us, that the Israelites were transported to Media and Persia,—(Antiq. ix. 14),—and the Talmud had not described the localities whither they were transported,—(Kiddushin 71, 72),—we could easily suppose that they were not deported beyond the limits of the Assyrian Empire. Hence the story of the lost ten tribes (actually only nine) would be debarred of every historical foundation. The Afghans, Lebians, and American Indians having in their turn been pointed out as the lost tribes of Israel, it is well to state here in advance of those who identified themselves not afterwards with the people of Judah, amalgamated among the pagans where they lived, or still exist in minor tribes about the Caspian Sea, on the Tartary mountains, or in the interior of Africa.

The localities to which the captives of Israel were deported are not distinctly enough described in the Bible—(I. Chron. v. 20 ; II. Kings xvii. 6)—to be discriminated at the first glance on the map, although the author of Kings tells us they were deported to Assyria. The author of Chronicles, who wrote after the return of the captivity, could, of course, not say, that those distant parts belonged still to Assyria.

We have mentioned above three distinct deportations from Israel, and our sources mention three distinct places, whither they were transplanted: *Halah, Kabor*, the river of *Gozan*, and the cities of Media, or *Hara*, as the author of Chronicles says. We maintain that the *Gozan* river, cities of Media and *Hara*, refer to the same place in Media.

The deportations from Damascus went to Kir,—(II. Kings xvii.9).— They were Israelites,—(Isaiah xxvii. 6). The second exiles (747 B. C.) were deported from Damascus to *Kir*, and from Israel to *Khabor*. A broad stream which falls into the Tigris about eighty miles north of Mosul, still retains the name of *Khabour*. The third and largest number of exiles from Israel, (721 B. C.) were undoubtedly dispersed to many different spots, but chiefly to those cantons at the south-western shores of the Caspian Sea, called afterwards Caspiani and Atropatena. The author of Chronicles calls this district *Hara*, so it was called Hé ré, which signifies, in the Pchlri language, a mountain land. It is evident that the Gozan river is this very district.

Exiles have no history; there may exist an account of their fate. In the case before us these accounts are very meagre. It is evident, that the localities to which they were deported, were in four countries which played a prominent part, in the history of two remarkable centuries (from Pal to Cyrus), two centuries of the most extraordinary revolutions, an uncommon change of empires. We refer to Assyria, Babylonia, and Medo-Persia. Hence the fate of the Hebrew exiles must have been as much changing and troubled as the history of those centuries is.

We have no accounts of the exiles during the life of Sargina. But when his successor Sanneherub met with an inglorious and disastrous defeat in Judea, under king Hezekiah, on his return the fate of the exiled Israelites was intolerable. Many of them were massacred every day, and their bodies exposed in the streets of Nineveh, and most likely also elsewhere, were refused a burial.

The Israelites, however, were soon relieved of the tyranny and cruelty of Sanneherub. Babylonia and Media revolted against the supremacy of Assyria. Merodach, king of Babylonia,—(Isaiah xxxix.)—in connection with the king of Susiana, the same man who cultivated the friendship of Hezekiah, king of Judah, fell into the Assyrian army and attacked Sanneherub. The war lasted eight years, and ended with the defeat of Merodach. Esar-Haddan, Sanneherub's son, was appointed viceroy of Babylonia.

The Israelites in Babylonia and Susiana must have been numerous, as Isaiah everywhere mentions them. Their hatred against Assyria, their long practice in warfare, and their tried bravery, together with the fact of Merodach's attempt to enter upon an alliance with Hezekiah, convinces us of the active part the Israelites played in this war. The sagacious Isaiah, perceiving at once the melancholy termination of this enterprise, prevented Hezekiah from an alliance with the kings of Babylonia and Susiana.

More successful than the former were the Medes, and it appears from the subsequent history, also the Armenians. It must be borne in mind, that in both countries many of the dispersed Israelites had settled. The exiles of Khabur, on the frontiers of Armenia, could and most likely did render them good services.

History records four distinct deportations from Judah to Babylonia. 1st—during the years 606, 605, 604, B. C., in the time of King Joachin; 2nd—during the years 597 and 596, B.C., with King Joachin; 3rd—in the years 589, 588, 587, and 586, before and after the destruction of Jerusalem, with King Zedekiah, and 4th—in the year 580, B.C., after the emigration of John and his followers to Egypt.

The first exiles, according to the united testimony of the books of Daniel, Baruch, and Susana, were deported to the City and Province of Babylon, where they existed as congregations, with their own laws and religion, administered by the officers of their own race. The Prophet Ezekial also testifies to the existence of Hebrew Communities in Babylon, to whom he spoke (xii. 24, 25). He calls that Province Chaldee, but he evidently referred to the one of which Babylon was the capital (xii., 11, 13). The distinction of the Provinces of Chaldee and Babylon was evidently unknown to Ezekiel. Daniel and his friends came with these exiles to Babylon.

The second exiles from Judah, with whom Ezekiel came, were located, as a prudent policy dictated, at the opposite end of the Babylonian Empire, in the north of the Messopotamia, and also as high up as the Western bank of the Tigris, so that they came near the exiles from Israel,—(Kiddushin, 72).

The third exiles appear to have been located between the two former, in Southern Messopotamia and Northern Babylon.

The fourth and last exiles went to unknown places, probably to Arabia, where many congregations were found during subsequent history. Many Hebrews maintained themselves in the Desert,—(Ezek. v. 2; x.

12'; Zach. xiii. 7 to 9 ; Ezek. xxx. 27 ; Isaiah li. 19),—while many others were sold as slaves,—(Nehem. v. 8 ; Joel iv. 6, 7, 8 ; Corp. Ezek. xxvii. 8).

The Hebrew settlements existing in Egypt and Ethiopia, were considerably augmented during the Assyrian and Babylonian invasions in Palestine. The emigrants who came with John and others settled on the side of their brethren in Daphna Pelusiæ, (Thapanhes), &c. Jeremiah uttered terrible oracles against the Hebrews of Egypt and the Egyptian king ; still the people remained there. They disappear altogether from history. Whether they amalgamated with the Egyptians, emigrated into the interior of Africa or to Greece, or returned to Palestine, cannot be ascertained. Their fate is entirely unknown. So is the fate of Jeremiah and Baruch. Some maintain, without a particle of evidence, that the patriotic prophet was killed in Egypt. Tradition says that both Jeremiah and Baruch went to Babylonia, where they died. The latter is said to have been the teacher of Ezra.

Among the first captives brought to Babylonia, there were many of the nobility of Judah and of the Davidian house. Nebuchadnezzar selected some of those young men to be placed under the particular care of *Asphenaz*, one of the high dignitaries, that they be instructed in the Chaldean language, art and science, in order to prepare them for official functions. Daniel Hananiah, Mishael and Azariah, were the most distinguished among the young Hebrews thus selected. They were so scrupulous in religious matters, that they would neither eat the dainties nor drink the wine which was offered them from the royal table. Their steward, at first, being afraid that frugality would impair their bodily vigor, refused to comply with their wish to subsist on grains and water ; but a trial to this effect having convinced him to the contrary, he allowed them their choice diet, which proved favorable to their physical condition.

Their time for instruction being passed, Aspheraz presented the Hebrew lads to Nebuchadnezzar, who was particularly pleased with Daniel, Hananiah, Mishael and Azariah. They proved to be very erudite in Chaldean literature, and Daniel understood especially well to interpret dreams, a science, then highly valued, of which we have no knowledge. Greek writers tell us that Pythagoras went to the Chaldeans to learn this science. The four Hebrews were retained at the royal court.

Daniel also rose in the estimation of his own people, by the following incident. Two judges and elders of the Hebrew congregation attempted in vain to beguile Susana, the beautiful wife of a man called Joakim.

Either to revenge themselves or to escape the punishment of the law, they appeared at the seat of justice as prosecutors and witnesses against Susana, accusing her of adultery. According to the law of Moses, Susana was sentenced to death. Daniel claiming the benefit of Israel's laws, as tradition presented them in behalf of the afflicted woman, caused her to be brought back to the court of justice, a new trial granted, when he cross-examined the malignant accusers, and by his sagacity entrapped them in contradictions, which established their guilt and Susana's innocence. She being exonerated, the penalty of the law fell upon the heads of the guilty men.

The sudden elevation of Daniel and his compatriots to high offices, is ascribed in our sources to the following cause: Nebuchadnezzar had a dream, which he forgot. None of his numerous savans could guess the dream or its interpretation, which cost them their lives. Daniel succeeded in guessing the dream, or at least in making the king believe so, and, like Joseph of old, giving a proper interpretation. This pleased the capricious monarch so well, that he paid homage to the God of Daniel. By request of the latter, he raised his three friends to the dignity of governors of the Province of Babylonia, made him rich presents, and retained him at court as a special favorite. Daniel was quite young then, for he outlived the Babylonian empire. His piety and wisdom were far-famed; so that he appears to his excellent cotemporary, Ezekiel, as one of the most pious and also the wisest man of his age,—(Ezekiel xiv. 13, 19 ; xxviii. 3),—but he was never considered a prophet.

It is evident that at one time the condition of the first exiles was quite tolerable, at least during the time that Daniel and his friends maintained their influence on the governing head of the country. Nebuchadnezzar contrived his warlike operations in the west of Asia long after the fall of Jerusalem. According to modern researches, he took Tyre in the year 573 B. C., and succeeded in subjecting finally Cœlo Syria, Ammon and Moab, in the year 572 B. C. It is doubtful that he ever succeeded in subjecting Egypt and Ethiopia; still Josephus mentions this as a fact, and the prophets appear to speak of it.

Elated with success, wealth, power, victory, and the homage paid to the mighty conqueror, Nebuchadnezzar turned so haughty and selfish that he became insane. Having erected a huge image of himself, or of the god whose name he preferred to his own, in the valley of Duro, all the officers of the state were invited to the dedication, and required to pay homage to the idol. The penalty of death was dictated to the disobedient. The officers obeyed, except the three friends of Daniel—Hananiah, Mishael, and

Azariah (Daniel most likely was not required to do it). The three disobedient Hebrews were thrown into a heated oven, from which, by unknown means, they went forth uninjured. Nebuchadnezzar considered their escape from death so marvellous, that he again professed the God of the Hebrews to be the greatest and most glorious.

Shortly after this, Nebuchadnezzar had another dream, which betokened already the deranged condition of his mind. Daniel again interpreted the dream to the satisfaction of the king. The prediction of the pious sage was fulfilled. Twelve months after this, Nebuchadnezzar was so completly insane and unconscious of himself, that he ate grass with the animals. This narrative is no mere invention, to show how God punished the haughty man, who destroyed His Temple and exiled His people; for Berosus, the Chaldean historian, tells nearly the same story. During his insanity, his wife, Semiramis, governed the Empire. After seven years, Nebuchadnezzar regained his health, and governed Babylonia to the end of his days. He died after a reign of forty-three years, (561 B.C.), leaving his empire to his son, Evilmerodach.

Evilmerodach released king Joachin from his prison, when the latter was about sixty years old, placed him first among the dethroned Kings, changed his vestment of captivity, let him eat at the royal table, and bestowed on him a rich annuity. Joachin was not kept in prison those forty years,—(I. Chron. iii. 16–17),—but he was kept confined. This change of government certainly had a favorable influence on the captive Hebrews; but they did not enjoy it long; for Evilmerodach was killed by his brother-in-law, Neriglesser, who mounted the throne after him, (559 B.C.) This King governed to the year 556 B.C., when he fell in battle. He was succeeded by the boy Labosordach, who was killed by a son of Nebuchadnazzar,—(Dan. v. 11; xiii. 8,)—whom Daniel calls Bellshatzar, and profane historians call him Nabo-Nadius; both names are nearly synonymous—(Isaiah xlvii. 6). He was the last king of Babylonia.

Daniel remained at court during these political changes, but exercised no influence on the kings. His friends disappear altogether from the historical record. There are traces in Isaiah of oppression which the Hebrews suffered during the reign of the last king—(Is. xlvii. 6).

Forty-eight or fifty years after the fall of Jerusalem, proud Babylonia was no more, as Israel's prophets had predicted. It fell by the very nations which they had named, and many of the captives of Judah lived to see the justice of Providence. Babylon with her proud palaces, temples and huge idols, was reduced to a small place, and the sons of the nations she had bereft of their home and liberty, threw the firebrand in her royal edifices. Whatever connection there existed between the Hebrews in the city of Babylon and the besieging army, their particular friends, those who avenged the wrongs of Israel; whatever part Daniel acted in this connection; how and why the mysterious writing and its expounding were produced, whether to show the direct interposition of Providence at so important a crisis of history, or to arrest the attention of the king and his officers while Cyrus executed his plan; whatever construction may be put upon the peculiar stratagems of Cyrus on this occasion, as recorded by Xenophon and Herodotus—the fact is certain, that Cyrus took the city by surprise, and made an end to the Babylonian Empire, and that both Cyrus and Darius were the friends of Daniel and his people.

Darius, the Mede, died in the year 556 B. C., and Cyrus, that great and good man, assumed the government of the largest empire in those days. He gave the Hebrews permission to return to Palestine and rebuild the Temple of Jerusalem.

In the Apocryphal book Esdras, which, although excluded from the sacred canon as an uninspired production, is, nevertheless, entitled to consideration, as stating much which in all probability is an indisputable fact; there is this information respecting them; "Those are the ten tribes which were carried away prisoners out of their own land, in the time of Osea the king, whom Shalmaneser, the King of Assyria, led away captive, and he carried them over the waters, and so they came into another land. But they took this counsel among themselves, that they would leave the multitude of the heathen and go forth into a further country, where never mankind dwelt, that they might there keep the statutes, which they never kept in their own land; and they entered into Euphrates by the narrow passages of the river. For the Most High then showed signs for them, and held still the flood till they were passed over. For through that country there was a great way to go, namely, of a year and a half. And the same region is called 'Arsareth,' (ch. xiii, 40–45), or Ararat, and which in Hebrew signifies the 'Curse of Trembling.'"

For the following we are indebted to an interesting paper "On the Ten Tribes," by the author of Letters to the Hebrew nation, in vol. i. of the "Christian's Pocket Magazine." "It is said that in the fifth century, Jerome has these words when treating of the dispersion of the Jews, 'unto this day, (5th century), the Ten Tribes are subject to the kings of the Persians, nor has their captivity ever been loosened,'" vol. vi, p. 7.

And again, "the ten tribes inhabit at this day, the cities and the mountains of the Medes." Vol. vi., p. 80.

In a curious and learned pamphlet published in London, Eng., in 1650, entitled "Jews in America; or Probabilities that the Americans are Jews, proposed by Thomas Thorowgood, B. D., one of the Assembly of Divines," the author observes, "That the Indians used strong knives, very sharp and cutting, like the Israelites of old in circumcision; and that Lerius affirms he saw some of those cutting stones or knives in Brazil." In "The Journal of a Two Months Tour in America," by Charles Beatty, A. M., (London, Eng., 1768,) the author says: "A Christian Indian informed me that an old uncle of his, who died about forty years ago, related to him several customs and traditions of the Indians in former times; and among others, that *circumcision* was practised long ago by them; but that their young men at length making mock of it, brought it into disrepute, and so it came to be disused."

The celebrated Dr. Robertson, and others, agree that the most of the Indians came originally from Tartary, and passed over into America from Behring's Straits. If this can be proved, it avails much to prove that many of the Indians are the descendants of the ten tribes, for Shalmaneser carried the ten tribes into Tartary.

It is a remarkable fact that the Indians pronounce the Hebrew word Yo-he-wah (Jehovah) more like the Jews, than do the English.

William Penn, who was governor of Pennsylvania, and must have consequently known much about the Indians, was decidedly of the opinion that they are descendants of the Israelites. He says: "They agree in *rites*, they reckon by *moons*, they offer their *first-fruits*, they have a kind of a *feast of tabernacles*, they are said to lay their altar on *twelve stones, their mourning a year, the customs of women*; with many that do not now occur."

James Adair, Esq., also, who lived as a trader among the Indians of North America for forty years, in his "History of the American Indians," thus expresses his conviction: "It is very difficult to divest ourselves of prejudices and favorite opinions, and I expect to be censured for opposing commonly received sentiments; but truth is my object, and from the most exact observation I could make in the long time I traded among the Indians in North America, I was forced to believe them to be lineally descended from the Israelites."

Hence it is probable that "the desert," or "further country," referred to by Esdras, "where never mankind dwelt," may be America, which country, indeed, would much better accord than any contiguous one could do, with that other representation which he makes of it, as a "great way to go, namely, of a year and a half." Esdras further says, "the same region is called Ararash, or Ararat;" and Dr. Boudinot says, "A gentleman of the first character of the city of New York, well acquainted with the Indians from his childhood, assured him, that when with them at a place called *Cohoch*, or *Owlflat*, now degenerated to *Cookhouse*, yet well known, they showed him a mountain to the west, very high, and that appeared from Cohoch, much as the Neversinks do from the sea, at first approaching the American coast, and told him that the Indians call it *Ararat*."

Mr. Bruce, the celebrated traveller, says, "There are Jews in Abyssinia as black as the original natives; which Jews," he says, "must be the descendants of the Ten Tribes." He further says, "the motto of the king of Abyssinia is, 'The lion of the race of Solomon and of the tribe of Judah hath overcome.'" According to Mr. B., the people of Abyssinia suppose that they are to bear a part in the final restoration of Jerusalem.

Upon the whole, then, I incline to conclude that at least a portion of the Ten Tribes are to be found in every country, and in every quarter of the globe, and that they are to be found especially in those countries mentioned in Is. xi. 11, namely, "Assyria, Egypt, Pathros, Cush, Elam, Shinar, Hamath, and the Islands of the Sea." Nor do I think it at all improbable that they may be existing in very considerable numbers where conjecture has placed them, particularly among the Afghans of Persia and the Red Men of North America. Ireland, too, has its share, for the physical features are in strong harmony with those of the Jews.

CHAPTER XI.

DEMONS AND EVIL SPIRITS.

Opinions of the heathen on Evil Spirits—Views held by the Reformed Jews—Doctrines taught by orthodox Jews.

The doctrine of the evil spirits taught by the heathen, has a double source. Either it was originated by the idea of the Egyptians, that there is a destructive power in nature, being represented by Typhon, or by the dualistic system of Zoroaster, who taught that there are two Deities, namely: Ormuzd, the author of all good, and Ahriman, the author of all evil. In the old Biblical Scriptures, however, there is not a shadow of all these notions to be found.

They say there is not a passage to be found in the Old Testament that proves the existence of a devil, with his kingdom of evil spirits.

The following are some of the passages they quote in proof of their belief:

Exod. xx. 5: "For I the Lord thy God am a jealous God, visiting the iniquity of the fathers upon the children unto the third and fourth generation of them that hate me, and showing mercy unto thousands of them that love me," etc. Here it is evidently said, that it is exclusively the omnipotent hand of God which rewards or punishes, giving fortune or misfortune, sorrow or happiness.

Again Ibid ii.: "For in six days the Lord made heaven and earth, the sea and all that in them is," etc. The whole universe, together with all its powers, are represented as "creatio primitira," a primitive creation and action of God, the sole primitive force. This alone shall be worshipped and adored; because this alone governs everything.

Ibid xxiii., 25, 26: "And you shall serve the Lord your God, and He shall bless your food and your beverage, and I will take sickness away from the midst of you. There shall nothing cast their young, nor be barren in the land. The number of thy days I will fulfil." To the influence of God alone it is here ascribed temporal wealth, as well as also the removing of sickness, pestilence, and epidemical diseases.

Furthermore, Ibid. xv. 26: "I will put none of those diseases upon you which I have brought upon the Egyptians; for I am the Lord thy physician." (See also Deut. vii. 12-15.)

Again, Deut. xxxii. 39: "See now that I, I alone am He, and there is no God with me; I kill and I make alive; I wound and I heal; neither is there any that can deliver out of my hand." It is here expressly said, that no kind of sickness, nor death, or life, can be engendered except by the will of God alone, and that no one exists who is able to alter this divine will.

Some theologians maintain that the word עזאזל Lev. xvi. 8, 10, 26, means an evil spirit or the devil. They declare this false, and try to prove it by the following:

1. It reads, Lev. xvii. 7: "And they shall no more offer their sacrifices unto devils," etc. "This shall be a statute for ever unto them throughout their generations." Consequently, a sacrifice which should be offered to an evil spirit in the desert, would be contradictory not only to the mentioned law, but also to the general religious principles of Mosaism, which repeatedly enjoins that God alone shall be adored and worshipped.

2. The definition of the word "Asasel," an evil spirit, is without any grammatical foundation. The word "Asasel" signifies either as the Septuagint rendered the same, namely, "apopompaios," "transportation," or as others maintain, that it is the name of a place in the desert, where the scape-goat was sent to.

The prophet Samuel said—(1 Sam. xii. 20, 21)—". . . . but serve the Lord with all your heart, and turn you not aside, for then should you go after vain things which cannot profit nor deliver, for they are vain."

Isaiah said—(xliv. 8)—"Is there a God beside me? yea, there is no divine power: I know not any." And Ibid xlv. 6, 7: "That they may know from the rising of the sun, and from the west, that there is none besides me. I am the Lord, and there is none else. I form the light and create darkness. I make peace and create evil. I the Lord do all these things," etc., etc.

The prophet Jeremiah, admonishing the Israelites not to contract the vicious habits of the Babylonians, and not to embrace their worship, said (chap. x. 3): "For the religious customs of the people are vain," etc., and Ibid, 15, 16: "They are vanity, and the work of errors," etc. It is true that we find sometimes in the Holy Scriptures the expression רוח רעה (Ruach Raah); but in order to get a true meaning of it, they endeavour to show by the following what was meant by a "Ruach," when spoken of by the ancient Hebrews.

It signifies—1st. Soul, (Numbers xvi. 22, etc.); 2nd. The talents and skilfulness, (Exodus xxviii. 3, etc.); 3rd. The disposition and emotions of the heart, (Genesis xxvi. 25; Exod. vi. 9, etc.; Ps. li. 12). The expression, רוּחַ רָעָה, (Ruach Raah), occurring in the Book of Judges ix. 23, means, consequently, not an evil spirit, but an evil mind. But just as little can be rendered, I. Sam. xvi. 15, רוּחַ אֱלֹהִים רָעָה, "An evil spirit from God;" because were Saul and his contemporaries believing that he was possessed by a demon, they had surely not tried to cure an evil of such a nature by the means of musical sports, and would rather have consulted a conjurer, and requested him to exorcise the evil spirit, just as Saul had taken refuge in his desperate political circumstances to a woman, whom he supposed to be a sorceress.

The passage, I. Kings xxii. 21: "And there came forth a spirit," etc., is by no means a proof that the notion of the existence of a Satan had been already prevailing among the Jews at the time of King Ahab: for there is not spoken of an evil spirit, but of a serving angel commissioned by the Lord to execute His decree of punishment, and especially as the diction of the whole narrative shows it has not been a real fact, but a metaphor used by the prophet in his vision.

This, then, is the Reformers' belief, that there are no devils or evil spirits, which is contrary to the Orthodox party, who believe in a Devil and evil spirits.

CHAPTER XII.

TRADITION OF THE JEWS.

The Unwritten Law—The Mode of its Transmission—"Making a Hedge for the Law"—Divisions of the Law.

Their traditions are three-fold; either those that they called and accounted " an unwritten law given to Moses at Sinai," and handed by tradition from generation to generation; or the practical glosses and canons, which were made upon that unwritten and traditional law in the several generations as they passed; both these were called the traditions of the fathers and of the elders.

The deliverers of the unwritten law (which they say came successively from Moses), they will name you, directly from generation to generation. "Moses (say they) received his traditional law from Sinai, and delivered it to Joshua, Joshua to the elders, the elders to the prophets, and the prophets to Ezra's great synagogue."

After the return of the captivity, they derive its pedigree thus: "Simeon, the Just, received it from Ezra; Antigonus of Saco, from Simeon; Joses, the son of Joezer, of Zeredah, and Joseph the son of Johanan, of Jerusalem, received it from Antigonus; Joshua, the son of Perrkiah, and Nittai, the Arbelite, received it from them; Judah, the son of Tabbai, and Simeon, the son of Shetah, received it from Joshua and Nittai; Shemaiah and Abtalion received it from Judah and Simeon; Hillel and Shamai from them; Rabban Simeon, the son of Hillel, and Rabban Jochanan Ben Zaccai received it from Hillel and Shammai; Rabban Gamaliel, called the old, (Paul's master), received it from Rabban Simeon, his father; Rabban Simeon, the son of Gamaliel, received it from Gamaliel, (he was slain at the destruction of the temple); after him, was his son Rabban Gamaliel, of Jabneh, who received it from his father; and after him, was Rabban Jochanan Ben Zaccai, who had received it from Hillel and Shammai," &c.

This is the tradition concerning the descent and conveyance of the traditional law, of which persons, and of which law, these two things are to be taken notice of :—1st. That all those that are named single in this succession, were the heads or presidents of the Sanhedrin; and where they are named double, or (Sugoth) " pairs," the first-named of the two was " Nasi," or president, and the second-named was " Abbethdin," or vice-president. 2nd. That this traditional law, whose conveyance they thus pretended from Moses, might not be disputed, as concerning the truth or certainty of it, though it received, in every generation, some illustration and practical gloss for the laying out of its latitude and extent.

They that fixed these positive practical senses upon it, were the elders of the great Sanhedrin, concluding thereupon in the council, and commenting this traditional law into particular laws and ordinances, as rules to the nation whereby to walk; and the Sanhedrin, of every generation, was adding something in this kind or other. And so they held, "That the great Sanhedrin, at Jerusalem, was the foundation of the traditional law, and pillars of instruction; and from them decrees and judgments went out unto all Israel; and whosoever believed Moses and his law, was bound to rest and lean upon them for the matters of the law.

The way or manner of their legislative determining upon this unwritten law, was thus:—1st. The general rule by which they went to work, was "to make a hedge to the law;" (Aseh Sejog Latorah,) that man should not break in upon it, to transgress it, and this was a special ground and rise, and a specious colour, for all their traditions; for they, pretending to make constitutions to fence the law from violation, and to rise the observance of it the higher—they brought in inventions and fancies of their own brains for laws; and so made the law, indeed, nothing worth. Take a pattern of one or two of their hedges, that they made to this purpose. The written law forbade, "Thou shalt not seethe the kid in her mother's milk." Now, to make sure, as they pretended, that this should not be broken in upon, they fenced it with the tradition, "Thou shalt not seethe any flesh whatsoever in any milk whatsoever." All things that were appointed to be eaten the same day, the command taught till the dawning of the next morning; if so, why do the wise men say but till midnight? Namely, to keep men far enough from transgressing.

2ndly. They divide the unwritten law into three parts or forms, "Tekanuth, Gezeroth, Hanhogoth," constitutions, decrees, and customs, or practices. The Sanhedrin, in several generations, made canons and constitutions to decide and determine upon all these particulars, as their own reason, knowledge, and emergencies, did lead them and give occasion.

As in one generation, they proscribed such and such times for morning and evening prayer. In process of time, they found these times allotted to be too strict; therefore, the Sanhedrin of another generation did give enlargement, as they thought best. "And in the days of Rabban Gamaliel (say they), heretics increased in Israel," and they vexed Israel, and persuaded them to turn from their religion. He, seeing this to be a matter of more import than anything else, stood up, he and his Sanhedrin, and appointed another prayer, in which there was a petition to God to destroy those heretics, and this prayer he set among the eighteen prayers, and ordained it to be in every one's mouth; and so the daily prayers were nineteen.

CHAPTER XIII.

ABSURD LEGENDS AND STORIES.

"R. Judah sat labouring in the law before the Babylonish synagogue in Zippor: there was a bullock passed by him to the slaughter, and it lowed." Because he did not deliver his bullock from the slaughter, he was struck with the tooth-ache for the space of thirteen years. "A certain traveller, who was a barber and an astrologer, saw by his astrology that the Jews would shed his blood," (which was to be understood of his proselytism, namely, when they circumcised him.) "When a certain Jew, therefore, came to him to have his hair cut, he cut his throat. And how many throats did he cut? R. Lazar Ben Jose saith eighty. R. Jose Ben R. Bow, saith three hundred." "When a hog was drawn up upon the walls of Jerusalem, and fixed his hoofs upon them, the land of Israel shook four hundred parsæ every way." "They say of Charina, that he, seeing once his fellow-citizen carrying their sacrifices to Jerusalem, cried out : 'Alas ! they every one are carrying their sacrifices, and, for my part, I have nothing to carry ; what shall I do ?' Straightway he betaketh himself into the wilderness of the city, and finding a stone, he cuts it, squares, and artificially formeth it ; and saith : 'What would I give that this stone might be conveyed into Jerusalem !' Away he goeth to hire some that should do it ; they ask him a hundred pieces of gold, and they would carry it. 'Alas !' saith he, 'where should I have a hundred pieces ? indeed, where should I have three ?' Immediately the Holy, Blessed God procureth five angels, in the likeness of men, who offer him, for five shillings, to convey the stone into Jerusalem, if himself would but give his helping hand. He gave them a lift ; and, of a sudden, they all stood in Jerusalem ; and when he would have given them the reward they bargained for, his workmen were gone and vanished." "A huge stone, of its own accord, takes a skip from the land of Israel, and stops up the mouth of the den in Babylon, where Daniel and the lions lay." Adam, when first formed, reached from earth to heaven ; and had a tail like an Ouran-Outang. Og, of Bashan, walked during the deluge, by the side of the ark, and sometimes rode astride it ; from one of his teeth, Abraham made a bedstead. The wings of the bird, Bar Juchne, when extended, causes an eclipse of the sun. One of her eggs, which fell from her nest, broke down three hundred cedars, and inundated sixty villages. Rabba, grandson of Channa, said: "I once saw a frog as large as the village of Akra, in Hagronia." But how large was that village? It contained sixty houses. There came a huge serpent, which swallowed the frog. But after that came a raven, which devoured the serpent. Rabba Papa answered: "If I had not seen it myself, I should not have believed it."

CHAPTER XIV.

JUDAISM NOT BORROWED FROM THE EGYPTIANS.

Many modern scholars have expressed the opinion that there is much in the Mosaic code borrowed from the Egyptians. They would willingly attribute to the Indians and to the Chinese the regulations and laws contained in the Holy Writings, if they could conceive or prove the least contact with these people by Moses and the Hebrews. For not only do these scholars deny the divine origin of the law, but they would, moreover, animated by a spirit of intolerance, deny to the Israelitish race all creative powers, or at least weaken it in attributing to other nations what is undeniably their work alone. As there is no other means of arriving at this end, they convert Moses into a disciple of Egyptian priests and of Egyptian learning. They do not recollect that there was one impassable barrier between the Hebrews and the natives; a contrast which prevented all approach, either real or simulated. On the other hand, from whatever point we consider the books of the holy legislation, we see the most striking contrast between this legislation and that of Egypt; so that since Egypt was the only country from which Israel could have borrowed ideas, the Israelitish origin of the Mosaic law is the more clearly demonstrated.

Not only polytheism and the grossest idolatry undoubtedly existed in Egypt, but there was not a single religion of antiquity so entirely addicted to animal worship as the Egyptian. Crocodiles, ibises, ichneumons, bulls, cats, dogs, hawks, and other animals, received divine honors, were placed as divinities in the temples, clothed and fed luxuriantly, embalmed after death, and buried in grottos in the rock. As the antipodes to these idols arose, the doctrine of the One God, who was not to be worshipped under any corporeal form or figure of any description, and this doctrine is so sublime, so grand, so clear, so positive, and so rational, that the religion of Israel is the most powerful opposition of ancient and modern paganism in general, and of Egyptian worship in particular. No nation has covered its country with so many temples and religious edifices as the Egyptian; that has devoted to the splendour of these buildings the lives of numerous generations, and all the power of the people; while from the commencement, and during all periods, only one place of worship was permitted to Israel for Divine worship, a place which only became a fixed temple five centuries after the conquest of Canaan; and while the Egyptian people were rigorously divided into castes, rising in order up to the sovereign and dominant caste of the priests, Israel was formed of one class of people, among whom liberty and equality completely reigned, among whom all industrial and spiritual labours were equally shared. In Egypt the military state was a separate caste, while among the Hebrews the numbering of the people at the going out of Egypt, is indicated by the total number of men capable of bearing arms. If we oppose the family of hereditary priests, who were appointed at the foot of Sinai, after the making of the golden calf, we must not forget that this is indicated in Scripture as a deviation from the general principle; that this sacerdotal family, in all things which do not concern worship, was placed exactly on the same footing as the rest of the people; that by their exclusion from a considerable territorial possession they were, from the very first, deprived of a large amount of influence, and the revenues which were assigned to them were free gifts offered from the religious feeling of individuals; while in Egypt this was compulsary tax. Thence the great poverty which the Israelitish priests often endured; and from this circumstance it was that the majority of the people, and some men particularly, were generally more pious than the priests, and that the latter only exercised temporary power during short periods, and under extraordinary circumstances. We must not forget, that while among other people, the priests made the religion, among the Israelites, the religion made the priests. Neither do the Mosaic laws of purification resemble those of the Egyptian. While among the Egyptians, the care bestowed upon the Egyptians was very great, it was very limited with the Israelites. Among the Egyptians, precisely those animals were prohibited to be eaten, which were considered as clean by the Israelites. Among the former, the dietary prohibitions extended to plants in general. We cannot forget that the laws regarding food for the Hebrews, did not exist before Moses.

It is thus that the religion of Israel, in its most ancient portions, forms an absolute contrast to Egyptian customs; and to endeavour to seek in the latter, the origin of the former, is an evident error. Modern researches have proved that the primitive alphabet is that of the ancient Hebrew, and that it has nothing in common with hieroglyphical writing, but was rather in complete opposition to it.

CHAPTER XV.

THE PRAYER "ALENU."

The closing prayer of the morning prayers, in private as well as public worship, is called "Alenu," from the first word with which that prayer begins, the meaning of which is, "On us."

This prayer is an excellent one; the only objection which might be made, is that the Jews speak of themselves as they *ought to be* and not as in fact they are. For the sake of its excellency, and in order to explain how it became the cause of persecution, we translate it, adding the clause which is ommitted in the present editions of the Jewish prayer book.

"It is on us (our special duty) to praise the Lord of all, to ascribe greatness to Him who created all things in the beginning, that He has not made us like other nations of the lands, and has not placed us like other families of the earth; for he has not given us a portion like theirs, nor our lot with all their multitudes. *For they kneel, worship and bow down before vanities and lifeless things*; *they pray and are not delivered;* but we kneel, worship and bow down before the Supreme King of kings, the Holy One, blessed be He. He who stretches out the heavens, and laid the foundations of the earth; the residence of His glory is in heaven above, and the dwellings of His power in the highest heavens. He is our God and none besides Him. Our King is Truth, and there is none like Him, as it is written in His law; 'Know, therefore, this day, and reflect it in thine heart, that Jehovah is the God in heaven above, and on the earth beneath, and there is none else.' Therefore we hope in thee, O Jehovah, our God, speedily to behold the glory and beauty of Thy power, to remove all abominations from the earth, and cause all idols to be utterly destoryed. To establish the world into a kingdom of the Almighty God, so that all flesh may invoke Thy name, and all the wicked on the earth turn unto Thee. May all the inhabitants of the earth know and acknowledge Thee, for unto Thee every knee must bow, and every tongue shall praise. Before Thee, O Jehovah, our God, they shall fall down and worship and ascribe honor to the glory of Thy name. They shall willingly take upon themselves the yoke of Thy dominion, and Thou shalt speedily be King over them for ever and ever.' And again it is said: 'And Jehovah shall be King over all the earth; at that time Jehovah shall be One and His Name One.'"

This is the prayer, "Alenu," and the italicized passages is that which caused not only persecutions and sufferings, but destruction of hundreds, and perhaps thousands, of lives of the Jewish people. But it was not that clause alone which caused so much indignation among the Gentiles of those dark ages, but the custom to *spit out* after having said those words. This obnoxious clause is omitted in all modern prayer books; but most of the orthodox teach their children to insert it by heart; and even the spitting is still practical in those dark corners of Europe, where pure gospel light has not penetrated, and where Jews and Gentiles are several centuries behind time.

What the Jews pray for when they say "Alenu,"—though not ten in a hundred understand what they say,—we, and all true Christians, long and pray for when we say, "Thy kingdom come, thy will be done on earth as it is done in Heaven."

PART SIXTH.

THE RELATION OF THE JEWS TO CHRISTIANITY.

CHAPTER I.

FALSE CHRISTS.

Accounts of false Christs who have arisen, A.D. 114 to A.D. 1862—Involves the principle of the ceaseless expectation of the Messiah—General remarks.

After the death of our Saviour, and immediately before the destruction of Jerusalem, false Christs ever and anon appeared, and deceived many. In the year 114, in Trajan's reign, *Andrew* arose, and was the death of thousands. Under Adrian, *Bar Cochab*, the son of a star, appeared, and vanished, as *Bar Cosibah*, the son of a lie. In the year 434, under Theodosius the Younger, *Moses* sprung up in Crete, and did not succeed so well in persuading his followers to ford the Mediterranean dry-shod. In the year 520, one *Danaan* cropped up in Arabia, and, committing grievous outrages upon the Christians of Nagra, was destroyed. In the year 529, *Julian* made his *entrée* in Palestine, and, drawing Jews and Samaritans into sedition, destroyed many. In the year 620, *Mohammed* appeared, and, in the first instance, drew after him Jews in multitudes, until the eternal law of ceremonies, of which the Jews boast themselves, took another shape under Islam, and the sixth and the seventh precepts of the decalogue received a fearful illustration. In the year 721, another false Christ arose, a Syrian by birth, and yet received Jews as followers. In the year 1157, the very century in which Aben Ezra, Maimonides, Jarchi, and Benjamin of Tudela flourished, the Jews arose in Spain under another Messiah, and were well-nigh exterminated. In the year 1167, ten years after, removed to Aifrca, in the Kingdom of Fez, they made a similar attempt at dominion, under yet another false Christ, and failed. In the same year, another pretended Christ made Arabia the scene of his exploits ; and being apprehended, and about to be put to death, was shrewd enough to predict, that if his head were cut off, he would be the subject of an immediate resuscitation : he was accordingly decapitated, and thus happily escaped the torture of being impaled alive. In the year 1174, the Jews, to their own destruction, were led into rebellion by a false Christ in Persia, and by another in Moravia, *David Almusar*, as he was called. In the year 1199, a great magician, *David Alroy*, otherwise rejoicing in the royal title of *David El David*, stood forth in Persia, and pleased the Jews for a while, and flickered and flashed as their Messiah, and expired. In the year 1222, a Jew, styled *The Son of David*, announced himself in Germany as the Messiah, and induced many of the Jews to follow him. In the year 1465, soon after Constantinople had been taken by the Turks, and the Saracens were teaching by the sword the degenerate nations of Christendom, Rabbi Abraham Avenaris, an astrologer, predicted the coming of the Messiah, from a conjunction of the planets Jupiter and Saturn, in the sign Pisces. The conjunction of Jupiter and Saturn in Pisces, it would appear, is a juncture in judicial astrology peculiarly favorable to Jewish dominion; for even Rabbi Isaac Abarbanel, who distinguished himself in this century, afterwards professed in his commentary on the book of Daniel, to deduce the period of the Messiah's appearance from this conjunction. Accordingly, Milton, with appropriate shrewdness, and not without a sly hint at Jewish astrology, has put similar calculations into the mouth of the Tempter, in his address to our Saviour in the wilderness.

> "Now contrary, if I read aught in heaven,
> Or heaven write aught of fate, by what the stars,
> Voluminous, or single characters,
> In their conjunction met, give me to spell,—
> Sorrows and labours, oppositions, hate,
> Attends thee, scorns, reproaches, injuries,
> Violence, and stripes, and lastly, cruel death ;
> A kingdom they portend Thee, but what kingdom,
> Real or allegoric, I discern not ;
> Nor when, eternal sure, as without end,
> Without beginning ; for date prefixt,
> Directs me, in the starry rubric set."

In the year 1497, *Ismael Sohpus* spread his victorious arms through Media, Persia, Mesopotamia, and Armenia; and the Jews for a while rested under his shadow, trusting him as their Messiah ; but he settled down as the head of a new sect among the Mahomedans. In the year 1500, Rabbi Asher Lemla gave himself out, in Germany, as the forerunner of the Messiah, who that very year, was to restore the Jews to Canaan. Public prayers and fasts were ordered and observed ; but the

Messiah did not appear, and the restoration was not effected. In the year 1534, a new Messiah made his appearance in Spain; but his success was similar to that of his impious predecessors; he was made the subject of an *anto da fé* under Charles V. In the year 1615, another false Messiah appeared in the East Indies. In the year 1624, yet another showed himself in Holland. In the year 1666, *Sabethai Zevi* in like manner, boasted himself to be a Messiah, with no small expectation of the Jews; but to save his life he became a Mahomedan. And, in the year 1682 many of the German Jews, and almost all those of Italy, owned *Rabbi Mardochai* as their Messiah; but his Messiahship also came to nought.

Those dates and facts, as given by Leslie, in his treatise on the Jews, are taken from the work of Johannes à Tent, printed at Herborn, in 1697, and confirmed by several Jewish Rabbis. They are not bare facts and dates, but involve a principle; they shew the ceaseless anticipation of a Messiah on the part of the Jewish nation; and now, after a course of nineteen centuries, might have taught the Jews that, in seeking the object of their search, they have proceeded in the wrong direction. Having rejected Jesus of Nazareth as the true Messiah, they have become the dupes of every wrongheaded and unprincipled imposter.

The fact is, more than one of the most learned among the Jews have denied that the Messiah is to be known by the working of miracles. He is simply to gather the Jews together to fight the Lord's battles, and conquer the world. And, in so far, modern Judaism, looks for the same weapon that was so effective in the diffusion of the Islam. The sword that made Mecca the centre of a new religion, is to make Jerusalem the metropolis of the world.

Yet, notwithstanding all their wanderings, in the midst of all their calamities, learned men have appeared among the Jews. Literature has been cultivated; schools and private societies have sprung up, and flourished, and still show their fruits, in a busy intermeddling with all knowledge; in strains of absorbing pathos, and deepest melancholy; in prayers and supplications, mingled with their paternal ceremonies; in keen, curt, and caustic exegesis of the inspired books; in proverbial sayings, and pithy apothegms; in quaint and curious stories, and hyperbolical enigmas; in strange and entrancing tales of surpassing wonder, that often leave the reader in doubt whether the narrator is imbued with the spirit of sorrowful earnestness, or is laughing in his sleeve at the dupe of his quaint humor and marvellous invention; and, we wish that we had not to add, sometimes, too, in the manifestation of a spirit, now wild and unsavory as "the vine of Sodom," now poisonous and deadly as " the fields of Gomorrha." The great Council at Jerusalem, with Ezra as its President, the names of Jafue, and Cæsarea, and Tiberias, are known as celebrated schools in Palestine, as those of Nahardea, and Sora, and Piombadutha were in the farther East, in Babylon. Such, if not the birth-place, were the cradles of the present Jewish literature; thence sprung up, or gathered strength, the *Masora*, the *Cabala*, and the *Talmud*.

CHAPTER II.

OFFICES AND TITLES OF THE MESSIAH AS TAUGHT IN RABBINICAL WRITINGS.

1. JEHOVAH.—In the book " Echa-Rabathi," fol. 59, the question is asked: What is the name of the Messiah? Rabbi Abba ben Chanania replies: Jehovah is his name; as it is written: "and this is his name by which he shall be called: *Jehovah our righteousness.*" Again, in Midrash Tehilim, fol. 40, the 10th verse in the 35th chapter of Isaiah is thus commented: "and the redeemed of Jehovah shall return, and come to Zion, with shouting and everlasting gladness upon their heads;" this means *the Redeemed of the Messsiah.*

2. MEMRA (Logos, or The Word).—In Genesis xxvi. 3: "And I shall be with thee," says the Targum, "my *Memra* shall support thee." Genesis xxxix. 2: "And Jehovah was with Joseph." The translation of the Targum is: "And the *Memra* of God was in the assistance of Joseph." Exodus iii. 8: "And I am come down to deliver them out of the hand of the Egyptians." The Targum says: "By my *Memra* I will deliver them out of Egypt." Num. xxiii, 21: "Jehovah his God with him: and the shouting of a king in him;" which Jonathan Ben Uziel translated: "The *Memra* of God is their help, and the trumpet of King Messiah shall be heard among them." The Targum Onkelos, however, says: "The *Memra* of God is their help, and the *Shekina* of their King among them."

SHEKINA.—Wherever the word "Chebod Jehovah," the "Glory of Jehovah," transpires in the Old Testament, the Targum translates it *Shekina*, a word which means the revealed, or rather the invisible God— God manifested in the flesh—because the root of the word *Shekina* is שכן *Shaken*, "to dwell." They derived this title from Exodus xxiv. 16: "And the glory of Jehovah *dwelt* upon Mount Sinai." Deut. xxxi. 3: "And Jehovah, thy God, shall go before thee." Jonathan Ben Uziel translates, "And the *Memra* of God, his *Shekina*, shall go before thee."

4. HAKADASH BARUCH HU—(The Holy One, blessed be He).— This we find in Sohar upon Genesis, fol. 63, "And the King Messiah, who shall also be called: *The Holy One, blessed be He.*"

ZEBAOTH.—Sohar upon Exodus, fol. 4, speaking of the 7th verse, 2nd chapter, of the Song of Solomon: "I charge you, O ye daughters of

Jerusalem, by the roes (which is in the Hebrew *Zebaoth*), and by the hinds of the field," he says, this means the King Messiah, who is called *Zebaoth*.

6. SON OF GOD.—The Midrash Rabbah on Exodus, fol. 133, says: In future all nations shall bring presents to the King Messiah, and God will say to him: take from them as it is written: " Princes shall come out of Egypt, Ethiopia shall soon stretch out her hands unto God." Psalms lxviii. 31: And also: " Kiss the *Son*, lest he be angry." Ps. ii. 12: also, Prov. xxx. 4: " Who has ascended up into heaven and descended? Who gathered the wind in his fists? Who has bound the waters in a garment? Who has established all the ends of the earth? What is His name, and what is the name of His *Son*, if thou knowest it?"

7. LIGHT.—On Isaiah lx. 1: "Arise, shine, for thy light is come,'' the Targum paraphrases; thy *salvation is come*. Tanchuma, fol. 75, says: The prophet speaks of the age of Messiah; and the *light* is the Messiah. The Midrash Rabbah, on Lamentation, says: The name of the Messiah is *light*; as it is written: " He revealeth the deep things, and the secret things; He knows what is in the darkness, and the *light* dwelleth with him."

8. MATRON.—Sohar, on Exodus, fol. 21, says: In the age of Messiah all those nations who would show themselves hostile to Israel, shall be delivered into the hands of *Matron*; as Isaiah said: "Who is he that cometh from Edom, with dyed garments from Bozrah, * * * For I will tread them in my fury, and their blood shall be sprinkled upon my garments." Then in another place, says the same book: the Shekina *is* the *Matronitha*.

9. YEER ANPIN, זְעִיר אַנְפִּין, "The little face." This title the Cabalists confer upon the Son, to distinguish him from the Father; and it is very frequently used in the Sohar, and other Cabalistic works.

10. JINON.

11. PHELEH.—(Wonderful).

12. JOETZ.—(Counseller).

13. EL-GIBOR.—(Mighty God).

14. ABI-AD.—(Everlasting Father).

15. SAR-SHALOM.—(Prince of Peace).

These are the names of Messiah in his Divine character. In his human character he has the following names:

1. BAR-ENOSH.—Son of Man. Sohar, on Genesis, fol. 85, says: It is written, "There came one, like a Son of Man, in the clouds of Heaven." Dan. i. 13: This is the King Messiah, and has the same signification as in the second chapter (of Daniel), verse 44, "and the God of Heaven shall set up a kingdom which shall never be destroyed."

2. DAVID.—Sohar on Exodus, fol. 93, says: As David was King in this world (or age), so shall David be the King in the age to come; which is the King Messiah.

3. ZEMACH.—Zechar vi. 12, it is written: "Behold the man whose name is ZEMACH, (the branch), and he shall grow out of himself, and he shall build the temple of the Lord." On which the Targum paraphrases instead of Zemach, Messiah. In Midrash Rabbah, on Lamentations, we find Rabbi Joshua Ben Levi says: The name of Messiah is ZEMACH, as it is written: I shall bring my servant ZEMACH. Zechar iii. 8. Rabbi Tanchuma, fol. 68, on the same passage in Zechariah: This is the King Messiah; as also the prophet Jeremiah says: "Behold the days come, saith the Lord, that I will raise unto David a righteous branch, ZEMACH, and he shall reign as a King, and shall prosper, and execute judgment and justice upon the earth."

4. BAR-NAFLI.—This is the name which the Talmud gave him, and is hardly to be translated in the sense in which it is understood by the scholar of the Talmud. The passage where we find this name is in Tract Sanhedrin, fol. 96, 2, and reads thus: Saith R. Nachaman to R. Isaac: Hast thou any information of the coming of BAR-NAFLI? The other replied: Who is Bar-Nafli? It is the Messiah, answered the first. Dost thou call the Messiah Bar-Nafli? Yes, he replied, for it is written: "In that day will I raise up the tabernacle of David, which is fallen." Amos ix. 11, The word Nafli has the same root as the word Nofeleth, "which is *fallen.*"

5. EHED.—Servant. In Isaiah xlii. 1; xliii. 10; Zechar iii. 8; Psalms lxxxvi. 16; Isa. lii. 14; liii. 11; and many other places, the Rabbins agree with Christians, that it is the Messiah.

The Messiah as King, Redeemer, and High Priest.

1. KING.—Hebrew, Melech, Cadean, Malka, Sohar, on Exodus, fol. 52, says: Wherever Scripture speaks of a MELECH, without special name, we have always to understand: King Messiah.

2. SHILO.—Talm. Tract Sanhedrin, fol. xcviii. 2, says: What is the name of the Messiah? R. Shila replied: His name is SHILO. Midrash Rabbah, on Genesis, says: "Until Shilo comes;" this means the King

Messiah. Targum Onkelos, as well as Targum Jerusalemi, translates this passage : Until King Messiah comes, to whom belongs the government.

3. GOEL.—Redeemer, Rabbi Berechiah says: Even as the first Redeemer, Moses, made himself known, as such, by his works, so the latter Redeemer, King Messiah, will be acknowledged by his works. The first brought down manna from Heaven ; so will the latter do ; as the Psalmist says, when prophesying of the Messiah, (72), that the corn will grow even upon the top of the mountains. The first gave the people water from the rock; the latter will do the same; as it is written in Joel iii. 18, "and it shall come to pass in that day, that the mountain shall drop down new made wine, and the hills shall flow with milk ; and the rivers of Judah shall flow with waters, and a fountain shall come forth from the house of the Lord, and shall water the valley of Shittim."

4. MALACH HAGOEL.—"The Redeeming Angel." Sohar Chadash on Gen. xlviii. 16, says: Who is the Redeeming Angel who shall bless the children ? It is Shekina, because no other can redeem, and no other can bless.

5. MALACH HA-BERITH.—" The Angel of the Covenant." This is derived from Mal. iii. 1, and the Sohar takes it as a rule, that wherever Scripture says, the Angel of the Covenant, it speaks of Jehovah.

CHAPTER III.

HOW THE FIFTY-THIRD CHAPTER OF ISAIAH IS EXPLAINED AMONG THE JEWS.

They say that the fifty-third chapter of Isaiah was looked upon by Christians as referring to the alleged sufferings of Jesus, and by the Cabalists and some Rabbies, as referring to the supposed Messiah from the tribe of Joseph, who would die previous to the advent of the right Messiah. They say that the greatest commentators of the Bible, Rashi, Ibn Ezra, and Redak, maintain this chapter refers only to the people of Israel.

It is our intention to give, in the present exposition, the opinion of these commentators.

They try to establish in the first place, that the author of the last twenty-seven chapters of Isaiah, viz., from xl. to lxvi., is not the same author to whom the other thirty-nine chapters of Isaiah can be ascribed. They establish this fact by the most rigid and impartial criticisms. The first is exclusively Israelitish, has an Israel and Judah, sinful kings and invading foreigners, while the last is a cosmopolitan, and possesses none of the above characteristics. He knows of no priesthood, no king, no sacrifices, and no temple: he mentions only ruins and hopes.

2nd. Therefore Israel appears to this prophet, not in a state of rebellion, as it did to other prophets, but in a state of suffering and oppression, and he is the great harbinger of hope and consolation. He starts, "console ye, console ye, my people, * * * * that her (Jerusalem's) iniquity is pardoned; for she has received of the hands of the Lord double for all her sins." This is the tenor of all his prophecies. It is evident that the Israelites fraternized everywhere with the Medo-Persians; hence their sufferings under the last king of Babylonia must have been intense."

3. Israel appears to this prophet as "the servant of the Lord"—"The chosen of God," whose mission it is to bring salvation to the nations in the three-fold form of "truth, justice, and virtue," (Jer. iv. 2.) The honorable epitaph of "servant of the Lord," formerly given to Moses only, is applied by this prophet to all Israel, to such an extent, that it becomes evident, wherever he says plainly, "my servant," or, "my chosen one," he could mean none else except the nation of Israel,

"the covenant people, the light of nations." Only once he applies this epitaph to himself, (Isaiah xliv. 1 to 6.)

4. Israel is called "the servant of the Lord," because it is the messenger of God, to bring to mankind the Divine lessons of truth, justice and virtue, the truth of religion, the principles of absolute justice to govern the societies of man. So, and not otherwise, can this be understood; because the same prophet says, "You are My witnesses, saith God, and My servant whom I have chosen, that you may know, and cause others to believe Me, and understand that I am He; before Me there was no creative power, and there will be none after Me."—"I have formed this people to Me, that they may narrate My glory." (Isaiah xliii. 10 to 21.)

"And nations will walk after Thy light, and kings after the radiance of Thy sun." (Ibid. lxi. 3.) The whole sixty-first chapter conveys this idea, and the sixty-second chapter again begins and ends with it. The concluding chapter, especially the 18th and 19th verses, again, clearly express this idea.

5. The doctrine of Gnostic, Christian and Cabalistic theology, which transfers the mission and excellency of all Israel to one Messiah, Christ, or Redeemer, according to inveterate conceptions of regal majesty, and therefore, call that one person "the chosen one," "the servant of the Lord," has not the least foundation in this prophet's words. He has not the remotest idea of a Messiah, Christ, or Redeemer. We let the prophet speak for himself. He says: "Thus saith God, the King of Israel, and its Redeemer, God of Hosts, I am the first and the last, and beside Me there is no Lord." (Ibid. xliv. 6.) " I, even I, am God, and beside me there is no Saviour." (Ibid. xliii. 11.) "Israel is saved by God, an everlasting salvation." (Ibid. xlv. 19.) " Am I not God, and none beside Me? a just Lord and Saviour, there is none beside me." (Ibid. xlv. 21., "Our Redeemer, God of Hosts is His name, the Holy One of Israel." (Ibid. xlvii. 4.) "And He (God) will come a Redeemer to Zion, and to those who turn from transgression in Jacob, saith God." (Ibid. xlix. 21.)

6. This prophet, like all others, never expresses anywhere the idea, that one should die for the sins of Israel, or any other nation. On the contrary, they thought, only punishment, or true repentance, brings full remission of sins. The prophet says, right at the start, that Jerusalem's sins are pardoned, because "she hath received, from the hand of God, a double portion for all her sins."—"I, even I, am He who extinguisheth thy transgressions for My sake, I will not remember thy sins." (Ibid.

xliii. 25.) "I have extinguished thy transgressions like mist, and thy sins like clouds; return to Me, for I have redeemed thee." (Ibid. xliv. 22.) "Let the wicked forsake his way, and the man of iniquity his thoughts, and let him return to God, and He will have mercy with him, and to our Lord, for he will increase pardoning (as the iniquity increaseth). (Ibid. lv. 7.)

7. Lastly, we have to premise this. Not only Ibn Ezra, and Don Abarbanel, but almost all modern critics, agree that the speech containing the fifty-third chapter of Isaiah begins with the thirteenth verse of the previous chapter: "Behold my servant will be prosperous." The object of the chapter or question is "my servant." The subject of this chapter can be none except the "many nations," or "the kings," with which the fifty-second chapter ends. The context will show, that the kings are imagined speaking of "my servant," as they do from liii. 1, to *Ibid*: 9. The last three verses are the Prophet's own words. Therefore the first nine verses are in the past tense, and the rest in the future tense.

These premises inform us:—

(*a*). "My servant," cannot refer to a Messiah, Christ, Redeemer or to any one who died for the iniquity of others; whereas all those ideas are foreign to the Prophet.

(*b*). This prophet calling "My servant," either himself or Israel, he could refer only to either.

(*c*) Israel appearing to the Prophet, suffering in the captivity, and being the messenger of God to the nations, it cannot be expected that the Prophet would speak of himself—in a manner as he does in the three concluding verses—"My servant," can refer to Israel only.

Take these few ideas as a guide, and the whole chapter reads right, is plain, and can be rendered literally.

Introduction—Isaiah, lii. 13, 14, 15.

13. Behold my servant will be prosperous; he will be elevated, exalted, and very high.

14. As the multitude were amazed at Thee (so disfigured by man, in his visage, and his form by the sons of man).

15. So shall He fill many people with joy; kings shall shut their mouths at him, for they saw what was not narrated to them, and they comprehended what they never heard. *

---

* These three verses form the introduction of the next chapter, and also contain the outlines of it. We are told that Israel will be great yet, (although it is now degraded in captivity), by the triumph of truth and justice which it brings the nations,

DESCRIPTION OF THE SUFFERINGS OF ISRAEL, BY THE KINGS—ISAIAH liii.

1. Who would have believed our report, and the arm of God—over whom it was revealed.

2. He rose like the sucker before Him, and like the root from a desert land, *which* has no form and no beauty. We saw him, and he had no appearance, and we should have desired him?

3. He was despised and forsaken by men, a man of sorrow and used to disease. Like one who hides the countenance before us, he was despised, and we regarded him not. *

THE CAUSE OF THE SUFFERINGS AS THE KINGS WILL CONCEIVE IT.

4. Verily he hath borne our sicknesses, and our sorrows—he hath carried them; and we considered him wounded, smitten by the Lord, and afflicted.

---

something which they never perceived. The commentators overlooked the fact, that the hopes of Israel, expressed in this and the next chapter, are in the future tense, while the sufferings (as here in verse 14), are expressed in the past or present tense; because the prophet speaks of a present state, which in some future time will be narrated as something past and gone. If he had intended to speak of Jesus and His sufferings, or of any other Messiah, the sufferings also must be stated in the future tense, which is not the case. The above three verses being rendered literally, we need not account for it. We rendered "Yaszeh" with Gesenius, "he shall fill with joy," and not "sprinkle," as the English version has it; because it is not followed by an object of a thing, but by an object of a person "many nations." Nations cannot be sprinkled, fluids may be sprinkled *upon* an object, as עליהם מי חטאת מזה. Still *Yaszeh* in the *hiphil* form must be transitive.

* The Hebrew scholar must admit, that our translation is literal in every point. The English version mutilated most unpardonably these three verses, so that there is no sense in them, ויעל is rendered there "for he shall grow up," when נגלתה, concluding the second verse, makes it evident that the *rav* is conversive. The same blunder is committed with ונראהו, which is rendered, there, "And we shall see him," although it is preceded and followed by a perfect tense. The rules of grammar were set aside to make a prophecy concerning Jesus in this chapter; but it was still in vain. Jesus was not used to disease, we are not told that he ever was sick; nor was he forsaken by men, on the contrary, we are informed that thousands went after him wherever he went.

יונק, in verse second, signified literally *sucker*, the shoot of a plant from the roots or the lower part of a stem. This is a figurative of Israel dispersed among nations, hanging like little suckers on large trees. So is "from the desert land," a reference to Israel's descending from a land then deserted and waste. The kings describe the suffering of the captive Israelites in brief but expressive terms.

5. And he is defiled by our transgressions, he is dispersed by our iniquities; the correction of our welfare is on him, and we were healed in his association.

6. We all, like sheep, went astray, every man turned his own way; and God caused to fall on him the iniquity of us all.

7. He was oppressed, he was afflicted, and he would not open his mouth; like the sheep dragged to the slaughter, like the ewe is mute before her shearers, he would not open his mouth.

8. Taken violently away from dominion and judgment, and who will ever convince his generation, that he was cut off from the land of life, was stricken for the transgressions of my people, (9) and gave his grave to the wicked, and his sepulchre to the rich; because he hath done no violence, and there was no deceit in his mouth. *

---

*The speech of the Kings ends as it began, with a question, stated in conclusion with other words. The Kings think Israel bears their injustice and conceived falsehoods, is oppressed by the consequence thereof, so that all the iniquities of kings and nations fall on the captive people, which brought them the doctrines of truth and the principles of absolute justice. "The connection of our welfare is on him." After the patient suffering of Israel is described in verse 7, it says in verse 8, that he was driven from his own land, leaving his home, his grave, his sepulchre, to strangers, because he is the bearer of justice and truth, which he must bring to the Gentiles, to which "my people," in verse 8, refers in opposition to "my servant," of whom the Kings speak. The kings, convinced of this truth, exclaim at the start, "Who would then have believed our report," and exclaims, in conclusion, "Who will ever convince his generation," that saw the people in its degradation, that it should be commissioned by Providence to bear and uproot the iniquities of all, by truth and justice? מחולל in verse 5, cannot be rendered "he was wounded," as the English version does, because it is the present participle of the *peal* form, and signifies profaning or defiling. See Ezek. xxxix. 7. The same is in the case with מדכא "bruised" in the E. V., while it actually signifies "very much crushed," "broken very small," "crushed to atoms." A nation is defiled by its being dispersed, or broken in small fragments. בחברתי is rendered by the E. V., as if a Dakesh forte was in the second beth, while the term can mean but one thing, society, company, or association. The Kings say they were healed by their injustice and fictions by their associations with Israel. The concluding sentence of verse 6, is rendered after Gesenius. לקח in verse 8, contains, in itself, the word "violently," being the passive of the *peal* form, עוצר "prison." in the E. V. must, on account of משפט be rendered in the same sense of עצר יורש Judges xviii. 7, and refers to the captivity of Israel. The same is the case with being "cut off from the land of life," (their home) and leaving their graves and sepulchres to others. במותיו in verse 9 parallel to קברו, rendered by the E. V., in His death, is derived from במה, as Rabe justly remarks, כי, "that" of verse 8, refers to all members of the period

THE PROPHET'S DEFENCE OF THE JUSTICE OF PROVIDENCE.

10. Did God desire his oppression, or to afflict him with disease? If thou wilt make His person an offering for transgression, He must see seed, (that) will live long, and the delight of God must prosper in His hand.

11. For the travail of his soul he shall see, he shall be satisfied with this knowledge, (that) He will bring the righteous to righteousness, He is my servant to the great, and He will carry their iniquities.

12. There, therefore, will I afford him a position with the great, and he shall divide the spoil with the mighty, because he hath exposed his person to death, and was counted among transgressors, while he bore the sin of the multitude, and he will always assail the transgressors.*

---

down to עַל, in verse 9; therefore we connected the two verses. The unprejudiced reader will easily observe, that there is not the least reference to Jesus or any other Messiah in any of these verses.

* The prophet asks whether God, (who is gracious to all,) should desire, or delight in the affliction of his servant, Israel? The *vav* of the beginning of verse ten, is a השאלה indicating a question. To this he answers, if God (Thou) afflictest him for others, he must be rewarded for it by seeing his seed, (children) living long, and the desire of God, (truth and justice) prosper in the hands of his seed, the greatest reward of a father. This idea is similar to that which concludes the book of Job; that is not all, says the prophet, that gives his suffering servant satisfaction and strength in the hour of affliction; but the consciousness, that he suffers for the welfare of the greatest and best in the world, who labor under the mistake of error and injustice, must give him srrength and satisfaction. The prophet, in conclusion, introduces God himself, promising a happy future to those who suffered for the fictions and injustice of others, and were auxiliary in removing these stumbling stones. This reward should be their own, they should be afforded a portion, &c. Having spoken of the Kings, he concludes with רבים עצומים, the great and mighty, who should acknowledge Israel as their equal. The prophet considers not the justice of Providence, and the sufferings of Israel, from a narrow individual point of view, but he does so from universal point of view. Israel, the bearer of truth and justice, suffers and patiently bears the oppression of the Kings and nations addicted to error and injustice; because "my servant" knows he is appointed to this mission, and will be triumphant at last with the triumph of truth and justice. בנפש, E. Version, "his soul," we translated person on account of הֶעֱרָה נַפְשׁוֹ לָמוּת, the soul dies not. In earlier Scripture the term *nephesh* signifies "life soul," but this prophet has the terms רוח נשמה. In verse 11, most all translators forget to pay attention to the measure which is צדיק

מֵעֲמַל נַפְשׁוֹ יִרְאֶה - יִשְׂבַּע בְּדַעְתּוֹ - יַצְדִּיק

עַבְדִּי לָרַבִּים - וַעֲוֹנֹתָם הוּא יִסְבֹּל—3, 2, 2, 2, 3, and so we translated.

CHAPTER IV.

DID CHRIST BORROW FROM THE RABBIES?

Use of the Rabbinical writings in explaining the New Testament—Several illustrative examples—Note on Christ's relation to truth, old and new.

A Christian writer says: Without some knowledge of Talmudical writings, we shall be unable to understand even the fundamentals of Christianity; since from these authorities, we learn that our Lord condescended to borrow even the sacraments of Baptism and Communion from the rites of His countrymen; and that even the prayer which was bequeathed us in contradistinction to the vain repetitions of the Jewish Doctors, is derived from expressions that had been long familiar in the schools and synagogues of Judea. *

We will give the reader but a few specimens which may be compared with each other:

SAYINGS OF RABBIES.	NEW TESTAMENT.
"Be deliberate in judgment. Judge all mankind favourably."	"With what judgment ye judge ye shall be judged."—Matt. vii. 2.
"Make a fence for the Law."	"Think not that I am come to destroy the law or the Prophets; I am not come to destroy, but to fulfil."—Matt. v. 17.

לרבים E. V., "many" having a *Kamaz* under the *Lamed*, the definite *hai* thus replaced, must be rendered precisely like ברבים, in verse 12, which the E. V. renders "with the great." יפגיע is rendered by the E. V., "and make intercession," while this is plainly in the future tense, and the same term in the same form, הפגיע, in verse 6 is rendered "hath laid on him." The error is conspicuous. W translate literally. These three verses cannot refer to Jesus; for He saw no seed long living, as He had no children, and the Bible no where has the idea of spiritual seed; he never was alloted a portion among the great, so he is said to have been very humble, nor did he divide spoil with the mighty. The whole chapter does not say, that "my servant" died or will die.

* It is said of Dr. Lightfoot, that he could not patiently hear the ancient records of the Rabbins too much aspersed, as proceeding, most commonly, from ignorance of their admirable use in explaining the Holy Scripture. When Rutherford, in the assembly of Divines, had said that there was no news of somewhat in controversy, but in the Rabbins, it was of a "cup," in the institution of the Passover, seeming to speak contemptibly of them; Dr. Lightfoot replied: "That there are divers things in the New Testament, which must be beholden to the Rabbins for the understanding of; or else we know not what to make of them."

SAYINGS OF RABBIES.

"He that doth alms in secret is greater than our master Moses himself."

Rabbi Jannai saw one giving money openly to a poor man to whom he said: "It is better you had not given at all than so to have given."

"Does any one give his neighbour a box on the ear, or a blow upon the cheek, let him give him two hundred zuzees." (Coins.)

"Be not like servants who serve their masters for the sake of receiving a reward; but be like servants who serve their masters without a view of receiving a reward; and let the fear of heaven be upon you."

"Be not prone to much discourse with women-kind. Whoever converses much with women, bringeth evil on himself, and at last will inherit hell. He who looketh upon a woman's heel, is as if he looked upon her belly; he that looks upon her belly, is as if he had laid with her; he that looks upon her little finger, is as if he looked upon her privy parts."

"Making peace between neighbours, is numbered among those things which bring forth good fruit in this life, and benefit in the life to come."

"Be cautious in thy words." Giving and receiving among the disciples of the wise men, was in truth and faith, by saying, "Yes, yes; no, no."

Hillel said: "Be of the disciples of Aaron, who loved peace and pursued peace; so that thou love mankind."

"Whoever is ambitious of aggrandizing his name, destroys his name."

NEW TESTAMENT.

"Do not your alms before men."—Matt. vi. 1. "Let not thy left hand know what thy right hand doeth."—Matt. vi. 3. "Do not sound a trumpet before thee as the hypocrites do in the synagogues and in the streets."

"Whosoever shall smite thee on thy right cheek, turn to him the other also."—Matt. v. 39.

"But he shall receive an hundred fold, now in this time, &c., &c., with persecutions; and in the world to come, eternal life."—Mark x. 30.

"For he had respect unto the recompence of the reward."—Heb. xi. 26.

"Whoever looketh on a woman to lust after her, hath committed adultery with her already in his heart."—Matt. v. 28.

"Whoremongers shall have their part in the lake which burneth with fire and brimstone."—Rev. xxi. 8.

"Blessed are the Peace Makers."—Matt. v. 9.

"Let your communications be yea, yea; nay nay."—Matt. v. 37.

"Live peaceably with all men."—Rom. xii. 18.

"And whoever shall exalt himself shall be abased."—Matt. xxiii. 12.

SAYINGS OF RABBIES.	NEW TESTAMENT.
"Whosoever brings his hands to the modest parts, let his hand be cut off unto his navel; it is better that his belly be cleft in two, than that he should descend into the well of corruption."	"If thy right hand offend cut it off and cast it from thee, for it is profitable for thee that one of thy members should perish, and not that thy whole body should be cast into hell."—Matt. v. 30.
The school of Shammai said: "A wife is not to be put away unless for filthiness, that is, adultery."	"Whosoever shall put away his wife, saving for the cause of fornication, causeth her to commit adultery."—Matt. v. 32.
"Let the fear of heaven be upon you."	"Who shall not fear thee, O Lord."—Rev. xv. 4.
"Neither is the study of the law the principle, but the practice thereof."	"Even so faith, if it hath not works, is dead, being alone."—James ii. 17.
"Say little and do much."	James ii. 15-16.
"Be also as careful of the observance of a light precept as a weighty one."	"Teaching them to observe all things whatsoever I have commanded you."—Matt. xxviii. 20. Also Luke xvi. 10.
"All thine actions are written in a book."	"And the dead were judged out of those things which were written in the books."—Rev. xx. 12.
"Abolish thy will for the sake of His will."	"Nevertheless not my will but Thine be done."—Luke xxii. 42.
Hillel said: "Separate not yourself from the congregation."	"Not forsaking the assembling of ourselves together."—Heb. x. 25.
"Have no confidence in thyself."	"And have no confidence in the flesh."—Philips. iii. 3.
"If he hath acquired a pure doctrine of the law, he hath obtained for himself immortal life in a future state."	"He that abideth in the doctrine of Christ, he hath both Father and Son."—2 John, verse 9.
"Have you ever seen beasts or fowls that had a workshop? and yet they are fed without trouble of mind."	"Behold the fowls of the air, &c.—your Heavenly Father feedeth them."—Matt. vi. 26.
"Whosoever hath but a small morsel in his basket, and said what have I to eat to-morrow, behold he is to be reckoned with those of little faith."	"Therefore take no thought—saying: What shall we eat?"—Matt. vi. 31. "O ye of little faith."—Verse 30.
"There is enough trouble in the very moment."	"Sufficient unto the day is the evil thereof."—Matt. vi. 34.

THE LORD'S PRAYER.

SAYINGS OF RABBIES.	NEW TESTAMENT.
"Let none pray in the singular number, but in the plural, say; Our Father which art in Heaven."	"Our Father which art in Heaven."
"Sanctify Thy name above all that do sanctify Thy name."	"Hallowed by Thy name."
"A prayer wherein is not mentioned 'Kingdom of God,' is not a prayer."	"Thy Kingdom come."
"What is the short prayer?' Rabbi Eliezer saith—"Thy will be done in Heaven, and give quietness of spirit to them that fear Thee on earth."	"Thy will be done on earth as it is in Heaven."
"Let it be Thy good pleasure to give every man what sufficeth him for his daily food."	"Give us this day our daily bread."
Rabbi Judah was wont to pray thus: "Let it be Thy good pleasure to deliver us from evil men, evil affection, and from Satan the destroyer."*	"Lead us not into temptation, but deliver us from all evil." *
"We therefore hope in Thee, O Lord our God, speedily to behold Thy glorious power, for the kingdom is thine. The Lord shall reign for ever."	"For thine is the kingdom, and the power and the glory, for ever. Amen."
"In the measure that a man measureth others measure to him." Hillel saw a skull floating on the water and said, "Because thou didst make others float, have they floated thee, and the end of those who made thee float, will be that they will also float."	"With what measure ye mete, it shall be measured to you again."—Matt. vii. 2.
When any (judge) said to another—"Cast out the mote out of thine eye," he answered, "Cast you out the beam out of your eye."	"How wilt thou say to thy brother, let me pull out the mote out of thine eye; and behold a beam is in thine own eye?"

---

* It was, and still is a law, a belief among the Jews, that men cannot expect forgiveness of their sins on the Day of Atonement, unless they forgive one another.

DID CHRIST BORROW FROM THE RABBIES?

SAYINGS OF RABBIES.	NEW TESTAMENT.
R. Tarphon said—"I wonder whether there be any in this age that will receive reproof. But if one saith to another, 'Cast out the mote out of thine eye,' he will be ready to answer, 'Cast out the beam out of thine own eye.'"	"Thou hypocrite; first cast out the beam out of thine own eye, and then shalt thou see clearly to cast out the mote out of thy brother's eye."—Matt. vii. 4, 5.
"Go forth and consider which is the good part for man to adhere to?" R. Eleazar said—"A good, benevolent and pure heart."	"Blessed are the merciful." "Blessed are the pure in heart."—Matt. v. 7, 8.
"Go forth and consider which is the evil way man should shun," "An evil heart," was the answer.	"For out of the heart proceed evil thoughts, murders, adulteries, fornications," &c., &c.—Matt. xv. 19.
A certain Gentile came to Shammai, and said: "Make me a proselyte, that I may learn the whole law, standing upon one foot." Shammai beat him with a staff that was in his hand. He went to Hillel and he made him a proselyte, and said: "That which is odious to thyself do it not to thy neighbour, for this is the whole law."	"Whatsoever ye would that men should do unto you, do ye even so to them—for this is the law and the Prophets."—Matt. vii. 12.
"Let all thine actions be in the name and to the glory of God."	"Whatsoever ye do, do all to the glory of God."—1 Cor. x. 31.
"A gourd is known by its branch."	"By their fruits ye shall know them."—Matt. vii. 20.
"In the day of the great judgment," is a form of speech very usual among the Jews, as well as "Kingdom of Heaven."	"Day of Judgment." "Kingdom of Heaven."
"Let the honour of thy associate be as dear to thee as thine own."	"In honour preferring one another."—Romans x. 12.
"Be not easily moved to anger."	"Be slow to wrath."—James i. 19.
"When thou art praying, consider not thy prayer as ordinary, but as supplicating mercy in the presence of God."	"And when thou prayest, thou shalt not be as the hypocrite."—Matt. vi. 5. (See parable, Publican and Pharisee.)—Luke xviii. 11-13.
"Be expeditious to study the law, that thou mayest know how to refute the epicurean."	"Be ready always to give an answer to every man," &c.—1 Peter iii. 15.

SAYINGS OF RABBIES.

"Consider in whose presence thou art labouring and in whose service thou art employed; who will pay thee the reward of thy labour."

"R. Tarphon said: "The day is short, but the labour is much, and labourers slothful; and the master of the house presseth for dispatch."

"As a drop of mustard."

"Consider in whose presence thou must in futurity render an account in judgment, even before the Holy Supreme King of Kings, blessed is He."

"A religious man who becomes a publican is to be driven out of the society of religion."

"Two or three who set together and discourse of the law, the Divine presence may be said to rest on them."

"Pray for the peace of the kingdom, for were it not in deference thereof men would swallow each other alive."

"Give unto God of His own; for for thou and all thou possessest are His."

"Laughter and levity accustom mankind to lewdness."

This was, and still is, the ordinary salutation among the Jews.

"Be exceedingly humble of spirit."

"It were better for him that he were not created." A usual way of speaking.

"Whosoever profaneth God's name in secret, will be punished openly."

NEW TESTAMENT.

"He shall reward every man according to his works."—Matt. xvi. 27.

"We are labourers together with God."—1 Cor. iii. 9.

"The harvest is plenteous, but the labourers are few. Pray ye therefore the Lord of the harvest, that he send forth labourers into his harvest."—Matt. ix. 37, 38.

"As a grain of mustard seed."

"For we all must appear before the judgment seat of Christ, that every one may receive the things done in his body," &c., &c.—2 Cor. v. 10.

"Let him be unto thee as an heathen and a publican."—Matt. xviii. 17.

"For where two or three are gathered together in My name there am I in the midst of them."—Matt. xviii. 20.

"Prayers to be made for kings, and for all that are in authority, that we may lead a quiet and peaceful life."—1 Timothy, ii. 1-2.

"Render unto God the things that are God's."—Matt. xxii. 21.

"What hast thou that thou didst not receive."

"Neither filthiness, nor foolish talking, nor jesting, which are not convenient, but rather giving thanks unto God."—Ephes. v. 4.

"Peace be unto you."—Luke xxiv. 36; John xx. 19.

"Be clothed with humility."—1 Peter, v. 5.

"It had been good for that man if he had not been born."—Matt. xxvi. 24.

"For there is nothing covered that shall not be revealed."

SAYINGS OF RABBIES.

"Repentance and good deeds are a shield before the Divine punishment."

The Rabbins say: "Thou shalt not hate thy brother in thy heart." Perhaps he does not beat him, he does not pull his hair; he does not curse him. The text says: "In thine heart," speaking of hatred in the heart. But whence is it proved that he that sees his brother doing some foul actions is bound to reprove him? Because it is said: "In reproving thou shalt reprove." He reproves, but he heareth not; whence is it proved he is bound to a second reproof? It says in reproving thou shalt reprove." "How long must we reprove?" Rabha saith: "Even to blows, that is, until he that is reproved strikes him that reproves." Samuel saith, "Until he is angry."

Samuel saith: "Whosoever sins against his brother, he must say to him, 'I have sinned against thee,' if he hear thee it is well, if not, let him bring others, and let him appease him before them."

"Whosoever lays on himself the yoke of the law, shall be relieved from the yoke of the kingdom, and the custom of the world."

"Everything is given to man on security, and a net is spread over every living creature; the shop is open, and the merchant credits; the book is open and the hand records; and whosoever chooses to borrow may come and borrow; for the collectors are continually going round daily, and obtain payment of man whether with his consent or not, as they have full authority to support them, and the judgment in true justice; and all are prepared for the feast."

NEW TESTAMENT.

"Except ye repent ye shall likewise perish."—Luke xiii. 5; Acts viii. 22.

Go and tell him his fault between thee and him alone, if he shall hear thee thou hast gained thy brother."—Matt. xviii. 15.

"If he will not hear thee, then take with thee one or two more." &c., &c.—Matt. xviii. 16.

"Take my yoke upon you, for my yoke is easy, and my burden is light."—Matt. xi. 29, 30.

Parables.

(See Matt. xxi. 33.
  "   xxv. 1.
  Mark xii. 1.
  Luke xv. 13.)

SAYINGS OF RABBIES.	NEW TESTAMENT.
"They do not show a man a palm tree of gold, nor an elephant going through the eye of a needle."	"A camel to go through the eye of a needle."—Matt. xix. 24.
"To what may he be likened whose wisdom exceedeth his good works? To a tree whose branches are multiplicious, and its roots scanty; so that the wind cometh and plucketh it up and overturneth it. But to what is he like whose good deeds exceed his wisdom? To a tree whose branches are few, and its roots multifarious, so that if the most violent tempest discharges its fury against it, it will not be able to move it from its place."	"Shall he be likened unto a foolish man which built his house upon the sand, and the rain descended, &c., &c." "Shall be likened to a wise man, which built his house upon a rock, and the rain descended, and the floods came, and the winds blew; and it fell not," &c., &c.—Matt. vii. 24-28.
"To what was R. Bon Bar Chaija like? 'To a king who hired many labourers; among which there was one hired who performed his work extraordinary well.' What did the king do? 'He took him aside and walked with him to and fro.' When even was come, those laborers came that they might receive their hire, and he gave him a complete hire with the rest. And the labourers murmered saying. 'We have laboured hard all day and this man only two hours, yet he hath received as much wages as we,' the King saith unto them, 'He hath laboured more in those two hours than you in the whole day.'"	"The kingdom of heaven is likened," &c., &c. "Who went out early in the morning to hire labourers," &c., &c. "They received every man a penny," &c., &c. "They murmured against the good man of the house." &c.—Matt. xx. 1-14.
"He that is wronged is forbidden to be difficult to pardon. But when the offender implores him once and again, and it appears he repents of his deed, let him pardon him, and whosoever is most ready to pardon is most praiseworthy."	"Shall I forgive him? Till seven times."—Matt. xviii. 21. "If thy brother repents, forgive him."—Luke xxvii. 3.
"Those that were more eminent for the profoundness of their learning, or the splendour of their virtues, were set out by such an expression as this: 'He is a rooter up, (or a remover) of mountains.'"	"But if ye say unto this mountain, 'Be thou removed and be thou cast into the sea, it shall be done.'"—Matt. xxi. 21.

DID CHRIST BORROW FROM THE RABBIES?

SAYINGS OF RABBIES.	NEW TESTAMENT.
"It was a custom among the Jews to invite poor travellers to feasts."	"Go ye into the highways, and as many as ye find bid to the marriage."—Matt. xxii. 9.
"Rabbi! Rabbi! It was customary, and they loved to be saluted with this honorable title, notwithstanding the dissembled axiom: 'Love the work, but hate the title.'"	"And to be called of men Rabbi! Rabbi!"—Matt. xxiii. 7.
"A king invited his servants, but did not appoint any set time. Those that were wise adorned themselves. Those that were foolish went about their own business. The king all of a sudden called for servants: those went in adorned; these undressed. The king was pleased with the wise, and angry with the foolish."	"And five were wise, and five were foolish," &c., &c.—Matt. xxv. 1-12.
"It was customary among the Rabbies to use the *jod* to signify some small or insignificant thing. Sometimes they called a little town ironically *jod*. In Talmud, tract kidushin, it is said: From a little *jod* I see arise a whole city."	"Till heaven and earth pass one *jot* or one *tittle*, shall in no wise pass from the law till all be fulfilled."—Matt. v. 18.
"Who is mighty? he who subdueth his evil imagination."	"Resist the devil, and he will flee from you."—James iv. 7.
"Run to the performance of the slightest precept, and flee from the commission of sin."	"Flee from these things, and follow after righteousness."—1 Tim. vi. 11.
"This world may be likened to a court-yard, in comparison with the future world; therefore, prepare thyself in the ante-chamber that thou mayest enter into the dining-room."	"We should live soberly, righteously and godly in the present world, looking for that blessed hope and the glorious appearing of the great God."—Titus ii. 12-13.
"One hour's refreshment in the future world is preferable to the entire life of this."	"For what shall it profit a man if he gain the whole world and lose his own soul."—Mark viii. 36.
"Look not at the flask, but at that which is therein, for there are new flasks full of old wine and old flasks which have not even new wine in them."	See Matt. ix. 17; Mark ii. 22; Luke v. 37.

SAYINGS OF RABBIES.	NEW TESTAMENT.
"Against thy will must thou hereafter render an account and receive judgment in the presence of the Supreme King of Kings, the Holy God, blessed be He."	"Every idle word that men shall speak they shall give an account thereof in the day of judgement."—Matt. xii 36.
"Let not thine evil imagination persuade thee that the grave is a place of refuge for thee."	"How can ye escape the damnation of hell?"—Matt. xxiii. 33.
"Pestilence cometh into the world for the commission of sins said to be punishable with death in the law."	"Because of these things cometh the wrath of God upon the children of disobedience." — Eph. v. 6; Col..iii. 6.
"He who saith, 'What is mine is thine, and what is thine is also thine,' is the custom of the pious."	(See Matt. xix. 21; Mark x. 21; Luke xviii. 12; also Acts iv. 32.)
"Samael* the wicked and head of all evil spirits, had no power over Moses, the servant of God. He waited, however, impatiently for the moment when Moses would breathe his last breath, and the people of Israel without their leader. He said to himself: 'O when will the time come, when I shall rejoice, and Michael, the patron of Moses, shall weep?' The time came when God said to Moses, 'Go up the mount Abarim, and die there;' and Michael said to Samael: 'Now rejoice, thou wicked one, and I shall weep because Moses my friend must die.' Again, Moses desired to enter the land of promise, and could not bear the idea that he must die before. The good angels refused to take the life of Moses; and Samael, who was ready to do it, had a hard combat with him."	"Yet Michael the archangel, when contending with the devil, he disputed about the body of Moses, &c."—Jude i. 9.
"The holy, blessed God saith concerning Israel : Those that belong to me, are as simple as doves, but amongst the nations of the world, they are subtle as serpents."	"Be ye therefore wise as serpents and harmless as doves."—Matt. x. 16.

---

* Samael is one of the names given to Satan by the Rabbins. It is compounded of Sam (poison) and Eli (God).

DID CHRIST BORROW FROM THE RABBIES?

SAYINGS OF RABBIES.	NEW TESTAMENT.
"May be compared to a king, that had a vineyard; and there were three, who were enemies to it. What were they? One cut down the branches. The second cut off the bunches. The third rooted up the vines."	"A certain man planted a vineyard." &c.—Mark xii. 1.
"About the time of the Messiah impudence should abound, and then son shall revile and ill-treat his father, the daughter shall rise against her mother, and the daughter-in-law against the mother-in-law, and man's foes shall be they of his own household."	Matt. x. 35. "And a man's foes *shall* be they of his own household."—Matt. x. 36.

NOTE.—With reference to the foregoing extracts, we may observe; first, that Christ came not to disparage truth already known to man, but to give it new life and power. Hence, wherever He found the truth, whether in the Law, the Prophets, or in the sayings of the Scribes and Elders who sit in Moses' seat; He added to it the authority of His testimony. Secondly, this synopsis probably containes all that can be gleaned from the Rabbies, which reappears in the New Testament. Hence, we may learn how truly original is the Gospel. It expands our views of old truth, and also brings to light things that are new. It completes the Revelations of former ages, by a new and perfect declaration of the will of God.—N. B.

CHAPTER V.

TESTIMONY CONCERNING JESUS FROM A REFORMED RABBI.

The manifold calamities—originating from the wickedness of the rulers, and increased by the wars, fought by Syrians and Egyptians upon the soil of Palestine—disposed a great many members of the Jewish Society to melancholy and dejection, while others were inspired with a martyr's faith in a glorious termination of all the existing misery. Nothing could shake their trust in a final, miraculous redemption. Thus their misery led a great many Jews to expect the Messiah. With many others, appeared Theudas, playing the part of the same. But all failed in securing the sympathy of the people. They answered neither to the cherished ideas of the Messiah, nor had they influence and mind enough to unite the nation, and produce the desired effect. *Jesus*, born of Mary, in Nazareth—the founder of the Christian religion—was more successful. He won a great many followers, clinging to the new faith with greater pertinacity in proportion as the Jews persecuted him. Religious persecutions, however, assist in exasperating the roused spirit of the parties—and instead of procuring a reconcilliation, will call forth hatred and discord, division and mutual aggression. Nevertheless, by the means of an allwise Providence, Christianity became the instrument of bringing a great many nations, absorbed in superstition and idolatry, nearer to the true God, the Creator of heaven and earth, and of kindling anew the zeal of the Jews in behalf of their religion. Many Jews became apostates, and especially among the Essenes, Sadducees, Samaritans, and Idumeans, and took a hostile position against Judaism; but this very apostasy contributed greatly in uniting the remaining large majority of the Jews, inspiring them with an unusual affection and love for their religion, and imbuing them with a national pride, indispensably necessary for the impending struggle.

CHAPTER VI.

ISRAEL'S STUMBLING-BLOCKS.

There is something intensely interesting in the past history and future destiny of the Jews. From whatever point viewed, they become to us a marvel and a study.

If we look at them in their *national* character, they present the most remarkable ethnic phenomenon in the history of the world. For no people have ever been dispersed among other people, without losing their national traits and characteristics; but the Jews, though scattered throughout the habitable globe for eighteen hundred years, still preserve their ethnic identity and peculiarities, and, though they mingle with every nation, blend with none.

If we look at them as an *historical* nation, they present greater points of interest than can be found in the annals of any other country. Their histories go back a thousand years beyond the birthday of the most renowned nations of antiquity, and unlike the fables and myths which hang like clouds around the origin of the Athenians and of the Romans, are clear, true, and God-inspired.

If we look at them as a *prophetical* nation, we see a nation about whom the first prophecy in Eden was uttered, and among whom existed a line of seers, extending through a period of twelve hundred years, before whose visions were presented, and by whose pens were written, the future destinies of the world.

If we look at them as a *literary* nation, we find them possessing a written language, history, odes, laws, and philosophy, at the time that Cadmus was introducing his letters into Greece, and six hundred years before the Wolf-nursling founded Rome; a people whose histories have never been excelled by Herodotus or Livy; whose poetry has never been equalled by the blind old man of Chios, or the Mantuan bard; whose biographies have never been surpassed by Plutarch or Tacitus; whose moralists far outstrip Plato and Seneca; and whose legal writers leave far behind them the theories of Aristotle, in his Nicomachean ethics, or the "de Republica" of Cicero.

If we look at them as a religious nation, we see a people having a knowledge of the one living and true God, and giving Him holy worship, and possessing His holy Word, and enjoying the ministration of a priest-

hood which He had instituted, and above all, the symbols of His Divin[e]
Presence and Sovereignty, when the rest of mankind are sunk in idolatr[y]
and superstition; and, not to enlarge on this comparison, if we look [at]
the Jews as the race to which was given the Divine law—to whom wer[e]
committed the oracles of God—"of whom, as concerning the flesh, Chri[st]
came"—and concerning whom Christ himself declared "salvation is [of]
the Jews"—then do we place this nation, outcast though it now is, an[d]
dispersed though it be, on a higher platform than can be occupied b[y]
the wisest, the richest, the greatest nations of the earth; centering i[n]
itself more wonders, and challenging for itself more study, than are four[d]
in or called out by, all the world beside.

Of the stumbling-blocks in the minds of nominal Christians, th[e]
first which we will mention is, their general prejudice against a Jew. I[n]
the works of learned historians, from Bede to Hallam; in the pages [of]
popular novelists, from Cervantes to Sir Walter Scott; in the verses [of]
the most popular poets, from Baccaccio to Southey, the Jew has bee[n]
drawn as an object of calumny, satire, and scorn; and when Shakspea[re]
would concentrate, in one character, subtlety, cunning, covetousness, an[d]
an overreaching avarice, he conjures up a Shylock, a Jewish mone[y]
lender, of Venice, and holds him up to the contempt of the Christia[n]
world, as the representative of the Hebrew race—so that the name [of]
Shylock and Jew are almost synonymous on Gentile lips. We hav[e]
thus been educated to despise the Jews, and so accustomed to see the[m]
mentioned with opprobrium, that we easily become imbued with th[e]
prejudice and act it out in our daily life. But this is unjust. What [is]
it that has made the Jew a wanderer, a usurer, a trader, an alien i[n]
every land, branded and persecuted with fire and sword? It is Chri[s]
tian intolerance! Christian avarice! Christian revenge! Genti[le]
nations have trodden them in the dust, and then reviled them becau[se]
they have fallen beneath their iron heel.

The *second* stumbling-block in the way, is the apathy of Christian[s.]
It is really lamentable to know how little hold the subject of promotir[g]
Christianity among the Jews has upon the Church of God. The ver[y]
persons who are deeply interested in missions to the heathen here fe[el]
but little sympathy; and yet every argument which can urge to foreig[n]
missions, comes with additional force when applied to the Jew. If it [is]
right to send missionaries to the heathen who know not God, much mo[re]
to send the Gospel to the Jews, who do worship Jehovah, and acknov[v]
ledge the Scriptures of the Old Testament. If it is right to send mi[s]
sionaries to idolaters, much more to the Jews who have never bowed th[e]

knee to wood and stone, but have ever directed their worship to the one living and true God.

This apathy is allied to a *third* stumbling block, viz.: a misunderstanding of the Biblical aspect of the subject. There is a great lack of Bible knowledge as to the real state of the Jews before God. We see them, indeed, a dispersed and down-trodden nation; shall we argue thence that God has cast them off, that He has ceased to love them? No. St. Paul declares, "God hath not cast away his people." They are still "beloved for their fathers' sake." Their present position is that of a disobedient and refractory child, lying under a father's displeasure. The child has offended his father, rebelled against him, set at nought his counsels; and the father, grieved and sad, puts the child under the ban of his displeasure, debars him a child's privileges until he repents and comes back to his filial duty. So the Jews, like sinful children, have rebelled against God, and cast out their Messiah; but God has still towards them a Father's love, still yearns over them with a Father's compassion. They are His children still, under the ban of his displeasure for a moment, but soon to be received back to His paternal favor and home. And were we to go to the house of a friend whose child was under the father's displeasure, should we think it right, just, or humane, because the child was in temporary disgrace, to beat and insult it also, to add our ill-treatment to a father's displeasure? So when we see the Jews, these suffering children of God, shall we, because God has for a moment hidden His face from them, revile and abuse them, and add our insults to His punishment?

A *fourth* stumbling-block in the minds of Christians in reference to this work is, that they judge of it by the standard of other missionary work. But it is entirely different from all other missionary work. It has to deal with a different class of people, a different religious faith, and a people, too, not compact in population and centralized in particular nations or states, but sprinkled about in patches of families here and there, all over the world. The missionary work to the Jews is unique; it is not a preaching but a teaching work, not a gathering of congregations, but personal conversations; it is a hand-to-hand contest with prejudices which borrow all their strength from the very Bible which we firmly believe, and with false hopes which root themselves in a misunderstanding of the very prophecies which we equally hold. The work of dismantling the mind of a single Jew of his national and Rabbinical prejudices, often involves more toil, learning, and faith, than it requires (humanly speaking) to convert a whole village of idolaters, or to bring back a corrupt church to a pure faith. The very nature of the work forbids the expectation of large and immediate results.

Turning from the stumbling-blocks in the minds of Christians, let us look at those which exist in the minds of the Jews. We will mention a few leading and peculiar ones.

First. Their hereditary hatred of the Gentiles. If you had been from the first dawnings of knowledge, taught to hate a certain class of men; if they had been represented to you as vile in themselves, in their belief, in their practices, as hostile to your parents and to their faith; if this hatred had been drawn in, not only with your mother's milk, and your father's teaching, but from the sacred books of your worship; and if all the deep religious sentiment of your soul had been shaped and warped by such moulding influences; then would few understand the depth and inveteracy of those prejudices which the Jews have against Christians. For this is their state towards us. They have been educated from infancy to regard Christians as their enemies, and the enemies of their faith. They have looked upon them as having no part in God's covenant mercy, as being outcasts and idolaters. This has been taught them by parents and Rabbies, in the house and in the synagogues, in their school books, and in their Talmuds; and this hatred has been perpetuated from generation to generation for nearly four thousand years. And when to this hereditary dislike of all the uncircumcised, you add their intense hereditary pride of descent from Abraham, and their pride of nation, as being God's favoured people, you can in some measure understand how thoroughly ingrained must be their enmity to the Gentiles, not only their persons (of which, in this country, at least, we see but little,) but especially to their religion, and to all attempts to bring them to their despised faith.

The *second* stumbling-block is the oppression and persecution of the Jews by professing Christian nations,

A more melancholy record cannot be found in the volume of history, than that which narrates the fate of this peeled and scattered people. Though the Gospel was first preached to the Jews, and not to the Gentiles, until the Jews had, as a nation, fairly rejected it; yet the Jews, as we learn from the Acts, were ever ready to stir up oppositions to the Christians, and incite persecutions against them. As the Gentile Christians increased, they soon began to avenge their injuries upon the Jews, and finding them immovable in their faith, soon made laws and edicts, which placed this unhappy people between the upper and nether mill-stones of oppression.

Every Christian nation in Europe has in turn persecuted and banished the Jew. The first persecuting law of a Christian Prince was by Constantine, in A. D. 325, against the Jews. In the fourth century they were banished from Rome, having first had their ears cut off. In the sixth century, they were compelled, in France, to embrace the dogmas of the Church, or leave the kingdom. In the seventh century the same edicts were enacted in Spain. In the eighth and ninth centuries they were made to wear badges of servitude, and denied many privileges. In the tenth century, they were driven out of Bohemia. In the eleventh century, they were subjected to the merciless persecutions of the crusaders, the chiefs of that first crusade, declaring that before they attacked the Mussulmans, they should destroy the nation which crucified the Son of God; and hence, there was a general massacre of the Jews in the cities on the banks of the Moselle and the Rhine. In the twelfth century, they were banished from France by Philip Augustus. His successor, St. Louis, twice expelled them; and Charles VI, in A.D. 1394, again banished them from the empire. In the thirteenth century, under Edward I, all Jews were required to depart from England. They were proscribed in Spain in the fifteenth century, and the last year of that century was signalized by their banishment from Portugal. One of the primary reasons for the establishment of the Inquisition was to root out what was called "the Jewish Leprosy."

To recount the barbarities which the Christian nations of Europe have inflicted on the Jews would fill volumes, and they should be written with tears, instead of ink, and on sackcloth, instead of parchment. Every species of annoyance, every diabolical torture, every debasing usage, every epithet of opprobrium, every manifestation of hatred and contempt has been exercised against them; their property was ever regarded as lawful prey; and their persons were never secure from ill-treatment. Their lives were at the mercy of ruthless rulers; everywhere they have been treated by the Christian nations of Europe with contumely and wrong. Laws of the most oppressive kind have been enacted against them. They could not testify against a Christian in the civil courts; they were forced to wear badges designed to mark them with disgrace; they were forbidden to institute suits against Christians in the courts of law. They were made the foot-ball of kings and princes, being spurned now hither, now thither, by the feet of petty despots. They were compelled to reside in certain sections of cities, and locked in at night. No Christian servants or nurse could stay with or attend them; no inn for travellers could receive or entertain them. They were in truth what prophecy declared they should be, "a by-word and a reproach among all nations." When Christian nations have thus maltreated and abused this ancient people, do we wonder at their prejudice against Christianity?

Thirdly. If Christian *nations* have dealt thus with them, the Christian *Church* has been equally culpable in placing another stumbling-block before them.

The councils of the Church, from that of Laodicea, in A.D. 350, through hundreds of years, have made canons against them. The festivals and fasts of the Church have been made occasions of assault upon them, and even Bishops, Archbishops, Cardinals and Popes, have urged the bigoted and the superstitious, to massacre and exterminate this everywhere hated seed of Jacob. Nor is this exercise of its persecuting power all the obstacle (great as it is) which the Church has put in the way of this people's conversion; for, *fourthly*, a greater stumbling-block than even this is found in the idolatry and superstition of the Greek and Roman Churches.

The Jews have been taught by God Himself to hate and abuse idols. They have been trained up in the worship of "the one living and true God." For their several aberrations into idolatry, they have been most sorely punished. Against such worship there stands the second commandment, the warnings of the prophecy and the threatenings of the Almighty. From infancy they are trained to hate idols and idol worship, and rather than submit to it, millions have endured cruel tortures, and millions more violent death. Yet what meets the eye of the Jew in nearly every nominal Christian land? Idolatry—image worship.

The larger part of the Jews, especially those on the continent of Europe, Asia Minor, and Syria, know nothing of Christianity, but what they see of it as displayed in the Greek and Roman Churches.

They have beheld only this corrupt form of our holy religion; they have witnessed the debasing idolatry of these idolatrous churches; they have seen the Virgin Mary elevated above the Lord of Hosts; Jewish apostates as they would term the apostles, made to be objects of worship; statues, pictures, altars, shrines, and the miserable tinsel worship of a meretricious ritual to take the place of simple devotion; and above all, they have seen the crucifix, everywhere kissed and caressed, prayed to and worshipped, and yet the very word by which they designate an idol, is that by which they designate the cross, so that the very language of the Apostle: "God forbid that I should glory, save in the cross of our Lord Jesus Christ," is to them equivalent to saying that Christians boast of their idolatry. In France, Germany, Belgium, Austria, Russia, Greece, Hungary, Spain, Portugal, Italy, what can the Jew know of a pure Christianity? They see little that does not militate against God's command, shock their religious sense, and carricature our holy religion; they see churches containing what to them are the abominations of the heathen; they see a priesthood bigoted, vicious, covetous, hypocritical and persecuting; they see a religion which only glosses crime and legalizes iniquity, and which teaches its followers to insult them, oppress them, and make their lives bitter with bondage. With such follies and superstitions, such mockery of God and deification of man, such intolerance and lust, such iniquitous lives, in priests and people, can we be surprised at the feeling of disgust which the Jew has against the Church, when the false and idolatrous church is the only one with which he is conversant? And when, in this age, such a case can occur as that of the child Mortara, at Bologna—when what is called the Church of Christ, through its priests, can go into the family of a Jew, and snatch from its mother's arms, and its parental home, a child of love, and force it away among strangers, that it may be brought up in a faith which the parents abhor. When the Pope sanctions such proceeding, and despite remonstrances and appeals, that should have melted a heart of stone, persists in keeping the child, what must the Israelite argue concerning a religion which can sanction such proceedings? What, but cherish against it bitter hatred? How would you feel towards a religion which taught its followers thus to deal with the child of your heart and home?

Fifthly. The Jews find a great stumbling-block in the way of their conversion, in the evil lives of Christians. "Let us confess with shame," says an English writer, "that in all probability the errors in doctrine and the errors in conduct, which the Jews have observed among the professors of Christianity, have tended as much as any other thing to prejudice and harden them against the religion of Christ. The influence of their Rabbies, and the prejudices of their education, close their eyes to every Christian book but one—the book of our profession and practice. And, alas! what an erroneous book has this been, in all ages and among all denominations of professors; not only as exhibited in the Church of Rome, but in the Reformed Churches also." The Rabbinical Jews, by far the larger part of the nation, attach two ideas particularly to the word Christian: *First,* Ungodliness; *Secondly,* Idolatry. They suppose that Christians live without God and solely for this world, and with most of the European Jews, (especially when they wish to express the utmost profligacy of life, to which one of their nation can debase himself), they say : " He lives just like a Christian."

Sixthly. No people on earth have such obstacles to contend with in becoming Christians as the Jews, more particularly those living in foreign lands. Few records are more exciting than those which tell of the struggles of Jewish converts in coming out from the synagogue, from the influence of their Rabbies ; from the intense family prejudices ; from the social surroundings, which, like meshes of iron, hem them in on every side. The very listening by a Jew to Christian teaching, is regarded as encouraging blasphemy ; the receiving of a Christian minister into his house is regarded as aiding national rebellion ; the taking and reading of the New Testament is esteemed a henious crime ; the entering a Christian church is equivalent to casting reproach on Judaism; and when the eyes of the poor Israelite begin to be opened, he is met by entreaties, by argument, remonstrance, invective, anger, violence, repulsion ; and if he still persists, stripes and imprisonment often await him. He is cursed ; he is turned out of the synagogue, he is disinherited ; he is stripped of his property ; he is placed under a fearful interdict, so that no Jew can go near him. His father turns him from his door, his mother forgetting a mother's love in a mother's faith, reproaches him as a reprobate ; brothers and sisters league against him ; wherever he turns he meets continually reproach, violence, and perhaps death. You have perhaps read the narrative of the conversion of some Jews, and painfully intense as they are, they are but specimens of what takes place in nearly every instance when an Israelite turns to Jesus as his Saviour. Indeed, the narratives are rather under-coloured than over-coloured. There are a hundred little circumstances which cannot be brought out ; there are crowds of tumultuous emotions which cannot be expressed. There is a silent suffering, known only to God, bitterer far than any outspoken grief ; and there are secret agonies endured in the privacy of the household or the chamber, which no pen can describe, but which are known by the sympathising heart of Jesus. Oh! it is not the tearing the flesh with pincers, it is not the breaking of the bones on the wheel, it is not the roasting of the soles of the feet before fires, it is not the cold, damp, dark, foodless, fœted dungeon, it is not alone these things that are the most cruel tortures. No! These eat only into the body ; these only waste and lacerate flesh and blood ; these only cripple limbs and maim members ; but the rack which breaks up a once symmetrical mind, the pincers which nip and twist, and tear away the sensibilities of the soul, the fires which burn out the life-blood of warm affections, which are found, not in Inquisitions, but in families, and which are inflicted, not by executioners, but by relatives; these are the fearful tortures which have ever met the Jewish converts in their whole course, from the first inception of a Christian idea, to the full development of the Christian faith.

But who can portray the glories of this regathered people, and the blessings consequent on their return to Palestine? Imagination folds its wings before the vast conception, and thought stands mute at the magnificent vista which opens before the eye of faith. With the conversion of the Jews is linked every great hope of the Christian world. With their Christianity is entertained the redemption of the whole earth; and the glories of the milennial day—second only to the glories of "the perfect day" in heaven—are reserved as the compliment, the filling up of a scene the preliminary act of which is the national conversion of Israel, and their restoration to their earthly Canaan.

> "Hail! glorious day, expected long,
> When Jew and Greek one prayer shall join—
> With eager feet one temple throng—
> With grateful praise one Christ adore."

CHAPTER VII.

SUFFERINGS OF THE JEWS.

Sufferings in the olden time—In Britain—On the Continent of Europe—From the wickedness of their own people—On account of false Messiahs—Accounted for from the WORD of GOD—Dawn of a better day—Notes on persecutions by Christians.

History has not shewn a more injured nation than Israel. This people, who may be styled the sole survivors of the really olden times, when mankind was in its infancy—this people, unmixed and unchanged in their belief and religious observances, and whose history, down to the present day, inseparably connects itself with those primeval and most sacred records, from which the civilized portion of mankind derives its faith, and on which it rests its hopes—this people has beyond all others exercised the most lasting influence on the human mind.

Every Bible reader must readily allow, that the dispersion of the Jews, ever since the time of the destruction of their Temple, and city of Jerusalem, is attended with such particular marks of reprobation, that man must be blind not to discern the hand of God in it. This dispersion is become a field fertile in miracles, prodigies, and invectives. The Christian and the Jew may equally reap their harvest therein, both may discover wonders there—and yet behold them in a different light. Some of the Christian expounders of the word of God, have from time to time, by the art of persuasion, found means to awaken in the minds of their audience an idea of the reprobation of the Jews. The opprobrious language with which that people are by the majority of other nations daily treated—the odious character they bear—the abolishment of those ceremonies which are the most essential to their religion—the whole dominion of their church subverted—their tribes and families confounded, and their sacrifices suppressed, are some of the visible marks of that fatal reprobation.

The Jews, on the other hand, find matter of glory and triumph in their very misfortunes, and proudly assert that *their* actions is the heart of the universe. Though the heart is the noblest part of the human body, yet, it is that which suffers most by its indispositions, that which is consumed by the passions, and tormented with anguish; no corruption, however, can be found in it, since it is endued, as it were, with an innate purity, and preserves to itself the power of discharging all such corrupt humours as destroy the other parts. That fine and delicate matter whereof the heart is composed, attracts indeed a number of distempers to it, which afterwards it expels by the strength of its constitution. The Jews assert, likewise, with the Prophet Amos, that no people on earth but themselves are the favorites of Heaven, and for that reason the Almighty visits them for their manifold sins and iniquities. But these sins and iniquities are transitory, because God will not suffer them to destroy the heart, as they formerly destroyed the people of Canaan. The Jews suffer by the depredations of their neighbours, and the heart suffers by the indispositions of the liver, spleen, stomach, &c. This plainly demonstrates, that the idea which they entertain of their disgraces and misfortunes, is very different from that of the Christians. A people, however, like the Jews, who once looked upon themselves as superior to all the nations upon earth, may, of course, be indulged in a few fabulous relations, and pardoned for their excess of pride and ostentation, so that being accustomed to miracles and prophecies, they presumed to think Providence neither could, nor ought, ever to speak or act but in their favour. But why not at the same time admit, that they have to be the monuments of God's justice? And, since our present aim is to give an adequate idea of the various calamities of the Jewish nation, through every age, since the time of our blessed Redeemer, we hope that we also will become acquainted, at the same time, with the different reasons thereof.

Religion is, for the most part, severely shocked by the decay and revolutions of kingdoms, and that man must have a more than common resolution, who sincerely professes a religion which is dispised and out of fashion, through the prevailing power of human passions. The destruction of Jerusalem by the Babylonians, was a fatal blow to the Jewish religion, and though some worthy men returned from that captivity, yet a great many wicked wretches also returned with them, who completed those evils which the impiety of their ancestors had begun, and mingled their own vices with those of the colonies which the King of Babylon had left in Judea; but that, indeed, was no more than the natural and general consequence of a mixture of various nations.

The Jews, after their return from captivity, began, insensibly, to deviate from the purity of their morals and their religious worship, when, at the same time, they grew more earnest and zealous for the observance of their rights and ceremonies. Might I be indulged with making one reflection here. I would observe that, for want of miracles and prophesies, which prevented them from taking that for religion, which was no more than the external part, the pomp and grandeur for it, the Jews gave blindly into the idle traditions of their formal doctors, who raised their own merits upon the ruins of prophesy, and thought the surface and externals of the law requiste for supporting the splendor of a difficult and troublesome discipline, which was no longer upheld by miracles; the whole form of the Jewish religion was, therefore, changed, and the Jews assumed the mask of hypocrisy. But though the ceremonies and customs of men appear never so incommodious, yet they are still infinitely more easy than the reformation of the heart.

In the midst of this corruption, Paganism triumphed over the weakness and decay of the Jewish religion, by the awful power of the Romans, and as the time of its destruction grew near, this corruption seemed to spread over the Jewish Church in equal proportion, and so ripened them into that rebellion which brought upon them the destruction of their State. The Roman emperors, under whose government the Jews were obliged to live, treated them after a very severe manner; but after the destruction of their great city, they were much less regarded. The Emperor Domitian loaded them with intolerable taxes, and exacted them so rigorously, that he caused those who were only suspected of Judaism to be stripped stark naked. Under the Emperor Adrian they were reduced to such extremities as to turn fortune-tellers for their daily subsistence.

The severe sufferings which the Jews endured under King Richard was the cause of the emigration of many. John I, shortly after the beginning of his reign, persuaded them to return, as their expatriation lessened his revenues. Trusting to his promise to build their synagogues, to appoint spiritual guides under the name of "Elders," and to allow them the acquisition of real estate, and to restore them all their former liberties, a great many returned to England, but they soon found out they had not come to an angel's land. The property which they brought back, was taken from them again, and the people continually clamored for their expulsion. But the English kings would not throw away such a valuable revenue as the Jews were. The revenue which they brought in, increased so fast, that a particular "treasurer of the Jews" was appointed. King John asked, at one time, 66,000 Marks, and as they could not collect at once such a sum, they were imprisoned and plundered till the required sum was forthcoming. Thus a Jew was taken prisoner in Bristol, because he could not pay, at the order of the King, the sum of one thousand Marks silver, and as he continued to refuse payment, one of his teeth was daily extracted, till he cashed the order on the eighth day of his imprisonment.

When in the year 1254, large sums were acquired from the Jews for prosecuting the war against Spain, and one Jew in London paid, during seven years, 30,000 Marks in the royal treasury—they asked permission to emigrate.

Richard, the king's brother, assured them of the good wishes of the king, and shewed them the uncertainty of a better fate in other countries. Thus they remained and enjoyed the humanity with which they were treated by Richard, to whom the Jews had been sold by the king. Edward I, 1273, issued an edict, which secured the safety of the Jews, settled the payment of regular yearly dues, and permitted them the acquisition of real estate. But in the year 1287 he acted very severely against them. He oppressed them in different ways, repealed many of their liberties, and accused them of many crimes. This was done to extort money, but in order to hide all appearance of greediness, he ordered the moiety of all confiscated moneys to be paid to Christian apostates. But few only made use of this bait. The year 1290 crowned Edward's inimical views. He sequestered all their property and commanded them to leave the country; travelling expenses only were permitted to be retained. And thus sixteen thousand Jews were forced to leave a country which they had helped in many an hour of need, and to sail with mariners who plundered and drowned them, and carried the rest to further persecutions.

Under Cromwell the Jews returned to England again, through the intercession of Manasse-ben-Israel from Portugal, well known as author, philologian, divine, and a friend to all mankind.

In Seville, Spain, the Jews were doomed to another terrible persecution. In 1391, the mob excited by the sermons of the Archbishop Niebla, destroyed the Jewish quarter, killed more than half of the 7,000 families living there, and forced the others to become converts. The same atrocities were committed in Valencia, Toledo, Cordova and Barcelona. By baptism only, could the Jews be rescued from the hands of the rabble, and more than 200,000 are reported to have submitted to baptism. But the large majority of these new converts in heart remained true to their former religion; in cellars and caverns, and at the risk of life, they still celebrated their Sabbath and holidays, and carefully avoided intermarriages with the Gentiles.

In Castile, too, the Jews suffered very much from the proscriptive laws, issued by the Antipope Benedict XII.; they had to submit to baptism, but in secret still observed their religious ceremonies. Ferdinand V. and Pope Pius II. being informed of the secret religious meetings, called on the officers of the Inquisition—the clerical court established by Ferdinand and Isabella for the purpose of exterminating all heresy in the Catholic Church—to enforce their rigid laws against these secret Jews. 2,000 of them were executed by command of this formidable and fanatic court; others cast into dungeons, and when released from prison, compelled to wear a red badge on their garments, as a sign that they had been condemned to the stake. Their property was confiscated; their children declared unfit to take possession of the paternal inheritance, and both parents and children were deprived of all their titles and privileges. The people were still dissatisfied with the appointment to public offices of even converted Jews; and in 1445 a revolt broke out in Toledo, where the inhabitants, complaining of this infringement on their privileges, ransacked the dwellings of the Jews and butchered the inmates. The revolt was quelled, and the government resolved to appoint no more converts as public officers. The Spanish clergy, and at their head the Dean of Madrid, opposed this measure with all their might, fearing that such a law would do away with a great inducement of the Jews to apostasy. The government, however, desirous of peace in their various states, was unwilling to yield to the remonstrances of the clergy, till Pope Nicolai threatened with excommunication all those who declared the Jewish converts unfit to hold public offices. But henceforth were persecuted and hunted down with remorseless cruelty those Jews who, publicly feigning to be Christians, still secretly adhered to the Jewish faith. Thomas of Torquemada, the great Inquisitor, enforcing the decrees of his predecessors, obliged the Rabbis to denounce all these renegades, and tired of his unavailing efforts of making the Jews converts to the Church, he caused, in the year 1492, the passage of the royal decree, by which all the Jews were excluded from Spain. A respite of four months was granted to them to sell their goods and estates. Under penalty of death they were forbidden to remain any longer in Spain, and the Spaniards were not even allowed to furnish them with the necessary stores of provisions.

It was in vain that *Don Isaac Abarbanal*, threw himself at the feet of Queen Isabella, imploring the revocation of this fatal decree. Knowing the covetousness of the king, he offered him a present of 30,000 ducats towards defraying the expenses incurred by the wars against the Moors, the audience was suddenly interrupted by Torquemada, who, rushing into the room, in which Don Abarbanal was imploring the grace of their majesties, lifted up his crucifix and exclaimed: Judas Iscariot sold his master for 30 silver pieces; your majesties intend to sell him for 30,000; here he is, take him, and barter him away. With these words he threw the cross on the table, and left the room. His words did not fail in their effect. Don Abarbanal was dismissed, and over 800,000 Jews were ordered to leave the country. They had to comply with this order, without receiving any indemnification for their property, as in the short terms granted to them, they were even constrained to barter a house against an ass, and a vineyard for some linen.

Most of these exiles emigrated into Portugal, Italy, France, the Levant, and also Africa; large numbers died of pestilence, in Italy, and still more in Africa, by the fury and greediness of the Moors who plundered and killed the fugitives, defiled their wives and daughters, and ripped up the bodies of others in hope of finding some pieces of gold swallowed by them. Many died of hunger in the open fields—a sojourn in the cities and villages having been refused them. Bowed down by these unheard of miseries, some returned into Spain and submitted to baptism. Since that time the Jews were not permitted to reside in this country.

A similar fate awaited the unfortunate exiles who had settled in Portugal. King Emanuel was informed by his mother-in-law, the Queen Isabella of Spain, that she was unwilling to have a son-in-law who tolerated in his country the enemies of Christ. Emanuel, who, in the beginning of his reign, had treated the Jews with all due forbearance, now changed his course, and, in 1405, issued a decree ordering the Jews to leave his kingdom. Eight months were granted them to prepare for emigration. Those who wished to remain had to choose between death, slavery, and apostasy. When the victims tarried in leaving their cherished country, the children were tore from their arms, dragged to the baptistry, and given away to Christians. In order to save them from apostasy, many parents killed their own children and then committed suicide, the others hurried away from Portugal, though the King, anxious for his revenue, tried to prevent their departure; but few remained in the country as slaves or feigned apostates, in order to retain their children and liberty. But here, as well as in Spain, the officers of the Inquisition soon discovered these pretented apostates, and handed them over to all the cruel proceedings of this Court. Thus they were once furiously attacked, while celebrating in their houses the Jewish Passover, and more than 2,000 were put to death. Soon afterwards, however, the Jews again obtained permission to return to Portugal, only according to a Decree of 1583, they had to wear a yellow hat, by which they were distinguished. And when, in 1821, the Inquisition was abolished, several Jews settled in Lisbon, under the protection of the British Government. At present, from 2,000 to 2,600 Jews are reported to live in Portugal, of whom about 600 reside in Lisbon. Most of them are from Gibraltar and the Barbary States, whither the Portuguese Jews often travel for commercial purposes. Some of them are engaged in manufacturing Turkish slippers, the majority in commercial pursuits with Africa, from whence they export wax, leather, gum, and other productions. In 1830, a small number emigrated from Lisbon to the Brazils; a few are living in Oporto. In Lisbon, there are three synagogues, in private houses, occupied partly by Christians and partly by Jews. But when the Christians were once masters of the Roman Empire, they did not show any indulgence to a nation who were looked upon as the inveterate enemies of Jesus Christ, they recollected that they had crucified the Messiah, and thought themselves in duty bound to avenge the indignities which he had suffered at their hands.

It is true that the Jews have suffered many persecutions, frequently grounded on enormous crimes imputed to them by the nakedness of some particular men, and which the illiterate vulgar, out of a misguided zeal, punished with all the rage and resentment that enthusiasm and bigotry could inspire them, but many times persons out of their own people have laid the foundation of their sufferings and persecutions.

One of the greatest crimes which was, and, still in some countries, is imputed to the Jews is, their crucifying of children; they have been and are still charged to meet privately on a Thursday before the Feast of the Passover, and at the same time sacrifice an infant, to testify their abhorence of the Christian religion. The cause of their banishment from France, in the reign of Philip Augustus, was an accusation of such a crime. It is very possible that some of the Jews might be so impious and inhuman as to commit so flagrant a crime, but it is not, and cannot be thought as sufficient grounds to charge the whole nation with it over and over, as some fanatic monks and Jesuits, even in our present age, are not ashamed to make their people believe, with an addition of the most odious and aggravating circumstances. But be that as it will, this pretended sacrifice of infants, has many times occasioned a great number of Jews to be massacred like animals; and at the same time this pretended sacrifice was of no small emolument to the Roman Catholic Church, who under that specious pretence seized on all the effects of the Jews.

The Jews have been likewise charged with an impious and profane abuse of the sacred Host, and scourging crucifixes; and, indeed, they are not absolutely to be justified upon all these articles of impeachment; but this, we think, we may venture to say, that several have imagined that it was for the interest of religion to lay such crimes to their charge, as for examples, at the beginning of the 14th Century, an Italian Monk having concealed a crucifix under a dunghill, imputed that sacrilege to the Jews, and caused them to be destroyed without mercy. They were likewise accused of having poisoned the waters of several springs and rivers, and thus caused a very great number of them to be destroyed. This accusation originated, or took its rise from a certain ceremony which the Jews perform on the feast of *their* New Year. On this day they wend their way to the river, and throw into it any small missiles they may have in their pockets, and pronounce the words: "And Thou wilt cast all their sins into the depth of the sea."

We shall now return to those kinds of sufferings, which so many times has befallen them through the hands and wicked calculations of their own people; yes, the most fatal blow which they suffered at the time when their Temple and City was destroyed, when above a million and a half of human beings perished, some writers in the Talmud ascribe to such causes. The Talmud, Tract Gittim, fol. 45, p. 2, contains a description of Jerusalem, and other cities of importance, among which Tur-Hanalkah (the light of the queen) and Bitter, which two cities were the scenes of the bloody wars. It says: "For the sake of Kameza and Bar-Kameza, came the destruction of Jerusalem; for the sake of a hen and a cock, came the destruction of Tur-Hamalkah; and for the sake of a pole of a carriage, the destruction of Bitter." It then goes on to enlarge upon these subjects, and gives the following stories: "One of the richest and most distinguished men in Jerusalem sent out his servants to invite all the noble families of the city, the high priests, and the members of the high court (Sanhedrin) to the wedding of his daughter. On the list of those who were to be invited, was a man with the name 'Kameza;' but there was another man in Jerusalem with the name 'Bar-Kameza;' and by mistake, the servant invited the latter instead of the former, and he came. The house was filled with guests, and all were already sitting around the tables, when the lord of the house appeared. In passing around, to review and salute his guests, he saw Bar-Kameza sitting among them, with whom he had had some quarrel long before that time. With indignation he bade him to leave his house immediately, as he had never invited him. Bar-Kameza replied, that he was invited; and thinking that his old friend desired again to have peace with him, he accepted the invitation and came. But the master of the feast said that he did not wish to be his friend any more, and he must therefore leave the house. Bar-Kameza offered him a sum of money which would pay half the expense of the feast; but in vain. The merciless man insisted that Bar-Kameza should leave, and he left it, with a bitter sting in his heart. Returning to his house, he said to himself: 'Because all the Rabbins, wise men, and priests sat at table, and made not even an attempt to reconcile that inflexible man; and I, deeply ashamed, was compelled to leave the house, I will go and put a stone in their way, upon which they shall stumble, and fall, and perish.' And off he went to the Emperor in Rome, and being permitted to appear before him, he said: 'Cæsar, my lord, the Jews rebel against thee.' The Emperor replied: 'How shall I know that thou sayest the truth? My vice-regent makes no mention of a rebellion in his last report.' Bar-Kazema said: 'It is still secretly preparing; but try them, send them a young heifer, a year old, without any blemish or spot, to be offered for thee as a burnt offering, and see whether they will accept and offer it.' The Emperor did so; he sent an heifer without blemish to the high priest in Jerusalem, through a special messenger, requesting that it should be offered upon the altar of Jehovah in his behalf. But Bar-Kameza, either in agreement with the messenger, or stealthily, made a small cut in the lips of the heifer; and, of course, she was not accepted. The messenger returned to the Emperor with the sad report that the Jews rejected his offering, upon which he commanded Vespasian to go up to Jerusalem, with a mighty army to punish the rebels; and thus the bloody war commenced which terminated in the destruction of Jerusalem and the Temple."

But we come now, to the other two stories, which follow immediately the one above related, "For the sake of a hen and a cock, Tur-Hamalkah was destroyed." It was customary among the Jews that they, on the occasion of a wedding, took a pair of chickens, as a symbol of fruitfulness, bearing them upon painted sticks before the procession, from the house of wedding to the synagogue, and back again; and then killing and preparing them as a meal for the young married couple. On such an occasion, a party of Roman soldiers passed through the city, and in their insolence, seized the fowls from the bearers, and mocked at the indignant Jews. But the people, who considered themselves offended in their religious liberty, crowded to the spot, and massacred the soldiers, of whom only a few escaped, to carry the sad news to the governor of the province. As soon as the Emperor received information of what the Jews had done, he sent a mighty army to punish them. One hundred thousand Romans with drawn swords entered at once the unhappy city, and began to massacre all who fell into their hands, so that the river which ran through the city was filled with two parts of blood and the third part of water; for the city was so great and so thickly populated, that while the Romans raged with death and destruction in several parts of it, they in other parts had no idea of it, and continued in their pleasures and entertainments, until the angels of death were ushered in upon them like the thunders-troke on a sunny day.

The third part of the story says: "For the sake of a pole of a carriage, Bitter was destroyed." There was again, in this case, a custom which became the fatal cause of the destruction of a large and densely populated city. It was the habit of the Jews to plant a tree at the birth of a child, and it was regarded as an especial favor of God, and a sign of blessing and the prosperity of that child, if the tree grew up without any injury, and, when the child married, or was given in marriage, the tree was splendidly adorned with ribbons and cords of all colours, and used as a chupah-stick. Now it happened, one day, just when a wedding took place, that a daughter of the Emperor, with her suite, passed the city of Bitter, and, in one of the crooked streets, she had the misfortune to break the pole of her carriage. Her attendants conceived the unhappy idea of taking one of the young trees, which had just the thickness required for a new pole, and which attracted their attention by being adorned with colors, and overspread with an adorned and gilded canopy.

The consequences were the same as in Tur-Hamalkah. The people, highly offended by such an attack upon their so much cherished religious customs, rushed in crowds, and well armed, to the spot where the offence was performed, and massacred the whole detachment of soldiers which accompanied the princess. She herself escaped safely, in consequence of the wise counsel of some old men, who possessed more prudence than the others. Bitter was then besieged and taken, and all, without respect to age, put to death in the most cruel manner.

But here we come to another subject which is very copious and extensive—it is the different persecutions and sufferings which the Jews had to undergo concerning their false Messiahs and imposters. One by the name of Bar Cochba, was the first of those imposters. He appeared the first among those false Messiahs. We mean the first after the true Messiah. And what was the consequence of his impostership? The blood of the poor Jews flowed like a stream into the ocean, and even carried in its force stones with it. "And do you think," says the record, "that the sea was very near to the city? No, it was a mile distant." There were many more imposters, as Hacam, Zedebias, Sabathy, and a certain Daniel; also, Tzeve, &c., &c. The result of all those false Messiahs was that not only did they pay for their crimes with their own lives, but unfortunately, the poor and wretched Jews suffered likewise. And now we come to those persecutions which the Jews suffered in almost every part of the world, where they had become dispersed.

First, the Jews suffered for their zeal in converting Heathens and Mohamedans to the Jewish faith. About fifty years afterwards, in Germany, at Worms, several thousands of Jews were massacred. At the same time a Hermit whose name was Rudolphus, sounded the alarm against them under the pretence that charity required the total extirpation of the enemies of the Christian religion. This man had doubtless assumed a mission which was by no means conformable to that of Jesus Christ, who had brought peace into the world, and reproved His apostles, who, through a misguided zeal, were for having the Samaritans destroyed by fire from heaven. The persecutions of the Crusades were general, and all European Jews felt the dreadful effects of them; but all those persecutions which we have already mentioned, have neither been so universal, nor so violent as those of Spain, where as already mentioned, thousands were burnt alive, thousands sold as slaves, children dragged away before their parents, &c.

We can with surety say, that not one generation from the time of our blessed Redeemer, has passed, without witnessing such horrible persecutions of the Jews—in short there is not a spot in the whole inhabited world where Jewish blood crieth not out from the ground, except that of the new world; for even in England the Jews were not treated with more humanity than in other Christian countries..

What we have already said, must be, I think, sufficient to give an idea to my Christian friends, of the persecutions which the Jews have suffered from time to time in all parts of the world, and although it must be confessed, that the Jews often brought themselves into trouble through different excesses which were equally criminal—yet the most of their persecutions were, however, frequently grounded on enormous crimes imputed to them by the wickedness of some particular man, and which the illiterate and vulgar out of misguided zeal, punished with all the rage and resentment that enthusiasm and bigotry could inspire them with.

And now, dear Christian friends, supposing the question were to be asked: Why are the Jews so much persecuted and afflicted? Is it the hand of God and his wrath which rests upon them, or is it a mere fate? Our answer is: We must be blind not to see in it the hand of

God, and seeing it we cannot but admire and adore it; for what other probable acccount can they themselves give for their long captivity, dispersion, and miseries, but that they have to be the monuments of God's justice. But is there not after all a *special* reason given us for their sufferings in the word of God? It is a question well worth the inquiry. There is, however, another important question which you will permit me to anticipate, and that is—Why are the Jews afflicted by God with a captivity wherein they are now, and which might be termed the perpetual wrath of God—for it does not seem to have an end? For more than 1700 years have elapsed since they were made captives by Titus. We know that their forefathers worshipped idols, killed prophets, and rejected the law of God. Now for all these transgressions they were kept only 70 years captive in Babylon, and after the period foretold by the prophets, God became propitious again to them, and led them back into their own land—although, according to Scripture the wrath of God was at this time even more violent than before, yet their punishment only lasted 70 years. But now we see the wrath of God wherewith he punishes them does not end, must it not necessarily follow from this, that they must have committed sins greater than those of their ancestors; and again, since God does not punish a whole nation except from a sin of which they are all guilty, it must follow, that the whole Jewish nation is guilty of one crime.

Let us then, therefore, cast a serious glance into the word of God, and see if we cannot find there some satisfactory answer. God spake by the prophet Amos (xii. 6): "For three transgressions of Israel, and for four, I will not turn away the punishment thereof; because they sold the righteous for silver." All those who study the sacred books are, and must be, well aware that the first of the four transgressions of Israel was the selling of Joseph by his brethren; the second sin points to the worship of the calf on Mount Horeb; the third to the killing of the prophets, for which they lived 70 years in captivity; but the fourth transgression, which even in its language is separately announced from the before-mentioned three, surely can be, and is no other crime, than the selling of Jesus Christ, who, in fact, was sold after the 70 years captivity; for were this not so, that is, that this selling of Jesus be the fourth transgression, we should assign various crimes to Israel before the selling of Joseph; this, however, we can by no means maintain, since the testimony of the book of Genesis is against us, for we find the selling of Joseph to be the first crime in numerical order laid on all the sons of Jacob; whilst the prophet Amos dwells distinctly on the fourth sin—

the selling of the just one; wherefore they were to come into this present captivity, out of which God threatens them not to return when he says: "And for the fourth I will not turn away the punishment thereof." In like manner we read the word of God, through the mouth of the prophet Isaiah, ch. lxv. 12-15: "Therefore will I number you to the sword, and ye shall all bow down to the slaughter; because when I called ye did not answer; when I spake ye did not hear; but did evil before mine eyes, and did choose that wherein I delighted not. Therefore, thus saith the Lord God: Behold my servants shall eat, but ye shall be hungry; behold my servants shall drink, but ye shall be thirsty; behold my servants shall rejoice, but ye shall be ashamed; behold my servants shall sing for joy of heart, but ye shall cry for sorrow of heart, and shall howl for vexation of spirit. And ye shall leave your name for a curse unto my chosen, for the Lord God shall slay thee, and call his servants by another name." There is no want of many more words to prove that for the selling and rejection of Him, who is our Great Teacher and Prophet, the unbelieving Jews suffer, and believers rejoice, for it is visible to all the world that the people of the Jews have been, and still are, severely punished for their infidelity and disobedience to that prophet, and those are blessed by God upon earth who received the other name. The prophecy is clear and expressive: Deut. xviii. 18,—"I will raise them up a prophet from among their brethren like unto thee, and will put My words in his mouth, and he shall speak unto them all that I shall command him, and it shall come to pass, that whosoever will not harken unto My words which he shall speak in My name, I will require it of him,"—that is, I will severely punish him, as the Hebrew word signifies. This prophecy evidently relates to Jesus Christ; and has not this terrible denunciation been fully executed upon the Jews, commencing soon after Jesus had finished his ministry among them, and His apostles had likewise preached in vain. We may be the more certain of this application, as our Saviour Himself not only denounced the same destruction, but also foretold the signs, the manner, and the circumstances of it; and those of the Jews, who believed in His name, by remembering the caution, and following the advice which he had given them, escaped from the general ruin of their country, like firebrands picked out of the fire. The main body of the nation either perished in their infidelity, or were carried captive into all nations; and have they not ever since persisted in the same infidelity, been obnoxious to the same punishment, and been a distressed and miserable people in the earth—the hand of God was scarce ever more visible in any of his dispensations. I, therefore, repeat once more, we must be blind not to see that they have long been monuments of God's Justice; but we believe they will become objects of His mercy again. And in the meantime we will say with the apostle Paul—"Our heart's desire and prayer to God for Israel is, that they may be saved."

But the question may be asked: how can God, who is a God of love, visit the iniquity of the fathers upon the children, if the fathers have eaten sour grapes, why shall the teeth of the children be set on edge? If the fathers hated the Lord, why should the children suffer for it? And which question becomes graver still, when we read in Holy Writ where it is distinctly stated: "The fathers shall not die for the children, neither shall the children die for the fathers." And when the prophet Ezekiel teaches in the word of God, "The son shall not bear the iniquity of the father, neither shall the father bear the iniquity of the son," our first answer may be that the children are as well unbelievers as their fathers were. But we are permitted, by contemplating our position in the material world, and comparing cause and effect in human life, to conceive the justice of God in this great question, and exclaim: Man thou standest perplexed and dejected on the portals of wisdom, and darest not set thy foot on the threshold of its sanctuary, because it seems shrouded in an impenetrable veil; but how, if within thyself, within thine own heart, thou possessest the key to this mystery? Cast a contemplating glance within thine own bosom, and ask thyself when, by voluptuousness and sensuality, thou hast impaired the faculties of thy mind, and weakened thy body, and brought upon thyself diseases which ruin thy constitution, and are inherited by thy children, must not the children suffer for the sins of their fathers, in dragging along an existence embittered by sickness and ill health? Or, when, by intemperance and extravagance, thou hast squandered away thy fortune, and spent a patrimony to which they have a rightful claim, and hast brought upon thyself want and poverty, which prevents thee from giving thy sons a proper education, which would entitle them to occupy an honorable position in society, and gain an honest living, and train up thy daughters to become ornaments to society, and an honor to their sex? Hast thou not handed over by thine own faults, thy children, and, perhaps, thy childrens' children, to an existence embittered by penury, to a life unblessed by education; does not the sin bear its bitter fruit from generation to generation! Or still, hast thou, through dishonesty, forfeited the confidence of the world, and branded the name which thou hast inherited from thine ancestors untarnished, and which it was thy bounden duty to leave to thy children after thee without stain? Hast thou not made them the inheritors of thy shame? Hast thou not bequeathed to them the contempt which thou has earned, and of which they in a certain degree may be innocent? Is not the iniquity of the fathers visited on the children in the unmerited disgrace which attaches to them? Or thinkest thou this an injustice? Foolish thought! Wouldst thou that God should subvert the order of things, and change for thy sake the eternal laws of cause and effect, which rule the material world? And as it is with this individual, so it is with whole nations. History teaches us how whole nations had to expiate the sins of their fathers; how empires great and powerful, vanished from the face of the earth by exterminating wars and fearful pestilences, through the crimes and the depravity of their ancestors; and yet God is just and full of love, who shows mercy unto thousands of them that love Him. And can this idea be difficult for us to comprehend? Must it not present itself clearly before our mind's eye, when we reflect on the fate of the Jewish nation, which for nearly 1800 years has bowed them down, and which the misdeeds of their ancestors have brought upon them? Have not the prophets, in flowing and soul-stirring language, portrayed to the fathers the future misery of their children, and the sufferings which the latter will have to endure for the sins of the former? And though the dispersion of the Jews, together with their sufferings, has been made instrumental in the hands of eternal wisdom, to erect it as a living standard, and to prove the truth of the word of God, their dispersions and sufferings are nevertheless the just punishment God has inflicted for the sins of their forefathers, who said: "Let his blood be upon us and our children."

And now we come to another point. The fortune and circumstances of the Jews have had their revolution also. According to the zeal of the people who were animated by the clergy, or by the political views of Christian princes, and since the Reformation, at the time of Luther and Calvin, circumstances have become more favorable to them. The Jews have, ever since, established themselves to advantage in several Protestant kingdoms. Holland was the first which received them more generously than any of the other Protestant countries. And now, the Jews are settled peaceably in all the Protestant countries. In short, ever since men have begun to throw off the trammels of prejudice, and the fetters of hatred and enmity, and wherever the dignity of human nature has been respected, wherever the iron hand of ignorance and bigotry has ceased to crush virtue, that dignifies mankind to the dust, and wherever contempt and oppression, that maketh a wise man mad, has vanished away; in a word, wherever pure Christianity has erected its banner, and the love of Christ was manifested and practiced, and only there, the Jew was, and is still permitted to prove that he likewise is made in the image of God, and that he has preserved many noble things, many noble feelings, inseparable from his former greatness.

And now my dear Christian friends, let us consider, therefore, the design of the rejection of my beloved people, and your adoption in their state, for in times past ye have not believed God, yet have now obtained mercy through their unbelief, even so have these also now not believed, that through your mercy they also may obtain mercy. Let us remember also, that "salvation is of the Jews," "who are Israelites, to whom pertaineth the adoption and the glory, and the covenants, and the giving of the Law, and the service of God, and the promises, whose are the fathers, and of whom as concerning the flesh Christ came who is over all, God, blessed for ever. Let us rejoice in the prospect of the Jews being grafted again into the good olive tree, if they continue not in unbelief, and may our prayer be to Him who is our Lord and Redeemer, that He may hasten the time, when their unbelief, together with their persecutions and sufferings, shall be taken away, when Jew and Gentile will walk hand in hand to the Temple of our Lord.

NOTE.—To recount the barbarities which the Christian nations of Europe have inflicted on the Jews, would fill volumes, and they should be written with tears instead of 'ink, and on sackcloth instead of parchment. Every species of annoyance, every diabolical torture, every debasing usage, every epithet of opprobrium, every manifestation of hatred and contempt has been exercised against them; their property was ever regarded as lawful prey; their persons were never secure from ill-treatment; their lives were at the mercy of ruthless rulers; everywhere they have been treated by the Christian nations of Europe with contumely and wrong; laws of the most oppressive kind have been enacted against them; they could not testify against a Christian in the civil courts; they were forced to wear badges designed to mark them with disgrace; they were forbidden to institute suits against Christians in the courts of law; they were made the foot-ball of kings and princes, being spurned now hither, now thither, by the feet of petty despots; they were compelled to reside in certain sections of cities, and locked in at night, and no Christian servants or nurse could stay with, or attend them, no inn for travellers could receive or entertain them; they were in truth, what prophecy declared they should be, "A byword and a reproach among all nations." When Christian nations have thus maltreated and abused this ancient people, do we wonder at their prejudices against Christianity.

NOTE 2.—Only a short time ago, a little peasant girl, in the village of Schawlau, was missed. Suddenly the report was spread that the child was kidnapped by the Jews in order to make use of its blood in the Passover ceremonies. A judicial enquiry was at once instituted, the houses of the neighboring Jews were thoroughly searched, but no trace of the girl could be discovered. A month afterwards her body was found under a mass of snow, which had begun to melt. The village priest then preached in the church that the Jews, after having drawn the blood from the child, had buried the corpse in the snow. The proprietor of the estate, equalling the priest in fanaticism, made the same assertion. The excitement of the ignorant peasautry against the unfortunate Jews, thus spread farther daily, and at last grew to such intensity that it became really furious. All intercourse with the Jews of the whole district was cut off, and every Jew that dared to show himself in the street was assailed with hatchets. Moreover, the leading Jews of Schawlan were at once thrown into prison, there to await their trial as murderers.

CHAPTER VIII.

THE RESTORATION OF ISRAEL.

Shall Israel be restored to their own land? Undoubtedly they shall if the promises of God are of literal fulfilment, as none can question, who see in the past the mirror of the future; or perhaps, we should say, who interpret promises concerning the future, by the precedent of those whose accomplishment has become matter of history. God gave them the land in promise, so long ago as the days of Abraham. "All the land which thou seest, to thee will I *give* it, and to thy *seed forever.*"—Gen. xiii. 14-17; xv. 18; xvii. 7, 8; xxvi. 2, 6: Exod. vi. 4: Deut. xxxiv. 1-5: Psalms cv. 1-5.

"In all parts of the earth," says a recent writer, "this extraordinary people, whose name and sufferings are in every nation under heaven, think and feel as one man on the great issue of their restoration." This belief and the desire, is almost universal among the Jews, and as far as Hebrew converts are concerned, there is scarcely one who differs from this belief. If it be enquired, how, or by what instrumentality this great event is likely to be accomplished, we say, through a signal interposition of Heaven.

The desire of their restoration is interwoven in all their prayers, more particularly those for their festivals. In their prayer for the feast of the Passover, it is repeatedly said: "This year we are here, at the next year we shall be in the land of Israel." Read the following predictions: Jer. xxx. 8, 11, 18; xxxi. 33-40: Zech. xii. 1-18: Is. xxvii. 12, 13: Ezekiel xi. 17: xx. 40, 42; xxxiv. 13; xxxvi. 14, 28: xxxvii. 21-28; xxxix. 28, 29: Hosea iii. 5: Amos ix. 14, 15; and Zech. xiv. 10, 11. Nor ought we to lose sight of the prediction of our blessed Jesus Himself, who said: "And Jerusalem shall be trodden down of the Gentiles until the time of the Gentiles be fulfilled."—Luke xxi. 24. Then the Jews will be converted, and return to their own land, and rebuild and inhabit Jerusalem, that is, they will return, in an unconverted state to their country, and then and there, "a nation will be born in a day."

I must confess that up to a short time ago, I was not a believer in a *temporal* but a spiritual restoration of the people of Israel. But the more I search the scriptures on this important subject, and my own experience in connection with the state of the church, as well as with the experience of converted Hebrews in the Christian Church, the more

I feel convinced that the Jews will be literally restored to their country.

"There is but one objection," says another Hebrew convert, "and that is, that if the Jews are to return to Canaan before their conversion, then it is needless to make exertion to promote their conversion." Does it follow that because we do not expect the national conversion of our people till after their restoration to Canaan, that therefore no individuals may be converted before that time? The Apostle Paul said and believed that my dear brethren, the sons of Abraham, would continue under the influence of spiritual darkness until the fulness of the Gentiles come in; yet that did not prevent him from going into the synagogue every Sabbath day, and reasoning with them from the Scriptures, that Jesus is the Christ, the Son of God."

CONCLUSION.

It is but rarely that Christian authors afford us an opportunity for expressing our satisfaction with the results of their researches in the field of Jewish literature. They generally view Jewish events and Jewish efforts through a distorted medium. In the most of their eyes modern Jewish history has only a value in as far as it serves to set off events in our Christianity. Comparison—the real use of which only consists in bringing out in bolder relief, either individual characteristics, or the distinguishing marks of occurrences—are alas too often only instituted by Gentile writers on Jewish history, for the purpose of exalting Gentile virtues and Christian proceedings, on the pedestal of Jewish vices, and Jewish misdoings. With the exception of one or two, we are not acquainted with a work in the English language narrating events subsequent to the Christian Era, in a dispassionate manner, ready to view and treat of Judaism independently of Christianity. However much such a cooked up history may be to the taste of some, it cannot but raise disgust in the minds of the unbiased Christian and Jew. A population like that of the Jews, existing in full vigour, numerous, and in the possession of mental faculties of acknowledged superiority, of means and influence equal to those enjoyed at any antecedent period, eighteen hundred and sixty-nine years after the object of its existence is supposed to have been attained, must have an independent value, and still a mission to fulfil. They may appeal to natural, profane and sacred history, alike for evidence bearing out the correctness of this view. The loveliest flower fades after it has produced seed; and the stateliest tree is stripped of its foliage as soon as it has yielded the fruit which its boughs were laden, and bare and naked it remains until the season comes for its renewed mission. No nation has remained on the stage of the world one moment beyond the period necessary for the realization of the idea of which it was the bearer. When its part is acted, it either decays, serving to prepare the ground for successors, or is suddenly absorbed by a vigorous assailant. The present Greeks do not equal their ancestors, either in classic taste, or philosophic acumen, or in valorous exploits. The virtues which distinguished the ancient Romans, have not been transmitted to any of their descendants, if such be anywhere still traceable. But the present Jews are actually more numerous now than those that were conquered by Titus. Their religion is substantially the same. The idea then represented by them, still forms the standard round which they rally, and no decay can be perceived in any of those virtues, and intellectual qualities, which marked them of old. If anything, the unparalelled calamities and sufferings of two thousand years, have freed them from some vices with which they were reproached of old; softened down some of their faults, and brought out to great advantage some other powers latent for centuries. A captivity of eighteen centuries has been a furnace through which they not only have passed unscathed, but which has actually refined them of much dross; yea, and prepared them for the accomplishment of a Divine purpose. Can this be said of any other nation? Have Assyrians, Egyptians, Greeks, or Romans shown forth to advantage, after the sword of the conqueror had passed through their countries? The stream may gain in size, yet not in purity, as it flows onwards. Yet this is the process exhibited by the Jews as they are borne onward by the wave of time.

Can Judiaism, therefore, forming as we know it does, the mainspring and life-blood of our Christianity, really be so effete and worn out as to be fit only to lay down and die? Can it be nothing else but mummy embalmed, and with all its former greatness, glory, predictions and promises bundled up, and buried eighteen hundred years ago, in the sepulchre out of which Christianity arose? Has Israel to play no part any more on the platform of events to come? Has the curtain over the prophecies of Old and New Testament Scriptures concerning them been dropped already? No! There is vigor and intense vitality still throbbing in every one of Israel's veins; its pulsations are as strong as ever. Blind they are, but not dead, for "blindness in part is happend to Israel, until the fulness of the Gentiles come in." And so all Israel shall be saved. Persecuted and hated they are, but not cast away. "God hath not cast away His people which He foreknew." Dispersed they are, but not forsaken: "For I am with thee, saith the Lord, to save thee, though I make a full end of all nations whither I have scattered thee, yet will I not make a full end of thee; but I will correct thee in measure, and will not leave thee altogether unpunished."—Jer. xxx. 11, 12.

Blind they are, but not dead!
But—" There is none to plead thy cause."
For—" All thy lovers have forsaken thee."
Therefore—" I will restore health unto thee, because they called thee an outcast."

Brethren, my heart's desire and prayer to God for Israel is, that they might be saved!

C. FRESHMAN.

GALT, March 12, 1869.

www.ingramcontent.com/pod-product-compliance
Lightning Source LLC
Chambersburg PA
CBHW051847300426
44117CB00006B/301